D1586990

Insolvency Law Handbook

THIRD EDITION

The University of Law
of **Law**
incorporating The College of Law

The University of Law, 14 Store Street, London WC1E 7DE
Telephone: 01483 216387 E-mail: library-bloomsbury@law.ac.uk

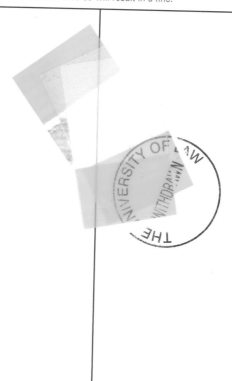

Birmingham ⏐ Bristol ⏐ Chester ⏐ Guildford ⏐ London ⏐ Manchester ⏐ York

INSOLVENCY LAW HANDBOOK

THIRD EDITION

Vernon Dennis

The Law Society

Crown copyright material is reproduced with the permission of the Controller of Her Majesty's Stationery Office

ISBN-13: 978-1-907698-43-9

First published in 2005
Second edition published in 2007
This third edition published in 2013 by the Law Society
113 Chancery Lane, London WC2A 1PL

Typeset by Columns Design XML Ltd, Reading
Printed by CPI Group (UK) Ltd, Croydon, CR0 4YY

The paper used for the text pages of this book is FSC® certified. FSC (the Forest Stewardship Council®) is an international network to promote responsible management of the world's forests.

Contents

Preface to the third edition

The first edition of this handbook was published in 2004 and was written in the shadow of the then newly enacted Enterprise Act 2002. The most significant reforms to insolvency law in a generation were introduced by this Act, with corporate insolvency reforms coming into force in September 2003 and the personal insolvency provision coming into force in April 2004. Writing a handbook at that time required a little bit of guesswork. What trends were likely to develop? How would the courts interpret the newly introduced provisions? Would there be a move by the judiciary and by insolvency practitioners to give effect to the spirit behind the new reforms? Would we see a change in economic behaviours; a more entrepreneurial dynamic 'rescue' culture with a reducing social stigma for personal insolvency?

By the time of the second edition in 2007, the reforms had been bedding in at a time of prolonged economic growth, fuelled by consumer and public spending. This spending pattern was causing an ever expanding debt burden and certainly at that time one could point to the large rise in consumer insolvency and the use of the pre-pack administration procedure as consequences of this over-indebtedness. The risks that these trends posed, however, were arguably countered by the continuing beneficial growth to the overall economy. For corporate businesses, an easy solution to financial difficulty at this time was to refinance and take on more debt. One could see that this would exhaust non-secured assets and returns for unsecured creditors in the event of insolvency, but problems could be postponed. If the financial problems were more fundamental, the availability of funding could fuel pre-packs, lenders being willing to provide funding to the business (and not the corporate) and funding 'new co' to purchase the business and assets of 'old co' free of debt. Individuals released from bankruptcy restrictions in less than one year were free to spend again. The debt burden was not reducing, simply being moved on by a non-stop merry-go-round.

This third edition is written against a very different backdrop. A liquidity bubble that had been growing for nearly 20 years burst. However, rather than lenders turning to borrowers to enforce security and obtain repayment, this time problems have mainly been focused on the lenders themselves, and this has caused unprecedented and unpredictable results.

In the lead-up to the credit crunch, investment banks had developed ever more complex financial instruments to trade in debt, and such trading had created expanding capital markets and availability of credit (by creation of debt). Unfortunately, many instruments masked the true assets/liability underpinning the trade, and banks thus had difficulty in making assessment of loss when it became apparent that defaults may occur, the trigger being the instability of the US housing market and its effect on the sub-prime mortgage market. Ultimately, this uncertainty caused a paralysis in the short-term money markets. The worldwide financial system was imperilled until huge governmental monetary intervention sought to restore liquidity to the markets. The cost of this, however, is still being felt. What was once a banking crisis is now a sovereign debt crisis, with those heavily indebted countries unsuccessfully seeking to cut costs (austerity measures) and increase revenue (tax) at a time of worldwide economic recession.

To encourage growth and lending, interest base rates have reached historic lows (0.5 per cent at the time of writing), but this has failed to provide the stimulus to the economy, which has alternated between very low and negative growth in each quarter since 2008, with the UK economy officially experiencing a 'double dip recession'.

One would think that against this background insolvency numbers would have escalated. At the time of writing, this is not the case, and throughout this book, but in particular in Chapter 14, some suggestions are given as to why this counterintuitive trend has occurred. Indeed, R3 (the Association of Business Recovery Professionals) in November 2012 estimated that as many as one in 10 businesses were unable to pay their principal debt and/or had been required to reach a compromise of some sort with their creditors. These companies have been termed 'zombies': insolvent businesses continuing to avoid an insolvency process. Whether this prolonged half life is preferable to a Darwinian fight for survival of the fittest, with waves of insolvency and possible economic depression, is a key question for policymakers. Is the pain of the credit crunch being prolonged by the distortions of economic forces?

Insolvency law lies at the heart of this debate. Do the processes and procedures unfairly distort market forces? Indeed, should they? These themes are picked up throughout the book and the reader is invited when considering 'what' the law may say, to consider at the same time 'why' it does so?

This bigger picture macro-economic analysis is clearly not the aim of this work. In this third edition I have continued my aim of providing a user-friendly overview of the practical implications of insolvency law and practice, while attempting to keep this work at a manageable length. This book remains neither an academic textbook nor a commentary on the principal statutes. Instead, it aims to provide a 'first port of call' for professional advisers, debtors and creditors alike, guiding each through the options that are available and the decisions that may be faced in any given insolvency situation. Wherever possible it thus seeks to provide guidance from the very different perspectives of the debtor and the creditor.

Part I of the book tackles the decisions faced prior to the commencement of any formal insolvency procedure; **Part II** looks at each major insolvency process; **Part III** examines the effect of insolvency procedures on debtor and creditor; and

Chapter 14 seeks to provide a 'look into the crystal ball'. Wherever possible, I have used flowcharts, checklists and reference tables to provide 'at a glance advice', while the text contains more detailed analysis of hurdles and pitfalls presented to both debtor and creditor in a situation of insolvency.

The book is written with the law as applicable in England and Wales as at the end of December 2012.

Vernon S. Dennis
December 2012
Partner HowardKennedyFsi LLP
Email: Vernon.dennis@hkfsi.com

About the author

Vernon Dennis is a partner at HowardKennedyFsi LLP solicitors where he is head of Corporate Restructuring.

Vernon's career in insolvency began in the early 1990s. Since that time he has acted for insolvency practitioners, creditors and debtors on a wide range of corporate recovery, reconstruction and business rescue issues. His practice also encompasses personal insolvency, and he acts on both domestic and cross-border issues.

He is a fellow of R3 (the Association of Business Recovery Professionals) and a member of the Turnaround Management Association. He regularly lectures and provides media commentary on insolvency issues and trends.

His first work was as co-author of *The New Law of Insolvency* (Law Society, 2003). Since then he has authored two editions of this work (Law Society, 2005 and 2007) and all three books in the Law Society's Insolvency Law Series: *Administration* (2010), *Liquidation* (2011) and *Bankruptcy* (2012).

Acknowledgements

Very many thanks to my colleague Katie Harding for her invaluable contribution in providing this updated version of the Handbook. Katie has been able to bring a fresh pair of eyes to the material and has assisted in refreshing the text, although any errors remain entirely my own.

I would also like to express all my love and heartfelt thanks to my wife, Sarah-Jane, and to our children, Tom and Emma. It is their patience, understanding and, most especially, their love and support that makes the writing of these books possible.

Table of cases

Table of statutes

Table of statutory instruments

Table of international legislation

Abbreviations

BRO	bankruptcy restrictions order
BRU	bankruptcy restrictions undertaking
CA 1985/1989/2006	Companies Act 1985/1989/2006
CDDA 1986	Company Directors Disqualification Act 1986
CDO	collateralised debt obligation
COMI	centre of main interests
CPR	Civil Procedure Rules 1998, SI 1998/3132
CVA	company voluntary arrangement
CVL	creditors' voluntary liquidation
DBIS	Department for Business, Innovation and Skills
DRO	debt relief order
DTI	Department of Trade and Industry
ECSC Treaty	Treaty establishing the European Coal and Steel Community, 1951
ETO	economic, technical or organisational
FCA	Financial Conduct Authority
FSA	Financial Services Authority (UK)
FSMA 2000	Financial Services and Markets Act 2000
FTVA	fast-track voluntary arrangement
HMRC	Her Majesty's Revenue and Customs
IA 1986/2000	Insolvency Act 1986/2000
IPA	income payments agreement
IPO	income payments order
IR 1986	Insolvency Rules 1986, SI 1986/1925
IVA	individual voluntary arrangement
LLP	limited liability partnership
LPA receiver	Law of Property Act 1925 receiver
MBS	mortgage backed securities
MVL	members' voluntary liquidation
QFCH	qualifying floating charge holder
SME	small and medium-sized enterprise
TUPE	Transfer of Undertakings (Protection of Employment) Regulations 2006, SI 2006/246
UNCITRAL	United Nations Commission on International Trade Law

CHAPTER 1

Preliminary considerations

1.1 WHAT IS INSOLVENCY?

Insolvent, bankrupt, broke, bust, ruined, failed, gone to the wall, wound up, on the rocks, in queer street, in receivership, up Carey Street, stony-broke, in liquidation, cleaned out, penniless – the descriptions are numerous; we all have an idea what they may convey, but it is often difficult to identify precisely what 'insolvency' means and when it has arisen.

Insolvency does not in itself denote a lack of money or assets; instead insolvency requires the existence of both credit and debt. The granting of credit is the provision of a resource (e.g. goods or services) in exchange for an agreement by the recipient to return the resource or provide 'repayment' at a later date, the agreement creating an obligation of debt owed to the supplier (the creditor) by the recipient (the debtor).

While poverty may arise from individuals possessing few of their own assets, insolvency is a factual status arising where the debtor owes a debt to a creditor and the debtor is unable to meet the obligation of repayment. This obligation of repayment can be assessed on either a 'cash flow test' or a 'balance sheet test', and if the debtor fails on either test he is technically insolvent. However, as we shall see, this does not mean that an insolvency process will necessarily follow just because a debtor is insolvent. What sets insolvency apart from poverty is that the debtor has in some way spent or utilised the money of a third party (creditor(s)) rather than just utilised his own resources.

Definitions

A **debt** is a legally enforceable liability, whereby a party known as a debtor can be compelled to render what is due at the insistence of a party known as a creditor.

A **debtor** is a person/company who owes money.

A **creditor** is a person/company who is owed money.

The **cash flow test** is a measure of whether a debtor is insolvent and is based on whether the debtor can pay his debts as they fall due.

> The **balance sheet test** is a measure of whether a debtor is insolvent and is based on whether the debtor's total liabilities exceed his assets.

The relationship of creditor and debtor is an essential feature of a developed economic system. Early economic activity most probably involved only a system of bartering. However, as civilisation has developed individuals within a given society perform ever more specialist roles or tasks, leading to the need to develop a system for individuals to trade with one another by establishing a system of transferable value. Money fulfils this role in most societies. Money dates back at least a hundred thousand years, with shells or ochre (clay pigments) apparently having been used as a means of exchange by civilisations in Africa and Australasia. More common was the use by early civilisations of goods which themselves had an intrinsic value, such as cattle, metals, spices or jewellery. It is interesting to see how often gold has been returned to as a means of exchange in times of economic monetary collapse. From 550 BC salt was used as a means of paying wages or 'salary', which explains the derivation of the phrase 'being worth one's salt'.

Trade conducted by monetary exchange increases economic activity, and increasingly sophisticated trading arrangements are likely to lead to a system where credit will be given and debt will arise. Credit introduces a degree of trust into any trading relationship; if the creditor cannot rely on the debtor's promise of repayment and/or enforce the debt obligation, credit will not be provided. As a result, a creditor's ability to enforce any debt obligation is of paramount importance in ensuring stable trading economic conditions. However, the provision of credit also introduces an element of risk for the creditor – the debtor may abscond or may be unable to pay the debt at the agreed time of repayment. The reward for the creditor taking that risk is that the debt obligation is usually of greater value than if the goods/services had been paid for immediately, with the most common form of risk return being interest paid on the debt. However, if the debt cannot be repaid, then nearly all economic systems have developed, often over many centuries, rules and regulations to deal with the steps that can be taken by creditors and debtors alike.

1.1.1 The historical roots of modern insolvency law

The ancient Greeks did not recognise bankruptcy as we would recognise it today (i.e. a collective enforcement remedy by an individual's creditors as a whole, against the property of the debtor). They did, however, employ the concept of 'debt slavery' whereby an individual citizen who was unable to pay his creditor could be put into slavery, together with his wife, children and servants, and forced to repay the debt through physical labour.

In ancient Rome, the reliance on trade and the rise of a significant merchant class meant that rather than such individual creditor self-help remedies, there soon arose a need for collective enforcement measures, i.e. action against a debtor for and behalf of all of his creditors. This led to rules governing the seizure and realisation of a debtor's available assets for his creditors as a whole and the distribution of these realised assets on a *pari passu* principle – a principle which still lies at the heart of modern insolvency law.

While Roman law developed to regularise and police the relationship between the creditors of a debtor, it is of note that a debtor could still be tortured or put to death, although following enactments of Julius Caesar, certain non-culpable trade debtors were allowed voluntarily to give up all of their property to their creditors to avoid such harsh sanction.

As the Roman Empire crumbled and medieval trade between Europe and the East flowed through the former areas of the Empire, medieval merchants trading in these areas developed a whole series of rules and regulations to deal with situations of merchant insolvency. It is here in the medieval 'law merchant' that the derivation of the word 'bankruptcy' is said to have arisen. A merchant in what is now modern Italy would have a bench (*banco*) in the trading exchange and if he could not pay his debts he could declare himself '*fallito*' and abandon his property to his creditors, in which case his bench would be broken (*banco rota*). Voltaire even wrote of a historical Italian custom that in certain circumstances the failed merchant could keep his property provided he seated himself bare bottomed and in view of all other merchants, showing us an early and very public form of financial rehabilitation. It is of note that the law merchant continued with the tradition of distinguishing trade debt from personal debt, with regulation applying only to tradesmen and merchants.

In England, a feudal society militated against significant trade; as a result the non-payment of a debt was seen as a sinful or criminal activity rather than treated as a necessary by-product of trading relationships. Indeed it was not until the sixteenth century that any statute was passed specifically to deal with insolvent debtors. The Bankruptcy Act 1542 addressed the problem of absconding trade debtors and allowed creditors to seize the debtor's property and make a rateable distribution from the proceeds of sale of the property between creditors, i.e. the *pari passu* principle. The Act also imposed the death penalty for fraudulent trading activity. In 1604, a new measure was introduced which allowed a creditor to cut off part of the debtor's ear to show his disreputable character; this is said to explain the derivation of the term 'earmarked'.

While bankruptcy law developed for merchants and tradesmen in England, the collection of a debt from a non-trader continued to be a matter of civil recovery. Akin to the ancient Greek process of debt slavery, a creditor could seize not only the property of the debtor, but also his person. The individual debtor could thus be imprisoned by his creditor until the debt was paid, generally by family or benefactors. The inequity and inefficiency of the arrangement was that the debtor was forced to rent space within the prison and was responsible for paying for his own food and clothing, remaining in prison until the debt was paid. Obviously without recourse to trade or employment the debtor was entirely dependent on his family, alms or the mercy of his creditors. Corruption was rife in such prisons and Victorian social reformers saw the need to abolish debtors' prisons as an important aspect of social reform. Although debtors' prisons had in theory been abolished by 1869, at the beginning of the First World War there remained a handful of debtors still resident in prison, having been unable to pay off their debts.

Reform of insolvency law continued, despite the existence of debtor prisons, with the enactment of the Statute of Anne Bankruptcy Act 1705, which for the first time introduced a concept of the honest non-culpable debtor who, on giving up all of his goods and assets, could obtain a release from debt if 80 per cent of his creditors were in agreement. In the Bankruptcy Act 1861 the distinction between trade and non-trade debtors was abolished and the Bankruptcy Act 1883 codified the bankruptcy regime and formed the basis of a modern bankruptcy system, which survived until the Insolvency Act 1985.

The 1883 Act firmly established that bankruptcy was a matter of public concern for the entire community. The administration of the bankrupt's estate was to be for the best interests of creditors as a whole and any misconduct by the bankrupt would be dealt with appropriately. Bankruptcy also offered an individual the chance of financial rehabilitation and protection from individual creditors. The bankruptcy system was and remains a careful balance between the rights of the debtor and the rights of the creditors.

It was not until the Insolvency Act 1976 that limited rights of automatic discharge from bankruptcy were first introduced. Prior to this date, bankrupts needed to apply to the courts for discharge, something in fact rarely done.

The Insolvency Act 1985 introduced a system of automatic discharge after three years. However, it should be noted that the implementation of the 1985 Act was delayed and its provisions were consolidated into the Insolvency Act (IA) 1986, which came into force on 29 December 1986.

For the first time, following the Enterprise Act 2002 reforms on personal insolvency law that amended IA 1986 (the reforms came into effect on 1 April 2004), there is now a two-tier system of bankruptcy, distinguishing between the culpable and the non-culpable, and leading to the automatic discharge of most bankrupts within 12 months.

As described above, personal insolvency law has a long historical ancestry; its roots can be traced from Roman law, through to the medieval mercantile law and the Tudor Bankruptcy Act 1542. Corporate insolvency law is a more recent creation. However, it should be remembered that it was only following the development of corporate legal personality that there was any need for a distinct body of law to deal with the insolvency of a company. As we shall see, this development has been surprisingly slow.

'Companies' of fellow knights, alderman and burgesses could by Royal Charter be granted special privileges. In reality this meant monopolies. These monopolies were exploited for commercial gain in certain territories of the world, to provide services or operate certain industry sectors. The first and most famous example of the privatisation of powers traditionally belonging to the monarch, in exchange for duties, taxes and investment return, was the East India Company established by Royal Charter on 31 December 1600.

Privateering gave way to the developing economic doctrines of mercantilism and the resultant huge expansion of international trade. Across Europe the seafaring nations saw the creation of new merchant classes who were increasingly being led into frenzied speculation on investment in corporate enterprises that could offer spectacular levels of return. In Holland, astronomical sums were spent on ventures developing new varieties of tulip bulbs. In England, riding high on this wave of investor confidence was the South Sea Company.

The company was founded in 1711 following the war of the Spanish succession, to provide investment opportunities to trade in Spain's South American colonies. It was seen in its day to be an investment opportunity not to be missed. The collapse of the so-called 'South Sea bubble' in 1720 and the personal ruination of hundreds of individual investors led to the Bubble Act 1720. This was effectively a ban on the use of corporations unless authorised by Royal Charter or Private Act of Parliament. The Bubble Act is said to have set back the development of company law in the newly formed UK by at least a century.

With the Industrial Revolution and the rise of a new industrial class, a critical need for new forms of corporate structure arose. Industrialisation and the growth of business undertakings, and ever larger building and project works required a lot of capital (and many investors). As a result, unincorporated companies formed by deed of settlement between shareholders and trustees sprang up, whereby the management of the business would be transferred to directors in whom the property of the company would be vested. Despite the separation of investment from management, and protections for investors (as between themselves) crucially on failure of the enterprise, the law treated these companies as no more than partnerships, the debts of the companies resting on their investors personally.

While it was increasingly acknowledged that for large public project works the risk to individual investors was too high (the many fraudulent and dishonest floatations during the railway boom and bust of the 1840s being a prime example), mid-era Victorian thinking was still greatly influenced by the *laissez-faire* economic principles of Adam Smith. He had argued that the limited liability afforded to the investors in a company should be a rare privilege, granted only to a limited number of enterprises and for a small number of activities. The state's role in company regulation and hence bankruptcy should be negligible. Commercial practice (i.e. the market) and personal vigilance (i.e. buyer beware) should be the regulators of corporate activity.

Following the losses that arose from the speculation in railways, within a decade, the new middle class investors, fearful of personal liability, were increasingly being led to speculate on fanciful schemes such as mining and grand public schemes with 'limited liability undertakings' in the United States and on continental Europe. This era of speculation, exploitation and loss was satirised by Anthony Trollope in his novel *The Way We Live Now*.

The desire to meet the demands of the investor classes in the UK led to the Joint Stock Companies Act 1844, but it was not until the Joint Stock Companies Act 1856 that the liability for personal contribution by shareholders in the event of corporate insolvency was limited. Even then, despite this reform, the corporate veil was not so much pierced as torn apart by the courts, which consistently determined that through 'rules of agency' an insolvent company was nothing more than the alter ego of its members and hence ultimate liability rested with the members. In addition, the corporate veil was often pierced on instances of fraud, an exemption to limited liability that exists to this day.

It was not until *Salomon* v. *Salomon and Co. Ltd* [1897] AC 22 that the House of Lords firmly established the doctrine of distinct corporate personality. As a result, despite company winding up through the courts being introduced as a creditor remedy in 1844 and voluntary winding up being introduced as a concept in 1856, it was not until the beginning of the twentieth century that corporate insolvency law could truly be said to come of age, and it was the process of company liquidation that led the way.

The Companies Act 1862 introduced the first specific regulation dealing with the procedure for winding up a company. This was followed by provisions in the Companies Acts 1908, 1929, 1948 and 1985. IA 1986 addressed the need for the development of corporate rescue techniques, where companies did not have the 'advantage' of a floating charge which allowed the appointment of an administrative receiver, by introducing company voluntary arrangements (CVAs) and administration procedures. The Act also gave statutory recognition to the receivership process, which during the 1960s and 1970s had developed as a means of rescuing the business of an insolvent company at the instigation of a secured lender, the procedure being identified as 'administrative receivership'.

However, the rescue procedures introduced in IA 1986 were underutilised and arguably failed to encourage a culture of corporate rescue. The Enterprise Act 2002 was the culmination of a long period of review by the government of this area, from 1997 onwards. One of the key findings was that the corporate rescue techniques introduced by IA 1986 had severe defects (some rectified by the Insolvency Act 2000) and that administrative receivership, particularly during the early 1990s, was seen more often than not as a hindrance to company rescue. This led to the corporate insolvency law reforms (which came into effect on 15 September 2003) which introduced the restriction of administrative receivership and the central role of administration, intended to encourage a greater incidence of corporate rescue.

As we have seen, deriving from differing historical legal roots, insolvency law in the UK continues to distinguish between the practice and procedures applicable to the insolvent individual debtor and those accorded to the insolvent corporate debtor. It remains an essential task for any adviser to determine whether creditor claims are against an individual or a corporate body.

1.2 WHO IS INSOLVENT?

Although most statutory provisions regarding both the process and procedures of personal and corporate insolvency law can be found within IA 1986, there are in fact two different codes contained within the statute, distinguished by terminology as well as practice and procedure. This is in contrast to many countries around the world. In the USA, a single bankruptcy code is applicable to both individuals and corporations.

'Insolvency' is a factual condition, whereas bankruptcy or liquidation is a legal condition and status. However, in common usage the terms 'bankrupt' and 'insolvent' are often used interchangeably.

In legal terms, however, an individual may only find himself:

- in bankruptcy; or
- subject to a debt relief order.

A company may only find itself in:

- liquidation/winding up (the terms are synonymous);
- receivership; or
- administration.

Both individuals and companies may be insolvent but come to an arrangement with their creditors (either formally, within the terms of a voluntary arrangement under IA 1986, by means of a scheme of arrangement under the Companies Act (CA) 2006, or informally by means of some form debtor/creditor agreement). Such arrangements may well stave off the procedures outlined above.

Paradoxically, both individuals and companies may be 'technically insolvent' but avoid any formal insolvency procedures, because, for instance, their creditors do not seek to enforce their claims at that particular time. However, as we shall see, it is dangerous for either companies or individuals to ignore the fact of insolvency.

It is also something of a misnomer to regard 'receivership' as an insolvency process. As we shall see, receivership is a means of enforcement by a secured creditor. Although often a cause of the debtor's demise, it does not follow that the debtor is insolvent and the receivership process has no direct collective effect on the creditors as a whole. However, it is a reminder that in the UK, terminology is often used interchangeably and incorrectly (e.g. the company is going bankrupt) and as a result one must be very careful to identify the legal personality of the debtor and the insolvency process that has arisen or may arise, before one can move on to consider the effects and consequences of 'insolvency'.

Definitions

Consumer/trade debtor: there is no legal distinction of consequence between an individual who is unable to pay his personal debts (often termed a 'consumer debtor') and an individual whose debts are incurred in respect of his business activities (often termed a 'trade debtor'). However, a distinction is often drawn for statistical purposes between consumer and trade debtors.

Firm/partnership: commonly defined as a group of individuals joined for the purpose of common profit. A partnership has no legal personality distinct from its individual members.

Proceedings for partnership debts can be taken against the individual partners or against the name of the partnership (firm).

Limited partnership: formed in accordance with and regulated by the provisions of the Limited Partnership Act 1907. The partnership has no legal personality of its own. It consists of at least one general partner and at least one limited partner and is registered pursuant to the Act. Limited partners cannot be concerned in the management or control of the partnership and are liable only to the extent of their contribution to the partnership.

Limited liability partnership (LLP): formed in accordance with and regulated by the provisions of the Limited Liability Partnerships Act 2000 and the Limited Liability Partnerships Regulations 2001, SI 2001/1090, which came into force on 6 April 2001. The LLP has a separate legal identity from its members and it is liable to the full extent of its assets, while the liability of its individual members will be limited.

Registered company: not defined in IA 1986; however, the Companies Act 1985 provides that a 'company' is one incorporated under that Act or earlier Companies Acts.

Unregistered company: includes any association or company not registered in the UK under any Companies Act, past or present.

For reasons of space, this book focuses on the most common forms of insolvency process likely to be encountered by the general practitioner – bankruptcy, liquidation and administration. However, it also outlines individual and company voluntary arrangements, debt relief orders, schemes of arrangement and receivership (in its various forms).

The book deals in general only with individual and registered company insolvency. Trade unions, municipal/ecclesiastical corporations and societies incorporated by Royal Charter all lie outside the provisions of IA 1986, and any insolvency of such a body is dealt with by its own special provisions. It should also be noted that there are special provisions which deal with the insolvency of partnerships and unregistered companies (which crucially include 'foreign' companies and therefore raise issues of cross-border insolvency). Specialist works should be referred to when tackling issues relating to the insolvency of such entities.

1.3   WHAT IS BANKRUPTCY?

Definition

Bankruptcy is the legal status of an individual debtor arising through due legal process.

Although commonly used as a term to denote when a debtor is unable to pay his debts, bankruptcy is a legal status afforded to an individual, where the duties, rights and obligations of the debtor and creditor(s) are governed by specific laws.

Unlike liquidation, the parallel corporate insolvency procedure to bankruptcy, in which the winding-up process of a company ends in its ultimate demise by dissolution, bankruptcy fulfils two concurrent functions; as a creditor remedy for recovery of debt and a means for debtor financial rehabilitation.

This dual nature of bankruptcy laws was not always the case. As we have seen in **1.1**, bankruptcy laws originally only governed creditors' remedies and the regulation of affairs as between the conflicting creditors. The debtor's release from debt is a much more recent advance in the law and indeed it remains the case that in some jurisdictions the release from the disabilities of bankruptcy arises only on repayment of the entire debt.

As shown from the historical development of bankruptcy, the system now in place in the UK continues to balance the demands of bankruptcy as a means of creditor recovery against the interests of the debtor and the requirement for economic rehabilitation. Indeed, while bankruptcy was initially viewed as a privilege, earned in certain circumstances, to protect the debtor from unjust and oppressive creditor recovery action, now it is seen more as a means of facilitating financial rehabilitation. The Enterprise Act 2002 reforms made it clear that the legislature took the view that no stigma should attach to the bankruptcy, and that for the majority of individuals bankruptcy was merely a consequence of general economic activity. Debtors should thus be given a 'second chance' and be released from debt as soon as just and practicable.

Bankruptcy thus offers an individual the chance of financial rehabilitation and protection from individual creditors' actions. The bankruptcy system was and remains a careful balance between the rights of the debtor and the rights of the creditors.

Conversely, the fact that an individual cannot pay his debts does not mean that he will be bankrupt. As we shall see, measures of insolvency, such as the ability to pay debts as they fall due (cash flow) or liabilities exceeding assets (balance sheet), may be important in establishing whether bankruptcy is appropriate for an individual; however, if such measures do indicate that an individual is insolvent, it does not inevitably mean that an individual will be adjudged bankrupt. It should also be noted that an individual may be solvent on one test of insolvency but could still be adjudged bankrupt. Indeed, as we shall see, a debtor who chooses to ignore or refuses to meet a statutory demand will be deemed to be unable to pay his debts as they fall due and could therefore be adjudged bankrupt, irrespective of his actual financial position.

Bankruptcy is by its very nature a collective procedure which seeks to ensure that creditors are dealt with fairly and equitably. Any distribution to creditors is in accordance with a statutory order of priority and on a *pari passu* basis between creditors of the same class. Bankruptcy provides an opportunity for the financial rehabilitation of the debtor and, as a result, bankruptcy differs from liquidation. The liquidation of a company ultimately sees its demise (the dissolution of the company); in contrast, bankruptcy (since the Bankruptcy Acts of 1883 and 1914) allows for the release of a debtor from the effects of a bankruptcy and provides an opportunity for the individual to be freed from debt.

1.4 WHAT IS LIQUIDATION?

The word 'liquidation' is derived from the medieval Latin term *liquidare*, meaning to melt, make liquid, to clear and clarify. While insolvency is a factual status, i.e. an inability to pay debt, it is the liquidation process that resolves the chaos and disorder between creditors and debtor. This is done by reducing to order the debts of the company and seeking the realisation of the company's assets to the extent that they are able to meet the company's debts.

Lord Hoffmann in *Buchler v. Talbot; Re Leyland DAF Ltd* [2004] UKHL 9, [2004] 2 WLR 582 (HL), provided the following succinct description of the process (at [28]):

> The winding up of a company is a form of collective execution by all its creditors against all its available assets. The resolution or order for winding up divests the company of the beneficial interest in its assets. They become a fund which the company thereafter holds in trust to discharge its liabilities . . .

The use of the word 'trust' is apt, although as a matter of legal theory the use of the term remains contentious. On winding up, the company is no longer deemed to be the beneficial owner of its assets (*Re Oriental Inland Steam Co.* (1873–74) LR 9 Ch App 557). The unsecured creditors do not, however, acquire any beneficial interests in the assets; rather they acquire a right to have the assets administered in accordance with the statutory scheme provided by IA 1986 and the Insolvency Rules (IR) 1986, SI 1986/1925 (*Mitchell v. Carter* [1997] 1 BCLC 673). Unlike in bankruptcy, where the bankrupt's estate vests in the trustee in bankruptcy (IA 1986, s.306), in liquidation the company's assets remain vested in the company and do not transfer and vest in the liquidator (note, however, the potential application that may be made to vest company property in the liquidator by his official name (IA 1986, s.145) in cases of compulsory liquidation). As a result, the relationship between the company, acting through its liquidator, and its creditors has been described as a form of quasi-trust (*Lyall (P) and Sons Construction Co. Ltd v. Baker* [1933] 21 OR 286).

A practical effect of the liquidation process means that the members of the company are disenfranchised, their interest solely being in the equity of redemption. While it is correct to say that, pre-winding up, a company does not hold assets on trust for its members (it has of course its own distinct legal personality), the directors of the company are holding and dealing with assets in accordance with the company's memorandum and articles of association in a manner likely to promote the success of the company for the benefit of its members as a whole (CA 2006, s.172(1)). Similarly, on winding up, the company does not hold the assets for its creditors; rather, the liquidator deals with the assets in accordance with the statutory scheme for the benefit of the company's creditors as a whole. As a result the liquidator, like a director, is not a trustee but a fiduciary agent of the company.

It should be borne in mind that the realisation of the company's assets by the liquidator is subject to any secured interest on those assets. This means that in general a secured creditor is unaffected by liquidation and can enforce its security as it sees fit during the liquidation process. Therefore, liquidation does not alter the secured creditor's rights (*Mineral and Chemical Traders Pty Ltd* v. *T. Tymczyszyn Pty Ltd* (1994) 15 ACSR 398), the winding-up process being conducted for the benefit of the unsecured creditors.

1.5   WHAT IS RECEIVERSHIP?

As set out in **1.1**, receivership has long historical antecedents, with the centuries-old power of the Court of Chancery to appoint a receiver being exercised as an equitable remedy to protect and safeguard property or interests. A receiver would be appointed where the court, in the exercise of its flexible discretion, considered the appointment necessary, just and reasonable in all the circumstances (e.g. protection of a minor's property until he came of age, partnership property pending resolution of a partnership dispute).

The modern jurisdiction relating to court-appointed receivership is found in the Supreme Court Act 1981 (now renamed the Senior Courts Act 1981), s.37 and the Civil Procedure Rules 1998, SI 1998/3132 (CPR), Practice Direction 69, with the powers and role of the court-appointed receiver determined by court direction. The court-appointed receiver is an officer of the court and is not an agent of the company or a trustee. Any party who interferes with the court-appointed receiver's control of the property will be guilty of contempt of court. The court-appointed receiver will thus, in general, perform a very different role from the more commonly encountered out-of-court/extra-judicial receiver. It is this latter type of receiver, which is a much more recent construct, that will be referred to in this book.

The emergence of the out-of-court receiver arose in the nineteenth century as a matter of contractual agreement, typically between lender and borrower, which would enable the lender to protect his security by means of the appointment of a receiver over property subject to a mortgage or charge, without reference to the court. This led to statutory acknowledgement in respect of mortgages for land in the Law of Property Act 1925, s.101.

However, it should be noted that the role of such a receiver is limited. In *Re Manchester and Milford Rly Co.* (1880) 14 Ch D 645 Sir George Jessel MR stated:

A 'receiver' is a term which was well known in the Court of Chancery, as meaning a person who receives rents or other income paying ascertained outgoings, but who does not, if I may say so, manage the property in the sense of buying or selling or anything of that kind.

11

As a result, although the terms commonly used are a receiver or sometimes a Law of Property Act 1925 receiver (LPA receiver), in reality one is more likely to encounter a receiver and manager, whose additional powers (such as trading a business) are derived from the terms of the mortgage or charge. Without such additional powers a receiver may only receive income (rent or profit on land) while it is a manager who can be seen to control and if necessary trade or carry on business, in addition to being given a power of sale (*Gloucester County Bank* v. *Rudry Merthyr Steam and Home Coal Colliery Co.* [1895] 1 Ch 629. However, although the debenture may not specifically provide for the appointment of a receiver and manager, if it provides for the receiver having power to carry on the business of the (borrower) company, the receiver is in reality a receiver and manager (*Re Odessa Promotions Pty Ltd (in liquidation)* (1979) ACLC 32).

It should be kept in mind that receivership is not a collective remedy; it is an enforcement remedy pursued solely at the behest of the secured creditor. As a result, it is not a process dealt with in detail in this book, although, as we shall see, receivership often dovetails with collective insolvency processes such as liquidation and administration.

The receiver need not be an insolvency practitioner and need only be a person not otherwise disqualified under any relevant statutory provision.

A private receiver is not an officer of the court, but either agent for the appointing party or, commonly, where so provided, the deemed agent for the borrower. The receiver owes his primary duty to the appointor both in contract and in tort (*Gomba Holdings Ltd* v. *Homan* [1986] 3 All ER 94). A duty is also owed to the company over whose property the receiver is appointed, although as agent of the company the receiver is appointed 'not to receive directions from the directors but to give directions' (*Meigh* v. *Wickenden* [1942] 2 KB 160). A receiver's duty has been equated to the duties of a mortgagee (*Medforth* v. *Blake* [1999] 2 BCLC 221 and *Silven Properties Ltd* v. *Royal Bank of Scotland* [2003] EWCA Civ 1409).

It should be noted that the receiver is under no duty to sell (*Routestone Ltd* v. *Minories Finance Ltd* [1997] BCC 180) and/or the timing of the sale may be such that it is to the disadvantage of the debtor (*Bell* v. *Long* [2008] BPIR 1211). While the duty owed to parties other than appointor in the conduct of any sale is often said to be limited to acting in good faith (*Kennedy* v. *De Trafford* [1897] AC 180), this is probably now viewed as an oversimplification, with the duty being expressed by Lord Moulton as being to 'behave in conducting such realisation as a reasonable man would behave in the realisation of his own property' (*McHugh* v. *Union Bank of Canada* [1913] AC 299; see also *Cuckmere Brick Co. Ltd* v. *Mutual Finance Ltd* [1971] Ch 949). This 'extended' duty is not, however, a common law tortious duty of care but is an equitable one arising out of the mortgage relationship and owed to those with an equity of exoneration (*Downsview Nominees Ltd* v. *First City Corpn Ltd* [1993] AC 295) and extended to those who have a given a guarantee of the debt (*Burgess* v. *Vanstock* [1998] 2 BCLC 478). The duty has more recently been referred to as one which requires the receiver to take reasonable precautions and to exercise due diligence (*Yorkshire Bank* v. *Hall* [1999] 1 All ER 879). This does not, however, extend to improving the property's value, e.g. by obtaining planning permission (*Silven Properties Ltd* v. *Royal Bank of Scotland* [2003] EWCA Civ 1409). While this duty has been said not to be owed to ordinary unsecured creditors (*Northern Development (Holdings) Ltd* v. *UDT Securities* [1977] 1 All ER 747), it is possible that if a surplus payable to unsecured creditors would have been achieved, but for the receiver failing to take reasonable precautions (e.g. accepting a bid without proper independent valuation of the property) it may be possible to claim on equitable principles.

A receiver may be liable to third parties in tort, such as trespass (*Re Goldburg (No.2)* [1912] 1 KB 606), and in this respect a receiver needs to ensure that he is validly appointed (namely the mortgagee has the ability to appoint) to avoid such liability being owed to the company, or for conversion (*Standard Chartered Bank Ltd* v. *Walker* [1982] 1 WLR 1410).

Receivers are also distinguished between those appointed as administrative receivers (IA 1986, Part III) and those appointed as private receivers (e.g. LPA receivers and non-administrative receivers). The concept of administrative receivership developed in the 1960s from the increasingly wide powers granted under debentures to receivers and managers, whereby control could be taken of all or substantially all of the assets of the company. Regulation and reform of this type of receivership was introduced in IA 1986, which at the same time as defining 'administrative receivership' (IA 1986, s.29) introduced the concept of administration for those companies that did not enjoy the advantages brought by a lender's floating charge.

An administrative receiver is defined as an office holder in IA 1986 and as a consequence has certain powers and responsibilities (IA 1986, ss.233–236). The Enterprise Act 2002 significantly reformed this area of the law, prohibiting the appointment of administrative receivers in respect of securities created after 15 September 2003, save in nine specific cases (IA 1986, ss.72B–72G).

1.6   WHAT IS ADMINISTRATION?

Administration is a legal process used to facilitate the 'rescue' of an insolvent company, and involves the appointment of an administrator.

The process is initiated by:

- court order;
- the filing of a requisite notice at the court (the out-of-court route) by a qualifying floating charge holder; or
- the filing of a requisite notice at the court (the out-of-court route) by the company or its directors.

The administrator is appointed to manage the company's affairs, business and property (IA 1986, Sched.B1, para.1(1)), and a company is deemed to be 'in administration' while the appointment of the administrator has effect.

The administrator is an officer of the court, whether appointed by the court, a qualifying floating charge holder, or the company or its directors (IA 1986, Sched.B1, para.5). This has a number of important consequences:

1. A third party may be guilty of contempt of court if it seeks unjustifiably to interfere with the performance of the administrator's duties (see *Re Paramount Airways Ltd* [1990] BCC 130 and *Re Sabre International Products Ltd* [1991] BCC 694), although it must be noted that this remains a rarely used remedy.

2. The administrator may seek the direction of the court if thought necessary to assist in the discharge of his duties. Conversely, the court retains an inherent jurisdiction to direct an administrator to take a particular course of action.

3. The administrator must act fairly and reasonably, in accordance with the so-called 'rule in *Ex parte James*' (see *Re Condon, ex p. James* (1873–74) LR 9 Ch App 609). Although somewhat ill-defined in scope, this 'rule' has been taken to mean that an administrator should be candid with the court (see *Re Ah Toy* (1986) 4 ACLC 480), providing evidence of all relevant circumstances, whether that assists the administrator or otherwise (see *Re Colt Telecom Group plc (No.2)* [2003] BPIR 324). The administrator should also not rely on the strict letter of the law, if it produces 'dishonourable', unfair or obtuse results and must act independently and impartially and be seen to do so (see *Re Intercontinental Properties Pty Ltd* (1977) 2 ACLC 488).

The administrator acts as agent of the company (IA 1986, Sched.B1, para.69) and may do anything necessary or expedient for the management of the affairs, business and property of the company (IA 1986, Sched.B1, para.59(1)).

Under these general provisions, and specifically under the powers listed in IA 1986, Sched.B1, the administrator has very wide discretionary powers. The court is unlikely to intervene on any question of commercial judgment exercised by the administrator, save in cases of manifest bad faith, irrationality or unreasonableness/ negligence (see *T&D Industries plc* [2000] 1 BCLC 471; *Re Transbus International Ltd* [2004] 2 All ER 911; *Re Lehman Brothers International Ltd* [2009] BCC 632).

The powers of an administrator over the company are wider than those conferred on a director of the company and extend to the management of the affairs of the company, including the power to remove/appoint directors (IA 1986, Sched.B1, para.61) and the ability to call a meeting of members or creditors (IA 1986, Sched.B1, para.62).

Like a director, the administrator owes fiduciary duties to the company (see *Oldham v. Kyrris* [2004] BPIR 165), although unless it is specifically so provided the administrator will not incur personal liability for contracts he enters into on behalf of the company. Importantly, the administrator can claim an indemnity from the company's assets for any liabilities incurred.

Under common law rules of agency a party dealing/contracting with the administrator in good faith and for value need not enquire into whether the administrator is acting within his powers (this is also expressly provided in IA 1986, Sched.B1, para.59(3)).

Most importantly, the administrator (unlike a receiver, whose duties are primarily referable to the secured creditor who has appointed him) has a responsibility to manage the company for the benefit of all creditors and all those interested in the estate (IA 1986, Sched.B1, para.3(2)).

The administration process is collective in nature. This is only modified in cases where the administrator is appointed by a qualifying floating charge holder, and the only likely return is that to the secured creditor who has appointed the administrator; even then the administrator must not act in a way which unnecessarily harms the interests of the creditors as a whole (IA 1986, Sched.B1, para.3(4)).

See *Zegra III Holdings Inc.*, sub nom. *BLV Realty Organization Ltd* v. *Batten* [2009] EWHC 2994 (Ch), where it was held that the duty to act in the interests of the creditors as a whole did not mean that treatment of those creditors needed to be in an identical fashion; 'unequal treatment' was not necessarily unfair where it was for sound commercial reasons. However, it should be noted that an administrator owes no general common law duty to a specific unsecured creditor absent the creation of some form of special relationship (*Charalambous* v. *B&C Associates* [2009] EWHC 2601 (Ch)).

A key feature of the administration process is the moratorium that comes into effect, which prevents a creditor during the administration period from enforcing the payment of debt or from exercising certain rights (proprietary or otherwise), whether by an insolvency or other legal processes. In theory, this allows the company breathing space in which calmly to evaluate its prospects, free from creditor pressure, with the hope of achieving financial rehabilitation via proposals formulated by the administrator and approved by the creditors. In practice, the rescue and survival of the debtor company is rare, the company exiting administration and being returned to its directors and members occurring in less than 5 per cent of cases.

1.7 WHAT IS A STATUTORY DEMAND?

In the case of both bankruptcy and insolvent liquidation, a common precondition for the commencement of the procedure by a creditor is the need to discharge an evidential burden demonstrating the debtor's inability to pay a debt (see IA 1986, s.267(2) (a condition for the presentation of a bankruptcy petition) and IA 1986, s.122(1)(f) (a ground upon which a company may be wound up)).

As we shall see, while this can be discharged in a number of ways, a common and convenient method available to the creditor is the service of a statutory demand on the debtor.

Definitions

A **statutory demand** is a formal demand for payment of a debt made by a creditor to a debtor under the terms of IA 1986 and in accordance with IR 1986.

If the debtor fails to comply with or contest the demand within three weeks of service, the debtor is deemed to be unable to pay the debt. This provides the creditor with evidence sufficient to present a bankruptcy petition (for individual debtors) or a winding-up petition (for corporate debtors).

A statutory demand is a demand for payment of debt which must be in a standard form as prescribed by IA 1986:

(a)   non-compliance with a statutory demand is one of the two ways in which a creditor can show that a personal debtor is unable to pay a debt (IA 1986, s.268(1)(a)); and

(b)   non-compliance with a statutory demand is one of the three ways a creditor can show that a corporate debtor is unable to pay a debt (IA 1986, s.123(1)(a)).

(See also Insolvency (Amendment) Rules 1987, SI 1987/1919, forms 6.1, 6.2 and 6.3 (individuals) and Form 4.1 (company).)

The statutory demand is not an insolvency process or procedure per se, but may act as a prelude to the formal insolvency procedures of bankruptcy and liquidation (*Re a Debtor (No.1 of 1987) (Lancaster)* [1989] 1 WLR 271). It could also be used to evidence a company's insolvency in cases where administration is being sought. If the statutory demand is not satisfied by the debtor, the debtor will be deemed unable to pay the debt and insolvency is therefore presumed.

The service of a statutory demand on a debtor is a right of action available to an individual creditor and does not bear any collective nature, contrasting with creditors' petitions for bankruptcy and winding up. There is no register of statutory demands, nor is a statutory demand a court process that requires approval before service. This contrasts with the former (pre-1986) bankruptcy notice procedure, where notice of debt and due payment was issued by the courts. A claim made by a statutory demand remains entirely a matter between the creditor and the debtor.

It should also be noted that it is possible to serve a statutory demand on an individual or a company out of the jurisdiction without the need to seek permission of the court. However, where a demand is to be served the creditor must carefully follow the procedure as set out in Practice Direction, Insolvency Proceedings Civil Procedure 2012, para.13.

If the demand is complied with, the matter rests there. If it is not complied with, it is a matter for the creditor to decide whether to proceed further; it is not obliged to do so. The demand remains effective for four months, after which time the creditor may proceed with the unsatisfied demand only after satisfying the court that it is right to do so. The creditor's reasoning for this is set out in the witness statement supporting the petition (see IR 1986, rule 6.12(7)). The creditor may decide that proceeding with a collective insolvency procedure (i.e. bankruptcy or compulsory winding up) is not in its best interests and/or that the costs of doing so will be disproportionate.

1.8 ADVISING A DEBTOR

Checklist

Advising a debtor

- Is the debtor actually insolvent?
- Can the debtor 'work out' his/its financial difficulties?
- What do the creditors know?
- What do the creditors want?
- Is an informal compromise available?
- Is financial reconstruction feasible?

1.8.1 Is the debtor insolvent?

Very often those facing financial difficulty are not best placed to assess their own situation. The stresses and strains that inevitably accompany financial problems may cause undue panic, or alternatively a 'head in the sand' mentality. Neither approach has much to commend it. Those advising insolvent debtors need to assess quickly whether the individual or company is truly insolvent. How much are the creditors owed? How many creditors are there? When are payments due?

This evaluation may be easier in some instances than in others. Where a judgment has been obtained against the debtor and it remains unsatisfied and/or where a statutory demand has been issued, the fact that a debtor has an inability to pay his or its debts as they fall due is more readily identifiable. In other instances, an independent assessment from an accountant may be required, which in certain circumstances may be best provided by an insolvency practitioner.

It should be remembered that in many small businesses, the way a bookkeeper has been maintaining the accounts may hide or mask insolvency (although this is not unknown in the largest multinational companies, e.g. Enron and Parmalat). This may be completely unintentional or a symptom of fraud by part or all of the management team, and the debtor may not become aware of his insolvency until creditor pressure has become acute. For reasons that we will explore in more detail, it is important that company directors take proper professional advice, which will reveal the true state of the finances of the company. Furthermore, with the introduction of bankruptcy restrictions orders (BROs) it is even more important for individuals to be aware of the true state of their finances, as those who are reckless and/or have no regard to their liabilities when taking on credit may be penalised.

From time to time an individual or a solvent company will avoid paying a debt, whether through oversight, because of a point of principle or because there is a genuine dispute and/or cross-claim. However, if execution on a judgment debt is returned unsatisfied and/or a statutory demand ignored, this is taken as evidence of an 'inability to pay debt' and allows a creditor to petition for bankruptcy or winding up. As we shall see, a creditor of a corporate debtor has an ability to petition for the winding up of a company without first serving a statutory demand. However, this is a more risky strategy and must be carefully thought through.

Checklist

Advising an individual debtor

Having established that:

(a)   the legal personality of the debtor is an individual; and

(b)   the individual debtor is in fact insolvent,

the legal adviser can then determine what options are available to the individual insolvent debtor.

Options available are:

- informal arrangements with creditors;
- deed of arrangement;
- contractual composition;
- individual voluntary arrangement; or
- bankruptcy.

Advising a corporate debtor

Having established that:

(a)   the legal personality of the debtor is a company; and

(b)   the corporate debtor is in fact insolvent,

the legal adviser can then determine what options are available to the insolvent corporate debtor.

Options available are:

- informal arrangements with creditors;
- Companies Act schemes of arrangement;
- CVA;
- receivership;
- administrative receivership;
- administration; or
- liquidation.

1.8.2 'Honesty is the best policy'

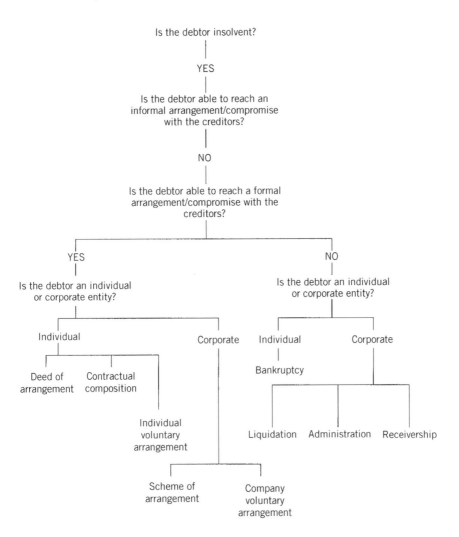

Figure 1.1   Options available to a debtor

Surprisingly, when a debtor faces financial crisis, the position the creditors may take is often overlooked. Have they been approached and appraised of the debtor's financial situation? It is remarkable how accommodating a fully informed creditor can turn out to be. Unfortunately, what is more common is that the debtor has avoided tackling its creditors, keeping them in the dark and providing increasingly unlikely excuses. It should be borne in mind that the opportunity to resolve the issue of an unpaid debt in a manner satisfactory to both parties reduces over time.

Debtor's excuses: good and bad

- The cheque is in the post.
- The cheque is waiting to be signed.
- What invoice?
- We've lost the invoice, send another.
- The goods haven't arrived yet.
- You've just missed our cheque run.
- Your goods/services are rubbish.
- We have ceased trading.
- The bill wasn't delivered at the right time.
- If I pay you I won't be able to pay my current bills.
- You spoke to me in a hateful manner, so I am not paying.
- I have better things to do than pay my debts.
- The owner has been buried with his cheque book.
- My ex-wife took your cheque to get even with me.
- The director went for an operation and never returned, as he ran off with the nurse.
- I do not speak English.
- We're in the middle of an armed robbery.
- All names are put in a hat. If yours is pulled out you will get paid. If not, it will stay in the hat until next week.
- Not now, it's the office party.
- Its not a valid debt as my vindictive ex-wife ran off with the company credit card.
- The director is in Barbados and cannot be disturbed.
- You will be paid if I make enough at the next car boot sale.
- The cheque flew out of the car window and on to the M25.
- I just got back from my luxury holiday; it cost more that I thought so I no longer have the funds to pay you.
- My wife has been kidnapped and I need the money to get her back.
- The director has been detained by customs officials at Heathrow.
- I have just been shot by an intruder. Can you call back later?

Sources: Bizarre excuses taken from **www.payontime.co.uk** from research conducted for The Better Payment Practice Company by Alex Lawrie, 16 February 1999, Press Release Credit Services Association Survey, **www.bbc.co.uk**, report 11 November 2002 and **www.realbusiness.co.uk** report August 2008.

Misinformation, or simply a failure to advise creditors, is a primary cause of eventual dispute. It is also much more difficult to persuade creditors to offer some degree of forbearance when they have not been informed of the debtor's true position.

When advising an insolvent debtor, one needs to assess the situation. Often, the first step is to discuss the matter with the debtor's principal creditors.

1.8.3   What does the creditor want?

What exactly do the principal creditors require? Blood out of a stone? Clearly, creditors' priorities will differ. It may be more important for some creditors to receive at least a proportion of the debt, but in time; for others, the amount paid may be more critical than the timing. For some creditors, the debt itself may be somewhat irrelevant, e.g. a supplier to a business may consider it preferable to continue supplying, perhaps on revised terms (e.g. cash on delivery) and leave the historic debts to one side for the time being. This type of arrangement may give a small business an opportunity to work out its difficulties and get back on an even keel.

There are also other non-monetary considerations that a creditor may take into account. Could an individual or a small business offer additional services in lieu of payment? Could the debtor company offer equity in exchange for debt?

The adviser must also consider the number of creditors. If there are only one or two creditors it may be relatively easy to undertake this type of exercise, establishing with them individually what their requirements are. Where there are a large number of creditors, each with an ability to force the insolvent debtor into a technical insolvency procedure, such an approach may be more problematic. This does not, however, mean that there are no alternatives for the insolvent debtor, although a more formal procedure/approach may be required.

While in theory debtors should be aware of their creditors and their demands, it is often the case that the debtor is unaware that a creditor is pressing for payment until served with a formal demand. A debtor may also wait for a final demand and/or have a policy of paying only after a specified number of days after payment becomes due. The formal demand may take the form of a letter before action (i.e. unless payment is received within a specified time legal proceedings will be commenced) or be in the form of a statutory demand.

1.9   ADVISING A CREDITOR

1.9.1   'Closing the stable door'

This book is concerned with the options available to a creditor who has given credit to a debtor who is or subsequently becomes insolvent. Outside times of severe economic recession the creditor will hope that this is a rare occurrence, but to avoid the possibility and/or to protect the creditor's position on giving credit the following safeguards could be considered.

Checklist

Creditor's safeguards

● Think twice about offering credit terms.

21

- Ask whether the customer/borrower is creditworthy and insist on proof.
- Offer only limited credit terms and keep a constant check on exposure.
- Provide incentives for early payment of debt.
- Obtain security, e.g. charge over debtor assets and/or guarantees from third parties.
- Revise terms and conditions, e.g. supply goods subject to a retention of title.
- Reach agreement that any debts arising are paid by regular instalments.
- Review the position of the debtor's other creditors; in the event of debtor insolvency will others get in first?
- When a debt is owed only supply further goods/services on condition of cash payment.
- Pry into the debtor's financial situation; if a debt arises understand what a realistic financial settlement is.
- Take up references and undertake commercial credit checks.
- Undertake investigations, possibly at Companies House, on the county court register of judgments and at the Land Registry.

Even the most prudent businesses can find themselves with 'bad debt'. In such circumstances the following questions need to be asked of the creditor.

Checklist

Advising a creditor with bad debt

- Is the creditor's claim against an individual or a corporate debtor?
- What is the nature of the creditor's claim?
- Is the debt disputed?
- Has a judgment been obtained in respect of the debt?
- Has the creditor taken any step to enforce payment of the debt?
- Has the creditor some form of security for the debt?
- Is the debtor insolvent?
- Is the debtor subject to any formal insolvency procedure?
- What is the creditor's attitude in regard to the debt and the debtor?

1.9.2   Legal personality of the debtor

The options available to a creditor depend on whether the creditor is secured or unsecured, the type of claim that it possesses against the debtor and the legal personality of the debtor (individual or corporate?). The options and procedures differ depending on the answers to these questions.

The fact that the debtor may be insolvent is not per se of concern to the creditor. Until such time as a formal insolvency procedure has been commenced, the creditor is free to seek payment of its debt by any legal means due. There is no collective responsibility to other creditors and the law allows those with rights against the debtor to take enforcement action on a 'first come, first served' basis. As we shall see, however, the completion of any execution must take place before the commencement of the insolvency procedure.

Ultimately, if the creditor is unable to obtain payment/enforce its debt, the options for the creditor are to do nothing and wait to see if the insolvency of the debtor leads to a formal insolvency process, or to take one of the following steps.

If the debtor is an individual:

- Petition for his bankruptcy.

If the debtor is a company:

- Apply for an administration order.
- Appoint an administrator (if the creditor holds a qualifying floating charge).
- Appoint an administrative receiver (if the creditor is a floating charge holder with security created before 15 September 2003).
- Appoint a receiver (if the creditor has fixed charge security).
- Petition for compulsory liquidation of the company.

Where the debtor is unable to pay its debts as they fall due it may be committing an offence by taking further credit, continuing to trade, etc. It is incumbent on the debtor to consider whether formal insolvency procedures should follow.

1.9.3 Nature of the creditor's claim

Before the creditor can be advised to commence any form of insolvency procedure in respect of the debt, the nature of the creditor's claim must be established.

If the creditor wishes to present a statutory demand as the precursor to bankruptcy or compulsory liquidation, the debt must be unsecured, over £750 and undisputed.

In the case of an individual debtor, there is provision for the debtor to apply to court for an order setting aside the statutory demand. Indeed, the statutory demand must state the court to which the debtor must apply if it disputes the demand.

In the case of a corporate debtor, where a statutory demand has been served, if the debt is disputed and the creditor refuses to withdraw the demand, the debtor may take injunctive proceedings to restrain the presentation of a winding-up petition. The creditor in such circumstances can be at risk of indemnity costs and damages should it act unreasonably by failing to withdraw an unmeritorious demand (see *Ross & Craig (a firm)* v. *Williamson* [2006] All ER (D) 139 (Mar)).

If the debt is disputed, the creditor's route is to apply to court for judgment. The debtor is placed in considerable difficulty if a bankruptcy petition or winding-up petition is based on the judgment debt. The court hearing the insolvency proceedings will usually not look behind the judgment debt; therefore it will be incumbent upon the debtor to apply to court to set aside the judgment. At best, the debtor can expect an adjournment of the petition pending the application to set aside the judgment/order.

A creditor obtaining a judgment debt also has the advantage that it can (prior to the commencement of an insolvency procedure) enforce the debt by the following means:

- writ of *fi fa*/warrant of execution;
- charging order;
- attachment of earnings (in the case of an individual); or
- third party proceedings (formerly known as garnishee proceedings).

The creditor has a carefully balanced decision as to whether to seek to enforce its debt or to move immediately to the insolvency procedure. This will depend on the creditor's attitude to the debt and the current position of the debtor.

Table 1.1   Pros and cons of taking enforcement proceedings

Pros	Cons
• Proprietorial nature of remedy – 'first in first out'	• Delay
• Potentially better result for creditor than in insolvency	• Reliance on court procedure/ mechanisms
• Failure to execute a judgment debt can provide a ground for petitioning for bankruptcy/ winding up which is not open to challenge	• Additional costs
	• Futile, if it is inevitable that the debtor will not pay

Table 1.2   Pros and cons of taking insolvency proceedings

Pros	Cons
• Speed of process	• Collective nature of insolvency procedure
• Finality	• No better return than other unsecured creditors
• 'Ultimate' enforcement action	• Delay in obtaining any payment (dividend)
• Simplicity	• Cost procedures or commencement of procedures
	• Cost of the insolvency procedures, eating into the debtor's estate

If the debtor is not subject to any existing insolvency procedure and there remains a possibility of recovery by means of enforcement by the creditor, this option should generally be pursued. This book does not extend to detailing forms of enforcement procedure, as the primary focus is on the situation where the debtor is insolvent and therefore 'unable to pay its debts'.

If, however, an enforcement procedure has been tried and failed, or it is inevitable that no payment will be received, the creditor is left with the option of commencing some form of insolvency procedure. As previously discussed, the procedure is generally initiated after the service of a statutory demand.

PART I

Pre-commencement considerations

CHAPTER 2

Advising a personal debtor

The general issues facing a debtor, whether an individual or a corporate debtor, were assessed in **1.8**. In this chapter we consider matters specific to an individual personal debtor, exploring options when faced with a statutory demand, bankruptcy and alternatives to bankruptcy.

2.1   STATUTORY DEMAND AND THE PERSONAL DEBTOR

2.1.1   Debtor's considerations on being served a statutory demand

---

Checklist

The debtor needs to consider:

1.   Is the debt demanded disputed?
2.   Can the demand be set aside/disputed on any other grounds?
3.   Irrespective of the answer to (1) or (2), is the debtor otherwise insolvent? If so, professional advice from an insolvency practitioner is almost certainly necessary and appropriate insolvency procedures should be considered.
4.   If the answer to (1) or (2) is no, can the debtor pay the debt demanded?
5.   If the answer to (4) is no, can the debtor make an offer to secure or compound the debt?
6.   If the answer to (4) and (5) is no, is the creditor going to proceed to take further action?
7.   If the answer to (6) is yes, the debtor should consider whether some form of alternative insolvency procedure is feasible and in the best interests of other creditors.
8.   If the answer to (7) is no, should the debtor do nothing?

On being served with a statutory demand the debtor must assess whether:

* the debt is disputed;
* there is a genuine or serious cross-claim; and
* he is able to pay the demand within the 21-day period.

The adviser should carefully discuss with the alleged debtor his attitude on being served a demand. Does the debtor admit the debt; is it a case of he would pay if he could? Are there other debts; is this the tip of the iceberg? Is the debtor prepared to go bankrupt?

The cautious debtor could legitimately take the view that even though he disputes the demand and/or has a cross-claim, to avoid any possibility of bankruptcy proceedings it may be wise to offer some form of security pending resolution of the dispute. This could involve the payment of the disputed sum into an account held in escrow.

A debtor who has a genuine dispute concerning the debt and/or a cross-claim will generally be best advised to demand the agreement of the creditor to 'withdraw' the demand (i.e. undertake not to present a petition based on the non-compliance with the statutory demand). If a creditor proceeds with a demand when it is known or should be known that the debt is disputed, the creditor can be punished with severe costs sanctions.

Consequently, notice of the dispute/cross-claim should normally be sufficient. The raising of a bona fide dispute on service of a statutory demand does not prevent the creditor from taking legal proceedings to establish the debt. However, as we shall see, if an agreement to withdraw the demand cannot be reached within 18 days, the debtor is obliged to make an application to court to set aside the demand.

However, if the debt is not disputed but the debtor cannot immediately pay, the debtor may be best advised to put an offer of compromise to the creditor. This may involve payment by instalments, or postponement of payment to a later date and/or an offer of security. Before making any such offer, the debtor does need to consider the position of other creditors – it is pointless seeking agreement with one creditor if another will be 'stepping into their shoes'. However, there is no obligation on the creditor to accept anything less than that which it is entitled to.

If the debt is not disputed and/or any offer of settlement has been refused, yet for some reason the creditor decides not to act on the demand, the debtor is in a difficult position: a presumption of insolvency has arisen. Consequently, if further credit is taken and/or losses are incurred at a time when the debtor knows he is insolvent, and the individual debtor is subsequently declared bankrupt, he may become subject to a BRO.

As a result, if a demand is served and the debtor cannot comply with it, irrespective of whether the creditor decides to proceed, the debtor is best advised to seek immediate professional guidance from an insolvency specialist, such as a lawyer or an insolvency practitioner. The same applies even if the debt is disputed but the debtor is unable to pay other debts falling due.

An individual served with a statutory demand may apply to court for an order seeking to set it aside (IR 1986, rule 6.4); as we shall see in **Chapter 3**, this remedy is not available to a corporate debtor. As the remedy available to the alleged debtor is exercised in the equitable discretion of the court, it is best that the alleged debtor acts fairly and reasonably by giving the creditor reasonable opportunity to 'withdraw' the demand. This will provide the alleged debtor with grounds for recovery of legal costs should it eventually need to commence legal proceedings.

Checklist

Setting aside a statutory demand – possible grounds

- The debt is disputed on substantial grounds.
- The debt is not payable immediately.
- Only part of the debt is admitted. (Note that it is prudent to pay/make an offer to pay the admitted part. A pending appeal procedure is not generally sufficient reason to set aside a demand, although the court would consider this as a factor on the hearing of the bankruptcy petition, which might well be adjourned pending the appeal.)
- A creditor holds security for the debt demanded.
- The debtor possesses a counterclaim, set-off or cross-claim for a sum equal to or exceeding the value of the claim.
- Execution on a court judgment has been stayed (*Re a Debtor (No.960 of 1992)* [1993] STC 218, although the fact that the debtor was appealing against a tax assessment did not justify the setting aside of a statutory demand).
- The statutory demand does not comply with the Insolvency Rules. A debtor relying on this ground must, however, take note that the court will now avoid excessive respect for the formalities which beset the previous insolvency regime. See IR 1986, rule 7.55 and *Oben* v. *Blackman* [2000] BPIR 302 where the failure of a creditor to comply with rule 6.8 (the failing to state the consideration of the debt) was an insufficient ground to justify the dismissal of a bankruptcy petition.
- The undisputed debt does not exceed £750 (*Re a Debtor (Nos.49 and 50 of 1992)* [1995] Ch 66 (CA). If the demand is partially disputed, leaving an undisputed amount below £750, the court will generally exercise its discretion and dismiss the petition.
- The claim is time-barred. (See *Re a Debtor (No.50A-SD-1995)* [1997] Ch 310, where a bankruptcy petition was dismissed, as it was founded on a judgment debt obtained over six years previously. The court held that the presentation of the petition was an 'action' within the meaning of the Limitation Act 1980 and hence time-barred. A statutory demand in respect of a debt which is time-barred by reason of the Limitation Act 1980 will be set aside.)
- Any other grounds (IR 1986, rule 6.5(4)(d)). (The Insolvency Rules do not specify what other grounds could be sufficient to set aside the demand.)

Listed above are some potential grounds, but others may well exist where the court considers it fair and reasonable to set aside the demand. However, it should be noted that the court is more likely to consider issues of equity and fairness on the hearing of the bankruptcy petition rather than on the hearing of an application to set aside a statutory demand.

In **Chapter 4** the process, procedure (see **4.1.5**) and considerations that arise on application to set aside a statutory demand are considered in full detail.

2.2 INFORMAL ARRANGEMENTS WITH CREDITORS

At the end of 2011, personal debt in the UK totalled £1.451 trillion. The Office for Budget Responsibility estimates that by 2017 personal debt in the UK will reach

£2.045 trillion, with an average debt per household of £78,669. With such a level of personal debt it is not surprising that there has been a proliferation of debt advisers specialising in providing advice and/or debt counselling services to individuals.

The advantage to the individual of employing the services of such advisers is the advisers' knowledge of the approach taken by some creditors, e.g. credit card companies and banks. The disadvantage is the cost which can be attached to their advice – realistically, the insolvent debtor may be better advised using that money to put forward a more advantageous proposal to his creditors. Furthermore, the area is currently under-regulated and many advisers are employed or work on high commissions for organisations offering debt consolidation loans or in some cases are specifically seeking to 'sell' debt management plans and/or individual voluntary arrangements (IVAs). More than ever before, a debtor must be wary of the advice being given and ensure that it is truly independent.

A difficult issue for any adviser to an insolvent debtor is to determine whether to 'front' any offer to the creditors. The creditors may feel that if the insolvent debtor can afford the services of a professional adviser he can afford to pay their debts. This is certainly more common where the debts are smaller. However, where there is a complex individual insolvency situation creditors often accept that it is right and proper for an individual to seek professional advice and would not be surprised if an adviser put forward proposals on behalf of his client. This is an issue, however, that requires careful thought and planning with the debtor.

2.2.1 Informal arrangements

Whether with the assistance of an adviser or, more likely, as a result of negotiation conducted solely by the debtor, the most common means of resolving a financial difficulty is for the individual to come to an informal agreement with creditors, or at least one or two of his major creditors.

An agreed repayment schedule may allow for the gradual discharge of the whole debt over a period of time or alternatively may guarantee a percentage return to the creditors. This latter option is often taken where the individual debtor can obtain funding from a third party. A common example of this is where a relative of the debtor offers money to the individual's creditors in return for their forbearance on the enforcement of the debt owed.

Table 2.1 Pros and cons of an informal arrangement with creditors

Pros of an informal arrangement with creditors	Cons of an informal arrangement with creditors
• Flexibility for the debtor – in time and content	• Creditors may take enforcement proceedings at any time

Pros of an informal arrangement with creditors	Cons of an informal arrangement with creditors
• Less costly	• A minority creditor could scupper plans which may be acceptable to the majority
• Less publicity	• Lacks independent scrutiny of the debtor's position
• Less third party cost may result in better return for the creditors	• Creditors' demands may cause undue hardship to the debtor, who may be better advised to seek immediate bankruptcy
• Provides the creditor with option to take action at a later date	• No formal moratorium is available while terms are being negotiated

An informal arrangement can be totally flexible (in both content and time). It will incur less cost than a formal insolvency proceeding and is a matter of private concern between the debtor and creditor(s). It has the attraction to the creditors that it may result in higher returns, particularly if a third party is willing to provide funds which would not otherwise be available through a formal insolvency procedure.

The single most significant drawback to reaching any informal arrangement is the fact that creditors are still left with a right to pursue their individual legal remedies. Consequently, while one creditor may be willing to accept a compromise put forward, another could scupper the plan by taking action to recover its debt and/or force the bankruptcy of the individual. As a consequence, where the debtor has a large number of individual creditors, an informal arrangement may be unattractive.

2.2.2 Deeds of arrangements/compositions

Alongside the procedures for IVAs introduced by IA 1986 there remains the possibility of an arrangement governed by the Deeds of Arrangement Act 1914. In practice, this procedure is cumbersome and little used. Indeed, by the time the Cork Committee reported in 1982, it recommended the repeal of the Act. Despite this, the Act still remains on the statute book.

An arrangement which requires acceptance by a simple majority of creditors can involve a composition of debt (*Re Lee* [1920] 2 KB 200) or an assignment of the debtor's property to a trustee, who would then deal with the creditors' claims in accordance with the terms of a scheme of arrangement (*Re Lipton Ltd* v. *Bell* [1924] 1 KB 701) in return for which the debtor would be released from his debt. The deed of arrangement requires registration within seven days with the Registrar at the Insolvency Service's Insolvency Practitioner Unit in Birmingham, the last deed being registered in 2004.

The procedure avoids the need to appoint a nominee and report to the court and may avoid the necessity of calling a creditors' meeting. However, in practice it has little to commend it compared with the IVA procedures available under IA 1986, particularly as the arrangement does not bind non-assenting creditors; those not bound by the scheme have the right to bring enforcement and/or bankruptcy proceedings against the individual debtor.

A further alternative to an IVA is a contractual composition between a debtor and his creditors. Such a composition could be any form of agreement leading to a multiparty contract governed by common law. This has advantages over arrangements under the Deeds of Arrangement Act 1914 since contracting creditors may be contractually prevented from taking steps to enforce their claims and/or force the bankruptcy of the debtor. It also has the advantages of avoiding publicity; of being flexible (in both content and term); and may be less costly than an IVA.

However, the problem remains that non-contracting parties are not bound by the terms of the agreement. They can take steps to enforce their claims and the insolvent debtor's property is not ring-fenced for the benefit of the creditors who are contracting parties, unless it is in some way written in trust.

For the creditors, a contractual composition has a distinct disadvantage, in that there is no opportunity for independent investigation, assessment of the insolvent debtor's position and policing of the arrangement, all of which are tasks dealt with by the nominee/supervisor of an IVA.

2.3 INDIVIDUAL VOLUNTARY ARRANGEMENTS (IVAS)

2.3.1 Introduction

Definitions

An **IVA** is a proposal put forward by a debtor to his creditors for a composition in satisfaction of debts or a scheme of arrangement of his affairs in accordance with the provisions of IA 1986. If approved by the requisite majority it acts as a statutory binding on the debtor's creditors.

A **composition** is an arrangement between a debtor and creditor under which a creditor compromises or releases their rights against the debtor in respect of a debt and in return receives whatever payment terms are being offered by the debtor.

A **scheme of arrangement** is an arrangement between a debtor and creditor which involves something other than a release or discharge of the creditor's debts, such as a moratorium or an agreed repayment plan, and may include the debtor handing over assets to be administered by the supervisor of the IVA in accordance with the proposals.

A **supervisor** is an insolvency practitioner or person licensed to administer the terms of the IVA, ensuring the debtor's compliance and dealing with creditors' claims once the IVA has been approved.

Recently there has been a very large rise in the numbers of IVAs (e.g. 3,002 in 1991; 6,269 in 2001; and 49,056 in 2011). This is in part a reflection of the success of the procedure since its introduction in 1986, but it also reflects the state of the economy, the large rise in personal debt levels and the aggressive marketing of the procedure by a new breed of firm.

Provided a bankruptcy petition has not been presented against the individual, or the court has not ordered (under IA 1986, s.273) the appointment of an insolvency practitioner to enquire into the debtor's affairs and report (IA 1986, s.253(5)), an individual may at any time initiate a proposal for an IVA with creditors. An enquiry into the debtor's affairs may be ordered by the court of its own volition, if the debtor has petitioned for his own bankruptcy and the court considers it necessary to explore alternatives.

An IVA is, at its simplest, a deal between an individual and his creditors and is generally used as an alternative to bankruptcy where the individual is insolvent. An IVA may be of use to a debtor who can satisfy the balance sheet test but does not have enough liquid assets to satisfy the cash flow test of insolvency. There is no technical requirement that the debtor must be insolvent to propose an IVA, although the proposal is unlikely to be acceptable to creditors if the debtor has an ability to pay his debts.

A concern often shared by creditors is that the debtor is seeking to avoid paying his debts in full and discloses debts which are either overstated or bogus. This may involve the collusion of third parties, that will put forward spurious claims. These third parties may have some business or social relationship with the debtor and will approve the terms of the proposal; thus 'connected' parties will bind the minority creditors. In these circumstances, however, it should be remembered that the unconnected creditors would probably be able to set aside the IVA on grounds of unfair prejudice and/or material irregularity (IA 1986, s.262(1)).

Although an IVA is deemed to be a statutory binding – binding an individual's creditors to the terms of the proposal – it is at heart a contract between the debtor and his creditors (see *Raja* v. *Rubin* [1999] BPIR 575).

The IVA may be either a composition in satisfaction of debt, in which an individual retains control of his assets and agrees to pay certain sums to his creditors, or a scheme of arrangement, whereby the individual hands over assets to a trustee who administers them in accordance with the terms of the scheme. In reality the flexibility of the voluntary arrangement proposal means that the distinction is blurred and is of little relevance to creditors – indeed the proposal may be a combination of the two types of arrangement outlined above. Such is its flexibility that it has been held that an IVA can still be valid despite the fact that no return is anticipated to unsecured creditors (see *Inland Revenue Commissioners* v. *Adam & Partners Ltd* [2002] BCC 247).

Since the introduction of the procedure in IA 1986, IVAs have proved very popular, certainly in comparison with the use made of the CVA procedure. For a debtor, the IVA avoids the restrictions and disabilities of bankruptcy. For the creditors, statistics show a better return than in bankruptcy.

Table 2.2 Comparison of bankruptcy and IVA numbers

Year	Total	Bankruptcy orders	Individual voluntary arrangements	Debt relief orders (6 April 2009)
1987	7398	6994	404	
1988	8493	7714	779	
1989	9362	8138	1224	
1990	13985	12058	1927	
1991	25634	22632	3002	
1992	36792	32106	4686	
1993	36695	31016	5679	
1994	30737	25634	5103	
1995	26319	21933	4386	
1996	26271	21803	4468	
1997	24441	19892	4549	
1998	24549	19647	4902	
1999	28806	21611	7195	
2000	29528	21550	7978	
2001	29775	23477	6298	
2002	30587	24292	6295	
2003	36328	28021	8307	
2004	46650	35898	10752	
2005	67898	47502	20396	
2006	107288	62956	44332	
2007	106645	64480	42165	
2008	106364	67248	39116	
2009	134142	74670	47641	11831
2010	135089	59173	50737	25179
2011	119941	41876	49056	29009

Source: Insolvency Service Statistical Directorate

Given the reforms of personal insolvency law which came into effect on 1 April 2004, there were some doubts that IVAs would continue to be as popular and widely used. The main reasons for this view are that the shortened period of bankruptcy could appear an attractive alternative to a debtor; an IVA may bind the debtor to repay sums over a much longer timescale and compliance may be seen as more onerous than bankruptcy; and also the introduction of a post-bankruptcy fast-track voluntary arrangement (FTVA) (IA 1986, ss.263A–263G, dealt with separately in **Chapter 10**).

What was not foreseen was that this area would be subject to a rise in entrepreneurial activity and venture capital investment, with specialist firms being set up solely to promote and run large numbers of 'standard' IVAs, benefiting from the economies of scale that such operations can produce. These firms will generally have a small number of insolvency practitioners overseeing the operation and nominally supervising the arrangements, and may run in parallel to sister companies offering other forms of personal debt assistance.

It is unlikely that the proliferation of such firms and the commoditisation of the IVA as a financial product could have been envisaged by Parliament when the IVA procedure was first introduced. As will be seen, the procedure seems to have been devised for trade debtors who wish to restructure their business in such a way as to keep trading while compromising debts. This is borne out by the fact that the debtor is responsible for putting forward a proposal that is then considered by an insolvency practitioner acting as nominee. In reality, the complexity of the procedure and the wish by many stakeholders (e.g. HM Revenue and Customs (HMRC), banks and credit card companies) to see standard provisions in each proposal has meant that almost invariably insolvency practitioners will take responsibility for the drafting of the proposal. While there is scope for trade debtors to have more individually crafted proposals, what has been evident is that consumer debtors have been especially targeted and the large growth in IVA numbers is attributable to the use of the procedure by this category of debtor. There is some disquiet, particularly within the banking industry, that the procedure is now used too regularly and that debtors are being encouraged to make IVA proposals too readily.

Table 2.3 Pros and cons of an IVA

Pros	Cons
• Flexibility	• Possible cost
• Availability of statutory moratorium	• Debtor may be bound to difficult terms
• Avoids restrictions/disabilities of bankruptcy	• Debtor may be bound for a long duration
• Less stigma	• Creditors may be sceptical that debtor has fully disclosed assets
• Greater return to creditors	• Creditors may be suspicious that debtor has overstated liabilities and/or that certain disclosed debts are bona fide
• Debtor may retain control of assets	
• Investigation and supervision by independent insolvency practitioner	• The debtor's credit record may still be adversely affected
• Ability to bind non-consenting creditors or creditors who have not received notice of the IVA	

2.3.2 IVA – process and procedure

Part VIII of IA 1986 (ss.252–263) deals with IVAs. Significant changes to the IVA regime have been brought about by IA 2000, s.3 and Sched.3 (the Act came into force on 1 January 2003). It should also be noted that the following section deals with IVAs as opposed to FTVAs, which are intended as an early exit from bankruptcy and were introduced by the reforms of the Enterprise Act 2002, which came into force on 1 April 2004. FTVAs are dealt with separately in **Chapter 10**.

Guide to procedure

IVA

1. Debtor selects an intended nominee.
2. Debtor considers with the nominee the terms of the proposal and whether an interim order is required. If required, follow steps (3)–(6), otherwise move directly to step (7).
3. Debtor prepares a proposal with the nominee and makes application to court for an interim order.
4. If necessary, debtor applies for stay of any proceedings, pending hearing of the application for an interim order.
5. Court will usually grant a 14-day interim order, with the application adjourned to 14 days from consideration of the nominee's report.
6. Debtor delivers statement of affairs to nominee.
7. Nominee files the proposal and the debtor's statement of affairs. Nominee must confirm in a report that in his opinion a meeting of creditors should be summoned.
8. Court will usually without further attendance from any party make a standard order summoning a creditors' meeting and adjourning to a date some three weeks after the creditors' meeting.
9. If no earlier interim order was required and the nominee has delivered the report with the initial application for an interim order a concertina order may be made, combining the 14-day interim order with the standard order referred to in step (8).
10. If no interim order is required at all, the court does not need to satisfy itself that a creditors' meeting should be held and, consequently, the filing of the nominee's report, the proposal and statement of affairs are purely procedural.
11. The creditors' meeting takes place; 75 per cent of the creditors voting are required to approve the arrangement.
12. The chairman of the meeting (the nominee) will report on the result of the meeting and file a copy of his report at court.
13. If approved, the nominee becomes the supervisor of the arrangement and will report to the Secretary of State.
14. Within 28 days from the date of filing of the report, an appeal may be made to court in respect of any decision of the chairman for the meeting of creditors.

The nominee

The role of the nominee in formulating a proposal with the debtor, for consideration by his creditors, is crucial. The nominee must have credibility with the creditors, evidencing professionalism and independence from the debtor's position. It must be remembered that an important aspect of the IVA procedure is that the insolvency practitioner (who has considered the debtor's proposal) will generally assume responsibility for the implementation of the arrangement. The supervisor (as the nominee is then called) will provide independent scrutiny, ensuring that the provisions of the IVA are performed and that the debtor conducts himself in accordance with the terms of the arrangement. The court has a much less active role in the IVA procedure than was the case within schemes of composition under the Bankruptcy Act 1914.

The nominee/supervisor acting as a 'policeman' for the creditors will therefore be responsible for ensuring the debtor's compliance with the terms of the IVA. If the debtor fails to comply with the terms, the supervisor of the arrangement may petition for the debtor's bankruptcy. Often this is expressly provided for in the IVA, with a term of the proposal ensuring that the supervisor will retain enough money to cover the costs of taking such a step.

The nominee/supervisor of an IVA is also under an obligation to report a debtor to the Secretary of State if it appears that the debtor is guilty of any offence in connection with the IVA. For example, if the debtor makes a false representation, or does or omits to do anything for the purposes of obtaining creditors' approval for the IVA, the debtor has committed a criminal offence.

This section applies even if the IVA is not eventually approved. If found guilty, the debtor will be liable to a fine and/or imprisonment (on indictment, punishable with up to seven years' imprisonment and an unlimited fine; on summary conviction, up to six months' imprisonment and a £5,000 fine (IA 1986, s.262A and Sched.10)).

Following the introduction of IA 2000, from 1 January 2003 it has been possible for individuals other than a licensed insolvency practitioner to act as the supervisor of the arrangement (IA 2000, s.4). In part, this was a reflection that in recent years there has been a great increase in the number of individuals specialising in 'turnaround' and providing debt solution advisory services. The government sought to open up the provision of voluntary arrangements to a wider range of professionals, with the intention of reducing cost by increased competition and increasing the use of the procedure.

During the reform process, this proposal met with stiff opposition, with the fear that unqualified and dishonest advisers might put forward unworkable proposals, to the disadvantage of the debtor, and/or seek to mislead creditors. To assuage these fears the government provided that only those individuals belonging to a professional body recognised by the Secretary of State as meeting the necessary standards of education and training would be considered. As a result, to date the market has not been opened to non-insolvency practitioners.

The proposal

One of the most advantageous aspects of the IVA procedure is the flexibility of the proposal which a debtor can present to his creditors. The proposal can be in the form of either a composition in satisfaction of debt or a scheme of arrangement of the debtor's affairs (see IA 1986, s.253(1); *Re Ravichandran* [2004] BPIR 814; *Demarco* v. *Perkins and Bulley Davey* [2006] BPIR 645 where it was held that an IVA cannot be proposed in respect of debts released on discharge from bankruptcy as there is nothing for the creditor to release).

The proposal will be discussed by the debtor with the proposed nominee before any application to court. The terms of the proposal will vary depending on the individual circumstances of the case, the assets and liabilities of the debtor and the position being taken by the creditors. The proposals may vary from a complete return to creditors within a matter of days, to no monetary return being proposed at all to unsecured creditors.

A proposed nominee may also take the time to 'sound out' the debtor's principal creditors, to find out if approval is likely on the proposed terms. There is little point in putting forward a proposal which has little prospect of success.

The decision as to whether to take this step very much depends on whether creditor pressure is being brought to bear on the debtor. Can the proposed nominee afford to wait?

A careful balance in the proposal needs to be made between making a reasonable return to creditors and ensuring that the conditions are not so onerous on the individual that the debtor is disincentivised and will not be able to comply with the terms of the arrangement.

The terms of the eventual proposal may not provide an 'easier' way out for the debtor and, in reality, bankruptcy may be a better medium-term option for the debtor. It should, however, be remembered that an IVA avoids the stigma, restrictions and disabilities of bankruptcy, something which may be of vital importance to debtors within certain professions. Following the Enterprise Act 2002 reforms and the introduction of the bankruptcy restrictions order procedure, the government has put pressure on professional bodies and associations to reconsider their professional rules so as to allow bankrupts to continue to practise unless subject to a bankruptcy restrictions order. It should be noted that the Law Society currently prohibits bankrupts from practising as solicitors, but members of Parliament can now remain sitting as MPs.

IA 1986 and its accompanying rules are framed in such a way to allow the debtor to prepare his own proposal and then approach an insolvency practitioner to act as a nominee. While this is entirely possible and may be a cheaper way for the debtor to proceed, as shown below, the proposal must contain a number of important details, so it is generally better for the debtor to seek professional advice before undertaking such a task.

In all cases the intended nominee must report to the court on the terms of the proposal (IA 1986, s.256). The proposal must contain enough information for the nominee to form a view as to the viability of the proposal and for him to make his report.

A proposal must provide a short statement as to why the debtor considers that an IVA is desirable and why the creditors may be expected to agree to the arrangement. For this reason, the proposal often contains a comparison between the returns expected in bankruptcy as against the returns expected in an IVA. As described previously, while it is not a mandatory requirement that the proposals under an IVA are better for the creditors than under bankruptcy, it does mean that, if this is the case, it is more likely that the creditors will accept the terms of the proposals.

The proposal must state, so far as it is within the debtor's knowledge:

(a) the debtor's assets, with estimation of value;

(b) the extent to which any assets are charged in favour of creditors;

(c) the extent to which any assets are to be excluded from the terms of the voluntary arrangement;

(d) particulars of any property, other than the assets of the debtor, which is to be included in the arrangement, the source of such property and the terms under which it is being made available for inclusion. This provision covers assets and property made available by third parties, which will only be made available if the voluntary arrangement is approved;

(e) the nature and amount of the debtor's liabilities;

(f) how it is proposed to deal with preferential creditors;

(g) how it is proposed to deal with secured creditors;

(h) how it is proposed to deal with associates of the debtor (being creditors);

(i) where the debtor is an undischarged bankrupt, whether to the debtor's knowledge claims have been made under s.339 (transaction undervalue), s.340 (preferences) or s.343 (extortionate credit transactions) or whether there are circumstances giving rise to the possibility of such claims. Where the debtor is not an undischarged bankrupt, whether there are any circumstances that could give rise to claims under ss.339, 340 and 343 if the debtor was to be adjudged bankrupt. In either case, if present, whether and if so how, the voluntary arrangement will make provision wholly or partly indemnifying the insolvent estate in respect of such claims;

(j) whether any guarantees have been given in respect of the debtor's debt and, if so, whether the guarantors are associates of the debtor. The proposal should set out how co-debtors/guarantors are to be dealt with – see *Johnson* v. *Davies* [1999] Ch 117;

(k) the duration of the voluntary arrangement;

(l) dates for distribution to creditors and estimates of potential amounts to be received;

(m) the amount to be paid to the nominee by way of remuneration and expenses;

(n) the manner in which it is proposed that the supervisor of the arrangement should be remunerated and how expenses are to be paid during the course of the arrangement;

(o) whether for the purposes of the arrangement any guarantees will be given by any third party and/or if any security is to be given or sought;

(p) the manner in which funds held for the purpose of the arrangement are to be banked, invested or otherwise dealt with pending distribution to creditors;

(q) the manner in which funds held for the purpose of payment to creditors (and not so paid on the determination of the arrangement) are to be dealt with. It is important that the proposal deals with how these sums will be dealt with if the arrangement fails, e.g. the sums are in trust for the creditors;

(r)   if the debtor has any business, the manner in which it is proposed to be conducted during the course of the arrangement;

(s)   details of any further credit facilities which it is intended to arrange for the debtor and how the debts arising under these credit arrangements are to be paid;

(t)   functions which should be undertaken by the supervisor of the arrangement;

(u)   the name, address and qualification of the person proposed to be the supervisor;

(v)   confirmation from the debtor that, so far as he is aware, the proposed supervisor is qualified to act; and

(w)   whether the EC Regulation on Insolvency Proceedings (Council Regulation 1346/2000/EC) will apply and, if so, whether they will be main, secondary or territorial proceedings.

With agreement in writing from the nominee, the proposal may be amended at any time up to the date of delivery of the nominee's report to the court (IA 1986, s.256).

Notice to intended nominee

The debtor is obliged to provide notice of the proposal to the intended nominee (IR 1986, rule 5.4(1)). As stated, however, it is often the case that the nominee has drafted the proposal on behalf of the debtor. As part of the procedure, if the intended nominee agrees to act, the nominee must endorse the date of receipt on a copy of the notice sent by the debtor when he has received a copy of the proposal. The copy of the notice must then be signed and returned to the debtor.

If the debtor intends to apply for an interim order, he is now in a position to do so.

Where the debtor is an undischarged bankrupt, notice of the proposal must be provided to the Official Receiver and any trustee in bankruptcy. It must contain confirmation that an insolvency practitioner has agreed to act as the undischarged bankrupt's nominee.

Interim order

Since 1 January 2003 and the coming into force of IA 2000, the debtor has had a choice as to whether to seek an interim order before putting an IVA proposal to his creditors. Prior to this date, the making of an interim order was a prerequisite of all IVAs (see *Fletcher* v. *Vooght* [2000] BPIR 435). This reform was introduced as the cost of bringing a court application was seen as a disincentive to some debtors and a cause of depletion of already limited resources.

However, the single most important reason why a debtor may wish to obtain an interim order is that while an interim order is in place, a bankruptcy petition cannot be presented against the debtor. No other proceeding, execution or other legal process may be commenced or constituted against the debtor's property without leave of the court (IA 1986, s.252(2), amended by IA 2000, Sched.3, para.2, to include proceedings by landlords and other persons to whom the rent is payable by forfeiture, peaceable re-entry or distress; this reverses the effect of *Razzaq* v. *Pala* [1997] 1 WLR 1336 and *McMullen & Sons Ltd* v. *Cerrone* [1994] BCC 25). This period of moratorium therefore allows the debtor time in which to put together the final detailed terms of the proposal, free from creditor pressure.

It should be noted that the moratorium is not absolute and creditors may apply for permission to enforce rights by commencing or continuing proceedings. In particular, the court will not restrain a secured creditor from enforcing security rights, as the proposal contained in any IVA cannot automatically affect those rights (IA 1986, s.258(4)). However, permission will not generally be granted to a creditor who is seeking to enforce a claim in preference to other unsecured creditors (see *Roberts Petroleum Ltd* v. *Bernard Kenny Ltd* [1983] 2 AC 192).

An interim order cannot remain in force, at least initially, for more than 14 days (IA 1986, s.255(6)). It is capable of being extended with a court order, but cannot be used to frustrate the legitimate claims of creditors (see *Re Cove (a Debtor)* [1990] 1 All ER 949).

The application for an interim order may be made by the debtor personally (IA 1986, s.253(3)(b)). This in turn leaves open the possibility that an application may be made on behalf of the debtor by an appointed representative. The application must exhibit a copy of the notice sent to the nominee (who, if the proposal is approved, will be responsible for supervising and implementing the terms of the voluntary arrangement) and a copy of the proposal given to the intended nominee (IR 1986, rule 5.5(2), as amended). If approved by the court, an interim order will be granted and the application will be adjourned for 14 days for consideration of the nominee's report.

It is usual, however, for the potential nominee already to have drafted a proposal with the debtor. As a consequence, a 'concertina order' can be sought, when the nominee's report and proposal are filed at the same time. (A concertina order combines an interim order with an order summoning the creditors' meeting and an order adjourning the hearing of the application to a date about three weeks after the creditors' meeting.)

The debtor applies to the court at which he would be entitled to present his own bankruptcy petition (see **2.7.5**). The application must be supported by an affidavit or witness statement, and must deal with:

- the reasons for making an application;
- the particulars of any execution or other legal process which has been commenced;
- confirmation that the debtor is an undischarged bankrupt or able to petition for his own bankruptcy;

- confirmation that no previous application for an interim order has been made in the last 12 months;
- confirmation that a nominee who is an insolvency practitioner is willing (or otherwise authorised) to act in relation to the proposal; and
- if the applicant intends to apply for a stay of any action, execution or legal process pending hearing of the application of the interim order, evidence in support of the stay.

The application must also be accompanied by a copy of the notice endorsed with the agreement of the intended nominee to act in relation to the proposal and a copy of the debtor's proposal to the nominee.

If the debtor is bankrupt, at least two days' notice of the intended application must be given to the Official Receiver/trustee in bankruptcy. If the debtor is not bankrupt, notice of application must be given to any creditor who has presented a bankruptcy petition against him (IR 1986, rule 5.7(4)). In all cases, notice of application must be given to the nominee. In the case of a debtor who is neither bankrupt nor has a bankruptcy petition pending against him, the nominee may waive the requirements for the two days' notice of application and the application may be heard immediately.

Pending the hearing of the application for an interim order, no landlord may exercise rights of forfeiture without leave of the court. The court may also forbid the levy of any distress or stay any action, execution or other legal process pending the hearing (IA 1986, s.254(1)). Any applicant seeking to obtain such a moratorium against such creditor action must specify the action, execution or legal process to be stayed. A separate supporting witness statement will not be required where necessary evidence has been included in the witness statement filed in support of the main application. Furthermore, any court in which proceedings are pending against the individual may stay those proceedings, or permit them to continue subject to terms (IA 1986, s.254(2)). The court will normally hear the application for the stay on the day on which the application for the interim order is filed.

Provided no bankruptcy order or outstanding petition exists, the court will be prepared to make a 14-day interim order, with the application also adjourned for 14 days for consideration of the nominee's report. In other cases, the court will hear the interim order application, with representations by the Official Receiver, trustee in bankruptcy and petitioning creditor (as appropriate).

An interim order is effective for 14 days beginning on the day after the making of the order unless otherwise extended by the court. The order may also provide for an extension of time for the filing of the nominee's report, together with consequential amendments extending the effect of the order and the date for considering the report.

The court may not make an interim order unless it is satisfied the debtor intends to make a proposal (IA 1986, s.255(1)) and is able to petition for his own bankruptcy (IA 1986, s.265(1)), namely the debtor can satisfy the domicile and residence requirements and is unable to pay his debts as they fall due (IA 1986, s.272(1)), the debtor has not made an application in the last 12 months (see *Hurst* v. *Bennett (No.2)* [2002] BPIR 102 re previous applications) and the nominee is an insolvency practitioner willing to act (IA 1986, s.255(1)(d); IR 1986, rule 5.7(1)(e)).

The court will also not grant a interim order unless the proposal is 'serious and viable' (see *Cooper* v. *Fearnley*; *Re a Debtor (No.103 of 1994)* [1997] BPIR 20; *Hook* v. *Jewson Ltd* [1997] BPIR 100; *Shah* v. *Cooper* [2003] BPIR 1018).

For a proposal to be serious it is not sufficient that the debtor considers the proposal is made with all due seriousness and is even bona fide. The court must consider whether the proposal is one of substance and would be seriously considered by the creditors and is not derisory (see *Knowles* v. *Coutts & Co.* [1998] BPIR 96).

It should be noted, however, that the court will not seek to conduct a mini-trial and will not second-guess the creditors. The court does not need to be satisfied that the creditors will approve the proposal, but simply needs to be satisfied that it is not impossible or strongly improbable that the creditors would do so. To this end the court will usually consider whether the voluntary arrangement provides a better return to creditors than bankruptcy. However, failure to provide better creditor prospects than under bankruptcy does not mean that the court and creditors will necessarily reject the proposal. The creditors may approve the proposal for reasons of charity or in order to keep the business trading and acquire better terms in the future (see *Greystoke* v. *Hamilton-Smith*; *Re a Debtor (No.140-IO of 1995)* [1997] BPIR 24). If such a proposal is put forward, it is advisable that evidence of possible acceptance is also put to the court.

The 'viability' of the proposal means that it is realistic and capable of being implemented and is not bound to be rejected if a creditor with over 25 per cent of the debt objects (see *Re a Debtor (No.140 of 1995)* [1996] 2 BCLC 429; *Knowles* v. *Coutts & Co.* [1998] BPIR 96).

The court will not grant an interim order where:

- the court is of the opinion that the debtor is using an interim order procedure as a blocking or stalling device (see *Re Cove (a Debtor)* [1990] 1 All ER 949, where an interim order was used continually to block bankruptcy proceedings);
- an interim order has been sought in the last 12 months (see above); or
- the court has ordered an insolvency practitioner to enquire into the debtor's affairs (IA 1986, s.273).

The court will also have regard to the credibility of the debtor and the honesty (or otherwise) that he has shown in putting forward the proposal (*Re a Debtor (No.2389 of 1989)* [1991] Ch 326; *Hurst* v. *Kroll Buchler Phillips Ltd* [2003] BPIR 872; *Davidson* v. *Stanley* [2005] BPIR 279).

The court may require an enquiry into the debtor's affairs where a debtor has presented his own bankruptcy petition and, rather than granting an immediate bankruptcy order, the court feels that an alternative is in the best interests of all parties. The reason for preventing an application for an interim order by the debtor in such circumstances is that the court may grant an interim order of its own initiative (IA 1986, s.274(3)(a)).

If the debtor is an undischarged bankrupt an interim order may be made, although the interim order may well contain provisions as to the continuing conduct of the bankruptcy, or the administration of the bankrupt's estate. However, if the debtor is bankrupt, the interim order will not relax or remove any of the requirements obliged to be performed under IA 1986, unless the court is satisfied that the continuation of the bankruptcy will result in a significant diminution in value of the debtor's estate (IA 1986, s.255(5)).

The interim order will cease to have effect at the end of 14 days beginning on the day after the making of the order, unless otherwise ordered by the court. Time is therefore of the essence in the nominee reporting to court (IA 1986, s.255(6); IR 1986, rules 5.6, 5.7).

Debtor's statement of affairs

Unless the debtor has already filed a statement of affairs in connection with a bankruptcy petition, the debtor must, within seven days of the proposal being delivered to the nominee (or such longer time as the nominee may permit), deliver a statement of affairs to the nominee (IR 1986, rule 5.5).

The statement of affairs must contain:

- details of the debtor's assets, divided into appropriate categories for easy identification, with estimated values;
- particulars of any secured property;
- the names and addresses of preferential creditors and amounts in respect of claims;
- the names and addresses of unsecured creditors with amounts for respective claims;
- particulars of any debts owed to, or from, associates of the debtor; and
- such other particulars as a nominee may in writing require.

See IA 1986, s.435 for the definition of associates – these include husband, wife, civil partner, relative, or husband or wife of a relative; employee, employer and certain trustees. Relatives include brother, sister, uncle, aunt, nephew, niece, linear ancestor or linear descendant, treating a relationship of the half blood as a relationship of the whole blood and an illegitimate child as a legitimate child of his mother and reputed father. Reference to husband and wife includes any former husbands or wives.

It should be noted that any material omission or inclusion of information that is false and misleading entitles the supervisor of the arrangement, or any persons bound by the arrangement, to present a bankruptcy petition against the debtor (IA 1986, s.276(1)). It is also potentially a criminal offence on the part of the debtor.

Nominee's report

Where an interim order has been made, the nominee must submit a report to court before the order ceases to have effect (IA 1986, s.256). The report should state the following:

(a) whether the voluntary arrangement has a reasonable prospect of being approved and implemented;
(b) whether a meeting of the debtor's creditors should be summoned to consider the debtor's proposals; and
(c) the date on which and the time at which the meeting should be held.

If the nominee is unable to complete the report on the basis of the information provided to him by the debtor in the proposal and statement of affairs, the supervisor may call upon the debtor to provide further information as to why he is unable to pay his debts, particulars of any previous proposals for a voluntary arrangement and any other relevant information (IR 1986, rule 5.6(1)).

The debtor is under a duty to provide the nominee with access to accounts and records and may be asked by the nominee if he has been concerned at any time in the affairs of an insolvent company, or adjudged bankrupt, or entered into any previous arrangement (IR 1986, rule 5.6(2)).

Where the nominee has failed to submit a report, the debtor may apply to court for a direction that the interim order continues, or, if it has ceased to have effect, that the order be renewed for a further period (IA 1986, s.256(3A)). Similarly, the nominee may apply for the period of the interim order to be extended, to have more time to provide a report. If the nominee considers that a meeting should not be called, he must give reasons for this (IR 1986, rule 5.11(3)).

The nominee will deliver to the court the report together with the debtor's proposal and summary of the statement of affairs provided by the debtor, not less than two days before the interim order ceases to have effect (IR 1986, rule 5.11(1)).

Where the debtor is an undischarged bankrupt, the nominee must send notice of the report, the proposal and the statement of affairs to the Official Receiver (IR 1986, rule 5.11(6)). If a person has presented a bankruptcy petition against the debtor, the nominee will send these papers to that petitioning creditor (IR 1986, rule 5.11(7)).

Provided there is no existing bankruptcy order, or outstanding bankruptcy petition, the court will usually be prepared to make the following orders without any further attendance from the nominee or debtor. Together these orders are referred to as the 'standard order':

(a) the interim order is extended to a date seven weeks after the date of the proposed creditors' meeting;
(b) a direction that the creditors' meeting be summoned is provided; and
(c) the hearing of the application is adjourned to three weeks after the date of the creditors' meeting.

Alternatively, a 'concertina order' may be granted, which combines an initial 14-day interim order and the standard order described above. Such orders will be made where the application for an interim order is accompanied by the nominee's report (which is usual practice).

As stated above, as a result of the reforms introduced by IA 2000 it is now possible for a debtor to make a proposal for an IVA without first seeking an interim order (IA 1986, s.256A). The consequence of the debtor failing to obtain an interim order is that there is no moratorium during the IVA process and creditors are free to take action to enforce claims until the meeting of creditors.

Where no interim order is sought, the procedure to be followed is somewhat different. To enable the nominee to prepare a report to court, the debtor must provide the nominee with the proposal, his statements of affairs and such information as may be required by the nominee.

After receiving these documents, if the nominee is satisfied he must submit a report to court stating that:

(a)   the voluntary arrangement has a reasonable prospect of being approved and implemented;
(b)   the debtor's creditors should be summoned to consider the proposal; and
(c)   a meeting should be summoned on a specified date, time and place.

On receipt of this report, the court is not under a duty to satisfy itself that the creditors' meeting should be held. The initiation of the whole procedure therefore relies upon the nominee's view that the proposals have a reasonable prospect of being approved and implemented.

Summoning of creditors' meeting

Where the nominee has reported to the court that a meeting of creditors should be summoned, the nominee must, unless the court otherwise directs, summon the meeting for the time, date and place proposed in the nominee's report. A creditors' meeting summoned before the court has considered the nominee's report is invalid (see *Vlieland-Boddy* v. *Dexter Ltd* [2004] BPIR 235).

The date, time and place for the creditors' meeting will be no less than 14 days from the date the report is filed, and no longer than 28 days from the date the report is considered by the court. The meeting should be held between 10 am and 4 pm on a business day at a place convenient for the creditors.

Notice of the meeting will be sent to all creditors named in the statement of affairs and other creditors of whom the nominee has become aware. The meaning of 'creditors' is widely defined: see *Re a Debtor: JP* v. *a Debtor* [1999] BPIR 206, where despite the fact that the debtor's ex-wife was owed money in respect of a lump sum order obtained on divorce (which would not constitute a provable debt in bankruptcy), the wife was entitled to receive notice of the meeting. The nominee must give at least 14 days' notice of the date fixed for the meeting (IR 1986, rule 5.17(2)).

Where the debtor is an undischarged bankrupt, the creditors include every person to whom the bankrupt owes a bankruptcy debt and any person who would be a creditor if the bankruptcy had commenced on the day on which notice of the meeting was given (IA 1986, s.257(3)).

The notice must:

- specify the court to which the nominee's report was delivered;
- state the requisite majorities which will be required for the passing of particular resolutions with respect to the voluntary arrangement; and
- enclose a copy of the proposal and the nominee's report on the proposal; the debtor's statement of affairs; a summary of the debtor's creditors with amount owed; and a proxy form.

The creditors' meeting

The purpose of the creditors' meeting is to consider the proposals put forward by the debtor. Every creditor who has been given notice of the meeting, or who has become aware of the meeting, may vote, or do so by proxy if unable to attend.

The nominee acts as the chairman of the meeting, although he may nominate another insolvency practitioner or employee who has experience in insolvency matters to act as chairman in his place (IR 1986, rule 5.19).

The chairman must decide on each creditor's entitlement to vote, which will usually require the submission by the creditor of some form of proof of debt. The procedure for accepting creditors' claims is less prescriptive than in the bankruptcy and liquidation process. However, written notice of the claim at or prior to the meeting is essential, and where this is not provided the claim will be excluded from the calculation (see *Calor Gas Ltd* v. *Piercy* [1994] BCC 69). For this reason the proposed chairman may have asked that creditors submit proofs of debt by 12 pm the day before the meeting. Indeed, it is often the case that by the date of the meeting the chairman may have received a sufficient number of proxy forms to make the voting at the creditors' meeting a mere formality.

The value of the debt is calculated as at the date of the meeting, unless the debtor is an undischarged bankrupt, in which case the value of the debt is as at the date of bankruptcy (IR 1986, rule 5.21(2)).

A creditor who possesses an unliquidated debt (e.g. a damages claim) or where the debt value has yet to be assessed may not vote unless the chairman agrees to put an estimated minimum value for the purposes of the voting (IR 1986, rule 5.21(3)). This decision to 'value' the debt is non-binding and will be altered as and when the value becomes ascertainable.

Any decision of the chairman made at the meeting will be subject to court appeal by any creditor or the debtor. The appeal must be made within 28 days of the date on which the chairman's report is filed at court.

One potential point of conflict at the creditors' meeting is between the chairman and a creditor possessing an unliquidated claim. In the absence of agreement, in order to progress the meeting, the chairman may impose a minimum value on the debt. The chairman must exercise genuine professional judgment in estimating the claim, and the debtor cannot compel the chairman to 'agree' the valuation (see *Re a Debtor (No.162 of 1993)* [1994] BCC 994, Knox J, affirmed by the Court of Appeal in *Doorbar* v. *Alltime Securities Ltd* [1995] BCC 1149; contrast these cases with the earlier decision of *Re Cranley Mansions Ltd*; *Saigol* v. *Goldstein* [1994] BCC 576 where Ferris J had held that some element of bilateral agreement was required between the chairman and the debtor).

If a dispute does arise regarding the valuation of any debt and/or there is any doubt as to whether to admit or reject a debt, the chairman may mark the debt as disputed and proceed with the meeting. If the debt is subsequently held invalid and/or the chairman's decision is reversed or varied, the court may either affirm the decision of the remaining creditors (if the invalid vote made no difference to the outcome), or summon a further meeting. The court will only order a further meeting if the matter gave rise to unfair prejudice or a material irregularity arose (IR 1986, rule 5.22(5)).

At the meeting the creditors may propose modifications to the IVA, although these will not become binding unless the debtor consents (see *Reid* v. *Hamblin* [2001] BPIR 929; *Re Plummer* [2004] BPIR 767). These could include the replacement of the proposed supervisor with another insolvency practitioner more acceptable to the creditors.

Secured creditors' rights are unaffected by any proposal, or modification, unless the secured creditors otherwise consent (*Joseph Manuel Rey* v. *FNCB Ltd* [2006] EWHC 1386 (Ch)). Secured creditors have no voting rights, save where their claim is only partly secured. In such cases the chairman may agree to put a valuation on the unsecured portion of their claim and the secured creditor may vote in respect of that unsecured portion of the debt (see *Calor Gas Ltd* v. *Piercy* [1994] BCC 69). Security may be revalued during the course of the arrangement.

The meeting should not approve any proposal or modification where any preferential debt is to be paid otherwise than in priority to the claims of creditors possessing non-preferential claims, or where the preferential creditors are treated less favourably. It should be noted, however, that the preferential creditors may consent to such treatment. This has less relevance since 15 September 2003, as the categories of preferential creditors are now limited, with only employees' claims being of general significance; the Crown does not enjoy preference in any IVA commenced after 15 September 2003 (IA 1986, s.386 and Sched.6).

Approval of any modification requires a majority in excess of three-quarters in value of the creditors present in person, or by proxy, and voting on the resolution (IR 1986, rule 5.23(2)). Any other resolution proposed during the course of the meeting requires a majority in value of creditors (IR 1986, rule 5.23(1)). If a modification makes a substantial alteration to the proposal of which creditors voting by proxy did not have notice, the chairman of the meeting may be best advised to adjourn the meeting to give due notice (IR 1986, rule 5.24).

If support of the requisite majority of creditors is not obtained, the chairman may adjourn the meeting for no longer than 14 days. Similarly, the creditors may resolve during the course of the meeting to adjourn. If the proposal is not approved at the final meeting it is deemed rejected. Notice of adjournment must be provided to the court by the chairman of the meeting (IR 1986, rule 5.24(4)).

It is possible that the creditors may wish a proposal to take effect, but to be supervised by some other insolvency practitioner. If that is the case, the person nominated by the creditors must produce written confirmation to the chairman that he is a licensed insolvency practitioner and has consented to act. This consent may be given orally at the meeting (IR 1986, rule 5.25(2)).

Report of decision to court

Within four days of the conclusion of the creditors' meeting, the chairman must file a report to court indicating the result of the meeting (IR 1986, rule 5.27(3)). The report must state whether the proposal was rejected or accepted with or without modification, the resolutions taken at the meeting and the decision of each one, a list of creditors present at the meeting and how they voted, whether the EC Regulation on Insolvency Proceedings applies and, if so, whether the proceedings are main or territorial proceedings and such further information as the chairman thinks fit (IR 1986, rule 5.27(2)).

Although it is not expressly provided, if an interim order was sought it is the usual practice for the court to convene a hearing to consider the report on the same day as the date provided for discharge/extension of the interim order. This hearing is often a formality and the attendance of any party may be excused (see Practice Direction on Insolvency Proceedings, para.16.1(4)). If no interim order is sought, the court will not consider the chairman's report unless an application is made for the court to do so (IR 1986, rule 5.27(5)).

Notice of the result must also be sent to persons who were sent notice of the meeting, such other creditors as the chairman is aware of and, if the debtor is an undischarged bankrupt, the Official Receiver and, if any, the trustee (IR 1986, rule 5.27(4)).

If the chairman reports that the meeting has rejected the proposal, the court may immediately discharge any interim order which is in force (see *Re Symes (a Debtor)*; *Kent Carpets Ltd* v. *Symes* [1996] 2 BCLC 651). Although the legislation provides that the court 'may' discharge the order, it is general practice for the interim order to be discharged, although the court may be persuaded to allow the interim order to run its course if it is anticipated that the debtor will challenge the decision of the meeting (see below) or seek an extension of the interim order. The discharge of the interim order will terminate a stay in any proceedings.

In the event of refusal of the IVA proposal it is open to the debtor to challenge the decision reached at the meeting of creditors (IA 1986, s.262). This might be on the ground of material irregularity, e.g. where the chairman has for some reason excluded a creditor who might otherwise have approved the proposal.

Approval of proposal

If the IVA has been approved, the chairman of the meeting, as well as filing at court the requisite report of the meeting (see above), must also report the following to the Secretary of State:

- The name and address of the debtor and the date upon which the arrangement was made.
- The name and address of the supervisor.
- The court in which the chairman's report has been filed (IR 1986, rule 5.29(1)).

The purpose of this report is for entry on to a public register of IVAs maintained by the Secretary of State. The approval of the arrangement by the creditors means that procedurally no further step is required to make the arrangement binding. The report by the chairman to the court seems therefore to be merely procedural.

The approved arrangement which takes effect as at the date of the meeting binds those:

- entitled to vote at the meeting (whether present or not); and
- who would have been entitled to vote at the meeting had they had notice (IA 1986, s.260(2), as amended by IA 2000).

IA 2000 has had the important effect of binding creditors to the terms of an arrangement even if they did not receive notice. Prior to IA 2000 (which came into effect on 1 January 2003) only those creditors who had received notice of the meeting were bound. Even if the debtor and the nominee had inadvertently failed to send notice to the creditor, that creditor would not be bound.

It should be noted, however, that any person who is bound without notice is able to claim payment which would otherwise be due to him following successful completion of the IVA and has a right to challenge the meeting's decision on grounds of a material irregularity or unfair prejudice within 28 days of becoming aware that the meeting has taken place. If the IVA has ceased to have effect as it has been successfully concluded, the creditor, on becoming aware of the arrangement, may only thereafter seek to challenge the arrangement on the grounds that it has unfairly prejudiced his interest (IA 1986, s.262(3)). Alternatively, the creditor can claim from the debtor such dividend as it would have received under the arrangement had it received notice and been duly admitted by the supervisor for dividend purposes (IA 1986, s.260(2A)).

It should be noted that on approval of the IVA both debtor and creditors are bound and the limitation period on any claim ceases to run (*Tanner* v. *Everitt* [2004] BPIR 1026).

Where the creditors have approved an IVA in respect of an undischarged bankrupt, the court has two courses of action, to be exercised either alternatively or cumulatively:

- to annul the bankruptcy order (see *Re Johnson* [2006] BPIR 987); or

- to give such directions for the conduct of the bankruptcy/the administration of the bankrupt's estate as thought appropriate to facilitate the implementation of the IVA.

The advantage for the debtor in the annulment of the bankruptcy is that it is treated as if the bankruptcy order had never been made – see **Chapter 10**. An IVA is likely to be substantially less expensive when compared with an application to annul on grounds that bankruptcy debts have been paid (under IA 1986, s.282(1)(b)), one reason being that *ad valorem* duty (a fee levied by the Secretary of State of 17 per cent on realisations paid into the Insolvency Service Account) does not need to be paid.

The annulment of the bankruptcy order should not take place:

(a)   before the end of 28 days beginning on the date on which the chairman's report was filed;

(b)   at any other time where an application under IA 1986, s.262 is pending;

(c)   if an appeal in respect of such application is pending; or

(d)   at any time in the period within which an appeal may be brought.

These provisions are to enable an appeal to be brought against the decision of the creditors' meeting.

2.3.3   Challenge to meeting's decision

Any decision made at the creditors' meeting is capable of being challenged within 28 days, beginning on the day upon which the chairman's report was submitted to court. Following the amendments introduced by IA 2000, and the statutory binding of creditors who have not been provided with notice of the IVA, such creditors have 28 days commencing on the day on which they became aware that the meeting had taken place (IA 1986, s.262(2), (3)).

An application may be made to court on one or both of the following grounds:

(a)   the voluntary arrangement has unfairly prejudiced the interest of a creditor of the debtor; and/or

(b)   there had been some material irregularity at or in relation to the meeting.

An application can be brought by any of the following:

- The debtor.
- A creditor who was entitled to vote at the meeting, or would have been if given notice of the meeting.
- The nominee or replacement nominee.
- If the debtor is an undischarged bankrupt, the trustee of the estate or the Official Receiver.

There is a limited power for the court to extend the 28-day period (IA 1986, s.376), but this will only be granted in limited circumstances (*Tager* v. *Westpac Banking*

Corporation [1997] BPIR 543; *Re Timothy* [2006] BPIR 329) and consequently a creditor aggrieved by the decision reached at the meeting must act quickly.

Unfair prejudice

'Unfair prejudice' to a creditor's position can mean unfair prejudice to a single individual creditor, or to a specific class, or to classes of creditor. However, the fact that one creditor would not be any less unfairly prejudiced than any other creditor of the same type appears to be irrelevant (see *Re Primlaks (UK) Ltd (No.2)* [1990] BCLC 234). Unfair prejudice means unfairness brought about by the terms of the IVA which affects the relationship between the various creditors. It should be asked whether the creditor is to be treated less favourably and/or whether the terms of that arrangement will unfairly affect the position of that creditor.

It should be noted, however, that it is not enough that the proposals treat a creditor less favourably than, say, if the debtor had been made bankrupt. The court will weigh up all the circumstances and consider the overall position of the creditors (see *Re a Debtor (No.259 of 1990)* [1992] 1 WLR 226; *Re a Debtor (No.222 of 1990), ex p. Bank of Ireland* [1992] BCLC 137; *Re a Debtor (No.87 of 1993) (No.2)* [1996] 1 BCLC 63; *Sisu Capital Trust Ltd* v. *Tucker* [2006] BPIR 154). If the creditors as a whole are put in a better position, the fact that one creditor may be disadvantaged/ prejudiced may not mean that the IVA is 'unfairly prejudicial'.

If in reality the creditor is questioning the validity of certain debts admitted by the chairman during the course of the creditors' meeting, which have the effect of binding him as a dissenting creditor in a manner which he considers unfairly prejudicial, the remedy for the creditor is an appeal against the decision of the chairman to allow the claim (see *Re a Debtor (No.259 of 1990)* [1992] 1 WLR 226; IR 1986, rule 5.22(3), (5)–(7)).

Examples

Unfair prejudice

- Where an arrangement provides that a co-debtor/guarantor of the debtor is also released from the debt (see *Johnson* v. *Davies* [1998] 3 WLR 1299).
- Where a spouse is forced to relinquish/compromise a matrimonial debt, which would not otherwise be released on bankruptcy (see *Re a Debtor (No.448-IO) of 1996*; *J P* v. *a Debtor* [1999] 2 BCLC 571).
- The compromise of a landlord's proprietorial rights under a lease (note that the landlord's rights in his capacity as creditor for rent arrears or in the right circumstances claims for future rent can be compromised – see *Re Naeem (a Bankrupt) (No.18 of 1998)* [1990] 1 WLR 48; *March Estates plc* v. *Gunmark Ltd* [1996] 2 BCLC 1).

Material irregularity

In order successfully to challenge the decision made at the creditors' meeting, the applicant must not only show there has been a material irregularity at, or in relation to, the meeting (or in respect of the preparatory documents: see *Re a Debtor (No.87 of 1993 No.2)* [1996] BCC 80; *Fender* v. *IRC* [2003] BPIR 1304), but also that had the vote or votes of the creditors, which were improperly allowed, been discounted, the outcome would have been different (see IA 1986, s.262(8); *Doorbar* v. *Alltime Securities* [1995] BCC 1149).

Examples

Material irregularity

- The provision of false or misleading information in the proposal or in the statement of affairs (see *Re a Debtor (No.87 of 1993) (No.2)* [1996] BCLC 63). It should, however, be noted that if this occurs, the creditor also has a right to petition for the debtor's bankruptcy under IA 1986, s.264(1)(c); the debtor may also be guilty of a criminal offence (IA 1986, s.262A) which is punishable on indictment by up to seven years' imprisonment and an unlimited fine.
- A decision by the chairman to exclude or undervalue a valid claim, or admit an invalid claim, or overestimate a claim (see *Re Cranley Mansions Ltd* [1994] 1 WLR 1610; *Roberts* v. *Pinnacle Entertainment Ltd* [2004] BPIR 208).

Consequences of court accepting allegation

If the court is satisfied that a creditor has been unfairly prejudiced, or there has been a material irregularity, it may:

- revoke the approval of the arrangement provided at the previous meeting;
- suspend the approval of the arrangement given at a previous meeting (i.e. where a material fact has not been disclosed);
- summon a further meeting;
- rule that the aggrieved party is not bound to the terms of the arrangement;
- provide directions in respect of any action taken pursuant to the terms of the proposal agreed at the initial meeting; or
- provide for costs.

If the court has made a direction summoning a further meeting and it becomes evident that in the time following that direction the debtor, perhaps by reason of having insufficient funds, does not intend to submit a proposal, the court may revoke the direction and any approval given at the previous meeting.

Where the court gives a direction for a further meeting it may if necessary extend the interim order. If the court is of the opinion that a meeting will be of little use it may refuse any further extension.

The court may, if it thinks fit, validate any step taken since the initial meeting and/or provide for supplemental directions in respect of anything done since the meeting pursuant to the voluntary arrangement.

If the court forms the opinion that the chairman's conduct at the meeting and exercise of judgment was unreasonable in the particular circumstances of the case, the chairman may become liable for the costs of the arrangement if set aside (see *Re a Debtor (No.222 of 1990), ex p. Bank of Ireland (No.2)* [1993] BCLC 233; *Re Cardona* [1997] BCC 697; *Fender* v. *IRC* [2003] BPIR 1304). Costs may also be awarded against the debtor.

In the event of a successful challenge, costs can be ordered to be paid by the insolvency practitioner (*Re a Debtor (No.222 of 1990), ex p. Bank of Ireland (No.2)* [1993] BCLC 233 where it was held that the chairman had wrongfully excluded certain creditors from voting).

False representations

If the debtor has for the purposes of obtaining approval of the IVA made any false representation or fraudulently does or omits to do anything, he commits an offence – if he is found guilty he is liable to imprisonment, a fine or both. (IA 1986, s.262A, introduced by IA 2000 provides that it is an offence irrespective of whether the proposal is approved, i.e. there was intent to defraud; IA 1986, Sched.10 provides that the maximum term of imprisonment is seven years on indictment and an unlimited fine, six months and/or up to £5,000 fine on summary conviction.)

In addition, it is open for both the supervisor and any creditor to petition for the debtor's bankruptcy (IA 1986, ss.264(1)(c) and 276(1)(b)) on the grounds that the approval of the IVA was procured through false or misleading statements or omissions in the proposal or statement of affairs, or in any document or in any other way provided to creditors in connection with the meeting (*Cadbury Schweppes plc* v. *Somji* [2001] 1 WLR 615, a case concerning failure to disclose a 'secret' deal with certain creditors; *Re Bradburn* v. *Kaye* [2006] BPIR 605, where the debtor failed to disclose the true extent of his debts).

Prosecution of delinquent debtors

A further change introduced by IA 2000 is to provide for the prosecution of debtors where it appears to the nominee or supervisor that the debtor has been guilty of an offence in connection with the arrangement for which he is criminally liable. In such cases, the nominee or supervisor must report the matter to the Secretary of State and provide such information as is necessary. The nominee/supervisor is under a duty to provide all assistance in connection with the prosecution that he is able. This section is intended to cover the situation where it is later discovered by the nominee/supervisor that the debtor has made a false representation, or has committed a fraudulent act (IA 1986, s.262B). The section therefore only applies where the IVA has been approved.

2.3.4 Implementation and supervision of approved IVA

Where a voluntary arrangement takes effect, the person previously referred to as the nominee becomes the supervisor of the voluntary arrangement.

During the course of the IVA, if the debtor, any creditor or any other person is dissatisfied with any act, omission or decision of the supervisor they may at any time apply to court for relief.

The court has the power to:

- confirm, reverse or modify any act or decision of the supervisor;
- give directions to the supervisor; and/or
- make any such order it considers appropriate.

The supervisor is also entitled to apply to court for directions at any time. The power to give directions does not, however, extend to permitting variations of the arrangement (see *Re Alpa Lighting Ltd* [1997] BPIR 341). The IVA should therefore make provision for minor amendments or variation of the arrangement with a mechanism for calling a further meeting of creditors to approve the variations if material amendments are proposed. The supervisor may, however, apply for directions to determine the construction of the IVA (*Welsby* v. *Brelec Installations Ltd* [2000] 2 BCLC 576); the effect of a subsequent bankruptcy (*Re NT Gallagher Ltd* [2002] 1 WLR 2380); or whether an IVA has failed and the supervisor is obliged to present a bankruptcy petition (*Re Maple Environmental Services* [2000] BCC 93).

The court is empowered at any time to make an order appointing a duly qualified individual to be the supervisor or to act in substitution for an existing supervisor, to fill a vacancy or to add to the number of supervisors.

It is unlikely that the court will give directions regarding matters of commercial judgment and/or take decisions normally taken by the supervisor such as deciding whether to present a bankruptcy petition where the debtor has defaulted.

When the arrangement has been fully completed or terminated, the supervisor must send to the debtor and all creditors bound to the arrangement notice that the arrangement has been completed, or terminated, together with a report showing receipt and payments made during the course of the arrangement, within 28 days.

If there is a difference between the proposal as approved by the creditors and that actually implemented, i.e. there is a difference in return to the creditors, this must be explained. Copies of the notice and report must be sent to the Secretary of State and the court (IR 1986, rule 5.34(3A)).

There is no requirement to hold a final meeting of creditors, nor is there any formal way for the supervisor to vacate office; instead, this should be provided for in the terms of the arrangement.

If the IVA is terminated due to a default of the terms of arrangement by the debtor, a procedure for dealing with the default will generally be provided for in the arrangement. This may include notice of default being sent to the debtor, requesting the breach is remedied within a period of days and/or the requisitioning of a creditors' meeting (or creditors' committee if appointed) to consider whether it is appropriate to issue a 'certificate of termination/failure'.

It should also be noted that IA 1986, s.264(1)(c) entitles a bankruptcy petition to be presented by a supervisor or by any person bound by the arrangement, where there has been a failure of the individual voluntary arrangement.

The court will make a bankruptcy order in the circumstances only if satisfied that:

(a)   the debtor has failed to comply with the obligations under the voluntary arrangement;

(b)   information which is false or misleading, or any material omission, was relevant to any statement prepared or the proposal; or

(c)   the debtor has failed to do all the things which are reasonably required of him by the supervisor.

The making of a bankruptcy order automatically terminates the IVA with the effect that any money or property in the hands of the supervisor becomes part of the debtor's estate and payable to the trustee in bankruptcy for distribution. As a result, it is often a provision of the IVA that any money held by the supervisor on termination of the proposal is held on trust for the benefit of the creditors bound by the IVA (see Figure 2.1).

2.4   DEBT MANAGEMENT SCHEMES

It should be noted that while the number of individuals entering bankruptcy (or becoming subject to a debt relief order, see below) continues to rise, the majority of individuals who are in financial difficulty resort to private service debt counselling firms which are likely to propose some form of debt management plan to the individual's creditors (it has been estimated that 59 per cent of all individuals in financial difficulty propose a debt management plan, as opposed to bankruptcy, IVA or a county court administration order: source Insolvency Service, *Improving Individual Voluntary Arrangements* (May 2007)).

A debt management plan is a non-statutory process and cannot bind dissenting creditors. Plans seldom include any element of debt forgiveness and can run for many years (20 years not being uncommon). The sector is largely unregulated and while charges may appear small at commencement of the plan, there are concerns that over the long duration of the plan they become 'excessive'. There is also concern that the advice being provided by these firms is not the best advice for the debtor and that there is too close a connection between organisations offering debt counselling advice, sub-prime lending/debt consolidation packages and/or IVAs.

Despite the disadvantages of debt management plans, they are popular with individuals as they avoid the stigma of bankruptcy. They may also be useful for those debtors who possess equity in their home. The terms of a 'standard' protocol-compliant IVA provide that the debtor's equity is re-evaluated after four years and any increase in value will be 'due' to the creditors bound by the arrangement. This

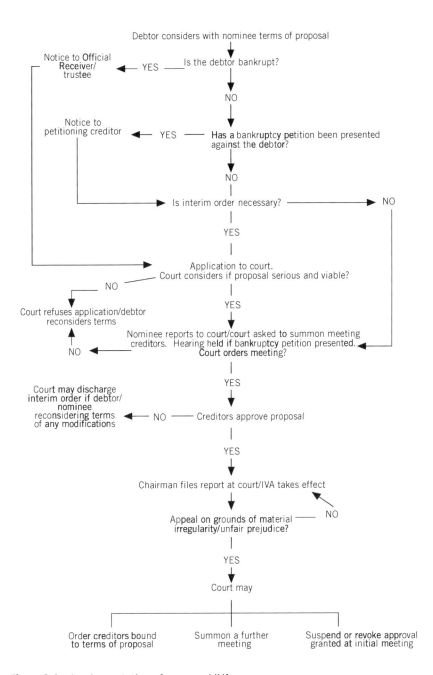

Figure 2.1 Implementation of approved IVA

creates an element of uncertainty for the debtor and his family and is a major reason why an individual debtor may wish to propose a debt management plan to creditors rather than an IVA.

The Tribunals, Courts and Enforcement Act 2007 led to the enactment of a series of proposals with regard to the regulation of debt management schemes. The Act introduced the concept of approved debt management schemes open to non-business debtors, whose debts and assets are under a prescribed maximum. The debtor would be able to make a request of an authorised scheme operator for a debt repayment plan to be arranged for him.

The scheme operator would act as the intermediary between the debtor and his creditors, seeking to obtain consensus on an agreed plan that would then be supervised by the scheme operator. If the plan were approved, on application to the court, the debtor would be discharged from the specific debts within the plan when all required payments have been made. In return, creditors within the plan would be unable to present bankruptcy petitions or seek a remedy to recover debts without the permission of the court.

A register of the plans was proposed, with creditors allowed a limited right of appeal in respect of the fact that a plan has been arranged, or where the treatment of a particular debt within the plan was unfair or the terms of that plan were unfair.

However, the measures have not been brought into force and at the time of writing it appears unlikely that they will be. In September 2009, a consultation paper headed *Debt Management Schemes: Delivering Effective and Balanced Solutions for Debtors and Creditors* was published and the results of the consultation process were released in October 2010. It was clear from the responses (see *Response to Consultation CP(R)09/09* (October 2010)) that there was little consensus within the industry, and the government's decision that a further review would be conducted within the context of consumer credit and debt was unsurprising.

2.5 DEBT RELIEF ORDERS

The emergence of the debt relief order (DRO) introduced in the Tribunals, Courts and Enforcement Act 2007 (the provisions relating to which came into effect on 6 April 2009) has had a significant impact on the treatment of debt and personal insolvency. It has removed at a sweep large numbers of debtors of low income and of low asset value (i.e. those that cannot pay and have no reasonable prospect of being able to pay their debts) from the rigours and associated costs of the bankruptcy process.

A DRO (see IA 1986, Part VIIA) is administered by the Insolvency Service through the Official Receiver's office. Akin to bankruptcy, the effect of a DRO is to provide a debtor relief from the enforcement of debts and discharge the individual from those debts after 12 months.

The development of the DRO arose from concern that bankruptcy had through its associated costs (e.g. the court fee and the Official Receiver's deposit) become unavailable to those on a very low income and that the county court administration order (see **2.6**) was of limited value. In addition, the one size fits all system of investigation and reporting dealt with those bankrupts, with few to no assets, inefficiently.

The DRO is thus available to debtors:

- owing less than £15,000;
- having less than £50 a month surplus income (taking into account reasonable domestic needs);
- having less than £300-worth of assets (motor vehicles are not included in this limit, provided the car is worth less than £1,000 or is needed because of disability);
- who live, run a business or own a property in England or Wales or have done so in the last three years; and
- who have not applied for a DRO in the last six years.

The debtor cannot apply for a DRO while being an undischarged bankrupt, while being subject to an IVA, or while a bankruptcy petition is pending (IA 1986, Sched.4ZA).

Debts that are not included are:

- secured debts;
- court fines;
- family maintenance payments;
- student loans; and
- debts created after the DRO has been issued.

While the DRO is still subject to a fee, required to cover the costs for initiation of the procedure, it is to be set at an affordable level (as at September 2011 it was set at a non-refundable £90).

The debtor submits an application for a DRO to the Official Receiver's office via an intermediary authorised by a competent authority (IA 1986, ss.251B, 251U). The approved intermediary is able to assess the liabilities, assets and income of the debtor and therefore his eligibility for the scheme or, if appropriate, consider alternatives. Since the DRO was introduced, competent authorities given the power to authorise intermediaries have included the Citizens Advice Bureau, the Consumer Credit Counselling Service, National Debtline and Payplan.

The debtor's application must include (see IR 1986, rule 5A.3):

- a list of debts to which the debtor is subject at the date of the application;
- details of any security held in respect of those debts;
- the amount of any income from any source;
- particulars of expenditure;
- the amount claimed as necessary to meet reasonable domestic needs;
- particulars of property and estimated value; and

- statements as to material antecedent transactions (e.g. possible preferential transactions and/or transactions at an undervalue).

The application is submitted in electronic form to the Official Receiver (IR 1986, rule 5A.4), who will consider the application and ensure that the requirements of IA 1986, s.251B, Sched.4ZA are met, that any queries have been answered and that the debtor has not made any false representations. If the Official Receiver refuses to make the DRO he must give written reasons (IR 1986, rule 5A.6(2)).

If a DRO is made it will be registered and a moratorium in relation to creditor enforcement action will come into effect. At the end of the DRO (it will last one year unless extended) the debtor is released from all qualifying debts.

A creditor has the right to challenge the making of a DRO on the grounds that it contained an error or omission, the debtor is in fact bankrupt or subject to an individual voluntary arrangement, or the Official Receiver was in error (IR 1986, rule 5A.14). Alternatively, a creditor may apply to vary or amend the DRO if dissatisfied with the Official Receiver's conduct in the determination of the application (IA 1986, s.251M).

Alternatively, the Official Receiver may, during the moratorium period, revoke the DRO if it is later discovered that the debtor has given misleading information or the DRO was obtained through an error or omission (IA 1986, s.251L).

2.6 COUNTY COURT ADMINISTRATION ORDERS

A county court administration order is available to individuals who are subject to a non-business related judgment debt obtained by a creditor in either the county court or High Court (see County Courts Act 1984, ss.112A–112AI). However, it is a remedy of decreasing importance due to the limitations in its use and the attractiveness of other personal insolvency processes.

To apply, the debtor must:

- owe less than £5,000 inclusive of interest and costs;
- owe money to two or more creditors;
- prove to the court that he can afford to meet regular payments; and
- be unable to meet the whole or part of a judgment debt.

On hearing the application, the court will decide what is reasonable for the debtor to pay, and how long the order (and obligation to pay instalments) will last. If it decides that the full debt cannot be paid, the court can order that an appropriate percentage is paid as part of a 'composition order'.

Provided the debtor meets the obligations imposed under the administration or composition order, no creditor (whose debt has been notified to the court and scheduled to the order) can take enforcement action against the debtor without permission of the court. An order can last up to five years, whereupon the debtor will be released from the debts in question.

In practice, for the debtor with few available assets and little income, the DRO offers a more realistic option. While it is noted that an administration order is available to those who have surplus income over and above reasonable domestic needs, whereas a DRO is for those with no such income, it must be rare to find a debtor who has surplus income yet is unable to meet debts of less than £5,000 (or at least unable to come to an agreement with his creditors). Proposals to remove the current limit on the maximum debt level and/or to replace it with a more realistic level, together with further amendments which would have overhauled the process, were mooted when the Tribunals, Courts and Enforcement Act 2007 was enacted. At the time of writing, these proposals do not seem likely to be progressed further.

2.7   BANKRUPTCY ON THE DEBTOR'S PETITION

2.7.1   Preliminary considerations

If neither a formal nor an informal arrangement with creditors is either practical or acceptable, the available options for an individual insolvent debtor are either a DRO (if available) or bankruptcy.

It should be remembered that an individual insolvent debtor will not necessarily become bankrupt unless he, a creditor, or any other person provided by statute petitions the court to make a bankruptcy order. Paradoxically, an individual may not in fact be insolvent, but could be adjudged bankrupt, e.g. where a debtor chooses to ignore a statutory demand or refuses to pay a due debt, or where the debtor's assets are insufficiently liquid to satisfy an immediate liability (so failing the cash flow test in insolvency).

Table 2.4   Debtor's petition for bankruptcy – why?

Pros of bankruptcy for a debtor	Cons of bankruptcy for a debtor
• Finality	• Loss of assets
• Protection from creditors' actions	• Loss of income
• Financial rehabilitation – a fresh start	• Restrictions
• Speed of process	• Disabilities
• Changing perception – the loss of stigma	• Historic 'stigma' attached

A significant feature of the English bankruptcy system is the financial rehabilitation of the debtor. Indeed, early legislation viewed bankruptcy as a privilege, a chance to avoid oppressive and continued enforcement action by creditors during the course of one's life and the potential at some point to start again with a 'clean slate'. This phrase is derived from Roman law, from which many concepts of modern bankruptcy law are derived – the 'slate' or tablets of a creditor's account could be ordered to be wiped clean, thus cancelling the debtor's liability.

While the modern bankruptcy regime has become progressively more liberal, in particular with the shortening of its duration, the balance between financial rehabilitation and the initiation of a collective enforcement process on behalf of creditors still lies at its heart.

An insolvent debtor may have been under incredible financial and emotional strain for a number of years, struggling to cope with multiple actions by a variety of creditors. The significant time and resources taken in fending off these creditors, who are each entitled to take their own enforcement action, places immense pressure on a debtor. For many, bankruptcy is a great fear, but in practice provides tremendous relief.

In return for giving up virtually the whole of his current property, the debtor will on discharge from bankruptcy obtain release and freedom from accumulated debt. The debtor has a fresh start, free from pre-bankruptcy debts and a chance to try again.

Once the debtor is declared bankrupt, creditors are subject to the collective process of bankruptcy, whereby a trustee in bankruptcy will collect such assets of the bankrupt as are available for distribution on a rateable basis in proportion to the debts owed (the *pari passu* principle). The creditors cannot individually continue to pursue the debtor.

A further significant factor, which has encouraged individuals to consider bankruptcy in even greater numbers since 1 April 2004, is the revised bankruptcy procedure introduced by the Enterprise Act 2002. IA 1986, s.279 provides that 'a bankrupt is discharged from bankruptcy at the end of the period of one year beginning with the date on which the bankruptcy commences'. The section goes on to provide that if during the period of one year the Official Receiver files at court a notice stating that investigation into the conduct and affairs of the bankrupt is unnecessary or has been concluded, then the bankrupt will be discharged earlier.

As a consequence, an individual may be discharged from the restrictions and disabilities of bankruptcy within a matter of weeks. The Official Receiver will seek to discharge his duties within a period of six to 12 weeks and therefore the majority of bankrupts are discharged within a period of 12 months.

While the assets of the individual will still vest in the trustee in bankruptcy (by virtue of IA 1986, s.306), the key advantage for the debtor is that he will be released from his accumulated debts due at the date of bankruptcy. He is free to start again. The intention of the government in introducing such a provision was to encourage financial rehabilitation, to give individuals a second chance and to further an entrepreneurial culture.

The release from debt enforcement, the shortened period during which the restrictions from bankruptcy apply, the greater its occurrence and thereby decreasing stigma of bankrupt are all factors which may cause a debtor to petition for his own bankruptcy.

The first step that the debtor will need to take in commencing the bankruptcy process is the presentation of a bankruptcy petition to a court with appropriate jurisdiction.

A bankruptcy petition may be presented by a debtor where:

- the individual is a debtor;
- the individual is domiciled in England or Wales, or is personally present in England or Wales on the day on which the petition is presented, or, at any time in the last three years ending with the day on which the petition is presented, has been resident in England or Wales, or has carried on business in England and Wales (IA 1986, s.265(1)).

Regard must also be had to the EC Regulation on Insolvency Proceedings before considering the commencement of any bankruptcy. If the debtor's centre of main interests (COMI) is in another European Member State, the bankruptcy should be opened in that state, or otherwise where the debtor has 'an establishment'.

2.7.2   Who may petition for a bankruptcy order?

A petition for a bankruptcy order to be made against an individual may be presented (IA 1986, s.264):

(a)   by one of the individual's creditors or jointly by more than one of them;
(b)   by the individual himself;
(c)   by a temporary administrator (within the meaning of Art.38 of the EC Regulation on Insolvency Proceedings);
(d)   by a liquidator (within the meaning of Art.2(b) of the EC Regulation) appointed in proceedings by virtue of Art.3(1) of the EC Regulation;
(e)   after default in respect of a voluntary arrangement by the supervisor or person bound to the arrangement; or
(f)   where a criminal bankruptcy order has been made against an individual by the Official Petitioner or any other person specified in the order under the Powers of Criminal Courts Act 1973, s.39(3)(b) (IA 1986, s.277).

In this section we are looking solely at the debtor's own petition.

2.7.3   Grounds for petition

The only ground on which a debtor may petition for his own bankruptcy is an inability to pay debt (IA 1986, ss.264(1)(b) and 272(1)).

IA 1986, s.382(3) defines 'debt' as being a debt or liability, present or future, certain or contingent, whether its amount is fixed or liquidated, or is capable of being ascertained by fixed rules or as a matter of opinion. The court will look to the commercial reality rather than the alleged book value of debt in assessing the debtor's financial position (see *Re Coney (a Bankrupt)* [1998] BPIR 333). However, there is no minimum debt level (although as we have seen above it may be more appropriate for the debtor to apply for a DRO under IA 1986, s.251A where the total level of debt owed is less than £15,000).

The petition itself does not need to be verified by affidavit, although the statement of affairs which must accompany the petition should be verified by affidavit or a witness statement that contains a statement of truth (IA 1986, s.272(2) and IR 1986, rule 6.41(1)).

Practical tips on completing Form 6.27

The references below are to those parts of Form 6.27 that need to be completed. The use of the prescribed form enables the debtor to ensure that all necessary information is contained in the petition (as set out in IR 1986, rules 6.38 and 6.39) and it is almost certainly quicker and more convenient to use the appropriate form. In practice, it is often the case that a debtor wishing to petition for his own bankruptcy will simply present himself at court, in which case the court staff are likely to assist him (providing easy to follow guidance leaflets) through the process of form filling. It may even be possible to complete the forms there and then before appearing before a district judge/bankruptcy registrar on the same day.

1. Debtor's personal details:

    (a) insert the debtor's name, place of business, residence and occupation (if any);

    (b) provide any other name used by the debtor or by which he is known;

    (c) insert former addresses at which the debtor may have incurred unpaid debts or unsatisfied liabilities;

    (d) insert trading name, or names, in which the debtor has carried on business; provide details of the nature of the business, and whether this has been carried on alone or with others;

    (e) provide details of any former business, the nature of the business, and whether this has been carried on alone or with others in respect of which the debtor may have incurred unpaid debts or unsatisfied liabilities;

    (f) provide details required under the EC Regulation on Insolvency Proceedings. In the majority of cases, the debtor's COMI will be where he resides and so 'conducts the administration of his interests on a regular basis'. In the case of business activity, the debtor may have an 'establishment' only if he resides elsewhere, but in the UK he has 'a place of operations where the debtor carries out a non-transitory economic activity with human means and goods'.

2. This section deals with the issue of court jurisdiction. The petition must contain sufficient information to establish that it is being presented to the appropriate court. The petition must be presented in:

Rule 6.37   Form 6.27

Debtor's Bankruptcy Petition
(Title)

(a) Insert full name, address and occupation (if any) of debtor

I
(a)_____

(b) Insert in full any other name(s) by which the debtor is or has been known

also known as
(b)_____

(c) Insert former address or addresses at which the debtor may have incurred debts or liabilities still unpaid or unsatisfied

[lately residing at
(c)_____

(d) Insert trading name (adding "with another or others", if this is so), business address and nature of the business

[and carrying on business as (d)_____

_____]

(e) Insert any former trading names (adding "with another or others", if this is so), business address and nature of the business in respect of which the debtor may have incurred debts or liabilities still unpaid or unsatisfied

[and lately carrying on business as (e)_____

_____

_____

_____]

(f) Delete as applicable

request the court that a bankruptcy order be made against me and say as follows:-

1. (f) [My centre of main interests is in England and Wales][I have an establishment in England and Wales.]

OR

I carry on business as an insurance undertaking; a credit institution; investment undertaking providing services involving the holding of funds or securities for third parties; or a collective investment undertaking as referred to in Article 1.2 of the EC Regulation.

OR

My centre of main interests is not within a Member State

Under the EC Regulation
(i) Centre of main interests should correspond to the place where the debtor conducts the administration of his interests on a regular basis.

67

(ii) Establishment is defined in the Council Regulation (No 1346/2000) on insolvency proceedings as "any place of operations where the debtor caries out a non-transitory economic activity with human means and goods"

2. I am (f)[not] resident in England and Wales. I am presenting this petition to the High Court because (f)[I have neither carried on business nor resided in England and Wales within the 6 months immediately preceding the presentation of this petition][I am a member of an insolvent partnership (f)[which is being wound up][in relation to which a winding-up petition has been presented which has not yet been disposed of]].

OR

I am (f)[not] resident in England and Wales. I am presenting this petition to the (f)[High Court][Central London County Court] because (f)[I carried on business in England and Wales within the 6 months immediately preceding the presentation of this petition and I carried on business within the area of the London insolvency district (f)[for the greater part of that period of 6 months][for a longer period than in any other insolvency district]][I have not carried on business in England and Wales but have resided in England and Wales within the 6 months immediately preceding the presentation of this petition and I resided within the area of the London insolvency district (f)[for the greater part of that period of 6 months][for a longer period than in any other insolvency district]] and the unsecured liabilities set out in the statement of affairs attached to this petition are (f)[£100,000 or more][less than £100,000].

OR

I am (f)[not] resident in England and Wales. I am presenting this petition to this county court because within the 6 months immediately preceding the presentation of this petition (f)[I carried on business in England and Wales and for the longest part of the period during which I carried on business in England and Wales within that 6 period of months, the (f)[principal] place of business was situated in the district of (f)[this][..........] county court][I have not carried on business in England and Wales but resided in England and Wales and for the longest part of the period during which I resided in England and Wales within that period of 6 months, I resided in the district of (f)[this][.............] county court]][and in order to expedite the presentation of this petition, I am presenting it to this court as it is the [nearest full time] court (f)[to my [principal] place of business][for the insolvency district in which I reside]].

3. I am unable to pay my debts.

4. (f) That within the period of five years ending with the date of this petition:-

(i) I have not been adjudged bankrupt

(j) Insert date

(k) Insert name of court

(l) Insert number of bankruptcy proceedings

OR

I was adjudged bankrupt on (j)   in the (k)

Court No. (l)

(ii) I have not (f) [made a composition with my creditors in satisfaction of my debts] or (f) [entered into a scheme of arrangement with creditors] (S16 BA1914)

OR

On (j)   I (f) [made a composition] [entered into a scheme of arrangement] with my creditors.

(iii) I have not entered into a voluntary arrangement

OR

On (j)   I entered into a voluntary arrangement

(iv) I have not been subject to an administration order under Part VI of the County Courts Act 1984

OR

On (j)   an administration order was made against me in the
(l)   county court.

5. A statement of my affairs is filed with this petition.

Date_____

Signature_____

Complete only if
petition not heard
immediately

> **Endorsement**
>
> This petition having been presented to the court on _____ it is ordered that the petition shall be heard as follows:-
>
> Date _____
>
> Time _____ hours
>
> Place_____

- the High Court if:
    - the debtor has not resided nor carried on business in England and Wales within the last six months;
    - the debtor is a member of an insolvent partnership being wound up/where a winding-up petition has been presented; or
    - the debtor has resided or carried on business in the London insolvency district for the greater part of six months and has unsecured liabilities of £100,000 or more;
- the Central London County Court if the debtor has resided or carried on business in the London insolvency district for the greater part of six months and has unsecured liabilities of less than £100,000;
- the 'debtor's own' county court if the debtor has resided or carried on business in the county court district for the greater part of six months. Not all county courts have jurisdiction to hear bankruptcy petitions and consequently the debtor may need to apply to a court in the insolvency district in which he resides (IR 1986, rule 6.9A(3)).

3.   A statement that the debtor is unable to pay his debts. This is of course mandatory and the only ground for a debtor to present a petition.

4.   This section deals with previous bankruptcy within the last five years (which may affect the ability to receive an automatic discharge) or any scheme of arrangement or IVA or county court administration order. If an IVA is in force, the petition must be presented in the court to which the nominee submitted his report; the particulars of the IVA and the name and address of the supervisor of the arrangement must be disclosed (IR 1986, rules 6.38, 6.39).

5.   The petition must be signed and dated and needs to be accompanied by a statement of affairs (Form 6.28). The court office on payment of the court fee and Official Receiver's deposit (as at October 2012, £175 and £525 respectively) will endorse the time and date of filing and provide a date for the hearing of the petition.

It can be seen that the requirements contained in IR 1986, rule 6.38 are intended to identify the debtor, where the debtor has resided and/or carried on business. They are also intended to clarify whether a previous bankruptcy order has been made, or whether the debtor has entered into some form of voluntary arrangement. This will assist the Official Receiver/trustee in bankruptcy to make appropriate enquiries and also establishes the appropriate court in which the bankruptcy petition is to be heard.

The debtor's petition must be accompanied by a statement of affairs in Form 6.28 (see IR 1986, rule 6.68). This form is of some considerable length and complexity and general guidance notes are supplied by the bankruptcy court to assist the debtor in completing a statement of affairs. While the court staff will in all likelihood assist the debtor in completing the petition, the debtor is entirely responsible for completing the statement of affairs. The statement must truly and accurately reflect the debts, liabilities and assets of the debtor and is verified by a statement of truth (IR 1986, rule 6.41(1)). Further information required to be set out in Form 6.28 includes details of:

- any dependants of the debtor;
- forms of distress that have been levied against the debtor;
- any court judgment or legal process currently outstanding;
- whether any attachment of earnings order is in place against the debtor;
- whether an attempt has been made to reach agreement with creditors regarding payment of debt;
- whether the debtor thinks it is possible that a voluntary arrangement would be accepted by his creditors; and
- the debtor's means, by way of a statement identifying income against expenditure of the debtor leading to a conclusion as to how much per month the debtor considers he is able to pay his creditors.

2.7.4   Procedure for presentation and filing

The petition and statement of affairs must be filed at court together with three copies of the petition and one copy of the statement of affairs (IR 1986, rule 6.42(1)).

On presentation of the petition and payment of the fees (see below), the court may hear the petition as soon as reasonably practicable (IR 1986, rule 6.42(2)). This may mean that the debtor is able to prepare the petition and statement of affairs on his first attendance at an appropriate court, with the hearing taking place on the same day as filing. If the court is unable to fix a date, or where an IVA exists, the court will fix a venue and date for hearing. Where an IVA is in place, 14 days' notice must be provided to the supervisor of the arrangement. The supervisor may appear and be heard at the hearing of the petition (IR 1986, rule 6.42(2A)).

It should be noted that IA 1986, s.264(1)(c) provides authority for the supervisor, or any creditor, to petition for the debtor's bankruptcy where there has been a failure of the IVA. Notable in its absence is any ability for the debtor to present a bankruptcy petition on the failure of the IVA. However, the Insolvency Rules make it clear that the debtor may present a petition when an IVA is in place. However, such a petition must be on the grounds of an inability to pay debts, not on the grounds that the IVA has failed.

Where a bankruptcy order is made on the debtor's petition and an IVA is in place, any expenses incurred in administration of the IVA shall be a first charge on the bankrupt's estate (IR 1986, rule 6.46A).

The debtor is required to pay a court fee and an Official Receiver's deposit (£175 court fee and Official Receiver's deposit on debtor's petition of £525 as at October 2012). There has been a challenge under Art.6 of the European Convention on Human Rights that this offends against the right of an individual to have access to justice (see *R. v. Lord Chancellor, ex p. Lightfoot* [1999] 4 All ER 583). In the case brought, the debtor contended that the requirement to pay fees in circumstances of financial impecuniosity deprived her of her fundamental right to justice. This argument was rejected by the Court of Appeal. While the court accepted that access to justice is a fundamental requirement for the rule of law, it did not consider that access to the bankruptcy scheme was a constitutional right. The legislature had provided for a deposit to meet the costs of administering the bankruptcy. This was reasonable, as the bankruptcy procedure was there not to adjudicate disputes, but to act as a scheme designed to ensure equality between creditors and debtors. With the introduction of DROs (see above) for those with few assets and little or no income, there is now a cheaper alternative in comparison with the 'expense' of bankruptcy, and moreover in some circumstances (e.g. where the debtor is on income support) the bankruptcy court fee may be waived.

An important point to note is that once the bankruptcy petition is presented, it cannot be withdrawn without leave of the court. This prevents a debtor from using a bankruptcy petition to avoid or 'buy time' from creditors' enforcement action. Even though the petition is presented by the debtor, once it is issued the court has control of the matter (i.e. it is not for the debtor simply to withdraw the petition).

Of the three copies of the petition:

(a)   one must be returned to the petitioner, endorsed with date, time and venue of the hearing;

(b)   another will be sent by the court to the Official Receiver (with a copy of the statement of affairs); and

(c)   the remaining copy will be retained by the court to be sent to any insolvency practitioner appointed by the court to report, in the case of a debtor with debts not exceeding the 'small bankruptcy level' (£40,000 under the Insolvency Proceedings (Monetary Limits) (Amendment) Order 2004, SI 2004/547), on whether an IVA as opposed to bankruptcy would be appropriate (IA 1986, s.273).

2.7.5   Presentation to appropriate court

The debtor should attend the local county court applicable to the district in which he has resided or carried on business for the longest period in the last six months.

It should be noted that not all county courts have insolvency jurisdiction. Furthermore, if for the greater part of six months the debtor has resided or carried on business in more than one insolvency district, the appropriate county court is that where he has spent the majority of his time. If the debtor has resided in one insolvency district and carried on business in another, the district in which he has carried on business takes precedence (IR 1986, rule 6.9A.40).

If the debtor has resided or carried on business in the London insolvency district for the greater part of six months immediately preceding the presentation of the petition, the petition must be presented at the High Court (if the petition debt is £50,000 or more) or the Central London County Court (if the petition debt is less than £50,000) (see IR 1986, rule 6.9A(1)).

If the debtor has for a longer period in those six months not resided or carried on business in any other insolvency district or, alternatively, where the debtor was not resident in England or Wales, the petition must be presented in the London insolvency district. In addition, the London insolvency district High Court has exclusive jurisdiction where the debtor is a member of an insolvent partnership being wound up/where a winding-up petition has been presented (see IR 1986, rule 7.10ZA).

In practice, the distinction between the issue of a petition in the High Court and issue in the Central London County Court will have less immediate impact following the changes that came into force on 6 April 2011 (see the London Insolvency District (Central London County Court) Order 2011, SI 2011/761) than first envisaged. The reason for this is that the petition can still be filed at, and will physically be heard in, the Royal Courts of Justice even though it will be heard by a district judge of the Central London County Court as opposed to a bankruptcy registrar.

If the debtor is subject to an IVA, the petition must be presented in the court to which the nominee's report under was submitted under IA 1986, s.256 (IR 1986, rule 6.40A(7)).

Where it is more expedient for the debtor to present the petition in the court where he resides, as opposed to trades, it is possible to present the petition at that court if there is a need to expedite the petition. Where either a district judge or bankruptcy registrar is not available to hear the case and/or an expedited hearing is not required, the petition must be filed at the nearest full-time court.

2.7.6 Hearing of the bankruptcy petition

If a bankruptcy registrar or district judge is unavailable to hear the petition immediately and/or the petition is not one requiring an expedited hearing, or if there is an IVA in place which requires notice to be provided to the supervisor, the court will appoint a date, time and place for the hearing of the petition.

The supervisor of the arrangement must be provided with not less than 14 days' notice. A copy of the statement of affairs is sent by the court to the Official Receiver. If the court hears the petition immediately, the court may require the debtor to deliver the statement of affairs directly to the Official Receiver.

The court has a general power to dismiss or stay the petition (IA 1986, s.266) and will refuse to make an order if it feels the petition is an abuse of process (*Re Painter* [1895] 1 QB 85, where a petition for bankruptcy was presented to avoid committal on a judgment summons).

It should also be noted that IA 1986, s.272(1) provides that a debtor's petition may only be presented on the grounds that the debtor is unable to pay his debts. If the debtor wishes to avoid a debt and makes himself bankrupt (for reasons of spite, illogical refusal, etc.) yet has an ability to pay, the court should refuse to make a bankruptcy order (see *Re a Debtor, ex p. Debtor* v. *Allen*, sub nom. *Re a Debtor (No.17 of 1966)* [1967] Ch 590).

On being made bankrupt, the debtor is required to attend before a court officer, who will direct the debtor to appear before the Official Receiver. In practice, a telephone call may be made from the court office by the debtor to the Official Receiver's office and a date for his appointment before the Official Receiver is set.

As stated above, it is possible, although unusual, for the court to order the appointment of an insolvency practitioner to prepare a report as to the appropriateness of putting forward an IVA to the debtor's creditors instead of making a bankruptcy order (IA 1986, s.273). The court will only do this if:

(a) the unsecured debts of the debtor do not exceed the small bankruptcy level (which is presently set at £40,000 by the Insolvency Proceedings (Monetary Limits) (Amendment) Order 2004, SI 2004/547);

(b) on the making of the bankruptcy order, the value of the bankrupt's estate would not exceed the minimum amount (set at £4,000 by SI 2004/547); or

(c) within a period of five years ending with the presentation of the petition, the debtor has neither been adjudged bankrupt, nor made a composition or scheme of arrangement with his creditors in satisfaction of debts.

These provisions are to ensure that bankruptcy remains a matter of last resort, particularly in cases where the amounts due to creditors are small and the estate itself is of insubstantial value.

The insolvency practitioner appointed by the court will report as to whether a meeting of the debtor's creditors should be summoned to consider a proposal for an IVA.

In considering the report, the court may, without application, make an interim order under IA 1986, s.252 for the purposes of facilitating the consideration and presentation of a proposal. If, after considering the report, the court does not consider it appropriate to summon a meeting of creditors, a bankruptcy order will be made.

Even after the making of an order, the court retains a power to annul a bankruptcy order, if it is of the opinion that the order should not have been made (IA 1986, s.282(1)(a)).

2.7.7   Post-petition steps

Following the making of the order, the court office will draw up the order, which will include:

- reference to the date that the petition was presented;
- the date and time of the order being made;
- a full description of the debtor as stated in the petition, including names, aliases, address(es) and business address(es);
- notice to the bankrupt that immediately on service of the order he must attend the Official Receiver's office; and
- the name, address, telephone number and reference of the bankrupt's solicitors (if appropriate).

The court will then send to the Official Receiver at least two sealed copies of the bankruptcy order and the Official Receiver will send a copy of the order to the bankrupt, and:

- send notice of the making of the order to the Chief Land Registrar for registration in the register of writs and orders;
- advertise in such newspapers as thought fit;
- cause notice of the order to be published in the *London Gazette*; and
- enter appropriate notice in the register of bankruptcy orders.

Debtor's petition for bankruptcy – procedure

Guide to procedure

Bankruptcy: debtor's petition

1.   Debtor prepares bankruptcy petition and statement of affairs verified by affidavit or witness statement.
2.   Debtor attends court. Court staff may assist debtor in preparing petition.
3.   Debtor pays court deposit as security for fees of Official Receiver and court fee.

4. File petition plus three copies and statement of affairs (in Form 6.28) plus two copies.
5. Hearing before bankruptcy registrar or district judge may take place on that day.
6. If no bankruptcy registrar/district judge is available and/or an expedited hearing date is not required, the court will endorse a copy of the petition with a date of hearing not less than 14 days hence.
7. At the hearing, the court may order the appointment of an insolvency practitioner to enquire into the debtor's affairs and report if a proposal for a voluntary arrangement is appropriate. More usually, however, a bankruptcy order is immediately made.

2.7.8   Debtor's bankruptcy petition – abuse of process

There remains a concern among creditors that a certain minority of debtors use the bankruptcy procedures as a means of preventing creditor enforcement action. On discharge from bankruptcy (or in some cases where an order is not made), the debtor will be able to continue with his previous 'dishonest' practices.

IA 1986 provides a number of ways by which dishonest conduct can be tackled, such as proceedings to set aside transactions at an undervalue, preferences and transactions taken to defraud creditors. Criminal offences may also be committed by individuals in respect of certain cases of misconduct.

An important point to note is that once the bankruptcy petition is presented, it cannot be withdrawn without leave of the court. This prevents a debtor from using a bankruptcy petition to avoid or 'buy time' from creditors' enforcement action. The court has overall control of the matter once the petition is presented.

Overarching these provisions is the fact that the court always retains the discretion to refuse the petition, where the presentation amounts to an abuse of legal process (IA 1986, ss.264(2), 266(3)). Furthermore, the court retains a power to annul a bankruptcy order, if it is of the opinion that the order should not have been made (IA 1986, s.282(1)(a)) (see **10.10**).

CHAPTER 3

Advising a corporate debtor

In this chapter we consider matters specific to a corporate debtor, exploring the options when faced with a statutory demand and the possible commencement of an insolvency procedure, in particular a CVA, company/director led administration and voluntary liquidation.

3.1 STATUTORY DEMAND AND THE CORPORATE DEBTOR

3.1.1 Debtor's considerations on being served with a statutory demand

---

Checklist

The corporate debtor needs to consider:

1. Is the debt demanded disputed?
2. Can the demand be disputed on any other grounds?
3. Are there sufficient grounds, evidence and resources to enable a challenge to the demand and ultimately the initiation of injunctive relief?
4. Irrespective of the answer to (1) or (2), is the debtor otherwise insolvent? If so, professional advice from an insolvency practitioner is almost certainly necessary and appropriate insolvency procedures should be considered.
5. If the answer to (1) or (2) is no, can the debtor pay the debt demanded?
6. If the answer to (5) is no, can the debtor make an offer to secure or compound the debt?
7. If the answer to (5) and (6) is no, is the creditor going to proceed to petition for the compulsory winding up of the company?
8. If the answer to (7) is yes, the debtor should consider whether some form of alternative insolvency procedure (such as voluntary liquidation, administration or CVA) is feasible and in the best interests of other creditors.
9. If the answer to (8) is no, should the debtor (and the directors) do nothing?

On being served with a statutory demand the debtor must assess whether:

- the debt is disputed;

- there is a genuine or serious cross-claim; and
- it is able to pay the demand within the 21-day period.

The adviser should carefully discuss with the company and its directors their attitude on being served a demand. Could the service of a demand and possibly a petition irredeemably harm the company's reputation and dissipate goodwill? Could it cause difficulties in the company's ability to continue to trade? As we shall see, one of the effects of the issue of a winding-up petition is the potential freezing of the company's bank account (IA 1986, s.127). In either event, will the company's banker, suppliers, landlords or other key stakeholders withdraw support? Is it worth the risk?

As a result, even though the company may dispute the demand and/or has a cross-claim, to avoid the possibility of any insolvency proceedings it may be best to offer partial payment of the sum demanded or some form of security pending resolution of the dispute. This could involve the payment of the disputed sum into an account held in escrow.

If, however, there is a genuine dispute and/or a cross-claim the alleged debtor company should demand that the alleged creditor 'withdraw' the demand (i.e. undertake not to present a petition based on the non-compliance with the statutory demand). If the creditor refuses, the company must apply to court to restrain the creditor from presenting a winding-up petition.

As the remedy of injunctive relief available to the alleged debtor is an exercise of the equitable discretion of the court, it is best that the alleged debtor is seen to act fairly and reasonably by giving the creditor reasonable opportunity to withdraw the demand rather than seeking immediate injunctive relief. Acting in this manner will provide the alleged debtor with grounds for the recovery of legal costs should it eventually be necessary to commence legal proceedings.

Alternatively, if a creditor proceeds with a demand, where it is known or should be known that the debt is disputed, the creditor can be punished with severe costs sanctions. Consequently, notice of the dispute/cross-claim and agreement to withdraw is normally sufficient. The raising of a bona fide dispute on service of a statutory demand does not prevent the creditor from taking legal proceedings to establish the debt.

If the debt is not disputed but the debtor cannot immediately pay, the debtor may be best advised to seek some form of agreed compromise with the creditor. This may involve payment by instalments, or postponement of payment to a later date and/or an offer of security. Before seeking any compromise, the debtor does need to consider the position of other creditors – it is pointless seeking agreement with one creditor if another will be 'stepping into their shoes'. However, there is no obligation on the creditor to accept anything less than that which it is entitled to.

If the debt is not disputed and/or any offer of settlement has been refused, yet for some reason the creditor decides not to act upon the demand, the debtor is in a difficult position: a presumption of insolvency has arisen. Consequently, if further credit is taken and/or losses are incurred at a time when the debtor knows it is insolvent (i.e. is unable to pay its debts as they fall due, which of course is the evidential burden discharged by the non-compliance with a statutory demand) and if the company is subsequently wound up, proceedings against the directors for wrongful or fraudulent trading could be undertaken, as could proceedings under the Company Directors Disqualification Act (CDDA) 1986.

As a result, if a demand is served and the company cannot comply with it, irrespective of whether the creditor decides to proceed, the directors are best advised to seek immediate professional guidance from an insolvency specialist, such as a lawyer or an insolvency practitioner. The same applies even if the debt is disputed but the debtor is unable to pay other debts falling due.

As we have seen in **Chapter 2**, a procedure is available to enable a personal debtor to apply to court for an order setting aside the statutory demand (IR 1986, rule 6.4). While the corporate debtor has no such equivalent, the potential grounds for setting aside a demand for an individual outlined in **2.1** are of equivalent application in the case of a company seeking to restrain the presentation of a winding-up petition based on a statutory demand, and should be considered.

3.2 INFORMAL ARRANGEMENTS WITH CREDITORS

3.2.1 Informal arrangement/workouts and turnaround

There are many different reasons for business failure; poor management, loss of market, supplier or customer insolvency, general economic conditions, lack of financial control and overtrading, to name but a few. What distinguishes business failure from insolvency is the inability of the company to meet the demands of its creditors. However, this does not necessarily mean that the company is insolvent and that a formal insolvency procedure is inevitable. Instead, steps can be taken to alleviate the problems faced by the business, to seek to avoid formal insolvency processes. Informal arrangements can vary from an individual creditor giving additional time for payment, to a range of measures under the umbrella terms of restructuring, turnaround and workout.

For a corporate debtor, in many cases the company's assets are subject to fixed and floating charge security. The co-operation of the secured lender is therefore often an essential ingredient in any reconstruction of the business (moratoriums and restructuring of debt with a secured lender are often termed 'workouts'). Ultimately, if co-operation is not forthcoming or agreement cannot be reached, refinancing and substitution with a new lender may be the corporate debtor's only option.

For unsecured creditors of a company, the fact that members of the company (save in exceptional circumstances) enjoy the benefits of limited liability means that their rights and chances of recovery of debt are often limited. As we have seen in **Chapter 1**, steps can be taken before the provision of credit to minimise the creditor's risk, but it is often the case that these steps have not been taken and an unsecured creditor may find that if it takes steps to enforce claims against the company, this could lead to the secured creditor taking steps to enforce its security (or to the company's directors inviting the secured creditor to do so).

If a company has available assets, the options open to the creditor are more varied and it may be best advised to seek to obtain judgment on its claim and then to enforce that judgment. In any case where the company has an undisputed debt which it is unable or unwilling to pay, the creditor can elect to seek the winding up of the company.

An attractive offer to creditors in these circumstances is the provision of third party funds, i.e. giving the creditors something that would not otherwise be available to them if they sought to enforce their debt/commenced insolvency proceedings. Payment to creditors could be made directly from the third party (e.g. a parent/sister company wishing to maintain goodwill with a key supplier) or through the company after refinance/restructure. The question remains, however, whether the company can obtain funding, perhaps from alternative banks, venture capitalists, private equity funds, new investors or asset-based lenders.

The techniques used to restructure corporate debt will differ if the company is a small owner-managed business rather than a multinational corporation.

For small owner-managed businesses, refinancing may mean that the directors have personally to introduce new capital to the company and/or offer creditors additional security, perhaps in the form of a personal guarantee or seeking new business 'partners'. The options available are virtually limitless, but will be constrained and eventually determined by the needs and demands of the creditors.

While the techniques used for larger companies appear complex and sophisticated, fundamentally they are the same as those for a small company, namely agreement by the creditors to allow the debtor time to refinance and/or restructure the business. This may involve an informal agreement that the creditor(s) will withhold taking enforcement action pending investigation of available financial options. Within this informal moratorium the options to restructure debt are again limitless, and range from offering equity for debt to consolidating debt, asset-based finance or agreeing to sell parts of the business.

Options to restructure and potentially refinance the company can be explored in a number of ways.

3.2.2 Company doctors

There are a number of individuals (and, increasingly, small niche firms), often with vast experience of dealing with businesses in financial difficulty, who are willing to look into the financial position of the company and advise on corporate strategy, funding routes and overall management. They can be brought into the company by the directors or by stakeholders such as the company's banker. Sometimes termed 'company doctors', they will often take a hands-on role, accepting a directorship in the company, the role of chief restructuring officer or some form of interim manager appointment. They will then instigate a process of identifying and then analysing the problems of the business and planning and implementing reconstruction of the business. Key to stabilising the business is improving its cash flow, which may involve reducing stock levels, improving the debtor book profile, and reducing staffing costs and other expenditure. It is trite point, but 'cash is king', and with an improved cash flow and stability the company can move forward to plan and implement reconstruction.

3.2.3 Turnaround professionals

Turnaround professionals range from company doctors to insolvency practitioners and will perform an advisory role rather than take a direct role in the business. They will look at all facets of the business, its management, strategy and profitability. In doing so, the turnaround professional may prepare a business plan with the existing management and consider refinance options and/or whether formal insolvency procedures are necessary. A great deal of skill and expertise in accounting and insolvency is required from these individuals. Often these turnaround professionals are introduced to the company by creditors themselves (in particular, banks may initially appoint an insolvency practitioner to review the affairs and ongoing viability of the business). While the business is undergoing so-called 'intensive care', the principal creditors may informally agree to withhold any enforcement action. This is particularly prevalent in medium to large companies or groups of companies, where there are a number of secured creditors. In small companies with a large number of small value creditors, formal procedures to effect a moratorium may be necessary.

3.2.4 Multi-bank workouts

Almost unique among central banks, the Bank of England has a long tradition of involvement in corporate restructuring. From the 1920s onwards, the Bank of England became involved in leading and formulating proposals for corporate restructuring, acting as 'an honest broker' between a number of banks and the money markets. The Bank of England's role was to facilitate discussions between the lenders and the debtor.

By the early 1990s, the Bank of England had increasingly moved away from direct involvement in the process and instead issued a set of guidelines to assist workout proposals in multi-bank situations. These principles became known as the 'London approach', and effectively allowed a period of review by an independent investigative accountant, during which time the banks would agree to withhold proceedings. Proposals would then be formulated and an assessment of the seniority of claims would take place with a view to sharing loss between the banks within the same category of lending. However, while the Bank of England lost its supervisory function over the UK banking industry, the importance and use of the London approach diminished.

Following the credit crunch and ensuing recession, the need to reform and regulate the banking industry has led to a number of amendments to legislation (in particular the Banking Act 2009 and the Investment Bank Special Administration Regulations 2011, SI 2011/245), although by virtue of the nature of the crisis these reforms have been more aimed at insolvent banks/investment firms than general corporate borrowers dealt with by the banks.

Turnaround procedures and multi-bank workout solutions still persist, not least because often they offer a higher rate of recovery for participating banks than would otherwise be available through formal insolvency procedures. There is also a great deal of flexibility available in the negotiation between the banks and distressed companies.

The distinct disadvantage in such schemes is that there is a requirement for unanimity. As global corporate financing becomes more complicated and there is an increasing trade in distressed debt, there is greater difficulty in persuading all interested parties to negotiate during a period of corporate reconstruction. The other considerable disadvantage which can arise from these informal workouts is the excessive demands on management time for both creditor and debtor. They also tend to be immensely expensive. The position of the unsecured creditors is often overlooked in these larger workout models.

3.2.5 Cross-border corporate reconstruction

There have been significant moves in recent years to introduce a worldwide set of agreed principles between creditors facing a multinational corporate insolvency. For example, the review on international insolvency by the United Nations Commission on International Trade Law (UNCITRAL) sought to tackle this issue. The resulting UNCITRAL model law (adopted on 30 May 1997) was brought into effect in the UK in modified form under the Cross-Border Insolvency Regulations 2006, SI 2006/1030 with effect from 6 April 2006. It has also been adopted in a number of other countries, including Japan, Poland, Romania, South Africa and the USA.

While informal workout models envisage a stand-still period which will stop major (secured) creditors taking action during a period of review, these procedures do not possess the degree of compulsion that is available from a statutory moratorium. The UNCITRAL model law, formulated after an exceptionally long gestation period, offers assistance in dealing with recognition of certain insolvency proceedings (and the office holder) in a foreign country, recognition of foreign insolvency office holders in a signatory country and protocols for co-operation between courts and competent authorities in differing jurisdictions. It does not, however, create an automatic enforceable moratorium in a situation of a multinational insolvency. Instead the moratorium needs to be sought in individual countries (e.g. Chapter 15 recognition in the USA), which will be subject to the statutory framework that that country has in place.

On a day-to-day basis, an adviser outside the City of London is not generally concerned in the negotiation of a global multi-bank workout or corporate reconstruction. This is a specialist area where political and economic considerations are as great as legal ones. However, despite the complexity involved, it should be remembered that in essence all that is happening is that the company is coming to an informal arrangement with its creditors to allow it time to refinance/restructure its business.

Table 3.1 Pros and cons of informal arrangements with creditors

Pros of informal arrangements with creditors	Cons of informal arrangements with creditors
• Flexibility in time and content	• Except in the case of larger companies, turnaround/workout techniques may be prohibitively expensive
• May attract less publicity	
• May be appropriate for global/multi-jurisdictional company group insolvencies	• May delay an inevitable formal insolvency process
• Keeps control in hands of key stakeholders/funders to the business	• Formal corporate rescue methods may be more attractive to the corporate debtor
• Consensual process involving debtor	• No formal moratorium is available

3.3 FORMAL ARRANGEMENTS WITH CREDITORS

3.3.1 Company Act schemes of arrangement

Part 26 of CA 2006, which replaced s.425 of CA 1985, provides for a 'compromise or arrangement' to be put by a corporate debtor to its creditors and can be used in a variety of reconstruction scenarios, such as:

- conversion of debt to equity;
- subordination of unsecured or secured debt; and
- conversion of a secured debt to an unsecured debt or vice versa.

There is no need for the company to be insolvent, although the procedure may be used by an administrator or a liquidator of the company. The procedure involves obtaining sanction of the court to a scheme approved by the requisite majority of creditors (three-quarters in value) in various specified classes. The creditors' meetings are convened by order of the court and each class of creditor must approve the proposal for the scheme of arrangement to take effect.

Many of the advantages of using a scheme of arrangement procedure have disappeared in the last few years. The significant advantage prior to IA 2000 was that a Companies Act scheme of arrangement could bind all creditors whether or not those creditors were actually identified (see *Barclays Bank plc* v. *British Common-wealth Holdings* [1995] BCC 19). A scheme of arrangement was also used where the administration procedure was unavailable, such as in respect of insurance undertakings. Reforms in this area have meant that administration is now available to insurance undertakings and this costly and cumbersome method of reconstruction appears less and less attractive. It remains of use, however, in large and complex reconstructions, where large numbers of stakeholders (members/creditors, secured and unsecured) may be involved and have competing interests requiring resolution.

Table 3.2 Pros and cons of formal arrangements with creditors

Pros of formal arrangement with creditors	Cons of formal arrangement with creditors
• Binds all creditors of any class	• Complexity
• Approval of reconstruction, such as reduction of capital, transfer of assets and liabilities available to the court	• Cost
	• No moratorium available
	• Cumbersome/lengthy procedures

3.3.2 Section 110 schemes

IA 1986, s.110 provides for a specific form of arrangement by the liquidator of a company in voluntary winding up who proposes to transfer the whole or part of the company's business or property to another company in exchange for shares, policies or other like interests. This procedure is not appropriate as a means of distributing assets other than in accordance with creditors' legal rights (see *Re Trix Ltd* [1970] 3 All ER 397).

The uses of the procedure are many and varied, including as a means of tax efficiently transferring assets across a corporate structure or effecting a split of the business to a number of new corporate vehicles, perhaps where the shareholders of the transferor company are in dispute. The company does not need to be insolvent, although in the case of a solvent liquidation before transfer of the assets the liquidator must ensure that the transferor has discharged all liabilities (actual, present or future) and has, if appropriate, obtained enforceable indemnities from the transferee companies in respect of contingent liabilities.

Sanction is required for members' voluntary winding up by a special resolution of the company; in the case of creditors' voluntary winding up, the court or liquidation committee must approve. Dissenting members of the company have the right to have their shareholding in the company bought out for cash if they comply with IA 1986, s.111(2) by writing to the liquidator within seven days of the passing of the special resolution.

3.4 COMPANY VOLUNTARY ARRANGEMENTS (CVAS) – INTRODUCTION

While the CVA is a creation of IA 1986, companies have had a statutory ability to enter into an arrangement with creditors since 1908 (Companies (Consolidation) Act 1908, s.120). Early company arrangements provided for a meeting of creditors and if the agreement of three-quarters in value of the creditors present at the meeting was obtained, this would bind all creditors and the company to the terms of the arrangement – sounds familiar! The number of statutory company arrangements pre-1986 was low, with the procedure being considered too slow, cumbersome and costly.

One of the main intentions behind IA 1986 was to encourage corporate rescue by the introduction of new procedures – namely administration and 'new style' CVA procedures. Unfortunately, CVAs have proved to be somewhat the bridesmaids of corporate rescue techniques and are used more to facilitate a distribution to creditors after another insolvency process (e.g. administration) than as a means of corporate rescue in themselves. Certainly, in comparison with the number of IVAs (also introduced in IA 1986), the number of CVAs entered into has been negligible. Despite higher returns offered to creditors, there are unfortunately few examples of CVAs being used to rescue trading companies, although a recent trend has seen their use in complex cross-border situations.

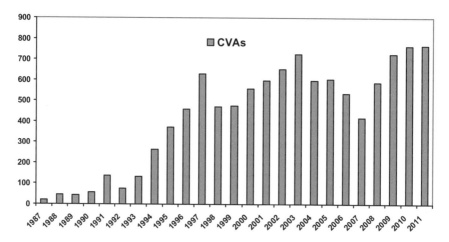

Figure 3.1   Number of CVAs 1987–2011

Source: Insolvency Service Statistical Directorate

As can be seen from Figure 3.1, while the number of CVAs has increased over the last few years, the procedure still remains relatively underutilised, in 2011 accounting for only 3.5 per cent of all corporate insolvency procedures.

A lack of familiarity and defects in the CVA procedures, such as a lack of moratorium against creditor action pending the proposal being put to creditors, may have explained the initial low rate of use of the procedure. However, while many of the defects were resolved by the reforms of IA 2000, which came into effect on 1 January 2003, no noticeable rise in the number has resulted. The reasons for this are many and varied, but include the perceived cost, the lack of speed in implementation, the attitude of creditors and the need to obtain the consent of such a high proportion of creditors to the arrangement. Furthermore, since the Enterprise Act 2002, administration offers in many cases an attractive, speedy and straightforward route for obtaining a moratorium against creditors' actions and a more flexible means to restructure and rescue the company or the business. CVAs therefore continue to be a useful exit route from administration, or in some cases liquidation, offering an efficient means of distribution; however, the use of the procedure in its own right still remains unlikely to become a principal means of effecting corporate rescue.

3.4.1 Nature of a CVA

A CVA is a statutory form of binding between a company and its creditors. There is no requirement that the company should be insolvent or unable to pay its debts. The CVA proposal may be made by the directors of the company and put to the company and its creditors (IA 1986, s.1(1)). Alternatively, a CVA may be proposed by the company's administrator or liquidator (IA 1986, s.1(3)). It should be noted, therefore, that the members of the company are also involved in the process.

A nominee is required to report to the court on the proposal and if the proposal is approved by the creditors and members the nominee will become the supervisor of the arrangement. IA 2000 introduced a reform allowing non-insolvency practitioner business recovery specialists to apply for a licence from the Department for Business, Innovation and Skills (DBIS) (formerly the Department of Trade and Industry (DTI)), allowing them to act as nominee/supervisors. Such licensing to non-insolvency practitioners has yet to occur, and as a result such arrangements are still supervised by an insolvency practitioner.

The directors of a foreign company may propose a CVA (IA 1986, s.426 and *Re Television Trade Rentals Ltd* [2002] BCC 807), but since the Insolvency Act 1986 (Amendment) Regulations 2005, SI 2005/879 (see IA 1986, s.1(4)) this option has been limited to:

- a company registered under the Companies Act;
- a company registered in a European Economic Area state; or
- a company registered outside the EU with a COMI within an EU Member State (other than Denmark) (see *BRAC Rent-a-Car International Inc* [2004] BCC 248 and *Re Sendo Ltd* [2006] 1 BCLC 395).

IA 1986, s.1(1) provides that a CVA may be either a composition in satisfaction of the company's debts (see *Re Bradley-Hole* [1995] 1 WLR 1097) or a scheme of arrangement of the company's affairs (see *March Estates plc* v. *Gunmark Ltd* (1996) 2 BCLC 1).

A composition will involve the company retaining control of its assets, probably with a continuation of business, with an agreement to pay agreed sums to discharge the creditor's debt. A scheme of arrangement differs as it will include provisions for company assets to be dealt with in accordance with a scheme possibly administered by the supervisor/trustee.

At its simplest, the CVA is a deal between the company and its creditors in the nature of a contract (see *Re Kudos Glass Ltd (in liquidation)* [2001] 1 BCLC 390). However, it should be remembered that creditors are bound by the terms of the CVA even if they have not accepted the terms, or even voted; hence it is a statutory binding instrument as opposed to a contract. Furthermore, after the IA 2000 reforms, creditors may be bound even if they did not receive notice of the proposed CVA (IA 1986, s.5(2)(b)(ii), as amended). If the company complies with the provisions of the CVA, creditors can look only to the funds realised by the supervisor for payment of their debts and cannot return to enforce the original debt against the company.

The 'creditors' who may be bound by the CVA are not expressly defined by statute, but IR 1986, rule 1.17(3) provides that a creditor may vote in respect of an unliquidated or unascertained claim which will be valued at £1 unless the chairman of the meeting places a higher value upon it. In the case of *Re T&N Ltd* [2006] BPIR 532 future tort claimants who were at risk of ill-health following exposure to asbestos, but as at the date of the CVA had no symptoms and thus no cause of action, were treated as contingent creditors for the purposes of a CVA and a scheme of arrangement and were therefore bound by the terms of settlement. See also *Newlands (Seaford) Educational Trust* [2006] EWHC 1511 (Ch) regarding the steps that the chairman of a creditors' meeting should take to evaluate a creditor's claim and the obligation to attribute a sum greater than £1 if he is satisfied he can safely do so and **5.2.6**.

As a procedure, the CVA's main advantage is its flexibility. Indeed, its flexibility was evidenced in the case of *Inland Revenue Commissioners* v. *Adam & Partners Ltd* [2001] 1 BCLC 222, where the Inland Revenue challenged the terms of a CVA as it provided no return at all to unsecured creditors. The Court of Appeal held that although the CVA could not therefore be a composition in satisfaction of debt, it could be a scheme of arrangement, and could thus constitute a valid CVA. This should be contrasted with the case of *Commissioners for the Inland Revenue* v. *Bland* [2003] BPIR 1274 where a CVA offering no return to creditors was treated as a nullity.

It should be remembered that the terms of a CVA cannot prevent a secured creditor from enforcing its security even if there is a clause purporting to prevent creditors from taking proceedings (*Joseph Manuel Rey* v. *FNCB Ltd* [2006] EWHC 1386 (Ch)). However, in certain circumstances a landlord's right to forfeit for non-payment of rent may be lost if a claim for unpaid rent has been subsumed into the CVA (*Thomas* v. *Ken Thomas Ltd* [2006] EWCA Civ 1504).

Table 3.3 CVAs – the pros and cons for the company debtor

Pros	Cons
• Flexibility	• Debtor may be bound to difficult terms
• Possible availability of statutory moratorium	• Debtor may be bound to a CVA of a long duration
• Provides possibility of trading through difficulties	• Cannot affect secured creditors' rights
• Cost advantages over liquidation process (realisation and investigation costs avoided)	• High level of creditor agreement is required
• Greater return to creditors	• Procedure may incur delay in implementing the rescue proposal
• Directors retain control of the management of the company	• Moratorium is available only in limited circumstances
• Investigation and supervision of CVA by an independent insolvency practitioner	• Negative view from customers and suppliers in the future
• Ability to bind non-consenting creditors	• Nominee's investigation prior to CVA may be insufficiently vigorous for creditors

3.5 CVA (WITHOUT MORATORIUM) – PROCESS AND PROCEDURE

Since 1 January 2003 and the coming into force of IA 2000, the CVA procedures can be divided between those where a moratorium is necessary and available and those without moratorium.

The provisions regarding a CVA without moratorium are still contained within IA 1986, Part 1. Procedures governing CVAs where a moratorium is sought are contained within IA 1986, Sched.A1. The section below considers the CVA procedures without moratorium.

Guide to procedure

CVA (without moratorium)

1. Directors instruct an insolvency practitioner to act as an intended nominee.
2. Directors consider and prepare with the nominee the terms of a potential proposal.
3. Directors prepare and deliver to the nominee the proposal which he endorses with receipt and returns to the directors.
4. Within seven days of delivering the proposals, the directors prepare and deliver to the

    nominee a statement of affairs made up to a date not earlier than two weeks before and confirmed as correct by two directors.

5.   Nominee reports to court, filing a copy of the proposal and statement of affairs within 28 days of receipt.
6.   Court endorses date of filing.
7.   Unless otherwise ordered, nominee summons meeting of members and creditors (not less than 14 days nor more than 28 days after filing).
8.   Meetings can be on different days, but creditors' meeting must be held in advance of members' meeting.
9.   At the meeting the creditors and members consider whether to approve the proposal with or without modification (75 per cent in value of creditors voting/50 per cent of members required).
10.   Chairman of meeting reports result of meeting to court within four days of the meeting and to those who had notice of meeting immediately thereafter.
11.   If approved, the nominee becomes the supervisor of the arrangement and sends a copy of chairman's report to Registrar of Companies.
12.   If applicable, the directors do all that is required to put the supervisor in possession of the assets subject to the arrangement.
13.   Supervisor puts voluntary arrangement into effect.

3.5.1 Nominee role and investigations

The CVA procedure introduced by IA 1986 talks of the directors of the debtor company preparing 'a document setting out the terms of the proposed voluntary arrangement'. Written notice of this proposal would then be sent to a proposed nominee, who would endorse upon it a confirmation of it being received. The proposed nominee should then be provided with information from the directors, such as a statement of affairs (within seven days of the notice) and such other information as the nominee sees fit. Within 28 days, unless that period is extended by a court order, the nominee is then expected to prepare a report to the court, providing an opinion as to whether the proposal put forward has a 'reasonable prospect of being approved and implemented' (IA 1986, s.2(2)(a)), whether a meeting should be summoned and, if so, the date of the meeting.

In practice, it is virtually impossible for the directors of the company to prepare a proposal without assistance, as the proposal needs to comply with all of the requirements set out in the Insolvency Rules and be sufficiently detailed for the nominee to report to the court on its prospects of success. As a result, the directors of the company should almost certainly seek the advice and assistance of an insolvency practitioner, who will help them formulate the proposal.

It is often the case that the directors may be aware that the company is in financial difficulty, but unaware of the options available to them. As a result, an insolvency practitioner is often called in to investigate the affairs of the company and make recommendations to the board of directors on an appropriate course, e.g. CVA, administration, liquidation. The involvement of the insolvency practitioner in providing such advice must be disclosed to the creditors and members of the company in the CVA proposal. The insolvency practitioner formally advises the court that a CVA is appropriate, but his role as 'nominee' in formulating the proposal is also crucial.

The nominee is not under a statutory obligation to investigate the affairs of the company, but should within the limits of reasonable time and financial constraints be satisfied that the proposals are based on reliable financial information. It must be remembered that in providing his opinion that the proposal has a reasonable prospect of being approved and implemented, the proposed nominee is an officer of the court and is accountable to the creditors. Maintaining professional integrity is of paramount concern to the insolvency practitioner's reputation among creditors (particularly secured creditors), and is vitally important. While the debtor company and its directors will with luck be facing unpaid creditors for the first and only time, the insolvency practitioner often finds himself negotiating with the same creditors/institutions. Consequently, while the nominee is entitled to rely on the information provided to him by the directors, the nominee should not merely act as a post box, accepting what he is told (see DTI, *Guidance Note to Insolvency Practitioners* (March 1995)).

The insolvency practitioner also has a duty in contract and tort in advising the debtor company (see *Pitt* v. *Mond* [2001] BPIR 624) and in formulating a proposal (see *Prosser* v. *Castle Sanderson and Geoffrey Martin & Co.* [2002] All ER (D) 507). It should be noted, however, that the court is more reluctant to impose private law duties on an insolvency practitioner as nominee, chairman or supervisor when he is fulfilling a public/statutory role. In such cases, statute imposes a means of enforcing such duties and these are generally deemed sufficient (see *King* v. *Anthony* (1998) 2 BCLC 517).

The insolvency practitioner can also find himself liable for adverse costs in the circumstances where a creditor challenges a proposal on the grounds of unfair prejudice or material irregularity, if the insolvency practitioner has failed to act fairly and reasonably (see *Re a Debtor (No.2220), ex p. Bank of Ireland (No.2)* [1993] BCLC 233).

The nominee will therefore make such enquiries as deemed necessary to satisfy himself that the proposal ought to be put to creditors. The nominee's duty is to report whether in his opinion the proposal has a reasonable prospect of being approved and implemented and whether a meeting of creditors and the company's members should be held. In reaching these conclusions, the court has laid down guidance providing that the nominee must be satisfied that:

(a)   the company's true financial position is not substantially different from that represented to creditors;
(b)   the proposal as represented to the creditors has a real prospect of success; and
(c)   on the basis of the information before him, no already manifest yet unavoidable prospective unfairness in relation to the function of admitting or rejecting claims is present.

(See *Greystoke* v. *Hamilton-Smith* [1997] BPIR 24. This case concerned an IVA, but is equally applicable to a CVA.)

If the nominee is not satisfied that any of the three conditions will be met, an explanation should be made to the court as to why a meeting of creditors should still be held. An explanation must also be provided as to how the nominee is still able to hold the opinion that there is a reasonable prospect of the voluntary arrangement being approved and implemented. A nominee is also required to report to court if he considers that a meeting should not be summoned. If a nominee fails to report he can, by court order, be replaced. Alternatively, he may on his own application be replaced if he finds it 'impracticable or inappropriate' to continue to act (IA 1986, s.2(4)).

If information comes to light which in some way alters the nominee's opinion on the factors outlined above, it should be circulated to all creditors (see *Cadbury Schweppes* v. *Somji* [2001] 1 WLR 615).

3.5.2 Proposal

The proposal for a CVA is made by the directors of the company. Accordingly, the proposal is made to the company, not by the company. As IA 1986 provides that the directors should put forward the proposal, it is arguable that all directors should agree to this course of action; indeed, IR 1986, rule 1.5(1) provides that 'the directors' shall deliver both the proposal and a statement of affairs to the nominee which shall be filed at court. The statement of affairs must be verified by a statement of truth made by at least one director (IR 1986, rule 1.5(4)). However, with reference to the debate regarding the need for unanimity/majority vote in respect of any resolution of the directors to put a company into administration (see *Minmar (929) Ltd* v. *Khalastchi* [2011] EWHC 1159 (Ch)), close regard should be had to the company's constitution and formalities to ensure that a decision made by the majority of directors is valid.

If the company is in administration, or is being wound up, a proposal may be made by the administrator or a liquidator. In such instances the office holder should try to structure the proposal so that there is a reasonable prospect of obtaining the requisite majority approval without unfairly prejudicing any creditor, seek to achieve a sufficient consensus among the majority of creditors, and put forward a proposal within a reasonable range and with a reasonable prospect of support (*Sisu Capital Fund Ltd* v. *Tucker* [2006] BPIR 154).

A proposal must contain (see IR 1986, rule 1.3):

- an explanation as to why in the directors' opinion a voluntary arrangement is desirable for the company and why creditors are expected to concur with the arrangement;
- a schedule of the company's assets and an estimate of respective values;
- the extent of any security granted by the company;
- the extent to which any particular asset is to be excluded from the voluntary arrangement;

- the particulars of any property, other than assets of the company, which it is proposed will be included in the arrangement;
- the nature of the company's liabilities;
- how secured and preferential creditors will be dealt with;
- an estimate of the value of the prescribed part, if there were to be an insolvent liquidation;
- how persons connected with the company (being creditors) are proposed to be treated;
- whether there are in the directors' knowledge any circumstances giving rise to the possibility, in the event the company enters into liquidation, of a claim under IA 1986, ss.238, 239, 244 and 245;
- whether any guarantees have been given of the company's debt by any person;
- the proposed duration of the voluntary arrangement;
- the proposed dates of distribution with estimated amounts;
- how it is proposed to deal with those persons bound by the arrangement who have not had notice of the arrangement;
- the amounts proposed to be paid to the nominee by way of remuneration and expenses;
- the manner in which the proposed supervisor of the arrangement will be remunerated;
- whether any guarantees are to be given by any directors or other persons;
- the manner in which the funds held for the purposes of the arrangement are banked, invested or dealt with, pending distribution to the creditors;
- the manner in which the funds held for the purposes of payment to the creditors and not so paid on termination of the arrangement are to be dealt with;
- the manner in which the business of the company is proposed to be conducted during the course of the arrangement;
- details of any further credit facilities which are intended to be arranged for the company and how debts which arise are to be paid;
- the functions which are to be undertaken by the supervisor of the arrangement;
- the name, address and qualification of the proposed supervisor; and
- confirmation that the EC Regulation on Insolvency Proceedings will apply and, if so, whether the proceedings will be main, secondary or territorial proceedings.

With a list of requirements as full and complete as this, it is no surprise that company directors do not draft their own proposals and instead rely on the professional assistance of insolvency practitioners.

The directors are under a duty to put relevant facts before the creditors 'so far as within the directors' immediate knowledge'. The making of any false representation or taking any fraudulent step with the purpose of obtaining approval of the arrangement is a criminal offence (IA 1986, s.6A), and a person guilty under this section is liable to imprisonment or fine or both (IA 1986, Sched.10: currently seven years' imprisonment and/or unlimited fine on indictment; on summary conviction, six months' imprisonment and/or maximum £5,000 fine).

Any arrangement made between the company debtor and a creditor, in addition to that which the creditor is otherwise entitled under the arrangement, is fraudulent and unenforceable (see *Mallalieu* v. *Hodgson* [1851] 16 QB 698). Arrangements which have the effect of preferring one creditor over another are possible, but must be disclosed in the terms of the arrangement (see *Cadburys Schweppes* v. *Somji* [2001] 1 WLR 615). For instance, a vital supplier may insist on prepayment, or a landlord who continues to hold a strong position in the insolvency process can engineer better terms.

3.5.3 Statement of affairs

The directors of the company are required to submit to the nominee a statement of affairs, which must provide details of the company's creditors, its debts, liabilities and assets and other prescribed information (IR 1986, rule 1.5(2)). The statement of affairs must be certified as correct by at least one director of the company (IR 1986, rule 1.5(4)). The purpose of the statement of affairs is to supplement or amplify, so far as is necessary, information regarding the company's affairs contained within the directors' proposals.

The statement of affairs should be made up to a date no earlier than two weeks before the date that notice was given to the nominee of the proposal, although it is possible for the nominee to allow an extension of time of no more than two months before the date, if necessary. If the nominee is prepared to give an extension of time, he must explain this in his report to the court. The directors of the company are compelled to provide the statement of affairs to the nominee at the same time as providing notice of the proposal (IR 1986, rule 1.5(1)).

In practice, the company is likely to have prepared a statement of affairs upon which the nominee and the directors are able to draft a proposal, not the other way around. As a result, the preparation of the statement of affairs is very often the first step that the insolvency practitioner requires the company directors to undertake. If the nominee feels unable to prepare a report upon the basis of the information given to him in the statement of affairs he may call upon the company directors to provide such further information as he sees fit and/or he can inspect the company records and accounts (IR 1986, rule 1.6(3)). The nominee is also entitled to call upon the company directors to provide him with details of any previous insolvency they have been involved in within the last two years, or whether any director has been adjudged bankrupt or entered into any arrangement with his creditors (IR 1986, rule 1.6(2)).

3.5.4 Nominee's report

The legislation provides that the nominee makes his report to court within 28 days of receiving notice of the proposal. Once filed, the proposal cannot be amended or varied until the meeting of members and creditors takes place.

The court endorses the report with the date of filing and any creditor is entitled to inspect the court file at reasonable times on any business day (IR 1986, rule 1.7(3)). The nominee must also send a copy of his report and any comments he has made to the company (IR 1986, rule 1.7(4)).

In the majority of cases, the court will not hold a hearing to consider the report. However, it should be noted that on filing the report the court has the power to direct that a meeting should not take place and can do so where there is no prospect of the proposal being approved (*Re a Debtor (No.83 of 1988)* [1990] 1 WLR 708) or where it has been demonstrated that the directors have failed to be honest and open (*Re a Debtor (No.2389 of 1989)* [1991] Ch 326)). It is possible that the court could summarily refuse to proceed further with the proposal, but it is more likely that a hearing would first be held with attendance by the company directors and nominee, if the court was inclined to refuse to proceed.

As a result of the general lack of judicial scrutiny, a great deal of responsibility is placed upon the insolvency practitioner. It should be noted that in certain cases the insolvency practitioner, owing as he does duties to the court and creditors, may potentially be in conflict with the company directors, who ultimately are sanctioning payment of his fees. It is a common concern of creditors that the proposed nominee acts as a 'mouthpiece' of the directors. In the majority of cases, however, an insolvency practitioner is able to balance the conflicts between the directors/company and the interests of the creditors. This careful balance continues throughout the period of the CVA, when the nominee becomes supervisor.

Once the report is filed the nominee is required to summon the meeting (IA 1986, s.3(1)). A meeting held without a report to court is a nullity (*Fletcher* v. *Vooght* [2000] BPIR 435).

Creditors who are concerned that the nominee is failing in his duties can seek to have him replaced. A procedure is available for replacement if the nominee fails to report to the court, or if the nominee finds it impractical or inappropriate to continue to act. The nominee or a creditor of the company may apply to court for a replacement (IA 1986, s.2(4)(b)). It is of course also open to the creditors at the creditors' meeting to replace the nominee with a supervisor of their own choice.

3.5.5 Creditor action pending creditors' meeting

In the absence of a moratorium, it is possible for a creditor to petition for the winding up of the company prior to the creditors' meeting being held. The court is likely to stay those proceedings until the creditors' meeting has been held. However, if that creditor holds more than 25 per cent of the company's total liabilities, the CVA has no prospect of success. As a result, a stay in these circumstances is unlikely. The court will, therefore, also look into the circumstances of the case and will make a winding-up order if it is reasonable to do so (see *Re Piccadilly Property Management Ltd* [1999] 2 BCLC 145).

3.5.6 The creditors' meeting

At least 14 clear days (see *Mytre Investments* v. *Reynolds (No.2)* (1996) BPIR 464) prior to the meeting of members and creditors, the nominee is required (IR 1986, rule 1.9) to send out:

- notice of the meeting (time and location);
- details of the effect of the rules on majority voting requirements;
- details of the court in which he has filed his report;
- a copy of the proposal;
- a statement of affairs (or summary);
- his comments on the proposal; and
- a form of proxy.

At the meeting, the members and creditors consider the proposal and any proposed modifications.

The CVA is approved when the proposal (with or without modification) secures approval of a majority in excess of three-quarters in value of the creditors present in person (or by representative) or by proxy voting (IR 1986, rule 1.19(1)). However, the resolution will be invalid if those voting against include more than half in value of the creditors, counting in this number only those:

- to whom notice of the meeting was sent;
- whose votes were not left out of account; and
- who are not connected persons, or associates of the debtor to the best of the chairman's knowledge and belief (IR 1986, rule 1.19(4)).

This provision provides a degree of protection for general unsecured creditors by ensuring that proposals cannot be pushed through by the debtor's 'friends'. The chairman of the meeting is therefore sometimes placed in the difficult position of assessing whether persons are 'connected' to the corporate debtor. Careful thought must be given to this issue, as any decision on this is subject to appeal to the court.

In the case of a CVA, a majority of the members voting in the company meeting must also approve the arrangement. It must be remembered that a company meeting is called if at least two members are present, in person or by proxy (IR 1986, rule 12.4A(2)). The voting rights of the members are as set out in the company's articles of association, as are the numbers of votes attaching to the shareholding.

The CVA takes effect if approved at both the creditors' and the members' meetings (IA 1986, s.4A(2)(a)). If the creditors and the members make different decisions, the decision of the creditors' meeting will take priority, subject to any order of the court (IA 1986, s.4A(6)).

A member wishing to challenge the decision of a creditors' meeting has 28 days in which to do so. These amendments were made by IA 2000, which came into force on 1 January 2003 (for more detail, see **5.2.7**). Creditors may challenge the approval of the voluntary arrangement, but not its rejection (IA 1986, s.6).

The creditors' meeting is chaired by the nominee, unless he is unable to attend (IR 1986, rule 1.14(1)). The nominee is entitled to nominate any person to chair the meeting in his place, provided that person is authorised to act in relation to the voluntary arrangement or is an employee of the nominee, or his firm, and experienced in insolvency matters. As a consequence, the chairman will remain independent from the directors/company.

At the meeting, one of the chairman's crucial roles is determining the creditors' entitlement to vote. Every creditor who has notice of the meeting may vote. Additionally, any creditor who has not been notified of the meeting but learns of it may also attend and vote, provided that he can satisfy the chairman that he is a creditor (see *Beverley Group plc* v. *McClure* [1995] BCC 751). At the creditors' meeting, votes are calculated in accordance with the amount owed to the creditor as at the date of the meeting (IR 1986, rule 1.17(2)). This differs in the case of liquidation, or administration where a moratorium has been in place, where debts are calculated at the commencement of the applicable process.

3.5.7 Modifications to the proposal

At the creditors' meeting, the proposal may be modified (and frequently is) on the proposed resolution of one or more creditors and/or the company. It is often the case that institutional creditors such as banks, credit card companies or, commonly, HMRC, which often faces CVA or IVA proposals in large numbers, have standard modifications which they wish to see effected.

The proposed modifications are subject to the agreement of the company and majority creditor approval. However, since IA 2000 came into force, the members of the company do not need to vote again on whether to accept the CVA if they voted prior to the modification.

There is no statutory power to amend a proposal after the meeting. As a result, if the creditors have voted to reject the proposal, the company must start again with the procedure and cannot simply put forward a revised proposal (*Re Symes* [1995] 2 BCLC 651).

It remains unclear what the effect of a proxy's vote in favour or rejection of a proposal is where there have been substantial modifications. In practice, it is for the chairman to determine whether that creditor would need further information on which to base his decision. As a result it is often best for a chairman faced with significant modifications to adjourn the meeting to allow the company and its creditors time to consider the revised proposal.

If the meeting has taken place, modifications to the proposals can only be effected if:

- in the case of a non-moratorium CVA, a second CVA with modifications is proposed which subsumes the creditors of the original CVA;
- there is unanimous consent of all the creditors affected by the modification (*Raja* v. *Rubin* (2000) Ch 274 (CA)); or
- there is a variation clause within the CVA which does not have the effect of affecting the rights of secured or preferential creditor (*Re Broome (a Debtor)* [1999] 1 BCLC 356).

3.5.8 Effect of approval

A CVA binds every person entitled to vote at the meeting (whether represented or not) or who would have been entitled to vote had he received notice (IA 1986, s.5(2)). Depending on the terms of the arrangement, it may operate as an absolute and unconditional release of the debt in question, hence relieving third parties of their liabilities in respect of the same debt (e.g. such as a guarantor: see *Johnson* v. *Davies* [1999] Ch 117). If there are circumstances where a creditor could be so affected, the creditor should ensure that the arrangement specifically excludes such a release, and/or if the creditor is bound against its will by the requisite majority, the creditor may seek to challenge the proposal on grounds of unfair prejudice.

As creditors who have not received notice of the meeting are now bound, their right to challenge the proposal on grounds of unfair prejudice runs from the day they become aware of the meeting being held. At that stage, when a creditor has not received a sum payable under the CVA, the company is liable to the creditor to the extent of that creditor's entitlement to a dividend or other due payment (IA 1986, s.5(2A)).

3.6 WHY HAVE CVAS PROVED RELATIVELY UNPOPULAR?

3.6.1 Lack of moratorium

Before IA 2000, which introduced a new procedure for obtaining a moratorium for certain types of small company, no moratorium was available. In the normal course of events, while the CVA is being negotiated with creditors, the company does not have the advantage of any moratorium from creditor action; this contrasts with the interim order provisions provided for an individual.

3.6.2 Better alternatives

Alternative insolvency procedures for the company, such as receivership, administration or, alternatively, liquidation, are often more effective. It should be remembered that an insolvent corporate debtor entering into a CVA is agreeing in some way to compromise and deal with its debts. There are various corporate rescue techniques which will avoid entirely the obligation of the business to discharge these debts and which will allow it to start afresh. A common practice is for the owner/directors of a business to purchase the business of the company from the insolvency practitioner. The practice of 'phoenix trading' has for a number of years caused concern to creditors. However, in recent years and in view of the growing acceptance of the need to rescue businesses, phoenix operations have obtained a degree of respectability as long as certain conditions on sale are observed. A sale of the business as a going concern to the existing management occurs on average in approximately 12 per cent of all insolvency processes (R3 Twelfth Annual Survey, January 2002–June 2003). The advantages for the creditors are that some return may be obtained and/or there may be a new customer. This form of corporate rescue effected through administration, administrative receivership and even liquidation may have more attractions to the directors of an insolvent company than a CVA.

3.6.3 Secured creditors

The rights of a secured creditor cannot be affected by the terms of the CVA without consent. The continuing rights of action that the secured creditor possesses may act as a 'sword of Damocles' over the company, and the inability of the company to deal with all of its debts may be a disincentive to restructure its debts through a CVA.

3.6.4 Creditor scepticism

The attitude of creditors has also militated against the success of CVAs. Concern over the Crown's response to CVA proposals was addressed during the reform and consultation process leading to the Enterprise Act 2002. The problem was partially acknowledged, and led to the formation of a joint Inland Revenue/Customs and Excise unit (the Voluntary Arrangement Service) in April 2001 specifically to deal with the approval or otherwise of CVAs. As a result, the Crown's approval rate for CVAs has significantly increased. However, anecdotal evidence continues to suggest that, while HMRC will more readily approve proposals, it does so only with stringent conditions attached and/or subject to its own standard modifications. This often means that despite the unit's approval of the proposal, the revised CVA is unlikely to succeed and/or is unattractive to the company and is not proceeded with.

There is also the problem of the scepticism of the general unsecured creditors, even though statistically CVAs appear to offer the best return to creditors (i.e. 17p in the pound compared with a 4p average for other insolvency procedures: R3 Twelfth Annual Survey). However, there remains concern that the nominee/supervisor will too readily seek the work involved in putting forward a proposal and side with the company rather than representing the creditors' interests.

3.6.5 Resolution of perceived defects?

Prior to the reforms introduced in 2003, the original 1986 legislation was criticised as failing to provide an adequate procedure to effect the corporate rescue of small and medium-sized businesses. Indeed, such companies tended towards liquidation, as formal rescue procedures (such as administration and CVA) were often seen as slow, costly and/or, in the case of the CVA, failing to provide relief from creditor action.

IA 2000 (which came into effect on 1 January 2003) sought to address these perceived weaknesses by tackling two major areas of concern, namely:

1. a lack of moratorium procedures to prevent creditors' actions while rescue proposals were formulated; and
2. the inability of a company to bind creditors who did not receive notice of the creditors' meeting.

3.7 CVA (WITH MORATORIUM) – PROCESS AND PROCEDURE

Guide to procedure

1. The directors instruct an insolvency practitioner to act as an intended nominee.
2. Both consider if the company is eligible/qualified for moratorium.
3. Directors consider and prepare with the nominee the terms of the potential proposal.
4. Directors prepare and deliver to nominee a statement of affairs.
5. Nominee prepares and submits a statement to the directors indicating:

    –   whether CVA has reasonable prospects;
    –   whether company has sufficient funds to trade during moratorium;
    –   whether a meeting should be summoned.

6. Directors file at court:

    –   proposal;
    –   statement of affairs;
    –   statement that company is eligible for moratorium;
    –   nominee consent to act;
    –   nominee's statement.

7. Moratorium comes into force on filing.
8. Notice of moratorium provided to nominee.
9. Nominee advertises moratorium/notifies Registrar of Companies.
10. Nominee summons meetings of members and of creditors (within 28 days of commencement of moratorium unless extended) providing at least 14 days' notice.
11. Meetings held. They can be on different days, but creditors' meeting must be held in advance of members' meeting.
12. Meetings consider proposal and modifications.
13. Approval of proposal required from 75 per cent in value of creditors voting/50 per cent of members.
14. Chairman reports result of meetings to the court (within four days) and to those who had notice of meeting, immediately thereafter.
15. If approved, supervisor sends copy of chairman's report of meeting to Registrar of Companies.
16. If applicable, the directors do all that is required to put the supervisor in possession of the assets subject to the arrangement.

17.   Supervisor puts voluntary arrangement into effect.

3.7.1 The effect of the moratorium and eligibility

The IA 2000 reforms provide that directors of eligible companies intending to propose a CVA are able to obtain a moratorium that will provisionally suspend the rights of the company's creditors (IA 2000, s.1 and Sched.1 inserts s.1A and Sched.A1 into IA 1986). The purpose of the moratorium is to allow the company time to put together a proposal and to prevent creditors from taking enforcement action during this period. Since the introduction of the reforms, in practice only a handful of companies have benefited from a moratorium prior to the CVA. The procedure is seen as onerous and burdensome on the nominee, and the availability of a moratorium via administration is seen as quicker and cheaper.

The moratorium is only available to those companies that meet the eligibility conditions and are not otherwise excluded (IA 1986, Sched.A1, para.2). A company is eligible if the following qualifying conditions are met:

- The company must satisfy two or more of the requirements for being a small company in the relevant period (CA 2006, s.382, which replaces CA 1985, s.247(3)). The relevant period is the year ending with the date of filing or the financial year of the company which ended last before that date (IA 1986, Sched.A1, para.3).
- The company's financial year is to be determined in accordance with CA 2006, s.390 (replaces CA 1985, s.223).

A 'small' company is one which fulfils two or more of the following criteria:

- Turnover no greater than £5.6 million.
- Assets on the balance sheet no greater than £2.8 million.
- No more than 50 employees.

This definition is provided in CA 1985, s.247(3), as amended by the Companies Act 1985 (Accounts of Small and Medium-sized Enterprises and Audit Exemption) (Amendment) Regulations 2004, SI 2004/16, which came into force on 30 January 2004. It is worth noting that the Secretary of State for Business, Innovation and Skills may amend the eligibility criteria by secondary legislation, so making the CVA moratorium available to more companies.

Eligible companies are excluded if, on the date of filing, an act or feature of insolvency is in place, e.g.

- an administrative receiver or a provisional liquidator has been appointed;
- an administration order is in force;
- the company is being wound up;
- a CVA is in place (IA 1986, Sched.A1, para.4).

There is also protection from 'serial' debtors seeking to use the moratorium procedure to avoid enforcement action, by virtue of the fact that if a moratorium has been in place in the last 12 months, further protection cannot be obtained.

Certain types of companies are not eligible to benefit from a moratorium (IA 1986, Sched.A1, paras.2(2) and 4A–4K), namely:

- insurance companies;
- banks;
- companies operating in the financial markets;
- a participant in, or any of whose property is subject to, a collateral security charge;
- a holding company which does not qualify as a small or medium-sized group in respect of the company's financial year which ended before the last date of filing (IA 1986, Sched.A1, para.3(4));
- a party to a capital market arrangement under which a party has incurred or is expected to incur a debt of at least £10 million;
- a project company of a project which is a public private partnership project which includes step-in rights; and
- a company which has incurred liability under an agreement of £10 million or more.

These provisions mirror situations where the ability to appoint an administrative receiver will still be available after 15 September 2003.

3.7.2 The role of the nominee

The directors of the debtor company must submit their CVA proposal document to the proposed nominee. This must contain essentially the same information as set out for a non-moratorium CVA (IR 1986, rule 1.3). It must be accompanied by a statement of the company's affairs containing details of its preferential and unsecured creditors, secured claims by creditors, debts secured against company assets and such other information as is necessary to supplement and amplify the details of the company's affairs already contained within the director's proposals (IR 1986, rule 1.37) in Form 1.6 at the same time as delivery of the proposal and made up no earlier than two weeks before the date of the proposal. As we have seen for a CVA without moratorium, given its procedural complexity it is highly unlikely that the directors will prepare a proposal without the prior assistance of an insolvency practitioner.

A nominee must then submit a statement to the directors within 28 days, indicating whether or not in his opinion:

- the proposed moratorium has a reasonable prospect of being approved and implemented;
- the company is likely to have sufficient funds available to it during the proposed moratorium period to enable it to carry on business; and

- meetings of the company and its creditors should be summoned to consider the proposal for the voluntary arrangement;

(IR 1986, rule 1.38 in Form 1.5 and annexing comments and consent to act in Form 1.8).

It should be noted that the procedure (thus far) for obtaining a CVA with moratorium is virtually the same as that for a CVA without moratorium, save importantly that the nominee must also assess whether there is likely to be sufficient funds to cover the company's period of trading during the moratorium. This may involve a discussion with funders, suppliers and customers or the company and may be a difficult exercise to perform with a necessary degree of confidentiality. The fact that a moratorium is required indicates creditor pressure; if word gets out that an insolvency practitioner is intervening in the company affairs this may provoke immediate enforcement action, scuppering any plans for rescue.

A nominee is entitled to rely on the information provided to him by the directors unless he has a reason to doubt its accuracy (IA 1986, Sched.A1, para.6(3)) (see also *Greystoke* v. *Hamilton Smith* [1997] BPIR 24). However, the nominee must make the statement on the basis of his own opinion and so should examine the affairs of the company and the proposed CVA with great care. This in itself raises a question of funding; the proposed nominee will require payment for his professional services in formulating the proposal and incur fees in performing his statutory duty to ensure that the CVA has a reasonable prospect of success and the company has sufficient funds to trade during the moratorium period. As a result, the costs are likely to remain relatively high, which makes the moratorium procedure unattractive to the very companies it has been introduced to assist.

3.7.3 Process and procedure

To obtain a moratorium, the directors of the company must use Forms 1.5, 1.7, 1.8 and 1.9 (IR 1986, rule 1.39) and file at court:

- the terms of the proposed CVA;
- a statement of the company's affairs;
- a statement that the company is eligible for a moratorium;
- a statement from the nominee that he has consented to act;
- a statement from the nominee that in his opinion:
  - the proposed CVA has a reasonable prospect of being approved and implemented;
  - the company is likely to have sufficient funds available to it during the proposed moratorium period in order for it to carry on business; and
  - a meeting of the company and its creditors should be summoned to consider the proposed CVA;
- a copy of any statement made by the nominee setting out the reasons why he has allowed the directors to prepare the company's statement of affairs which is not

in accordance with IR 1986, rule 1.37(3), i.e. statement of affairs prepared to a date between two weeks and two months before the filing of the documents; and

- four copies of a schedule listing the submitted documents. These must be filed at court within three working days of submission of the nominee's statement in Form 1.5.

The moratorium automatically comes into force when these documents are filed at court, with three copies of the schedule endorsed with the date of filing being returned to the person filing the documents (IA 1986, Sched.A1, para.8 and IR 1986, rule 1.39(3)). There is no judicial scrutiny of whether the moratorium is appropriate.

In reality, the moratorium does not allow the company time to formulate a proposal; rather, it allows the company a breathing space before the creditors' meeting. For instance, it can be used where there is an outstanding winding-up petition against the company. In the absence of such a moratorium, creditors can take such enforcement action as they think fit, which could immediately defeat the intention of the CVA.

The moratorium lasts for a maximum of 28 days, unless extended by the agreement of the shareholders and creditors. The extension can be for a maximum of two months from the date of the first meeting, which must be convened within the first 28-day period (IA 1986, Sched.A1, para.8).

The moratorium comes to an end on the day on which the shareholders and the creditors meet to approve the proposals for the CVA (or otherwise reject the proposals). If a meeting is not called or held, the moratorium period ends on the 29th day after filing.

Before any decision is made to extend the moratorium period, the nominee is under a duty to inform the shareholders and creditors how he will continue to comply with the duty to monitor the company's activities. The nominee must also inform the meeting of the cost of his actions to date and his expected costs to continue. If the expected costs are not approved by the shareholders' and creditors' meetings, the moratorium comes to an end. Any decision to extend or further extend the moratorium must be registered at Companies House and the court must be notified.

3.7.4 Challenge to any extensions of the moratorium period

If a creditor or member of the company is dissatisfied with any act or omission of the directors during the moratorium period, that creditor or member may apply to the court during or after the moratorium period for an order on one of the following grounds:

(a) the company's affairs, business or properties are being or have been managed by the directors in a manner which is unfairly prejudicial to the interests of its creditors or the members in general, or at least some of the creditors or members, including the petitioner; or

(b)   any act or proposed act or omission of the directors is, or would be, prejudicial (IA 1986, Sched.A1, para.40(1)–(3)).

The court may make such order as it deems fit, including but not limited to:

- adjourning the hearing conditionally or unconditionally;
- regulating the management by the directors of the company's affairs, business and property during the moratorium period;
- requiring the directors to refrain from doing, or continuing to perform, an act complained of by the petitioner;
- requiring the directors to carry out an act which the petitioner has complained of, or they have omitted to do;
- requiring the summoning of a meeting of creditors or members for the purposes of determining matters as set out by the court;
- bringing the moratorium to an end; and
- making such consequential provisions as the court thinks fit.

In making an order to end the moratorium, the court must have regard to the need to safeguard the interests of the persons who dealt with the company in good faith and/or for value during the period of the moratorium (IA 1986, Sched.A1, para.40(6)).

The moratorium will also come to an end if a nominee withdraws his consent to act. The nominee is obliged to withdraw consent to act if:

- he considers that the proposed CVA, or proposed modifications, have no reasonable prospect of being approved or implemented;
- he considers that the company will not be able to fund the continuance of the business during the remainder of the moratorium;
- he becomes aware that on the date of filing for the moratorium, the company is not eligible; or
- the directors fail to comply with all statutory duties.

The moratorium will also come to an end if a director, creditor or member of the company affected by the moratorium obtains a court order to that effect.

3.7.5   From moratorium to members'/creditors' meeting

When the moratorium comes into force, the directors are under an obligation to notify the nominee of the commencement of the moratorium by sending the nominee two copies of the schedule endorsed by the court (IR 1986, rule 1.40(1); IA 1986, Sched.A1, para.9).

The nominee must advertise the moratorium to creditors (in the *Gazette*) and such newspapers as appropriate (IA 1986, Sched.A1, para.10(1); IR 1986, rule 1.40(2) in Form 1.10).

The nominee must notify:

- Companies House;
- the company;
- any creditor who has presented a winding-up petition before the beginning of the moratorium (IA 1986, Sched.A1, para.10(2); IR 1986, rule 1.40(3) in Form 1.11);
- any sheriff charged with execution or legal process against the company; and
- as far as the nominee is aware, any person who has distrained against the company (IR 1986, rule 1.40(4)).

Thereafter any order form or business letter issued on behalf of the company must bear the nominee's name and a statement that the moratorium is in force. If the company does not comply with this rule, the transaction will not be void or unenforceable against the company, although the company and any officer who authorises or permits the default may be fined (IA 1986, Sched.A1, para.15).

During the period of moratorium:

- no winding-up petition may be presented against the company;
- no meeting of the company may be called without the consent of the nominee, or the court's permission;
- no resolution to wind up the company may be passed;
- no administration application may be presented;
- no administrator may be appointed under Sched.B1, para.14 or 22;
- no administrative receiver may be appointed;
- no landlord can exercise rights of forfeiture;
- no creditors can take steps to enforce security;
- no proceedings or legal process may be commenced, or continued, without leave of the court (IA 1986, Sched.A1, para.12); and
- the company may not obtain credit or more than £250 from any persons without informing them that a moratorium is in force (IA 1986, Sched.A1, para.17).

This provision, while understandable, is potentially restrictive, making it difficult for a company to continue its business. Will suppliers still continue to trade with the company? Will they demand cash on delivery? Such a change in terms can have severe effects on planned cash flow and make the transition into the CVA difficult, if not impossible, during the period of moratorium. However, a company that wilfully contravenes these provisions is liable to a fine and an officer of the company will be liable to imprisonment.

During the moratorium the company may only dispose of property which is free from secured interests if there are reasonable grounds for believing that disposal will benefit the company and if the proposed disposal is approved by the creditors' committee or nominee. This provision does not apply to disposals by the business in the ordinary course of its trading (IA 1986, Sched.A1, para.18(2)).

A further weakness of the procedure is that funding during the moratorium may be difficult to obtain as the granting of security is subject to a test that it must be believed, on reasonable grounds, that it would benefit the company (IA 1986, Sched.A1, para.14). Lenders may well be discouraged by the risks inherent in this approach.

If the company wants to dispose of charged property, i.e. property subject to security, hire purchase, etc., it must obtain the consent of the charge holder or the court's permission. If the court grants permission, the order must be filed at Companies House within 14 days.

Public utility companies cannot refuse to supply services unless outstanding debts are paid, but they can require the nominee personally to guarantee payment for supplies during the moratorium period. This potential liability is a significant disincentive to insolvency practitioners unless they are assured that sufficient funds are in place. They may ask the directors to provide personal guarantees in such circumstances.

A moratorium committee may be established by a resolution at either the creditors' or members' meeting and is only likely to be needed if the moratorium is to be extended. The reason for this is that creditors and members will not have met prior to the moratorium period being entered into; they will only meet if the moratorium needs to be extended.

The nominee is under an obligation to monitor the company's affairs (IA 1986, Sched.A1, para.24) and needs to be assured that:

- the proposed voluntary arrangement continues to have a reasonable prospect of being approved and implemented; and
- the company continues to have sufficient funds to enable it to carry on business.

As stated previously, the nominee is under a duty to withdraw consent if the arrangement is no longer capable of being achieved or if there are insufficient funds to carry on business (IA 1986, Sched.A1, para.25).

The actions taken by the nominee may also be challenged by creditors, during the moratorium or after it has ended. If a creditor considers that an act, omission or decision of the nominee has resulted in a loss for the company and the company is not intending to pursue a claim against the nominee, the creditor may apply to the court for an order that the nominee compensates the company, or such order as is thought fit. The court will not make an order if it is satisfied that the nominee has acted reasonably in all circumstances (IA 1986, Sched.A1, para.27(3)).

If the nominee fails to comply with any duty imposed upon him or dies, the directors may apply to court to have him replaced by another person qualified to act as an insolvency practitioner. In addition, if it becomes impracticable or inappropriate for the nominee to continue to act, the directors or the nominee may make an application in court for his replacement.

3.7.6 Consideration and implementation of CVA with moratorium

A nominee is required to summon the meeting of creditors and the company within 28 days of the commencement of the moratorium (see IA 1986, Sched.A1, para.29).

At the meeting, the creditors may resolve to adjourn the meeting and extend the moratorium with or without conditions (IA 1986, Sched.A1, para.32), although this is subject to a two-month limit. The nominee must inform the meeting of the steps taken to monitor the company, the costs incurred and the anticipated future costs, which remain subject to the creditor's approval.

The meeting may also resolve to appoint a moratorium committee, with the consent of the nominee, to assist as deemed necessary in the decision on whether to dispose of company property other than in the ordinary course of business.

However, if and when a decision approving a voluntary arrangement is reached either at the initial meeting or at any adjourned meeting, the voluntary arrangement comes into effect on that day. The effect of the approval is the same as for a non-moratorium CVA and is dealt with in **3.5**.

Once approved, the CVA can be challenged on grounds of unfair prejudice or material irregularity and the provisions are virtually identical to those for a non-moratorium CVA and are dealt with in **3.5**, and in more detail in **5.2.7**.

3.7.7   The future for CVAs with a moratorium

During the statutory reform process, some commentators felt that the burdens and obligations imposed on the nominee would make any potential appointment an unattractive proposition for an insolvency practitioner. Whether the low take-up rate of new-style CVAs with moratorium is as a result of this, or the late coming into force of the provisions, is difficult to determine. (The provisions came into force on 1 January 2003, with the Enterprise Act 2002 reforms and new-style (and easily obtained) administrations coming into force shortly afterwards on 15 September 2003.) In reality it is most probably a combination of both factors.

While the CVA moratorium procedure remains open to small companies, it is almost certain that the company can enter into administration (and obtain the benefit of the moratorium) more quickly and cheaply; thereafter it is open to the company to propose a CVA to creditors. In practice, the CVA with moratorium was a long overdue reform which came far too late and was quickly superseded by the Enterprise Act 2002 provisions. As a result, only a handful of companies have proposed a CVA with moratorium.

3.8   THE USE OF THE ADMINISTRATION PROCESS BY THE CORPORATE DEBTOR

3.8.1   The introduction and reform of the administration process

The administration process was first introduced in IA 1986 to encourage corporate rescue where a company was not subject to a floating charge, or where the floating charge holder had no interest, or saw no benefit, in appointing an administrative

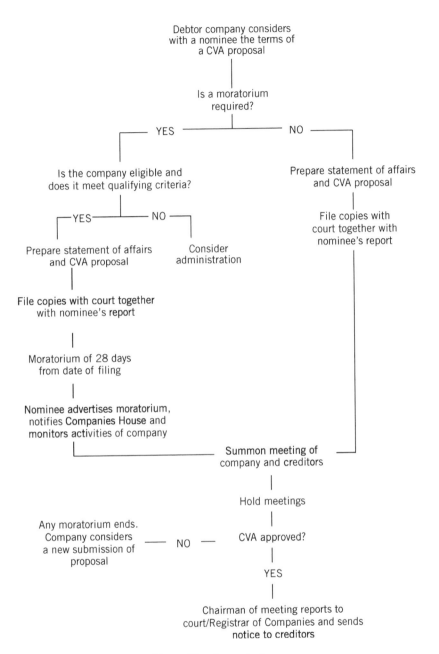

Figure 3.2   CVA procedure with or without moratorium

receiver. Administration was therefore a procedure designed to complement administrative receivership, not to replace it. After the introduction of IA 1986 and the economic recession of the early 1990s, the new procedures for corporate rescue, namely administration and CVA, were sorely tested. However, the number of appointments made remained small, with only approximately 200 administration appointments a year for the first 10 years after the process was introduced, and the number of administrative receivership appointments by far exceeded the number of administration appointments.

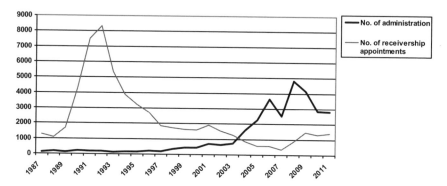

Figure 3.3   Number of receiverships compared with administrations 1987–2011

Source: Insolvency Service Statistical Directorate

While this may have been due to familiarity with the administrative receivership procedure, there was also criticism that the administration process was legalistic, cumbersome, inflexible, overly complex and costly. The principal reason for this was that administration was designed as a court-led process, whereby justification for an order was required, which required significant evidence and was thus criticised as being an unattractive option for small companies.

One of the principal intentions behind the Enterprise Act 2002 was to reform the administration procedure to create an efficient, less costly and streamlined process:

- with a clearer focus on company rescue;
- to secure a better return to creditors as a whole where company rescue is not practical;
- with a clearer timescale to ensure that the administration is not drawn out at the expense of creditors; and
- to ensure that an administrator owes wider duties to creditors as a whole.

These objectives were outlined in the House of Lords on the second reading of the Enterprise Bill (2 July 2002), by Lord Sainsbury, Parliamentary Under Secretary of State for Trade and Industry.

As well as introducing two out-of-court routes for appointment, which will be examined below, the Enterprise Act 2002 also relaxed some of the requirements in regard to obtaining a court order and, in theory, made this route less cumbersome and costly.

3.8.2 The purpose of administration

In order to commence an administration process, an insolvency practitioner must be satisfied that the single overriding purpose for administration as contained in IA 1986, Sched.B1, para.3(1) will be achieved, namely:

(a) rescuing the company as a going concern;
(b) achieving a better result for the company's creditors as a whole than would be likely if the company were wound up (without first being in administration); or
(c) realising property in order to make a distribution to one or more secured or preferential creditors.

The old (pre-Enterprise Act) administration regime had four differing purposes for administration (formerly IA 1986, s.8(3), as amended); since the reform there is one purpose with a hierarchy of objectives. It should be noted therefore that the administrator does not now need to state which of the objectives will be fulfilled; indeed he may take the appointment considering that restructuring and rescuing the company is possible but move to sell the assets of the business. In deciding which objective to pursue, the administrator retains a wide discretion based on his subjective opinion, which will only be capable of challenge in instances of bad faith or irrationality; there is no objective test as to which statutory objective should be pursued (*Unidare plc* v. *Cohen and Power* [2005] BPIR 1472).

Administration is justifiable as long as the purpose remains reasonably capable of achievement (IA 1986, Sched.B1, para.79(2)) and where it is achieved the administrator must take steps to bring the administration to an end (IA 1986, Sched.B1, para.80(2)).

It does not matter by what means and by whom the administrator was appointed; in every case the administrator must perform his functions with the objective of achieving the purpose of administration, for the interests of the company's creditors as a whole (IA 1986, Sched.B1, para.3(2)). The only exception to this overriding duty to the company's creditors is where the administrator is simply realising property to make a distribution to one or more secured or preferential creditors. In those limited circumstances, the administrator must not unnecessarily harm the interests of the creditors as a whole.

The first objective for any administrator is to rescue the company as a going concern, which should generally be pursued unless the administrator thinks it is not reasonably practicable. However, it should be remembered that the company is no more than the legal entity that owns the business. It is the business of the company that is made up of goodwill, its employees and its tangible and intangible assets.

Accordingly, it is the business that holds the value of the company. It may therefore be open to some question whether the rescuing of the company is of importance to the creditors of the company. Those who have an interest in the preservation of the company are its shareholders, not its creditors, and it is often noted that the short-term rescue of the company may hide the structural difficulties which are faced by the business. The company has become insolvent and the continued operation of the company by its failed management and/or stakeholders may be at odds with the interests of the creditors. As a result, rescuing the company may not be in the long-term interests of the creditors or employees.

In such circumstances, if the administrator considers that he could realise the company's property (with a view to obtaining a better result than on winding up) and that effecting a sale on a break-up basis would achieve a better result for the company's creditors as a whole, then the administrator should proceed to the second objective (IA 1986, Sched.B1, para.3(3)).

This second objective is most likely to occur on the sale of the whole or, more often, part of the business as a going concern, or the sale of the business on a break-up basis. What should be noted is that the decision is one for the administrator's commercial judgment, and must be reviewed on a subjective basis, i.e. what the administrator thinks is achievable, rather than an objective standard, i.e. what a reasonable administrator would have thought. However, the fact that this is a subjective opinion does not leave the administrator free from criticism from creditors or stakeholders, who retain a right of action if the administrator has acted negligently. Furthermore, any creditor or member of the company dissatisfied with the administrator's decision may apply to the court, claiming that the administrator has acted or proposes to act in a way that would unfairly harm the interests of the applicant, whether alone or in common with other members and creditors (IA 1986, Sched.B1, para.74(1)).

The courts, however, remain reluctant to intervene or criticise the exercise of an administrator's commercial judgment (see *T & D Industries plc (In Administration)* [2000] 1 BCLC 471 (pre-Enterprise Act); see also *Re Transbus International Ltd* [2004] 2 All ER 911 (post-Enterprise Act)). Consequently, challenges regarding the exercise of the administrator's judgment as to what is reasonably practicable and what is in the best interests of the creditors as a whole are unlikely to succeed unless bad faith, improper motive or irrationality in the decision-making process can be shown.

Two contrasting cases show the courts' approach to instances where administration orders are sought on the basis that administration offers a better return to creditors than winding up. In *Re Logitext UK Ltd* [2005] 1 BCLC 326 it was held that the offer of an unsecured creditor to fund the administrator to investigate the company and if appropriate commence claims in circumstances where that funding would not be available if the company were liquidated justified an order, whereas in *Re Dollarland (Manhattan) Ltd* [2005] All ER (D) 371 it was felt that the independent examination of the case by the Official Receiver was of greater benefit to creditors as it could not be shown that administration would result in a greater financial return to the creditors. In both cases an administrator had provided a statement that in his opinion the purpose of administration could be achieved; the cases show that the courts will question this. However, it should be noted that these were court applications and not out-of-court appointments, where in practice the administrator's opinion is open to less scrutiny.

Table 3.4 Why use administration?

Advantages	Disadvantages
• Appointment easily and quickly obtained	• Tax position
• Moratorium	• Problems of funding during the administration
• Flexibility – in content and duration of proposals	• Problem of rates as payable expenses
• Gives the administrator an ability to sell assets of the business/ restructure business	• Problem of funding pre-appointment costs
• Speed and efficiency of the procedure	• Lack of control of the process by existing management

3.8.3   Advantages of the administration process

The key advantage of commencing the administration process is to give the management and owners of the company time in which to consider the company's options, as a moratorium against creditor action is imposed. Together with the administrator, the directors can then consider the best option for the company, be that reconstruction, sale of part of the company's assets, a scheme of arrangement, a CVA, or, ultimately, liquidation. Administration was traditionally viewed as an interim insolvency procedure (i.e. another procedure was likely to follow); the reforms introduced by the Enterprise Act 2002 have made it possible for administration in certain circumstances to lead to the company being returned to its existing management, distributions made to creditors and/or the dissolution of the company, thus being the sole insolvency process used.

The reformed procedures are intended to be speedy and cost-effective, as it is possible for the company and/or its directors to appoint the administrator by an out-of-court route. While reforms have been also been made to the procedure for appointments by court order, this method still remains relatively time-consuming and costly. The introduction of the out-of-court route of appointment has revolutionised the administration procedure and makes it much more attractive to smaller companies.

Following the Enterprise Act 2002 reforms, in the majority of cases the administration process will now be initiated by the directors of the company using the out-of-court process of appointment (see IA 1986, Sched.B1, para.22(2)). As we shall see, this out-of-court process offers a quick and easy route to commencement, although it is subject to strict procedural conditions.

It is also possible for the directors/company to apply to court for an administration order, and this route may be followed if one or more of the conditions for the out-of-court route cannot be met (e.g. where a petition for the winding up of the company has been presented but not yet disposed of: IA 1986, Sched.B1, para.25(a)).

The directors or the company may appoint an administrator (see IA 1986, Sched.B1, para.22(1)), although the company is subject to the same restrictions regarding an out-of-court appointment as are the directors. A resolution at a general meeting must be passed for the company to appoint an administrator. While an informal unanimous decision made by all the shareholders following the '*Re Duomatic* principle' (*Re Duomatic Ltd* [1969] 2 Ch 365) may be treated as a resolution (a provision which may assist smaller owner-managed private companies), the need to attach a copy of the written resolution of the intention to appoint/notice of appointment may make it easier and/or more certain for owner-managers to commence the process in their capacity as directors. As will be discussed in detail below, regard must be had to the constitution of the company to ensure that any decision reached by the directors is valid (see *Minmar (929) Ltd* v. *Khalatschi* [2011] EWHC 1159 (Ch)).

Once commenced, one of the key features of the administration process is its inherent flexibility and the ability of the administrator to deal swiftly and efficiently with the assets. This extends to an ability to sell the assets prior to any creditors' meeting (whether through pre-pack on or about the date of appointment or indeed any sale prior to first meeting).

3.8.4 Disadvantages of the administration process

In advising the directors of the insolvent company, it must be borne in mind that administration will lead to a loss of management control. In the USA, Chapter 11 procedures provide for 'debtor in possession', which means continuing control and management by the board during the reconstruction process. In the UK, control and management of the company transfer to the administrator, although the administrator may well delegate back some powers to existing management. However, such decisions will be entirely dependent on the nature of the business and what the result of the administration is likely to be. For example, the existing management is only likely to be involved in the process if there is a possibility that the business may be saved, either by trading through its difficulties or by selling on to a third party. The reluctance of management to hand over control to a third party remains one of the stumbling blocks to greater use of the administration procedure.

The administrator must also ensure that during the course of the administration, the position of the unsecured creditors is not worsened. Effectively this means that the administrator will not allow the company to continue in administration if it is going to trade at a loss and further damage will be suffered by creditors. As a result, it is often necessary to ensure that sufficient funding is in place to cover the period of administration and ensure that losses are not incurred and/or will be covered. In the USA, this is dealt with by s.364 of the Bankruptcy Code, which provides for 'debtor in possession financing'. This means that, with court approval, the company can obtain further credit and the court may order:

(a) the creditor will be granted 'super-priority' over all administrative expenses in respect of additional credit provided;

(b) the creditor will be granted a lien on unencumbered property, or a junior lien on encumbered property; or

(c) in special circumstances, the creditor can be granted a lien in priority over any existing lien.

The absence of such a provision in the UK administration procedure has been criticised. Indeed, this matter was much debated during the reform process, although the government rejected calls for super-priority funding on the basis that banks and other lenders would continue to assess the commercial viability of administration and, if satisfied, would be willing to provide additional funding. It is therefore left to private sector lenders to vet administration proposals and support only those with a sufficient chance of success, themselves taking a large commercial risk in providing further funding to an insolvent company.

The courts, however, have provided some relief for those seeking to fund administrators. In *Bibby Trade Finance Ltd* v. *McKay* [2006] All ER (D) 266 (Jul) it was held on appeal that an administrator was entitled to deduct as an expense of the administration additional monies that had been advanced by a financier post administration and which had enabled the company to complete a valuable contract. The court felt that this accorded with the flexible approach to administration expenses as set out in *Centre Reinsurance International Co.* v. *Freakley* [2005] EWCA Civ 115, namely that an expense was recoverable if it was incurred in furtherance of the purpose of the administration.

If the directors consider that the company can produce sufficient returns to cover ongoing costs, or can find a funder willing to cover the costs of the administration process, then administration remains a viable option. Of course, the administrator on being appointed could take the decision to lay off staff, cut back on expenses of the business and close unprofitable parts of the business, which might provide the company with sufficient funding to cover ongoing expenses. In effecting a rescue of the business it is a truism that 'cash is king', and obtaining healthy reserves of cash is often a vital first step for any administrator. This is a matter which requires careful planning and discussion with the proposed administrator.

One issue that has caused difficulty since 15 September 2003 is the question of whether an administrator is entitled to recover as an expense of the administration the costs incurred in advising and assisting the company prior to the commencement of the administration. Before the Enterprise Act 2002, when a company sought to obtain an administration order it was common practice to ask the court for an order that the costs of preparing the rule 2.2 report and the costs of applying to the court for the order should be treated as an expense of the administration.

The position unfortunately become less clear following the Enterprise Act. The Insolvency Service issued guidance (*Dear IP*, no. 24, September 2005) suggesting that pre-administration costs could be paid by the company either prior to entering into administration or where they had been incurred in completing the Form 2.2B statement (i.e. the statement of the administrator that in his belief the purpose of administration can be achieved). This latter guidance accords with IR 1986, rule 2.67(1)(c), which provides for the recovery of 'costs and expenses of the appointor in connection with the making of the appointment'. It was, however, unclear whether this covers pre-appointment advice in its wider sense, such as the costs of investigations that may have been needed by the insolvency practitioner to assess whether the company is suitable for administration. Almost certainly, the rule does not provide for the recovery of costs incurred in taking strategic advice, planning and reconstruction. This is of great significance in the case of a 'pre-pack adminis-tration' sale of the business where a great deal of work will be carried out by the proposed administrator before his appointment. In such cases the administrator will need to ensure that he is paid by the company, obtains an agreement from the purchaser that it will pay pre-administration costs in addition to the purchase price of the company's business and assets or obtain creditor approval (post expenditure) pursuant to IR 1986, rule 2.67A.

The continued uncertainty as to the recoverability of pre-appointment costs means that the administration may be less attractive or, alternatively, strategic planning of reconstruction will occur after administration rather than beforehand, which may not necessarily be advantageous to the company or its creditors.

A further problem with administration is the disadvantageous tax position. After 15 September 2003, a company going into administration is subject to a new tax accounting period ending on the day that the company ceases to be in administration (Taxes Management Act 1970, s.108(3)(a)). As a result, the administrator is responsible for making a tax return for his period in office, although he may still delegate this to the company's directors. Tax arising on income during the period of administration is treated as a necessary disbursement (*Re Toshuku Finance plc* (2002) 3 All ER 961) and, as a consequence, is payable as an expense of the administration. Where a chargeable gain arises on the sale of a property it is treated as a sale by the company and not the administrator personally, irrespective of whether the sale is by the administrator, a secured creditor or receiver; however, the chargeable gain is also payable as an expense of the administration (IR 1986, rule 2.67(1)(j)). The tax position in administration is to be contrasted with administra-tive receivership, where such tax liabilities remain with the company rather than being treated as an expense of the administrative receivership.

The advantage of receivership (at very least in regard to the better return offered) for secured creditors has been further amplified by the decision in *Exeter City Council* v. *Bairstow* [2007] EWHC 400 (Ch), a case concerning the Ciro Citterio menswear retail chain. The court held that non-domestic rates arising on properties occupied (and most probably unoccupied) by the company in administration were to be treated as an expense of the administration (IR 1986, rule 2.67(1)(f)). This decision, followed by *Goldacre (Offices) Ltd* v. *Nortel Networks UK Ltd* [2009] EWHC 3389 (Ch), continues to cause alarm among some commentators, who fear that potential administrations for companies which hold a significant amount of property are now imperilled. In some instances an insolvency practitioner advising the company may be unaware of the extent of the company's property portfolio and the liabilities that are incurred by the company as a result. The administrator may find funding from secured creditors particularly difficult as a result of this additional expense. In contrast, the administrative receiver is not personally liable for rates as an expense of the receivership and as a result and contrary to Parliament's intention it may encourage charge holders to appoint (if possible) receivers rather than administrators.

3.8.5 Timing of the decision process

If the directors of the company have determined that the company is insolvent and have received suitably qualified professional advice that the purpose of administration is reasonably likely to be achieved, they can move forward to consider when to commence the process.

The timing of the commencement of the process will be dependent on:

(a)   finding an insolvency practitioner prepared to act;
(b)   obtaining a cost/benefit analysis for the company and its creditors as a whole, of administration as against alternative solutions/insolvency processes;
(c)   getting 'buy in' from key stakeholders (e.g. secured creditors and key creditors such as landlords, HMRC and suppliers); and
(d)   getting ready for administration – ensuring funding during the administration process and/or possibly finding a buyer.

As we shall see, the process cannot be commenced without an insolvency practitioner agreeing to act and providing a statement (in Form 2.2B) to court that he is authorised to act as an insolvency practitioner and that in his opinion the purpose of administration is reasonably likely to be achieved.

Although this is a simple statement, its provision should not be undertaken lightly. In reaching an opinion the insolvency practitioner will need to have satisfied himself, based on the information he has seen and the meetings held with the directors, that the purpose of administration is reasonably likely to be achieved and that this is 'best advice'. Prior to the Enterprise Act 2002 reforms, the application to court needed to be accompanied by a so-called 'Rule 2.2 Report' from an insolvency practitioner (generally the proposed administrator) evidencing that administration was in the best interests of the creditors as a whole. This report would often provide an estimated financial comparison between administration and other processes, in providing justification for the order being sought. While this formality is no longer required, this type of exercise should still be undertaken by the insolvency practitioner as part of his advice to the directors. In turn, the directors can take comfort that they have acted in the proper discharge of their duties to the company and its creditors by pointing to such advice having been sought.

Obtaining such advice will take time and in practice the directors may feel it important to speak to a number of different insolvency practitioners, who may have a different approach to the company's financial difficulties, possess different depths of resources and cost base proportionate to the debtor company, all of which are factors that should be borne in mind in reaching a decision as to whom to appoint.

Once an insolvency practitioner is retained by the company to advise, it is often the case that he will outline the plans for the company to key stakeholders. Obtaining support may be vital to achieve the purpose of administration, although care must be taken to ensure that prior disclosure does not lead to precipitous action by creditors. For example, a supplier may be key to the business and the proposed administrator may feel it appropriate to ensure that the supplier will continue to support the business when it is in administration. The supplier is not compelled to assist and may, on hearing of the plan, withdraw credit terms, refuse to supply and, if applicable, seek to enforce any retention of title. Actions by landlords and HMRC (such as forfeiture and/or distraint) may also follow if they learn of the company's difficulties and act before a moratorium comes into effect on the commencement of the process. As a result, it may be the case that the insolvency practitioner considers it is not appropriate to approach certain stakeholders prior to the commencement of the process.

As we shall see, any creditor with a floating charge must be given notice of the company's intention to commence administration. In practice, any creditor with fixed charge security over significant company assets is also likely to be approached by the proposed administrator as part of the pre-planning stage, as on appointment the administrator cannot deal with these assets without consent (or leave of the court). Consequently, as a matter of form and practice the major secured creditors holding fixed charges are also likely to be approached, although, as noted previously, the company's principal lenders are likely to have both fixed and floating charge security in any event.

Lastly, the success of the administration will be dependent on ensuring adequate cash flow/funding during the process. If there is a risk that the administration process will deplete available assets, funding/indemnities will need to be obtained to ensure that the process will not worsen the creditors' position. The inherent risk of worsening the creditors' position (and the costs and expense rule in administration) has led to the use of so-called 'pre-pack administration sales'. As a result, an administration often will not be commenced until a buyer is found and negotiations regarding the purchase of the company's business and assets are concluded.

3.9 APPOINTMENT OF ADMINISTRATOR BY COURT ORDER

Checklist

An administration application to court may only be made by:

- the company;
- the directors of the company;
- one or more creditors of the company (including both contingent and prospective creditors);
- the justice and chief executive of the magistrates' court in the exercise of powers conferred by the Magistrates' Courts Act 1980, s.87(A) (i.e. fines imposed on the company); or
- a combination of the persons above (IA 1986, Sched.B1, para.12(1) in compliance with IR 1986, rule 2.4).

3.9.1 Grounds for application to court

The court may make an administration order in relation to a company only if it is satisfied that:

- the company is or is likely to be unable to pay its debts; and
- the administration order is reasonably likely to achieve the purpose of the administration (IA 1986, Sched.B1, para.11).

The use of the word 'satisfied' was addressed in the case of *Re Colt Telecom Group plc (No.2)* [2003] BPIR 324. In this pre-Enterprise Act case a creditor was seeking an administration order pointing to the likelihood that, in the future, the company would be unable to pay sums due to the particular applicant/creditor. The creditor's motive for the administration was that a sale of the company's business at that time was in the creditor's own best interest. In dismissing the creditor's petition, the court held that 'insolvency' must be established on the 'balance of probabilities'. See also *Re AA Mutual Insurance International Insurance Co. Ltd* [2005] 2 BCLC 8 where the position is seen to be unchanged after the Enterprise Act 2002 reforms.

The wording 'unable to pay its debts' is also found in IA 1986, s.123. It is specifically provided that the reference in para.11 is to have the same meaning as that in s.123 (IA 1986, Sched.B1, para.111(1)). As a result, the court can have regard to either the 'cash flow' test (see *Re Business Properties Ltd* (1988) 4 BCC 684) or the 'balance sheet' test of insolvency (see *Re Dianoor Jewels Ltd* [2001] 1 BCLC 450). Importantly, in assessing the balance sheet test regard is to be had to future, contingent and prospective liabilities (see *Re AA Mutual International Insurance Co. Ltd* [2005] 2 BCLC 8) but contingent and prospective assets are not to be considered (see *Byblos Bank SAL* v. *Al-Khudhairy* [1987] BCLC 232). The tests are mutually exclusive and while a company may be solvent on one basis, if it is not solvent on the other a finding that the company is or is likely to be unable to pay its debts will be made.

In making an administration order, the court needs to be satisfied that it is reasonably likely to achieve the purpose of the administration. In reaching this conclusion the court needs to be satisfied that there is a 'real prospect' that the purpose of administration will be achieved (see *Re Harris Simons Construction Ltd* (1989) 5 BCC 11 and *Re Redman Construction Ltd* [2004] All ER (D) 146 (Jun)). More recent authorities have perhaps watered down the concept of 'real prospect' and it is been held that this does not necessarily equate to more than a 50 per cent probability (see *DKLL Solicitors* v. *Revenue and Customs Commissioners* [2007] BCC 908).

The court will, however, still be mindful to guard against the commencement of fanciful, speculative administrations, which could risk worsening the creditors' position. It will also guard against administration being improperly used to simply prevent enforcement action (see *Doltable Ltd* v. *Lexi Holdings plc* [2006] 1 BCLC 384 where directors unsuccessfully sought to obtain a moratorium to prevent a secured creditor from realising its security over assets at a price objected to by the directors).

Each case depends on its own circumstances but it should be remembered that the court is not equipped to, and is unlikely to, indulge in speculation as to what is at heart a commercial judgment. As a result, in reaching its decision the court is likely to have primary regard to professional (expert) opinion.

As we shall see, as in the case of an out-of-court appointment, an insolvency practitioner, in consenting to act, must in a prescribed form (Form 2.2B) state that in his opinion it is reasonably likely that the purpose of administration will be achieved (IR 1986, rule 2.3(5)(c)).

Under the previous regime, in reaching its decision the court paid close regard to the so-called 'Rule 2.2 Report' which was provided by an insolvency practitioner (often the proposed administrator) as 'expert evidence' to the court (see *Re Colt Telecom Group plc (No.2)* [2003] BPIR 324). This report provided specific information (much of which is now to be found in the witness statement that needs to be filed in support of the administration petition: see IR 1986, rules 2.2–2.5) and an expert assessment as to whether the purposes of the administration were likely to be achieved. This form of report is no longer required. As a result, in simple non-contested cases the court may be willing to accept the administrator's statement made in Form 2.2B alone. However, where there is likely to be a conflict (e.g. the company/directors are applying to court because a creditor is seeking a winding-up order) the applicants would be well advised to outline in some detail why it is thought that an administration order is appropriate and why it offers the best option for the creditors as a whole and show that this is supported by professional opinion. This could be achieved by attaching as an exhibit to the witness statement accompanying the application any report or letter of advice provided by an insolvency practitioner outlining his advice to the company.

Ultimately the making of the order remains a matter of discretion for the court. The court will have primary regard to the interests of the creditors as a whole. As a result, even if it were to find that the purpose of administration is reasonably likely to be achieved, if it were found that on comparable grounds other possible insolvency procedures would produce a better result and/or the creditors would be likely to reject the administrator's proposals, the court might not make an order. It should always be remembered, however, that the cases are fact sensitive.

In *Re Land and Property Trust Co. plc (No.2)* [1991] BCLC 849 an order was refused where the creditors were likely to object to a proposed course; contrast this with *DKLL Solicitors* v. *Revenue and Customs Commissioners* [2007] BCC 908 where the largest (majority) creditor unsuccessfully objected to the order being sought.

In *The Oracle (North West) Ltd* v. *Pinnacle Financial Services (UK) Ltd* [2009] BCC 159 there was a dispute between the directors of the insolvent company and the largest creditor as to the choice of administrator. In this case the court resolved in favour of the creditor, for whose benefit the administration was being commenced. Regard to the interests and benefit of administration to the unsecured creditor was also important in *Re Kayley Vending Ltd* [2009] EWHC 904 (Ch), where the costs and expenses incurred pre-administration in the negotiation of a pre-pack sale were ordered to be costs and expenses of the administration as the sale was to an independent third party and not to the existing management and was 'cleared' of benefit to the creditors as a whole.

3.9.2 Who may make the application?

An administration application to court may only be made by:

- the company;
- the directors of the company;
- one or more creditors of the company (including both contingent and prospective creditors);
- the justice and chief executive of the magistrates' court in the exercise of powers conferred by Magistrates' Courts Act 1980, s.87A (i.e. fines imposed on the company); or
- a combination of the persons above (IA 1986, Sched.B1, para.12(1) in compliance with IR 1986, rule 2.4).

The wording of the section seems to prohibit other parties from applying to court. Parties other than those listed above under differing statutory provisions may apply for an administration order. Such parties will bring an application for and on behalf of the company and are specifically empowered to do so by appropriate statutory authority (e.g. a liquidator by virtue of IA 1986, Sched.B1, para.38; a supervisor of a CVA may do so pursuant to IA 1986, s.7(4)(b), see IR 1986, rule 2.2(4); the Financial Conduct Authority (FCA) by virtue of the Financial Services and Markets Act 2000, s.359).

While the members may, after passing the appropriate resolution, apply to court on behalf of the company for an administration order, individual members are not entitled to apply to the court for an administration order (see *Re Chelmsford City Football Club (1980) Ltd* [1991] BCC 133).

It should be noted that if the application is made by the directors, it is to be stated as being made under IA 1986, Sched.B1, para.12(1)(b), but from the date of making the application it is to be treated for all purposes as if it were an application of the company (IR 1986, rule 2.3(2)).

As discussed in **5.3.9**, an application can be made by a creditor of the company.

One or more creditors may apply for an administration order (IA 1986, Sched.B1, para.12(1)(c)) and if there are multiple creditors each must be specifically identified (IR 1986, rule 2.3(4)). The court will only make an order if it is satisfied that the company is, or is likely to become, unable to pay its debts (i.e. the debtor company's insolvency) and the order is reasonably likely to achieve the purpose of administration (IA 1986, Sched.B1, para.11). The court will not make an order if there are grounds for belief that there is a genuine or substantial dispute in respect of the creditors' claim (*Re British American Racing (Holdings) Ltd* [2005] BCC 110).

There is some debate as to the standard of proof required to establish the debtor company's insolvency on a creditor's petition, as presumably it will be made in the face of opposition by the company. In *Re Colt Telecom Group plc (No.2)* [2002] EWHC 2815 (Ch), a case under the old administration regime, the applicant sought to argue that the debtor company was insolvent by reason of large contingent and prospective liabilities. The court ruled that 'likely' to be unable to pay its debts in this context meant 'more probable than not' and being 'satisfied' was measured on the balance of probabilities. As post-Enterprise Act legislation provides that it must be 'likely' that the company is unable to pay its debts and it is 'reasonably likely' that purpose of the administration will be achieved, it is suggested that a less stringent test applies to the latter than to the former.

3.9.3 Administration application

Guide to procedure

Administration order

- File at court:
    - application (in Form 2.1B);
    - affidavit in support (or witness statement) (IR 1986, rule 7.57);
    - written statement from proposed administrator (in Form 2.2B).

- Interim moratorium takes effect.
- Give not less than five days' notice of hearing to:
    - any person who has appointed/may appoint an administrative receiver;
    - any qualifying floating charge holder who may appoint an administrator;
    - such other persons as necessary (e.g. petitioning creditor, the company administrative receiver or supervisor or CVA);

    −   the proposed administrator.

- File certificate of service (IR 1986, rule 2.9(2)).
- Hearing takes place and administration order may be made (in Form 2.4B).

The Insolvency Rules that govern the court appointment regime specifically provide that the administration application *shall* (emphasis added) be in Form 2.1B (IR 1986, rule 2.2(1)); as a result this form should be used and amended if required.

In completing the application, regard must be had to what is the appropriate court in which to issue the application. This may be guided by convenience to the applicant/company and/or regard to the efficiency of the court and ability to hear the application quickly. A county court can be used where the company's share capital does not exceed £120,000 provided the company's registered office is situated in the jurisdiction of the particular court. However, it is common for practitioners to use the High Court because of the court's greater resources, familiarity with the process and ability to check that a winding-up petition has not been issued prior to issue of the administration applications (by attendance at the Companies Court general office to search the central registry of winding-up petitions, although a search by telephone on 020 7947 7328 is now available). This is especially important in respect of an appointment by the out-of-court route, where an administrator's appointment by the company/directors will be invalid if a winding-up petition has been presented and has not been disposed of (see *Re Blights Builders Ltd* [2007] 3 All ER 776).

Practical tips on completing Form 2.1B

The numbers and letters in the list below follow those as set out on Form 2.1B.

1.   (a) Insert the name of the company, the actual names of the directors or the creditor making the application.

     (b) Only needs to be completed on a creditor application and if the application is supported by other creditors.

     (c) Only needs to be completed if the application is by a qualifying floating charge holder. The reference to para.35 is to IA 1986, Sched.B1, para.35, which provides that a qualifying floating charge holder may apply to court (rather than appoint out of court) in special cases, perhaps where the security may be susceptible to challenge or if an administrative receiver or provisional liquidator is in office. The reference to para.37 is to IA 1986, Sched.B1, para.37, which provides that a qualifying floating charge holder has applied to court because the company is already in compulsory or voluntary liquidation, so presenting an out-of-court appointment where there is no need to establish insolvency.

2.   (d) Insert name of company subject to application.

Rule 2.2

Form 2.1B

Administration application

Name of Company	Company number

In the	For court use only
[full name of court]	Court case number

1. The application of (a) _____ being

*(i) the company, in reliance on paragraph 12(1)(a) of Schedule B1 to the Insolvency Act 1986 ("the Schedule")

*(ii) the directors, in reliance on paragraph 12(1)(b) of the Schedule

*(iii) a creditor / a creditor presenting this application on behalf of himself and the following creditors of the company: (b) _____ , in reliance on paragraph 12(1)(c) of the Schedule

*(iv) a holder of a qualifying floating charge, in reliance on paragraph 35 of the Schedule: (c)
_____

*(v) a holder of a qualifying floating charge, in reliance on paragraph 37 of the Schedule: (c)
_____

*(vi) the liquidator of the company, in reliance on paragraph 38 of the Schedule

*(vii) a justices' chief executive for a magistrates' court, in the exercise of the power conferred by section 87A of the Magistrates' Courts Act 1980

*(viii) the supervisor of a company voluntary arrangement, in reliance on section 7(4)(b) of the Insolvency Act 1986

2. (d) _____ ("the company") was incorporated

on (e) _____ under the Companies Act 19   , and

the registered number of the company is (f) _____ .

3. The registered office of the company is at (g) _____
_____

4. The nominal capital of the company is (h) £_____ divided into ___ shares of £____ each. The amount of the capital paid up or credited as paid up is (j) £_____

5.   The principal business which is carried on by the company is:
_____

122

*Delete as applicable

6. The company *is / is not *an insurance undertaking / credit institution / an investment undertaking providing services involving the holding of funds or securities for third parties / or a collective investment undertaking under Article 1.2 of the EC Regulation.

7. For the reasons stated in the witness statement in support of this application it is considered that the EC Regulation *will / will not apply. If it does apply, proceedings will be

(k) Insert whether main, secondary or territorial proceedings

(k) _____ proceedings as defined in Article 3 of the EC Regulation.

*Delete as applicable

8. *The applicant(s) believe(s) that the company is or is likely to become unable to pay its debts for the reasons stated in the witness statement in support attached to this application.
(* Delete this paragraph if application is in reliance on paragraph 35 of Schedule B1)

9. The applicant(s) propose(s) that during the period for which the order is in force, the affairs, business and property of the company be managed by

(l) Insert full name(s) and address(es) of proposed administrator(s)

(l) _____

_____

whose statement(s) in Form 2.2B is / are attached to this application.

10. A witness statement in support of this application is attached.

*Delete as applicable

(m) Insert address for service - where applicant is company or directors this must be the registered office of the company unless special reason to contrary

11. The *applicant's / applicant's solicitor's address for service is (m)

_____

_____

_____

12. The applicant(s) therefore request(s) as follows:-

(1) that the court make an administration order in relation to (d) _____

(n) Insert full name(s) of proposed administrator(s)

(2) that (n) _____

be appointed to be the administrator(s) of the said company

(o) Insert details of any ancillary orders sought

(3) (o) _____

_____

or

(4) that such other order may be made as the court thinks appropriate.

*Delete as applicable

Signed

*Applicant / applicant's solicitor
(If signing on behalf of firm or company state position or office held)

Dated _____

<table>
<tr><td colspan="2">Endorsement to be completed by the court</td></tr>
</table>

Endorsement to be completed by the court

This application having been presented to the court on _____ will

(p) Insert name and address of Court/District Registry

be heard at (p) _____

_____ on

(Date) _____ at

(Time) _____ hours
(or as soon thereafter as the application can be heard)

The solicitor to the applicant is:—

Name

Address _____

_____

Telephone No: _____

Reference _____

[Whose Agents are:—

Name _____

Address _____

_____

Telephone No. _____

Reference _____

(e)   Insert date of incorporation.

(f)   Insert registered number.

3.   (g)   Insert registered office. In IA 1986, s.117(6) in regard to the issue of a winding-up petition the place the company has its registered office is said to be where it has been longest in the last six months. This is of note in view of the practice of cross-border 'forum shopping', where a foreign company may wish to restructure its business under the UK administration process.

4.   (h)   Provide details of company's nominal share capital.

(j)   Provide details of company's paid-up share capital.

5.   Provide details of the company's principal business. To obtain the information to enable successful completion of this section and (d) to (h) above, a company search should be obtained, including the company's memorandum and articles of association and its last annual return.

6.   Delete 'is/is not' as appropriate. Note, however, that if the company is an

insurance undertaking, credit institution, an investment undertaking providing services involving the holding of funds or securities for third parties, or a collective investment undertaking under Art.1.2 of Council Regulation 1346/2000/EC of 29 May 2000 on Insolvency Proceedings then a different insolvency regime will apply and specialist works should be consulted. Such companies will also not be subject to the EC Regulation.

7.   Delete 'will/will not' as appropriate, although again if the EC Regulation does not apply then a different regime is likely to be in operation.

    (k)   The proceedings are main proceedings provided the registered office/ COMI lies in the UK. This will need to be expanded upon further in the witness statement in support of the application (see definition of main or secondary proceedings provided below for further details).

8.   The applicant must state that he believes the company is unable to pay its debts unless the application is being made by a qualifying floating charge holder in the special cases described above.

9.   Insert name and address of proposed administrators. As Form 2.2B needs to be attached, the prospective insolvency practitioner must have reviewed the affairs of the company and concluded that administration is appropriate.

10.   An affidavit/witness statement in support must be filed.

11.   (m)   The address for service of the applicant/applicant's solicitors is inserted. If the directors have made the application then the registered office of the company must be used unless special circumstances described in the witness statement are shown.

12.   (n)   Insert name of proposed administrator(s).

    (o)   Include any other orders being sought; give thought to whether any issue of service needs to be specifically dealt with, any special issue regarding the commencement of administration proceedings or regarding ancillary matters such as dealing with any outstanding winding-up petitions, etc.

Definitions

Main or territorial proceedings and EC Regulation on Insolvency Proceedings

The EC Regulation on Insolvency Proceedings (Council Regulation 1346/2000/EC, 29 May 2000) came into effect throughout the EU (excluding Denmark) on 31 May 2002. The Regulation is limited to setting out how office holders will perform their function in relation to companies with interests in more than one EU Member State. The Regulation applies to all collective insolvency proceedings (Art.1.1 includes administration, but not an administrative receivership).

The Regulation distinguishes between main and territorial (or secondary) proceedings (Art.3). This distinction is vital as main proceedings will have 'universal scope' and 'aim at encompassing all the debtor's assets' (Recital 12). Territorial/secondary proceedings have more limited scope and are subservient to any main proceedings.

The main proceedings are commenced in the Member State in which the debtor's COMI is situated. Unfortunately, the term is not expressly defined, although in the Recitals to the Regulation it is stated to be the place where the debtor conducts the administration of its interests on a regular basis. In the case of a company, there is a rebuttable presumption that this will mean the company's registered office (Art.3.1).

As a consequence, the definition straddles the two concepts used across the differing jurisdictions in Europe. In certain countries, including the UK, the place of incorporation of the corporate entity is deemed *prima facie* evidence in determining jurisdiction. In other countries, a real seat doctrine has been adopted, where the courts consider that where the assets are held, business carried on or decisions taken should determine jurisdiction.

As a rule, therefore, in completing an application if the registered office of the company is situated in the UK, it can be assumed that the proceedings will be 'main proceedings'. However, further consideration may need to be given if the administrative centre of the company is situated elsewhere.

3.9.4   Witness statement to be filed with the application

The administration application in Form 2.1B must be accompanied by a witness statement in support which must be filed with the court and comply with IR 1986, rule 2.4.

If the administration application is made by the company or by the directors, the witness statement should be made by one of the directors (IR 1986, rule 2.2(2)). The director should state the basis of his authority to make the application, perhaps by reference to a board resolution which confirms both the board's decision to bring the application and the authority given to the individual to make the witness statement.

If the administration application is made by a creditor, the witness statement should be made by a duly authorised person, stating the nature of his authority and the means of his knowledge of the matters contained within the witness statement (IR 1986, rule 2.2(3)).

If the application is made by a qualifying floating charge holder in the special circumstances of IA 1986, Sched.B1, para.35 (e.g. where there may be some concern as to possible challenge), sufficient details must be provided in the witness statement to allow the court to conclude that the qualifying floating charge holder would be entitled to appoint under IA 1986, Sched.B1, para.14 (IR 1986, rule 2.4(3)). Presumably this could cover a situation where a floating charge holder was aware of possible challenge to the validity of the security and sought to persuade the court that the security was valid. It must be remembered that in making the order the court can have regard to all circumstances and, if it is deemed to be in the interests of the creditors as a whole, could make the order on the basis that the applicant was in any event an unsecured creditor (see *Re G-Tech Construction Ltd* [2007] BPIR 1275 for an example of how the court overcame a procedural defect where the notice of intention to appoint was in Form 2.5B as opposed to the correct form of Form 2.10B and where the court allowed a revised application to appoint to be issued).

The affidavit/witness statement in support must contain:

(a) a statement of the company's financial position, specifying to the best of the applicant's knowledge and belief the company's assets and liabilities, including contingent and prospective liabilities;

(b) details of any securities known (or believed) to be held by creditors of the company;

(c) in a case where a security confers the power upon the shareholder to appoint an administrative receiver or an administrator, a statement as to whether an appointment has been made;

(d) details of any insolvency proceedings in relation to the company including any petition that has been presented for the winding up of the company;

(e) if more than one person is to be appointed administrator, a statement specifying the functions to be exercised for the persons acting jointly and what functions if any are to be exercised by any or all of the persons appointed (IA 1986, Sched.B1, para.100(2)); and

(f) any other matters which in the opinion of those making the application will assist the court in deciding whether to make an order.

The affidavit should also state whether in the opinion of the person making the application, the EC Regulation on Insolvency Proceedings will apply and if so whether the proceedings will be main or territorial proceedings.

The EC Regulation on Insolvency Proceedings (Council Regulation 1346/2000/EC of 29 May 2000) came into effect throughout the EC (excluding Denmark) on 31 May 2002. The Regulation distinguishes between main and territorial (or secondary proceedings) (Art.3). This distinction is vital as main proceedings will have 'universal scope' and 'aim at encompassing all the debtor's assets' (Recital 12). Territorial/secondary proceedings have more limited scope and are subservient to any main proceedings, applying only to the debtor's assets situated in the local jurisdiction.

Main proceedings are commenced in the Member State in which the debtor's COMI is situated. Unfortunately, the term is not expressly defined, although in the Recitals to the Regulation it is stated to be the place where the debtor conducts the administration of its interests on a regular basis. In the case of a company, there is a rebuttable presumption that this will mean the company's registered office (Art.3.1).

As a rule, therefore, for the purposes of completing an application, if the registered office of the company is situated in the UK, it can be assumed that the proceedings will be 'main proceedings'. However, further consideration might need to be had where it is thought that the 'administrative centre' of the company may be situated elsewhere.

The application must also crucially be supported by a statement from the proposed administrator consenting to act and stating that the purpose of administration is reasonably likely to be achieved (in Form 2.2B).

For Form 2.2B, see **www.insolvency.gov.uk/forms/englandwalesforms.htm**.

3.9.5 Notice of application

The application and supporting documents should be filed at court with a sufficient number of copies for service (IR 1986, rule 2.5(1)), which will be sealed by the court and issued to the applicant for service (i.e. it is for the applicant to consider by reference to IA 1986, Sched.B1, para.12(2) and IR 1986, rule 2.6(3) the number of parties who may require service of the proceedings) (see below for guidance on who may need to be served).

As soon as reasonably practical after making the administration application, the applicant shall serve as directed by the court (IR 1986, rules 2.6(2), 2.8) the notice of application and evidence filed in support not less than five days before the hearing date on the following:

1. Any person who has appointed an administrative receiver of the company.

    It should be noted that the court must dismiss an administration application in the case where an administrative receiver is already in office (IA 1986, Sched.B1, para.39(1)) unless the appointor consents or the court is satisfied that the floating charge is liable to be released or discharged under IA 1986, ss.238–240 (transaction at an undervalue and preference) or IA 1986, s.245 (avoidance provisions relating to a floating charge).

2. Any person who is, or may be, entitled to appoint an administrative receiver of the company.

    In general, IA 1986, s.72A prohibits a floating charge holder from appointing an administrative receiver unless it is one of the specially listed exemptions to that section or the charge was created prior to 15 September 2003. In cases where a floating charge holder still has an ability to appoint an administrative receiver, notice must be given to the potential appointor, who could, providing the floating charge in question is not challengeable (e.g. under IA 1986, ss.238–240 or s.245), decide to appoint an administrative receiver, bringing into effect the consequences of IA 1986, Sched.B1, para.39(1) previously described.

3. Any person who is or may be entitled to appoint an administrator of the company.

    As a result of the post-Enterprise Act 2002 restrictions in administrative receivership, in most cases the floating charge holder will no longer have an ability to prevent the company entering into administration by the appointment of an administrative receiver. However, provided that the floating charge in question is not challengeable (e.g. under IA 1986, ss.238–240 or s.245), the charge holder will have the ability to intervene in the proceedings and make an appointment of his own nominated administrator under IA 1986, Sched.B1, para.36(1). The charge holder's nomination will be accepted by the court unless the court thinks it right to refuse the application because of particular circumstances of the case (IA 1986, Sched.B1, para.36(2)). We are still waiting to see whether there are circumstances in which a court will refuse to make an appointment where it is considered that the administrator would be too 'secured creditor friendly', e.g. where the interests/wishes of all the other creditors would prefer an administrator following an alternative strategy which may be perceived as less beneficial to the secured creditor.

If the floating charge holder applies to court under this section, he is required to produce to court the written consent of all prior floating charge holders, written statement of consent to act and opinion as to the likely achievement of the purposes of administration (in Form 2.2B) and evidence of entitlement to appoint (IR 1986, rule 2.10). This latter condition therefore requires the floating charge holder to disclose the nature of the loan agreement, the security and ability to appoint an administrator thereunder.

4.   If there is a pending petition for the winding up of the company, the petitioning creditor.

It may be the case that on being provided with notice the petitioning creditor opposes the administration and seeks the winding up of the company. The court will, however, have regard to all the circumstances and the fact that the majority creditor opposes the appointment and has indicated that it would object to the proposals put forward by the administration is not in itself enough to prevent the court making an administration order (see *DKLL Solicitors* v. *Revenue and Customs Commissioners* [2007] BCC 908).

If there is a conflict between the choice of the company's/directors' nominee as administrator and that of any other party (generally the unsecured creditors), the court will exercise its discretion after review of all the relevant circumstances. Almost certainly, both proposed administrators will be seen as competent to act. The court will therefore take into account such factors as the knowledge of the case and work already carried out by one of the proposed administrators compared with the other. In *Re World Class Homes Ltd* [2005] 2 BCLC 1 prior involvement was seen as an advantage. Contrast this with *Clydesdale Financial Services* v. *Smailes* [2009] EWHC 1745 (Ch) where an administrator was removed from office as he was perceived to have been so closely involved in the negotiations of a pre-pack sale that another administrator should be appointed to conduct an independent review. See also *The Oracle (North West) Ltd* v. *Pinnacle Services (UK) Ltd* [2008] EWHC 1920 (Ch) where a conflict between directors' and major unsecured creditors' choice of appointment was resolved in favour of the creditors, particularly as the administration was intended for their benefit.

5.   If there is any provisional liquidation order in place, the provisional liquidator.

6.   A liquidator who has been appointed in another Member State as part of main proceedings in relation to the company.

7.   The person proposed to be administrator.

8.   The company, if the application is made by anyone other than the company.

9.   If a CVA is in place, the supervisor.

10.   If the company is regulated by the FCA.

The applicant must also, as soon as reasonably practicable after filing the application, give notice to any High Court enforcement officer (the formerly named 'sheriff') or officer who to his knowledge is charged with execution or other legal process against the company or its property and any person who to his knowledge has distrained against the company or its property (IR 1986, rule 2.7).

The document is served by leaving it with the recipient or sending it by first-class post (IR 1986, rule 2.8(6)). The service of the application will be verified by a certificate of service, specifying the date on which and the manner in which service was effected and all other information as set out in IR 1986, rule 2.9(1A). The certificate of service and a sealed copy of the application exhibited to it must be filed at court as soon as reasonably practicable after service, and in any event, not less than one day before the hearing of the application (IR 1986, rule 2.9(2)).

3.9.6 Hearing of application

At the hearing of the administration application (and irrespective of whether the parties have been served with the application) the following may appear or be represented:

- The applicant.
- The company.
- Any one or more of the directors.
- If an administrative receiver has been appointed, that person.
- Any person who has presented a petition for the winding up of the company.
- Any person appointed or proposed to be appointed as administrator.
- Any Member State liquidator who has been appointed in main proceedings in relation to the company.
- Any person who is a holder of a qualifying floating charge.
- A supervisor of any CVA in respect of the company.
- With the permission of the court, any other person who appears to have an interest justifying that appearance (IR 1986, rule 2.12).

On hearing the application, the court may:

- make an administration order;
- dismiss the application;
- adjourn the application conditionally or unconditionally;

- make an interim order;
- treat the application as a winding-up petition and make an order to wind up the company; or
- make any other order as it thinks fit.

If the court makes an administration order it will be in Form 2.4B.

For Form 2.4B, see **www.insolvency.gov.uk/forms/englandwalesforms.htm**.

The costs of the applicant and any other person allowed by the court are payable as expenses in the administration (IR 1986, rule 2.12(3)). The court will also as soon as reasonably practicable send two sealed copies of the order to the person who made the application. That applicant must then send a sealed copy of the order as soon as reasonably practicable to the person appointed as administrator (IR 1986, rule 2.14).

An interim order may be made where, e.g., the company's property is considered to be in immediate jeopardy. In such cases, the court may appoint an appropriate person (who may or may not be the intended administrator) to take control of the company's property and manage its affairs pending determination of the substantive matter. In such circumstances, the court may restrict the powers of the directors or the company (IA 1986, Sched.B1, para.13(3)).

It should be noted that an application for an administration order can be treated as a winding-up petition and the court can make an order winding up the company in circumstances where the administration application is weak and unmerited. This introduces a degree of judicial intervention and some degree of uncertainty. However, it is likely that the procedure will be used sparingly by the court in cases where the company is clearly insolvent and the administration has no prospect of success. In such circumstances, it would be preferable to wind up the company immediately, rather than allow a further period of uncertainty (IA 1986, Sched.B1, para.13(1)(e)). An example of the court exercising this power was in the case of a Delaware registered corporation in *Re Ci4net.com.Inc* [2005] BCC 277.

If the court makes an administration order on the application of a qualifying floating charge holder where a winding-up order is in place (IA 1986, Sched.B1, para.37) or on the application of the liquidator (IA 1986, Sched.B1, para.38), the order must include necessary consequential directions, including as appropriate the removal of the liquidator from office, provisions relating to release, payment of expenses, indemnity and the handling or realisation of company assets in the hands of the liquidator (IR 1986, rule 2.13).

It should be remembered that an application for an administration order may not be withdrawn without permission of the court (IA 1986, Sched.B1, para.12(3)). The courts have been consistent in their attempts to dissuade creditors from using insolvency procedures as a means of debt collection or debt avoidance and an administration application will be regarded in the same light (see *Doltable Ltd* v. *Lexi Holdings plc* [2006] 1 BCLC 384 where administration was being used to obtain a moratorium and thwart a secured creditor's enforcement action). It is a reminder that administration is a collective remedy not to be undertaken lightly and not to be used to further the interests of the applicant at the expense of the company and, more importantly, its creditors as a whole.

3.10 OUT-OF-COURT APPOINTMENT OF AN ADMINISTRATOR BY COMPANY/ DIRECTORS

The introduction of a new streamlined method for the appointment of an administrator, by the so-called 'out-of-court route', was one of the most radical introductions brought in by the Enterprise Act 2002 reforms. Originally, a company could only be placed into administration by order of the court. Since 15 September 2003, an appointment of an administrator can be made by the company, its directors, or by a qualifying floating charge holder (QFCH) by an out-of-court route. This has proved to be a very successful measure resulting in a large growth in the number of administrations.

Table 3.5 Benefits of out-of-court administration appointments

Advantages	Disadvantages
• Speed	• Unavailability in certain circumstances, e.g.
• Efficiency and simplicity of procedure	– previous CVA/administration moratorium in the last 12 months
• No court hearing required	– winding-up petition presented
• Judicial intervention at a minimum	– administrative receiver in office
• A moratorium can be obtained out of court hours	– the company wishes to challenge the floating charge holder's choice of administrator
	– lack of scrutiny

In this section we shall deal with why and how the company and/or its directors may put the company into administration.

The process is initiated by either:

- the company – the members must pass an appropriate (ordinary) resolution at a general meeting (or unanimous informal agreement as per common law or CA 2006, s.288, which replaced CA 1985, s.381A); or
- the directors of the company (see below for discussion on the formalities of appointment).

A distinction between the ability to appoint by the company and its directors is necessary in cases where the members may not wish to put the company into administration, but the management of the company is concerned with its own position (i.e. trading while insolvent). It may also be more convenient for the directors immediately to commence the procedure rather than to call a general meeting. However, once the procedure is initiated by the directors it is treated as if it were an appointment by the company.

On a directors' appointment careful note must be taken of the judgment in *Minmar (929) Ltd* v. *Khalatschi* [2011] EWHC 1159 (Ch) (April 2011). In this case the High Court held that an out-of-court appointment of administrators was invalid on two counts:

- The directors' decision was not made in accordance with the company's articles and there was no valid board resolution.
- There was no notice of intention to appoint served on the company at its registered office.

Dealing with the first point, IR 1986, rule 2.22 provides that a directors' notice of intention to appoint an administrator must be accompanied by a record of the directors' decision to make the appointment. The use of the word 'record' had generally been taken to signify that a formal meeting and resolution of the board was not necessarily required, provided that the majority of the directors were in agreement with the decision.

In *Minmar* the record suggested that only one individual attended the directors' meeting and did so on behalf of a newly appointed director, who as part of a board room coup had purportedly taken control and management of the company. On the facts, it transpired that no notice was given to any of the three existing directors of this purported meeting; as a result the meeting was not called with due notice as required by Minmar's articles of association and there was no quorum at the meeting. The applicant directors therefore argued that the meeting was a sham and that the appointment was invalid.

The new director sought to rely on rule 2.22 and on IA 1986, Sched.B1, para.105, which states that:

> A reference in this Schedule to something done by the directors of a company includes a reference to the same thing done by a majority of the directors of a company.

It was argued that the legislation did not require a board meeting to be properly convened and that instead a simple majority was sufficient. The judge, Sir Andrew Morritt (the Chancellor), residing over the case disagreed. The court considered the background of para.105 and its general application in some detail. The judge held that the legislation did not remove the need to comply with the usual requirements in a company's articles to obtain valid board resolutions at meeting properly convened with notice.

In the *Minmar* case there was no quorum, no valid board meeting and hence no valid decision of the board; the administrator's appointment was therefore declared invalid. The judge took the view that the directors of a company lacked authority to make an out-of-court administration appointment unless authorised to do so in accordance with the company's articles of association. In this case, the articles of

Minmar Ltd required the directors to act unanimously or with the authority of a formal resolution of the board. As the appointing directors had neither, they lacked authority to make the appointment.

The decision has made it very clear that the internal constitution of the company cannot be ignored and the formalities required to effect a decision of the directors must be followed carefully. Extreme caution must be exercised if there is any question of shareholder/director dispute and indeed in such circumstances the prudent advice may be to apply to court for an administration order, as opposed to seeking to rely on the out-of-court route of appointment.

The issue of failure to serve notice of intention and the steps that can be taken to rectify this error are considered in the section below.

See the example of a board resolution to place the company in administration at the end of **3.10.3**.

Guide to procedure

Appointment of administrator out of court

- Where the company is subject to a floating charge, prepare notice of intention to appoint in Form 2.8B.
- If the directors are to appoint, prepare a notice of intention to be served on the company, adapt Form 2.8B as appropriate.
- Attach to Form 2.8B the record of company resolution/directors' decision regarding administration.
- File notice of intention at court within five days of making statutory declaration contained in notice.
- Interim moratorium takes effect (10 days maximum duration).
- Serve notice of intention on QFCH giving at least five business days' notice.
- Additionally, send notice of intention to:

    - any High Court enforcement officer (sheriff) charged with execution;
    - any creditor who has distrained;
    - any supervisor of a CVA;
    - the company (if appointed by directors);
    - the FCA, if applicable.

- If there is a QFCH and they:

    - consent to appointment; the company/directors can complete statutory declaration contained in notice of appointment (Form 2.10B);
    - fail to respond to notice, the company/directors can after five days complete statutory declaration contained in notice of appointment (Form 2.10B); or
    - object and/or make appointment of their own choice of administrator or appoint an administrative receiver (if the option is available), the company/directors can take no further step.

- If no QFCH, prepare notice of appointment in Form 2.9B.

- Notice of appointment (Form 2.9B or 2.10B) is then filed at court with administrator's statement (in Form 2.2B) (if no notice of intention was required, a record of company resolution regarding the commencement of the administration must be attached).
- Administration commences.

3.10.1   Restrictions on appointment

The company or its directors may only appoint an administrator if:

(a)   an administrator has not been appointed by the company or its directors, nor was the company subject to a moratorium in respect of a voluntary arrangement, in the previous 12 months (IA 1986, Sched.B1, para.23(2));

(b)   the company is, or is likely to be, unable to pay its debts (this contrasts with an appointment made by a qualifying floating charge holder where, as we have seen, the company need not be insolvent);

(c)   no petition for winding up, nor any administration application, has been presented or is outstanding in respect of the company (IA 1986, Sched.B1, para.25);

(d)   the company is not in liquidation or provisional liquidation;

(e)   no administrator is in office;

(f)   no administrative receiver is in office.

If any of the above restrictions apply, it may be open to the company to apply to court for an administration order (see, however, *Chesterton International Group plc* v. *Deka Immobilien Inv GmbH* [2005] BPIR 1103; in the absence of any circumstances rendering the security invalid or suspect, where an administrative receiver was already in office, the court felt that it lacked jurisdiction to make an administration order).

The most common prohibition against an out-of-court appointment by the directors is the prior presentation of a winding-up petition. Understandably in such circumstances, the company needs to make an administration application to court, to serve it on the petitioning creditor and to persuade the court that, irrespective of any objection by the creditor, it is in the best interests of the creditors as a whole that an administration order should be made rather than a winding-up order.

Before commencing the administration process, it is therefore essential to check that a winding-up petition has not been presented. If one has been presented, any purported appointment of an administrator will be invalid. The purported administrator will be deemed a trespasser liable for damages to the company (see IA 1986, Sched.B1, para.34 regarding the potential indemnity from the appointor in such circumstances).

The difficulties that can arise if a company makes an appointment were fully illustrated in the case of *Re Blights Builders Ltd* [2007] BCC 712. In this case a winding-up petition had been posted to court, and was stamped and dated but not sealed and issued for service by the petitioning creditor. In the meantime, the company appointed an administrator using the out-of-court route. After it came to light that a petition had been in existence at the time of the appointment, the administrator sought direction as to the validity of his appointment. The court held that the winding-up petition was presented as and when it was filed at court. It was irrelevant that the company was unaware of the petition and that it was not registered at the central registry of petitions maintained by the Companies Court. This type of problem would be compounded yet further if the winding-up petition was filed at a county court. Although sympathetic, the court held that it could not validate the appointment.

Consequently, a search at Companies Court of the register of outstanding petitions should be undertaken and where there is a risk of an imminent winding-up petition, enquiries should be made of the creditor as to their intention. If the situation is explained to the creditor and it is indicated that an administrator will be appointed, which will be more advantageous than liquidation, the creditor may be persuaded to desist. In cases of doubt, however, the company may be well advised to make an application rather than risk commencement using the out-of-court route.

The company is also prevented from using the out-of-court route for appointment if in the previous 12 months the company has already been in administration or subject to a CVA. This provision is to prevent the company/its directors from using (and abusing) the process to obtain a moratorium solely to hinder creditor claims. In these circumstances, the company can still seek to obtain an administration order, but the application will need to be accompanied by persuasive evidence and careful explanation, which is likely to be closely scrutinised.

3.10.2   Notice of intention to appoint

The ability of the company to make an out-of-court appointment is tempered by the requirement that before the appointment can be made at least five business days' notice of any proposed appointment must be given to the holder of any qualifying floating charge, who is entitled to appoint an administrative receiver and/or administrator (IA 1986, Sched.B1, para.26). The notice of intention must be in Form 2.8B, and on this being filed at court an interim moratorium period takes effect (IA 1986, Sched.B1, para.44). The effect of the interim moratorium is discussed in more detail in **Chapter 7**.

Practical tips on completing Form 2.8B

The numbers and letters in the list below follow those set out on Form 2.8B.

1.   (a) Insert the name and registered office of the company. IA 1986, s.117(6) provides that in regard to the issue of a winding-up petition the place the company has its registered office is said to be where it has been longest in the last six months. This is of note in view of the practice of cross-border forum shopping, where a foreign company may wish to restructure its business under the UK administration process.

Rule 2.20

Notice of intention to appoint an administrator by company or director(s)

Name of Company	Company number

In the [full name of court]	*For court use only* Court case number

(a) Insert name and address of registered office of company

1. Notice is given that, in respect of (a) _____

_____ ("the company")

*Delete as applicable

* the company / the directors of the company ("the appointor") intend to appoint

(b) Give name(s) and address(es) of proposed administrator(s)

(b) _____

as administrator(s) of the company.

2. This notice is being given to the following person(s), being person(s) who is / are or may be entitled to appoint an administrative receiver of the company or an administrator of the company under paragraph 14 of Schedule B1 to the Insolvency Act 1986:

(c) Insert name and address of each person to whom notice is given

(c)

_____

3. The company has not, within the last twelve months:

(i) been in administration
(ii) been the subject of a moratorium under Schedule A1 to the Insolvency Act 1986 which has ended on a date when no voluntary arrangement was in force
(iii) been the subject of a voluntary arrangement which was made during a moratorium for the company under Schedule A1 to the Insolvency Act 1986 and which ended prematurely within the meaning of section 7B of the Insolvency Act 1986.

4. In relation to the company there is no:

(i) petition for winding up which has been presented but not yet disposed of
(ii) administration application which has not yet been disposed of, or
(iii) administrative receiver in office.

*Delete as applicable

5. The company *is / is not *an insurance undertaking / a credit institution / an investment undertaking providing services involving the holding of funds or securities for third parties / or a collective investment undertaking under Article 1.2 of the EC Regulation.

(d) Insert whether main, secondary or territorial proceedings

6. For the following reasons it is considered that the EC Regulation *will / will not apply. If it does apply, these proceedings will be (d) _____ proceedings as defined in Article 3 of the EC Regulations._____

*Delete as applicable

7. Attached to this notice is *a copy of the resolution of the company to appoint an administrator / a record of the decision of the directors to appoint an administrator.

PRE-COMMENCEMENT CONSIDERATIONS

(e) Insert name and address of person making declaration

I (e) _____
(If making the declaration on behalf of appointor indicate capacity e.g. director/solicitor)

hereby do solemnly and sincerely declare that:

(i) the company is or is likely to become unable to pay its debts
(ii) the company is not in liquidation, and
(iii) the statements in paragraphs 3 and 4 are, so far as I am able to ascertain, true,

and that the information provided in this notice is to the best of my knowledge and belief true,

AND I make this solemn declaration conscientiously believing the same to be true and by virtue of the Statutory Declarations Act 1835

Declared at _____

Signed _____

This _____ day of _____ 20

before me _____

Note: This form now to be sent to all those required to be sent the form by Rule 2.20(2)

A Commissioner for Oaths or Notary Public or Justice of the Peace or Solicitor or Duly Authorised Officer.

Consent of Floating Charge Holder to Appointment of Administrator(s)
(Do not detach this part of the notice)

(f) Appointor to insert address

If, having read this notice, you have no objection to the making of this appointment you should complete the details in the box below and return a copy of this notice as soon as possible, and within five business days from receipt of this notice, to the appointor at the following address: (f) _____

_____

If your consent has not been given within five business days the appointor may make the appointment notwithstanding that you have not replied.

(g) Insert name and address

(g)

_____

being the holder of the following floating charge over the company's property:

(h) Give details of charge, date registered and (if any) financial limit

(h) _____

_____

consents to the appointment of the administrator(s) in accordance with the details of this notice.

Signed _____ Dated _____
(If signing on behalf of a firm or company state position or office held)

Endorsement to be completed by court

(j) Insert date and time

This notice was filed (j) _____

(b)   Insert names and addresses of the proposed administrators. While at this stage Form 2.2B (i.e. the consent to act form, etc.) does not need to filed, the fact that insolvency practitioners are named in the notice would suggest that by this stage the company/its directors should have obtained advice and agreement from an insolvency practitioner to so act. The use of Form 2.2B simply to obtain an interim moratorium and/or to file a notice of intention on multiple occasions may well amount to an abuse of process (see below), as potentially would be naming insolvency practitioners who had not (at very least in principle) agreed to act. While there are no rules governing any change of proposed administrators between the provision of the notice and then the appointment, in view of the fact that the notice is primarily one to the floating charge holder, who has the choice to object/appoint their own nomination, in practice their consent to any change should be sought.

2.   (c)   Insert name and address of qualifying floating charge holder. The proper address for service is likely to be found in the loan agreement/facility letter/security documentation. If this is not provided, in the case of a bank (which is likely to have multiple sites, etc.), the address should be where the company has maintained its bank account, or if no such office is known, the registered office, or if no such office, the last known usual address (IR 1986, rule 2.8(5)).

3.   The declarant is required to confirm that the company has not within the last 12 months: been in administration; been subject to a moratorium arising from court order pending the calling of a meeting of creditors to consider a CVA (at present this being available only to 'small' companies); been the subject of a CVA (which was obtained following a moratorium period) which has terminated early (see IA 1986, Sched.A1).

4.   The declarant is required to confirm that no winding-up petition has been presented but has not been disposed of (it is therefore vital to check with the court that no petition has been issued and not yet served), no administration application has yet to be disposed of, and no administrative receiver is in office.

5.   Delete 'is/is not' as appropriate. Note, however, that if the company is an insurance undertaking, a credit institution, an investment undertaking providing services involving the holding of funds or securities for third parties or a collective investment undertaking under Art.1.2 of Council Regulation 1346/2000/EC of 29 May 2000 on Insolvency Proceedings, a different insolvency regime will apply and specialist works should be consulted. Such companies will also not be subject to the EC Regulation.

6.   Delete 'will/will not' as appropriate. Again if the EC Regulation does not apply, a different regime is likely to be in operation.

(d)   The proceedings are deemed 'main' proceedings provided the registered office/COMI lies in the UK (see definition of main or secondary proceedings provided in **3.9.3** for further details). The reasons why the proceedings are main proceedings must be stated on the form.

7.   Attach a copy of the company's resolution to appoint, or the record of the directors' decision to appoint. Note that the resolution is in respect of the intention to appoint; it is not a resolution to file a notice of intention, again emphasising that the notice of intention is a prelude to the appointment of an administrator and should not be used solely as a means of obtaining an interim moratorium against creditor action.

    (e)   Insert details (full name and address) of the individual who is making the statutory declaration contained on the remainder of the form. This must be someone duly authorised by the appointor, such as one of the directors or the company's solicitor. However, the statutory declaration must not be undertaken lightly, as it is a sworn declaration that none of the statutory restrictions on appointment apply (see below), that there are no outstanding insolvency proceedings (such as an outstanding winding-up petition, administration application or administrative receiver in office) and that the company is insolvent and is not in liquidation. It is an offence to make a statement that is false and/or that is not reasonably believed to be true (IA 1986, Sched.B1, para.27(4)). Because of the importance and unique nature of the knowledge pertaining to the declaration, the declarant should probably be a director or senior officer of the company duly authorised by the board to make the declaration. This declaration, which should be sworn before an independent solicitor (or commissioner for oaths, notary public, justice of the peace or officer of the court, each of whom will charge a fee of £7), should not be made more than five business days before the date it is filed at court (IA 1986, Sched.B1, para.27(2); IR 1986, rule 2.21).

    (f)   The address of the appointor/appointor's solicitors to which the floating charge holder should apply is provided.

    (g)   This section is for completion by the floating charge holder who should provide its name and address for service.

    (h)   This section is for completion by the floating charge holder to give details of the charge, date registered and financial limit (if any).

In practice, sections (g) and (h) may be completed beforehand by the appointor, leaving the floating charge holder to provide a duly authorised signatory to endorse the form with consent. It should be noted that the form does not provide for rejection of the proposed administrator or notice of an alternative administrator; in practice, in such circumstances the appointment is likely to be contested leading to correspondence, negotiation and/or a contested court application and hearing.

    The endorsement is to be left blank and is completed by the court on filing. A date and exact time are given, essential to assess when the administration is deemed to have commenced.

It should be noted that Form 2.8B is drafted in such a way to suggest that the notice is first filed at court, endorsed and then served on the floating charge holder. In fact, IA 1986, Sched.B1, para.26 provides that written notice (in the prescribed form, i.e. Form 2.8B) is first served and IA 1986, Sched.B1, para.27 provides that as soon as reasonably practicable after service of the notice a copy of the notice will be filed at court. While an interim moratorium comes into effect on filing (and not on service), this may be of little practical consequence to the charge holder, as IA 1986, Sched.B1, para.44(7) provides that the interim moratorium does not prevent the appointment by the charge holder of an administrator by out-of-court route, or the appointment of an administrative receiver (in respect of a floating charge created pre-15 September 2003 or where a special exemption applies). It should be noted, however, that other legal processes would be prevented, so presumably the company and/or its directors may prefer to first file the notice of intention and serve the duly endorsed copy upon the floating charge holder.

As well as to the floating charge holder, a copy of the notice of intention must also be given to:

(a)   any enforcement officer who to the knowledge of the person giving the notice is charged with execution or other legal process against the company;
(b)   any person who has distrained against the company or its property;
(c)   any supervisor of any CVA in place in regard to the company; and
(d)   the company, if the company is not making the appointment (IR 1986, rule 2.20(2)).

Service on the company is at its registered office, and service on any other person is by delivering the requisite documents to their proper address. The proper address is that which has previously been notified as an address for service and if this is not appropriate, then delivery should be to the last known address (IR 1986, rule 2.8). See *Re Sporting Options plc* [2005] BCC 88 which rules out service by email, although regard may be had in the future to changes to service on companies provided in CA 2006.

In *Minmar (929) Ltd* v. *Khalatschi* [2011] EWHC 1159 (Ch) the Chancellor, Sir Andrew Morritt, in his judgment held that the directors proposing to appoint administrators out of court have to give notice, not just to qualifying floating charge holders, but also to such other persons as may be prescribed (IA 1986, Sched.B1, para.26(2)), irrespective of whether there was or was not a qualifying floating charge holder and the failure, in this case to serve the company with a notice of intention, invalidated the appointment *ab initio*.

The notice must be provided, presumably in the form of the prescribed notice of intention to appoint, even where there is no qualifying floating charge holder and no mention is made on that form of these other parties.

The judge suggested that in the absence of any prescribed statutory period of notice (save in respect of the qualifying floating charge holder), 'a reasonable period of notice' should be given.

It was no surprise to find that following the *Minmar* judgment there was a rush of applications to court by administrators concerned that they may be invalidly appointed. One of the first was *Re Derfshaw Ltd* [2011] EWHC 1565 (Ch), determined on 2 June 2011.

The court has power to make appointments effective from an alternative date to any administration order it makes for those appointments under IA 1986, Sched.B1, para.13(2)(a) and it was under this provision, assuming that the out-of-court appointment was invalid, that an application was made for an administration order to take effect retrospectively.

Before making an administration order, the court has to be satisfied that:

(a)   the company is insolvent; and
(b)   the purpose of administration is reasonably likely to be achieved.

If the court is satisfied of these, it has jurisdiction to make the order and could then move on to provide that the order took effect from an earlier date (see the judgment of Hart J in *G-Tech Construction Ltd* [2007] BPIR 1275). In *Re Derfshaw* Hart J considered that a retrospective administration order would be the most practical solution in terms of speed, expense and certainty. However, Hart J said that such a jurisdiction should be exercised 'with extreme caution'.

The judge's approach therefore in light of *Minmar* was to grant the administration orders retrospectively to the moment when the purported appointments out of court were intended to take effect and so validate all the steps taken by the administrators in the intervening period. It was clear to the court that it was appropriate for administrators to have been appointed over the company at the time they were purportedly appointed.

It should be noted that following *G-Tech* a retrospective order can only be made up to 364 days before the hearing. The logic of this is that an administration period expires after one year's duration; it is therefore only possible to go back one year from the date of the application for a retrospective order, as on the same date one will also need to provide for an extension of the administration period. Furthermore, in this case and some previously, judicial unease with the use of the *G-Tech* authority was expressed, although the desirability of making the order outweighed these concerns.

One issue that was not discussed in the *Derfshaw* judgment was whether on making an administration order it was appropriate to assess whether the purpose of administration would be achieved, as at the date of the application for a retrospective order, or as at the date that the administration order is sought to take effect from. In *Derfshaw* all the seven companies were still in a position that as at the date of the application the purpose of administration was reasonably likely to be achieved; what would be the situation where the purpose had already been achieved and the claims of creditors could just as equally be dealt with through a liquidation process, or where no further distributions were envisaged such that the company could be dissolved?

In the case of *Frontsouth (Witham) Ltd and Another* [2011] EWHC 1668 (Ch) (determined on 30 June 2011) the applicants were unable to rely on *G-Tech* and *Re Derfshaw*, as in this case the invalidity of appointment stemmed from a failure, just before the expiry of the first anniversary of the appointment, to obtain the consent of the requisite creditors. The administrators had obtained the consent of the bank but had no response from a second charge holder who was securing a contingent claim under an overage clause.

The administrators accepted that the lack of sufficient creditor consent meant that the administration had expired on the first anniversary of their appointment. As a result the applicants needed to seek a different means by which to remedy an invalid administration appointment, using the 'slip rule' to correct defects in insolvency proceedings.

Rule 7.55 provides that: 'No insolvency proceedings shall be invalidated by any formal defect or by any irregularity, unless . . . substantial injustice has been caused . . .'.

The administrators and the company therefore applied to court for an order on one or more of the following terms:

- That the administrator's appointment remained in effect despite the failure to obtain the requisite creditor consent, as the failure to obtain proper consent was a remediable defect in insolvency proceedings, within the meaning of rule 7.55.
- That the acts of the administrators in the period of the defective extension were valid despite the defect in their appointment (IA 1986, Sched.B1, para.106).
- That, as per *G-Tech*, the court make an administration order in respect of the company with effect from the expiry of the administration (IA 1986, Sched.B1, para.13(2)(a)).

The court, in light of *Minmar* and *Derfshaw*, held that:

- Where an administrator was not in office, either because he was invalidly appointed or because his term of office had expired, there were no 'insolvency proceedings' within the meaning of rule 7.55. Accordingly, the court could not make an order under that provision.
- Similarly, an invalidly appointed administrator, or one whose term of office has expired, is not the subject of a defective appointment, but rather his appointment is a nullity. Consequently, acts undertaken by the administrator while purportedly in office cannot be validated under IA 1986, Sched.B1, para.104.
- The court cannot make an administration order on the application of a company, unless the making of that application was authorised in accordance with the provisions of its articles of association. In this case, a shareholder resolution was insufficient authorisation, as the articles of association provided that the company's powers were exercisable by its directors.

On 7 October 2011, Mr Justice Norris handed down judgment on the case of *Care Matters Partnership Ltd* [2011] BCC 957, a case in which the two sets of applicants sought a declaration as to the validity of the purported appointment by the directors of the company of an administrator by the out-of-court process and, if appropriate for an administration order to be granted with retrospective effect, backdated to the time of the purported out-of-court appointment.

In the case of *Care Matters Partnership Ltd*, Norris J felt unable to make a retrospective administration order. The reason for this was that he felt that as at the date of the administration application one must be satisfied that the purpose of administration is reasonably likely to be achieved (i.e. future tense). If the purpose has already been achieved or it cannot be achieved, an administration order cannot be granted and as a result one cannot then move on to determine whether the administration order will take effect from an earlier date.

Norris J gave very strong indication that the case of *G-Tech Construction Ltd* [2007] BPIR 1275 should be used with extreme caution. Interestingly, he also referred to his earlier decision in *Re Blights Builders* [2006] EWHC 3549 (Ch) and the potential use of IA 1986, Sched.B1, para.104, which provides: 'An act of the administrator of a company is valid in spite of a defect in his appointment or qualification.' If this remedy had been pursued, it might have found favour.

In December 2011, judgments in the cases of *Virtualpurple Professional Services Ltd* [2012] BCC 254 and *Brezier Acquisitions Ltd* [2011] EWHC 3299 (Ch) were delivered by Norris J.

In *Brezier* (as in *Virtualpurple*) notice of intention had not been served on the company, but as the solicitors instructed by the company dealt with the filing of the notice of intention, it was deemed that the company had sufficient notice. Norris J stressed that focus needs to be on the consequences of non-compliance and on posing the question, taking into account the consequences, whether Parliament intended the outcome of total invalidity.

This rationale was repeated in *Virtualpurple*, a case differing from *Brezier* in that no notice of intention was prepared; the facts in *Virtualpurple* were that a sole director appointed the administrators by use of Form 2.10B as there was no QFCH (and hence no notice of intention was served on the company).

In answer to the question, 'What are the requirements of IA 1986, Sched.B1, para.26 with which the appointor must comply?', Norris J disagreed with the Chancellor's observations in *Minmar* and held that there was no requirement to notify the company of the intention to appoint the administrators, if, as in the *Virtualpurple* case, the appointor was able to make an immediate appointment.

Norris J noted that the earlier judgment of *Hill* v. *Stokes* [2011] BCC 473 had not been referred to the Chancellor. In the *Hill* v. *Stokes* case, McCahill J determined that the draftsman had made a mistake, he said:

> I conclude that, in paragraph 28(1) of Schedule B1 of the Insolvency Act 1986, the reference in the second line to paragraph 26 should be a reference to paragraph 26(1).

McCahill J therefore determined that it is not necessary to serve those other parties (in this case a landlord who had distrained) if there was no QFCH.

Both the *Hill* v. *Stokes* and the *Virtualpurple* judgments reflect the fact that the out-of-court procedure was introduced to promote speed and efficiency of appointment and allows the appointment of an administrator to be made immediately if there is no QFCH. The purpose of serving those listed in IR 1986, rule 2.20 was, it was argued in *Virtualpurple*, to give those creditors who have taken enforcement action over the company's property the right to apply to court for leave to continue to enforce. The effect of the interim moratorium created by the notice of intention is to necessitate service on those parties at that stage. Their right to seek leave to continue to enforce is the same whether a notice of intention is served upon them or a notice of appointment. It seems to us therefore unnecessary to serve a notice of intention on those same parties if there is no QFCH. It is also noted that such parties have no say in whether the appointment takes place (unlike the QFCH).

In the *Virtualpurple* judgment, Norris J posed a second question. Irrespective of the answer to the above question, what are the consequences of non-compliance? Norris J's answer was to hold that even if there was a requirement to give a notice of intention to the company (e.g. where notice of intention had been filed and served because there was a qualifying floating charge), a failure to give this notice does not necessarily render the administrator's appointment invalid.

In determining this second point, Norris J focused on the consequences of non-compliance, i.e. where the company was aware of the board's decision, no mischief could be caused by the failure to serve notice on the company.

However, clarity in this area was short-lived. On the same day that the *Virtualpurple* judgment was handed down, Warren J in *Natwest* v. *Masada Group* [2012] BCC 226 held that the failure to serve was fatal.

In *Ceart Risk Services Ltd* [2012] EWHC 1178 (Ch) the directors' failure to obtain the prior approval of the Financial Services Authority (FSA) as it then was (see Financial Services and Markets Act 2000, s.362A) was considered. Section 362A imposes on FSA-regulated companies the requirement to obtain FSA consent to an administrator being appointed by the out-of-court route by directors and that this consent together with the notice of intention must be filed. In *Ceart Risk Services*, although subsequent FSA consent was obtained, the FSA had not been served with a notice of intention and, by analogy to *Minmar*, it was argued that the appointment was invalid. Here, Arnold J considered that the FSA's subsequent consent cured the defect in the form of appointment (the appointment becoming effective when the consent was filed at court), that Norris J's reference to para.104 in *Care Matters* was to be preferred to that of Hart J in *G-Tech Construction* and that it should be applied where there was a curable defect in the appointment.

On service of the notice of intention to appoint, the qualifying floating charge holder may agree to the appointment or seek to appoint its own choice of administrator. It is only in respect of pre-15 September 2003 securities that the floating charge holder will retain the option to appoint an administrative receiver rather than an administrator.

Although it is not expressly stated, if the floating charge holder gives notice within the five days that it objects to the administration, but does not wish to appoint an alternative administrator (perhaps because it considers that liquidation is more appropriate), this could also amount to an effective veto. The reason for this is that in the notice of appointment (Form 2.9B), the appointor is required to state that the qualifying floating charge holder has either consented or failed to reply. If the directors still wished to appoint an administrator in the face of objection from the floating charge holder, the matter would need to be resolved on application to the court, the court weighing up what would be in the best interests of the creditors as a whole. A theoretical conflict could well arise in a situation where a fully secured creditor wanted to realise its security via a break-up sale through a liquidator rather than see an administrator appointed, who would seek to achieve the rescue of the company or at least a going concern sale. In practice, the court, seeking to follow the legislature's promotion of a rescue culture, would in all likelihood look more favourably on the administration application provided that the purpose of administration was reasonably likely to be achieved (perhaps this evidence being tested by the secured creditor). In circumstances where the secured creditor objects, it is more likely to appoint its own nominee as administrator, who perhaps would be more likely to make proposals suitable to the charge holder. Moreover, an insolvency practitioner may be unwilling to take an appointment in the face of such opposition for fear of loss of reputation and also possible dispute as to the cost, expenses and fees associated with the administration in the event of insufficient recovery to discharge the secured creditor in full.

If no response of any kind is received from the floating charge holder after five business days have elapsed, the appointor may move to make the appointment of the administrator no later than 10 business days after filing of the notice of intention to appoint (IA 1986, Sched.B1, para.28(2)).

3.10.3 Notice of appointment

Where either a notice of intention has been served as above, or where the company/ directors does/do not need to serve notice of intention as the company is not subject to a qualifying floating charge, the company/its directors may proceed to appoint an administrator, such appointment taking effect upon the filing at court of the requisite documentation (IA 1986, Sched.B1, para.31).

The appointment of an administrator by a company or its directors shall be by prescribed form (Form 2.9B (prior notice of intention given) or 2.10B (no prior notice of intention)).

Practical tips on completing Form 2.9B

The numbers and letters in the list below follow those as set out on Form 2.9B.

1.　(a)　Insert the name and registered office of the company. IA 1986, s.117(6) provides that in regard to the issue of a winding-up petition, the place the company has its registered office is said to be where it has been longest

Rule 2.23   Form 2.9B

Notice of appointment of an administrator by company or director(s)

(where a notice of intention to appoint has been issued)

Name of Company	Company number

In the [full name of court]	*For court use only* Court case number

(a) Insert name and address of registered office of the company

1. Notice is given that, in respect of (a)

_____

_____

_____

_____
_____ ("the company")

*Delete as applicable

* the company / the directors of the company ("the appointor") hereby appoints

(b) Give name(s) and address(es) of administrator(s)

(b)

_____
_____

_____

_____

_____
as administrator(s) of the company.

*Delete as applicable

2. The written statement(s) in Form 2.2B *is / are attached.

3. The appointor is entitled to make an appointment under paragraph 22 of Schedule B1 to the Insolvency Act 1986.

4. This appointment is in accordance with Schedule B1 to the Insolvency Act 1986.

*Delete as applicable

5. The company *is / is not *an insurance undertaking / a credit institution / an investment undertaking providing services involving the holding of funds or securities for third parties / or a collective investment undertaking under Article 1.2 of the EC Regulation.

(c) Insert whether Main, secondary or territorial proceedings

6. For the following reasons it is considered that the EC Regulation *will / will not apply. If it does apply, these proceedings will be (c) _____ proceedings as defined in Article 3 of the EC Regulation: _____

_____

147

7. Where there are joint administrators, a statement for the purposes of paragraph 100(2) of Schedule B1 to the Insolvency Act 1986 is attached.

8. The appointor has given written notice of the intention to appoint in accordance with paragraph 26(1) of Schedule B1 to the Insolvency Act 1986 and a copy of that notice was filed at court on (d)

(d) Insert date

_____

and *(a) five business days have elapsed from the date of the notice, or
    * (b) each person to whom the notice was sent has consented to this appointment.

*Delete as applicable

I (e)

(e) Insert name and
address of person
making declaration

_____ do

solemnly and
(If making the declaration on behalf of appointor indicate capacity e.g. director/solicitor)

sincerely declare that

(i) the information provided in this notice and
(ii) the statements made and information given in the notice of intention to appoint

are, and remain, to the best of my knowledge and belief, true,

AND I make this solemn declaration conscientiously believing the same to be true and by virtue of the Statutory Declarations Act 1835.

Declared at _____

Signed _____

This _____ day of _____ 20

before me _____

A Commissioner for Oaths or Notary Public or Justice of the Peace or Solicitor or Duly Authorised Officer

Endorsement to be completed by court
This notice was filed (f)_____

(f) Insert date and time

in the last six months. This is of note in view of the practice of cross-border forum shopping, where a foreign company may wish to restructure its business under the UK administration process.

Delete the company/the directors as appropriate. See above re choice and process and procedure for each.

(b) Insert names and addresses of the proposed administrators.

2. Form 2.2B (i.e. consent to act, etc.) needs to filed for each administrator who is being appointed.

3. The declarant is required to confirm that the appointment is in accordance with the provisions of IA 1986, Sched.B1, para.22, namely that the company has so resolved, or the directors by majority have decided, to appoint the administrator. It follows that all of the statement contained within the notice of intention to appoint (Form 2.8B) remains true and accurate (e.g. no winding-up petition has been issued, no administrative receiver is in office; although owing to the fact that a moratorium came into effect on the notice of intention being filed these steps should not have occurred).

4. The appointment must be in accordance with Sched.B1 (see in particular the provisions of paras.23–30 and the completion of all formalities) and the declarant is required to confirm the same.

5. Delete 'is/is not' as appropriate. Note, however, that if the company is an insurance undertaking, a credit institution, an investment undertaking providing services involving the holding of funds or securities for third parties or a collective investment undertaking under Art.1.2 of Council Regulation 1346/2000/EC of 29 May 2000 on Insolvency Proceedings then a different insolvency regime will apply and specialist works should be consulted. Such companies will also not be subject to the EC Regulation.

6. Delete 'will/will not' as appropriate. Again, if the EC Regulation does not apply, a different regime is likely to be in operation.

(c) The proceedings are deemed 'main' provided the registered office/COMI lies in the UK (see the definition of main or secondary proceedings provided in **3.5.2** for further details). The reasons why the proceedings are main proceedings must be stated on the form.

7. Where more than one person is to be appointed administrator, a statement specifying the functions to be exercised for the persons acting jointly and what functions, if any, are to be exercised by any or all of the persons appointed (IA 1986, Sched.B1, para.100(2)) must be attached. This is of significantly greater importance where the insolvency practitioners are from different firms and the functions split between the two (e.g. management of business/marketing and sale of business and assets/investigation and report on directors' conduct, etc.). However, in practice, while such agreement may be reached the administrators may not wish their powers to be fettered.

8. (d) Insert date that notice of intention was filed at court.

(e) Insert details (full name and address) of the individual who is making the statutory declaration contained on the remainder of the form. This must be someone duly authorised by the appointor such as one of the directors or the company's solicitor. The statutory declaration provides that the appointor may make the appointment (i.e. no restrictions apply and that therefore the information contained in Form 2.8B remains accurate), that a notice of intention has been filed and that five business days' notice have elapsed and/or consent has been obtained to the appointment. It is an offence to make a statement that is false and/or that is not reasonably believed to be true (IA 1986, Sched.B1, para.29(7)). Because of the importance and unique nature of the knowledge pertaining to the declaration, the declarant should probably be a director or senior officer of the company duly authorised by the board to make the declaration. This declaration, which should be sworn before an independent solicitor (or commissioner for oaths, notary public, justice of the peace or officer of the court, each of whom will charge a fee of £7), should not be made more than five business days before the date it is filed at court (IA 1986, Sched.B1, para.29(6); IR 1986, rule 2.21).

The endorsement is to be left blank and is completed by the court on filing. A date and exact time are given, essential to assess when the administration is deemed to commence.

Practical tips on completing Form 2.10B

The numbers and letters in the list below follow those as set out on Form 2.10B.

1. (a) Insert the name and registered office of the company. IA 1986, s.117(6) provides that in regard to the issue of a winding-up petition the place the company has its registered office is said to be where it has been longest in the last six months. This is of note in view of the practice of cross-border forum shopping, where a foreign company may wish to restructure its business under the UK administration process.
   Delete the company/the directors as appropriate. See above re choice and process and procedure for each.
   (b) Insert names and addresses of the proposed administrators.

2. Form 2.2B (i.e. consent to act, etc.) must be filed for each administrator who is being appointed.

3. The declarant is required to confirm that the appointment is in accordance with the provisions of IA 1986, Sched.B1, para.22, namely that the company has so resolved or the directors by majority have decided to appoint the administrator.

4. The appointment must be in accordance with Sched.B1 (see in particular the

Rule 2.23   Form 2.10B

Notice of appointment of an administrator by company or director(s)
(where a notice of intention to appoint has not been issued)

Name of Company	Company number

In the [full name of court]	*For court use only* Court case number

(a) Insert name and address of registered office of the company

1. Notice is given that, in respect of (a) _____

_____

_____ ("the company")

* Delete as appropriate

* the company / the directors of the company ("the appointor") hereby appoints

(b) Give name(s) and address(es) of administrator(s)

(b) _____

_____

as administrator(s) of the company.

*Delete as applicable

2. The written statement(s) in Form 2.2B * is / are attached.

3. The appointor is entitled to make an appointment under paragraph 22 of Schedule B1 to the Insolvency Act 1986.

4. This appointment is in accordance with Schedule B1 to the Insolvency Act 1986.

5. The company has not, within the last twelve months: -

(i) been in administration
(ii) been the subject of a moratorium under Schedule A1 to the Insolvency Act 1986 which has ended on a date when no voluntary arrangement was in force
(iii) been the subject of a voluntary arrangement which was made during a moratorium for the company under Schedule A1 to the Insolvency Act 1986 and which ended prematurely within the meaning of section 7B of the Insolvency Act 1986.

6. In relation to the company there is no:

(i) petition for winding up which has been presented but not yet disposed of
(ii) administration application which has not yet been disposed of, or
(iii) administrative receiver in office.

*Delete as applicable

7. The company *is / is not* an insurance undertaking / a credit institution / an investment undertaking providing services involving the holding of funds or securities for third parties / or a collective investment undertaking under Article 1.2 of the EC Regulation.

151

(c) Insert whether main, secondary or territorial proceedings

8. For the following reasons it is considered that the EC Regulation *will / will not apply. If it does apply, these proceedings will be (c) _____ proceedings as defined in Article 3 of the EC Regulation:

*Delete as applicable

9. Attached to this notice is *a copy of the resolution of the company to appoint an administrator / a record of the decision of the directors to appoint an administrator.

10. Where there are joint administrators, a statement for the purposes of paragraph 100(2) of Schedule B1 to the Insolvency Act 1986 is attached.

(d) Insert name and address of person making declaration

I (d) _____

(If making the declaration on behalf of appointor indicate capacity e.g. director/solicitor)

hereby do solemnly and sincerely declare that:

(i) the company is or is likely to become unable to pay its debts
(ii) the company is not in liquidation, and
(iii) the statements in paragraphs 5 and 6 are, so far as I am able to ascertain, true,

and that the information provided in this notice is to the best of my knowledge and belief true,

AND I make this solemn declaration conscientiously believing the same to be true and by virtue of the Statutory Declarations Act 1835.

Declared at _____

Signed _____

This _____ day of _____ 20

before me _____

A Commissioner for Oaths or Notary Public or Justice of the Peace or Solicitor or Duly Authorised Officer

---

(e) Insert date and time

Endorsement to be completed by the court
This notice was filed (e)

provisions of paras.23–30 and the completion of all formalities) and the declarant is required to confirm the same.

5. The declarant is required to confirm that the company has not within the last 12 months: been in administration; been subject to a moratorium arising from a court order pending the calling of a meeting of creditors to consider a CVA (at present, this is available only to small companies); been the subject of a CVA (which was obtained following a moratorium period) which has terminated early (see IA 1986, Sched.A1).

6. The declarant is required to confirm that no winding-up petition has been presented but has not been disposed of (it is therefore vital to check with the court that no petition has been issued and not yet served), no administration application has yet to be disposed of, and no administrative receiver is in office.

7. Delete 'is/is not' as appropriate. Note, however, that if the company is an insurance undertaking, credit institution, an investment undertaking providing services involving the holding of funds or securities for third parties or a collective investment undertaking under Art.1.2 of Council Regulation 1346/2000/EC of 29 May 2000 on Insolvency Proceedings then a different insolvency regime will apply and specialist works should be consulted. Such companies will also not be subject to the EC Regulation.

8. Delete 'will/will not' as appropriate. Again, if the EC Regulation does not apply, a different regime is likely to be in operation.

(c) The proceedings are main proceedings provided the registered office/ COMI lies in the UK (see definition of main or secondary proceedings provided in **3.9.3** for further details). The reasons why the proceedings are main proceedings must be stated on the form.

9. Attach a copy of the company's resolution to appoint, or the record of the directors' decision to appoint.

10. Where more than one person is to be appointed administrator, a statement specifying the functions to be exercised for the persons acting jointly and what functions if any are to be exercised by any or all of the persons appointed (IA 1986, Sched.B1, para.100(2)) must be attached. This is of significantly greater importance where the insolvency practitioners are from different firms and the functions split between the two (e.g. management of business/ marketing and sale of business and assets/investigation and report on directors' conduct, etc.). However, in practice, while such agreement may be reached the administrators may not wish their powers to be fettered.

(d) Insert details (full name and address) of the individual who is making the statutory declaration contained on the remainder of the form. This must be someone duly authorised by the appointor, such as one of the directors or the company's solicitor. The statutory declaration provides that the appointor may make the appointment (i.e. none of the statutory restrictions on appointment apply, that there are no outstanding insolvency proceedings (such as an outstanding winding-up petition, administration application or administrative receiver in office) and that the company is insolvent and is not in liquidation). It is an offence to make a statement that is false and/or that is not reasonably believed to be true (IA 1986, Sched.B1, para.29(7)). Because of the importance and unique nature of the knowledge pertaining to the declaration, the declarant should probably be a director or senior officer of the company duly authorised by the board to make the declaration. This declaration, which should be sworn before an independent solicitor (or commissioner for oaths, notary public, justice of the peace or officer of the court, each of whom will charge a fee of £7), should not be made more than five business days before the date it is filed at court (IA 1986, Sched.B1, para.29(6); IR 1986, rule 2.21).

The endorsement is to be left blank and is completed by the court on filing. A date and exact time are given, essential to assess when the administration is deemed to commence.

Form 2.2B (the administrator's statement) must contain the following:

- Consent to the appointment.
- A statement that in his opinion the purpose of the administration is reasonably likely to be achieved.
- The disclosure of any prior professional relationship with the company.

This latter provision is one the administrator will consider where there is a potential conflict and he has acted in accordance with regulatory provisions in taking such an appointment. An appointment cannot be taken up if the firm has been auditor to the company and/or provided material advice and services apart from recent advice on insolvency issues.

In making the statement, the administrator is entitled to rely on the information supplied by the directors of the company, unless he has reason to doubt its accuracy. Although the insolvency practitioner no longer has to provide evidence that his appointment would be likely to achieve one of the purposes of administration (as was the case under the old administration regime, which required the preparation and filing of a so-called 'Rule 2.2 Report' by the insolvency practitioner), the administrator must go through many of the steps that were previously required to satisfy himself that the administration is reasonably likely to achieve the purpose of the administration. This will require investigation of the company's affairs and an assessment of the merits of administration against other insolvency processes in the light of how this will affect the creditors as a whole.

As soon as reasonably practicable thereafter, the appointor should notify the administrator and other prescribed persons of the appointment (IA 1986, Sched.B1, para.32). Further details of the notice provisions and other steps to be taken after appointment are dealt with in **Chapter 5** which details the administration process.

Example of board resolution to place company in administration

[NAME OF COMPANY] LIMITED

(Company No. [ ])

(the 'Company')

Minutes of a meeting of the board of directors of the Company held at [place]

On [*date*]

Present

[*Name*]   [*Position*]

[Apologies for absence received from]

1.   Chairperson

       [*Name*] was appointed chairperson of the meeting.
2.   Notice and quorum

       The Chairperson reported that due notice of the meeting had been given and that a quorum was present. Accordingly the Chairperson declared the meeting open.
3.   Declaration of interest

       3.1 [The relevant directors declared the nature and extent of their interest in the matters to be considered at the meeting in accordance with section 177 of the Companies Act 2006 and the Company's articles of association; as follows]
       [*Provide details of such if any direct or indirect interests had in the proposed administration*]
       OR
       [Each director confirmed that they had no direct or indirect interest in any way in the proposed transaction [and other arrangements] to be considered at the meeting which they were required to disclose in accordance with section 177 of the Companies Act 2006 and the Company's articles of association.]
       3.2 It was noted that the articles of association of the Company entitled a director to be counted in the quorum of directors and to vote on any matter on disclosing the nature and extent of his material interest.
       3.3 It was further noted that, among his other duties, a director is required by statute to act in the way he considers, in good faith, would be most likely to promote the success of the Company for the benefit of its members as a whole, having regard, among other things, to the matters listed in section 172(1) of the Companies Act 2006.

4.   Business of the meeting

       The Chairperson reported that the business of the meeting was to consider the financial affairs of the Company and to determine whether to take steps to place the Company into administration.
5.   Resolutions

       5.1 After consideration of the financial affairs of the Company the board concluded that the Company was insolvent in that it had an inability to pay its debts as they fell due. Following further consideration of advice provided by [*name of insolvency practitioner*] on the options available to the Company and to the matters referred to in section 172(1) Companies Act 2006 IT WAS RESOLVED that such steps as prove necessary should be taken immediately to place the Company into administration.

5.2 IT WAS FURTHER RESOLVED that [*name of insolvency practitioner*] be authorised to do all such acts and agree to execute on behalf of the board and/or on behalf of the Company all necessary documentation including but not limited to the preparation and filing at court of a notice of intention to appoint administrators.

6.   Close

There being no further business the Chairperson declared the meeting closed.

....

Chairperson

....

Dated

3.11 VOLUNTARY LIQUIDATION – INTRODUCTION

> The winding up of a company is a form of collective execution by all its creditors against all its available assets. The resolution or order for winding up divests the company of beneficial interest in its assets. They become a fund which the company thereafter holds in trust to discharge its liabilities …
>
> (Lord Hoffman in *Buchler* v. *Talbot (Re Leyland DAF Ltd)* [2004] UKHL 9 at [28])

This succinct definition explains the purpose and effect of the procedure known as winding up, or liquidation. Whether being instigated by the directors/company itself or by a creditor, it is a procedure for the benefit of all creditors, ensuring that they are treated fairly and equally and, as we have seen in **Chapter 1**, is the oldest form of corporate insolvency procedure.

Liquidation results in the realisation of the company's assets (i.e. turning them into cash) and then distribution of the cash proceeds to creditors in an order of priority as set out in statute. It is a collective process carried out for the benefit of all creditors and in general will end the creditors' individual rights of action against the company. Rather than have a multitude of various different creditors, each attempting to enforce their claims, insolvency legislation dating from the nineteenth century has intervened to provide mechanisms and procedures whereby creditors' claims can be dealt with collectively by a liquidator.

The winding up of the company is the beginning of its end; after distribution of the proceeds of sale, the company will be dissolved and struck off the register of companies. The corporate entity will cease to exist.

Definitions

A **company** may be wound up under the provisions of IA 1986, Part IV. A **company** includes:

- registered companies;
- unregistered companies (IA 1986, s.220);
- insolvent partnerships (Insolvent Partnerships Order 1994, SI 1994/2421; IA 1986, s.420); and
- limited liability partnerships (Limited Liability Partnerships Regulations 2001, SI 2001/1090, reg.5(1)(a)).

The alternative methods of winding up are:

- members' voluntary liquidation, commenced by the company when it is able to pay its debts, also referred to as a solvent liquidation;
- creditors' voluntary liquidation, commenced by the company when the company is insolvent although control of the process rests with the company's creditors; and
- compulsory liquidation, commenced by order of the court.

Liquidation remains the most commonly used corporate insolvency procedure, accounting in 2011 for some 77 per cent of all cases of corporate insolvency. There was, however, an interesting development after the Enterprise Act 2002 reforms, when creditors' voluntary liquidations declined, matched by an equivalent rise in the number of administrations. This trend has largely abated in recent years as the novelty of the administration process has worn off, the drawbacks to the use of the process became evident (cost and expenses rule/Transfer of Undertakings (Protection of Employment) Regulations 2006, SI 2006/246 (TUPE), etc.) and, for smaller companies in particular, the use of the liquidation process was just as effective in transferring business and assets to a new trading entity.

Circumstances where a company may be wound up

- Where the company is insolvent, either on a balance sheet or cash flow basis.
- Where the company is likely to become insolvent.
- Where the period of duration for the company as specified in the articles of association has expired.
- Where the purposes as set out in the articles of association have been fulfilled.
- Where there is no purpose to be served for the company continuing in existence.
- Where the shareholders wish to realise value from their equity investment.
- On grounds of public interest.

The first two circumstances cover situations where the company is insolvent. In such cases, a creditors' voluntary liquidation will follow, so called as the creditors have control of the insolvency procedure.

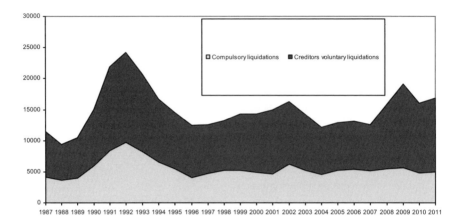

Figure 3.4   Number of insolvent liquidations 1987–2011

Source: Insolvency Service Statistical Directorate

The further four instances where a company may be wound up occur if the company remains solvent. In that case, the liquidation procedure is generally a members' voluntary liquidation, so called as the control of the liquidation is exercised by the members. This procedure can only be followed where the company is able to pay its debts in full and continues to be able to do so during the course of the liquidation. Members' voluntary liquidation is often used where the shareholders wish to realise their investment or where, for the purposes of wider tax/corporate reorganisation, it is best that the company ceases to exist. It is often used in conjunction with a s.110 scheme of reconstruction (IA 1986, s.110: see **3.3.2** for further details). As a members' voluntary liquidation is a solvent liquidation, it is not dealt with in detail in this book, although a short guide to the procedure follows.

Guide to procedure

Members' voluntary liquidation

1. Where the directors of a company are able to provide a statutory declaration of solvency, the company may be placed into members' voluntary liquidation. The importance of this is that the members of the company will effectively control the process, i.e. choice of liquidator, etc.

   The statutory declaration must:

   - confirm that in the directors' opinion, after making full enquiry of the company's affairs, the company is able to pay its debts (and any statutory interest) within a period not exceeding 12 months from the commencement of the winding up (IA 1986, s.89(1));
   - be made within five weeks of the resolution to wind up the company (IA 1986, s.89(2));

- include, as near as possible to the date of the statutory declaration, the company's statement of affairs; and
- be delivered to the Registrar of Companies within 15 days (in Form 4.70).

The making of a statutory declaration by the directors is a serious matter. If the directors have no reasonable grounds for making the declaration, they are guilty of an offence and liable to a fine and/or imprisonment (on indictment punishable with two years' imprisonment and an unlimited fine; on summary conviction, six months' and/or a fine up to £5,000 (at time of writing the statutory maximum)).

The directors can rely upon a third party's commitment to provide funds (this may be the case in circumstances where a parent company has agreed to discharge the liabilities of the subsidiary). However, the directors must have reasonable grounds to justify the belief that the commitment will be honoured.

2.   Within five weeks of the statutory declaration being made, the company may by special resolution in a general meeting resolve to liquidate the company and by ordinary resolution appoint one or more liquidators for the purposes of winding up the company's affairs and distributing its assets. Generally, the appointment of a liquidator will be made at the same meeting.

3.   On appointment by the members, the directors' powers cease except so far as sanctioned at the general meeting or by the liquidator.

4.   If the company remains solvent and creditors are paid in full, the liquidator will move on to distribute any surplus funds to the members.

If, however, during the winding up of the company, the liquidator is of the opinion that the company is unable to pay its debts, the liquidator must:

- call a meeting of creditors within 28 days;
- give the creditors at least seven days' notice of the meeting;
- advertise the meeting in the *Gazette* and at least two local newspapers;
- provide any information required to the creditors;
- prepare a statement of affairs complying with the requirements under IA 1986, s.95(4);
- lay down the statement of affairs at the creditors' meeting; and
- attend and preside at the creditors' meeting.

(IA 1986, s.95(2)).

When the creditors' meeting is held, the declaration of solvency is deemed never to have been made and the creditors' meeting is held as if it was the commencement of a creditors' voluntary liquidation. Accordingly, a different liquidator may be appointed and/or a creditors' committee established at the meeting.

5.   In any other circumstances, a general meeting of the company must be held in every year in which the liquidation continues, with a final meeting being held after the realisation of assets and distribution of proceeds has been completed.

6.   The final meeting will be advertised in the *Gazette* and final returns filed by the liquidator. If no person shows cause, the Registrar of Companies will strike off the company after three months and the company will thereby be deemed dissolved.

The last ground for winding up is on the petition to court by the Secretary of State for Trade and Industry (IA 1986, s.124A) following appropriate regulatory or criminal investigation. See *Re Supporting Link Ltd* [2004] BCC 764 for a review of authorities on this section.

3.12   WHICH LIQUIDATION PROCEDURE SHOULD BE INITIATED?

An insolvent liquidation may be initiated by the company or its creditors. The remainder of this chapter deals with a situation where the company initiates the procedure. The company by its directors or members has a choice whether to initiate a creditors' voluntary liquidation, or otherwise petition for the winding up of the company by court order (compulsory liquidation).

Table 3.6   Voluntary liquidation

Advantages	Disadvantages
• Convenience	• Possible lack of scrutiny
• Economy	• Requirement for members' resolution
• Control over timing	• Cost of funding private sector – are there available liquidator assets/ funding to cover fees? The liquidation process is carried out
• Speed	
• The control and management of the company by liquidator; on initiation of the process, management power is removed from existing directors	• Cost of funding private sector – are there available liquidator assets/ funding to cover fees?
• The management of the company may be able to dictate the choice of liquidator	
• Court and Official Receiver not directly involved in the process companies	
• Not available for unregistered companies	

Table 3.7   Compulsory liquidation

Advantages	Disadvantages
• Directors can initiate process without members' approval	• Cost in initiating procedure
• Judicial scrutiny	• Delays in commencing procedure
• Liquidation process will be dealt with by Official Receiver in case of company with no assets/funding to cover costs of private sector liquidator	• Difficulties for the company operating between time of petition and the hearing of winding-up petition
	• Increased cost to creditors of procedure/realisations

Advantages	Disadvantages
• Involvement of Official Receiver and obligation to investigate affairs of company	
• Liquidator able to commence proceedings in respect of past conduct (IA 1986, ss.214, 215 (wrongful trading)). See also CDDA 1986	

The liquidation of a company may follow another insolvency procedure such as a CVA or administration; it may run concurrently with a continuing administrative receivership or LPA receivership but not an administration.

Commonly the directors of the company and others who are in effective control of the company will recognise the financial difficulties facing the company and seek advice. While it is possible that the directors, without third party advice, could call a meeting of the company and thereafter for the members to pass a resolution which would have the effect of placing the company into voluntary winding up, it is more likely that the directors will require some assistance from an insolvency practitioner in taking these steps.

The insolvency practitioner is likely to advise them on whether liquidation is the most appropriate course of action and may assist in calling the meeting of creditors, at which time an appointment of the liquidator will be made.

Creditors' voluntary liquidation is so called as the appointment of the liquidator is ultimately by the creditors. The company may well have used the services of an insolvency practitioner to assist in the convening of the creditors' meeting and indeed that insolvency practitioner is likely to be present at the creditors' meeting, which must be chaired by a director of the company (the s.98 meeting).

For the directors of the company, there is considerable advantage in having already nominated an insolvency practitioner, as any creditors' apathy may mean that no alternative is put forward. There is also a perception that the liquidators who are appointed by the company may perhaps give the appointors (i.e. in reality the directors of the company) an 'easier ride' than if their appointment had been initiated by the creditors. Section 98 creditors' meetings can be boisterous affairs, where the reasons why the company has passed into liquidation can be gleaned by creditors from questions put to the directors of the company. If the directors are to be investigated and proceedings initiated, the choice of an appropriate liquidator is often vital. Creditors are often represented by insolvency practitioners and this can lead, sometimes, to a jockeying for position (and creditors' votes) to obtain the appointment as liquidator 'from the floor'. If the company/directors have taken the initiative and nominated a liquidator, this may prevent creditor scrutiny and interest in the process.

One aspect that may militate against the initiation of a creditors' voluntary liquidation procedure is the necessity to fund a private sector insolvency practitioner to act as liquidator. The insolvency practitioner will need to be satisfied that the company has sufficient assets, free from secured interests, to cover the liquidation costs and expenses (see IA 1986, s.176ZA regarding the payment of such expenses from floating charge realisations). If sufficient funds are unlikely to be realised the liquidator will need to have in place third party funding and/or appropriate indemnities. In some instances this will not be available, so while the initiation of the compulsory liquidation procedure may be more expensive (i.e. the costs of the petition and the Official Receiver's deposit (£1,165 at time of writing) need to be paid) than commencing creditors' voluntary liquidation, it is a short-term fixed cost, rather than a long-term variable cost.

The directors of the company may also consider applying to court for a winding-up order if the members of the company are unwilling to resolve to place the company into voluntary liquidation, or where it is not possible for a meeting to be convened (i.e. the members may have been missing or absent). In the circumstances, the directors of the company may well have regard to their own position and the possibility that they might be guilty of wrongful trading should the company continue to trade/or not pass into an appropriate insolvency procedure. It is more usual, however, for compulsory liquidation to be initiated by a creditor or creditors of the company. As a result, this commencement of and thereafter the practice and procedure of compulsory liquidation is dealt with separately in **5.5**.

3.12.1 Voluntary winding up – procedure to commencement

Guide to procedure

Creditors' voluntary liquidation

- Meeting of members called on 14 days' notice or less if possible.
- Notice given of intended resolution to wind up company provided to QFCH (at least five business days).
- If no objection/appointment of an administrator by QFCH meeting convened and members pass special or extraordinary resolution to wind up the company (75 per cent of those voting).
- Liquidation commences on the day the resolution is passed.
- If not held on the same day, a meeting of creditors must be held within 14 days (seven days' notice of meeting must be given and it must be advertised).
- Resolution is registered at Companies House and advertised in the *London Gazette*.
- At the meeting of creditors, the creditors may approve the company's nomination of liquidator or may propose an alternative (voting is by simple majority in value), who will replace the company's nominee.

Under the provisions of CA 2006, registered companies may use the voluntary liquidation procedure to effect the winding up of the company's affairs (IA 1986, s.84):

(a) where the articles provide for dissolution on a given event, or after a certain elapse of time and the company so resolves by ordinary resolution of a general meeting; or

(b) the company resolves by a special resolution that it be wound up voluntarily.

Unregistered/foreign companies may only be wound up by the court (IA 1986, s.221(4)).

Five business days' notice of the intended resolution must be provided to the holder of a qualifying floating charge to which IA 1986, s.72A applies (IA 1986, s.84(2A), inserted by the Enterprise Act 2002 (Insolvency) Order 2003, SI 2003/2096 with effect from 15 September 2003). The requirement to provide notice of an intended winding up therefore applies only to a QFCH who possesses security created after 15 September 2003.

This provision affords a QFCH the ability to appoint an administrator rather than see the company go into liquidation and was deemed required as, in respect of securities created after 15 September 2003, in the majority of cases a QFCH will be unable to appoint an administrative receiver to realise its security. In contrast, prior to the reform a QFCH could always appoint an administrative receiver even where the company was already in liquidation.

If the QFCH fails to respond, the company is free to proceed with the general meeting at which the resolution to wind up the company will be put. If the company is to be wound up, following an event specified in the articles as one on which the company is to be dissolved, an ordinary resolution is required (i.e. by majority of the members) otherwise a special or extraordinary resolution is required (i.e. by three-quarters of members).

The company meeting to pass the requisite resolution should normally be convened by the directors, one of whom should act as chairman at the creditors' meeting (IA 1986, s.99(1)(c)).

The members should be given 14 days' notice of the resolution (CA 2006, s.307). However, a shorter period of notice can be provided if 95 per cent of the members agree in writing beforehand (CA 2006, s.307(4)) or 90 per cent if a private company has passed a resolution reducing the required majority for short notice from 95 per cent to 90 per cent. A defect in the notice provisions can be cured if there is unanimous consent to the resolution or subsequent ratification (*Re Duomatic Ltd* [1969] 2 Ch 365).

A private company can pass the resolution in writing, which takes effect when the company's auditors have notice of it, who must in any other case be given notice of the members' forthcoming meeting (CA 2006, s.288). In most circumstances the members and creditors will meet on the same day and, in any event, the creditors' meeting is usually called before the winding-up resolution is passed (IA 1986, s.98(1)).

A statement of affairs in Form 4.19 must be sworn by the directors, or one of them, and put before the creditors (IA 1986, s.99(1)(b)).

Between the date of the board resolving to call a company meeting and the initial meeting of creditors, the directors should consider instructing an insolvency practitioner to assist in the interim and consider the company's banking arrangements and how the business and affairs of the company are to be wound down causing the least possible loss for the company's creditors. It is advisable for the directors to seek professional advice when taking these steps.

What are the powers of the liquidator nominated by the company prior to the s.98 meeting? If no liquidator has been nominated, what powers are retained by the company's directors?

The 1960s case of *Centrebind Ltd* [1966] 3 All ER 889 brought this issue to prominence, after judicial approval was provided to the liquidator who had in the exercise of his discretion disposed of the business and assets prior to the creditors' meeting. Although this was for totally legitimate reasons, this practice, which became known as 'centrebinding', led to more flagrant abuses by directors and unscrupulous (and at that time unlicensed) insolvency practitioners in an attempt to deprive creditors of an opportunity to participate in the insolvency process. Licensing and greater regulation of the insolvency profession followed the introduction of IA 1986 in an attempt to discourage these practices, as well as the introduction of a number of safeguards:

1. Where no liquidator has been nominated, the powers of the directors of the company cannot be exercised without permission of the court, except:

    (a) to secure compliance with the legislative provisions regarding the calling of the creditors' meeting and preparation of a statement of affairs;

    (b) to dispose of perishable goods;

    (c) to dispose of other goods whose value is likely to diminish unless immediately disposed of; and/or

    (d) to do such things as are necessary for the protection of the company's assets.

    (IA 1986, s.114.)

2. Where a liquidator has been nominated by the company, the liquidator must not exercise the powers contained in s.165 without the permission of the court, except:

    (a) to take into custody or control company property;

    (b) to dispose of perishable goods;

    (c) to dispose of other goods whose value is likely to diminish unless immediately disposed of; and/or

(d)   to do such things as are necessary for the protection of the company's assets.

(IA 1986, s.166.)

IA 1986, s.165 provides the liquidator with the powers exercised by the directors and other necessary powers.

These two provisions taken together should ensure that centrebinding is stamped out, although there is anecdotal evidence that prior to the Enterprise Act reforms (and the ease of administration) the procedure was re-emerging, with justification for a sale of business assets prior to the s.98 meeting being that the purchaser would otherwise disappear.

3.12.2   Voluntary winding up – procedure post-commencement

Once the resolution has been passed:

- it must be registered at Companies House within 15 days (IA 1986, s.84(3));
- it must be advertised in the *Gazette* within 14 days (IA 1986, s.85(1));
- the voluntary winding up is deemed to commence (IA 1986, s.86);
- the company must cease business except in so far as may be required for its beneficial winding up (IA 1986, s.87); and
- no share transfer/alteration of the members' status can be made without liquidator sanction (IA 1986, s.88).

Once the resolution is passed it cannot be rescinded (*Ross* v. *PJ Heeringa* [1970] NZLR 170) as the liquidation is deemed to have commenced (IA 1986, s.86).

The voluntary winding up commences on the passing of the company's resolution; this remains the case even if subsequently the company passes into compulsory liquidation (IA 1986, ss.86, 129(1)).

On the passing of the resolution the company must:

- summon a meeting of creditors (a so-called s.98 meeting) within 14 days;
- send notice of the meeting to creditors, giving at least seven days' notice;
- advertise the meeting in the *Gazette* and two local newspapers;
- prepare a statement of affairs;
- place the statement of affairs before the creditors at the s.98 meeting.

(IA 1986, ss.98, 99.)

The notice to creditors must give the name of any insolvency practitioner nominated by the company who can provide additional information to the creditors or, in the absence of such person, a place where a list of company creditors can be inspected.

The notice should also state the time and place for the filing of proofs and proxies to be lodged and be sent at least seven days before the meeting and be advertised in the *Gazette* and two local newspapers (IR 1986, rule 4.51).

The directors must attend the s.98 meeting and one of their number must act as chairman (IA 1986, s.99(1)(c), although in practice the nominated insolvency practitioner will act as *de facto* chairman). The liquidator nominated by the company will act thereafter to wind up the affairs of the company, unless the creditors nominate an alternative, in which case their nomination will take precedence (IA 1986, s.100(2)).

The creditors' resolution for appointment is passed by a simple majority in value of those voting in person or by proxy (IR 1986, rule 4.63). A quorum is present if at least one creditor votes in person or by proxy.

If dissatisfied with the creditors' decision the directors, members or other creditor may apply to court for relief within seven days of the s.98 meeting. The court may thereafter direct that the liquidator is the person nominated by the company, appoint some other person or direct a joint appointment of the person nominated by the creditors and the company (IA 1986, s.100(3)).

It should be noted, however, that in the majority of cases the meeting of members and the meeting of creditors will be held on the same day. This avoids the problematic issue of what steps can be taken prior to the s.98 meeting, and is more convenient and cheaper and therefore preferable, especially where the result of the members' meeting can be guaranteed.

On the passing of the resolution to wind up the company, the company will cease business so that further losses are not incurred. However, the liquidator appointed can exercise commercial judgment to see if completion of certain works (e.g. contracts, etc.) may be beneficial to the winding up (IA 1986, s.87(1)). This discretion may be exercised where the continuation of business may either reduce losses and/or increase returns. Such powers (IA 1986, s.165(3) and Sched.4, para.5) are, however, exercised cautiously and if a sizeable period of trading is thought appropriate, it is almost certainly more advisable for the company to be placed into administration.

3.12.3 The use of creditors' voluntary liquidation and 'phoenix trading'

Despite the process of a creditors' voluntary liquidation being controlled by the company's creditors, the initiation of the liquidation process rests with the company. As we have seen, the process is commenced by the passing of a resolution by the members of the company, who will nominate a liquidator. The liquidator is from the private sector; the courts and Official Receiver will not be directly involved in the process. The liquidator is likely to assist in the calling of a creditors' meeting and will be present at the meeting seeking his appointment from the creditors themselves.

This has important tactical advantages for the existing management, who may be able to put forward a liquidator to the creditors. Often that liquidator is willing to follow the directors' wishes for the business; he may also have been involved in providing advice on the appropriate procedures that the company should follow. A common situation is that directors will seek to purchase the principal assets of the business from the liquidator. Although there remains some public disquiet with such a concept, there is nothing to prevent the liquidator carrying out such a sale if it is in the best interests of the creditors as a whole. It should also be remembered that the directors of the company are often best placed to make an offer – they know the value of the assets and may be the only party likely to make an offer. Provided the liquidator has sought proper valuations and advertised or otherwise adequately marketed the assets for sale, the fact that the directors are making the best or only offer should not be of concern. The abuses of phoenix trading (i.e. serial failures and use of the procedures for a pre-planned purchase of assets at a discount) are avoided partly by statutory provision and partly by the independence and professionalism of the insolvency practitioner.

IA 1986, s.216 restricts the reuse of the company name or some name that is similar without permission of the court. CDDA 1986 provides a mechanism to police serial failures. It should also be noted that the preservation of the business and saving of jobs is a guiding aim of much insolvency legislation. Furthermore, as demonstrated above, historic failings of the insolvency regime have also been addressed, which makes abuse less likely. For example, IA 1986, ss.114 and 166 are designed to prevent centrebinding practices.

There is concern, however, that the ease in which directors can appoint an administrator and effect a pre-pack administration sale (i.e. one that is pre-agreed and the terms negotiated prior to the commencement of the administration) or control the liquidation process has seen a return to centrebinding by the back door.

CHAPTER 4

Advising a creditor in the case of an insolvent personal debtor

4.1 STATUTORY DEMAND AND THE CREDITOR

4.1.1 Purpose of a statutory demand

A bankruptcy petition presented by a creditor against an individual must be in respect of one or more debts owed by the debtor to the petitioning creditor (IA 1986, s.267(1)).

As we shall see (in **4.3**), there are four further conditions for the presentation of a petition as set out by IA 1986, s.267(2), including the condition that the debt which is the subject of the bankruptcy petition is one that the debtor is either unable to pay or has no reasonable prospect of being able to pay (IA 1986, s.267(2)(c)).

While, in respect of a corporate debtor, the petitioning creditor may seek to satisfy the court evidentially that the corporate debtor is unable to pay its debts as they fall due in a number of possible ways, in the case of an individual debtor this statutory hurdle can be overcome by only one of two methods (IA 1986, s.268), namely:

(a) the debt is one where execution or other process issued in respect of the debt on a judgment or order of any court in favour of the petitioning creditor has been returned unsatisfied in whole or in part; or

(b) the petitioning creditor has served a demand (known as a statutory demand) and three weeks have elapsed and the demand has not been met, or, alternatively, the debtor has not sought to set aside the demand.

As an alternative to obtaining a judgment and then seeking unsuccessfully to enforce by means of a warrant of execution or other process (which could be time-consuming and costly), the use of a statutory demand is a considerably more convenient method and thus has a central role in the bankruptcy process.

A statutory demand is a formal demand for payment of a debt made by a creditor to a debtor under the terms of IA 1986 and in accordance with IR 1986. The demand must therefore be in a prescribed form (IR 1986, rules 6.1 and 6.2; see also Forms 6.1, 6.2 and 6.3).

If the debtor fails to comply with or contest the demand within three weeks of service, the debtor is deemed to be unable to pay the debt, thus fulfilling the statutory condition for the presentation of a bankruptcy petition. The unsatisfied statutory demand is sufficient evidence in itself to show that the debtor is unable to pay, or has no reasonable prospect of being able to pay the debt, and the creditor may thereby proceed with the presentation of a bankruptcy petition.

It should be kept in mind, however, that a statutory demand is not an insolvency process or procedure per se (*Re a Debtor (No.1 of 1987) (Lancaster)* [1989] 1 WLR 271). Instead, the service of a statutory demand upon a debtor is an option available to an individual creditor; it does not bear any collective nature, contrasting with a creditors' petition for bankruptcy. There is no register of statutory demands, nor is it a court process which requires approval before service. This contrasts with the former (pre-1986) bankruptcy notice procedure, where notice of debt and due payment was issued by the court. A claim made by a statutory demand remains entirely a private matter between the creditor and debtor. The service of a statutory demand does not mean that the creditor is obliged to present a bankruptcy petition.

It should also be noted that, as the statutory demand is neither an insolvency, nor part of a court process, it is possible to serve a statutory demand on an individual out of the jurisdiction without the need to seek permission of the court. However, where a demand is to be served the creditor must carefully follow the procedure set out in the Practice Direction on Insolvency Proceedings, para.13.

If the debtor complies with the demand, the matter rests there. If the demand is not complied with, it is entirely a matter for the creditor to decide whether to proceed further; a creditor is not obliged to proceed with a bankruptcy petition.

The demand remains effective for four months, after which the creditor may only proceed with the unsatisfied demand after satisfying the court that it is right to do so. The creditor's reasoning for this is set out in the affidavit or witness statement that supports the petition (see IR 1986, rule 6.12(7)). For instance, the creditor may decide that proceeding with a collective insolvency procedure is not in its best interests and/or the costs of doing so will be disproportionate.

Creditor's considerations before serving a statutory demand

Checklist

Creditor's considerations before serving a statutory demand

1. Is the debt a liquidated and due debt?
2. Is the debt likely to be disputed?
3. Does the debtor possess a genuine cross-claim?
4. Is the creditor unwilling to proceed with a formal collective insolvency procedure in the event of non-payment?
5. If the answer to (2) (3) or (4) is yes, the creditor should almost certainly proceed to enforce payment of the debt by some other means.

A creditor must have primary regard to the type of debt that is owed. As we shall see, not only can adverse cost consequences befall a creditor who has served a misconceived demand, but also a strategic initiative can be lost and time wasted.

While a creditor might have the right to serve a demand, the creditor needs to think very carefully whether it should do so. What will be the effect? Will the debtor seek immediate bankruptcy protection? Is there a possibility of dissipation of assets? Is the creditor willing (and able) to follow up non-compliance with a demand with a bankruptcy petition? Bankruptcy is of course a collective remedy; is the creditor willing to share returns (if any) on a *pari passu* basis? Has the creditor explored and exhausted all other forms of enforcement remedy?

Creditors' considerations after serving a statutory demand

If the demand is challenged by the debtor, by reason of a dispute as to the debt claimed or the debtor alleges he has a serious cross-claim or set-off, the debtor will probably seek the agreement of the creditor that the demand be withdrawn. If the creditor fails to agree, the individual debtor may apply to court to set aside the demand.

In view of the cost penalties that can be imposed on a creditor proceeding with a statutory demand where there is a bona fide dispute, the creditor must think very carefully when being asked to withdraw a statutory demand. There is no formal procedure to withdraw the demand, but an undertaking or written agreement may be sought from the creditor that it will not present a petition based on the demand.

If, after serving the statutory demand, no response is received from the debtor, the creditor may proceed to petition for the bankruptcy of the debtor. In doing so, however, the creditor must recognise that the insolvency process is a collective one, i.e. conducted for the benefit of all creditors. The petitioning creditor is put in no better position and will receive payment of its debt *pari passu* with other unsecured creditors. As we shall see, the costs of the petitioner are paid in priority to creditors' claims, but often the creditor needs to 'gamble' that there will be sufficient assets available even to cover these costs. Against this is the fact that the creditor may similarly waste time and effort in pursuing other enforcement methods and may consider it better to find out sooner rather than later that the debtor is a 'man of straw'.

The decision on whether to proceed with the statutory demand rests with the creditor who has served the demand. The creditor could therefore elect not to take action after serving the demand, regarding it as a failed method of obtaining payment of its debt. However, in abusing the demand process in this way, the creditor must recognise that the service of the demand may have serious consequences for the debtor, who may regard the non-compliance with the demand as sufficient warning to cease trade and/or seek protection by some form of insolvency process, such as bankruptcy or an IVA.

Table 4.1 Pros and cons of a statutory demand for creditors

Pros of serving a statutory demand for creditors	Cons of a statutory demand for creditors
• Inexpensive	• Hollow threat if not acted upon
• Quick	• May lead to expensive legal challenge
• Establishes debtor's ability to pay insolvency procedures (better to find out early)	• Ultimate remedy on non-compliance is collective
• No court involvement in preparation and service	• Evidential burden to dispute is light/sympathy of the court may lie with the debtor
	• Open to challenge

4.1.2 Nature of claim made by a statutory demand

A statutory demand can only be presented in respect of an undisputed debt.

If the debt is likely to be disputed by the debtor, or the debtor possesses a genuine cross-claim, the creditor should almost certainly proceed to enforce payment of the debt by some other means. It should also be at the forefront of the creditor's mind that bankruptcy is a collective enforcement action, regulating the actions of creditors and their rights and ability to recover as between each other. As a consequence, where the creditor is unwilling to be treated on a *pari passu* basis in the event of debtor non-payment, the creditor should not use bankruptcy as a means of enforcement of a debt.

In every case where the debtor's bankruptcy is sought at the behest of a creditor, it should be noted that the making of a bankruptcy order remains a matter left to the court's overriding discretion. The serious nature of the sanction means that the creditor's claim will be carefully considered; only certain debts can form the basis of a bankruptcy petition, and these are considered below.

- *The debt must be undisputed.* In the case where there is a dispute as to whether the debt is due and owing, it is open to the individual debtor to apply to the court for an order setting aside the statutory demand. Indeed, the statutory demand must state the court to which the debtor must apply if he disputes the demand. As we shall see, to proceed on the basis of a debt where it is known to be disputed may amount to an abuse of process. The issue of 'dispute' is reviewed more closely in the discussion at **4.1.5** as to when a statutory demand may be set aside.
- *The debt must be liquidated.* The debt must be a liquidated sum based on a claim in contract or tort (see *Re Humberstone Jersey Ltd* (1977) 74 LSG 711). However, a claim in tort will be for unquantified loss or damages, which

requires some degree of assessment or agreement. Accordingly, a court judgment or binding settlement is required before the creditor can proceed with a statutory demand in respect of a debt that has arisen from a claim in tort. Similarly, an order that costs are payable by one party cannot be subject to a statutory demand until those costs have been assessed or agreed (*Galloppa* v. *Galloppa* [1999] BPIR 352).

- *The debt must be or will become due for payment.* IA 1986, s.267(2)(b) provides that the debt must be 'for a liquidated sum payable ... immediately or at some certain, future time'.

IA 1986, s.123(1)(a) speaks of a 'due' debt. As a result, the debt claimed must be for a sum which is due and payable immediately and/or where liability in respect of the debt is 'existing', i.e. it is or will become due.

A statutory demand can therefore be presented in respect of a debt which is payable in the future, although the court will require evidence that the debtor will be unable to pay that debt when it is due and payable. See **4.4.4** for consideration of contingent claims, which cannot be the subject of a statutory demand.

Interest payable on the debt can be claimed if interest is due under the terms of the contract or statute (see the Late Payment of Commercial Debts (Interest) Act 1998), but should be calculated only to the date of the demand, the demand being the date at which the debt is due and payable.

- *The debt must be unsecured.* IA 1986, s.267(2)(b) provides that a debt must be 'unsecured'. It is often the case, however, that a secured creditor has some proportion of the debt which is owed that is unsecured, e.g. where the current value of a particular secured property means that the creditor's security is insufficient to cover the whole debt. In such cases the secured creditor can participate in the bankruptcy for the proportion of its debt which is unsecured. It is also open to the secured creditor to value its own security and to present a statutory demand and/or petition for bankruptcy for the unsecured element of its debt, provided the debt is in excess of £750. In doing so, the value of security is best assessed on a forced sale basis (see *Platts* v. *Western Trust & Savings* [1996] BPIR 339).

The secured creditor must be careful when taking such a step, as unless its claim in the bankruptcy is carefully constructed, the creditor can be seen to forgo its secured rights by taking such action. As a consequence, the adviser to a secured creditor must balance the advantages and disadvantages of proceeding with a collective insolvency process against those of commencing proceedings in respect of the creditor's own security.

Generally, it is advisable to pursue the remedy provided by the security first and then determine the balance of the debt, which will be unsecured. However, in some cases, a secured creditor may wish to abandon its security, as the creditor may consider it advantageous for a collective process to be initiated, where rights of action vest only in a trustee in bankruptcy (see transactions at an undervalue and preference actions, IA 1986, ss.239, 240).

The rights which a creditor may possess in respect of the security will depend on the terms of the charge or other form of security. The creditor remains free to exercise its right of security at any time until an insolvency procedure commences. It should be noted that the rights of secured creditors are unaffected by the collective nature of the insolvency procedures.

Even where the insolvency procedure has been commenced, namely the administration of the bankrupt's estate, the rights of a secured creditor cannot be adversely affected. As we shall also see, a secured creditor's rights cannot be prejudiced, save where that creditor has consented, in the case of an IVA.

Therefore, the secured creditor may well retain the right to proceed with its own remedy to recover debts, irrespective of the debtor's insolvency. In the case of a secured creditor of an individual, this may be enforcement against the individual's property subject to the security, e.g. their home.

- *The debt must be in excess of the bankruptcy level.* The debt claimed (in any statutory demand or petition) must be in excess of the bankruptcy level (IA 1986, s.267(2)(a)), which is currently £750 (IA 1986, s.267(4)).

While any debt in excess of £750 can be claimed pursuant to a statutory demand and thus form the basis of a bankruptcy petition, due to the serious consequences that arise, the courts will not look favourably on petitions that are based on debts only slightly in excess of £750 (see *City Electrical Factors Ltd* v. *Hardingham* [1996] BPIR 541). The value of the debt is a factor likely to be considered by the court in the exercise of its discretion on the hearing of the petition for bankruptcy; as a result, despite the creditor's entitlement to present the petition, the court may refuse to make an order.

If the debt claimed is slightly in excess of £750, the adviser should warn the creditor that in such circumstances the bankruptcy of the individual is not a foregone conclusion.

- *The debt may be assigned.* The debt may be assigned to a creditor under an effective legal assignment and the assignee is free to issue a statutory demand. In such circumstances, details of the assignment must be provided to the debtor.
- *The debt may be the sum of various claims.* If there is more than one debt owing, these must be separately identified and a description of the basis upon which liability arises provided for each (see *Bennett* v. *Filmer* [1998] BPIR 444). Subject to this, it is possible to present an aggregated demand for payment.
- *The debt must not be statute-barred.* A statutory demand and/or bankruptcy petition cannot be based on a debt which is statute-barred (see *Re Karnos Property Co. Ltd* (1989) 5 BCC 14; *Jelly* v. *All Type Roofing* [1997] BCC 465; and *Bruton* v. *IRC* [2000] BPIR 946).

4.1.3 Validity of a statutory demand

A statutory demand is a demand in the prescribed form (IR 1986, rule 6.1, Form 6.1, 6.2 or 6.3) requiring the debtor to pay a debt, or to secure or compound for it to the satisfaction of the creditor, and to establish that there is a reasonable prospect that the debtor will be able to pay the debt when it falls due (IA 1986, s.268).

A statutory demand must be dated and authenticated either by the creditor himself or by a person stating himself to be authorised to make the demand on the creditor's behalf (IR 1986, rule 6.1). A person 'authorised' means someone who in fact did have authority in law to make the demand. In practice, this may mean a director or an authorised officer of the creditor, or a solicitor (see *Horne* v. *Dacorum Borough Council* [2000] BPIR 1047).

The statutory demand must make clear whether the debt is payable immediately (IA 1986, s.268(1)(a)) or whether the debt is one which, while not payable immediately, is one which the debtor has no reasonable prospect of paying (IA 1986, s.268(2)). This latter form of demand covers future debts but not contingent or conditional debts.

Practical tips on completing Form 6.1

The references below are to those parts of Form 6.1 that need to be completed. The use of the prescribed form enables the creditor to ensure that all necessary information as set out above is included, and while a statutory demand can be drafted in the form of a written demand, it is almost certainly quicker and more convenient to use the appropriate form:

1.   *To*: The demand should be addressed to the individual debtor, providing as full a name as the creditor is aware of. As described below (in **4.1.5** on setting aside a demand), while some small errors (e.g. of spelling) may not invalidate the demand, it must be clear to whom the demand is being made.

2.   *Address*: The individual's address should be stated, the creditor having regard to the debtor's place of residence, place of business or other address for service. While the demand is likely to be served personally on the debtor, the creditor needs to consider which court will have jurisdiction to hear the bankruptcy petition and/or any application to set aside the demand (see below).

3.   *Name*: Insert the name of the creditor. This is the party with ownership of the debt, not the party seeking payment for and on behalf of the creditor (such as a legal representative). However, if the creditor is entitled to the debt by way of assignment, the details of the original creditor and any other party who has held the debt by way of assignment until it came into the hands of the creditor should be included in Part C.

4.   *Address*: Insert creditor's address.

5.   *The creditor claims that you owe*: Insert the sum being claimed. Full particulars need to be provided on page 2. The sum must be payable immediately,

Form 6.1

Rule 6.1

Statutory Demand under section 268(1)(a) of the Insolvency Act 1986. Debt for Liquidated Sum Payable Immediately

Notes for Creditor

- If the creditor is entitled to the debt by way of assignment, details of the original creditor and any intermediary assignees should be given in part C on page 3.
- If the amount of debt includes interest not previously notified to the debtor as included in the debtor's liability, details should be given, including the grounds upon which interest is charged. The amount of interest must be shown separately.
- Any other charge accruing due from time to time may be claimed. The amount or rate of the charge must be identified and the grounds on which it is claimed must be stated.
- In either case the amount claimed must be limited to that which has accrued due at the date of the demand.
- If the creditor holds any security the amount of the debt should be the sum the creditor is prepared to regard as unsecured for the purposes of this demand. Brief details of the total debt should be included and the nature of the security and the value put upon it by the creditor, as at the date of the demand, must be specified.
- If signatory of the demand is a solicitor or other agent of the creditor the name of his/her firm should be given.

*Delete if signed by the creditor himself

Warning

- This is an **important** document. You should refer to the notes entitled "How to comply with a statutory demand or have it set aside".
- If you wish to have this demand set aside you must make application to do so **within 18 days** from its service on you.
- If you do not apply to set aside **within 18 days** or otherwise deal with this demand as set out in the notes **within 21 days** after its service on you, you could be made bankrupt and your property and goods taken away from you.
- Please read the demand and notes carefully. If you are in any doubt about your position you should seek advice **immediately** from a solicitor, a Citizen Advice Bureau, or a licensed insolvency practitioner

Demand

To _____

Address _____

_____

This demand is served on you by the creditor:

Name _____

Address

_____

The creditor claims that you owe the sum of £_____, full particulars of which are set out on page 2, and that it is payable immediately and, to the extent of the sum demanded, is unsecured.

The creditor demands that you pay the above debt or secure or compound for it to the creditor's satisfaction.

[The creditor making this demand is a Minister of the Crown or a Government Department, and it is intended to present a bankruptcy petition in the [High Court][Central London County Court].][Delete as appropriate]

Signature of individual _____

Name _____
(BLOCK LETTERS)

Date

*Position with or relationship to creditor _____

_____
*I am authorised to make this demand on the creditor's behalf.

Address _____

_____

Tel. No._____ Ref. _____

N.B. The person making this demand must complete the whole of pages 1, 2 and parts A, B and C (as applicable) on page 3.

Particulars of Debt

(These particulars must include (a) when the debt was incurred, (b) the consideration for the debt (or if there is no consideration the way in which it arose) and (c) the amount due as at the date of this demand.)

Notes for Creditor
Please make sure that you have read the notes on page 1 before completing this page.

Note:
If space is insufficient continue on page 4 and clearly indicate on this page that you are doing so.

176

Form 6.1 contd.

Part A
Appropriate Court for Setting Aside Demand

Rule 6.4(2) of the Insolvency Rules 1986 states that the appropriate court is the court to which you would have to present your own bankruptcy petition in accordance with Rule 6.40A. In accordance with those rules on present information the appropriate court is [the High Court][the Central London County Court][or]

[County Court]
(address)

Any application by you to set aside this demand should be made to that court.

Part B

The individual or individuals to whom any communication regarding this demand may be addressed is / are:

Name
_____

(BLOCK LETTERS)

Address
_____

_____

_____

Telephone
Number_____

Reference
_____

Part C
For completion if the creditor is entitled to the debt by way of assignment

	Name	Date(s) of Assignment
Original creditor		
Assignees		

How to comply with a statutory demand or have it set aside (ACT WITHIN 18 DAYS)

If you wish to avoid a bankruptcy petition being presented against you, you must pay the debt shown on page 1, particulars of which are set out on page 2 of this notice, within the period of **21 days** after its service upon you. Alternatively, you can attempt to come to a settlement with the creditor. To do this you should:

- inform the individual (or one of the individuals) named in part B above immediately that you are willing and able to offer security for the debt to the creditor's satisfaction; or
- inform the individual (or one of the individuals) named in part B immediately that you are willing and able to compound for the debt to the creditor's satisfaction.

If you dispute the demand in whole or in part you should:

- contact the individual (or one of the individuals) named in part B immediately.

If you consider that you have grounds to have this demand set aside or if you do not quickly receive a satisfactory written reply from the individual named in part B whom you have contacted you should **apply within 18 days** from the date of service of this demand on you to the appropriate court shown in part A above to have the demand set aside.

Any application to set aside the demand (Form 6.4 in Schedule 4 to the Insolvency Rules 1986) should be made within 18 days from the date of service upon you and be supported by a witness statement (Form 6.5 in Schedule 4 to those Rules) stating the grounds on which the demand should be set aside. The forms may be obtained from the appropriate court when you attend to make the application.

Remember! – From the date of service on you of this document

(a) you have only 18 days to apply to the court to have the demand set aside, and

(b) you have only 21 days before the creditor may present a bankruptcy   petition

---

undisputed and unsecured. If the debt includes interest not previously identified to the debtor, details of the grounds for the interest claimed should be set out separately (page 2 particulars). Where the debt is not payable immediately but instead payable in the future, Form 6.3 must be used.

6. *The creditor is a Minister of the Crown*: Delete the section stating that the demand is made by the Crown, etc. Note that different rules of jurisdiction apply to Crown debt, i.e. the petition will be heard in London (High Court if debt in excess of £50,000; the Central London County Court if under that amount).

7. *Signature of individual*: The demand is required to be authenticated by the creditor himself or someone authorised to make the demand on behalf of the creditor. As a result, where the creditor is corporate, or an institution, the demand will be signed with the name of an individual, who must print his name in block letters and is required to state the position with or relationship to the creditor (e.g. director, office holder, agent or solicitor) and that he is authorised to make the demand on the creditor's behalf.

8. *Date*: The date that the demand is made is inserted. This is not necessarily the date that the demand will be served.

9. *Address, telephone number and reference*: While the details of someone to whom communications regarding the demand may be sent must be included, these need not necessarily be the same as the details provided at page 1. It could be the case that a solicitor makes the demand on behalf of the creditor, but that if the debtor wishes to enter into correspondence or communication he may be directed to contact someone directly at the creditor's offices, whose details are found at page 3, Part B.

10. *Particulars of debt:* It should always be remembered that the true purpose of the demand being made is to establish an inability to pay debt; it should not be regarded as a debt collection method. Akin to a statement of case, the demand must include details of (a) when the debt was incurred; (b) the consideration

for the debt or, if none, how the debt arose; and (c) the amount due as at the date of demand. The particulars should set out the liability and, if appropriate, separately set out the grounds for any interest or charges claim. Details as to how the debt arose, etc. must be adequate to allow the debtor to identify the debt with sufficient certainty (see above for grounds of dispute). To avoid any technical argument, it is therefore best to include as much detail as possible. If there is any doubt as to an element of the debt, that element should be excluded. The reason for this is that it may give the debtor an opportunity to apply to set aside the demand on grounds of dispute, and in extreme cases the demand could be seen as an abuse of process. If a bankruptcy order is eventually made, the creditor is not stopped from proving his debt for the higher sum by reason of making a lower demand.

11. *Part B*: include details as to whom communications regarding the demand must be sent. The claimant must afford the debtor the possibility to correspond and set out any grounds of dispute, or allow him to propose terms of compromise or settlement within 21 days after service. The notice at the end of the demand sets out the debtor's options.

12. *Part C*: insert details of any assignment. If the creditor is entitled to the debt by way of assignment, the name and details of the original creditor and the date of the assignment should be provided. If appropriate, the chain of assignments must be provided.

4.1.4 Service of a statutory demand on an individual debtor

A creditor is under an obligation to do all that is reasonably practical to bring the statutory demand to the debtor's attention and, if practicable in the particular circumstances of the case, cause personal service of the demand to be effected (IR 1986, rule 6.3(2); Practice Direction on Insolvency Proceedings (1999, [2007] BCC 842); and see also *Anderson* v. *Kas Bank* [2004] BPIR 685; *Takavarasha* v. *Newham Borough Council* [2006] BPIR 311).

Whether a creditor has done all that is 'reasonably practical' is a question of fact to be determined by the court. Those attempting personally to serve a statutory demand will generally be required to make a number of attempts to effect service on the debtor. Visits may be required at different times of the day, at the debtor's home and at his workplace.

If, in the circumstances, personal service has not proved to be practicable, service may be effected by other means, such as first-class post, or insertion through a letterbox. The steps taken must be such as would satisfy the court that on the balance of probabilities the demand has come to the attention of the debtor. In most cases, the following steps should be taken.

- A personal call should be made to such residence and place of business of the debtor as is known, or at either of such places as is known (see *Regional Collection Services Ltd* v. *Heald* [2000] BPIR 661, where a statutory demand was set aside due to the failure of the creditor's agent to visit the debtor's known business premises).

- Where the debtor has more than one residential/business address, a personal call should be made at all known addresses.
- If, after taking these steps, the creditor cannot effect service, a first-class prepaid letter should be sent or a letter hand-delivered to the debtor's last known residence/business address specifying that a call was made and its purpose, stating that there had been a failure to meet the debtor and adding that a further call will be made for the same purpose on a specific date and time. At least two days' notice should be given of this appointment and copies of the letters sent to all known addresses of the debtor (Practice Direction on Insolvency Proceedings, para.13.3 and see *Takavarasha* v. *Newham Borough Council* [2006] BPIR 311 for a case concerning substituted service).

The appointment letter should also set out some other similarly convenient time and place in the event that the time and place proposed are not convenient. If the debtor fails to keep the appointment, the letter will go on to say that the creditor intends to serve the debtor by advertisement or by post through the letterbox and that if a petition is issued the creditor will argue that the statutory demand has been validly served as it was sufficiently brought to the attention of the debtor.

If the statutory demand is served by post, service is deemed to be effected on the seventh day after posting (Practice Direction on Insolvency Proceedings, para.11.5). It is possible that in some cases the demand can be served on the debtor's solicitor (*Re a Debtor (Nos.234 and 236 of 1991)* (1992) *Independent*, 29 June).

In the case of an individual debtor, if the statutory demand is based upon a judgment or order of the court and the creditor knows or has reasonable cause to believe that the debtor has absconded or is keeping out of the way with a view to avoid service and there is no reasonable prospect of the sum being recovered by execution or other process, the demand may be advertised in one or more newspapers (see *Lilly* v. *Davison* [1999] BPIR 81, where the court allowed the demand to be served by advertisement in the *London Evening Standard* on proof that the debtor lived in London). The time for compliance with the demand runs from the date of advertisement (IR 1986, rule 6.3(3)).

If a bankruptcy petition is presented based on non-compliance with the demand, the statutory demand must be filed at court with a certificate proving service (IR 1986, rule 6.11(1)). If the creditor has not been able to effect personal service of the statutory demand, or it has not been acknowledged by the debtor or persons stated to be authorised to accept service on behalf of the debtor, the certificate must set out the steps that were taken to effect service, satisfying the court that these steps taken to serve the demand would justify an order for substituted service being made in respect of the service of a petition (IR 1986, rule 6.11(6)).

The creditor must therefore take all reasonable steps validly and effectively to serve the statutory demand. If the creditor has done anything less, such as simply posting the demand through a letterbox, without making any attempt to effect personal service, it does not invalidate the demand per se; the debtor may well acknowledge the statutory demand. The problem is in proving service of the statutory demand if no response is received. The creditor must therefore give very careful thought as to how to effect service. The use of process servers or agents who have a good working knowledge of the Insolvency Rules is therefore essential.

4.1.5 Setting aside a statutory demand

Guide to procedure: disputing a statutory demand

An individual debtor

1. An individual served with a statutory demand may apply to the appropriate court to set it aside. The statutory demand should set out how and where the debtor should apply to set aside the demand.
2. The individual must within 18 days of service of the statutory demand prepare and file an application supported by an affidavit or a witness statement.
3. The individual should state when the statutory demand came into his hands, state the grounds on which it is disputed and exhibit a copy of the demand.
4. The court may dismiss the application without hearing if insufficient cause is shown or set a date, time and place for hearing, giving at least seven days' notice to the individual and the creditor.
5. On hearing the court may summarily determine the application, adjourn it or give directions.
6. The court will grant the application to set aside the demand where:

    (a) the debtor has a genuine dispute;
    (b) the debtor has a valid counterclaim, set-off or demand equal to, or exceeding, the value of the debt;
    (c) it appears that the creditor holds security not otherwise disclosed or properly valued, which exceeds the value of the debt; or
    (d) the court is otherwise satisfied on grounds that it should be set aside.

A document is treated as a statutory demand unless or until it is set aside (*Re a Debtor (No.1 of 1987)* [1989] 1 WLR 271). It is open to any person served with a demand to apply to the court for an order setting aside the statutory demand (IR 1986, rule 6.4). As the remedy available to the alleged debtor is exercised in the equitable discretion of the court, it is best that the alleged debtor acts fairly and reasonably by giving the creditor a reasonable opportunity to withdraw the demand before proceeding with the application. This will provide the alleged debtor with grounds for recovery of legal costs should he eventually need to commence legal proceedings.

If the creditor agrees that the debtor has raised a bona fide dispute with regard to the debt demanded in the statutory demand, there is no formal procedure for withdrawing the demand. In practice, an undertaking or written agreement from the creditor or his legal representatives that they will not proceed to present a bank-ruptcy petition on the basis of the demand is usually sufficient.

It should be kept firmly in mind, however, that the individual debtor has only 18 days from the date of service to apply to the court to set the statutory demand aside. The date of personal service is the date of actual service if service takes place before 4 pm; if after 4 pm, service is deemed to have taken place the next day. Where the demand is advertised in a newspaper under IR 1986, rule 6.3, the date of service is the date of the advertisement (IR 1986, rule 6.4(1)).

When an application to set aside is issued, the time limit provided for compliance with the statutory demand ceases to run (subject to any order of the court). This stresses the importance for the debtor to deal with the demand promptly.

If the debtor has not applied to set aside the demand within the first 18 days, after 21 days the creditor is free to issue a bankruptcy petition. If the debtor fails to apply to set aside the demand before the issue of the petition, the right is lost.

If the debtor fails to apply to set aside the demand within 18 days but subse-quently decides that he will seek to set aside the demand, he must apply to the court for an extension of time. After 21 days and until the hearing of the debtor's application, the creditor has the right to proceed with the issue of a petition. In the circumstances, unless agreement to withhold the issue and service of a petition can be obtained from the creditor, the debtor is forced to apply to the court for injunctive relief to restrain the creditor from presenting a petition until the hearing of the application for an extension of time and, if granted, the hearing of the application to set aside the demand.

Although the debtor is not prevented from using the same arguments on the hearing of a bankruptcy petition as those used on the hearing of an application to set aside a demand, the chances of being successful on a second attempt are very much diminished. It is therefore important that the debtor is fully prepared and has properly marshalled his arguments, as the court generally takes the view that the correct time to challenge the basis of the claim is on an application to set aside the demand (see *Barnes* v. *Whitehead* [2004] BPIR 693).

The application to set aside the statutory demand must be supported by an affidavit/witness statement which:

- specifies the date on which the demand came into the applicant's hands;
- states the grounds on which the applicant claims the demand should be set aside (see below); and
- attaches a copy of the statutory demand (IR 1986, rule 6.4(4) and (5)).

The court to which the debtor should apply to set aside the demand is the one where the debtor would present his own bankruptcy petition (under IR 1986, rule 6.40). The address and details of the court should be provided in the statutory demand. Where the demand is issued by a minister of the Crown or government department pursuant to a judgment or order of the court, and the demand so specifies, the appropriate court to apply to is the High Court (IR 1986, rule 6.4(2A)).

The court will grant an application to set aside the statutory demand if:

(a)   the debtor appears to have a counterclaim, set-off or cross-demand which equals or exceeds the amount of the debt or debts specified in the statutory demand;

(b)   the debt is disputed on grounds which appear to the court to be substantial;

(c)   it appears that the creditor holds some security in respect of the debt claimed in the demand, and either IR 1986, rule 6.1(5) is not complied with in respect of it or the court is satisfied that the value of the security equals or exceeds the full amount of the debt; or

(d)   the court is satisfied on other grounds that the demand ought to be set aside (IR 1986, rule 6.5(4)).

These grounds are considered below.

Debtor's counterclaim, set-off or cross-demand

A creditor will be prevented from proceeding where the debtor possesses a genuine and serious counterclaim which exceeds the petition debt or reduces the undisputed debt to below £750 (see *Re Bayoil SA* [1998] BCC 988, although this case concerned a corporate debtor; and *Re a Debtor (No.87 of 1999)* [2000] BPIR 589). The important point for the debtor is to show that the counterclaim raises a genuine triable issue (*Stone* v. *Vallance* [2008] BPIR 236, contrasting with the unsuccessful argument in *Gustavi* v. *Moore* [2004] BPIR 268).

A cross-demand has a wider meaning than counterclaim or set-off (see *Hofer* v. *Strawson* [1999] BPIR 501 and *Popely* v. *Popely* [2004] EWCA Civ 463). As a result, the court will not treat technically complex legal arguments regarding whether a counterclaim is precluded by law or contract with great regard (*Re a Debtor (Nos.4449 and 4450 of 1998)* [1999] All ER (Comm) 149). Rather, it is a question of equitable discretion as to whether it is fair and reasonable in all the circumstances to allow a petition to proceed if the debtor may have a genuine claim (of some form) against the petitioning creditor.

The debtor does not need to have previously raised or litigated the claim, nor does the claim need to be precisely quantified (*Garrow* v. *Society of Lloyd's* [1999] BPIR 885). Indeed, even if the claim has been raised in proceedings, whether successfully or unsuccessfully, it remains a matter for the bankruptcy court to determine whether it is fair and reasonable for the petitioning creditor to proceed. However, it should be acknowledged that where a court has already determined that a counterclaim has no prospect of success, the bankruptcy court will understandably be slow to set aside a demand on the basis of an alleged counterclaim (*Society of Lloyd's* v. *Bowman* [2004] BPIR 324).

While it may be reasonable for a debtor to raise a cross-demand in a different capacity from that in which he is being pursued (*Re a Debtor (No.87 of 1999)* [2000] BPIR 589), with regard to any counterclaim, at least, there appears to remain a requirement to show mutuality (see *Hurst* v. *Bennett* [2001] BPIR 287).

Disputed debt

Although the use of a statutory demand as a debt collection technique is often said to be frowned upon, if the debt is bona fide and in excess of £750 there is no sanction to prevent a creditor from proceeding in this manner (see *Re a Company (No.0012209 of 1991)* [1992] 1 WLR 351, in which the use of a statutory demand by a non-judgment creditor was described as a 'high risk strategy').

Petitions founded on debts which are subject to a bona fide dispute may be regarded as an abuse of process and will be followed by costs penalties (see *Ross & Craig (a firm)* v. *Williamson* [2006] All ER (D) 139 (Mar)). However, the demand offers the creditor a quick and inexpensive route to find out whether the debtor will pay the debt. The creditor may decide it is better to discover at an early date that the debtor is unable to pay, rather than proceed with a legal action and then fail to enforce any subsequent judgment.

Although it has been held that it is not improper to proceed with a statutory demand where the creditor is unaware of any dispute to the debt, the service of a statutory demand must be treated with caution (see *Cannon Screen Entertainment Ltd* v. *Handmade Films (Distribution) Ltd* [1989] BCLC 660). If there is a bona fide dispute, the fact that the debtor has neglected to pay does not mean that the creditor is justified in proceeding further (*Re a Company (No.003729 of 1982)* [1984] 1 WLR 1090). Criticism and costs penalties may, however, arise where the debt is genuinely disputed and almost certainly if the dispute to the debt is known by the creditor prior to the issue of the demand. (See *Re a Company (No.006798 of 1995)* [1996] 1 WLR 491, where a solicitor who swore an affidavit in support of a winding-up petition alleging a company's inability to pay a debt without basis was ordered to pay the company's costs personally. See also *Re a Company (No.003689 of 1998)* (1998) *The Times*, 7 October, where a director was liable for costs where he had caused statutory demands to be issued erroneously against a company.)

It should be noted that a determination of the General Commissioner of Inland Revenue is final and the court will not allow the matter to be reopened (see *Cullinane* v. *Inland Revenue Commissioners* [2000] BPIR 996).

It is not enough for the debtor to state that the debt is disputed; the court must be satisfied that there is a genuine dispute on substantial grounds (*Re a Company (No.006685 of 1996)* [1997] BCC 830). If the court is satisfied that there is a dispute, the creditor will not be permitted to proceed and the creditor is then left to pursue the payment of the debt by the usual means, i.e. litigation (see Practice Direction on Insolvency Proceedings (1999, [2007] BCC 842), para.13.4.4: 'Where the debtor … disputes the debt … the court will normally set aside the statutory demand if, in its opinion, on the evidence there is a genuine triable issue').

The burden is on the debtor to prove to the satisfaction of the court that there is a dispute to the creditor's claim. This burden is less onerous than that faced by a defendant resisting an application for summary judgment under CPR Part 24, where the defendant has to show that there is a real prospect of successfully defending the claim. The bankruptcy courts treat the matter somewhat differently; they will not conduct a mini-trial on the issues and the benefit of the doubt is more likely to be given to the debtor. However, a debtor must be careful as the court is likely to treat with some scepticism an application supported by voluminous material necessary to establish that a dispute exists. A clear and simple dispute speaks for itself; conversely, a complex technical defence may fail to impress.

Examples of disputes:

- *The debt is not due.* A statute-barred debt cannot form the basis of a bankruptcy petition, so reliance upon it in a statutory demand would result in the demand being set aside (see *Re Karnos Property Co. Ltd* (1989) 5 BCC 14). As previously noted, debts in respect of a contingent liability where the contingency has not yet arisen (*JSF Finance & Currency Exchange Co. Ltd* v. *ARMA Solutions Inc.* [2001] 2 BCLC 307) are not debts regarded as due and similarly cannot be relied upon. The debt must be 'due' at the time of the demand (*Re Synthetic Oil Pty Ltd* (1989) 1 ACSR 187) and the demand cannot be made before an agreed period of credit has expired (*Re Briton Medical and General Life Association Ltd* (1886) 11 OR 478). As we have seen, however, where the creditor wishes to rely on a future debt and adduce evidence that it will not be paid, Form 6.3 should be used and credible evidence of inability to pay the debt when it fall due must be advanced.

- *An incorrect amount of debt claimed.* A creditor will generally not be prevented from proceeding even if the debt claimed is not precisely accurate, provided the debtor can identify the debt and is not otherwise prejudiced. If the debtor considers that a debt has been overstated, then the debtor is best advised to pay that part of the debt which is admitted (see *Cardiff Preserved Coal and Coke Co.* v. *Norton* (1867) LR 2 Ch App 405 and *Re a Debtor (No.657 SD of 1991)* [1993] 1 BCLC 180).

  However, this is subject to the debtor's ability to ascertain readily and distinguish what is the correct undisputed element of the claim and the creditor's acceptance that this is the correct amount payable within the time limit (*Re Trinity Insurance Co. Ltd* [1990] BCC 235). For example, just because a debtor has accepted and offered to pay part of the debt, it does not mean that the creditor is bound to accept the offer of part payment and thereafter agree not to proceed with the bankruptcy petition, if the balance left unpaid remains due and payable and is in reality undisputed.

  It should be noted that if a demand is grossly overstated, despite the admission as to part of the debt, the court in exercise of its discretion could refuse to allow the creditor to continue with the petition (see *Re a Company* [1985] BCLC 37, where Norse J held that it was no means certain that a demand for £161,000 could be relied on, where the 'debt' was £83,000, as 'the discrepancy between the figures is so enormous').

- *The debt claimed is subject to existing litigation.* The fact that the debtor has been given leave to defend an action does not necessarily mean that the court will find that the debt is disputed on substantial grounds (*Re Tweeds Garages*

Ltd [1962] Ch 406). However, the creditor would need to show exceptional reason why they were proceeding on a seemingly disputed debt, which is neither admitted nor established by court judgment.

- *Debt founded on court judgment.* The Practice Direction Bankruptcy Court: statutory demand ((No 1 of 1987) [1987] 1 All ER 607) provides that:

> Where the statutory demand is based on a judgment or order, the Court will not at this stage look behind the judgment or order and inquire into the validity of the debt nor, as a general rule, will it adjourn the application to await the result of an application to set aside the judgment or order.

In seeking to establish to the satisfaction of the court that there is a genuine dispute, a debtor would be best advised to apply to set aside any judgment obtained in default prior to the hearing of any application to set aside the demand and/or hearing of the bankruptcy petition. This would at least evidence the debtor's commitment to disputing the claim and may assist the purported debtor at any petition hearing where the courts exercise a wider discretion.

It should be remembered that a judgment is not determinative of the issue. Previously, the court would only 'look behind the judgment' if it was obtained by fraud; in more recent times, the court is more relaxed and will consider whether there is a bona fide dispute to a judgment debt where it is considered right to do so. In *Woods of Winchester Ltd* v. *Sinclair*, LTL, 31 October 2003, it was held on the hearing of a bankruptcy petition that the court had wide discretion, extending to looking behind a judgment of a court of competent jurisdiction. However, this case should be contrasted with the stricter test applied in *Dawodu* v. *American Express Bank* [2001] BPIR 983, where to set aside a statutory demand based on a judgment it was held that the court would need to be satisfied that, had there been a properly conducted judicial process, the court would have found or would have been likely to have found that no debt was due.

- *Debt founded on court judgment which is being appealed.* An appeal against a judgment by the debtor will not prevent the creditor proceeding with a statutory demand (see *El Ajou* v. *Dollar Land (Manhatten) Ltd* [2007] BCC 953). However, in exercising its discretion on the hearing of the petition, the court may consider it just to stay the petition until the appeal is heard, provided no prejudice is caused to the creditor by this course of action. There is also some authority to suggest that if the debtor offers security for the judgment pending appeal, the petition should be stayed (*Re Douglas Griggs Engineering Ltd* [1963] Ch 19; *Woods of Winchester Ltd* v. *Sinclair*, LTL, 31 October 2003), although note the comments below regarding the use of such practice.

Creditor possesses security for the debt

A debt is secured to the extent that the person to whom the debt is owed holds security for the debt (whether a mortgage, charge, lien or other security) over any property of the person by whom the debt is owed (IA 1986, s.383(2)). Security does not include a lien on books, papers or records except to the extent that they consist of documents which give title to property and are held as such (IA 1986, s.383(4)), and security provided by a third party (perhaps as guarantor of the principal debt) is not taken into account (*Re a Debtor (No.310 of 1988), ex p. Debtor v. Arab Bank Ltd* [1989] 2 All ER 42).

It should be kept in mind that a secured creditor has the alternative remedies to enforce payment of the debt that are provided for in the terms of its security. The creditor will usually be provided with the ability to enforce and realise (the secured) property of the debtor without regard to the collective interests of the creditors as a whole.

It is often the case, however, that a secured creditor may have some proportion of the debt owed that is unsecured, e.g. where the current value of a particular property means that the creditor's security is insufficient to cover the whole debt (see **4.1.2**).

Whatever insolvency procedure has been commenced, the rights of a secured creditor cannot be prejudiced, save where that secured creditor has consented, e.g. in the case of an IVA.

Other grounds to set aside a demand

The court can consider all the circumstances of the case and may set aside the demand as it thinks fit.

Common grounds argued by the debtor include:

- *Offer to secure or compound the debt.* If the debtor is unable to pay the debt demanded within the statutory demand, the debtor may offer to 'secure or compound for a debt in respect of which the petition is presented'. Indeed, IA 1986, s.271(3) provides that where acceptance of such an offer would result in the dismissal of the petition and the offer has been 'unreasonably refused', the court will dismiss a bankruptcy petition.

  It should be noted, however, that the 'reasonableness' of any offer is a matter for the creditor; it is not an issue for the court to determine prior to the hearing of a bankruptcy petition. Although the notes which accompany a statutory demand (in Form 6.1) served upon an individual provide that should the creditor fail to accept an offer of compromise made by the debtor, the debtor may within 18 days apply to the court for an order to set aside the demand, the creditor is under no obligation to reply to any offer. It should also be remembered that an offer to secure or compound the debt is a means of complying with the demand; the fact that an offer has been made is not in itself a ground for setting the demand aside (*Re a Debtor (No.415 SD of 1993)* [1994] 1 WLR 917).

  However, the reasonableness of an offer will be considered on the hearing of the petition, when the court has a wider discretion to consider whether a bankruptcy order is appropriate in all the circumstances. If the court considers that a reasonable offer has been made, it may refuse to make a final order. The existence of this discretion should not, however, be relied upon too heavily by a debtor. The court will primarily take note of the fact that a debt is unpaid and, *prima facie*, the creditor will be entitled to its order. Only where the offer is such that it is to all intents and purposes a full payment of the debt is the discretion likely to be exercised in favour of the debtor (*Re a Debtor (No.51-SD of 1991)* [1992] 1 WLR 1294).

It used to be common practice, often with the consent of the creditor, to agree payment of the debt at a future date and ask the court to adjourn the hearing of the petition. This practice is discouraged. As described above, the collective rights of creditors come to the fore. If a debtor is insolvent, he has been seen to have an inability to pay his debts as they fall due. This is a matter which the court will be compelled to deal with, not least to protect the interests of other creditors and possible future creditors of the debtor. As a result, successive adjournments will not generally be granted save in exceptional circumstances.

In practice, even when a debtor cannot pay the sum demanded it remains important to put the best possible offer to the creditor. Although the offer may be short of full and/or immediate payment, the creditor may accept it, or the court may, when exercising its discretion, refuse to make a final order on the petition and/or may adjourn to a future date.

- *Confusing or perplexing demand.* Under the pre-1986 provisions a bankruptcy notice could be set aside if it was deemed 'perplexing'. It is now apparent, however, that a creditor will not be prevented from proceeding with a demand if, despite any apparent confusion, the debtor can identify the debt and is not otherwise prejudiced (*Re a Debtor (No.1 of 1987) (Lancaster)* [1989] 1 WLR 271; *Re a Debtor (No.490 SD of 1991)* [1992] 1 WLR 507).

- *Technical error in the demand.* Under the pre-1986 insolvency law, a technical error in the bankruptcy process (e.g. in a bankruptcy notice, which was the precursor to the statutory demand) would often be fatal to the creditor's position. Since 1986, however, the courts have become more relaxed. IR 1986, rule 7.55 provides: 'No insolvency proceedings shall be invalidated by any formal defect or by any irregularity, unless the court before which objection is made considers that substantial injustice has been caused by the defect or irregularity, and that the injustice cannot be remedied by any order of the court'; although it should be noted that as technically a statutory demand is not an insolvency proceeding, this rule does not expressly apply.

If, however, there is an error in the demand, provided that no prejudice is caused to the debtor, the creditor is unlikely to be restrained from proceeding further on grounds of technical error or omission (see *Re a Debtor (No.1 of 1987)* [1989] 1 WLR 271, where the Court of Appeal refused to set aside a demand on the grounds that the amount claimed was overstated; *Re a Debtor (No.106 of 1992)* [1996] BPIR 190, where there was an error in the degree of security enjoyed by the creditor; and *Oben* v. *Blackman* [2000] BPIR 302, where a failure to specify the consideration for the debt was not considered fatal).

However, this latitude is not to be taken as allowing the creditor to be slipshod in the preparation of the demand; the demand for payment must be clear and provide enough information to enable the debtor to identify the debt and, where appropriate, meet the demand. A demand which failed to give 21 days in which to pay was held invalid (*Re Manda Pty Ltd* (1991) 6 ACSR 119 (VICSC)).

4.1.6 Hearing of the application

The time limit for compliance with a statutory demand ceases to run from the date on which the application to set aside a statutory demand is filed (IR 1986, rule 6.4(3)).

On receiving the application, if satisfied that the debtor has failed to show sufficient cause, the court may immediately dismiss the application and will do so without giving notice to the creditor (IR 1986, rule 6.5(1)). If the application to set aside the statutory demand is dismissed in this manner, the time limit for compliance with the statutory demand immediately starts to run again.

If the application is not dismissed, the court will give at least seven days' notice of the venue for hearing the application to:

(a) the applicant, or solicitor acting for the applicant; and
(b) the creditor, or any person named in the statutory demand to whom communication should be sent.

The first hearing of the application should be a short summary hearing, at which the court will consider the evidence before it (i.e. the application and affidavit in support) and either summarily determine the application or adjourn and give such directions as thought appropriate.

If the issues to be resolved are obviously complex and/or there is a significant divergence of evidence, the court will be more inclined to set aside the statutory demand there and then. The bankruptcy court will be reluctant to determine the worth of prospective claims; it should be remembered that the court needs simply to adjudge whether there is a 'substantial dispute' to the debt; if there is 'genuine' cross-claim; and/or whether there are other valid grounds for setting aside the demand. If the matter looks as if it will require significant cross-examination of witnesses, or the interpretation of a significant number of documents, the court is more likely to consider that the matter should be determined through the normal litigation channels, and will be more inclined to set aside the demand.

At the hearing of the application, if the creditor holds any security in respect of the debt and the court is satisfied that the security is undervalued, it may require an amendment of the demand accordingly. This does not, however, prejudice the right of the creditor to present a bankruptcy petition by reference to the original demand.

Where a demand is made by a creditor holding undervalued security, the court could:

(a) order that the creditor should not present a bankruptcy petition within a specific number of days, during which the debtor would have a further period to comply with the demand based upon the amended security;

(b) set aside the statutory demand, if the debtor had previously offered to pay an amount equal to or exceeding the revalued unsecured debt; or

(c) authorise the presentation of a bankruptcy petition forthwith, if the debtor was simply taking a technical point.

If the debt is genuinely disputed, or there is a genuine and serious cross-claim which exceeds the petition debt (or reduces the undisputed debt to below £750), the statutory demand will in all likelihood be set aside. However, the court's jurisdiction is discretionary; the court 'may' set aside the demand (IR 1986, rule 6.5(4)) and as a result the court is not obliged to make such an order if in all the circumstances and in the interests of all creditors it is just and equitable to allow the bankruptcy petition to proceed (see *Re a Debtor (No.106 of 1992)* [1996] BPIR 190 and *Coulter* v. *Chief of Dorset Police* [2005] BPIR 62, where the demand was defective but the creditor was permitted to proceed).

Surprisingly, it has been somewhat unclear whether a statutory demand can be set aside conditionally. In the past, as on the hearing of an application for summary judgment, where the court felt that there was some doubt as to the bona fides of the dispute or genuineness of the cross-claim, it might order that a part payment was made or security provided (see *Re Douglas Griggs Engineering Ltd* [1963] Ch 19). The balance of recent authorities suggests that there is little place for treating disputes akin to 'shadowy defences' in summary judgment applications (*Re a Debtor (No.490-SD of 1991)* [1992] 1 WLR 507; *Re a Debtor (No.32-SD of 1991)* [1993] 1 WLR 314). Indeed, in *Higgins* v. *Valambia* [2004] BPIR 876, it was held that a court must allow or dismiss a statutory demand; it had no authority to make a conditional order.

From a practical point of view, however, the offer of security and/or other evidence to show that the debtor is not insolvent will be very useful to the debtor seeking to resist a bankruptcy order.

Where the application to set aside the statutory demand is dismissed, the court will make an order authorising the creditor to present a bankruptcy petition immediately or on a specified date. A copy of the order will be served on the creditor (IR 1986, rule 6.5(6)).

The court could consider ordering the postponement of the date on which the creditor can present a bankruptcy petition if there is a real prospect that the debtor would be able to comply with the statutory demand or there is an intended appeal.

With the consent of both parties, orders may be made without the attendance of the parties, either dismissing or withdrawing the application to set aside the statutory demand.

4.2 ALTERNATIVES TO BANKRUPTCY

This book does not deal with the enforcement of debt against a solvent debtor. However, a creditor in possession of a judgment debt or order of the court should consider:

- issuing a warrant of execution;
- applying for an attachment of earnings order;
- seeking a charging order;
- seeking a third party debt order (formerly a 'garnishee proceeding'); or
- applying for an oral examination of the debtor.

Certain creditors, such as landlords and secured creditors, may have their own unique rights of action, which are considered in detail in **Chapters 12** (personal insolvency) and **13** (corporate insolvency). However, for the unsecured creditors of an insolvent personal debtor, the options are stark. Unless they can come to an informal arrangement for payment of the debt (or agree to accept only part of the debt), the only action they can take against an insolvent debtor is to proceed with a bankruptcy petition.

The creditor may, however, conclude that proceeding with a bankruptcy petition is both costly and at best speculative; the petitioning creditor is placed in no better position than any other creditor in respect of its debt. Bankruptcy is a collective process for the enforcement of debt for the benefit of all the bankrupt's creditors; the bankruptcy assets will be collected in, realised and then after payment of expenses applied *pari passu* in satisfaction of debt. Bankruptcy should therefore not be regarded as a debt collection measure except as a means of last resort.

If the creditor decides not to proceed with bankruptcy, the debtor is left with a choice of:

- obtaining approval of an IVA;
- petitioning for his own bankruptcy; or
- doing nothing.

As we have seen in **Chapter 2**, an insolvent debtor who takes no action bears a risk, although this is not an uncommon situation (see also **10.3**, which looks at BROs). A creditor may decide to wait to see whether the debtor takes a positive step or whether other creditors take action. It is advisable for the creditor to re-evaluate the debtor's situation periodically, perhaps by oral examination, to see whether enforcement action and/or bankruptcy is a commercially viable option for the creditor.

4.3 BANKRUPTCY ON A CREDITOR'S PETITION

4.3.1 Introduction

It could be the case that the debtor has an inability to pay the debt/debts by reason of some cash flow problem. The debtor may have plenty of assets, but those assets

191

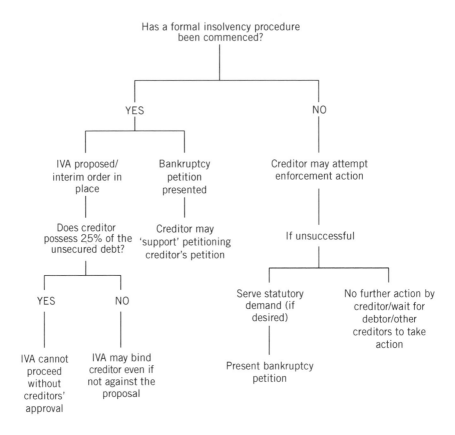

Figure 4.1 Advising the unsecured creditor of an individual insolvent debtor

remain illiquid, with the debtor being unable to release their value at the time of demand. One example of this is where the bankrupt resides in a house with substantial equity but has been unwilling or unable to remortgage.

An inability to pay a debt of over £750 as it falls due (proved after service of a statutory demand or after an unsatisfied warrant of execution on a judgment debt) justifies the presentation of a bankruptcy petition despite the fact that the debtor may well be solvent on a balance sheet basis. As a consequence, the creditor needs to think very carefully about the nature of the debtor's assets, why he has been unwilling to pay the debt and whether bankruptcy will be an effective method of obtaining payment of the debt.

The creditor may take the view that taking other enforcement action, such as obtaining a court judgment and then attempting to enforce it, will simply waste time and money, and that it is better to proceed to bankruptcy as a once-and-for-all method of finding out whether the debtor will be able to pay. Alternatively, if there are available assets, the creditor may be better advised seeking to enforce a judgment against those assets (e.g. by charging order or third party debt proceedings).

Creditors are also occasionally guided by either personal antipathy towards the debtor or some form of moral obligation to ensure that the debtor does not obtain credit from others. These more personal factors would not generally be considered by a professional adviser, but are often key factors in the creditor's eventual decision.

4.3.2 Creditor's petition

Guide to procedure

Bankruptcy petition by a creditor

1. Prepare bankruptcy petition (in Form 6.7 where failure to comply with statutory demand for a liquidated sum payable immediately).
2. Prepare affidavit/witness statement verifying truth of statements in petition (in Form 6.13).
3. File at appropriate court:

   - petition exhibited to affidavit /witness statement;
   - two copies of the petition;
   - affidavit of personal service of statutory demand (in Form 6.11).

4. Pay court fee (£220) and Official Receiver's deposit (£700) (fees correct as at the time of writing).
5. Court fixes venue, date and time for hearing and endorses this on petition and copies with date and time of filing.
6. Arrange for personal service of the petition forthwith (must be within 14 days of date of hearing).
7. File certificate of service of petition annexing sealed copy of petition.
8. At hearing file list of creditors who have given notice of intention to appear and whether they support or oppose the petition.
9. Bankruptcy registrar/district judge in chambers hears petition and may make bankruptcy order, give directions, adjourn or dismiss petition as sees fit.

A creditor may present a bankruptcy petition against an individual debtor where the debt or debts are:

- undisputed;
- unsecured (or if the debt is secured, the creditor's petition contains a statement that the creditor is willing to give up security in the event of the debtor's bankruptcy – see IA 1986, s.269);
- for a liquidated sum in excess of the bankruptcy level (as at 30 April 2007, the bankruptcy level is £750 – IA 1986, s.267(4));

- the debtor appears unable to pay or appears to have no reasonable prospect of being able to pay; and
- the debtor has not applied to have any statutory demand served in respect of the debt set aside.

The petition can be for a single debt or multiple debts and it is possible for more than one creditor to petition in respect of more than one debt (a multi-creditor petition), although this is rare.

In respect of an individual debtor, an inability to pay a debt for a liquidated sum payable immediately is established where the debtor has:

(a)   failed to comply with a statutory demand; or
(b)   execution or other legal process in respect of the debt arising from a judgment or order of the court has been returned unsatisfied in whole or part.

There is only one method of establishing that the individual debtor has no reasonable prospect of being able to pay a debt which is immediately payable, namely the failure of the debtor to comply with a statutory demand.

It should be noted that the position in respect of a corporate debtor differs: a creditor is entitled to petition for the winding up of the corporate debtor if it can establish to the satisfaction of the court that the company is unable to pay its debts as they fall due (IA 1986, s.123(1)(e)). This means that the creditor does not need to first serve a statutory demand or to have been unsuccessful in the execution of a judgment debt.

4.3.3   Procedure

A bankruptcy petition may be presented against an individual by a creditor or by a number of creditors jointly (IA 1986, s.264(1)(a)). Petitions can also be presented:

(a)   by the debtor;
(b)   by a temporary administrator (within the meaning of Art.38 of the EC Regulation on Insolvency Proceedings (Council Regulation 1346/2000/ EC));
(c)   by a liquidator (within the meaning of Art.2(b) of the EC Regulation appointed in proceedings by virtue of Art.3(1) of the Regulation; or
(d)   after default in respect of a voluntary arrangement by the supervisor or person bound to the arrangement.

The debtor's petition was discussed in **2.7**. This section looks solely at the process and procedure applicable to a creditor's petition.

A creditor may present a petition alone or with other creditors, in a multi-creditor petition in respect of a single debt owed to them jointly or in respect of separate debts (see *Re Allen*; *Re a Debtor (No.367 of 1992)* [1998] BPIR 319). This might be considered:

(a) where the individual creditors are owed less than the minimum unsecured petitioning creditor's debt (i.e. £750) but together are owed in excess of this sum;

(b) to save costs in the proceedings; and/or

(c) where one creditor who wishes to petition may have a non-provable bankruptcy debt.

A creditor with a non-provable debt may petition but is unlikely to succeed on the hearing of the petition unless there are exceptional circumstances, such as where the petition is presented by a number of creditors each with separate debts (see *Levy* v. *Legal Service Commission* [2000] BPIR 1065) or where the powers of a trustee in bankruptcy in safeguarding the bankrupt's assets from dissipation and investigating his affairs are thought necessary (see *Russell* v. *Russell* [1998] BPIR 259 in the context of divorce proceedings).

4.3.4 The petition

The bankruptcy petition (in Forms 6.7, 6.8, 6.9 and 6.10) should contain sufficient information to identify the debtor and provide information which will assist other creditors in submitting claims and to assist the Official Receiver/trustee in bankruptcy in their investigations if a bankruptcy order is made.

The petition must state, in so far as it is within the petitioning creditor's knowledge:

- the name, place of residence and occupation of the debtor;
- the name or names under which he carries on business;
- the nature of the debtor's business and the address or addresses at which he carries on business;
- any other names, other than the debtor's true name, under which the debtor has carried on business, at or after the time the debt was incurred, and whether he has done so alone or with others;
- any address at which the debtor has resided or carried on business at or after the date the debt was incurred and the nature of that business;
- whether the debtor has his centre of main interests or an establishment in another Member State (IR 1986, rule 6.7).

Carrying on a business refers to the business including a trade or profession undertaken by the debtor with some degree of management or control (*Graham* v. *Lewis* (1889) 22 QBD 1).

The petition must also contain sufficient details of the debt owed in order for the debtor adequately to identify the debt and, if possible, pay it. With reference to every debt claimed the petition must set out:

- the amount of the debt and consideration for it (or, if there was no consideration, the manner in which the debt arose and the fact that it is owed to the petitioner);

- when the debt was incurred or became due;
- any interest or charges claimed, separately identified, and the grounds upon which they are claimed;
- where the debt is a liquidated sum payable immediately, that the debtor would appear unable to pay it;
- where the debt is for a liquidated sum payable at a certain future time, that the debtor appears to have no reasonable prospect of being able to pay it;
- confirmation that the debt is unsecured;
- if the debt is one on which a statutory demand has been served, the date and the manner of service of the statutory demand and confirmation that the demand has not been complied with or set aside; and
- if the debt is based upon a judgment or order of court and the execution has been returned unsatisfied, details of the court from which the execution process was issued and particulars relating to the return (IR 1986, rule 6.8).

4.3.5 Court in which petition should be presented

A bankruptcy petition should not be presented under IA 1986, s.264(1)(a) or (b), i.e. by a creditor or debtor, unless the debtor:

- is domiciled in England and Wales;
- is personally present in England and Wales on the day upon which the petition is presented; or
- at any time in the period of three years ending with that day:
    - has been ordinarily resident, or has had a place of residence, in England or Wales; or
    - has carried on business in England and Wales.

These provisions are designed to ensure some connection or interest for the creditor(s) in commencing English bankruptcy proceedings (see *Geveran Trading Co.* v. *Skjevesland* [2003] BCC 209). A place of domicile is determined by a common law test. A domicile of origin can change by permanent residence in another country (*Whicker* v. *Hume* (1858) 7 HL Cas 124). IA 1986, s.265 expressly provides that the section is subject to Art.3 of the EC Regulation on Insolvency Proceedings. As a result, since 31 May 2002 if a debtor's centre of main interests is in another EU state (see *Shierson* v. *Vlieland-Boddy* [2005] EWCA Civ 974), bankruptcy proceedings can only be commenced in England or Wales if there is some 'establishment' of the debtor within the jurisdiction (i.e. assets/carrying on business). In such circumstances, the English bankruptcy proceedings will only have the limited role of dealing with the assets in this jurisdiction (so-called 'territorial proceedings'). If 'main' proceedings are then commenced in the other Member State, the territorial proceedings will be termed secondary proceedings and are subservient to the main proceedings. As a result, the creditor may need to think carefully about whether to commence proceedings against an individual in another Member State, where the full effects and powers of the Regulation may apply.

Under IR 1986, rule 6.9A, the court to which the petition is sent can be the High Court if:

(a)   the petition is presented by the Crown;
(b)   the debtor resided or carried on business within the London insolvency district for a greater part of the six months immediately preceding the presentation of the petition, or for a longer period in those six months than in any other insolvency district and the petition debt exceeds £50,000;
(c)   the debtor is not in resident in England or Wales; or
(d)   the petitioner is unable to ascertain the residence of the debtor or his place of business.

In all other cases the petition should be presented in the county court with appropriate insolvency jurisdiction where the debtor resided or has carried on business for the longest period during the last six months (IR 1986, rule 6.9A(4)). Not all county courts possess an insolvency jurisdiction and reference should be made to the debtor's local county court to check this issue. If the debtor has carried on business in one insolvency district but has resided in another, the insolvency district where the debtor has carried on business takes precedence (IR 1986, rule 6.9(3)). The petition must contain appropriate and sufficient information to establish that the proceedings have been commenced in the appropriate county court (IR 1986, rule 6.9A(7)).

The question of the appropriate court in which to issue the petition is likely to have been addressed by the creditor when completing a statutory demand, as the statutory demand must provide information to the debtor on where he is able to apply to set aside the demand.

4.3.6 Verification of bankruptcy petition

The petition must be verified by a statement of truth and filed at court (IR 1986, rule 6.12(1)). This must state that the evidence in the petition is true to the best of the deponent's knowledge, information and belief. If the petition is brought by a number of creditors (a multi-creditor petition), the debts of each creditor must be separately verified (IR 1986, rule 6.12(2)).

The petition must be exhibited to the affidavit or witness statement verifying it (IR 1986, rule 6.12(3)).

The statement must be made by the petitioner or by:

(a)   a director, company secretary or company officer, or solicitor who has been concerned in the matters giving rise to the presentation of the petition by the creditor; or

(b)   some other responsible person duly authorised to make the statement and who has the requisite knowledge of the matters (IR 1986, rule 6.12(4)).

If the deponent is not the petitioner himself, the petition must state the capacity in which he has authority to make the statement and has means of knowledge of the matters sworn in the affidavit (IR 1986, rule 6.12(5)).

If the petition is based on a statutory demand and more than four months have elapsed between the service of the demand and presentation of the petition, the petition must state the reasons for the delay (IR 1986, rule 6.12(7)). This provision ensures that old statutory demands are not generally relied upon and guards against instances where the debtor's financial position may have altered. It is possible that the creditor and debtor may have been undergoing lengthy negotiations which have subsequently failed. For this reason, there may be some justification for presenting a petition based on a statutory demand after four months, although this will be a matter for the court in the exercise of its discretion on hearing the petition.

4.3.7   Presentation of a bankruptcy petition

Once presented to court, the bankruptcy petition cannot be withdrawn without permission of the court (IA 1986, s.266(2)). This remains the case even if the debtor has paid the creditor's debt or they have otherwise reached agreement. The two parties cannot simply agree to withdraw the petition from the hearing list as other creditors have the right to attend the hearing and apply to take carriage of the petition (IR 1986, rule 6.31).

Because of this, the creditor must think very carefully about the consequences of issuing a petition. If a statutory demand is not complied with, this is a matter for the creditor alone; once a bankruptcy petition is issued, important collective rights arise. Other creditors, such as financial institutions, may make a search of petitions issued against individuals and withdraw credit facilities/freeze accounts. The debtor is also prohibited from disposing of assets, save in certain circumstances.

In such circumstances, a debtor may find himself unable to pay the debt claimed, even if he has available assets, without application to the court. Furthermore, when a petition has been issued, it may be supported by other creditors. Unlike a company winding-up petition, a bankruptcy petition is not advertised, although it is not unknown for creditors to hear of and to support the petition. Therefore, even if an agreement is reached between the debtor and the creditor, carriage of the petition may be moved to another petitioner and/or an order for substitution may take place. Any deal which has been concluded between the debtor and creditor could poten-tially be set aside as a preference if the debtor is subsequently made bankrupt (IA 1986, s.340). There is therefore considerable risk to the creditor if it is bringing a bankruptcy petition simply to put further pressure on the debtor and force payment of a debt. The collective nature of the bankruptcy moves the determination of matters away from the sole control of the creditor issuing the petition.

In addition to the payment of a court fee of £220, the petitioning creditor also needs to pay the Official Receiver's deposit of £700 (as at time of writing). This sum covers the initial investigation costs incurred by the Official Receiver's office. Payment is required as in many cases the debtor will have insufficient assets even to cover the costs of the Official Receiver. There are considerable cost implications for the creditor when presenting a bankruptcy petition.

Together with the petition, a copy of the petition must be delivered to court for service on the debtor (IR 1986, rule 6.10(3)). When an IVA is still in place, a further copy is required, to be served upon the supervisor.

The court will endorse on the petition the date and time of filing and fix a venue for hearing, which is also endorsed on the petition (IR 1986, rule 6.10(4), (5)).

Where a bankruptcy petition is based on the non-compliance with a statutory demand, an affidavit of service of the demand, exhibiting a copy of the statutory demand which was served on the debtor, must also be filed (IR 1986, rule 6.11). The procedure for the service of the statutory demand has been dealt with in **4.1.4**.

When the bankruptcy petition is filed, the court will send notice of the petition forthwith to the Chief Registrar, together with a request that it is noted on the register of pending actions. It is a search of this register by creditors which may lead to the debtor being prevented from obtaining further credit and/or disposing of assets.

4.3.8   Service of petition

The petition should be served personally on the debtor (IR 1986, rule 16.14(1)). A certificate of service evidencing when, how and by whom this was effected should be filed at court immediately after service (IR 1986, rule 6.15(A)).

If, however, the court is satisfied on affidavit or on other evidence that personal service cannot be effected because the debtor is keeping out of the way in order to avoid service of the petition or another legal process, the court may order substituted service to be effected in such manner as it thinks fit (IR 1986, rule 6.14(2)).

4.3.9   Substituted service

This may include service:

- by postal delivery;
- at the last known residence of the debtor;
- at the last known business address of the debtor;
- upon a third party agent (such as a solicitor);
- by newspaper advertisement.

If the debtor dies before service of the petition, the court may order that service is effected on the debtor's personal representatives, or such other person as it thinks fit (IR 1986, rule 6.16). For greater detail see para.14.7 of the Practice Direction on Insolvency Proceedings.

4.3.10 Hearing

Prior to the hearing, the petitioner should have filed:

- a certificate of service of the statutory demand (exhibiting the statutory demand if applicable);
- a statement verifying the petition (exhibiting the petition);
- a certificate of service of petition;
- a list of creditors intending to appear (IR 1986, rule 6.24, Form 6.21). This should be handed to the court before commencement of the hearing; and
- a certificate of continuing debt, confirming the debt is still due and owing (taking into account any sums paid since the presentation of the petition).

The hearing should not take place until 14 days have elapsed since service of the demand (IR 1986, rule 6.18(1)). As a consequence, the petitioning creditor should ensure that service of the petition is promptly effected immediately after issue. The petitioning creditor should bear in mind that it often takes some time to arrange for service and the debtor may seek to avoid service. If the creditor acts promptly, it may avoid the need to adjourn the hearing of the bankruptcy petition and/or need to apply to court for a substituted service order, keeping to the original date of the bankruptcy petition hearing while enabling 14 days' notice to be given.

The court does, however, have a discretion to allow the hearing to take place with less than 14 days' notice being provided if:

(a) it appears the debtor has absconded or the court is satisfied it is a proper case for an expedited hearing;

(b) the debtor consents to short notice; or

(c) there is a serious possibility that the debtor's property or the value of his property will be significantly diminished (IR 1986, rule 6.18(2); see also IA 1986, s.270 regarding the presentation of a petition before the expiry of 21 days from the date of service of a statutory demand).

If it can be shown that the debtor was deliberately avoiding service, it may also be possible to persuade the court to allow a shorter period of notice.

4.3.11 Attendance at the hearing

Under IR 1986, rule 6.18(3), the following may attend the hearing of the petition:

- The petitioning creditor.
- The debtor.
- The supervisor of any existing IVA in force in respect of the debtor.
- Any creditor who has given requisite notice.

Any creditor of the debtor may attend the hearing, but must first give to the petitioning creditor notice by 4 pm the day before the hearing of its intention to do so. In that notice to the petitioning creditor, the third party creditor must provide details of:

- its name and address;
- contact details;
- the amount of the debt; and
- whether it intends to support or oppose the petition.

Any creditor who fails to comply with the above provisions may only appear at the hearing on a bankruptcy petition with permission of the court (IR 1986, rule 6.23(4)). The petitioning creditor must prepare a list of those creditors who have provided such notice, which must be handed to the court before commencement of the hearing (IR 1986, rule 6.24 in Form 6.21).

Any creditor who attends the hearing may make such representations as it thinks fit in support of or in opposition to the petition. Attendance may be something the creditor considers, if it believes that the debtor and the petitioning creditor may come to some form of deal prior to the hearing which could lead to a withdrawal, postponement or dismissal of the petition. In such circumstances the supporting creditor may wish to take carriage of the petition, or seek to be substituted as petitioner. If the court is aware of the other creditor's position, it may adjourn the hearing of the bankruptcy petition and/or make subsequent directions. If no attendance is made, the court is more likely to dismiss the petition. Consequently, if acting for a creditor who is not the petitioning creditor, and that creditor wishes to seek the bankruptcy of the debtor, it is advisable that it attends and/or is represented at the bankruptcy hearing.

4.3.12 Court's decision on hearing

The court may:

- make a bankruptcy order;
- stay the petition;
- adjourn the hearing;
- extend time for the hearing;
- substitute the petitioning creditor for another creditor;
- change carriage of the petition; or
- dismiss the petition.

Each option is considered below.

Bankruptcy order

The court will make a bankruptcy order if the petitioning creditor has filed the correct papers (see above) and the court is satisfied that:

(a)   the statements in the petition are true; and

(b)   the debt on which the debt is founded has not been paid, secured or com-
       pounded for.

The payment of the debt must be unconditional, so it is not treated as material if it is
dependent on the dismissal of the petition (see *Smith* v. *Ian Simpson & Co.* [2000]
BPIR 667). This can pose practical difficulties if third parties are willing only to pay
the debt on condition that the petition is dismissed. A means of overcoming this
might be for the debtor's solicitors to hold the funds to the order of the third party
with an unconditional undertaking from the third party to allow release of the funds
to the creditor if the petition is dismissed. This arrangement will, however, require
the co-operation of the creditor.

   If there has been a technical error by the petitioning creditor, such as the failure to
file a certificate of service, the court may, if thought fit, accept an undertaking that
this error will be rectified forthwith. For example, if the debtor is present and/or
service can otherwise be proved, despite the fact that a certificate of service has not
been filed, the court is likely to overlook the technical error.

   On a practical point of procedure, generally a bankruptcy petition is listed with a
short time estimate (normally five minutes). Bankruptcy is, however, treated
seriously by the court and if a debtor is objecting to the petition on substantive
grounds, the court is likely to adjourn the hearing with a longer time estimate and
give further directions.

   The court also has a general discretion which it can exercise and is entitled to
dismiss the petition even if the debt is one over £750, if it thinks appropriate. In
making its assessment the court will consider whether all debts of the debtor,
including contingent and prospective liabilities, have been or are likely to be settled.
The court may dismiss the petition:

(a)   where the debt is only just over £750;

(b)   where it is evident that the debtor is solvent, a reasonable proposal for
       repayment has been made and evidence is available to show that payment will
       be made promptly, e.g. a remortgage has been effected and an undertaking
       provided that on the remortgage being provided the debt will be paid (IA
       1986, s.271(3) – the court may dismiss the petition if satisfied that the debtor
       is able to pay all of his debts); or

(c)   if the court is satisfied that the debtor has made an offer to secure or compound
       for the debt, the acceptance of which would require the dismissal petition and
       that such offer has been unreasonably refused.

The latter provision seems to envisage that payment has not been made in full and/or
for at least part of the debt an offer of payment in the future has been made.
However, it is unlikely that the creditor will ever be compelled to accept anything
less than the full payment of its petition debt.

   In *Re a Debtor (No.32 of 1993), ex p. Commercial Union Life Assurance
Company* [1994] 1 WLR 899, it was held that unreasonableness means 'beyond the

range of any possible reasonable reaction in these circumstances'. The fact that one creditor or another may have accepted the offer is not in itself conclusive (see also *Re Gilmartin (a Bankrupt)* [1989] 1 WLR 513; *Inland Revenue* v. *a Debtor* [1995] BCC 971).

The court can also order amendment of the petition to omit any creditor or debt, and continue with the petition on the basis of the remaining creditors or debts (IA 1986, s.271(5)). This power enables multi-creditor petitions to be amended, or changes in the carriage of the petition to be effected.

It should be noted that if the petitioning creditor fails to appear at the hearing and the petition is dismissed, that creditor is prohibited from issuing a subsequent bankruptcy petition against the same debtor, in respect of the same debt, without the leave of the court in which the previous petition had been presented (IR 1986, rule 6.26).

Stay of petition

A petition may be stayed if the debt claimed within the petition is a judgment debt which is subject to appeal or if execution of that judgment has been stayed (IR 1986, rule 6.25(2) – see *Heath* v. *Tang*; *Stevens* v. *Peacock* [1993] 1 WLR 1421). The bankruptcy court will look carefully at the appeal and may determine whether it has a reasonable prospect of success (see *Westminster City Council* v. *Parkin* [2001] BPIR 1156). It is, however, possible for the creditor to appeal against any bankruptcy order that is made at a later date if circumstances change (e.g. after a successful appeal – see *Re a Debtor (No.799 of 1994), ex p. Cobbs Property Services Ltd* [1995] 1 WLR 467).

Adjournment of petition

The court may adjourn the hearing of the bankruptcy petition for any number of reasons. These may range from technical failures/omissions on the part of the petitioning creditor, e.g. a failure to serve the debtor within 14 days of the hearing, to where a proposal is being put forward by the debtor either informally to the creditor(s) or as part of an IVA.

Even if there has been a failure to pay any part of the debt by the date of hearing, the court can order an adjournment if it is persuaded that the debt can be paid in the near future (*Re Gilmartin* [1989] 1 WLR 513). However, good evidence of when and how payment will be effected is required (*Dickins* v. IRC [2004] BPIR 718). Furthermore, in recent years the court has clamped down on repeated adjournments (*Judd* v. *Williams* sub nom. *Williams (a Bankrupt)* [1989] BPIR 88) and will generally look wherever possible to make an order or dismiss the petition, stressing that bankruptcy proceedings are collective rather than being a 'debt collection' matter between the debtor and one creditor.

If the petition is adjourned, the petitioning creditor, unless the court orders otherwise, must send to the debtor, and any creditor who has provided notice but was not present, the order for the adjournment and notice stating when and where the adjourned hearing will take place (IR 1986, rule 6.29(2), Form 6.24).

Extension of time for hearing

If the debtor has not been served with the petition, the petitioning creditor may apply for a further hearing date. However, the application for a further hearing will require the petitioning creditor to state the reasons why the petition has not been served. It could of course be accompanied by an application for substituted service. If another date is provided for the hearing, the petitioning creditor must notify any creditor who has provided it with notice (IR 1986, rule 6.28).

Substitution of petitioner

Under IR 1986, rule 6.30, where the petitioner:

- has presented a petition but is subsequently found not to have been entitled to do so;
- consents to the withdrawal of its petition;
- allows the petition to be dismissed;
- consents to an adjournment of the petition;
- fails to appear to support the petition; or
- does not seek an order in the terms of the petition,

the court may on such terms it thinks fit order for there to be a substitution of the petitioner. A creditor entitled to be substituted is one who:

- has provided notice of intention to appear at the hearing (IR 1986, rule 6.23, Form 6.20);
- is desirous of prosecuting the petition; and
- was on the date the petition was presented entitled to present a bankruptcy petition in respect of a debt owed by the debtor (IR 1986, rule 6.30(2)).

The fact that the creditor seeking substitution must have been entitled to present a bankruptcy petition as at the date that the original petition was presented means that the creditor must:

(a) have served a statutory demand on the debtor 21 days before it was found not to be complied with; or

(b) have sought execution of his debt which had been returned unsatisfied in whole or in part.

The substitution of the petitioner will require amendment of the petition, such as an insertion of a new petitioner and a new debt. As a result, directions are likely to be given regarding amendment to the petition, re-service and then further hearing.

Change of carriage of petition

A creditor who has given notice to appear at the hearing may apply to court for an order giving it carriage of the petition in place of the original petitioning creditor (IR 1986, rule 6.31). This order may be sought if the original petitioning creditor intends to postpone, adjourn or withdraw the petition or does not intend to prosecute the petition diligently or at all.

An order cannot be made if the petitioning creditor's debt has been paid, secured or compounded for with money or assets provided by some person other than the debtor, or where the debtor has done so from his own assets with approval of the court. As a consequence, the debtor is prevented from coming to a deal with the petitioning creditor using his own assets if this will prejudice the position of other creditors. This once again stresses the collective nature of the bankruptcy petition. The advantage to the creditor is that no amendment of the petition is required and the change of carriage order may be made whether or not the petitioning creditor appears at the hearing. If an order is made, the 'new' creditor is entitled to rely on all evidence previously adduced in the proceedings.

Dismissal of the petition

Where the petitioning creditor applies to court for the petition to be dismissed, or for leave to withdraw the petition, unless the court orders otherwise it must file a witness statement specifying the grounds upon which the application is made and all surrounding circumstances (IR 1986, rule 6.32(1)).

If after the petition has been issued a payment has been made to the petitioning creditor, it must state whether this was in settlement of whole or part of the debt, and whether dispositions of property have been made for the purposes of settlement and, if so, whether the disposition of any property of the debtor has been ratified by the court.

No order giving leave to withdraw the petition will be given before the petition is heard. This once again stresses the fact that there are other creditors who may wish to appear at the hearing and the rights of the petitioning creditor are subject to the collective rights of other creditors.

In practice, the court is likely to grant leave to withdraw the petition if the petitioning creditor has yet to serve the petition and will do so without the requirement of submitting witness statement evidence in most cases. If, however, the petition has been served and other creditors have given notice, the court will be concerned to find out why the petitioning creditor is seeking dismissal of the petition and may need to decide whether other creditors will apply for a change of carriage of the petition or substitution of petitioner.

If the petition is withdrawn by leave, or dismissed after payment of the petition debt, the petitioning creditor is entitled to costs of the proceedings (see *Re a Debtor (No.510 of 1997)* (1998) *The Times*, 18 June).

It is of course open to the debtor to dispute the petition debt. If no application to set aside the statutory demand was made, this right is unfettered (*Barnes* v. *Whitehead* [2004] BPIR 693); however, leaving the matter until hearing of the bankruptcy petition is a dangerous tactic for the debtor to pursue as it might be seen as opportunistic and if the challenge is unsuccessful bankruptcy will result. If arguments have been unsuccessfully raised on the application to set aside the demand, the debtor cannot simply re-phrase the argument with additional evidence, unless such evidence was unavailable at the application to set aside the demand (see *Turner* v. *Royal Bank of Scotland* [2000] BPIR 683; *Atherton* v. *Ogunlende* [2003] BPIR 21; and *Coulter* v. *Chief Constable of Dorset Police (No.2)* [2006] BPIR 10).

A petition will also be dismissed if the debtor is able to satisfy the court that he is able to pay all of his debts, although the question would then arise why the debtor has not paid the petition debt. Even if the debtor is balance sheet solvent, the fact that he is unable to pay his debts as they fall due will mean that he is deemed insolvent and a bankruptcy order will be made. Alternatively, the debtor could seek dismissal of the petition on ground that he has made an offer to compound or secure the debt which the creditor has unreasonably refused. However, as explained above, it is difficult to foresee circumstances where it could be seen as unreasonable for the creditor to refuse anything less than its entitlement to full and immediate payment.

4.3.13 After the hearing

The bankruptcy order is settled by court and must provide:

- the date and time that the petition was issued;
- the date and time of making the order;
- a notice requiring the bankrupt forthwith after service of the order upon him to attend the Official Receiver (IR 1986, rule 6.33);
- for a stay on any action of the proceedings against the bankrupt, if appropriate (enforcement procedures specified in IA 1986, s.346);
- where the petitioning creditor has been represented by solicitors, details of the solicitors' name, address, telephone number and reference.

Two sealed copies of the bankruptcy order will be sent to the Official Receiver, who will thereafter send one to the bankrupt. The Official Receiver will then send notice of the order to the Chief Land Registrar for registering the bankruptcy notice.

The bankruptcy will be advertised in such newspapers as the Official Receiver thinks fit and the *London Gazette*.

The court may, on application of the bankrupt, order the Official Receiver to suspend such action pending further hearing, e.g. where an annulment application is being made on the grounds that the order should never have been made.

At any time after making the bankruptcy order, the Official Receiver or trustee may apply to court to amend the title of the proceedings. This is essential if further information has been given as to the name, identity and business occupation of the bankrupt. This may lead to amendment by the Chief Land Registrar of the bankruptcy notice and/or re-advertisement.

CHAPTER 5

Advising a creditor in the case of an insolvent corporate debtor

5.1 STATUTORY DEMAND AND THE CREDITOR OF A CORPORATE DEBTOR

Checklist

Creditor's considerations before serving a statutory demand

1. Is the debt a liquidated and due debt?
2. Is the debt likely to be disputed?
3. Does the debtor possess a genuine cross-claim?
4. Is the creditor unwilling to proceed with a formal collective insolvency procedure in the event of non-payment?
5. If the answer to (2) (3) or (4) is yes, the creditor should almost certainly proceed to enforce payment of the debt by some other means.

5.1.1 Nature of the debt that can be demanded

While a statutory demand should not be regarded as a debt collection technique (see *Re a Company (No.012209 of 1991)* [1992] 1 WLR 351, in which the use of a statutory demand by a non-judgment creditor was described as a 'high risk strategy' and *Cannon Screen Entertainment Ltd* v. *Handmade Films (Distributors) Ltd* [1989] BCLC 660), if the debt demanded is due and payable and in excess of £750 there can be no criticism of a creditor for proceeding in this manner.

In order to be deemed 'due and payable', the debt demanded must not be:

- in respect of a contingent liability where the contingency has not yet arisen (*JSF Finance & Currency Exchange Co. Ltd* v. *Akma Solutions Inc.* [2001] 2 BCLC 307);
- for an unliquidated amount (*Reinsurance Australia Corp. Ltd* v. *Odyssey Re (Bermuda) Ltd* [2000] NSWSC 1118);
- statute-barred (*Re Karnos Property Co. Ltd* (1989) 5 BCC 14); or
- subject to a bona fide dispute (*Ross & Craig (a Firm)* v. *Williamson* [2006] All ER (D) 139 (Mar)). Indeed, where there is a bona fide dispute, even though the

debtor may have neglected to pay, it does not follow that the creditor is justified in proceeding further (see *Re a Company (No.003729 of 1982)* [1984] WLR 1090).

It should be noted, however, that a statutory demand provides a creditor with a quick and inexpensive route to ascertain whether the debtor will pay the debt demanded. The creditor may decide it is better to discover at an early stage whether the debtor is unable to pay, rather than proceed with a legal action and then fail to enforce any subsequent judgment.

However, it should be kept firmly in mind that where the debt is known to be genuinely disputed prior to the issue of the demand, severe costs sanctions can be imposed (see e.g. *Re a Company (No.006798 of 1995)* [1996] 1 WLR 491, where a solicitor who swore an affidavit in support of a winding-up petition alleging a company's inability to pay a debt, without basis, was ordered personally to pay the company's costs; also *Re a Company (No.003689 of 1998)* (1998) *The Times*, 7 October, where a director was held personally liable for costs where he had caused statutory demands to be issued knowing there was a dispute).

It should also be noted that a determination of the General Commissioner of Inland Revenue is final and the courts will not allow the matter to be reopened (see *Cullinane* v. *Inland Revenue Commissioners* [2000] BPIR 996; and also *Re D&D Marketing (UK) Ltd* [2003] BPIR 539, regarding an appeal for a VAT assessment of a 'disputed' HMRC assessment).

The debt must be for a sum which is due and payable immediately and/or where liability in respect of the debt is existing; IA 1986, s.123(1)(a) speaks of a 'due' debt. A statutory demand cannot be made in respect of contingent debt (see *Re Miller* [1901] 1 QB 51) where the contingency has yet to arise (see *JSF Finance & Currency Exchange Ltd* v. *Akma Solutions Inc.* [2001] 2 BCLC 307), although it should be noted that a contingent creditor is recognised as a 'creditor' possessing a 'debt' as defined in both IA 1986 and IR 1986 (see IR 1986, rule 13.12). A statutory demand cannot be served on a guarantor unless non-payment of the principal creditor has been established (see *Re a Debtor (No.1594 of 1992)* (1992) *The Times*, 8 December).

Interest payable on the debt can be claimed if interest is due under the terms of the contract or statute (see Late Payment of Commercial Debts (Interest) Act 1998), but it must be calculated only to the date of the demand.

The debt must be for a sum in excess of £750. However, due to the serious consequences that arise, the courts will not look favourably on petitions that are based on debts only slightly in excess of £750 (see *City Electrical Factors Ltd* v. *Hardingham* [1996] BPIR 541). The value of the debt is a factor likely to be considered by the court in the exercise of its discretion on the hearing of the petition (for bankruptcy or winding up); despite the creditor's entitlement to present the petition, the court may refuse to make an order. However, the fact that the debt is only just over £750 should not prevent a creditor from serving a statutory demand.

Rather, it is a matter for the adviser to warn the creditor that in such circumstances the liquidation of the company is not a foregone conclusion.

The debt may be assigned to a creditor under an effective legal assignment and the assignee is free to issue a statutory demand. In such circumstances, details of the assignment must be included in the statutory demand.

If there is more than one debt owing, they must be separately identified and a description of the basis on which liability arises provided for each (see *Bennett* v. *Filmer* [1998] BPIR 444). Subject to this, it is possible to present an aggregated demand for payment.

A statutory demand cannot be based on a debt which is statute-barred (see *Re Karnos Property Co. Ltd* (1989) BCC 14; *Jelly* v. *All Type Roofing* [1997] BCC 465; and *Bruton* v. IRC [2000] BIPR 946).

A debt claimed in a statutory demand must be for a liquidated sum, based on a claim in contract or tort (*Re Humberstone Jersey Ltd* (1977) 74 LSG 711). However, a claim in tort will generally be for unquantified loss or damages, which requires some degree of assessment or agreement. Accordingly, a court judgment or binding settlement is required before the creditor can proceed with a statutory demand in respect of a debt which has arisen from a claim in tort. Similarly, an order that costs are payable by one party cannot be subject to a statutory demand until those costs have been assessed or agreed (*Galloppa* v. *Galloppa* [1999] BPIR 352).

IA 1986, s.267(2)(b) provides that the debt 'is for a liquidated sum payable ... immediately or at some certain future time and is unsecured'. IA 1986, s.123(1)(a) speaks of a 'due' debt. A statutory demand can, however, be presented in respect of a debt which is payable in the future, although the court will require evidence that the debtor will be unable to pay that debt when it is due and payable.

In contrast to the position in personal insolvency, there is nothing to prevent a secured creditor from issuing a statutory demand (*Re Cushing Sulphite Fibre Co. Ltd* (1905) 37 NBR 254) or initiating winding-up proceedings (*Re Lafayette Electronics Europe Ltd* [2006] EWHC 1006 (Ch)). A secured creditor does, however, have the alternative remedies as laid down in the terms of its security, which will usually provide the ability to enforce and realise property of the debtor without regard to the collective interests of the creditors as a whole; winding up is thus generally the preserve of the unsecured creditors. It should be noted that when the debtor company is wound up, the secured creditor will need to elect whether it will be relying on its security (*Re Carmarthenshire Anthracite Coal and Iron Co.* (1875) 45 LJ Ch 200).

It is often the case that some proportion of the debt which is owed to a secured creditor is unsecured, e.g. where the current value of a particular property means that the creditor's security is insufficient to cover the whole debt. In such cases, the secured creditor can participate in the eventual liquidation for the proportion of its debt that is deemed unsecured. It is also open to the secured creditor to value its own security and to present a statutory demand and/or petition for winding up for the unsecured element of its debt, provided the debt is in excess of £750. In so doing, the value of the security is best assessed on a forced sale basis (see *Platts* v. *Western Trust and Savings* [1996] BPIR 339).

The secured creditor must be mindful in taking such a step as, unless the claim is appropriately constructed, the creditor can be seen to forgo its secured rights. As a consequence, the adviser to a secured creditor must balance the advantages and disadvantages of proceeding with a collective insolvency process against those of commencing proceedings in respect of the creditor's own security.

Generally, it is advisable to pursue the remedy provided by the security first and then determine the balance of the debt which will be unsecured. However, in some cases, a secured creditor may find it advantageous to abandon its security. The effect of IA 1986, s.176A may mean that a guaranteed return to unsecured creditors is a better option for a creditor whose security ranks low in priority and who may have little prospect of payment for its security. The creditor may also consider it advantageous for a collective process to be initiated, where rights of action vest only in the liquidator or administrator. (See transactions at an undervalue and preference actions, IA 1986, ss.238, 239.)

The rights which a creditor may possess in respect of the security will depend on the terms of the charge/debenture or other form of security. The creditor remains free to exercise its right of security at any time until any insolvency procedure commences. It should be noted that the rights of secured creditors are unaffected by the collective nature of the liquidation process. However, in contrast, where the debtor company enters into administration, enforcement rights are only exercisable with the permission of the court or consent of the administrator.

Whatever insolvency procedure has been commenced, the rights of a secured creditor cannot be prejudiced, save where that secured creditor has consented, e.g. in the case of a CVA.

Therefore, the secured creditor may well wish to retain the right to proceed with its own enforcement remedy to recover its debt. The secured creditor may then proceed with the alternative procedures of administration, administrative receivership or receivership, as opposed to taking part in the liquidation.

5.1.2 The nature and effect of serving a statutory demand

A statutory demand is a formal demand for payment of a debt made by a creditor to a debtor under the terms of IA 1986 and in accordance with IR 1986.

A statutory demand is not an 'action' (*Re a Debtor (No.88 of 1991)* [1993] Ch 286), a 'proceeding' (*Cornick Pty Ltd* v. *Brains Master Corporation* [1995] 60 FCR 565) or an insolvency process (*Re a Debtor (No.1 of 1987) (Lancaster)* [1989] 1 WLR 271). As described above, non-compliance with a statutory demand is a method by which a company's inability to pay its debts for the purposes of winding up can be established (IA 1986, s.122(1)(f)). As a result, if the debtor fails to comply with, or to contest, the demand within three weeks of service, the debtor is deemed to be unable to pay its debts. In *Cornhill Insurance plc* v. *Improvement Services Ltd* [1986] 1 WLR 114, it was held that where the debtor failed to pay a debt, which was not disputed, it could be relied on as evidence of insolvency notwithstanding clear evidence of substantial balance sheet solvency (assets exceeding liabilities).

Non-compliance with a statutory demand is, however, only one of the three ways a creditor can show that a corporate debtor is unable to pay a debt (IA 1986, s.123(1)(a) for a registered company and s.222(1)(a) for an unregistered company). However, it is a quick, convenient and relatively inexpensive method and therefore commonly used by creditors.

Prior to serving the statutory demand, the creditor is under no obligation to investigate first whether the debtor is willing or able to pay the debt (*Dooney* v. *Henry* [2000] HCA 44), nor is the creditor obliged to make some other form of prior demand.

It should be noted that while the service of a statutory demand is not a mandatory requirement in order to issue a winding-up petition, and the failure to comply with the demand does not automatically lead to a winding-up petition, the service of a statutory demand has important consequences for the debtor and creditor alike. If the demand is undisputed and cannot be paid, this can be relied upon by other third party creditors as a ground to substantiate a winding-up petition on grounds of inability to pay (*Brinds Ltd* v. *Offshore Oil NL* (1986) 2 BCC 98916). In addition, the unsatisfied demand may be relied on as an event of default under the debtor's banking facilities, which could have the effect of hastening the company's demise.

Alternatively, where the demand is for a debt which is disputed, if the creditor refuses to withdraw the demand, the 'debtor' can seek injunctive relief (and adverse costs) against the 'creditor', ensuring that no further proceedings can be taken. However, as the statutory demand is not an 'action' or 'proceeding', the service of the demand in itself is not an abuse of process; rather, it is the threat of action by means of a winding-up petition that is the actionable abuse of process (*James Estates Wires Pty Ltd* v. *Widelink (Aust) Pty Ltd* [2003] NSWSC 744).

The service of a statutory demand on a debtor is a step available to an individual creditor; it does not bear any collective nature, in contrast to the creditors' petition for winding up. There is no register of statutory demands, nor is it a court process that requires approval before service. This contrasts with the former (pre-1986) bankruptcy notice procedure, where notice of debt and due payment was issued by the courts. A claim for payment of a debt due and owing made by a statutory demand remains entirely one between the creditor and debtor.

It should also be noted that it is possible to serve a statutory demand on a company out of the jurisdiction without the need to seek permission of the court. However, where a demand is to be served, the creditor must carefully follow the procedure as set out in Practice Direction on Insolvency Proceedings [2007] BCC 842, para.13.2.

If the demand is complied with, the matter rests there. If it is not complied with, it is a matter for the creditor to decide whether to proceed further; a creditor is not obliged to do so. A creditor needs to remain aware of the fact that the non-compliance with the demand could be relied upon by another creditor, or have the consequence that the board of the debtor company concludes that the company is insolvent and that an insolvency process (be that creditors' voluntary liquidation or administration) should be commenced.

If the debt is not disputed, the creditor may find that if the debtor cannot immediately pay, the debtor may make an offer to compromise the debt. This may involve payment by instalments, or postponement of payment to a later date and/or an offer of security. Before accepting any offer, the creditor may need to consider the position of other creditors, e.g. it is pointless reaching an agreement if other creditors are likely to take action and scupper the ability to recover the debt over time. It should be remembered that the creditor is under no obligation to accept anything less than that which it is entitled to.

If the debt is not disputed and/or any offer of settlement has been refused, yet for some reason the creditor decides not to act on the demand, the debtor is in a difficult position; a presumption of insolvency has arisen. Consequently, if further credit is taken and/or losses arise at a time when the debtor knew it was insolvent, and the company is subsequently wound up, proceedings against the directors for wrongful or fraudulent trading could be undertaken, as could proceedings under CDDA 1986.

Accordingly, if a demand is served and the debtor company cannot comply with it, irrespective of whether the creditor decides to proceed or indeed whether the debt is disputed, the debtor company's directors may well seek immediate professional guidance from an insolvency specialist, ultimately leading to the initiation of a voluntary insolvency procedure. The creditor needs to think carefully if this may be an (unintended) consequence of the service of a demand.

5.1.3 Creditor considerations on debtor disputing the statutory demand

A statutory demand must be based on the liability to pay an undisputed debt. However, if the debt is disputed by the alleged corporate debtor, there is no set procedure or court application available to set aside the demand. Instead, the alleged debtor's remedy, in the absence of agreement to withdraw the demand by the 'creditor', is to apply for injunctive relief to restrain the presentation of a petition in the court having jurisdiction to wind up the company, or apply to restrain the advertising of the petition in the court where the petition is pending (IR 1986, rule 4.6A).

Where, following demand and then negotiation, the creditor agrees that the debtor has raised a bona fide dispute as to the debt demanded in the statutory demand, there is likewise no formal procedure for withdrawing the demand, but an undertaking or written agreement may be sought/provided from the creditor or its legal representatives that they will not present a petition based upon the demand.

It is not enough for the debtor simply to state that the debt is disputed; the court will not restrain the creditor from proceeding unless it is satisfied that there is a genuine dispute on substantial grounds (*Re a Company (No.006685 of 1996)* [1997] BCC 830). However, even when it is persuaded that there is a genuine dispute, the court may, in the exercise of its discretion, still allow a petition to proceed, e.g. if there is no other appropriate remedy available to the creditors as a whole (see

Parmalat Capital Finance Ltd v. *Food Holdings Ltd* [2009] 1 BCLC 274). In the normal course of events, however, the creditor is left to pursue the payment of the debt by the usual means, i.e. litigation (see *Re Richbell Strategic Holdings Ltd* [1997] 2 BCLC 429, where a court refused to make a winding-up order on the grounds that there was a genuine dispute).

Severe costs penalties can also be imposed on a creditor proceeding with a petition where there is a bona fide dispute and an earlier opportunity arose for the creditor to withdraw the demand. As a result, the creditor needs to think very carefully if the debt is disputed. Is it a bona fide dispute? Has the dispute been raised in the past? Is the debt wholly or partially disputed?

In establishing whether a dispute arises, the burden of proof is upon the alleged debtor, although this burden is less onerous than that faced by the defendant resisting an application for summary judgment under CPR, Part 24, where the defendant has to show that there is a real prospect of successfully defending the claim. The Companies Court will treat the matter somewhat differently; it will not conduct a mini-trial on the issues and the benefit of the doubt is more likely to be provided to the debtor. As a word of caution, however, the courts will look with some scepticism at voluminous material produced by a debtor seeking to establish that a dispute exists. A clear and simple dispute speaks for itself; conversely, a complex technical defence may fail to impress. In considering whether to grant injunctive relief, the court will consider the same factors as it would consider on an application by an individual to set aside a statutory demand.

Various examples of disputes in the context of the service of a demand upon a personal debtor are considered in detail in **4.1.5**. These have application to a dispute in regard to a corporate debtor.

Where time permits, rather than commence what may be expensive and costly injunctive proceedings, the alleged company debtor that disputes the demand (e.g. on grounds of disputed debt) is, however, best advised immediately to write to the creditor seeking its confirmation that the statutory demand will be withdrawn (i.e. it will not be proceeded with). As the injuctive remedy is available to the alleged debtor at the equitable discretion of the court, it is best that the alleged debtor acts fairly and reasonably by giving the creditor reasonable opportunity to withdraw the demand. This will provide the alleged debtor with grounds for recovery of legal costs should it eventually need to commence legal proceedings.

If the court is persuaded that the debt is genuinely disputed, or there is a genuine and serious cross-claim which exceeds the petition debt (or reduces the undisputed debt to below £750), save in exceptional circumstances, the 'creditor' will be restrained from petitioning (see *Cannon Screen Entertainment Ltd* v. *Handmade Films (Distributors) Ltd* (1989) 5 BCC 207).

In the past, as on the hearing of application for summary judgment, where the court felt that there was some doubt as to the bona fides of the dispute or genuineness of the cross-claim, it might order that a part payment was made or security provided (see *Re Douglas Griggs Engineering Ltd* [1963] Ch 19). Recent authorities suggest that there is little place for treating disputes on demands, made in the context of insolvency proceedings, akin to 'shadowy defences' in summary judgment applications (*Re a Debtor (490-SD-1991)* [1992] 1 WLR 507; *Re a Debtor (32-SD-1991) (No.2)* (1994) *The Times*, 3 May). Indeed, in *Higgins* v. *Valambia* [2004] BPIR 876 it was held that a court must allow or dismiss a statutory demand; it had no authority to make a conditional order.

A document is treated as a statutory demand unless or until it is set aside (*Re a Debtor (No.1 of 1987)* [1989] 1 WLR 271).

5.1.4 Content of a statutory demand

The provisions dealing with statutory demands on corporate debtors are contained in IA 1986, s.123(1)(a) and IR 1986, rules 4.4–4.6. The criteria necessary for a valid statutory demand are:

- the demand (in Form 4.1) must be in writing;
- the demand must be dated and authenticated by the creditor, or the person authorised by the creditor (IR 1986, rule 4.4(3));
- the debtor must be indebted to the creditor for a sum in excess of £750 (this is the current level and may be substituted by the Secretary of State by statutory instrument);
- the creditor must be an unsecured creditor for at least £750 of its debt;
- the demand must state the amount of the debt and the consideration for it (i.e. how the debt arose) (IR 1986, rule 4.5(1));
- any interest (not previously notified to the debtor) being claimed must be separately identified and the grounds claimed set out;
- the amount claimed must be limited to the date of the demand (IR 1986, rule 4.5(2));
- the demand must include an explanation of the purpose of the demand and the fact that if not complied with (within 21 days) proceedings may be instituted for the winding up of the company;
- the demand must state the methods open to the company to respond to the demand and set out the debtor's right to apply to court for injunctive relief (IR 1986, rule 4.6(1));
- information must be provided as to how an officer or representative of the debtor company may enter into communications with one or more named individuals with a view to securing or compounding the debt to the creditor's satisfaction; and
- where an individual is named in the demand, an address and telephone number (if any) must be provided (IR 1986, rule 4.6(2)).

Practical tips for completion of Form 4.1

The use of the prescribed form enables the creditor to ensure that all necessary information (as set out above) is included, and while a statutory demand can be

Rule 4.5

Statutory Demand under section 123(1)(a) or 222(1)(a) of the Insolvency Act 1986

Warning
• This is an **important** document. This demand must be dealt with **within 21 days** after its service upon the company or a winding-up order could be made in respect of the company.   • Please read the demand and notes carefully.

Notes for Creditor

- If the Creditor is entitled to the debt by way of assignment, details of the original creditor and any intermediary assignees should be given in part B on page 3.

- If the amount of debt includes interest not previously notified to the company as included in its liability, details should be given, including the grounds upon which interest is charged. The amount of interest must be shown separately.

- Any other charge accruing due from time to time may be claimed. The amount or rate of the charge must be identified and the grounds on which it is claimed must be stated.

- In either case the amount claimed must be limited to that which will have accrued due at the date of the demand.

- If signatory of the demand is a solicitor or other agent of the creditor the name of his/her firm should be given

*Delete if signed by the creditor himself.

DEMAND

To

Address

This demand is served on you by the creditor:

Name

Address

The creditor claims that the company will owe the sum of £ full particulars of which are set out on page 2.

The creditor demands that the company do pay the above debt or secure or compound for it to the creditor's satisfaction.

Signature of individual

Name
(BLOCK LETTERS)

Date

*Position with or relationship to creditor

*I am authorised to make this demand on the creditor's behalf

Address

Tel No   Ref.

N.B. The person making this demand must complete the whole of this page, page 2 and parts A and B (as applicable) on page 3.

Particulars of Debt
(These particulars must include (a) when the debt was incurred, (b) the consideration for the debt (or if is there is no consideration the way in which it arose) and (c) the amount due as at the date of this demand).

Notes for Creditor
Please make sure that you have read the notes on page 1 before completing this page.

Note:
If space is insufficient continue on reverse of page 3 and clearly indicate on this page that you are doing so.

Part A

The individual or individuals to whom any communication regarding this demand may be addressed is/are:

Name

Address

Telephone Number

Reference

Part B

For completion if the creditor is entitled to the debt by way of assignment

	Name	Date(s) of Assignment
Original creditor		
Assignees		

How to comply with a statutory demand

If the company wishes to avoid a winding-up petition being presented it must pay the debt shown on page 1, particulars of which are set out on page 2 of this notice, within the period of **21 days after** its service upon the company. Alternatively, the company can attempt to come to a settlement with the creditor. To do this the company should:

- inform the individual (or one of the individuals) named in part A above immediately that it is willing and able to offer security for the debt to the creditor's satisfaction; or

- inform the individual (or one of the individuals) named in part A immediately that it is willing and able to compound for the debt to the creditor's satisfaction.

If the company disputes the demand in whole or in part it should:

- contact the individual (or one of the individuals) named in part A immediately.

REMEMBER! **The company has only 21 days after the date of service on it of this document before the creditor may present a winding-up petition.**
NOTE: The company has the right to make an application to the court(*) for an injunction restraining the creditor from presenting a winding-up petition or from advertising it.

(*) The court to which an application should be made is the court having jurisdiction to wind up the company under section 117 of the Insolvency Act 1986.

drafted in the form of a written demand, it is almost certainly quicker and more convenient to use Form 4.1. The matters listed below refer to completion of the various parts of Form 4.1.

1. Insert name and address of the debtor company. As stated above, while some small errors (e.g. of spelling) may not invalidate the demand, it must be clear to whom the demand is being made. Accordingly, the demand should set out the name, registered number and registered office of the company in order to avoid any confusion. IA 1986, s.117(6) provides that the registered office is the place at which the company has had its registered office for the longest period in the last six months.

2. Insert name and address of the creditor.

3. Insert amount of claim. If the claim includes interest not previously identified to the debtor as being included in the debt being claimed, details of the grounds for the interest claimed and amount due should be set out separately. It should be remembered that the true purpose of a demand is to establish inability to pay a debt; it is not to be treated as a debt collection device. Accordingly, if the payment of interest (perhaps under the Late Payment of Commercial Debts (Interest) Act 1998) is a motivating factor, the claimant is best advised to use a litigation route to obtain judgment (and interest). The amount claimed under a demand should be an undisputed liquidated amount.

4. Signature of the demand and details of person signing. This must be the name of an individual person, who if appropriate needs to state the nature of the authority to sign on behalf of the creditor, e.g. as director or solicitor, together with contact details such as address, telephone number, reference, etc.

5. Particulars of demand. Akin to a statement of case, the demand must include details of (a) when the debt was incurred; (b) the consideration for the debt or if none how the debt arose; and (c) the amount due as at the date of demand. The particulars should set out the liability and, if appropriate, separately set out the grounds for any interest or charges claimed. Details as to how the debt arose, etc. must be adequate to allow the debtor to identify the debt with sufficient certainty (see **4.1.5** for grounds of dispute). To avoid any technical argument it is therefore advisable to include as much detail as possible.

6. At Part A include details concerning to whom communication regarding the demand must be sent. The claimant must give the debtor the possibility to correspond and set out any grounds of dispute or allow the debtor to propose terms of compromise or settlement within 21 days after service. The notice at the end of the demand sets out the debtor's options.

7. At Part B insert details of any assignment. If the creditor is entitled to the debt by way of assignment, the name and details of the original creditor and the date of the assignment should be provided. If appropriate, the chain of assignments must be set out.

5.1.5 Service of a statutory demand

IA 1986, ss.123(1) and 222(1) provide that the company is deemed unable to pay its debts if a statutory demand has been served upon the company 'by leaving it at the company's registered office' or 'its principal place of business' (in the case of an unregistered company) and thereafter the company has for three weeks neglected to meet the demand.

This would apparently rule out service by post, fax or email (see *Re a Company* [1985] BCLC 37). In addition, IA 1986, s.436B(2)(f) seems to suggest that the statutory demand must be in hard copy and cannot be in electronic form.

The question of whether service of a hard copy by post is an appropriate method of service was considered in *Re a Company (No.008790 of 1990)* [1992] BCC 11, where Morrit J observed that the statute does not specify who is to leave the demand at the company's registered office, and thus the creditor's agent – which could include the Royal Mail – could be deemed to have properly served the demand. Irrespective of this, Morrit J further held that if a company admitted that the statutory demand had been received, even if by post, the demand had been 'left at' the office and therefore properly served. In a more recent case it has been held that if no response was received in regard to a demand served by post, service cannot be proved (see *Re Galaxy Electro-Plating Factory Ltd* [2000] 1 HKLRD 876).

As a consequence, the creditor is best advised to serve the statutory demand at the company's registered office by the means which it would employ if it were serving a winding-up petition (IR 1986, rule 4.8(2)). This means that the premises of the registered office of the company should be attended and the demand:

(a)   handed to a person acknowledging himself to be a director;

(b)   handed to an officer or employee of the company authorised to accept service of documents on the company's behalf; or

(c)   left at the registered office in such a way that it is likely to come to the notice of such persons attending the office.

If none of the above methods of service are possible, or if the company is unregistered and has no registered office, a statutory demand may be served by leaving it at the company's last known principal place of business, in such a way that it is likely to come to the attention of any person attending there, or by delivering it to the company secretary, director, manager or principal officer of the company, wherever that person may be found.

If a process server or agent is being used, it is important that they have a good working knowledge of IR 1986 regarding service.

On being served, the debtor has 21 days in which to meet the demand, secure or compound it to the reasonable satisfaction of the creditor, persuade the creditor to withdraw or suspend the demand, or apply for injunctive relief to restrain the presentation of a petition based upon the demand. If the debtor company does nothing, it is deemed to be unable to pay its debts (IA 1986, ss.123(1)(a) and

222(1)); which is a ground on which the court may wind up the company (IA 1986, ss.122(1)(f) and 221(5)(b)).

The 21-day period begins after the day of service and consists of entire calendar days (*Re Lympne Investments Ltd* [1972] 1 WLR 523). A petition presented within the 21-day period where based on non-compliance with the demand will be dismissed (*Sri Hartamas Development Sdn Bhd* v. *MBf Finance Bhd* [1992] 1 MLJ 313).

The decision as to whether to proceed with the statutory demand and commence winding-up proceedings rests with the creditor who has served the demand, although, as stated above, evidence of non-compliance could be relied upon by another creditor, the directors, members or contributories to justify the presentation of a winding-up petition or voluntary winding up.

The creditor could therefore elect not to take any action after serving the demand, regarding it as a failed method of obtaining payment of its debt. However, in abusing the process in this way, the creditor must recognise that the service of the demand may have serious consequences for the debtor, who may regard the non-compliance with the demand as sufficient warning to cease trading and/or seek protection by some form of insolvency, or it may lead creditors such as secured creditors, lenders or landlords to take action.

The creditor can rely on the non-compliance with the demand at any time after the expiry of the demand (i.e. 21 days after service), but the longer the period between expiry of demand and the petition, the less likely the court will be to make a winding-up order. See *Deputy Commissioner of Taxation* v. *Cye International Pty Ltd (No.2)* (1985) 10 ACLR 305, where the presumption of deemed insolvency was said to elapse after six months (although this 'rule' was rejected in *Australia Card Services Pty Ltd* v. *JS Wallboards Pty Ltd* (1991) 5 ACSR 274); and also note that in personal insolvency, the rules specifically provide that evidence is required as to why the demand was not proceeded with within four months (IR 1986, rule 6.12(7)).

The option available to the creditor on the debtor's failure to satisfy or effectively challenge the demand, namely the compulsory winding-up petition, is discussed in **5.5**.

5.2 COMPANY VOLUNTARY ARRANGEMENTS (CVAS)

5.2.1 Creditor's position generally

The first a creditor may know of a proposed CVA is when it receives notice of a forthcoming creditors' meeting sent by an insolvency practitioner. With that notice the creditor will receive:

(a) an explanation of the rules governing the majorities required to approve the CVA;

(b) a copy of the directors' proposal;

(c)   a copy of the company's statement of affairs or, if the nominee thinks fit, a summary to include a list of creditors and the amounts of debt due;

(d)   the nominee's comments on the proposal; and

(e)   a form of proxy.

(See IR 1986, rule 1.9(3) (CVA without moratorium), rule 1.48(4) (CVA with moratorium).)

It is also not uncommon for the insolvency practitioner to send a proof of debt form with the notice, in order that the creditors may submit their claims. This is not a mandatory requirement, but it is a convenient method by which the insolvency practitioner can begin to assess whether a creditor will have a right to vote at the meeting and, if so, the respective value that is to be put on its claim/voting right.

Notice must be provided at least 14 days prior to the meeting and not more than 28 days from the date that the nominee's report was filed (unless an extension of any moratorium in place is obtained or the court orders otherwise).

The meeting must take place between 10 am and 4 pm on any business day in a place which is convenient for the creditors. Where the meeting of members is held on a different day from the meeting of creditors, it must be held first and no more than five business days in advance of the creditors' meeting. If it is held on the same day, the meeting needs to be in advance and in the same location (IR 1986, rule 1.13, as amended, Insolvency (Amendment) Rules 2003, SI 2003/1730 and Insolvency (Amendment) Rules 2010, SI 2010/686).

Checklist

Creditor's considerations on receiving a CVA proposal

- Is a moratorium in place? If not, is there time to take enforcement action?
- Is enforcement action commercially viable?
- Does the creditor possess security?
- What is the value of the creditor's debt?
- Has the creditor submitted a proof of its debt prior to the creditors' meeting?
- How has the chairman assessed the creditor's voting rights?
- Can the creditor determine the outcome of the creditors' meeting?
- Is it worthwhile for the creditor to approach other creditors?
- Can modifications to the proposal be put forward?
- Can the creditor challenge the outcome of the creditors' meeting?

Certain creditors may be approached by the insolvency practitioner, or the debtor, prior to the notice being sent. This informal 'sounding out' is a way for the insolvency practitioner to assess whether there is any possibility of the CVA being implemented. If the creditor is the majority creditor or one whose debts exceed 25 per cent of the total debt, this is a crucial step. If the creditor shows little inclination to accept the proposal, it is highly questionable whether the company and the insolvency practitioner should persist with the proposal.

On receiving either formal or informal notice of a proposed CVA, the creditor must assess the strength of its position and consider whether it is still possible for it to take action to enforce payment of its debt.

If a moratorium is in place, the creditor will be unable (except with leave of the court) to:

- take any form of enforcement proceedings;
- present a winding-up petition;
- make an administration application; or
- appoint an administrative receiver.

If no moratorium is in place, the creditor must decide whether there is enough time to take enforcement action prior to the creditors' meeting. However, if a winding-up petition is issued, the court is likely to stay that petition pending the meeting of creditors. There is also the issue of whether it is commercially viable to take enforcement action knowing that the company is probably unable to pay its debts. However, if the creditor is in a particularly strong commercial position and can force payment, perhaps because it is a key supplier to the company, it is possible that it can improve upon its position. The creditor therefore needs to consider the proposal carefully and assess how it will be treated, factoring into its decision its strength in terms of the voting rights at a meeting, i.e. is the creditor owed in excess of 25 per cent of the total debts? Will it be able to influence the outcome of the meeting?

The creditor may also wish to approach other creditors to see whether together they can exert control over the process and/or force modifications to the proposal. It should be remembered that modifications can be approved by the majority of creditors, although any modification will obviously require the consent of the company.

5.2.2   CVA and a secured creditor's position

A secured creditor continues to be entitled to enforce its security notwithstanding the existence of the CVA. It should be remembered that the CVA is concerned with the claims of unsecured creditors and the company cannot compromise the rights of a secured creditor without its consent.

The only instance where secured creditors' rights are affected is when a moratorium is obtained. A secured creditor obtains no prior notice of the company's intention to obtain a moratorium and while it is in place the consent of the court is required before enforcement action can be taken (IA 1986, Sched.A1, para.12). Furthermore, for the duration of the moratorium the crystallisation of any floating charge is suspended, as is any provision in the terms of the security which would impose on the company a restriction on its ability to dispose of property subject to the floating charge (IA 1986, Sched.A1, paras.13 and 43). These provisions at least allow the company time in which to structure a proposal to both unsecured and secured creditors.

'Security' as defined in IA 1986, s.248 means any mortgage, charge, lien (*Trident International Ltd* v. *Barlow* [2000] BCC 602 concerning a warehouseman's lien) or other form of security. A secured creditor is entitled to vote at the creditors' meeting if part of its debt remains unsecured. It is for the secured creditor to value its security and this is usually contained within the proof of debt form submitted to the nominee. The nominee as chairman of the meeting will consider the valuation and admit as he sees fit the partially unsecured debt, with appropriate voting rights.

If a secured creditor fails to disclose its security on a proof of debt it will be deemed to have surrendered its security for the general benefit of creditors unless the court relieves it from the effects of IR 1986, rule 4.96 on the grounds that the omission was inadvertent or the result of an honest mistake. This rule highlights the care that needs to be taken by a secured creditor in completing a proof of debt if it intends to gain some benefit from the terms of a CVA being put forward to unsecured creditors.

Most CVA proposals will contain provisions regarding how secured and partially secured creditors will be treated. However, the value attached to the security can be altered with the consent of the supervisor, or the leave of the court, even if the CVA is silent on the issue (see IR 1986, rule 4.95, and *Khan and Khan* v. *Mortgage Express* [2000] BPIR 473). The fact that a secured creditor has already received a dividend in respect of an anticipated shortfall does not preclude that creditor from later realising its security. This is particularly relevant to any bank holding a charge over a property which may well have risen in value from the date of the CVA to the date of eventual realisation. In such circumstances, the bank will simply give credit for the dividend received against the total debt.

It should be noted that in respect of any resolution to extend the moratorium or terminate it, secured and partially secured creditors can vote for the gross value of the claim without deducting the value of their security (IR 1986, rule 1.52(3)). As this shows, a creditor with security has a distinct advantage in the CVA procedure (which is replicated in much insolvency legislation), as collective rights and obligations are often superseded by proprietorial rights.

The strong position of the secured creditor is such that, in practical terms, the directors and insolvency practitioners are likely to consult closely with the secured creditors before putting forward any proposal. This may be commercially necessary to ensure that the secured creditor will not enforce its secured rights, making the continuation of the company's trading difficult, if not impossible. It should be remembered that often the terms of the security provide that an arrangement/compromise with a creditor is an event of default, entitling the secured creditor to realise its security.

Any security granted by a company while a moratorium is in force is unenforceable unless there are reasonable grounds for believing that it would benefit the company (IA 1986, Sched.A1, para.14). This provision, while in theory permitting new credit (and security), provides a disincentive to any party wishing to fund a company in such circumstances.

5.2.3 CVA and creditors in a unique position

Execution attachment

A creditor that has levied execution is not treated as having security. Generally, a creditor that has levied execution is not entitled to retain the benefit unless the execution is completed prior to commencement of a winding up (IA 1986, s.183). Similarly, a creditor that has obtained the benefit of execution will not be entitled to retain that benefit if the execution had not been completed prior to the commencement of the CVA moratorium. Completion of the execution is also the subject of an additional 14-day period in the case of chattel assets that have been seized and sold, i.e. if winding up or the moratorium is commenced within 14 days of such seizure and sale, the creditor is not entitled to retain the benefit. When the company is subject to a moratorium, the creditor is not entitled to continue with/complete any form of execution or distress.

Landlords

The law in this area has been significantly developed in recent years, due to rising levels of tenant financial distress, the depressed state of certain sectors of the real estate market and the clash between landlords and tenants seeking to restructure and, where possible, reduce leasehold liabilities.

In the case of *Thomas* v. *Ken Thomas Ltd* [2006] EWCA Civ 1504 the Court of Appeal had to determine whether a tenant company's attempt to bind its landlord into the terms of a CVA in respect of unpaid rent was effective. On the facts of the case, the Court of Appeal accepted the tenant's case that the landlord had waived his right to forfeit by accepting rent paid subsequently (despite the continuing existence of arrears). However, the court went on to consider the effect of the CVA on the landlord's right to forfeit.

The Court of Appeal considered two first instance decisions, that of *Re Naeem (a Bankrupt) (No.18 of 1988)* [1990] 1 WLR 48 and *March Estates plc* v. *Gunmark Ltd* [1996] 2 BCLC 1. In both instances, the court had determined that the CVA did not affect the landlord's proprietary right to forfeit.

However, the Court of Appeal held that a CVA is concerned with obligations not remedies. If the rent obligation is consumed within the CVA then all remedies must be modified. To allow the landlord the right to commence proceedings for forfeiture in respect of sums payable within the terms of a CVA was inconsistent with a rescue culture. The effect of the CVA (i.e. a statutory binding) means that the rent is no longer deemed owing from the tenant to the landlord and there is therefore no right to forfeit. Furthermore, as a landlord's right to forfeit is not a secured right (see *Re Lomax Leisure* [2000] BCC 352) as an unsecured creditor, a landlord could be bound within the terms of the CVA.

In respect of future rent, Mr Justice Neuberger felt that to bind a landlord in respect of future rent in a CVA was potentially unreasonable and unfairly prejudicial.

This case was followed by that of *Prudential Assurance Co. Ltd* v. *PRG Powerhouse Ltd* [2007] EWHC 1002 (Ch), where an insolvent electrical retailer proposed to save 53 stores using a CVA. Under the terms of the CVA, employees, local authorities and other creditors (including landlords) of the closed stores would share a pot of money provided by the parent company of £1.5 million. The remaining creditors would be paid out of the trading receipts of the reconstructed business.

The reasoning behind this proposal was that the business was hopelessly insolvent and the landlords would receive nothing from liquidation due to the very large deficiency owed to the parent company, which had made significant secured loans to the retail chain. The £1.5 million payment therefore allowed the landlords time to re-let the stores to be closed and saved the core of the company's business. Importantly for some of the landlords, the CVA proposals also sought to release the parent company from liability in respect of guarantees given on granting of the lease to its subsidiary. It was argued that if the guarantees were called upon the parent might be unable to support the newly reconstructed business.

At the creditors' meeting, the CVA was approved but the landlords of the closed stores immediately challenged it. The court was asked to determine two preliminary issues:

1. Were the guarantees given by the parent released by reason of the CVA?
2. If so, was this unfairly prejudicial?

It was common ground that IA 1986 does not deal expressly with the position of guarantors and co-debtors. The position is, however, reasonably clear under common law. Once a debt is released, a guarantor will no longer be liable to discharge it (*Commercial Bank of Tasmania* v. *Jones* [1893] AC 313). However, if the guarantee contains an express provision that the guarantee would be unaffected by indulgence/release of principal debtor, there is no automatic release.

The treatment of guarantors under the terms of a voluntary arrangement was considered in *Johnson* v. *Davies* [1999] Ch 117. This case established the principle that a voluntary arrangement did not have the effect of automatically releasing a co-debtor, but that the terms of a voluntary arrangement could be such as to effect the release of a guarantee without the creditor's consent. The practice since then has therefore been to look closely at the terms of the CVA to see how guarantors are treated.

It was held, however, that each creditor was a party to the CVA as a creditor of the company and that a CVA is a special form of contract between the debtor and the creditors. It is not a contract between one creditor and another or between a creditor and a third party. As a result, the terms of the CVA cannot affect the rights and obligations between a creditor and a third party; the terms of the CVA did not therefore give rise to an automatic release of the guarantees.

The court held, however, that it is entirely possible for a CVA to provide that a creditor cannot take steps to claim from a third party where that third party may have a right of recourse against the debtor, i.e. the fact that the guarantor could then claim repayment from the debtor may defeat the purpose of the CVA. While such a clause has no direct effect as between the creditor and the third party, it could in theory be enforced by the debtor to block claims against the guarantor.

In *Powerhouse*, after determining that the CVA did indeed release the parent company from its guarantees, the court went on to question whether this was unfairly prejudicial, affording the landlords a right of challenge capable of over-turning the CVA. The court held that there was no single test for unfairness and instead it needed to look at all circumstances of the case in exercise of its discretion. Etherton J carried out both a vertical comparison (i.e. what is the effect of the CVA as opposed to other insolvency procedures?) and a horizontal comparison (i.e. what is the treatment of other creditors under the CVA?).

Generally, the debtor needs to establish that the CVA offers the best available alternative and that creditors are being treated fairly. The fact that one creditor is being treated differently is not in itself enough for the CVA to be deemed unfair; instead the court should move on to balance the interests of that creditor against the interests of the creditors as a whole.

In the *Powerhouse* case it was held that the landlords of the closed stores were left in a worse position: in the case of liquidation they had lost a potential valuable guarantee against a solvent third party (namely the parent company guarantor); in respect of a s.425 Companies Act scheme of arrangement they would have been treated as a separate class of creditor. They were also being treated unfairly when compared with other creditors in that their dividend was calculated without reference to the value of the guarantees. The effect of the CVA was therefore held to be unfairly prejudicial.

In the case of *Cotswold Company Ltd* [2009] EWHC 1151 (Ch) the tenant company owed arrears of rent and service charges when it vacated its leasehold premises. In order to try to re-let the premises, the landlord was prepared to enter into a deed of surrender, releasing the tenant company from all claims under the lease except the right to claim within the CVA (which was being proposed to the tenant's creditors).

The CVA was approved and the landlord submitted a proof of debt, claiming full rent and service charges for an anticipated void period, one year's rent (representing the anticipated rent-free period that would be needed to induce a new tenant), rent to the end of term less discount and a dilapidations claim.

The supervisor rejected the claim, save for arrears up to the date of the surrender, on the basis that the deed had extinguished the lease and therefore the tenant's future obligations under it.

The landlord's appeal against this decision was successful on the grounds that its rights to claim in the CVA had been expressly reserved, despite the fact that the deed had put an end to the lease and the covenants within it. The court found that the landlord had accepted the surrender solely to mitigate the loss caused by the tenant's insolvency. The court went on to hold that although the final sum for future rent, etc. depended on the ability of the landlord to re-let, the landlord's claim could be admitted into the CVA and compromised. The claim would need to be assessed by the supervisor (in the usual manner re future, prospective and contingent claims); it was irrelevant that the claim was unliquidated and unascertained at the date of the CVA.

Despite the result, this case shows that specific provision must be included in any deed of surrender to ensure that a landlord retains a right to claim future rent and obligations in the CVA. Care is required when drafting a deed of surrender in the context of a tenant's insolvency, and likewise a nominee/supervisor may need to have regard to possible claims that could be brought by an ex-landlord, even where the lease has been extinguished by deed of surrender.

In *Mourant & Co. Trustees Ltd* v. *Sixty UK Ltd (in administration)* [2010] EWHC 1890 (Ch), Miss Sixty, a women's fashion retail chain, proposed a CVA as an exit route from administration. This was challenged on the grounds of unfair prejudice and material irregularity by the landlords of two retail units.

The CVA sought to distinguish open store landlords, that would effectively have been unaffected by the proposal, from closed store landlords, that would receive a sum in the CVA which should have been a genuine estimate of the surrender value of the leases.

As in the *Powerhouse* case, the parent company, which had provided guarantees to the landlords, was willing to fund the CVA provided it was released from the guarantees for a one-off compensatory payment of £300,000 (it said this represented the company's liability on surrender).

At the hearing, Henderson J applied the vertical and horizontal analysis provided in *Powerhouse*, finding that:

1. In the event of liquidation, the landlords of the closed stores would have had a continuing ability to call on the parent company guarantee and hence the CVA was unfairly prejudicial to their position (vertical analysis).

2. In contrast with other creditors (the parent and connected companies were not bound by the terms of the CVA), the landlords of the closed stores were treated unfairly (horizontal analysis).

The judge was very critical of the administrators (who did not attend the hearing), saying that the compensation figure was not a genuine estimate of the value of the company's liability on surrender and the administrators had misled creditors into believing that this was a figure reached after professional advice. The case followed the *Powerhouse* approach, but is also a salutary reminder to insolvency practitioners to remain objective and to consider the interests of all the creditors in putting forward a proposal, not to be led by the commercial imperative of the funding party.

We are left, post-*Powerhouse/Sixty UK Ltd*, with an analysis of CVA terms on a case-by-case basis, i.e. how does the CVA treat arrears of rent/future rent and guarantees and are the terms unfair to the landlord?

It should be noted that *Powerhouse* did not rule out the possibility that parent company guarantees can be avoided through the use of a CVA (a fact noted in *Sixty UK Ltd*). The cases establish no more than the need to take account of the value of landlord's claim and treat the landlord fairly.

In any corporate reconstruction involving leasehold property, the matter of consensual compromise remains one within the commercial judgment of the landlord, which may be willing to discuss with the nominee revised (reduced) terms of payment if there is a real possibility of the tenant's insolvency and/or inability easily to re-let the premises. In such circumstances, they may be prepared to consider claims being compromised within the CVA. This calls on the nominee to negotiate with the landlord rather than seeking to bind this creditor into the CVA against its will.

An example of an unsuccessful attempt to use a CVA by an insolvent tenant to bind its landlords to a plan of reconstruction was seen in early 2009 in Stylo plc, the owners of the Barratts and Shoeless retail chains. Landlords objecting to their treatment as ordinary trade creditors voted down the CVA proposal, probably more in fear of setting a precedent which would see tenanted retail chains ditch unprofitable stores than as a judgment on the commercial terms of the proposal.

It was against this background that there was a rise in use of administration and, in particular, pre-pack administration sales in this area (indeed, this is exactly what occurred in the case of Stylo after the rejection of the CVA). In such cases the administrator would often provide the purchaser of the business with an (unlawful) licence to occupy the premises without referring to the landlord, which is then prevented from acting upon any breach of the lease without the consent of the administrator or leave of the court. This practice was seen in a number of high-profile retail cases (in e.g. Whittards, Officer's Club, Card Warehouse, Oasis, Karen Millen) and has been heavily criticised by some landlords.

An administrator will, however, now need to think very carefully about taking such action – as where the property is being used for the benefit of the creditors/purpose of the administration, rent falling due as and when the 'administrator' is in occupation will be a cost and expense of the administration (contrast the discretionary approach to rent as a cost and expense in *Innovate Logistics* v. *Sunberry Properties* [2008] EWCA Civ 1321 with the mandatory approach of *Goldacre (Offices) Ltd* v. *Nortel Networks UK Ltd (in administration)* [2009] EWHC 3389 (Ch)). This change has once again encouraged the use of the CVA as a means of restructuring a tenanted property portfolio where, as we have seen, careful drafting and negotiation with the landlords is necessary to ensure that the treatment of the landlords in the CVA is not seen to be unfairly prejudicial and capable of being set aside.

5.2.4 CVA and a connected creditor's position

The chairman of the meeting must also consider whether any creditors are connected to the debtor. It should be remembered that the majority required at the creditors' meeting to approve the proposal is over 50 per cent of the unconnected unsecured creditors that have given notice of their claim to the chairman and 75 per cent of the value of all unsecured creditors.

The purpose of this is to ensure that creditors connected with the debtor do not overreach the decision of the majority of unconnected creditors. The chairman, in deciding whether a person is connected to the debtor, is entitled to rely on the information contained in the company's statement of affairs (IR 1986, rules 1.19(5) and 1.52(6) (CVA with moratorium)). The chairman's decision on whether the creditor is connected to the debtor is subject to appeal (IR 1986, rule 1.19(7)).

A person is deemed connected to the company if he is a director, shadow director or associate of the company (IA 1986, s.249). 'Associate' is widely defined (IA 1986, s.435) to include a husband, wife, civil partner, relative, employee or partner, and also includes connected companies, i.e. one where the same person has control of both debtor and creditor or one associate has control of one or other (IA 1986, s.435(6)). A company holding shares on a bare trust under which the beneficiary directs the voting rights is not deemed to be an associate by reason of the shareholding (*Unidare plc* v. *Cohen and Power* [2005] BPIR 1472).

5.2.5 CVA and a guarantor's position

A guarantor of a debtor is a contingent creditor of the debtor. Therefore, notice of the creditors' meeting must be given to the guarantor as well as to the principal creditor. The question that remains is how to treat the voting rights of the principal creditor and the guarantor, if in fact it is the same debt. This can lead to difficult questions for the chairman when determining voting rights. He may need to consider whether the guarantor has paid/will pay the debt in full, whether the guarantor has rights of subrogation and/or whether the principal creditor will receive an anticipated dividend.

This assessment is tied to another question which needs to be addressed, namely whether the potential compromise of the principal debt within the CVA has any effect on the guarantor's liability. It was initially thought that the CVA could not affect the creditor's right against the third party, as the CVA is a statutory binding agreement as opposed to a consensual one (*RA Securities Ltd* v. *Mercantile Credit Co. Ltd* [1994] 3 All ER 581). However, in the case of *Johnson* v. *Davies* (1998) BPIR 607 it was held that as there was deemed creditor consent to the CVA, whether there was a release of a guarantor was in each case dependent on the terms of the CVA. If the CVA operated as an absolute and unconditional release of the debt in question without reservation, the guarantor could be released. It should be noted, however, that in such circumstances the creditor might lose a valuable right of action against a solvent third party and hence could seek to challenge the CVA on grounds of unfair prejudice. (See *Prudential Assurance* v. *PRG Powerhouse* [2007] EWHC 1002 (Ch) for an example of such a successful challenge.) As a result, the standard conditions of a CVA often provide that a guarantor's liabilities are not released. It is of course open to the debtor to deal with how the guarantee is treated in the proposal, i.e. the guarantor could waive the right to dividends. It should also be remembered that a guarantor would not be liable to receive a dividend unless it had paid all of the guaranteed debt, as rights of subrogation do not arise until the full debt is paid.

5.2.6 Valuation of the creditor's claim

The directors of the company will inform the nominee/proposed supervisor of the meeting of the company's creditors. Details of creditors have to be contained in the statement of affairs, which will also include the directors' valuation of each debt. It is, however, for the creditors to establish their debt with the insolvency practitioner, providing as much information as is possible in order for the chairman of the meeting to put a value on the debt (*Re Hoare* [1997] BPIR 683). The debt is calculated as at the date of the meeting or at the commencement of the liquidation or administration if the CVA is proposed by a liquidator or administrator (IR 1986, rule 1.17(2)).

However, it may often be difficult to quantify the creditor's claim. This may be as a result of a genuine dispute as to the amount owed, or the debt may in some way be contingent or as yet unliquidated. It should of course be noted that the creditor's claim for voting rights can be different from the value of the claim at the time that a dividend is payable. However, some creditors with a prospective unliquidated debt may feel aggrieved that the CVA may be approved contrary to their wishes, as their claim has yet to be established. As explained below, some relief may be available to such aggrieved creditors.

In the past, a creditor could not vote if a claim was unliquidated or uncertain, except where the chairman agreed to put on an estimated minimum value for the purpose of entitlement to vote (IR 1986, rule 1.17(3)). The rules now provide that the creditor of an unliquidated or uncertain debt should have the debt valued at £1 (for voting purposes only), unless the chairman of the meeting agrees to put a higher value on it (see *Re Cranley Mansions Ltd* [1994] BCC 576 and *Doorbar* v. *Alltime Securities Ltd* [1996] 1 WLR 456). The creditor's consent to this valuation is not required, although the chairman should take reasonable steps to investigate the claim and, if satisfied that he can safely attribute a sum greater than £1, he should do so (*Newlands (Seaford) Educational Trust* [2007] BCC 195). The chairman is not, however, a lawyer and should not speculate on likely results at a hypothetical trial.

If a creditor is dissatisfied with the value placed on the claim for voting purposes, and it is the case that a higher value could be determinative of the proposal, he can appeal (IR 1986, rule 1.17A(3)) to court or present a challenge on grounds of material irregularity (IA 1986, s.6(1); see **5.2.7**).

Where there is a genuine dispute to the debt (either by the company or by other creditors), the claim ought to be admitted but marked as disputed (IR 1986, rule 1.17A(4)). If it is clearly apparent to the chairman there is no real dispute the claim should be admitted, whereas if it is clear that the claim is bad it should be rejected.

The chairman is not, however, obliged to perform a quasi-judicial role in assessment of claims and is therefore best advised where there is any doubt to mark the claim as disputed (*Re a Debtor (No.222 of 1990)* [1992] BCLC 137).

5.2.7   Challenge to approved CVA

Any creditor aggrieved by a decision of the chairman on the question of voting rights has 28 days from the filing of the chairman's report at court to appeal (IR 1986, rule 1.17A(6)) (see *Tager* v. *Westpac Banking Corporation* [1997] BPIR 543 on allowing extensions of time to appeal). If on appeal the chairman's decision is reversed or varied, the court may order another meeting to be summoned or make such other order as thinks fit (IR 1986, rule 1.17A(5)).

In this section we look more closely at other grounds of challenge which may overlap with this right of appeal, namely the statutory rights of challenge (IA 1986, s.6) on the basis of unfair prejudice or material irregularity.

Guide to procedure

Challenging an approved CVA

1. Within 28 days (of the report of the meeting being filed or creditors being aware of the meeting), applicant issues originating application (in Form 7.1) on grounds of unfair prejudice and/or material irregularity supported by evidence in a witness statement.
2. If the applicant is the liquidator or administrator, the application can be without notice.
3. If the applicant is a nominee, no notice will need to be given unless the company is in liquidation or subject to administration.
4. If the applicant is a person entitled to vote at the creditors' meeting, notice will be provided to the nominee, who will generally be the respondent acting as agent for the debtor company.
5. The applicant serves a copy of the sealed application endorsed with a date of hearing on the respondent not less than 14 days prior to hearing.
6. The applicant files a witness statement and/or affidavit serving a copy on the respondent not less than 14 days prior to hearing.
7. The respondent files any witness statement in reply and serves a copy upon the applicant, not less than seven days before hearing.
8. The applicant and respondent attend the hearing, at which the registrar may give such directions as he thinks fit and/or adjourn the matter to a judge in court.
9. The applicant lodges copy application and original application in court for use by the judge.
10. The applicant and respondent attend adjourned application in court.
11. The court hears the application and makes such an order as it thinks fit.
12. The court draws up the order and sends a copy to the applicant.
13. The applicant serves order upon the:

    (a) supervisor of the CVA;
    (b) directors of the company (or administrator/liquidator, if applicable); and
    (c) if the court directs a further meeting, on whoever is required to summon the meeting.

14. The directors (administrator/liquidator, if applicable) give notice of order to all persons given notice of the meeting.
15. Within seven days, the directors (administrator/liquidator if applicable) give notice to the court of intention to make revised proposal.
16. Within seven days, applicant delivers copy of the order to the Registrar of Companies.

A possible challenge to the decision reached at a creditors' meeting can be made by:

(a) any person entitled to vote at the meeting;
(b) any person who would have been entitled to vote had he received notice;
(c) the nominee, or any person replacing the nominee; or
(d) the liquidator or administrator of the company, if it is being wound up, or is in administration.

The circumstances in which the challenges are made are many and various, e.g. by a creditor:

- aggrieved at the valuation of its claim and subsequent approval of the arrangement;
- which failed to receive notice of the proposal and objects to the terms of the arrangement;
- which considers that it is being unfairly treated/prejudiced when compared with other creditors;
- which has a unique financial position *vis-à-vis* the debtor company which has been unfairly compromised;
- which considers that approval has been obtained by fraud, deceit, use of connected parties' voting rights; or
- which considers that the meeting was conducted unfairly.

However, the challenge must fall within one or other of two legal grounds:

(a) That the voluntary arrangement which had been approved unfairly prejudices the interests of a creditor, member or contributory of the company; and/or
(b) That there has been some material irregularity at or in relation to either of the meetings (IA 1986, s.6(1)).

An application must be made within 28 days beginning on the date on which the reports of the meeting were filed at court. This remains the case even if it subsequently transpires that there was some irregularity in the conduct of the meeting itself, or a creditor only subsequently considered that it had been prejudiced. It is possible that the creditor did not actually fully comprehend how it might be prejudiced when the arrangement was put forward.

Since creditors may be bound to the terms of the arrangement, even if they have not had notice of the meeting, if a person was not first given notice of the creditors' meeting, that person has 28 days beginning on the day on which he became aware that a meeting had taken place (IA 1986, s.6.3(b)).

If the court is satisfied on either of the grounds set out in IA 1986, s.6(1), it may:

(a) revoke or suspend any decision approving a voluntary arrangement; and/or
(b) give directions as to further summoning of meetings (IA 1986, s.6(5)).

A challenge is less likely to be successful if the creditor did not possess sufficient voting power to affect the outcome of the meeting. Furthermore, when considering whether a creditor has been unfairly prejudiced, the court has to look beyond whether the creditor is receiving less than it would have done on the liquidation and have regard to the position of the creditors generally.

The person who has applied to court under this section must serve copies of the application on the supervisor and/or directors of the company (or, if appropriate, the liquidator or administrator). A copy of the order must also be sent to the Registrar of Companies (together with Form 1.2) within seven days of the date of the order.

Unfair prejudice

The issue of unfair prejudice has been considered in the specific situation of tenant insolvency (see **5.2.3**, Landlords). The term 'unfair prejudice', however, is not defined within IA 1986 and IR 1986.

It should be remembered that the terms of the CVA may in some way legitimately prejudice the interests of some creditors over others. Indeed, any arrangement which entails creditors receiving less than their total debt due could be seen to be prejudicial. To be capable of challenge, however, the prejudice must in some way be regarded as unfair (*Swindon Town Properties Ltd* v. *Swindon Town Football Club Co. Ltd* [2003] BPIR 253).

'Unfair prejudice' may occur if there is differing treatment of creditors which would otherwise rank *pari passu*, although it is not always unfair to make a differentiation in the treatment of members of the same class (see *Re Cancol Ltd* [1996] 1 All ER 37; *Inland Revenue Commissioners* v. *Wimbledon Football Club Ltd* [2004] BCC 638; and *HMRC* v. *Portsmouth City FC* [2011] BCC 149, the later two cases involving the preferential treatment afforded to 'football creditors' and also evidencing the courts' reluctance to interfere with the commercial realities facing the insolvent company).

A successful challenge was seen in *Re Gatnom Capital & Finance Ltd* [2010] EWHC 3353 (Ch), where the court found that a certain creditor's claim should have been excluded as the transactions on which the claims were based were a sham, so the CVA was unfairly prejudicial to the other creditors. A challenge may also occur when a creditor's rights over and above those enjoyed by other creditors are curtailed (such as rights against an insurer: *Sea Voyager Martime Inc* v. *Bielecki* [1999] 1 All ER 628, or a guarantor: *Johnson* v. *Davies* [1998] BPIR 607; *Prudential Assurance* v. *PRG Powerhouse* [2007] EWHC 1002 (Ch); and *Mourant* v. *Sixty UK Ltd* [2010] BCC 882).

The court needs to weigh up the prejudice caused to the individual creditor against the collective advantage to the company and the rest of its creditors, to assess whether the prejudice is 'unfair'.

Material irregularity

Examples of irregularities which could occur during the course of the meeting are many and various. There could be a failure to notify one or more creditors of the meeting or a mistake in the assessment of voting rights, i.e. admitting a debt which is not otherwise due or vice versa (*Roberts* v. *Pinnacle Entertainment Ltd* [2004] BPIR 208). The provision of false or misleading information or an omission of material information may amount to a material irregularity (*Cadbury Schweppes plc* v. *Somji* [2001] 1 WLR 615 and *Re Bradburn* v. *Kaye* [2006] BPIR 605). It should also be remembered that the making of false representations by an officer of the company in order to gain approval of a CVA is an offence punishable by fine or imprisonment (IA 1986, s.6A).

To prevent a deluge of applications based on technical errors in the meeting, an irregularity must be 'material', i.e. one which, objectively assessed, would have made a difference to the voting at the creditors' meeting (see *Re a Debtor (No.259 of 1990)* [1992] 1 WLR 226 and *Trident Fashions plc*, sub nom. *Anderson* v. *Kroll Ltd* [2004] EWHC 351 (Ch)).

However, the fact that a sole creditor may have been omitted from voting at the creditors' meeting and even if it had been given notice of the meeting, could not have altered the outcome of the vote, does not necessarily render the irregularity immaterial. It all depends upon the circumstances of the case, e.g. whether the excluded creditor could have persuaded other creditors to change their minds. While many creditors will have made up their minds and will submit proxies, a number of creditors attend creditors' meetings and are swayed by the arguments put forward there.

Procedure

An application to challenge the approval of the CVA is made by a party (i.e. those specified in IA 1986, s.6(2)) issuing an originating application supported by evidence. The application will be heard by a registrar or district judge, unless the case is complex, in which case it will be adjourned to a judge in open court. The court may direct that any relevant party attend court for cross-examination and may make orders for disclosure for further information to be provided.

If the application is on grounds of unfair prejudice, the nominee and other creditors should not normally be the respondents to the application, although it is particularly important to give the nominee notice of the application (see *Re Naeem (a Bankrupt) (No.18 of 1998)* [1990] 1 WLR 48).

The costs of a successful application will be paid out of the debtor's estate unless there has been some conduct on the part of the nominee which will justify a costs order being made against them.

If the ground upon which the application is successful is that there was a material irregularity at the meeting, the nominee/chairman of the meeting may be ordered to pay the wasted costs (see *Harmony Carpets* v. *Chaffin-Laird* [2000] BPIR 61) and a direction made that at any subsequent meeting he should be replaced (*IRC* v. *Duce* [1999] BPIR 189). However, where a chairman has acted in good faith and has simply made an error, usually no order will be made against him (see *Re Cranley Mansions Ltd* [1995] 1 BCLC 290).

Where a court makes an order revoking or suspending the CVA, the applicant is required to, within seven days, serve sealed copies of the order on:

(a)   the directors, liquidator or administrator (according to who put forward the proposal);
(b)   the supervisor of the CVA;
(c)   the person required to summon the meeting of creditors (if different); and
(d)   the Registrar of Companies.

The company's directors must within seven days of receiving the order revoking the arrangement give notice to the court as to whether or not they intend to submit a revised proposal and/or summon a further hearing. If they fail to do so the matter ends there.

The court may revoke or suspend any decision approving the CVA with or without giving directions for the summoning of a further meeting. If the court orders a revocation of the original CVA, it remains open to the debtor company to propose a fresh scheme. The court may, however, direct any person to summon a further meeting. This does not necessarily mean that the original nominee will put forward the new proposal and indeed the court could order another insolvency practitioner to summon this meeting (*IRC* v. *Duce* [1989] BPIR 189).

The court does not have the power to grant proposals subject to modifications or propose modifications for the proposal (*Re Alpa Lighting Ltd* [1997] BPIR 341). It should be remembered that the proposals are always made by the directors to the company and it remains for the company to accept or reject a proposal with the modifications suggested by the creditors. However, if the company refuses to accept the modifications, there will be no CVA.

Any creditor (or other person) dissatisfied with any act, omission or decision of the supervisor may apply to court for relief (IA 1986, s.7(3); see *County Bookshops Ltd* v. *Grove* [2002] BPIR 772).

Once the CVA is approved, its implementation is largely governed by the terms of the arrangement. It is open to the supervisor to apply to the court for directions on any matter arising under the CVA (IA 1986, s.7(4)), but as set out above this is in respect of issues of construction and application of the arrangement being proposed; the court cannot direct variations to the proposals.

If the arrangement is deemed to have failed, the supervisor may apply to wind up the company in the name of the company (IA 1986, s.7(4)(b); see *Re Arthur Rathbone Kitchens Ltd* [1998] BCC 450; and on the treatment of the CVA and its creditors post winding up, see *Re NT Gallagher & Sons Ltd* [2002] 1 WLR 2380).

5.3 ADMINISTRATION

5.3.1 Introduction

The considerations that a creditor should bear in mind when claiming a debt were dealt with in **5.1.3**. The remainder of this chapter concentrates on the circumstances where enforcement procedures and/or the service of a statutory demand has failed to elicit payment of the debt and focuses on the initiation by a creditor of the three key corporate insolvency procedures: administration, administrative receivership and liquidation.

Checklist

Considerations by creditor on possibility of corporate debtor's insolvency
Adviser's checklist

1. Has the debtor company disputed or admitted liability in respect of the unpaid debt?
2. Has the debtor made any proposals for payment?
3. Does the creditor possess security for the debt?
4. Is the security valid?
5. What is the nature of the security?
6. Does the security cover the full value of the debt?
7. Does the creditor want the security discharged?
8. Does the security entitle the creditor to appoint an administrative receiver?
9. Does the security entitle the creditor to appoint an administrator?
10. What is the position of other creditors, both secured and unsecured?
11. If the creditor is unsecured, what is the possibility of there being any recovery from the liquidation of the debtor company?

On bringing a claim for payment, particularly where a statutory demand has been served and not complied with, the insolvent company may of its own initiative commence insolvency proceedings. This scenario is dealt with in **Chapter 3**. However, it is very often the case that the directors of the company bury their heads in the sand and hope that creditor claims will go away. Alternatively, the company may be able to pay, although it may need to liquidate some assets, but may remain unwilling to do so. It may require the commencement of an insolvency procedure in order for it to realise assets to pay off the creditor's claim. However, using an insolvency procedure to collect debt is a high-risk strategy. Administration and liquidation are collective procedures, conducted for the general benefit of creditors.

The fact that a creditor has initiated the procedure does not put it in any better position than any other unsecured creditor and it will not ensure payment of the principal debt. Furthermore, once the procedure is initiated, the creditor will lose some or all control of the process (particularly relevant in the case of compulsory liquidation). As a consequence, the return to the creditor of any of its debt by initiation of an insolvency procedure is uncertain.

The position of unsecured creditors should be contrasted with that of secured creditors. In the UK, considerable weight in the insolvency process is held by those who possess security for their debt. This is in respect of both the initiation of remedies deriving from their security (e.g. receivership) and their power and control over other insolvency procedures (e.g. administration and liquidation).

However, it should be remembered that receivership is not strictly an insolvency procedure, as it lacks a collective approach to the problems of corporate insolvency. It remains a remedy open solely to secured creditors and is a method of realising secured assets in settlement of the debt. The roots of receivership lie in equitable remedies granted by the courts in the sixteenth century. In more modern times, receivership has almost exclusively been a matter of contractual agreement, a development which arose due to the practice in the nineteenth century of including provisions in charge documentation which permitted a lender to appoint a receiver without reference to the court. The appointment of a receiver by private remedy therefore quickly overtook the use of court-appointed receivers.

The Enterprise Act 2002 reforms have meant that (save in very limited circumstances), in respect of security created after 15 September 2003, it is no longer possible for secured creditors to appoint an administrative receiver. As a result, we have seen a dramatic fall in the use of administrative receivership, which has been accompanied by a rise in use of the new administration procedure. As we shall see, despite reform of the insolvency regime the powers to appoint a non-administrative receiver remain unaffected and, although strictly outside the scope of this work (as it is an enforcement method as opposed to insolvency procedure), this option is discussed further in **5.4**.

5.3.2 Out-of-court appointment by a qualifying floating charge holder

Guide to procedure

1. If appropriate, the holder of a qualifying floating charge (the appointor) should prepare and file at court a notice of intention to appoint an administrator (in Form 2.5B).
2. At the same time as filing the notice of intention, two days' notice must be provided to any prior floating charge holder, giving them two clear days' notice of the proposed appointment.
3. If the prior floating charge holder consents or fails to reply, the appointor will prepare a notice of appointment of an administrator (Form 2.6B).
4. The appointor or representative must provide a statutory declaration (contained in Form 2.6), which cannot be made more than five days prior to appointment.

5. The notice of appointment is filed at court with three copies.
6. The notice of appointment should be accompanied by:

   • an administrator's statement (in Form 2.2B); and
   • evidence that notice has been given.

7. The court will issue two sealed copies of the notice of appointment to the appointor, who must as soon as reasonably practicable send one to the administrator.
8. If the appointment is sought out of court hours, notice of appointment will be by Form 2.7B.

Following the Enterprise Act 2002 reforms, from 15 September 2003 the holder of a qualifying floating charge may appoint an administrator by the out-of-court procedure set out IA 1986, Sched.B1, paras.14–21; see also IR 1986, rules 2.15–2.18.

These provisions are in large part a replacement of the previous ability of a holder of a floating charge to appoint an administrative receiver (see IA 1986, s.72(A)(1)), and offer a quick and efficient means by which a debtor company can be placed into administration. However, as we shall see, there are some risks in using the procedure and disadvantages to the secured creditor:

1. The statutory purpose of administration has a three-tier layer of objectives. It is only after the first two objectives have become not reasonably practicable that the administrator can simply realise property to make a distribution to the secured creditors.
2. In discharging his general duties, the administrator must act in the interests of the company's creditors as a whole (subject to the above caveat). An administrative receiver's primary duties are owed to the appointor.
3. The administrative receivership procedure is still regarded as quicker and cheaper than administration. Despite legislative improvements, this generally remains the case.
4. The administrator's actions/decisions are open to a wider degree of challenge from the general body of creditors than is the case with an administrative receiver.
5. Prior to IA 1986, s.176ZA coming into force, liquidation expenses could not be recovered from floating charge realisations (see *Buchler* v. *Talbot; Re Leyland DAF Ltd* [2004] UKHL 9). Administration expenses can be recovered from the floating charge realisations.
6. There are tax disadvantages to sale in administration as opposed to administrative receivership, namely any chargeable gain (IR 1986, rule 2.67(1)(j)) or income (Taxes Management Act 1970, s.108(3)(a)) is taxable and payable as an expense of the administration.
7. Non-domestic rates are payable as an expense of the administration (*Exeter City Council* v. *Bairstow* [2007] EWHC 400 (Ch)); they are not an expense of administrative receivership or a non-administrative receivership.

8.   The inflexibility and application of the costs and expense rule in administration.

These drawbacks may explain why in practice there has been some reluctance to use the process (research indicates that where there is an effective choice between a directors' or floating charge holder appointment, fewer than one in five appointments are made by secured creditors).

5.3.3   Does the appointor possess a qualifying floating charge?

As we shall see below, the use of the out-of-court route (as the description implies) involves little or no judicial intervention. As a result, despite the fact that the due process for appointment may have been followed and all parties have assumed that the administrator's appointment is valid, if the security pursuant to which the appointment is made is not a qualifying floating charge, the appointment is void *ab initio*.

There are three important considerations to determine whether the appointor does possess a qualifying floating charge:

1.   Does the secured creditor possess a floating charge?
2.   Is it a 'qualifying' floating charge?
3.   Is the qualifying floating charge enforceable?

Each is examined below.

What is a floating charge?

The statutory definition of a floating charge (IA 1986, s.251: 'floating charge' means a charge which as created was a floating charge) is singularly un-illuminating.

In practice, one will find a debenture containing both fixed and floating charges over the borrower company's assets. The statutory definition does, however, confirm that the fact that the floating charge may well become fixed on crystallisation is irrelevant, as it is defined by reference to its nature at the date of creation. It should always be remembered that whether the company's assets are secured by fixed or floating charge is a matter of substance, not form.

In determining whether the asset is subject to a fixed or floating charge, one can first look to the classic formulation, provided by Lord Justice Romer in the case of *Re Yorkshire Woolcombers Association Ltd* [1903] 2 Ch 284. In this case a floating charge was described as one:

*   which attaches to a class of assets of the company, present and future;
*   where that class of assets changes from time to time; and
*   where the company is entitled to carry on business and deal with those assets unless or until some step is taken by the chargee.

In the landmark decision of *National Westminster Bank plc* v. *Spectrum Plus Ltd* [2005] UKHL 41 it was held that in determining whether a charge was fixed or floating, the court should be engaged in a two-stage process:

1.   The intention of the parties in entering into the charge must be construed according to the language used. The object is not to discover whether the parties intended to create a fixed or floating charge, but to ascertain the rights and obligations which the parties intended to grant each other in respect of the charged assets.

2.   Once this is determined, the court should categorise the charge by reference to those rights and obligations, not by reference to what the parties may or may not have intended. Consequently, if the parties have granted borrower's rights which were inconsistent with the nature of the fixed charge, the charge cannot be fixed, however so described (see also *Re Brumark Investments Ltd*, sub nom. *Agnew* v. *Inland Revenue Commissioner* [2001] 2 BCLC 188).

Despite the fact that the majority of the company's assets may be charged under a fixed charge, providing there is a floating charge over the remainder of the company's assets, the appointment will be as administrator (see *Re Croftbell Ltd* [1990] BCLC 844, a case concerning the appointment of an administrative receiver). Indeed, it is often the case that the floating charges are no more than so-called lightweight charges 'over all other assets of the company'. In reality, the realisable value of these other assets may be negligible, but it will give the floating charge holder the option of appointing an administrator. If, however, the appointment is under the fixed charge element of the security, despite contrary description, the appointment cannot be as an administrator (see *Meadrealm Ltd* v. *Transcontinental Golf Construction*, Vinelott J (unreported, ChD, 29 November 1991)).

What is a qualifying floating charge?

IA 1986, Sched.B1, para.14(2) provides that a qualifying floating charge is one which:

(a)   states that IA 1986, Sched.B1, para.14 applies to the floating charge;

(b)   purports to empower the holder of the floating charge to appoint an administrator of the company;

(c)   purports to empower the holder of the floating charge to make an appointment which would otherwise be an appointment of an administrative receiver within the meaning given by IA 1986, s.29(2); or

(d)   purports to empower the holder of the floating charge in Scotland to appoint a receiver who on appointment would be an administrative receiver.

This wide definition therefore covers 'security documentation' which:

(a)   specifically refers to para.14, i.e. post-Enterprise Act 2002 terminology;

(b)   specifically provides for the appointment of an administrator;

(c)   contains pre-Enterprise Act terminology, such as a reference to 'administrative receiver', which has not been updated and does not specifically reflect the ability to appoint an administrator; or

(d)   relates to a security created before 15 September 2003 where the charge holder will have a choice of appointing either an administrator or an administrative receiver.

The security instrument (debenture, charge or other form of security) must relate to the whole or substantially the whole of the company's property, and if the potential appointor holds more than one debenture, charge or other form of security, the assets secured thereunder must together relate to the whole or substantially the whole of the company's property and at least one instrument must be a qualifying floating charge (IA 1986, Sched.B1, para.14(3)).

A charge holder that possesses a charge over only part of the company's assets (which does not amount to substantially the whole of the company's property) and/or that does not possess a floating charge cannot appoint an administrator by an out-of-court route, but can apply for a court order seeking the appointment of an administrator as a 'creditor'.

Could the charge be unenforceable?

It is also appropriate where there is some doubt as to validity of the floating charge (i.e. consider effect of IA 1986, s.245 and the invalidity of a floating charge created within two years of the onset of insolvency save to the extent of any 'new monies' provided at the time of creation) to use the court application route for appointment rather than use the out-of-court process.

Significant difficulty can arise in circumstances where, after challenge, the charge may eventually be found to be unenforceable, e.g. where it could also be avoided (under IA 1986, s.245), or found to be invalidly executed, or where it could be set aside (under IA 1986, ss.238–239). In such circumstances, despite the administrator's appointment and performance of duties, if the charge is found to be unenforceable the appointment will be deemed to be invalid (*BCPMS (Europe) Ltd* v. *GMAC Commercial Finance plc* [2006] All ER (D) 285 (Feb)). To avoid the significant difficulties that can arise in such circumstances, an application to challenge the validity of the security/appointment should be made promptly (see *Fliptex Ltd* v. *Hogg* [2004] BCC 870). In addition, if the administrator considers that the security may be invalid it is incumbent on him to seek immediate directions (see *Lovett* v. *Carson Country Homes Ltd* [2009] EWHC 1143 (Ch) where the charge document was held enforceable despite the forgery of one of the directors' signatures). Where there is possible invalidity, on application by a suitable party for an administration order (e.g. the company/its directors) the court may effect the appointment of the administrator commencing the appointment from a date deemed suitable to avoid complications (i.e. a retrospective order as in *Re G-Tech Construction Ltd* [2007] BPIR 1275).

However, the risk remains that where an administrator is appointed invalidly, he will be liable to the company as a trespasser. As a result of this possible liability where an appointment is made by a private debenture holder (as opposed to a major lender/bank), it is not uncommon for the insolvency practitioner to ask for an indemnity, guarantee or other form of security against such risk. It is, however, highly uncommon for a bank or other financial institution to be willing to give such an indemnity. In these circumstances, the purported administrator may need to apply to court for an order that the appointor indemnify him in respect of any liability which has arisen (IA 1986, Sched.B1, para.21(2); see *Hans Brochier Holdings Ltd* v. *Exner* [2007] BCC 127 for an example of invalid appointment).

To avoid these complications and with due regard to the fact that the court will not have reviewed the security and sanctioned the appointment, it is vital that a proper assessment is made by the appointor and the proposed administrator pre-appointment as to whether the security in respect of which the appointment is to be made is one by which the administrator will be validly appointed. See also Forms 2.5B, 2.6B and 2.7B, each of which requires the appointor to state that he is the holder of a qualifying floating charge which is now enforceable. Despite the inherent risk of making/accepting the appointment without due checks, it is common practice to find that a security review and assessment as to the validity of the appointment is conducted post appointment, in some cases some weeks after appointment. Whether this is a hangover from the previous practices which developed in regard to receivership is difficult to tell.

The insolvency practitioner will therefore need to be assured (preferably prior to appointment) that the appointor's security is valid and enforceable. In determining this question the following should be considered:

- Does the company have the requisite capacity to borrow and create the debenture?
- Do the company's directors have the requisite power to execute the debenture?
- Was the debenture validly executed?
- Was the debenture registered within the 21-day time limit as set out in CA 2006, s.860?
- Does the debenture secure the whole or substantially the whole of the company's property?
- Has the power to appoint an administrator under the debenture arisen? This may require consideration of the loan agreement, whether default has arisen and demand properly made.
- Is the debenture capable of attack by any party or by the liquidator appointed at the relevant time on any of the following grounds:

    - as a transaction undervalue (IA 1986, s.238);
    - as a preference (IA 1986, s.239);
    - as an extortionate credit transaction (IA 1986, s.244);
    - if the floating charge was created to secure past indebtedness within 12 or

24 months (depending on whether it was granted to a connected person) from the onset of insolvency (IA 1986, s.245);

– that the transaction was entered into at an undervalue with the intention of putting assets beyond the reach of a person who was making a claim and might otherwise make a claim, or where the transaction prejudiced that party's position (IA 1986, s.423)?

5.3.4 Restrictions on appointment

A floating charge holder may not appoint an administrator by an out-of-court route:

- without first giving two clear days' written notice to the holder of any prior floating charge, where the holder of the prior floating charge has an entitlement to appoint an administrator or administrative receiver. The prior floating charge holder may, however, give consent, thereby dispensing with the need to give two days' notice (IA 1986, Sched.B1, para.15(1)(b));
- where the floating charge is not enforceable (IA 1986, Sched.B1, para.16);
- where the company is in voluntary liquidation (IA 1986, Sched.B1, para.86 – note, however, that where voluntary liquidation is proposed, notice must now be provided to any qualifying floating charge holder that at that stage has an ability to appoint an administrator);
- if a provisional liquidator has been appointed (IA 1986, Sched.B1, para.17(a));
- if an administrative receiver is in office (IA 1986, Sched.B1, para.17(b)); or
- if an administrator is in office (IA 1986, Sched.B1, para.7).

The floating charge holder is not entitled to appoint an administrator by an out-of-court route if there is already an administrator in office, a provisional liquidator appointed or an administrative receiver in office (IA 1986, Sched.B1, para.17). However, the floating charge holder has an ability to appoint an administrator if a winding-up petition has been issued, unless the winding-up petition is based on a public interest ground (IA 1986, Sched.B1, para.40(1)(b)).

Where an order for winding up has been made, the qualifying floating charge holder may apply to court for an order discharging the winding-up order and making in its place an administration order, with such directions as thought fit (IA 1986, Sched.B1, para.37). In contrast, where a company is in voluntary liquidation the only party who may apply for an administration order is the liquidator (IA 1986, Sched.B1, para.38). It is for this reason that five days' notice of an intended voluntary liquidation must now be given to the holder of a qualifying floating charge which at that point retains an ability to appoint an administrator (IA 1986, s.84(2A)).

As we have seen, the existence of any of the above factors may not prevent the secured creditor from applying to court for the appointment of an administrator.

It is also worth noting that as the Enterprise Act 2002 has removed the right for most qualifying floating charge holders to appoint an administrative receiver in respect of post-15 September 2003 security (IA 1986, s.72A), the purpose of administration includes the objective of 'realising property in order to make a distribution to one or more secured or preferential creditors' (IA 1986, Sched.B1, para.3(1)(c)). If it is not reasonably practicable to achieve the other two objectives, the administrator need not act in the best interests of the creditors as a whole, but must act (which will mean there is no possibility of company rescue or return to unsecured creditors) in a way which does not unnecessarily harm the interests of the creditors. In *Bank of Scotland plc* v. *Targetfollow Properties Ltd* [2010] EWHC 3606 (Ch) a company unsuccessful challenged the bank's appointment of an administrator on the grounds that the administrator had previously been advising the bank and was therefore not independent. The court held that it had no reason to question the professionalism and independence of the appointment taker, and that the company and other creditors had remedies available if the appointment taker did not display impartiality.

It should be remembered that, in general, the holder of a floating charge may appoint an administrator out of court only if there is an existing right to exercise the powers granted by the terms of the security (which is likely to be underpinned by a default under the terms of a loan agreement/facility). It should, however, be noted that the circumstances of default in the terms of security documentation are generally very widely drawn and a charge holder can find an ability to realise their security in most cases (e.g. threat of insolvency, possible impairment of security, a petition for winding up being presented).

The situation could arise that the only creditor likely to receive any distribution is the secured creditor or alternatively, in the other extreme, the company may be in default of the terms of the loan agreement but otherwise solvent (e.g. in breach of a loan to value covenant). In either case, the other creditors are not directly affected and in such circumstances the charge holder needs to be able to evince that the charge is enforceable but does not need to show that the company is insolvent/has an inability to pay its debts as they fall due. As a consequence, the appointment procedure available to a floating charge holder remains similar to the power to appoint an administrative receiver.

5.3.5 Notice to holder of prior floating charge

A floating charge holder may not appoint an administrator by an out-of-court route without first giving two clear days' written notice to the holder of any prior floating charge, where the holder of the prior floating charge has an entitlement to appoint an administrator or administrative receiver. Failure to give such notice invalidates the subsequent administration appointment (see *Re Eco Link Resources Ltd (in CVL) (Case No.8326 of 2012)* Birmingham District Registry, 2 July 2012).

The prior floating charge holder may, however, give consent, thereby dispensing with the need to give two days' notice (IA 1986, Sched.B1, para.15(1)(b)).

Under IA 1986, Sched.B1, para.15(2) a floating charge is deemed 'prior' if:

(a)   it was created first; or

(b)   it was treated as having priority by agreement of the charge holders.

As a result, the appointor needs to have regard to any agreement/deed of priority that has been entered into by the different charge holders as the interpretation of who may be a 'prior' charge holder may be dictated by such agreement.

In the absence of clear express agreement, the wording 'prior floating charge holder' is open to some degree of interpretation. Does this mean that the first charge holder in time and/or as per the order contained in the register of charges at Companies House? What is the effect if a charge was created first but later ranked subservient to a later charge by virtue of the agreement in the deed of priorities? In *OMP Leisure Ltd* [2008] BCC 67 Hodge J expressed the view that there is no obligation to provide notice to a prior (senior) charge holder where that charge would never become enforceable. However, due to the prejudice and possible invalidity of appointment that can be caused for failing to provide requisite notice, it would be prudent to provide notice to any senior charge holder, irrespective of whether it is believed that the charge has been satisfied. In cases of urgency, it would also be wise to ensure that in any deed of priority entered into giving the second charge holder priority over the first, the second charge holder (i.e. in time) should be granted a power of enduring attorney from the first charge holder to appoint an administrator.

As there may be a delay in providing such notice, the appointor is able to serve a notice of intention to appoint in Form 2.5B. On filing of a notice of intention, an interim moratorium comes into effect for five days (IA 1986, Sched.B1, para.44(2)(b)). There is no requirement for the appointor to file notice of intention, which contrasts with the position of the company and its directors. If notice is given other than in accordance with Form 2.5B, a moratorium will not come into effect. An interim moratorium takes effect on the filing of the notice at court, which should take place at the same time as written notice is sent to the prior floating charge holder (IR 1986, rule 2.15).

If the prior floating charge holder determines that it does not wish to accept the administrator proposed by the company/its creditors, it may appoint its own choice of administrator or administrative receiver (if the security was created pre-15 September 2003). If it does not consent to the appointment of an administrator (perhaps preferring the company to pass into liquidation), the appointor is left in a difficult position. In contrast to the Form 2.9B notice of appointment which is filed by the company/directors after a notice of intention has been served and provides that the floating charge holder has not replied within five days or has consented, Form 2.6B simply provides that notice has been given. Does this mean that where the prior floating charge holder does not consent, but does not wish to appoint its own choice of nominated administrator, the subsequent charge holder can move to make the appointment? If there is no deed of priority, or it is silent, it may be the case that the prior floating charge holder should move to restrain the appointor from moving the company into administration and/or if there is a conflict between both charge holders over the future direction of the company the appointor may be best advised seeking court direction in regard to the appointment.

Practical tips on completing Form 2.5B

The numbers and letters in the list below follow those as set out on Form 2.5B.

1. (a) Insert the name and address of the holder of the floating charge.
    (b) Insert names and addresses of the proposed administrators. It should be noted that Form 2.2B (consent to act) does not need to be filed at this stage. However, for all practical purposes the administrator should have already agreed that it is reasonably likely that the purpose of administration will be achieved and have consented to act.
    (c) Insert name and registered office address of company subject to the appointment. In IA 1986, s.117(6) in regard to the issue of winding-up petitions the place the company has its registered office is said to be where it has been longest in the last six months.
2. (d) Give details of the charge, date registered and financial limit if any. In doing so the appointor needs to state (supported by the statutory declaration) that the charge is enforceable. This issue has been discussed at length above and may require consideration of the loan agreement/facility as well as the security. Consider whether there been a default making the security enforceable.
3. (e) Give details, names and addresses of any holders of any prior floating charges together with details of each charge. This will entail consideration of the register of charges and enquiries as to whether there is any priority given to any other charge holder subsequently registered in time.
4. (f) Insert details of any current insolvency proceedings. This would be limited to a winding-up petition, since if the company is already in administration, administrative receivership, provisional liquidation or liquidation the floating charge holder cannot use the out-of-court route.
5. Delete 'is/is not' as appropriate. Note, however, that if the company is an insurance undertaking, a credit institution, an investment undertaking providing services involving the holding of funds or securities for third parties or a collective investment undertaking under Art.1.2 of Council Regulation 1346/2000/EC of 29 May 2000 on Insolvency Proceedings, a different insolvency regime will apply and specialist works should be consulted. Such companies will also not be subject to the EC Regulation.
6. Delete 'will/will not' as appropriate. Again, if the EC Regulation does not apply a different regime is likely to be in operation.

    (g) The proceedings are 'main' proceedings provided the registered office/

Rule 2.15   Form 2.5B

Notice of intention to appoint an administrator by holder of qualifying floating charge

Name of Company	Company number

In the [full name of court]	*For court use only* Court case number

(a) Name and address of holder of qualifying floating charge

1. (a) _____

_____

_____ ("the appointor"), gives notice that it is the appointor's intention to appoint

(b) Give name(s) and address(es) of proposed administrator(s)

(b)

_____ as administrator(s)

of

(c) Insert name and address of registered office of company

(c) _____

_____ ("the company")

in accordance with paragraph 14 of Schedule B1 to the Insolvency Act 1986.

2. The appointor is the holder of the following qualifying floating charge which is now enforceable:

(d) Give details of charge relied on, date registered and (if any) financial limit

(d) _____

_____

3. This notice has been given to the following person(s), who is / are each understood to be holder(s) of (a) qualifying floating charge(s) in respect of the company's property, the said charge(s) being (a) prior floating charge(s) in accordance with paragraph 15(2) of Schedule B1 to the Insolvency Act 1986:

(e) Insert name(s) and address(es) of holder(s) of qualifying floating charge(s) and details of charge(s) held

(e) _____

_____

4. The company *is / is not at the date of this notice subject to insolvency proceedings,

(f) Give details of any current or outstanding insolvency proceedings

(f) _____

_____

*Delete as applicable

5. The company *is / is not *an insurance undertaking / a credit institution / an investment undertaking providing services involving the holding of funds or securities for third parties / or a collective investment undertaking under Article 1.2 of the EC Regulation.

(g) Insert whether main, secondary or territorial proceedings

6. For the following reasons it is considered that the EC Regulation *will / will not apply. If it does apply, these proceedings will be (g) _____ proceedings as defined in Article 3 of the EC Regulation: _____

_____

Signed _____
(If signing on behalf of appointor indicate capacity
e.g. director/solicitor)

Dated _____

Consent of Floating Charge Holder to Appointment of Administrator
(Do not detach this part of the notice)

If, having read this notice, you have no objection to the making of this appointment you can indicate your consent either by completing the details in the box below and returning a copy of this notice as soon as possible, and within two business days from receipt of this notice, or by sending details, as set out in Rule 2.16 (5), of your consent in writing to the appointor at the following address:

(h) Appointor to insert address

(h) _____

_____

If your consent has not been given within two business days the appointor may make the appointment notwithstanding that you have not replied.

(j) Insert name and address

(j) _____

_____

_____

being the holder of the following floating charge over the company's property:

(k) Give details of charge, date registered and (if any) financial limit

(k) _____

_____

consents to the appointment of the administrator(s) in accordance with the details of this notice.

Signed _____   Dated _____
(If signing on behalf of a firm or company state position or office held)

Endorsement to be completed by the court

(l) Insert date and time

This notice was filed (l)

COMI lies in the UK (see **3.5.2** for further details regarding 'main' or 'secondary' proceedings).

The second part of the form deals with the notice to be completed if consent is to be granted by the floating charge holder. Alternatively, the prior floating charge holder may provide written notice of consent, but this must comply with IR 1986, rule 2.16(5). It is noteworthy that this contains a significant amount of detail and to ensure compliance the appointor may well prefer to use Form 2.5B to avoid ambiguity. In this section, insert details of address for return of form/written consent. This is likely to be the solicitors acting for the appointor.

- (h) Insert name and address of appointor.
- (j) Give details of the appointor's charge, date registered and financial limit if any.
- (k) The endorsement is to be left blank and is completed by the court on filing. A date and exact time are given, essential to assess when the interim moratorium comes into effect.

5.3.6 Notice of appointment

The appointment of an administrator takes effect when Form 2.6B is filed at court. The notice should be accompanied by two copies (the original to be retained by the court, one to be served upon the administrator and one for the appointor). Form 2.6B must be accompanied by Form 2.2B, completed by the administrator (i.e. the consent to act, acknowledgement that the purpose of administration is reasonably likely to be achieved) and where there is a joint appointment this form must be accompanied by a statement as to the exercise of powers (IA 1986, Sched.B1, para.100(2)).

Practical tips on completing Form 2.6B

The numbers and letters in the list below follow those as set out on Form 2.6B.

1. (a) Insert the name and address of the holder of the floating charge.
   (b) Insert the names and addresses of the proposed administrators (with Form 2.2B attached).
   (c) Insert the name and registered office address of company subject to the appointment. In IA 1986, s.117(6), in regard to the issue of winding-up petitions, the place the company has its registered office is said to be where it has been longest in the last six months.
2. Form 2.2B needs to be attached.
3. (d) Give details of the charge, date registered and financial limit, if any. In

Rule 2.16   Form 2.6B

Notice of appointment of an administrator by holder of qualifying floating charge

Name of Company	Company number

In the [full name of court]	*For court use only* Court case number

(a) Name and address of holder of qualifying floating charge

1. (a) _____

_____

_____ ("the appointor")

(b) Give name(s) and address(es) of administrator(s)

gives notice that (b) _____

(c) Insert name and address of registered office of company

_____ is / are hereby appointed as administrator(s) of (c) _____

_____ ("the company")

*Delete as applicable

2. The written statement(s) in Form 2.2B *is / are attached.

3. The appointor is the holder of the following qualifying floating charge:

(d) Give details of charge relied on, date registered and (if any) financial limit

(d) _____

_____

4. The above charge is enforceable at the date of this appointment.

+Delete if not applicable

*Delete as applicable

5. + [The appointor has given at least two business days' written notice to the holder of any prior qualifying floating charge(s), and a copy of that notice, *(which was filed at _____ court on _____ (date)) is attached.]
OR
+ [all the holders of any prior qualifying floating charges have consented in writing to the making of this appointment and copies of the written consents are attached.]
OR
+ [there are no prior qualifying floating charges.]

*Delete as applicable

(e) Give details of any current or outstanding insolvency proceedings

6. The company *is / is not, at the date of this notice, the subject of insolvency proceedings:
(e) _____

_____

7. The company *is / is not *an insurance undertaking / a credit institution / an investment undertaking providing services involving the holding of funds or securities for third parties / or a collective investment undertaking under Article 1.2 of the EC Regulation.

*Delete as applicable

(f) Insert whether main, secondary or territorial proceedings

8. For the following reasons it is considered that the EC Regulation *will / will not apply. If it does apply, these proceedings will be (f) _____ proceedings as defined in Article 3 of the EC Regulation:

9. This appointment is in accordance with Schedule B1 to the Insolvency Act 1986.

10. Where there are joint administrators, a statement for the purposes of paragraph 100(2) of Schedule B1 to the Insolvency Act 1986 is attached.

(g) Insert full name and address of person making declaration

11. I (g) _____

of _____

_____

(If making the declaration on behalf of appointor indicate capacity e.g. director/solicitor)

do solemnly and sincerely declare that the information provided in this notice is, to the best of my knowledge and belief, true,

AND I make this solemn declaration conscientiously believing the same to be true and by virtue of the provisions of the Statutory Declarations Act 1835.

Declared at _____

Signed _____

This _____ day of _____ 20

before me _____

A Commissioner for Oaths or Notary Public or Justice of the Peace or Solicitor or Duly Authorised Officer.

(h) Insert date and time of filing

Endorsement to be completed by the court
This notice and the attached documents were filed
(h)

doing so the appointor needs to state (supported by the statutory declaration) that the charge is enforceable. This issue has been discussed at length above and may require consideration of the loan agreement/facility as well as the security. Consider whether there has been a default making the security enforceable.

4. The appointor needs to confirm that the charge is enforceable.
5. Delete as applicable depending on whether there were prior floating charge holders, and if so whether a notice of intention in Form 2.5B was filed, written notice provided and consent to the appointment obtained. If notice of intention to appoint in Form 2.5B was filed at court, this needs to be attached. As discussed above, it is not necessary to file Form 2.5B at court and written notice may simply have been provided; if so, this needs to be attached. In cases where a consent has been obtained, i.e. within two clear business days of service of written notice, the written consent must be attached to Form 2.6B.
6. (e) If appropriate, insert details and any current insolvency proceedings. This would be limited to a winding-up petition, since if the company is

       already in administration, administrative receivership, provisional liquidation or liquidation the floating charge holder cannot use the out-of-court route.

7.   Delete 'is/is not' as appropriate. Note, however, that if the company is an insurance undertaking, credit institution, an investment undertaking providing services involving the holding of funds or securities for third parties or a collective investment undertaking, Art.1.2 of Council Regulation 1346/2000/EC of 29 May 2000 on Insolvency Proceedings, a different insolvency regime will apply and specialist works should be consulted. Such companies will also not be subject to the EC Regulation.

8.   Delete 'will/will not' as appropriate. Again, if the EC Regulation does not apply a different regime is likely to be in operation.

    (f)   The proceedings are deemed 'main' proceedings provided the registered office/COMI lies in the UK (see definition of main or secondary proceedings provided in **3.5.2** for further details).

9.   The appointment must be in accordance with Sched.B1 (see in particular the provisions of paras.15–17 and the completion of all formalities) and the declarant is required to confirm the same.

10.   Where more than one person is to be appointed administrator, a statement specifying the functions to be exercised for the persons acting jointly and what functions, if any, are to be exercised by any or all of the persons appointed (IA 1986, Sched.B1, para.100(2)) must be attached. This is of significantly greater importance where the insolvency practitioners are from different firms and the functions are split between the two (e.g. management of business/marketing and sale of business and assets/investigation and report on directors' conduct, etc.). However, in practice, while such agreement may be reached the administrators may not wish their powers to be fettered.

11.   (g)   Insert details (full name and address) of the individual who is making the statutory declaration contained on the remainder of the form. This must be someone duly authorised by the appointor, such as a senior bank officer or the charge holder's solicitor. The statutory declaration must not, however, be taken lightly, confirming (to the best of the declarant's knowledge and belief) that the charge is enforceable as at the date of appointment, etc.

The endorsement is to be left blank and is completed by the court on filing. A date and exact time are given, essential to assess when the administration is deemed to commence.

Form 2.6B contains a statutory declaration. This declaration should be sworn before an independent solicitor (or commissioner for oaths, notary public, justice of the peace or officer of the court, each of whom will charge a fee of £7) and should not be made more than five business days before the date it is filed at court.

The statutory declaration will provide confirmation that:

(a)   the appointor holds a qualifying floating charge over the whole or substantially the whole of the company's property;

(b)   the charge is enforceable at the date of appointment;

(c)   the appointment is in accordance with IA 1986; and

(d)   notice has been provided to any prior floating charge holder.

The notice must be accompanied by the proposed administrator's written consent to the appointment in Form 2.2B, containing a statement that in his opinion the purpose of the administration is reasonably likely to be achieved (see *Re Colt Telecom Group plc (No.2)* [2003] BPIR 324 for consideration of administrators' duties of independence and impartiality in providing this assessment). Where there is more than one administrator, a statement setting out the respective roles and responsibilities of each must be provided (IA 1986, Sched.B1, para.100(2)).

The appointment of the administrator will commence when the papers are filed at court (IA 1986, Sched.B1, para.19), the court endorsing on the copies of Form 2.6B the date and time of filing. One of the copies must then be served on the administrator as soon as reasonably practicable (IR 1986, rule 2.17(2)). In practice, the filing of the papers is undertaken after close coordination with the administrator, who will want to be ready to take over control and management of the company immediately on appointment. If a company has multiple sites, this can require careful planning to ensure representatives of the administrator are on hand at each site to explain the process and procedure of the administration to staff, as well as providing an early indication as to the intentions of the administrator.

5.3.7   Out-of-hours appointment

In exceptional circumstances it is open to the holder of qualifying floating charge to make an appointment when the court office is closed, perhaps before 10 am or after 4.30 pm, or at the weekend, or on a bank holiday. It should be noted that notice to any prior floating charge holder is still required, as is the need to ensure that the administrator consents to act and is of the opinion that the purpose of administration is reasonably likely to be achieved (this, however, is endorsed on Form 2.7B as opposed to having a separate Form 2.2B).

Form 2.7B must also be accompanied by a notice providing the full reasons why the appointment needed to be made out of hours and why it would be 'damaging to the company and its creditors not to have so acted' (IR 1986, rule 2.19(8)).

Form 2.7B contains a statutory declaration which is required to be sworn by an individual duly authorised, so it should be remembered that an independent solicitor should be on hand (overnight/at the weekend) to administer the oath.

For Form 2.7B see **www.insolvency.gov.uk/forms/englandwalesforms.htm**.

Form 2.7B is then sent by fax or email to a specially designated number/email provided by the Court Service (IR 1986, rule 2.19(3)). It should be noted that this out-of-court and out-of-hours option is not available to the company and its directors. It is a mark of the flexibility of the UK system that in cases of extreme urgency and importance it may be possible to liaise with the court and the judge's clerk to find a judge prepared to hear an administration application outside normal court hours, and possibly even outside a court room (e.g. at the judge's home).

Details of the fax number and email are published on the Insolvency Service website (**www.insolvency.gov.uk**) and are currently fax: 020 7947 6607 and email: rcjcompanies.orders@hmcts.gsi.gov.uk.

The appointment takes effect on the date and time of the fax transmission. In case of email, a hard copy of the email must be created showing the time, date and address sent to, together with the attachment of the Form 2.7B sent. On the next day the court is open, the appointor must file three copies of the notice of appointment that was faxed or emailed, together with a transmission report showing the date and time the form was faxed and/or the hard copy email with all necessary supporting documents (IR 1986, rule 2.19(7)).

Two sealed copies of the notice of appointment are sent to the appointor, who must, as soon as reasonably practicable, send one sealed copy to the administrator. It is of crucial importance to note that an offence is committed if the appointor fails to comply with these provisions and the appointment will cease to have effect (IA 1986, Sched.B1, para.20(b) and IR 1986, rule 2.19(10)).

5.3.8 Court appointment sought by a holder of a floating charge

It should be noted that despite the out-of-court route available to the holder of a floating charge, a court appointment may be sought where:

(a)   a winding-up order is in place (IA 1986, Sched.B1, para.37);
(b)   there is some doubt as to the enforceability of the security and/or ability to appoint;
(c)   the company/directors have put forward a proposed administrator to whom the secured creditor objects; or
(d)   a prior floating charge holder has objected to the appointment of an administrator.

5.3.9 Court appointment sought by unsecured creditor

One or more creditors may apply for an administration order (IA 1986, Sched.B1, para.12(1)(c)). The court will only make an order if it is satisfied that the company is, or is likely to become, unable to pay its debts and the order is reasonably likely to achieve the purpose of administration (IA 1986, Sched.B1, para.11). The court will not make an order if there are grounds for belief that there is a genuine or substantial dispute in respect of the creditors' claim (*Re British American Racing (Holdings) Ltd* [2005] BCC 110; see, however, *Hammonds (a firm)* v. *Pro-fit USA Ltd* [2007] EWHC 1998 (Ch)).

There is some debate as to the standard of proof required to establish the debtor company's insolvency on a creditor's petition, as presumably it will be made in the face of opposition by the company. In *Re Colt Telecom Group plc* [2002] EWHC 2815 (Ch), a case under the old administration regime, the applicant sought to argue that the debtor company was insolvent by reason of large contingent and prospective liabilities. The court ruled that 'likely' to be unable to pay its debts in this context meant 'more probable than not' and being 'satisfied' was measured on the balance of probabilities. As the reformed legislation provides 'likely' in respect of the ability to pay debts and 'reasonably likely' to achieve the purpose of the administration, it is suggested that a less stringent test applies to the latter than to the former.

5.4 RECEIVERSHIP

5.4.1 Introduction

Receivership is a remedy solely available to a creditor possessing security for its debt, be that in the form of debenture, legal charge or mortgage. It is by nature a proprietorial enforcement remedy, possessed by one creditor, as opposed to a collective remedy available to all creditors (collectivism being the hallmark of an insolvency procedure). Receivership, however, has a place in any work on insolvency due to its historical significance and the fact that in practice the appointment of a receiver often leads to the eventual insolvency of the company and thereafter to another insolvency procedure, most commonly liquidation.

On appointment, a receiver appointed by a secured creditor will 'receive' the income generated from any asset and use the income to clear the secured debt. Sir George Jessel MR in *Re Manchester and Milford Rly Co.* (1880) 14 Ch D 645 at 653 providing the classic definition of a receiver being:

> a person who receives rents or other income paying ascertained outgoings but who does not, if I may say so, manage the property in the sense of buying or selling or anything of that kind.

There is thus a distinction between a receiver and a manager, although pursuant to the powers granted in the security instrument the receiver is highly likely to be a receiver and manager, thus able to carry on the business of the borrower and sell the borrower's assets. As a result, it has become commonplace to ignore the distinction between a receiver and a receiver *and* manager and instead simply to refer to the appointee as a receiver.

A receiver may be further distinguished between an LPA receiver (one appointed under a mortgage for land) and a non-administrative receiver, sometimes referred to as a fixed charge receiver. Again, these distinctions are rarely referred to, the term receiver being used for both.

It is possible, in the absence of an express or implied power of appointment, for the receiver to be appointed by court order, although in the majority of cases a receiver is appointed out of court as a privately appointed receiver and rather than just simply receive income, will move to sell the secured assets (provided that this power is granted to the receiver within the security instrument) to discharge the debt.

Save in limited circumstances (IA 1986, ss.72B–72GA), it is only creditors in possession of a floating charge security created prior to 15 September 2003 (generally, a charge is deemed created on the date of execution) that will be entitled to appoint an administrative receiver (Insolvency Act 1986, Section 72A (Appointed Date) Order 2003, SI 2003/2095). The distinction between a receiver and administrative receiver is set out in **5.4.2**.

There are some considerable advantages for the secured creditor in appointing a receiver rather than consenting to the appointment of an administrator (see below). As a result, it was felt prior to the Enterprise Act 2002 reforms coming into force that lenders may have sought to take assignments of pre-Enterprise Act security to preserve their right to appoint an administrative receiver. The fall in number of receiverships since 2003 does not, however, suggest that this practice has been widely adopted. While administration has in recent years been less attractive (not least due to the costs and expense rule) and we have seen a rise in the use of receivership, as a proportion of total corporate insolvencies the use of receivership when compared with other insolvency processes is still well below pre-Enterprise Act 2002 levels and far below levels seen in the early 1990s.

Table 5.1 Receivership appointments as a percentage of all corporate insolvencies 1987–2012

	No. of receivership appointments	Total no. of corporate insolvencies	Per cent (%)
1987	1265	12856	10
1988	1094	10766	10
1989	1706	12340	14
1990	4318	19632	22
1991	7515	29685	25
1992	8324	33004	25
1993	5362	26316	20
1994	3877	21028	18
1995	3226	18297	18
1996	2701	16831	16
1997	1837	15263	12
1998	1713	15724	11
1999	1618	16813	10
2000	1595	16907	9
2001	1914	18181	11
2002	1541	19140	8

	No. of receivership appointments	Total no. of corporate insolvencies	Per cent (%)
2003	1261	16915	7
2004	864	15255	6
2005	590	16348	4
2006	588	17786	3
2007	337	15774	2
2008	867	21811	4
2009	1468	24778	6
2010	1309	20954	6
2011	1397	21858	6
2012	1222	20731	6

Source: Insolvency Service Statistical Directorate

Receivership has had an important role in the development of corporate rescue. Central to development of a rescue culture throughout the 1960s and 1970s, it fell from government favour in the late 1990s – the remedy was perceived to have been overused by lenders and to have created economic recessionary pressure. This was exemplified by the economic recession of the early 1990s, which was generally property-led; as property prices fell more receivers were appointed, which depressed the market still further. This recessionary spiral was seen as one which should be avoided in the future.

As a consequence, the Enterprise Act 2002 introduced reforms, which saw predominant position of administrative receivership in corporate rescue decline in favour of administration. Despite this, receivership remains an important tool for charge holders to realise their security and the ability to appoint a receiver to realise assets subject to a fixed charge (LPA receiver) is unaffected by the 2002 reforms.

The choice of whether to appoint a receiver or an administrator is therefore often a difficult one, assessing likely recoveries versus costs. Generally, however, a bank holding security over a business whose prime asset is its property (a hotel, restaurant, etc.) may well appoint an LPA receiver, who will run the business to ensure that a sale as a going concern can be achieved. For the management and owners of the debtor company, there is little distinction between the appointment of an LPA receiver, an administrator and an administrative receiver.

Checklist

Advantages to secured creditor of (administrative) receivership over administration

- The principal obligation of a receiver is to the appointor; in administration it is to the creditors generally.
- The appointment of an administrator is open to greater challenge by unsecured creditors.

- A direct challenge to the appointment of an administrative receiver is not available.
- The capital gains tax consequences of administration are a distinct disadvantage.
- Non-domestic business rates are an expense of administration.
- The expenses of administration are recoverable from floating charge realisations.
- High costs of administration are likely.
- Control of the administration process generally rests with the creditors as a whole.

The principal characteristic of receivership is that the receiver's primary obligation and duty is to the appointor (*Downsview Nominees* v. *First City Corporation* [1993] AC 295). Receivers are appointed to realise the security of the appointor (*Gomba Holdings Ltd* v. *Homan* [1986] 1 WLR 1301, Hoffmann J: 'his primary duty is to realise the assets in the interest of the debenture holder, and his powers of management are really ancillary to that duty'). A receiver is therefore under no obligation to continue to trade a business to see if it can be rescued and need only act in good faith in exercising a power of sale; he need not have obtained the best possible price (*Cuckmere Brick Co. Ltd* v. *Mutual Finance Ltd* [1971] 2 All ER 633 (CA)).

A receiver (and administrative receiver) does owe a duty of skill and care to the company (*Medforth* v. *Blake* [1999] 3 All ER 97), to other secured creditors (*Midland Bank Ltd* v. *Joliman Finance Ltd* (1967) 203 Estates Gazette 1039) and to a guarantor (*Standard Chartered Bank* v. *Walker* [1982] 1 WLR 1410). Importantly, however, there is no general duty owed to the unsecured creditors of the company (*Northern Development (Holdings) Ltd* v. *UDT Securities* [1977] 1 All ER 747 and *Lathia* v. *Dronsfield Bros* [1987] BCLC 321). See *Natwest* v. *Hunter* [2011] EWHC 3170 (Ch) for an example of an unsuccessful challenge by a borrower of the receiver's sale of a property by auction.

In contrast, an administrator, whether appointed by a floating charge holder or otherwise, owes his primary obligation and duty to the creditors as a whole (IA 1986, Sched.B1, para.3(2)). An administrator must carry out his functions to fulfil the statutory purpose of administration. In exercising this function his actions could conflict with the interests of the secured creditor, e.g. rescuing the company may not be in the secured creditor's commercial interests as it may postpone effective enforcement of the security.

On the secured creditor appointing an administrator, the choice and motivation for the appointment may be challenged (IA 1986, Sched.B1, para.81(2) – improper motive). Although the likelihood of the secured creditor's appointee being removed from office is remote, it does provide further reason for the secured creditor to prefer the appointment of a receiver.

Expenses of the administration are recoverable from the floating charge realisations; these could include tax on income (*Re Toshuku Finance UK* [2002] UKHL 6) and payment of non-domestic rates (*Exeter City Council* v. *Bairstow* [2007] EWHC 400 (Ch)). While a receiver's costs will also be borne from the realisations, the role is more limited and control of those expenses (including remuneration) rests with the secured creditor. In the case of an administration, the unsecured creditors will set the rates of remuneration, unless no distribution is likely to be made to them (IR 1986, rule 2.106). A statement to this effect needs to be made by the administrator pursuant to IA 1986, Sched.B1, para.52(1).

Capital gains arising on the sale of company property are also treated as an expense of the administration and therefore accorded priority over floating charge realisations (IR 1986, rule 2.67(1)(j), from 15 September 2003). This contrasts with the pre-Enterprise Act 2002 position where sales by either an administrative receiver or an administrator were treated as company gains which were unsecured claims in any subsequent liquidation.

The role of the creditors, and particularly the creditors' committee, is central to agreeing the proposals for administration and determining how the administrator exercises his functions in accordance with the proposals. While an administrative receiver may form a creditors' committee, the committee has no power or specific function unless agreed by the administrative receiver.

As a result of the above factors, secured creditors will need to think carefully about whether they wish to appoint an administrator or allow the company to do so in circumstances where the secured creditor retains the right to appoint an administrative receiver, or more probably a fixed charge receiver.

An explanation of the powers and responsibilities of receivers is set out in **Chapter 8**, although, as receivership is an enforcement remedy, in the main the powers are dictated by the terms of contractual agreement between lender and borrower rather than by insolvency legislation. As has been noted, despite the fact that power and control of the company is retained by the existing management during the receivership process, this is subject to the terms of the security, which may severely curtail the directors' rights. A receiver is appointed, 'not to receive directions from the directors but to give directions' (Viscount Caldecote CJ, *Meigh v. Wickenden* [1942] 2 KB 160 at 166) and the receiver may in practice take over the control and management of the business of the entire company if the fixed charge encompasses land and the business thereon. A practical consequence of receivership over the key or main assets of a company is that liquidation is likely to result sooner or later.

5.4.2   Receivership and administrative receivership distinguished

Where a debtor is in breach of the terms of a loan facility, that breach may trigger rights under the security documentation to appoint a receiver, administrative receiver or administrator. The office taken by the eventual appointee depends on the contractual terms of the loan and in some cases the choice made by the appointor.

The loan may be secured by a fixed charge over specific identifiable assets, such as the company's premises, or a floating charge over assets which will vary during the lifetime of the company, such as stock or work in progress. The distinction between whether an asset is secured by a fixed and floating charge is important in respect of:

- the distribution of assets according to a statutory order of priorities; and
- the ability of the secured creditor to appoint a receiver and the functions the receiver can perform.

To ensure maximum potential recovery it is often necessary that asset values are preserved by continuation of the business during the receivership process. Assets realised from a trading company will probably realise more than assets from a company that has closed down its business, and almost inevitably in the case of certain assets (e.g. goodwill). In such circumstances, the receiver will be appointed as receiver and manager (if this is provided for in the security), entitling him to carry on the business of the company. A receiver is, however, under no obligation to continue to trade the business (*Re B Johnson & Co. (Builders) Ltd* [1955] Ch 634) and certainly is under no obligation to see whether the company (and its business) can be rescued (see *Medforth* v. *Blake* [1999] 2 BCLC 221 for extent of duty).

Example

A secured lender who possessed security created before 15 September 2003 comprising fixed and floating charge over a company, whose assets included a portfolio of properties each carrying on a restaurant/pub business, could appoint an administrator or an administrative receiver over the entire company or a receiver and manager to trade and then sell one or all of the businesses separately. The decision would rest on a number of different commercial factors, such as whether the entire business was worth more as a group or as separate units and what the costs and expenses of the various procedures would be.

However, it is often to the advantage of the secured creditor who possesses a floating charge to appoint an administrative receiver. An administrative receiver is defined by statute as:

(a)   a receiver or manager of the whole or substantially the whole of a company's property, appointed by or on behalf of the holders of any debenture of the company secured by a charge which, as created, was a floating charge, or by such a charge and one or more other securities; or

(b)   a person who would be a receiver or manager, but for the appointment of some other person as receiver of part of the company's property (IA 1986, s.29(2)).

As can be seen from the above definition, the ability to appoint an administrative receiver is dependent on the secured creditor possessing a floating charge as created. The fact that the floating charge may well become fixed on crystallisation is irrelevant.

An administrative receiver must be an insolvency practitioner, while a receiver can be any suitable person who is not otherwise disqualified from acting under any relevant statutory provision (e.g. a body corporate (IA 1986, s.30) or an undischarged bankrupt (IA 1986, s 31) cannot be appointed a receiver).

Furthermore, an administrative receiver is a receiver and manager of the whole (or substantially the whole) of the company's property. It should be remembered that the nature of the appointment is determined by the facts of the case, irrespective of any terminology applied by the lender and borrower and even the intentions of the parties. Whether the assets are secured by fixed or floating charge is a matter of substance, not form. Despite the fact that the assets may also be charged under a fixed charge, providing there is a floating charge over the remainder of the assets of the company, the appointment will be as administrative receiver (*Re Croftbell Ltd* (1990) BCLC 844). If, however, the appointment is under the fixed charge element, despite contrary description, the appointment will not be as administrative receiver (*Meadrealm Ltd* v. *Transcontinental Golf Construction* (unreported, 29 November 1991, Vinelott J)).

As a secured creditor that possesses a fixed charge will have advantages in respect of the priority of distribution, the fixed charge elements of debentures have been widely drafted to include as many assets as possible. The floating charges are often no more than so-called lightweight charges 'over all other assets of the company'. In reality, the realisable value of these other assets may be negligible, but it gives the floating charge holder an option to appoint an administrative receiver (or, in respect of security created since 15 September 2003, an administrator). One type of asset at the heart of this debate and subject to much recent controversy has been book debts.

5.4.3 Book debts – fixed or floating charge?

In June 2001, *Agnew and Beardsley* v. *Inland Revenue Commissioners (Brumark Investments Ltd)* [2000] 1 BCLC 353 (*Brumark*) marked a fundamental turning point in the consideration as to when and where fixed charges can be created over book debts. While *Brumark* was a Privy Council decision and technically non-binding in England, it marked a shift in judicial thinking which reached its logical conclusion in June 2005 with the House of Lords decision in *National Westminster Bank plc* v. *Spectrum Plus Ltd* [2005] UKHL 41.

It was, however, not a straightforward issue, with the judgment at first instance ([2004] 1 All ER 981, determined in January 2004 by Vice Chancellor Sir Andrew Morritt) being overturned by the Court of Appeal ([2004] EWCA Civ 670) only for that decision to be reversed by the House of Lords. For four years a great deal of uncertainty was created; however, *Brumark* and *Spectrum Plus* have not completely settled this area of law. The court in both cases stressed that the possibility of a fixed charge being created over book debts was not ruled out and that the decisions only related to the effectiveness of certain formulations of charges. The effectiveness of the fixed charge continues to depend upon the way that the security agreement ensures that the charge over book debts is fixed, i.e. what element of control exists over the charged assets.

The court in *Brumark* looked at the type of clause which had been used and adopted as standard bank security following the case of *Re New Bullas Trading Ltd*

[1994] BCC 36. This case provided authority for a proposition that fixed charges could exist over book debts, while a floating charge could exist over the proceeds. The Privy Council in *Brumark* considered that while the debts and proceeds formed two distinct separate assets, the proceeds were merely traceable assets of the debt and simply represented their value. Any attempt to distinguish the two made no commercial sense. As a consequence, the Privy Council determined that *New Bullas* was wrongly decided, a decision followed in the House of Lords in *Spectrum Plus*.

Instead, in determining whether a charge was fixed or floating, it has been held that the court should be engaged in a two-stage process.

It must construe the instrument or charge and seek to ascertain the intentions of the parties from the language that they have used. The object is not to discover whether the parties intended to create a fixed or floating charge, but to ascertain the rights and obligations which the parties intended to grant each other in respect of the charged assets.

Once determined, the court should then categorise the charge by reference to those rights and obligations, not by reference to what the parties may or may not have intended. Consequently, if the parties have granted borrowers rights which are inconsistent with the nature of the fixed charge, the charge cannot be fixed, however so described.

In the *Spectrum Plus* case an overdraft facility was secured by debenture in standard form which included 'by way of specific charge over book debts and other debts … now and from time to time due or owing to the company'. The company was required to pay into the company's account with the bank all monies received for such debts and there were covenants restricting the company's ability to sell, factor, discount, charge or assign the debts. This type of clause had been used by the major clearing banks following the 1979 decision of *Siebe Gorman* v. *Barclays Bank* [1979] 2 Lloyd's Rep 142, and consequently how it was construed was of major significance.

In determining whether the asset is subject to a fixed or floating charge, one can look to the classic formulation, provided by Lord Justice Romer in the case of *Re Yorkshire Woolcombers Association Ltd* [1903] 2 Ch 284.

A floating charge is one:

- which attaches to a class of asset of the company, present and future;
- where that class of asset changes from time to time; and
- where the company is entitled to carry on business and deal with those assets unless or until some step is taken by the chargee.

Looking at the *Siebe Gorman*-type charge in the *Spectrum Plus* case, the bank argued that the control over book debts was sufficient to categorise it as a fixed charge and was present in the operation by a borrower of a standard clearing bank account with the secured lender. This argument was rejected, with the court finding no distinction between the operation of an account in credit and one in debt within an agreed overdraft facility.

The question the court was next asked is whether the book debts were under the control of the bank or the company, both in contract and in practice. If the company was free to deal with the book debts and withdraw book debt realisations from the account held at the bank, without the bank's consent, the bank could not be said to exercise a sufficient degree of control over the book debts necessary to categorise the relationship as one where the bank possessed a fixed charge over the assets.

The court held that the availability of book debts to a company as a source of cash flow was inconsistent with the existence of a fixed charge. However, what was not answered is what degree of control is necessary for the court to find that the charge is fixed over book debts.

While further guidance is awaited, the following general principles may be of some guidance in determining whether a charge over book debts would be enforceable:

(a) An arrangement requiring book debts and proceeds to be paid into an account on which the company has an unfettered right to draw will not constitute sufficient control.

(b) To constitute sufficient control, the proceeds should be paid into a designated account on which the company is not free to draw, or cannot draw without the specific authority of the bank (this element of control is not present in the operation of a standard current account with a clearing bank).

(c) Where a designated account is used to fund a current account on which the company is free to draw, the authority and basis for the transfers between the designated account and the current account will need to be established.

(d) If the transfer requires some positive act or decision-making process from the charge holder, this is likely to constitute sufficient control.

(e) If the transfer requires neither action, nor a decision-making process on the part of the charge holder and/or the company has a right to request and obtain the transfer, it is unlikely that sufficient control will be deemed to exist.

Despite *Spectrum Plus* it is still open to question whether the decision-making process is one which must be exercised each time a transfer is required, or whether it can be fixed, or a standard policy automatically operates, e.g. transfers up to £1,000 are authorised without specific consent.

Major implications arise as a result of these decisions, such as a reduction in the assets available to secured creditors. As we have seen, the order of priorities dictates that the costs of the administration receivership/administration come from floating charge realisations; also preferential creditors are paid before the floating charge realisations. Despite the abolition of Crown preference introduced by Enterprise Act 2002 reforms in insolvencies after 15 September 2003, preferential creditors still exist (such as employee claims). More importantly, IA 1986, s.176A (the ring-fenced sum) applies and can reduce the recovery for the floating charge holder.

The *Spectrum Plus* decision has encouraged asset-based lenders, invoice discounters and factors, which can provide alternative funding on book debts. What is important here is that the debt is assigned to the factor and is no longer company property which would be dealt with in the insolvency. In recent years, it is also clear that post-credit crunch banks have become more prudent in their lending practices, seeking further personal guarantees from company directors.

In the wake of the credit crunch and the consequent global financial crisis, unfortunately there followed a rash of bank and other financial institution insolvencies, a major issue arising in many of these insolvencies being the need to determine ownership of funds in hand and/or security interest. The cases of *Gray* v. *G-T-P Group Ltd* [2010] EWHC 722 (Ch) and *Re Lehman Brothers International (Europe) Ltd (in administration)* [2012] EWHC 2997 (Ch) are noteworthy in that both point to the necessity to show possession and control rather than mere custody in order to qualify as a security financial collateral arrangement (see Financial Collateral Arrangements (No.2) Regulations 2003, SI 2003/3226), which has obvious parallels to the finding as to whether a secured interest is a fixed or floating charge.

5.4.4 Prohibition on the appointment of an administrative receiver

Save in the case of the exceptions detailed below, the holder of a qualifying floating charge in respect of the company's property may not appoint an administrative receiver of the company (IA 1986, s.72A). A qualifying floating charge is one which is created by debenture which:

(a) states that IA 1986, Sched.B1, para.14 applies to the floating charge;
(b) purports to empower the holder of the floating charge to appoint an administrator of the company;
(c) purports to empower the holder of the floating charge to make an appointment which would be an appointment of an administrative receiver within the meaning given by IA 1986, s.29(2); or
(d) purports to empower the holder of a floating charge in Scotland to appoint a receiver who would on appointment be an administrative receiver (IA 1986, Sched.B1, para.14(2)).

The prohibition against the appointment of an administrative receiver applies in all cases except where:

(a) the debenture was created before 15 September 2003; or
(b) the appointment falls within one of the specific statutory exemptions provided in IA 1986, ss.72A–72GA and/or a further statutory instrument.

The first exemption to the general prohibition is by far the most important in the general course of business. The other exemptions are in respect of specific cases, where it was felt by the government that administrative receivership should continue as a result of very specific needs for corporate finance. Interest groups involved in various corporate finance areas lobbied the government hard and obtained important exceptions, which are mirrored in the exemptions to the CVA moratorium procedure as set out in IA 2000.

It is also important to note that the Secretary of State may:

- create additional exemptions;
- provide that an existing exemption will cease to have its effect; and
- vary or amend the exemption (IA 1986, s.72H).

An order of the Secretary of State to fulfil any of these purposes may be made by statutory instrument, although there is provision that if the Secretary of State exercises his power under this section, the order will be subject to possible annulment pursuant to the resolution of the Houses of Parliament. The Secretary of State's ability to add, delete, vary or amend the exemptions could in theory provide scope for the growth in the number of administrative receiverships and the reintroduction of administrative receivership as a major tool for secured lenders. The return of administrative receivership by statutory instrument must, however, be considered unlikely.

A full exploration of the specific exemptions and examples of where these administrative receivership procedures might be used is of specialist interest and outside the scope of this book. Briefly, the exemptions set out in IA 1986, ss.72B–72GA are as follows.

Capital market exemptions

An agreement is or forms part of a capital market arrangement (as defined by IA 1986, Sched.2A, para.1) if:

(a) a party incurs or is expected to incur a debt of at least £50 million under the arrangement; and
(b) the arrangement involves the issue of a capital market investment (as defined by IA 1986, Sched.2A, paras.2 and 3).

Public private partnership

This is a project company (as defined by IA 1986, Sched.2A, para.7) where the project company is a public private partnership project and includes step-in rights (IA 1986, Sched.2A, para.9).

Step-in rights are those where the person providing the finance (including an indemnity) for a project has the right to take sole or principal contractual responsibility for carrying on all or part of the project on the occurrence of certain agreed events or to make arrangements for the carrying out of all or part of the project.

It should be noted that there is no monetary threshold applicable to this exemption and it is interesting to see that where the government is seeking to extract private finance to assist in public projects, an exemption is retained. The government's justification is that administrative receivership is required to protect public service developments, e.g. the building of new schools and hospitals which would otherwise be delayed by administration, an exception it is not willing to provide generally.

Utilities

This exemption covers a project company, where the project is a utilities project and includes step-in rights.

A utility project means a project designed wholly or mainly for the purposes of regulated business. The regulated businesses are as defined in statute (IA 1986, Sched.2A, para.10).

Urban regeneration projects

This exemption covers a project company which is designed wholly or mainly to develop land which at the commencement of the project is wholly or partly in a designated disadvantaged area outside Northern Ireland and includes step-in rights ('urban regeneration projects' as defined by the Finance Act 2001, s.92).

Project finance

This exemption covers a project company where the project is a finance project which includes step-in rights and where a debt of at least of £50 million is incurred, or expected to be incurred, for the purpose of carrying out the project.

This exemption is therefore intended to cover large project finance developments not otherwise covered by the public private partnership or utilities exemptions and was subject to much scrutiny during the reform process. The commercial property industry lobbied hard for these additional exemptions and argued that the threshold should be lowered for property finance projects, from £50 million to between £5 million and £10 million. This call was supported by the Association of Property Bankers, the Royal Institution of Chartered Surveyors and the British Bankers Association. It was feared that the lack of administrative receivership as an available rescue mechanism and the important ability to step in and continue the project would cause great difficulty for commercial property developers. It appears, however, that small to mid-market commercial property developments have not been adversely affected as a result of the loss of administrative receivership.

The meaning of 'financed project' and 'step-in rights' was considered in *Cabvision Ltd* v. *Feetum, Marsden and Smith* [2006] BPIR 379, a case which held that the prohibition against appointment also applies to limited liability partnerships.

Financial markets

This exemption covers a company by virtue of the market charge, a system charge or a collateral security charge (see CA 1989, s.173; Financial Markets and Insolvency Regulations 1996, SI 1996/1469; Financial Markets and Insolvency (Settlement Finality) Regulations 1999, SI 1999/2979).

Registered social landlords

Registered social landlords (generally meaning a housing association) are exempt, and those who provide low-cost housing who have generally taken over responsibility for such housing from the local authority (defined in the Housing Act 1996, Part 1).

Other exempt businesses

Other exempt businesses include:

- protected railway companies;
- a water company (holding an appointment under Chapter 1 of Part II of the Water Industry Act 1991);
- a transport company (being a 'licence company' within the meaning of the Transport Act 2000, s.26).

5.4.5 Appointment of a receiver

Checklist

Secured creditor considerations prior to appointment

- Is the borrower in default?
- Is the security enforceable?
- What assets have been secured?
- If appointed, what are the receiver's powers?
- Over what assets does the creditor wish to appoint?
- Is there any reason why the secured creditor may wish to have control over the borrower company and not just the assets of the borrower?

  - If so, does the security instrument contain a floating charge created before 15 September 2003 entitling the creditor to appoint an administrative receiver, or a qualifying floating charge created after 15 September 2003 entitling the creditor to appoint an administrator?
  - If not and if applicable, does the receiver have sufficient powers to manage any business of the borrower operated at the secured premises?

- Has a letter of demand been sent?
- How has the borrower responded to the demand?
- Has a letter (notice or deed) of appointment been prepared in accordance with the security instrument?
- Is the proposed insolvency practitioner or receiver ready to accept the appointment?

There is no statutory form of appointment for a receiver and consequently the mode and power of appointment of a receiver will be dictated by the formalities set out in the security instrument (legal charge, debenture, etc.). If the instrument requires that an appointment needs to be made in writing or under hand, an oral appointment, or one made by telex, will not suffice (*Re a Company* [1985] BCLC 37). This means that the wording of the instrument must be carefully considered, although it is noted that most security instruments provide that 'in writing' means all electronic communication, etc.

Again, depending on the terms of the security instrument, the notice of appointment can be in any form (e.g. letter) and need not be by deed. The appointment document may set out the appointor's details, the events giving rise to the appointment and the powers of the receiver (often more simply conveniently referring to the powers as set out in security instrument). While the appointment document may deal with the receiver's remuneration and any indemnity from the appointor, it is often more appropriate for this to be dealt with separately as between the two parties.

As discussed, an administrative receiver may only be appointed under a floating charge, which must have been created before 15 September 2003 (IA 1986, ss.29(2), 72A(4)) or where the appointment falls within one of the specific statutory exemptions. In most cases, therefore, the secured creditor with a fixed and floating charge debenture will have the option of appointing either an administrator (over the company and all of its undertaking) or a receiver (over that element of the company's assets that are secured). In practice, a lender may well have both a debenture and specific legal charges over fixed property; the choice of administration versus receivership is therefore determined on where the value is to be found weighed against the costs of dealing.

The debtor is generally best advised to approach the debenture holder some time prior to any impending financial difficulty and/or potential default in the terms of the security. This may lead to a payment holiday, an offer to refinance and/or give assistance in business restructuring. The closer involvement of the debenture holder (most typically a bank) may lead to the appointment of an investigating accountant. Appointed on the instruction of the bank, this accountant will assess the business and make recommendations to the bank as to future steps, which could include the appointment of an administrative receiver. There is nothing to prevent the insolvency practitioner or his firm from acting as both investigating accountant and administrator, administrative receiver or non-administrative receiver (*Bank of Scotland plc* v. *Targetfollow Properties Ltd* [2010] EWHC 3606 (Ch)).

There has been some concern that this practice encourages a greater use of administrative receivership than would otherwise be the case, given the perception that the investigating accountant may provide biased advice influenced by self-interest. During the consultation period leading up to the Enterprise Act 2002, proposals were mooted which would have restricted the ability of an investigating accountant to take the appointment as administrative receiver. These proposals did not find their way on to the statute book, with Parliament considering that, at present, this remains a matter for professional regulation. It is, however, an issue which may be reviewed in the future.

On the basis that the investigating accountant has recommended the appointment of an administrative receiver, the appointment must still be based on some default by the borrower, breach of the terms of the loan facility, giving rise to rights of enforcement under the terms of the security instrument. It should be noted, however, that loan facility agreements and debentures are drawn extremely widely to cover a wide variety of scenarios. It is the wide drafting of appointment clauses which has made the court-appointed receiver a rare beast. In the majority of cases, however, the default is one related to a failure to meet repayment terms.

Guide to procedure

Appointment of a receiver or an administrative receiver

- The borrower falls into arrears/defaults on term/is in breach of covenant.
- A letter of demand is sent providing the borrower a reasonable time to remedy the breach/default, which can be a short period – in certain circumstances as little as an hour (see *Cripps (Pharmaceuticals) Ltd* v. *Wickenden* [1973] 2 All ER 606; *Sheppard & Cooper Ltd* v. *TSB Bank plc (No.2)* [1996] BCC 965).
- In the absence of the borrower remedying the breach/default, the floating charge holder sends in writing a notice of appointment to an insolvency practitioner qualified to act (IA 1986, s.230(2)) or the fixed charge holder sends notice of appointment to a proposed receiver who is not disqualified from acting (IA 1986, ss.30, 31).
- A deed of appointment is not necessary, although it is often common practice (*Phoenix Properties Ltd* v. *Wimpole Street Nominees Ltd* [1992] BCLC 737).
- The appointment must be accepted by the proposed appointee before the end of the next business day after the notice has been received (IA 1986, s.33(1)(a)).
- Subject to the above, the appointment is deemed to commence at the time when the instrument of appointment is received (IA 1986, s.33(1)(b)).
- On appointment the receiver must:

  - ensure that the debenture holder will within seven days of appointment file notice of appointment at Companies House (CA 2006, s.871(1));
  - ensure that the company's website and every invoice, order for goods and services, and business letter issued on behalf of the company contains a statement that a receiver has been appointed (IA 1986, s.39(1));
  - ensure that an account of receipts and payments is sent to the Registrar of Companies within one month after the expiration of 12 months from appointment and every subsequent six months (IA 1986, s.38).

- On appointment, the administrative receiver must:

  - immediately send to the company notice of appointment (IA 1986, s.46(1)(a); IR 1986, rule 3.2(2));
  - publish notice of appointment in the *Gazette* and advertise in such other manner as the administrative receiver thinks fit (in Form 3.1A) (IR 1986, rule 3.2(3));
  - ensure that the appointor has sent notice within seven days to Companies House (CA 2006, s.871);
  - within 28 days, send notice to the company's creditors (IA 1986, s.46(1)(b) – unless the court otherwise directs);
  - ensure that an account of receipts and payments is sent to the Registrar of

> Companies within two months after the expiration of 12 months from appoint-
> ment and every subsequent 12 months (IR 1986, rule 3.32).

If the appointment is invalid (whether by virtue of the instrument of appointment or otherwise), the court may order the receiver to be indemnified against liability arising solely by reason of the appointment (IA 1986, s.34). This is important as the insolvency practitioner is personally liable for losses to the company as a result of trespass (see *OBG Ltd* v. *Allan* [2005] QB 762 and the subsequent House of Lords decision which deals with the limits of that liability). An appointment is not, however, invalidated simply because the amount demanded is not stated or the amount is overstated (*Bank of Baroda* v. *Panessar* [1987] Ch 335).

The insolvency practitioner will take steps to check the validity of the appointment and may seek a written indemnity from the appointor to cover any losses suffered (not just those relating to the appointment). This could cover losses as a result of any acts of negligence by the proposed administrative receiver. It is unlikely that a bank or institutional appointor would be willing to give such an indemnity, although it is more common in the case of a private debenture holder. The court will be reluctant to entertain applications challenging the validity of the appointment after a reasonable lapse of time (see *Secretary of State* v. *Jabble* [1998] BCC 39).

A receiver may apply to the court for directions in relation to matters arising in connection with the performance of his function (IA 1986, s.35; see *Re Cheyne Finance plc* [2008] BCC 182).

The practice and procedures followed by a receiver and/or administrative receiver after appointment are detailed in **Chapter 8**.

5.5 COMPULSORY LIQUIDATION

5.5.1 Preliminary considerations for creditors

The compulsory winding up of a company can only arise following a court order. As we have seen in **Chapter 1**, this remedy has older historical antecedents than voluntary winding up. Although initially it could only be commenced at the instigation of a creditor as a means of enforcement, where the debtor company was unable to pay a debt due and owing to the creditor, it now has wider application.

As we will see in more detail, a winding-up order can now be made on the application of:

(a)   a company and/or its directors;
(b)   a creditor or creditors;
(c)   a contributory or contributories;

(d) a liquidator or temporary administrator appointed in main proceedings in another EU Member State (Council Regulation 1346/2000/EC on Insolvency Proceedings);

(e) a designated officer of the magistrates' court in exercise of powers conferred by the Magistrates' Courts Act 1980, s.87A;

(f) the Secretary of State (on, *inter alia*, public interest grounds);

(g) the FCA;

(h) the Regulator of Community Interest Companies;

(i) the Official Receiver;

(j) a foreign representative appointed in main proceedings or foreign non-main proceedings;

(k) the Director of Public Prosecutions;

(l) the Attorney General against a company formed for charitable purposes (see Charities Act 1993);

(m) an administrator (see IA 1986, Sched.B1, para.60);

(n) the supervisor of a CVA (see IA 1986, s.7(4)(b));

(o) an administrative receiver;

(p) in certain circumstances where empowered by the charge, an LPA receiver; and

(q) the Bank of England (against an authorised institution, see Banking Act 2009).

The most common form of compulsory petition, however, remains that issued by an unsecured creditor of the debtor company. Before commencing proceedings, the creditor should question whether the issue of a winding-up petition will be an effective means of enforcing the debt owed (see below).

Checklist

Considerations before petitioning for the winding up of a debtor company

1. Is the debt secured?
2. Are there alternative proceedings available?
3. Is the debt guaranteed?
4. Has an offer of compromise/settlement been made and/or could an informal arrangement be engineered?
5. Is the sum undisputed?
6. Is the sum claimed over £750?
7. Has a statutory demand been served?
8. Have all alternative enforcement remedies been exhausted?
9. Has the creditor proof of the company's insolvency?
10. Is the creditor aware of other creditors' claims?
11. What assets does the debtor company possess?
12. Are there assets available to realise funds sufficient to discharge the creditor's claim?

Winding up is a collective enforcement procedure; once initiated, for the reasons that are explored below, the creditor may find it difficult to stop the process. This remains the case even though the creditor's individual interests may be best served by the dismissal of the petition following an offer to settle or compromise the debt.

As we have seen, a creditor may seek to recover a debt (e.g. by serving a statutory demand); however, it is far from certain that on being served with a demand the company will pay. Often it is the case that, faced with a demand or a series of demands, the debtor company takes matters into its own hands and initiates a voluntary liquidation process. However, if the debtor takes no action, in the absence of the creditor possessing security that might provide an alternative remedy, the unsecured creditor's ultimate remedy is to issue a winding-up petition against the debtor.

A petition to wind up a company and/or the threat of the process may be enough to elicit a swift response and settlement of the debt. Against this, however, it should be remembered that where a winding-up order is made, in most cases the unsecured creditor can only expect to receive a small proportion of its debt through the payment of a dividend. In addition, it should be remembered that a petitioning creditor's debt has no greater priority than any other debt owed to another unsecured creditor. While the costs of the petition may be recovered as an expense of the liquidation and therefore paid in priority to other unsecured claims, the petitioning creditor's debt is treated equally (*pari passu*) with other claims.

The petitioning creditor's control over the process is also quickly lost. As compulsory liquidation is a class remedy, it should not be used by one creditor to gain advantage over another. This message has been consistently repeated by the courts (see *Re a Company* [1983] BCLC 492). The Practice Direction on Insolvency Proceedings [2007] BCC 842, para.11.5.1 states that the requirement to advertise a winding-up petition: 'must be complied with (unless waived by the court); it is designed to ensure that the class remedy of winding up by the court is made available to all creditors, and is not used as a means of putting improper pressure on the company to pay the petitioner's debt or costs'.

As a result of this court practice, if a petitioner fails to advertise the petition without good reason it may lead to summary dismissal of the petition. Furthermore, the exercise of the court's discretion to allow an adjournment has to be on condition that the petition is advertised; no further adjournments for the purpose of allowing late advertisement will normally be granted. Advertisement of the petition allows other creditors to join the class remedy and allows them to be heard at the petition hearing. Accordingly, the court will not allow the petitioning creditor to consent to an adjournment of the petition hearing simply to allow the debtor company time to negotiate and settle with the petitioning creditor alone. Instead, the advertisement of the petition will mean that other creditors are alerted and can support the petition. The claims of such supporting creditors will then also need to be dealt with by the debtor company if it is to seek and obtain dismissal of the petition. The effect of advertisement is also to ensure that the dismissal of the petition can only be obtained after a court hearing and cannot be granted on an earlier application *ex parte*.

The winding-up process is initiated by the issue of a winding-up petition, and this has severe practical consequences for the debtor company. As we will see in **Chapter 9**, the effects of liquidation are deemed to commence on the issue of the petition. Accordingly, on learning that a petition has been issued, a debtor company's bank may withdraw facilities, contracting parties of the debtor company may terminate contracts as a result of 'an event of insolvency', leasehold property may be subject to forfeiture and the company may find it impossible to trade pending the hearing of the petition (see IA 1986, s.127).

The practical consequence of the above will be that it is difficult for the debtor company to settle the debt of the petitioning creditor, even if the debtor company has the ability, and is offering to pay 100 per cent of the debt prior to the petition hearing. The reasons for this are twofold: first, other creditors may support the petition and their debts will also need to be dealt with; secondly, the debtor company may find it difficult to realise property and/or use funds to discharge the debt.

It remains the case, however, that a creditor may feel it has little option other than to issue winding-up proceedings where a statutory demand has first been served and/or other enforcement methods have proved unsuccessful.

5.5.2 Grounds for winding up a company

A registered company may be wound up if one of the grounds set out in IA 1986, s.122(1) is present, although this list is not exhaustive (e.g. public interest petitions: IA 1986, s.124A).

IA 1986, s.122(1) provides that a registered company may be wound up if:

(a) the company has by special resolution resolved that the company be wound up by the court;

(b) the company is a public company which was registered as such on incorporation, but has not been issued with a trading certificate under CA 2006, s.761 (requirement as to minimum share capital) and more than one year has elapsed since it was so registered;

(c) it is an old public company, within the meaning of the Companies Act 2006 (Consequential Amendments, Transitional Provisions and Savings) Order 2009, SI 2009/1941, Sched.3;

(d) the company does not commence its business within one year of incorporation or suspends business for a whole year;

(e) except in the case of a private limited company limited by share or guarantee, the number of members is reduced to below two;

(f) the company is unable to pay its debts;

(fa) a moratorium under IA 1986, s.1A (i.e. company subject to a CVA) is in place and no voluntary arrangement is approved in relation to that company; or

(g) the court is of the opinion that it is just and equitable that the company should be wound up.

IA 1986, s.221(5) provides that a unregistered company may be wound up if:

(a)   the company is dissolved or has ceased to carry on business, or is carrying on business only for the purposes of winding up;

(b)   the company is unable to pay its debts; or

(c)   the court is of the opinion that it is just and equitable that the company should be wound up.

As can be seen from the above, only one ground for the winding up of a company relies solely on the company being insolvent, namely its inability to pay its debts, although the provision allowing for a winding-up petition where a moratorium has been in place but where a CVA was not approved also possesses an insolvency connotation.

On the hearing of every petition, the court has a discretion as to whether to make a winding-up order, and will consider whether it is right to do so in all the circumstances. Indeed, even if no petition is presented, if in the matter before the court one or more circumstances set out in IA 1986, s.122(1) apply, the court may in exceptional circumstances make a winding-up order of its own motion (see *Lancefield* v. *Lancefield* [2002] BPIR 1108 and *Lavin* v. *Swindwell* [2012] EWHC 2398 (Ch)).

In view of the court's overriding discretion, it is therefore common to include in any creditor's petition the additional ground that as well as the company being unable to pay its debts, it would also be just and equitable in the circumstances for the company to be wound up. The court in the exercise of its overriding discretion (see *Re Walter L. Jacob Ltd* [1993] BCC 512) may refuse to make a winding-up order if an alternative process or resolution appears more appropriate (see *Re Harrods (Buenos Aires) Ltd (No.2)* [1991] BCC 249). The 'just and equitable' ground is also used as a sole ground for winding up by contributories, or less commonly by contingent creditors (*Re Millennium Advanced Technology Ltd* [2004] 1 WLR 2177).

Examples of its use include:

- by shareholders in small companies, where each of the shareholders has legitimate expectations in the management (i.e. it is a quasi-partnership – see *Ebrahimi* v. *Westbourne Galleries Ltd* [1973] AC 360);

- if the main objects for which the company were formed can no longer be performed (*Re Red Rock Gold Mining* (1889) 61 LT 785 and *Davis & Co. Ltd* v. *Brunswick (Australia) Ltd* [1936] 1 All ER 299);

- if management cannot carry on effectively (such as where there is deadlock) and/or one party has been unfairly removed from the control and management of the company (see *Re Yenidje Tobacco Co. Ltd* [1916] 2 Ch 426 and *Re Zinotty Properties Ltd* [1984] 1 WLR 1249)); and

- if the affairs of the company are being conducted in a manner which is unfair or oppressive to the petitioner (*Loch* v. *John Blackwood* [1924] AC 783).

A winding-up petition on just and equitable grounds is also often allied to a CA 2006, s.994 petition, although it should be noted that the jurisdiction under IA 1986, s.122(1)(g) is no wider than that under s.994 (*Re Guidezone Ltd* (2000) 2 BCLC 321).

However, the majority of compulsory winding-up petitions (approximately 95 per cent) are presented by creditors on the basis that the company is unable to pay its debts. Although 'creditor' is not defined in the statute, 'debt' is widely defined in IR 1986, rule 13.12.

Definitions

Provable debt

All claims by creditors are provable as debts against the company, whether they are present or future, certain or contingent, ascertained or sounding only in damages, except where otherwise provided in IR 1986, rule 12.3(2).

Debt (as defined by IR 1986, rule 13.12(3))

For the purposes of reference to a debt or liability in any provision of IA 1986 or IR 1986 about winding up, it is immaterial whether the debt or liability is present or future, whether it is certain or contingent, or whether its amount is fixed or liquidated, or is capable of being ascertained by fixed rules or as a matter of opinion.

Liability

Means a liability under any enactment, any liability for breach of trust, any liability in contract, tort or bailment, and any liability arising out of an obligation to make restitution (IR 1986, rule 13.12(4)).

As a result of the wide definition of 'debt', contingent or prospective creditors may petition (*Tottenham Hotspur plc* v. *Edennote plc* [1994] BCC 681), although the claim must be one which is capable of constituting a debt capable of legal enforcement, meaning that statute-barred debts cannot be relied upon (see *Re Karnos Property Co. Ltd* (1989) 5 BCC 14). The debt need not, however, be a provable debt (see *Woodley* v. *Woodley (No.2)* [1994] 1 WLR 1167).

As a consequence of this, certain fines and maintenance/lump sum orders made in family proceedings, which are not provable debts, can still form the basis of a winding-up petition. The debt may also have been assigned to the petitioning creditor (see *Re Paris Skating Rink Co.* (1887) 5 Ch D 959).

The petition must be in a prescribed form (commonly Form 4.2, see **5.5.5** for further details). The petition must detail how the debtor company's liability to the creditor arose. It is insufficient simply to describe the petitioner as 'creditor' (see *Re*

Palais Cinema Ltd [1918] VLR 113). A creditor's petition will usually be on the basis that the debtor company is unable to pay its debts (IA 1986, s.123(1)(f) or s.221(5)(b)).

The debtor's inability to pay its debts could be on a cash flow or balance sheet basis, both measures of insolvency being included in IA 1986, s.123, which defines when a company is deemed to be unable to pay its debts.

A company is 'deemed' to be unable to pay its debts:

(a)   when it is served with a statutory demand and within 21 days the company has neglected to pay or secure the debt to the reasonable satisfaction of the creditor (i.e. a cash flow test);

(b)   if an execution or other legal process issued on a judgment or order of the court has been returned unsatisfied in whole or in part (i.e. a cash flow test); or

(c)   if it is proved to the satisfaction of the court that the company is unable to pay its debts as they fall due (i.e. a cash flow test), or where it is proved to the court's satisfaction that the value of the company's assets is less than the amount of its liabilities, taking into account its contingent and prospective liabilities (i.e. a balance sheet test) (IA 1986, s.123(2)).

The second ground (item (b) above) on which inability to pay debts may be proved is where execution has been levied but remains unsatisfied in whole or in part (IA 1986, s.123(1)(b) or s.224(1)(a)). However, it is not a requirement that a judgment creditor must first attempt to levy execution. If the ground is relied upon, it must be shown that the execution has been returned unsatisfied by the High Court enforcement officer.

The inclusion of the third ground (item (c) above), i.e. proved to the satisfaction of the court, means that there is no mandatory requirement in the case of a corporate debtor for a creditor to first serve a statutory demand or obtain a judgment (see *Taylor's Industrial Flooring Ltd* v. *M&H Plant Hire (Manchester) Ltd* [1990] BCC 44 (CA)). It is, however, still expected that demand for payment has been made by the creditor prior to presentation (*Re a Company (No.001573 of 1983)* [1983] BCLC 492). Although specific pre-action protocols do not apply to the issue of winding-up petitions, 'reasonable' pre-action behaviour is expected of a petitioner (see the Practice Direction on Pre-Action Conduct, which came into force on 6 April 2009; the current version is available at **www.justice.gov.uk/courts/procedure-rules/civil/rules/pd_pre-action_conduct.htm**). This is generally taken to mean that the 'debtor' company must be given the opportunity of disputing (or paying) the debtor. Accordingly, some form of written demand, allowing a reasonable time in which to respond, could be expected, save where it is clearly evident that the debt is undisputed and will not/cannot be paid (*Cornhill Insurance plc* v. *Improvement Services Ltd* [1986] 1 WLR 114).

It should be remembered that a debt is deemed undisputed if a statutory demand has been served and remains unsatisfied, whereas a demand in any other form could be disputed at any time. If in any doubt, the creditor is best advised first to issue a statutory demand. It should also be noted that a petition in respect of a debt of less than £750 can be presented, although it would be unusual for the court in the exercise of its discretion to make a winding-up order (*Re World Industrial Bank Ltd* [1909] WN 148).

The balance sheet test of insolvency provides an additional ground for winding up on grounds of inability to pay, which is not present where a creditor is seeking the bankruptcy of an individual. It leaves open a wider possibility for the petitioning creditor to issue a winding-up petition, if credible evidence exists as to the company's inability to meet its liabilities.

In assessing a company's inability to meet its liabilities, the court will look at the company's existing liabilities (*Re European Life Assurance Society* (1869–70) LR 9 Eq 122) although previously its contingent liabilities were not taken into account (*Byblos Bank SAL* v. *Al-Khudhairy* [1987] BCLC 232).

This issue was reconsidered in *BNY Corporate Trustee Services Ltd* v. *Eurosail UK* [2010] EWHC 2005 (Ch) where the nature of the test of insolvency as set out in IA 1986, s.123(2) was considered in detail. The court held that the balance sheet test is not simply a matter of straightforward analysis of the company's accounts as stated. Instead, assets should be valued as at the present time; this should not take into account contingent and prospective assets. In contrast, when considering liabilities, both contingent and prospective liabilities should be taken into account. This leads to a 'worst case scenario' conservative assessment of the company's balance sheet, which ultimately affords greater creditor protection.

In the context of wrongful trading (see **Chapter 11**), a former (now abandoned) test for assessing the directors' reasonableness in continuing to trade was the so-called 'silver lining test', i.e. was it reasonable to assume that the dark clouds of insolvency would be lifted? Such a test, taking into account optimistic forecasts of possible improvement, is almost diametrically opposed to the court's thinking in the *Eurosail* case, which favours a 'here and now' approach to the test of insolvency.

The *Eurosail* case is clearly in line with earlier authorities that had established that the company's inability to pay is assessed as at the date of hearing, but it also included a requirement that the company was unable to pay as at the date of issue of the petition. See further *Re Fildes Bros Ltd* [1970] 1 WLR 592, and the requirement for the petition to be accompanied by a statement of truth, i.e. that the company is insolvent as at the date of the petition.

Some form of admission by the debtor company of its insolvency may also be relied upon by a creditor in an attempt to persuade the court that the debtor is unable to pay its debts. The creditor should evidence any oral or written statements and could rely on the debtor's failure to pay other creditors' demands, e.g. unsatisfied county court judgments (see *Re Fortune Copper Mining Co.* (1870) LR 10 Eq 390; *Re Yates Collieries and Limeworks Co.* [1883] WN 171, for examples of where a debtor's declaration that it was unable to pay its debts was relied upon).

Where an unmerited petition is issued, it is treated as an abuse of court process and an injunction may be issued to restrain the petitioner from proceeding further with the petition, e.g. an injunction may restrain the advertisement of the petition. Furthermore, the petitioning creditor (and even the legal adviser conducting the proceedings) can be penalised by an indemnity costs order (see *Re a Company (No.010656 of 1990)* [1991] BCLC 464; *Re a Company (No.000751 of 1992), ex p. Avocet Aviation Ltd* [1992] BCLC 869; *Re a Company (No.007356 of 1998)* [2000] BCC 214).

If a debt is clearly undisputed, there might be a considerable tactical advantage in proceeding on the grounds of inability to pay a demand (other than a statutory demand) as there is no necessity to wait for the three-week period provided for in the statutory demand. However, for the reasons outlined above, it is a tactic that must be very carefully thought through.

Brief guide to procedure

Compulsory winding-up proceedings

1. Prepare petition in Form 4.2.
2. Prepare witness statement verifying the petition, attaching the petition as an exhibit.
3. Carry out search of Register of Petitions held at Companies Court to ensure there is no outstanding petition.
4. Pay Official Receiver's deposit (£1,165) and court fee (£220) and obtain receipted petition (fees as at time of writing).
5. File petition at court with two copies (IR 1986, rule 4.7(4) – two copies are required, one for service upon the company and one to be attached to the certificate of service).
6. Obtain the copies of the petition sealed and endorsed with a hearing date.
7. Serve company with copy of petition.
8. File certificate proving service immediately after service (Form 4.4) and not less than five business days before hearing.
9. Advertise petition in Form 4.6 in the *London Gazette*, not less than seven days after service, not less than seven days before hearing.
10. Prepare certificate of compliance (Form 4.7) and file at court at least five business days before hearing.
11. Prepare list of creditors (Form 4.10) which have given notice of intention to appear at the hearing.
12. Before commencement of the hearing, hand to the court a list of creditor appearances.

5.5.3 Jurisdiction to wind up a company by court order

Registered (IA 1986, s.117) and unregistered (IA 1986, s.221) companies and LLPs (see Limited Liability Partnerships Regulations 2001, SI 2001/1090) may be wound up following court order, subject to the provisions of Council Regulation 1346/2000/EC on Insolvency Proceedings, i.e. where main proceedings have been or could be commenced in another EU Member State.

Other corporations may be wound up where the court is given jurisdiction to do so (see *Lunn* v. *Cardiff Coal Co.* [2002] 171 FLR 430), e.g. building societies under the Building Societies Act 1986, s.86(1); European public LLPs under Council Regulation 2157/2001/EC; incorporated friendly societies under the Friendly Societies Act 1992; societies registered or deemed registered under the Industrial and

Provident Societies Act 1965; European co-operative societies under Council Regulation 1435/2003/EC.

A petition can also be presented for the winding up of an insolvent partnership as an unregistered company under the Insolvent Partnerships Order 1994, SI 1994/2421.

Companies which cannot be wound up include:

(a)   those already being wound up by a court;
(b)   where special insolvency regimes apply (e.g. water companies, railway companies, certain public private partnerships, air traffic service licence companies, protected energy companies);
(c)   a European Economic Area (EEA) insurer (see Insurers (Reorganisation and Winding Up) Regulations 2004, SI 2004/353);
(d)   EEA credit institutions (see Credit Institutions (Reorganisation and Winding Up) Regulations 2004, SI 2004/1045);
(e)   institutions of sovereign states (see State Immunity Act 1978, s.1(1));
(f)   certain international organisations established by treaty by sovereign states (see *Re International Tin Council* [1989] Ch 309);
(g)   illegal associations;
(h)   unincorporated member clubs; and
(i)   unincorporated societies.

The winding-up petition should be issued in the High Court, although if the company's share capital does not exceed £120,000, the petitioning creditor has the option of commencing proceedings in the county court appropriate to where the registered office of the debtor company is situated (IA 1986, s.117(2)). The registered office is the place where the company has had its registered office for the longest period during the last six months (IA 1986, s.117(6)).

It is common practice for practitioners acting for creditors to use the High Court, due to the court's familiarity with the process and the ease with which a date for hearing can be obtained. Furthermore, it is convenient to check that a petition has not already been presented by personal attendance at the Companies Court general office just prior to issue, as this is where the central registry for winding-up petitions is kept. While county court petitions should also be recorded on this register, in reality there is often a delay, which could cause the practical problem of two petitions being presented at the same time (see *Re Audio Systems Ltd* [1965] 1 WLR 1096 and *Re Filby Bros (Provender) Ltd* [1958] 1 WLR 683). A check can also be made by telephone (presently 0906 754 0043).

However, it will not invalidate the proceedings if the winding-up petition has been issued in the wrong court (IA 1986, s.118(1)). See *Re Pleatfine Ltd* [1983] BCLC 102 and *Re Sankey Furniture Ltd* [1995] 2 BCLC 594 for examples of the exercise of the court's wide discretion, which can include allowing proceedings to continue in the 'wrong' court (see IA 1986, s.118(2)), and transferring the matter to the correct court or striking out the proceedings (see IR 1986, rule 7.12).

5.5.4   Who may petition for the winding-up order?

A petition for the winding up of a company may be presented by the company or its directors. Where a receiver, administrator or supervisor of a CVA petitions for the winding up of a company, it also does so in the name of the company.

In addition, the following may apply together or separately to wind up a company (IA 1986, s.124):

- A creditor.
- A number of creditors jointly.
- A contingent or prospective creditor or creditors.
- A contributory or contributories.
- A liquidator (within the meaning of Regulation 1346/2000/EC, Art.2(b)) appointed in proceedings by virtue of Art.3(1)).
- A temporary administrator (within the meaning of Regulation 1346/2000/EC, Art.38).
- The clerk of a magistrates' court in exercise of the powers conferred by the Magistrates' Courts Act 1980, s.87A (enforcement of fines).
- The Secretary of State on grounds that:

    (a) the company is a public company which was registered as such on its original incorporation, and has not been issued with a trading certificate under CA 2006, s.761 (requirement as to minimum share capital) and more than a year has expired since it was so registered (IA 1986, s.122(1)(b));

    (b) it is an old public company within the meaning of the Companies Act 2006 (Consequential Amendments, Transitional Provisions and Savings) Order 2009, SI 2009/1941, Sched.3 (IA 1986, s.122(1)(c));

    (c) it is in the public interest (IA 1986, s.124A);

    (d) under the European Public Limited-Liability Company Regulations 2004, SI 2004/2326, it is a *Societas Europaea* whose registered office is in Great Britain and is not in compliance with Regulation 2157/2001/EC, Art.7 on the statute for a European company (location of head office and registered office) (IA 1986, s.124B);

- The FCA, where a European co-operative society whose registered office is in Great Britain is in breach of Regulation 1435/2003/EC, Art.73(1) (winding up by court of competent authority, see IA 1986, s.124C), or Art.6 (location of head office and registered office).
- The Regulator of Community Interest Companies, where a case falls within the Companies (Audit, Investigations and Community Enterprise) Act 2004, s.50 (IA 1986, s.124(4A)).
- The Official Receiver (or other authorised person), where a company is being wound up voluntarily. The court will not make a winding-up order unless satisfied that the voluntary liquidation cannot be continued without due regard

to the interests of the creditors or contributors (IA 1986, s.124(5)). In exercising its discretion, the court will be guided but not bound by the wishes of the majority in value of the company's creditors (*Re Southard & Co. Ltd* [1979] 1 WLR 1198). The court will have regard to whether impartial investigation of the directors' conduct is required, although it will always be reluctant to call into question the professional integrity and independence of a qualified insolvency practitioner, however so appointed (see *Re Gordon & Breach Science Publishers Ltd* [1995] BCC 261 for an example of a case where a compulsory liquidation superseded an existing voluntary liquidation).

Where a company is being wound up on the grounds that the moratorium for the company under a CVA has come to an end, a winding-up petition may only be presented by one or more creditors (IA 1986, s.124(3A)).

5.5.5 Nature and content of a winding-up petition

A company can only be wound up by the court under IA 1986 following the issue, service and hearing of a petition (IA 1986, s.124) (see *Re Osea Road Campsites Ltd* [2005] 1 WLR 760, where the court held that it had no power to make an order in the absence of a petition).

A petition must set out the necessary allegations detailing one of the circumstances in which a court may wind up a company and provide sufficient information for the court to make an order. Although similar in nature, it is not a statement of case or pleading for the purposes of the CPR. The petitioner must check that there is not an existing 'live' petition by personal attendance at the Companies Court or by telephoning (presently 0906 754 0043). The petitioner must be a party entitled to petition by virtue of the applicable legislation applying to the debtor company (see *Mann* v. *Goldstein* [1968] 1 WLR 1091 and *Re MTI Trading Systems Ltd* [1998] BCC 400).

The petition must be prepared in accordance with the prescribed form (see Form 4.2 for a creditor's petition, Form 4.4 for a contributory's petition and special forms for petitions under the Insolvent Partnerships Order 1994, SI 1994/2421). The most common type of petition, namely a creditor's petition, is explored further.

Practical tips for completion of Form 4.2

The matters listed below refer to completion of the various parts of Form 4.2. The letters in square brackets refer to the corresponding notes set out in Form 4.2.

1. The petition must be entitled 'IN THE MATTER OF [*name of debtor company*] Limited', and quote the registered number of the debtor company; and 'IN THE MATTER OF THE INSOLVENCY ACT 1986'.
2. The petition should be addressed to 'Her Majesty's High Court of Justice [or County Court]', verified by statement of truth (see below) and filed in court (IR 1986, rule 4.7(1)). [a]

Rule 4.7   Form 4.2

Winding-Up Petition

(Title)   **(Registered No.   )**

(a) Insert title of court   To (a)

(b) Insert full name(s)   The petition of (b)
and address(es) of
petitioner(s)

(c) Insert full name   1. (c)
and registered no. of
company subject to
petition

                             (hereinafter called "the company") was incorporated on

(d) Insert date of   (d)
incorporation

                             under the Companies Act 19

(e) Insert address of   2. The registered office of the company is at (e)
registered office

(f) Insert amount of   3. The nominal capital of the company is (f) £
nominal capital and   divided into   shares of £   each. The amount of the capital paid up or credited
how it is divided   as paid up is (g) £
(g) Insert amount of
capital paid up or
credited as paid up

                             4. The principal objects for which the company was established are as follows:

                             and other objects stated in the memorandum of association of the company

(h) Set out the   5. (h)
grounds on which a
winding-up order is
sought

(j) Delete as   6. The company (j) is/is not an insurance undertaking; a credit institution; an investment
applicable   undertaking providing services involving the holding of funds or securities for third
                             parties; or a collective investment undertaking as referred to in Article 1.2 of the EC
                             Regulation.

(k) Insert name of   7. For the reasons stated in the statement of truth of (k)   filed in
person making the   support here of it is considered that the EC Regulation on insolvency proceedings (j)
statement of truth   will/will not apply (j) and that these proceedings will be (l)_____
                             proceedings as defined in Article 3 of the EC Regulation
(l) Insert whether
main, secondary or
territorial proceedings   (7A) (j)[A statutory demand was served on the company on (ll). More than 4 months
                             have elapsed between the service of the statutory demand and the presentation of this
(ll) Insert date of   petition for the reasons set out in the statement of truth of (k)
service   filed in support hereof.]

284

8. In the circumstances it is just and equitable that the company should be wound up
The petitioner(s) therefore pray(s) as follows:-

(1) that (c)

may be wound up by the court under the provisions of the Insolvency Act 1986
or
(2) that such other order may be made as the court thinks fit

(m) If the company is the petitioner, delete "the company". Add the full name and address of any other person on whom it is intended to serve this petition

Note: It is intended to serve this petition on (m)
[the company] [and]

Endorsement

This petition having been presented to the court

(n) Insert name and address of Court

on _____ will be heard at (n) [Royal Courts of Justice, Strand, London, WC2A 2LL] [(n) _____ County Court
_____]

(o) Insert name and address of District Registry

[(o) _____ District Registry
_____]

on:

Date _____

Time _____ hours
(or as soon thereafter as the petition can be heard)

The solicitor to the petitioner is:-

Name _____

Address _____
_____

Telephone no _____

Reference _____

(j) [Whose London Agents are:-

Name _____

Address _____
_____

Telephone no. _____

Reference _____

---

3.   Insert full name and address of petitioner(s). [b]

It should be noted that the petitioner does not need to sign or endorse the petition, although a statement of truth (see **5.5.6**) is required to be signed by the petitioner or someone authorised to make the statement on behalf of the petitioner.

4.   Insert name and registered number of debtor company. [c]

As stated above, while some small errors (e.g. of spelling) may not invalidate the petition, it must be clear to whom the petition is addressed.

5.   Insert date of incorporation of the company [d], including as appropriate whether that was under CA 1948, 1985 or 2006.

6.   Insert registered address of the debtor company. [e]

7.   Provide details of the company's nominal share capital (i.e. its authorised share capital) and how it is divided into shares and the amount of the capital paid up or credited as paid up. [f] and [g]

This information is obtained from Companies House, searching the original constitution of the company and then checking whether subsequent to that there have been any changes to share capital. This is generally of historical significance only, as the available share capital is there to meet the demands of the company's creditors. In the early development of limited liability corporate activity, the capital would have needed to be high, but modern times have seen the development of trading activities that have little reliance on this form of creditor protection, and indeed, as from 1 October 2009, a registered company is no longer required to have an authorised share capital (the requirements of CA 1985, s.2(5)(a) being repealed by CA 2006 from that date). Amendments to Form 4.2 are therefore likely.

8.   Provide details of the principal objects of the company.

This information is obtained from review of the company's memorandum of association and can be a précis of what is often a long list of general objects. It should be noted that as from 1 October 2009 (see CA 2006, s.31), a registered company's objects are no longer restricted unless specifically provided for in its articles. Amendments to Form 4.2 are again likely.

9.   Set out the grounds on which the petition is based and a winding-up order sought. [h]

This should be as detailed as is necessary to justify standing and entitlement to petition and the basis of the debtor's liability (or other grounds as appropriate).

10.   Is the company an insurance undertaking, credit institution, investment undertaking or collective investment undertaking? [j]

If the company is one of the above, taking account of the provisions of Council Regulation 1346/2000/EC on Insolvency Proceedings, Art.1(2), a different specialist insolvency regime will apply. Such companies will not be subject to the general Regulation.

11. Insert name of the person providing statement of truth. [k]

For details regarding the statement of truth, see below. Explanation as to why Regulation 1346/2000/EC will apply needs to be given in the statement of truth. This may need to detail complex arrangements which go to establish the COMI as a matter of fact.

12. Does Regulation 1346/2000/EC apply? [j] If so will these proceedings be main or secondary proceedings as defined in Regulation 1346/2000/EC, Art.3? [l]

Based on the information contained within the statement of truth, the liquidation will be a main proceeding if the registered office/COMI is in England and Wales. Where the company is offshore/an unregistered (foreign) company, the proceedings may be secondary proceedings.

13. If the petition is based on the failure to satisfy a statutory demand, retain the appropriate paragraph and state the date that any statutory demand was served upon the debtor.

14. If the statutory demand was served more than four months before the presentation of the petition, retain this paragraph and refer to statement of truth where more details can be provided. [k]

Where reliance is placed on a statutory demand and more than four months have elapsed, justification for the delay and the reasoning not only as to why the debt is still due and owing, but also why the company could still be regarded as unable to pay its debts must be provided. This could include reference to continuing admission of debt, or unsuccessful negotiations to compromise or secure the debt.

15. In the prayer, the petitioner asks that the debtor company be wound up [c] or for such other order as the court thinks fit.

16. Details as to on whom the petition will be served need to be provided [m] (see below).

17. In the endorsement to the petition, details of the time and location of the hearing are filled out by the court official with the time and date of the filing of the petition (this is important as being the commencement date of the winding up (IA 1986, s.127)).

18. Details of the name, address and telephone number of the petitioner's solicitors (and London agents) are provided within the endorsement.

5.5.6 Statement of truth

The petition presented for filing must be verified by an affidavit or witness statement, which contains confirmation for and on behalf of the petitioning creditor that the petition is true to the best of the petitioner's knowledge, information and belief. The witness statement converts the allegations in the petition to evidence in chief (see *Re Wallace Smith and Co. Ltd* [1992] BCLC 970).

As detailed above, the statement will also deal with the facts relied upon to establish the debtor's COMI and application of Regulation 1346/2000/EC. If appropriate, it will also state the reasons why any statutory demand was not relied upon within four months of service.

The statement must be made by the petitioner, or person with requisite authorisation and knowledge of the matters giving rise to the petition. The statement must be made within 10 business days of the date of the filing of the petition (and statement) at court.

5.5.7 Filing and issue of the petition

The original petition must be attached as an exhibit to the statement and sufficient copies filed of the petition to enable service (see IR 1986, rule 4.7 and **5.5.8**).

A deposit is payable before the petition can be issued (as at time of writing this is £1,165). This deposit is payable to the Official Receiver and provides security for the performance of the Official Receiver's duties and responsibilities upon a winding-up order being made. If the petition is withdrawn or dismissed, the deposit is refunded to the petitioning creditor. The court fee payable (currently £220) is not refundable.

On issue, the court seals the petition and endorses it with a hearing date. While the petitioning creditor may wish to move matters along as quickly as possible, it should still have regard to the requirements to properly serve the petition and thereafter advertise it (see **5.5.8** and **5.5.9**). The process may take a number of days and consequently, as a rule of thumb, the petitioning creditor should seek to obtain a date not less than three weeks hence.

In cases of urgency, where it is considered that the assets of the company may be dissipated, the petitioning creditor may apply to court for the requirements of service and advertisement to be shortened. However, in cases of such urgency, the petitioning creditor should also consider an application to appoint a provisional liquidator (see **5.6**).

5.5.8 Service of the petition

The service of the petition is effected by serving the company at its registered office, by handing the petition to a person acknowledging himself to be a director, employee or officer of the company, or by handing it to a person who acknowledges they are authorised to accept service of documents on behalf of the company. Alternatively, the petition may be served by depositing it at the company's registered office in such a way as it is likely to come to the attention of the persons attending the office (IR 1986, rule 4.8). The petition may not be served by post or electronic means without court approval or direction (*Re a Company* [1985] BCLC 37).

Service of the petition is a fundamental requirement and the petition will be set aside if service cannot be proved (*Craig* v. *Kanssen* [1943] KB 256).

The petition must be served at least seven business days before it is advertised and the advertisement must appear at least seven days before the hearing (see **5.5.9**). Thus, the petition must be served at least 14 days before the date of the hearing.

If for any reason personal service on the company at its registered office is not practical, or the company has no registered office or is an unregistered company, the petition may be served by leaving the petition at the company's last known place of business in such a way that it is likely to come to the attention of a person appearing there. Alternatively, the petition may be delivered to a secretary or some director, manager or principal officer of the company, wherever that person may be found (IR 1986, rule 4.8(4)). A petition may be served upon the debtor's solicitors if they are instructed to accept service (IR 1986, rule 13.4).

If service is for any other reason impractical, the court may direct that a petition may be served in any other manner, e.g. service by advertisement in the local paper. An application must be made to court for permission on an *ex parte* basis, with a witness statement stating the steps that have been taken in order to serve the document and why it has proved impractical to serve the petition (IR 1986, rule 4.8(7)). In practice, the petitioner will need to satisfy the court that it has taken proper steps to serve the debtor, although in the case of service upon a company this is generally easily established by attending and delivering the petition to an identifiable registered office.

After effecting service, the petitioning creditor should prepare a certificate verifying the date, time and manner of service, which should be filed as soon as reasonably practicable after service and in any event not less than five business days before the hearing of the petition (IR 1986, rule 4.9A(4)).

5.5.9 Advertisement of the petition

Unless the court orders otherwise (e.g. on grounds of public interest: see *Re Golden Chemical Products Ltd* [1976] Ch 300), the petition must be advertised in the *London Gazette* not less than seven clear business days (i.e. excluding Saturdays, Sundays and public holidays) after it has been served on the company and not less than seven clear days before the day fixed for a hearing (IR 1986, rule 4.11).

The advertisement must be in Form 4.6. The use of this form ensures that the advertisement contains the matters prescribed in the Insolvency Rules (IR 1986, rule 4.11). The purpose of the advertisement is to gather the responses from any creditors or contributories of the company as to whether they support or oppose the petition.

A copy of the advertisement must be filed at court with the certificate of compliance (IR 1986, rule 4.14).

As previously discussed, the failure to advertise can be fatal and may result in the dismissal of the petition unless good reason is shown (IR 1986, rule 4.11(6)). Except in exceptional circumstances, the court will only allow the adjournment of the hearing of a petition if the petition is thereafter advertised. This discourages the use of the petition as a debt collection method at the behest of a sole creditor. As detailed below, once advertised the public hearing of the petition will take place and prior (*ex parte*) dismissal/withdrawal of the petition is not permissible.

A creditor receiving notification in this manner is given the opportunity to contact the petitioning creditor or its solicitors and give notice of its intention to appear at the hearing. Notice to the petitioner must be in Form 4.9. The notice of intention to appear must reach the creditor and/or solicitors not later than 4 pm on the business day before the date appointed for the hearing. Any person who fails to comply with this rule may only appear at the hearing with leave of the court.

A petitioning creditor should ensure that the advertisement is as accurate as possible. An error may invalidate the advertisement and the court may dismiss the petition, or order an adjournment and re-advertisement. However, if it is a small error and the creditors were not potentially misled and no prejudice is caused, the court may overlook the error (*Re Garton (Western) Ltd* (1989) 5 BCC 198). If the petition is not advertised in accordance with IR 1986, the court may dismiss it (IR 1986, rule 4.11(5), and see *Re Signland* [1982] 2 All ER 609 where the winding-up petition was advertised prior to service and was struck out).

5.5.10 Certificate of compliance

At least five business days before the hearing, the petitioning creditor or solicitor must file at court a certificate of compliance in Form 4.7 (IR 1986, rule 4.14). This certificate shows:

- the date the petition was presented;
- the date fixed for hearing;
- the date or dates upon which the petition was served; and
- the date upon which the petition was served and advertised.

A copy of the advertisement should be filed with a certificate of compliance. Non-compliance with this provision may mean that the court will dismiss the petition (IR 1986, rule 4.14(3)), although in practice the petition is likely to be adjourned (but only once) to allow time for the omission to be rectified. The time for filing a certificate of compliance has been extended to no later than 4.30 pm on the Friday preceding the date upon which the petition is to be heard (see Practice Direction on Insolvency Proceedings [2007] BCC 842).

The certificate is primarily to assist the court in determining that all of the formalities regarding the petition have been complied with. Although failure to submit can result in dismissal of the petition, it is not to be seen as abandonment of the petition. In practice, if through administrative error this certificate has not been filed and no prejudice will be caused, the court may grant a short adjournment to allow this error to be rectified. The court will not, save in exceptional circumstances, make an order where it cannot be shown that the certificate has been filed.

5.5.11 Leave to withdraw

Up to five days before the hearing, the petitioning creditor may, on *ex parte* application (and strictly on the condition that the petition has not been advertised), apply for leave to withdraw the petition (IR 1986, rule 4.15).

The court will grant such an application if satisfied that:

- the petition has not been advertised;
- no notice in support or opposition has been received by any other creditor; and
- the company consents to an order being made.

This enables the petition to be withdrawn in the case where the company is able to pay the petitioning creditor's debt prior to advertisement, or come to a suitable compromise with the petitioning creditor. However, the exercise by the court of this power is discretionary and the court can refuse the application to withdraw if it considers this appropriate. In any event, once the petition has been advertised, the application to withdraw the petition can only be heard at the hearing of the petition.

This stresses the collective nature of insolvency proceedings and points out the dangers to a petitioning creditor. Once the petition is issued, the matter can move outside the petitioner's control, despite any agreement with the company as to payment or postponement of the debt. The collective rights of the creditors need to be considered by the court, not just those of the petitioning creditor (*Re a Company* [1983] BCLC 492). See also Practice Direction on Insolvency Proceedings [2007] BCC 842.

5.5.12 Hearing of the petition

The petitioning creditor must prepare a list of those persons and creditors who have given notice of appearance, and this list must be handed to the court before commencement of the hearing (IR 1986, rule 4.17). If the company wishes to oppose the petition, it must file evidence in opposition not less than five business days before the date fixed for hearing (IR 1986, rule 4.18).

The hearing of the petition will be in open court. In the normal course of events in the High Court, the petition is usually listed for hearing with a large number of other winding-up petitions before a registrar or district judge. Petitions will be dealt with quickly and winding-up orders are usually made with minimal judicial scrutiny, provided all necessary papers have been filed.

The registrar may be asked to adjourn the hearing (perhaps while settlement proposals are put forward or a CVA is proposed), but the court is unlikely to adjourn more than once. Adjournments may also be sought to rectify some defect on the part of the petitioning creditor (i.e. failure to advertise properly, file notice of compliance).

If the petition is opposed, it is likely that the petition will be referred to a judge and further directions may be granted.

Only the petitioner and the company, creditors and contributories have the right to be heard, although the court may hear submissions for and on behalf of persons who have given notice of intention to appear (see *Re Bradford Navigation Co.* (1869–70) LR 5 Ch App 600).

The court may in the exercise of its discretion:

- dismiss the petition with or without costs;
- adjourn the hearing conditionally or unconditionally;
- make an interim order; or
- make any order as it thinks fit (IA 1986, s.125(1)).

If the petitioning creditor fails to appear at the hearing, the petition will normally be dismissed.

When the winding-up order is made, the court will send notice of this to the Official Receiver's office (IR 1986, rule 4.20(1)). When the winding-up order has been made and sealed by the court, it should be sent to the Official Receiver's office and the Official Receiver will then send one copy to the company, another to the Registrar of Companies and advertise the order in the *London Gazette* and in such other manner as it thinks appropriate.

The winding-up order is a final order (*Re Reliance Properties Ltd* [1951] 2 All ER 327).

Save where the winding-up order is made on the application of an administrator or supervisor of a CVA, the Official Receiver will be liquidator of the company by virtue of his office. The court does not have power to make a direct appointment of a private practice liquidator (IA 1986, s.136), although, as we shall see, the Official Receiver may call a meeting of creditors, or make a 'Secretary of State appointment' if persuaded that the majority of creditors support the appointment of a nominated office holder.

5.6 PROVISIONAL LIQUIDATION

Before the making of a final winding-up order, a provisional liquidator may be appointed (IA 1986, s.135 and see *Re a Company (No.00315 of 1973)* [1973] 1 WLR 1566).

An application in Form 7.1 to appoint a provisional liquidator may be made by:

- the petitioner;
- a creditor of the company;
- a contributory;
- the company;
- the Secretary of State;
- a temporary administrator;
- a liquidator appointed in main proceedings (as defined by Regulation 1346/2000/EC) in another EU Member State; or

- any person who under any enactment would be entitled to present a petition for the winding up of the company.

The reason why a provisional liquidator may be appointed is generally to ensure the preservation of the company's assets and to prevent prejudice pending the hearing of the winding-up petition. An order may be made where a company is already in voluntary liquidation (see *Re Pinstripe Farming Co. Ltd* [1996] 2 BCLC 295).

An application will thus be sought in unusual circumstances, such as where there is a possibility that the directors may abscond and/or remove company property prior to the winding-up order, although recent cases suggest that the court will not seek to confine the application of the section too narrowly (see *MHMH Ltd* v. *Carwood Barker Holdings Ltd* [2006] 1 BCLC 279). An order appointing a provisional liquidator will only be made if it can be shown that a winding-up order is likely to be made (*Re Treasure Traders Corporation Ltd* [2005] EWHC 2774 (Ch)). It may be made without notice to the company, but the court must be satisfied that the applicant will be prejudiced by delay, and/or actions are likely to be taken by the company if the order is not made, and lastly that an undertaking as to damages by the petitioner may be adequate compensation to the company if a winding-up order is not made (see *Re First Express Ltd* [1991] BCC 782).

Where an order is made, the provisional liquidator will act independently at the direction of the court and is not seen to represent a creditor, or class of creditors (*Re Bank of Credit and Commerce International SA (No.2)* [1992] BCLC 579).

The application must be supported by affidavit, detailing:

(a) the ground upon which the provisional liquidator should be appointed;
(b) if it is proposed that any person other than the Official Receiver is to be appointed, confirmation that the person has consented to act and is qualified to act as an insolvency practitioner in relation to the company;
(c) whether the Official Receiver has been informed of the application and furnished with a copy of it;
(d) whether to the applicant's knowledge there is in place a CVA, administrator or administrative receiver in office, or a liquidator appointed by resolution of the company in voluntary liquidation; and
(e) the applicant's estimate of the value of the assets of the company.

The appointment is generally made to preserve the status quo pending the hearing of the winding-up petition and the provisional liquidator will not have authority to wind up the company or distribute assets (*Re Hammersmith Town Hall* (1877) LR 6 Ch D 112). It is intended to be a short-term measure (*Re ABC Coupler and Engineering Co. Ltd (No.3)* [1970] 1 WLR 702), although it has been used for longer periods in exceptional circumstances, e.g. a scheme of arrangement for an insurance company (*Jacob* v. *UIC Insurance Co. Ltd* [2006] EWHC 2717 (Ch)).

The provisional liquidator may carry out such functions as ordered at the direction of the court (IA 1986, s.135(4)). Consequently, the provisional liquidator's powers are limited by the court order. If, however, there is a need to continue the business of the company pending the winding-up petition, the court may, on application, appoint any person to be a special manager of the business or the property of the company (IA 1986, s.177(1)) (see *Re Pinstripe Farming Co. Ltd* [1996] BCC 913). This application may be made by the liquidator or provisional liquidator in cases where it appears that the nature of the business or property of the company, or the interests of the company's creditors or contributories or members generally, require the appointment of a person to manage the company's business or property pending winding up. This is, of course, an unusual requirement in the case of a liquidation, as generally the company will cease to trade in order to prevent further losses prior to realisation of assets and dissolution of the company.

There is no requirement that the special manager needs to be a qualified insolvency practitioner. The powers of the special manager are determined by the court on a case-by-case basis. It is possible for the directors to be appointed as special managers, where appointment of a liquidator or provisional liquidator would have otherwise terminated their powers.

The effect of the appointment of a provisional liquidator is dramatic. The powers of the directors will cease (*Re Mawcon Ltd* [1969] 1 WLR 78) and it will terminate the authority of any agents appointed by the company (*Pacific and General Insurance* v. *Hazell* [1997] BCC 400), although notice of termination is required.

The court may order that information is circulated to creditors (*Equitas Ltd* v. *Jacob* [2005] BPIR 1312). Once an order has been made, actions or proceedings cannot be continued against the company except with leave of the court (IA 1986, s.130(2)).

PART II

The insolvency process

CHAPTER 6

The bankruptcy process

Irrespective of how a bankruptcy commences (by a debtor's petition; see **2.7** or a creditor's petition; see **4.3**), once the procedure has been commenced, it does not matter who initiated the process; the procedures are the same, with the trustee in bankruptcy being appointed for the benefit of the creditors as a whole.

6.1   INTRODUCTION

Guide to procedure

The bankruptcy process

1. Bankruptcy order made.
2. Court sends two sealed copies of order to Official Receiver.
3. Official Receiver sends copy to bankrupt and Chief Land Registrar.
4. Order advertised in *London Gazette* and, if appropriate, a local newspaper.
5. Bankrupt attends Official Receiver's office as and when required/delivers up books/ records.
6. Bankrupt prepares statement of affairs.
7. Within 12 weeks of order, Official Receiver reports to creditors on whether he has determined that a creditors' meeting should be held.
8. If no meeting is to be held, Official Receiver reports to creditors on the bankrupt's assets and liabilities/results of any initial investigations and gives creditors 28 days to respond.
9. If no objection received, Official Receiver will file notice of bankrupt's discharge.
10. If Official Receiver calls meeting or creditors requisition meeting, 21 days' notice provided and request for forms of proof and proxy to be completed by creditors.
11. Official Receiver or person nominated acts as chairman. Resolutions may include appointment of a trustee in bankruptcy.
12. Official Receiver puts trustee in possession of bankrupt's estate.
13. Trustee realises bankrupt's available assets.
14. Trustee distributes proceeds to creditors.
15. Irrespective of the progress of steps (13) or (14), after the expiry of 12 months from the date of bankruptcy, the bankrupt will be discharged automatically, unless prior discharge or application to suspend discharge, etc. has been sought.

As set out in the introduction to this book (see **1.3**) bankruptcy is a process for both creditor and debtor.

For the creditors, it offers a collective procedure which ensures fair and equitable treatment. Where a distribution is made to creditors, it will be in accordance with a statutory order of priority and on a *pari passu* basis (on a rateable basis between creditors of the same class).

For a debtor, bankruptcy provides an opportunity for financial rehabilitation and thus differs from liquidation. The liquidation of a company ultimately sees its demise (the dissolution of the company); in contrast, bankruptcy (since the Bankruptcy Acts of 1883 and 1914) allows for the release of a debtor from the effects of a bankruptcy and provides an opportunity for the individual to be freed from bankruptcy debt.

Early legislation provided release only after the public examination of the bankrupt and after a favourable report by an Official Receiver on the bankrupt's conduct. These procedures, which allowed a debtor to apply to court for a 'certificate of misfortune', were an earlier attempt to distinguish between culpable and non-culpable bankrupts. However, the use of this release procedure was rare and it was not until the Insolvency Act 1976 that limited rights of automatic discharge from bankruptcy were introduced.

IA 1986 introduced a system of automatic discharge after three years, with no distinction between the culpable and non-culpable bankrupts. Interestingly, the Cork Committee (the Review Committee on Insolvency Law and Practice set up in 1976 to review insolvency law and practice, chaired by Sir Kenneth Cork), when considering the bankruptcy regime, recommended a framework for recovery in which commercial morality was policed by investigation, disciplinary measures and restrictions. The committee's recommendation was for the bankrupt's conduct to be reviewed after five years, leading to discharge unless there was opposition by the Official Receiver (Report of the Review Committee on Insolvency Law and Practice, Cmnd 8558, 1982). The Cork Committee also recommended an early discharge procedure within 12 months, although the onus would be on the bankrupt to prove that discharge was warranted. These proposals were rejected on the basis that the economic costs of introducing such a system of investigation would be prohibitive. By 2002, matters had come full circle and among the reforms introduced by the Enterprise Act 2002 was the establishment of a distinction between culpable and non-culpable bankrupts, with early release for those whose conduct did not merit a further period of restriction.

One of the fundamental purposes of the reforms introduced on 1 April 2004 was the intention to reduce the stigma and disabilities of bankruptcy for the non-culpable bankrupt. The incoming Labour government of 1997, when reviewing the bankruptcy regime, determined that the strictness of the regime and the stigma of bankruptcy prohibited an entrepreneurial culture in the UK. It was felt that the UK bankruptcy regime caused entrepreneurs to be risk averse, which contrasted with the position in the USA, where there was a greater level of owner/manager businesses, with employees and employers sharing in the business risks and rewards of enterprise.

Coupled with this political motivation for change, evidence provided by the Official Receiver's office seemed to show that the majority of individuals became bankrupt through no fault of their own (see consultation paper, *Bankruptcy: A Fresh Start* (Insolvency Service 2000), section 7).

The government's White Paper preceding the Enterprise Act 2002 was entitled *Insolvency: A Second Chance* (Insolvency Service, 2001). It re-emphasised the government's commitment to the reform process and the aim that the reforms should allow both businesses and individuals a 'second chance' after business failure. The Enterprise Act 2002 reforms marked a fundamental shift in the attitude towards bankruptcy, with the reforms intended to reduce its stigma, restrictions and disabilities.

Since 2004, the numbers of individuals entering bankruptcy have rocketed. Whether the rise in numbers can be attributed at least in part to the reform of the legislation is open to debate. However, it is noted that over the last 20 years there has been a rising trend in personal insolvency levels irrespective of economic conditions. Explanations for this are many and various, but one cause may be the huge increase in personal debt levels. The rising acceptance of a credit culture, the taking of risk and the unsustainability of many individuals' borrowings (with some blame being attached to those financial institutions lending record levels of unsecured credit) all contribute to financial failure and bankruptcy. There is also a perception that with the stigma of bankruptcy diminishing and the example of other individuals' use of the procedure there is a greater encouragement for individuals to take on debt and then seek (an easy and quick) release from its burden.

It should, however, be kept in mind that the way that bankruptcy is commenced, whether by creditors' or the debtor's petition, is immaterial and, more importantly, the role and responsibility of the trustee in bankruptcy in collecting available assets is also unchanged by the reforms (save in respect of reforms which have been introduced regarding the family home). In this chapter we focus on the bankruptcy process itself – what happens and when it happens.

6.2 ADMINISTRATION OF THE BANKRUPTCY ESTATE

Once a bankruptcy order is made, it does not matter if the bankruptcy was commenced on the petition of the debtor or a creditor; the procedures and processes to be followed are the same, with the Official Receiver/trustee being appointed to fulfil the statutory functions of bankruptcy and in so doing acting for the benefit of the creditors as a whole.

The function of the trustee is to get in, realise and distribute the bankrupt's estate in accordance with the statutory provisions as set out in IA 1986, ss.305–355. In carrying out the functions and the management of the bankrupt's estate the trustee is entitled, subject to the relevant statutory provisions, to use his own discretion (IA

1986, s.305(2)). The court will also be reluctant to interfere in the commercial judgment that may be exercised by a trustee in fulfilling his functions, although the trustee should act fairly, reasonably and independently (see *Re Condon, ex p. James* (1874) 9 LR 79 Ch App 609 and *Re Ng* [1997] BCC 507).

The trustee is also responsible, before the bankrupt's estate is distributed, for identifying the persons to whom the estate will be distributed, and for quantifying the claims that such persons may have against the bankrupt or against the property of the bankrupt (e.g. whether the person has security or some other right over property of the bankrupt).

In acting, the trustee is often called upon to balance the interests of the bankrupt (and his family) against the interests of the creditors. While we shall look at this issue in more depth when considering the rights in respect of the family home, it should be noted that the bankruptcy process and the administration of the bankrupt's estate do not constitute a violation of an individual's human rights (see e.g. European Convention on Human Rights, Art.6, under which an individual is entitled to determination of civil rights and obligations at a fair and public hearing conducted within a reasonable time), as bankruptcy is not a process that results in the determination of civil rights and obligations (see *Foyle* v. *Turner* [2007] BPIR 43). It is also not an abuse for the trustee to continue to realise assets solely in order to pay the trustee's costs and remuneration where no financial benefit will be conferred on the unsecured creditors (*Thornhill* v. *Atherton (No.2)* [2008] BPIR 691).

6.3 DURATION OF BANKRUPTCY

The bankruptcy commences on the day on which the bankruptcy order is made and continues until the bankrupt is discharged (IA 1986, s.278).

In the majority of cases, a bankrupt will, at the latest, be automatically discharged from bankruptcy at the end of one year, the period of bankruptcy beginning on the date upon which the bankruptcy commences (IA 1986, s.279(1)).

However, the Official Receiver may file at court a notice providing for earlier discharge, where he considers that an investigation of the bankrupt's conduct and affairs is unnecessary, or has been effectively concluded, discharge being effected on the filing of the notice (IA 1986, s.279(2)). Where the Official Receiver intends to file a notice he is obliged to write to all creditors and any appointed trustee. A recipient then has 28 days in which to object, giving reasons for the objection.

If no objection is received and provided the Official Receiver remains satisfied that the investigations are unnecessary and/or concluded, after expiry of the notice period, he may file notice providing for the bankrupt's early discharge (see IR 1986, rule 6.214A, Form 6.82). A copy of the notice endorsed with date and filing will be returned to the Official Receiver, who will send this to the (former) bankrupt.

If an objection is received, the Official Receiver will consider it and will either agree to postpone the discharge until further investigations are undertaken or give notice of the reasons for rejecting the complaint. The complainant then has 14 days in which to appeal against this determination (IR 1986, rule 7.50(2)); after the expiry of this period or after the appeal has been determined, the Official Receiver may file notice of discharge (in Form 6.82).

Alternatively, the Official Receiver may apply to suspend the automatic discharge provisions and obtain a court order that the bankrupt will not be discharged until a specific date or after fulfilling a special condition (IA 1986, s.279(3)).

This could occur where the bankrupt has failed to co-operate with the Official Receiver and/or meet one of the many obligations imposed on the bankrupt, such as disclosure of assets, delivery up of property, etc. (see *Shierson* v. *Rastogi* [2007] BPIR 891). In practice, it is often the failure by the bankrupt to comply with the reasonable request of a trustee, rather than failure to co-operate with the Official Receiver, that leads to this application and the report/request by a trustee to the Official Receiver prompting the application to suspend automatic discharge. However, it is also open to the trustee to apply directly to the court to suspend the automatic discharge (IR 1986, rule 6.215). In either situation, the Official Receiver's report and the trustee's evidence (if applicable) must be served on the bankrupt at least 21 days before the hearing, and the bankrupt may within five business days of the hearing file a notice specifying any statement made by the Official Receiver or trustee which he intends to deny or dispute. If the court makes an order suspending the discharge, the order (in Form 6.72) will be sent to the Official Receiver, the trustee and bankrupt.

It should be noted that where the conduct of the bankrupt so merits (e.g. prior bankruptcy within six years of the current bankruptcy), it may be more appropriate for a BRO to be imposed rather than a suspension of the automatic discharge. The Official Receiver/trustee needs to consider what may be achieved through suspension of the discharge (e.g. a possible public examination) as opposed to the punitive imposition of a BRO.

The bankrupt may at any time apply to have the suspension lifted (IR 1986, rule 6.216). The Official Receiver (and trustee if applicable) may attend the hearing and may file evidence in support of matters that they consider should be drawn to the attention of the court.

6.4   ROLE OF THE OFFICIAL RECEIVER

The Department for Business, Innovation and Skills (DBIS) has responsibility for the administration of insolvency in England and Wales, and its insolvency work is undertaken by the Insolvency Service.

Official Receivers are appointed by the Secretary of State (IA 1986, s.399) and they (and an office) are attached to the High Court and/or at least one county court having bankruptcy jurisdiction. In 2011, there were 42 Official Receivers, who are authorised to investigate the conduct and affairs of every bankrupt in England and Wales. The Official Receiver should consider the conduct of the bankrupt pre- and post-bankruptcy and may report to the court if he thinks fit (IA 1986, s.289). This duty of investigation is no longer a mandatory requirement and may be dispensed with if the Official Receiver considers it unnecessary. The Official Receiver is, however, under an obligation to report to the court if the bankrupt makes an application for discharge (see above). The Official Receiver, in fulfilling this public function, is immune from suit in respect of any statement made acting within his powers and duties in the course of the bankruptcy, even if such a statement may have amounted to a negligent misstatement (*Mond* v. *Hyde* [1998] 3 All ER 833).

To assist the Official Receiver in the exercise of his duties, the bankrupt is under a duty to (IA 1986, s.291):

(a) deliver possession of his estate to the Official Receiver;
(b) deliver up all books, papers and records of which he has possession or control and which relate to his estate and affairs;
(c) do all such things as are necessary to protect property that is not delivered up;
(d) provide an inventory of estate and information; and
(e) attend on the Official Receiver as may reasonably be required.

The Official Receiver will also act as receiver and manager of the bankrupt's property until the appointment of a trustee in bankruptcy. In many cases, the Official Receiver will continue to act as trustee, generally where there are few (if any) assets to realise and where investigations are unlikely to result in legal proceedings (e.g. an action to set aside an antecedent transaction). It has been evident that in recent years the Official Receiver's office has been more inclined to retain control and conduct of the bankruptcy where there is likely to be a simple realisation, e.g. where the bankrupt's spouse is willing to purchase the trustee's interest in the matrimonial property. This ensures that the Official Receiver is able more readily to subsidise the costs of investigations which can be run without undue cost to the Exchequer.

On the making of a bankruptcy order, the bankrupt will be interviewed shortly afterwards by one of the staff of the Official Receiver. If the debtor has made himself bankrupt he may be instructed by the court officials to contact the Official Receiver's office by telephone on that day to arrange a meeting, otherwise the information will be sent to the bankrupt informing him of his duties and obligations *vis-à-vis* the Official Receiver and penalties (contempt of court, arrest and imprisonment) should he fail to comply.

Prior to the interview, the bankrupt will be asked to complete a long and wide-ranging questionnaire, which will be discussed at the interview. If the bankruptcy was on a creditor's petition, the bankrupt will also be required (within 21 days unless otherwise permitted) to submit a statement of affairs verified by a statement of truth (IR 1986, rule 6.59, Form 6.33A) to the Official Receiver. This statement of affairs will be filed at court by the Official Receiver. The Official Receiver may at any time ask the bankrupt to clarify, amplify, modify or explain any matter in the statement of affairs (IR 1986, rule 6.66) and/or provide an account of his affairs of such nature and for such period as may be specified (IR 1986, rule 6.64).

If the bankrupt is unable to provide a statement of affairs, or makes a request for assistance, the Official Receiver may at the expense of the estate employ a person to assist (e.g. the bankrupt's former accountant) (IR 1986, rule 6.63).

The Official Receiver must, at least once after the making of the bankruptcy order, send a report to creditors (known to the Official Receiver) with regard to the bankruptcy proceedings and the state of the bankrupt's affairs (IR 1986, rule 6.73(1)). Where a statement of affairs has been produced, a summary may be attached with comments and observations. The Official Receiver may apply to the court to be relieved of any duty to report, etc. and may do so if, e.g., there are insufficient funds in the estate. (Note that the Official Receiver's deposit is either £525 or £700 (as at time of writing), depending on whether it is a debtor's or creditor's petition and will consequently cover only a limited amount of work.) In addition, the Official Receiver is relieved of the responsibility to report where the bankruptcy has been annulled (IR 1986, rule 6.78).

In order to further any investigations being undertaken, the Official Receiver may at any time before the discharge of the bankrupt apply to the court for the public examination of the bankrupt (IA 1986, s.290). In practice, it is often due to non-co-operation and the possible sanction of public examination that the Official Receiver may apply to court to suspend the automatic discharge. The court will make an order on the application of the Official Receiver, unless it is satisfied that no proper questions can be put to the bankrupt (*Re Casterbridge Properties Ltd (in liquidation); Jeeves* v. *Official Receiver* [2003] 4 All ER 1041).

The Official Receiver can also be compelled to apply for the public examination of the bankrupt if required to do so by the majority of the creditors (by value) (IA 1986, s.290(2)). The request must be in writing, accompanied by a list of supporting creditors, with the value of their claims set out and the reasons why the creditors consider it appropriate to make the request (IR 1986, rule 6.173). The creditor making the request must provide a deposit to cover the costs of the Official Receiver if so ordered.

At the public examination, questions can be put to the bankrupt by the Official Receiver, the trustee (if appointed), any person appointed as special manager of the bankrupt's estate or business, or any creditor who has tendered proof in the bankruptcy. If the bankrupt fails to attend, he is guilty of contempt of court and liable to a fine or imprisonment and cannot plead that attendance or answers to certain questions may be self-incriminatory (*Re Paget* [1927] 2 Ch 85 and *Bishopsgate Investment Management Ltd (in provisional liquidation)* v. *Maxwell* [1992] BCC 222; although the court will have regard to issues arising from the European Convention on Human Rights: see *Re Rottmann* [2009] BPIR 617). In addition, where the bankrupt is suffering from a mental or physical disability which renders him unfit to be examined, the court will order a stay (IR 1986, rule 6.174). An order can be made against a person ordinarily resident outside the jurisdiction (*Re Seagull Manufacturing Co. Ltd* [1993] BCC 241).

The public examination is conducted in open court and any person permitted to question the bankrupt can do so through solicitor or counsel (IR 1986, rule 6.175).

The bankrupt may, at his own expense, employ counsel, who can put questions to the bankrupt in an attempt to clarify or explain any answers given. There will be such written record of the examination as the court thinks proper and this is read over to the bankrupt, who will be required to authenticate and verify his statements. This written record can then be used in evidence against the bankrupt, although it should be noted that where criminal proceedings have already been instituted and the court is concerned the public examination may prejudice a fair trial, the hearing may be adjourned (see IR 1986, rule 6.175(6); and for further comment on the interplay between questioning permissible by statute/regulatory authority and the defendant's right to a fair trial, see *Saunders* v. *United Kingdom* [1998] 1 BCLC 362).

For the purposes of a public examination, the court may order HMRC to produce to the court any return, any account submitted by the bankrupt, any assessment or determination made or any correspondence with the bankrupt (IA 1986, s.369). In practice, such applications are often by consent, and HMRC must, at least five business days prior to the hearing, indicate whether it consents or objects to the application (IR 1986, rule 6.194).

The Official Receiver also has the ability to request that the court order the private examination of the bankrupt, the bankrupt's spouse or former spouse, civil partner or former civil partner or any person known to have property in the bankrupt's estate, or be indebted to the bankrupt, or to have information concerning the bankrupt's dealings, affairs or property (IA 1986, s.366).

Where the bankruptcy exceeds a period of one year, a progress report should be sent to creditors (IR 1986, rule 6.78A).

6.5 ROLE OF THE TRUSTEE

6.5.1 Appointment of the trustee in bankruptcy

A trustee may be appointed by (IA 1986, s.292):

(a) a general meeting of the bankrupt's creditors;
(b) the Secretary of State; or
(c) the court,

although this list is not exhaustive (see *Donaldson* v. *O'Sullivan* [2008] BPIR 288).

Appointment by the court

The appointment of a trustee by the court may be made in circumstances where the supervisor of a failed IVA seeks appointment (IA 1986, s.297(5)). Alternatively, the court may order the appointment of an insolvency practitioner who has reported to the court following a debtor's petition in accordance with the provisions of IA 1986, s.274.

Where a trustee in bankruptcy has been appointed by the court, the trustee will give notice to the bankrupt's creditors of his appointment, or if the court so allows, he may advertise his appointment in accordance with directions of the court, setting out whether he will be summoning a meeting of creditors (IA 1986, s.297(7)).

Appointment by the Secretary of State

In other cases, as soon as is practicable and within 12 weeks of the bankruptcy order being made, the Official Receiver should determine whether it is right to summon a meeting of the bankrupt's creditors for the purposes of appointing a trustee (IA 1986, s.293(1)).

If the Official Receiver decides that there is no reason to summon a creditors' meeting and therefore no reason to appoint a trustee, notice of this determination will be sent to the creditors. From that date, the Official Receiver will be the trustee of the bankrupt's estate (IA 1986, s.293(3)). Prior to that date, the Official Receiver is the receiver and manager of the bankrupt's estate (IA 1986, s.287).

It should be noted that the determination as to whether it will be of benefit to appoint a trustee will principally be influenced by the assets possessed by the bankrupt (including choses in action). The reason for this is that the overriding purpose of the appointment of the trustee is to realise available assets for the benefit of creditors; the Official Receiver retains the function of investigating and, if necessary, reporting to the court and/or the role of prosecutor. As previously stated, in practice in recent years, the Official Receiver's office has been inclined to be more involved in seeking realisations, meaning that such steps are no longer the sole preserve of the private practice licensed insolvency practitioner.

As an alternative to holding a meeting, the Official Receiver may request that the Secretary of State appoints a trustee in place of the Official Receiver (IA 1986, s.296). The Secretary of State has discretion as to whether to make the appointment, but it would generally be expected that a Secretary of State's appointment would be made in such circumstances. In practice, this process is followed in one of two cases:

1. Where it is evident that a creditor(s) holds the majority of the debt owed by the bankrupt and supports the appointment of a particular nominated private practice insolvency practitioner. As a result, on making the bankruptcy order it is often useful for the petitioning creditor and any other significant creditor to make representations to the Official Receiver's office as to whether they favour the holding of a creditors' meeting and/or would prefer the immediate appointment of a trustee.

2. Where either the Official Receiver has called a meeting of creditors and they have failed to appoint a trustee (IA 1986, s.295) or the Official Receiver considers that the holding of a meeting would not further the interests of the creditors (i.e. it would delay matters/waste money) and wishes to appoint a private practice insolvency practitioner 'off the rota'. Akin to a cab rank rule,

those insolvency practitioners on the Official Receiver's rota will generally have to accept the Secretary of State's appointments as and when they are made.

Where a Secretary of State's appointment has been made, the trustee is obliged to give notice to the creditors of his appointment and advertise the appointment in accordance with the court's direction. The trustee must state in the notice or advertisement whether he is to summon a meeting of creditors in order to establish a creditors' committee, or alternatively set out to the creditors their power and ability to summon a meeting (IA 1986, s.296).

Two or more persons may be appointed as trustees, but such appointment must make provision as to the circumstances in which the trustees must act jointly and/or severally (IA 1986, s.292(3)).

The appointment of the trustee takes effect only if the insolvency practitioner accepts the appointment. Subject to this condition, the appointment takes effect at the time specified in the notice of appointment (IA 1986, s.292(4)).

Appointment at a creditors' meeting

Where the Official Receiver has decided within 12 weeks of the bankruptcy order to summon a meeting of creditors (IA 1986, s.293(1)), a venue for the meeting will be fixed not more than four months after the date of the bankruptcy order (IR 1986, rule 6.79(1)). Notice of the meeting must be given to the court and every creditor that is known to the Official Receiver and/or identified in the bankrupt's statement of affairs. The creditors must be given at least 14 days' notice of the meeting (IR 1986, rule 6.79(3)).

The chairman of the meeting will be the Official Receiver where he has convened the meeting, or a person nominated by him (IR 1986, rule 6.82). If the meeting has been convened by a creditor, the chairman will be a person nominated by the convener of the meeting and must be either a qualified insolvency practitioner or an employee of the proposed trustee who has experience in insolvency matters (IR 1986, rule 6.82(2)).

The notice of meeting must specify a time and date, not later than midday on the business day before the date fixed for a hearing, by which creditors should lodge a proof of debt and, if applicable, a proxy form (IR 1986, rule 6.79(4)). Notice must also be advertised in the *London Gazette* and may be otherwise advertised as the Official Receiver sees fit (IR 1986, rule 6.79(5)), and will contain information on the purpose of the meeting, the venue and the date and time by which creditors must lodge proxies and proofs, in order to be entitled to vote at the meeting (IR 1986, rule 6.79(5A)).

The chairman of the meeting can, however, still allow a creditor to vote even if no proof or proxy has been filed; and/or the proof or proxy was filed late; and/or the proof or proxy was deficient and did not comply with the provisions of the Insolvency Rules, provided that the chairman is satisfied that the reason for the failure was beyond the control of the creditor (IR 1986, rule 6.93A). Where a creditor wishes to appeal against the chairman's decision, he has 21 days from the date of the relevant creditors' meeting (IR 1986, rule 6.94(4A)).

If the Official Receiver has decided not to summon a meeting of creditors, the creditors can still request the Official Receiver to summon a meeting, provided that the request is with the concurrence of not less than one-quarter in value of the bankrupt's creditors (IA 1986, s.294(2)) and provided a deposit of security for the expenses of the meeting is provided (IR 1986, rule 6.87(3)).

Where a proper request has been made for a meeting the Official Receiver must (IR 1986, rule 6.79(6)):

(a) withdraw any notice that previously provided that a meeting would not be summoned;
(b) fix a venue for the meeting not less than three months from the date of the receipt of the creditors' request; and
(c) thereafter send notice to the creditors giving at least 21 days' notice of the meeting, advertise the meeting and provide for the lodgement of proofs and proxies (in Form 6.34 for the first meeting of creditors).

At the first meeting of creditors, no resolution may be taken other than resolutions for the following (IR 1986, rule 6.80):

(a) The appointment of the trustee in bankruptcy.
(b) Establishment of a creditors' committee.
(c) The settling of the basis for the trustee's remuneration.
(d) Where there are more than two trustees, as to whether acts are to be done jointly or severally.
(e) Where the meeting has been as a result of the creditors' requisition, a resolution authorising payment, as an expense of the bankruptcy, of the costs of summoning and holding a meeting.
(f) The adjournment of the meeting for not more than three weeks.
(g) Any other resolution which the chairman thinks right to allow for special reasons.

Thereafter, the Official Receiver or trustee may at any time summon a meeting of creditors to discuss matters relating to the bankruptcy and, importantly, obtain the consent of the creditors as to future actions; 14 days' notice of the meeting must be given (IR 1986, rules 6.81 and 6.83, as amended by the Insolvency (Amendment) Rules 2010, SI 2010/686, Form 6.35). Where any meeting of creditors is summoned, notice of the meeting must also be given to the bankrupt (IR 1986, rule 6.84, Form 6.36).

The meeting will be fixed at a venue which is convenient for the creditors (IR 1986, rule 6.86(1)) and will be held between 10 am and 4 pm on any business day, unless the court otherwise directs (IR 1986, rule 6.86(2)). However, it is now possible for the trustee to obtain a resolution of the creditors by correspondence and without the need to hold the meeting; this course is likely to be followed in the majority of cases (IR 1986, rule 6.88A).

A resolution can be passed in correspondence if:

(a) the trustee sends notice of the resolution to all creditors who would be entitled to attend a creditors' meeting;

(b) the notice includes a closing date for responses, giving at least 14 days' notice for a response; and

(c) within five days of the notice at least 10 per cent (in value) of creditors have not requested that an actual meeting is held.

The trustee will count the votes received by the closing date, and adjudicate on each proof and entitlement to vote. One vote will be sufficient to pass a written resolution, although if no vote is received the trustee will be required to call an actual meeting.

Where a meeting is summoned other than by the Official Receiver or trustee, the expenses of that meeting will in the first instance be paid by the convener of the meeting from the deposit provided to the trustee or the Official Receiver (IR 1986, rule 6.87(1)). The sum to be deposited will be that deemed appropriate by the trustee or Official Receiver (IR 1986, rule 6.87(2)).

However, where a meeting is summoned by a creditor(s), the creditors may vote that the expenses of summoning the meeting are payable out of the estate as an expense of the bankruptcy and the deposit paid by the convener of the meeting may also be repaid (IR 1986, rule 6.87(3), (4)).

Where a creditor has requisitioned a meeting, the request will be accompanied (if needs be) by a list of creditors concurring with the request and a statement of the purpose of the proposed meeting (IR 1986, rule 6.83, Form 6.34).

At the meeting of creditors, a resolution is passed when a majority in value of those present and voting, in person or by proxy, have voted in favour of the resolution (IR 1986, rule 6.88). With regard to the appointment of a trustee, where there are more than two nominees an alternative vote system applies, with the nominee with the least votes dropping out until one nominee emerges with the support of the majority (IR 1986, rule 6.88(2)). It is, of course, possible for two nominees to be appointed jointly. In practice, this is often the case where the nominees are from the same firm and wish to provide cover in the absence of one or the other. Alternatively, the creditors sometimes think it appropriate to appoint insolvency practitioners from different firms, perhaps with one taking primary responsibility for sales/realisations and the other for investigations/claims work.

In practice, the position to be taken by various creditors at the meeting is often canvassed by a number of insolvency practitioners. Some insolvency practitioners have arrangements with creditors, such as financial institutions and credit card companies, etc., which will ensure that they will attend the creditors' meeting free of charge with a view potentially to seeking appointments. As a result, the initial creditors' meeting can be a boisterous affair, with the meeting being attended by various insolvency practitioners indicating the routes that they propose to take in respect of the bankrupt in order to attract creditors' votes. There are, however, provisions against the use of improper solicitation and the court can order that no remuneration shall be allowed out of the bankruptcy estate where such solicitation was exercised (IR 1986, rule 6.148).

During the meeting, the chairman may in his discretion, but only once without adjourning the meeting, declare the meeting suspended for a period of up to one hour (IR 1986, rule 6.90). This may enable any issue to be resolved, such as confirming a creditor's entitlement to vote or seeking urgent instructions from a creditor on a revised resolution.

Alternatively, the chairman may in his discretion adjourn the meeting to such time and place as is appropriate in the circumstances (IR 1986, rule 6.91(1)). If within 30 minutes of the meeting being held, a quorum is not present, the chairman may similarly adjourn the meeting. Adjournments should not be for more than 14 days (IR 1986, rule 6.91(3)).

If no chairman is present at the meeting within 30 minutes of the time appointed, it is automatically adjourned for seven days (IR 1986, rule 6.91(4A)). If the adjournment would mean that the meeting would next fall on a non-business day it is adjourned to the day immediately following (IR 1986, rule 6.91(4A)).

In the case of any other meeting, i.e. called after the initial meeting by a trustee, the adjournment must be within 14 days of the original meeting; the meeting is adjourned to the business day immediately before the day that falls seven days after the date of the adjourned meeting (IR 1986, rule 6.91(4C)).

A creditor is entitled to vote only if, by the time and date specified in the notice, he has duly lodged a proof of debt. This proof must also have been admitted by the Official Receiver/chairman for the purposes of entitlement to vote and any proxy requisite to that entitlement (IR 1986, rule 6.93(1)). In exceptional circumstances the court can order that a creditor, or class of creditor, is entitled to vote without being required to prove for their debt.

A dispute may arise if a creditor is claiming an unliquidated amount, or the claim is in respect of a debt where the value is not ascertained. In such a case the chairman will put a minimum value on the entitlement to vote (possibly £1) and it is treated as a proof for voting purposes at this level (IR 1986, rule 6.93(3)). A secured creditor is entitled to vote only in respect of the balance of the debt after deducting the value of the security (IR 1986, rule 6.93(4)). Furthermore, the chairman is entitled to admit or reject the creditor's proof in respect of the whole or any part of the proof (IR 1986, rule 6.94).

If the chairman is in doubt as to whether the proof should be admitted or rejected, he should mark it as objected to and allow the creditor to vote subject to the vote being subsequently declared invalid if the objection to the proof is sustained (IR 1986, rule 6.94(3)). If on appeal the chairman's decision is reversed or varied, or the vote declared invalid, the court may order another meeting to be held. An appeal from any decision of the chairman must be made not later than 21 days after the date of the meeting (IR 1986, rule 6.94(4A)).

The chairman must keep a minute of the meeting together with a list of all creditors who attended the meeting (IR 1986, rule 6.95).

6.5.2 Vesting of bankrupt's estate

The bankrupt's estate vests immediately in the trustee on appointment or on the Official Receiver becoming a trustee (IA 1986, s.306(1)), without the need for any conveyance, assignment or transfer and wherever it is located (*Pollard* v. *Ashurst* [2001] BPIR 131 which dealt with assets located abroad, although consideration of the EC Regulation on Insolvency Proceedings is now required when the debtor is domiciled abroad and has assets located in another country).

The trustee thereafter realises the assets contained in the bankruptcy estate for the benefit of creditors, a process which continues irrespective of whether the bankrupt has or has not been discharged. As we shall see, creditors are assessed as at the date of commencement of the bankruptcy, i.e. the debtor's liabilities are crystallised as at that date; at the same time, the debtor's assets are those vesting in the estate as at the date of commencement (subject also to the possible addition of after-acquired property vesting during the duration of the bankruptcy (IA 1986, s.307)). The effect is a crystallisation of debts/liabilities and assets as at that date, meaning that a debtor can be made bankrupt for a second time in regards to debts incurred post bankruptcy and that the creditors in the second bankruptcy do not have access to the assets vesting in the first bankruptcy estate.

It is a common misconception that a discharge from bankruptcy will release the bankrupt from the process and consequences of bankruptcy – this is not the case. The trustee continues to realise available assets for the benefit of the creditors for so long as it is necessary. It should also be borne in mind that assets vesting in the bankruptcy estate may rise in value post bankruptcy (e.g. shares). This rise in value will generally be a windfall to the creditors whenever it arises. The one exception to this is the realisation of the bankrupt's interest in the family home (IA 1986, s.283A). Since 1 April 2004 in respect of any individual made bankrupt, the bankrupt's family's home will vest back to the bankrupt unless the trustee has within three years taken any step to realise his interest.

It should be remembered that the effect of discharge is to release the individual from the restrictions of bankruptcy and release him from possible proceedings by creditors possessing claims as at the date of bankruptcy. Post bankruptcy, the creditors' rights are against the bankruptcy estate not the bankrupt himself. This allows the bankrupt a second chance free from bankruptcy debt, financial rehabilitation remaining a key component of the bankruptcy system.

6.5.3 Realisation of the bankruptcy estate

A bankruptcy estate consists of all property belonging to, or vested in, the bankrupt at the commencement of the bankruptcy and any property which, by virtue of the statutory provisions, will be treated as such (e.g. after-acquired property, surplus income) (IA 1986, s.283(1)).

'Property' is said in IA 1986, s.436 to include 'money, goods, things in action, land and every description of property wherever situated and also obligations and every description of interest, whether present or future or vested or contingent, arising out of, or incidental to, property'.

This statutory definition of property is not meant to provide an exhaustive description; indeed, the inclusion of the word 'include' shows that it is open to interpretation. Instead, it reflects public policy that property of 'whatever kind or nature' (*Hollinshead* v. *Hazelton* [1916] 1 AC 428) should be made available to creditors. It also means that the court may from time to time be called upon to decide what property is to be regarded as included in the bankruptcy estate and what is not. For example, the following have been held to be included in the bankruptcy estate:

- Property held abroad (*Pollard* v. *Ashurst* [2001] 2 All ER 75).
- Causes of action, including the right to bring/continue proceedings in the bankrupt's name (*Young* v. *Hamilton* [2010] BPIR 1468).
- A power exercised in an individual capacity by the bankrupt over property which is capable of being within the bankrupt's estate, e.g. an option (*Clarkson* v. *Clarkson* [1994] BCC 921).
- The benefit of stocks and shares (*Gemshore Investment plc* v. *Stewart* [2002] All ER (D) 120 (Jan), where the bankrupt was the 100 per cent owner of shares and the company's sole director, the assets of the company were deemed to be part of the bankrupt's estate).
- The right to the proceeds of a disability insurance claim (see *Cork* v. *Rawlins* [2001] 3 WLR 300, although contrast with *Ord* v. *Upton* [2000] Ch 352 which follows long-established dicta that causes of action for damages to compensate pain and suffering in respect of the body, mind or character of the bankrupt are not included in the bankrupt's estate).
- The right of the bankrupt to proceed with a tax appeal (*Ahajot* v. *Waller* [2005] BPIR 82).
- The bankrupt's right to an account and share of a partnership (*Wilson* v. *Greenwood* (1818) 1 Swans 471).
- An assignable pre-emption right over property (*Dear* v. *Reeves* [2001] 1 BCLC 643).
- A waste management licence under the Environmental Protection Act 1990 (*Re Celtic Extraction Ltd* [1999] 4 All ER 684).

Despite the wide definition given to property, in *Haig* v. *Aitken* [2000] BPIR 462 it was held that personal correspondence (notwithstanding its public interest and possible value, as it related to the former MP Jonathan Aitken) does not vest in the trustee. In **Chapter 10** we shall look at special provisions and considerations that apply when considering and determining the bankrupt's interest in the family home and provisions applicable to a bankrupt's pension.

It should also be kept in mind that property held on trust, property which may be subject to a retention of title, and/or, most importantly, which is subject to the secured rights of a third party, is not property included in the bankrupt's estate. The trustee is looking to whether the bankrupt has a beneficial interest in property as opposed to a legal one.

The bankruptcy estate does not include:

(a) such tools, books, vehicles, and other equipment as are necessary to the bankrupt for use personally by him in his employment, business or vocation; or

(b) such clothing, bedding, furniture, household equipment and provisions as are necessary for satisfying the basic domestic needs of the bankrupt and his family (IA 1986, s.283(2)).

As is self-evident, this statutory exemption is drawn to ensure that the bankrupt is not deprived of his livelihood (e.g. a piano owned by a piano teacher: *Boyd Ltd* v. *Bilham* [1909] 1 KB 14).

The more modern inclusion of 'vehicle' within the definition of excluded property means that if a car is necessary for the bankrupt to travel to work, then subject to the trustee's right to require a reasonable replacement, if no surplus would result from sale (IA 1986, s.308), the bankrupt is allowed to keep the car. In addition, the bankrupt (and his family) should not be reduced below an 'acceptable standard of living' (*Re Rae* [1995] BCC 102). We shall look at this issue more closely in the context of a bankrupt's right to income in **Chapter 10**.

Where the trustee considers that any excluded item could be reasonably replaced and a surplus produced, he may serve notice on the bankrupt within 42 days of becoming aware of the property in question (IA 1986, s.309). This notice period is strict: the trustee cannot apply to court to serve out of time (*Solomons* v. *Williams* [2001] BPIR 1123) and the court will also look closely if the notice is served some time after the trustee's appointment (*Franses* v. *Oomerjee* [2005] BPIR 1320).

Upon service of the notice on the bankrupt, the property is deemed to vest in the bankruptcy estate, depriving the bankrupt of the ability to deal with it. Except where there has been a bona fide purchaser for value, the trustee's title to that property relates back to the commencement of the bankruptcy (IA 1986, s.308(2)). This prevents the bankrupt from transferring valuable household items/antiques to members of his family after the presentation of the petition.

The trustee must apply sums realised from the sale of the item to fund the reasonable replacement. In practice, and often to the consternation of creditors who may consider that a bankrupt continues to enjoy a lavish lifestyle, this provision is one rarely invoked by the trustee. The reason for this is often the difficulty in establishing the bankrupt's ownership or interest in the item in question, and in practice the low return on sale/the costs of sale, etc.

The Housing Act 1988 introduced additional exemptions from the bankrupt's estate, namely assured tenancies, assured agricultural tenancies, protected tenancies and secure tenancies which cannot be assigned (IA 1986, s.283(3A)). It is, however, possible for the trustee to provide notice that such tenancies vest in the bankruptcy estate, although such notice is ineffective as against a purchaser in good faith, for value and without notice of the bankruptcy (IA 1986, s.308A).

An important additional exemption with regard to the trustee's ability to deal with the bankrupt's property is in respect of assets which may be subject to criminal recovery action (see Proceeds of Crime Act 2002, Sched.11 and IA 1986, ss.306A, 306B and 306C). Where property is subject to a restraint or confiscation order, it is excluded from the bankruptcy estate. In practice, the victim of a crime may often be a creditor of the bankrupt, particularly true in the case of white collar crime, where the bankrupt may be in possession of proceeds of crime and may have mingled this with his own money or money held for and on behalf of intended victims. In this area there is a strong overlap between insolvency and criminal law. Indeed, a receiver or administrator of property subject to a confiscation order is often an insolvency practitioner, chosen because he is well versed in investigation and asset tracing. The provisions in IA 1986 make it clear that where there is a discharge or quashing of the restraint order, or where the property realised through confiscation is sufficient to settle the order, the property will vest in the trustee as part of the bankrupt's estate.

When the trustee has realised all available assets from the bankrupt's estate, the proceeds will be applied in the priority of distribution listed below.

6.5.4 Distribution to creditors

Checklist

Priority of distribution

1. Expenses of bankruptcy.
2. Pre-preferential debts.
3. Preferential debts.
4. Unsecured debts.
5. Interest (since commencement of bankruptcy).
6. Postponed debts.
7. Surplus to bankrupt.

The expenses of the bankruptcy will be treated as a first charge against any realised funds. IR 1986, rule 6.224(1) sets out an order of priority for the payment of bankruptcy expenses.

There are some unusual, largely historical, provisions which ensure that certain creditors have priority over the generally recognised class of preferential creditors. By virtue of IA 1986, s.348, apprentices or articled clerks of the bankrupt who have paid a premium for apprenticeship will have repaid to them such sum as the trustee in bankruptcy thinks reasonable. The trustee may, however, transfer the apprenticeship to some other person.

Where the bankrupt has in his possession money or property of a friendly society, the trustees of the friendly society have a first right of recovery in respect of the money (Friendly Societies Act 1874, s.59; see *Re Miller* [1893] 1 QB 327).

If the bankrupt has died, the cost of reasonable funeral, testamentary and administration expenses are treated as pre-preferential debts (Administration of Insolvent Estates of Deceased Persons Order 1986, SI 1986/1999).

Preferential debts remain as set out in IA 1986, Sched.6, which has been substantially amended following the Enterprise Act 2002 reforms (which came into force on 15 September 2003). There are now three remaining categories of preferential debt:

- Contributions to occupational pension schemes (Pension Schemes Act 1993, Sched.4).
- Remuneration of employees (see **Chapter 13**).
- Levies on coal and steel production (Treaty establishing the European Coal and Steel Community, 1951 (ECSC Treaty), Arts. 40(3), 49, 50).

The major change has therefore been the removal of Crown debt priority, which has had significant impact on bankruptcies commenced after 15 September 2003. The preferential debt must have been due at the date of the bankruptcy order or in the more unusual circumstances where an interim receiver was in office, when he was first appointed (IA 1986, s.387(6)). The payment to unsecured creditors is to those who have proved for their debt in the bankruptcy and they will receive distribution on the *pari passu* basis.

Interest is payable on all preferential and unsecured debts at a prescribed rate (currently 8 per cent) or the rate applicable to the debt apart from bankruptcy, whichever is the higher (IA 1986, s.328(5)).

Postponed debts include the following.

- *Debts between spouses.* Where a loan was provided by a person who was the spouse of the bankrupt (or civil partner: see Civil Partnership Act 2004, s.263(10)(b) from 5 December 2005), as at the commencement of the bankruptcy, the debt is only payable after all other creditors' claims have been dealt with. This provision operates irrespective of whether the loan was given for personal or business reasons (IA 1986, s.329).
- *Loans falling with the Partnership Act 1890.* Where a loan is made and repayable according to the profits of the business or a share of the profits is paid as interest, or a share of profits is to be paid in consideration of a sale of the goodwill of the business, the lender's debt is postponed. (See *Re Meade* [1951] Ch 774 where it was expressly held that the lender need not be a partner of the business nor share directly in profits provided there is some element of 'investment' on the part of the lender.)
- *The claims of beneficiaries under settlement avoided under IA 1986, s.339.*

After all of the above claims have been satisfied in full, any surplus is available to the bankrupt. This is unlikely, although it is possible if realisations of assets have been greater than was anticipated. In such cases, the individual could seek annulment of the bankruptcy (see **Chapter 10**). If realisations appear likely to exceed liabilities, the bankrupt would be better advised to seek the approval of creditors to an IVA proposal during the course of the bankruptcy.

The process and procedure for a creditor proving for a debt and receiving a dividend is looked at more closely in **Chapter 12**.

6.6   REMOVAL, RESIGNATION AND VACANCY IN OFFICE

6.6.1   Removal of trustee

Removal at general meeting of creditors

The trustee may be removed from office by order of the court or by the creditors at a general meeting convened for that purpose (IA 1986, s.298(1)).

Where the Official Receiver is the trustee, or a trustee has been appointed under a Secretary of State's appointment, or the trustee was appointed by the court, a general meeting of the bankrupt's creditors will be summoned for the purposes of removing the trustee only if the trustee thinks fit, or if the court directs, or if the meeting is requisitioned by 25 per cent or more in value of the creditors for the purpose of removing the trustee (IA 1986, s.298(4)).

Where a meeting is summoned, the notice (in Form 6.35) convening the meeting must specify the purpose of the meeting and draw attention to the statutory provisions governing the release of the trustee (IA 1986, s.299). A copy of the notice must also be sent to the Official Receiver (IR 1986, rule 6.129).

At the meeting, a person other than the trustee may be elected chairman. The chairman must within three business days of any creditors' resolution send notice to the Official Receiver if the creditors have resolved to remove the trustee, to appoint a new trustee and/or that the trustee is not due to receive a release.

A resolution is effective as and when the Official Receiver files a certificate of removal of the trustee at court (IR 1986, rule 6.131(2)).

Removal of trustee by court order

Where an application is made to the court for removal of a trustee (see IR 1986, rule 6.132, Form 6.48), the court may summarily dismiss the application if the applicant has failed to show sufficient cause. The court will provide five business days' notice of its intention to do so to the applicant, who is entitled to make further representations. Where a court thinks a hearing is appropriate, the trustee must be provided with at least 14 days' notice of the hearing. While the court may order the removal of the trustee, the court does not have jurisdiction under these provisions to appoint a new trustee (*Donaldson* v. *O'Sullivan* [2008] BPIR 1288). The court does, however, enjoy a wide discretion on the hearing of an application and although there should be good reason justifying the removal, there does not need to be evidence of misconduct (see *Re Edennote* [1996] BCLC 389; *Re Buildhead Ltd* [2004] BPIR 1139; and *Finnerty* v. *Clark* [2011] EWCA Civ 858).

It is common for a trustee to be replaced because he has resigned from a firm and is not taking his insolvency appointments to his new firm. Despite an insolvency appointment being unique to an individual in office, it is common practice for an insolvency practitioner to be attached to a specific firm and it is the staff of that firm who may have day-to-day conduct of the insolvency process. In the circumstances where the trustee moves from one firm to another, it may be considered administratively convenient (issues as to costs between the respective firms arise) for the case to remain at the original firm. As a result, the trustee may be removed in a block transfer, with a replacement also being provided for (see *Re Equity Nominees Ltd* [1999] 2 BCLC 19; IR 1986, rule 7.11(4) for transfers to the High Court; IA 1986, s.298(1) regarding the court's power of removal; and IA 1986, s.303(2) regarding the court's power of replacement). As in these circumstances a replacement is made without a creditors' meeting, the creditors are given notice of the transfer and are provided with liberty to apply.

Removal of trustee by Secretary of State

A trustee appointed by the Secretary of State may be removed by the Secretary of State (IA 1986, s.298(5)).

If the Secretary of State intends to do this, he must provide notice to the trustee specifying the grounds for removal in order to allow representations to be made (IR 1986, rule 6.133).

6.6.2 Vacancy in office

If there is a vacancy in office, e.g. the appointment has failed to take effect or the trustee is no longer qualified to act (IA 1986, s.298(6)), the Official Receiver will act as trustee (IA 1986, s.300). The Official Receiver will thereafter call a creditors' meeting to fill the vacancy.

The trustee must vacate office after the final meeting is held where the bankruptcy is annulled (IA 1986, s.298(8)).

6.6.3 Resignation of the trustee

Where a trustee suffers ill health or intends to cease practising as an insolvency practitioner, or where there is a conflict of interest or a change in personal circumstances which precludes the trustee from continuing in office or makes it impractical for him to do so, the trustee may resign (see **6.6.1** regarding block transfers and resignations; see also IA 1986, s.298(7); IR 1986, rule 6.126(3) and *Re Alt Landscapes Ltd* [1999] BPIR 459).

Before resigning, the trustee must call a meeting of creditors for the purpose of receiving his resignation. The notice of the meeting will be accompanied by an account of the administration of the estate, including a receipts and payments account.

If at the meeting no quorum is present, the meeting is deemed to have accepted the resignation and the creditors are deemed not to have resolved against the trustee having his release (IR 1986, rule 6.126(5)). If at the creditors' meeting it is resolved by the creditors not to accept the resignation, the trustee may apply to the court for permission to resign (IR 1986, rule 6.128).

6.6.4 Release of the trustee

Where an Official Receiver or trustee is released he will, with effect from the time of the release, be discharged from all other liabilities in respect of his administration of the estate otherwise than in relation to his conduct as trustee (IA 1986, s.299(5)).

However, the release will not prevent any application under IA 1986, s.304 where the trustee may have misapplied, retained or become accountable for the bankrupt's property or the estate has suffered loss or damage due to the trustee's misfeasance and/or breach of fiduciary or other duty in respect of the bankruptcy estate and the carrying out of the trustee's functions.

It should be noted that after the trustee has been released, permission is required from the court in order for there to be any action commenced against the trustee (IA 1986, s.304(2); *Brown* v. *Beat* [2002] BPIR 421).

Release of the trustee during the course of the bankruptcy

Where the Official Receiver is replaced as the trustee, he is released from the time he gives notice of his replacement to the court (IA 1986, s.299(1)).

A trustee who has died or has been removed by the creditors at a general meeting where the creditors have not resolved against his release, is deemed to have been released when the notice of removal is provided to the court (IA 1986, s.299(3)(a)).

A trustee who has been removed pursuant to a court order or by the Secretary of State, or who has vacated office on ceasing to be qualified, is released by the Secretary of State following an application by the former trustee. Where at a creditors' meeting the creditors have resolved not to release the trustee, the trustee is also not required to apply to the Secretary of State for release (IA 1986, s.299(3)(b)).

The trustee is released as and when the resignation becomes effective (IA 1986, s.299(3)(c)).

Release of the trustee on completion of the administration of the bankruptcy estate

If the Official Receiver is the trustee and gives notice to the Secretary of State that the administration of the estate is completed, for practical purposes, he has his release as and when the Secretary of State determines (IA 1986, s.299(2)). Before giving notice to the Secretary of State, the Official Receiver must give notice of his intention to seek release to the creditors who have submitted a proof of their debt, and to the bankrupt (IR 1986, rule 6.136). The notice must be accompanied by a summary of the receipts and payments made into the bankruptcy estate, although on application to the court the Official Receiver can be relieved of this duty (IR 1986, rule 6.137A).

In other cases, the trustee must give at least 28 days' notice of the final meeting to creditors in Form 6.35. Notice must also be sent to all creditors of whom the trustee is aware, and to the bankrupt (IR 1986, rule 6.137(1)).

On application by the trustee, the court may relieve the trustee from his obligations to send out notice and authorise him to carry out his duty in a way other than required by rules 6.136 or 6.137, having regard to costs and proportionality and the interests of the creditors (IR 1986, rule 6.137A).

The notice to the creditors must also include a summary of the trustee's receipts and payments, including details of remuneration and expenses, and of the basis fixed for the trustee's remuneration. The statement must also be reconciled with the trustee's account with the Insolvency Service (i.e. use of the Insolvency Service account, into which the trustee is obliged to pay all realisations).

At the final meeting, the trustee must give an opportunity for the creditors to question him on any matter in his report and it is open for the creditors to resolve against the trustee's release.

If the creditors resolve against his release the trustee may apply to the Secretary of State for release.

If there is no quorum at the final meeting, the trustee must report this to the court and indicate that a final meeting has been deemed to have been held and the creditors have not resolved against the trustee's release (IR 1986, rule 6.137).

6.7 DETERMINATION OF BANKRUPTCY

6.7.1 Final meeting

The trustee may send out notice of the final meeting of creditors (IA 1986, s.331) at the same time as providing notice of whether a final distribution will be made to creditors (IA 1986, s.330). At the final meeting the trustee must report on the administration of the estate and the creditors must determine whether to provide the trustee with a release. The release discharges the trustee from liability for his acts or omissions in the administration of the estate and otherwise in relation to his conduct as trustee (IA 1986, s.299(5)), subject to rights of action in respect of misfeasance or breach of fiduciary duty (IA 1986, s.304; see *Brown* v. *Beat* [2002] BPIR 421). Upon release, the role of trustee reverts to the Official Receiver until discharge of the bankrupt.

6.7.2 Suspension of the bankruptcy period

On the application of the trustee in bankruptcy, or the Official Receiver, the court may order that the calculation of time attributable to the one-year period ceases to run until the end of a specified period or on the fulfilment of a specified condition (IA 1986, s. 279(3)).

The court will do so if the bankrupt has failed to comply with any statutory obligations, e.g. if he has failed to make a complete disclosure of assets or failed to assist in the trustee's investigations. An application to suspend must be brought before the expiry of the one year (IR 1986, rule 6.215). If an interim order is to be made pending full hearing the term of the extension must be short (*Re Jacobs (a Bankrupt)* [1999] 1 WLR 619) and there must be reasonable grounds to allow the conclusion that an order would be made on full hearing (*Bagnall* v. *Official Receiver* [2004] BPIR 445 (CA)). The court's power to annul (as opposed to discharge) the bankruptcy order is unaffected by the existence of any suspension of the bankruptcy period (IA 1986, s.279(7)).

The law applying to a criminal bankrupt remains largely unchanged, and application to court for discharge can only be made five years after the date the bankruptcy commences (IA 1986, s.280).

6.7.3 Effect of discharge

When a bankrupt is discharged, the discharge releases the bankrupt from all bankruptcy debts and frees the individual from the restrictions and disqualifications of bankruptcy debts unless a BRO or undertaking is in place. As has already been explained, this has no effect on the trustee carrying out his functions in realising available assets. Furthermore, the discharge does not affect:

- the right of any creditor to prove in the bankruptcy for any debt from which the bankrupt is released (IA 1986, s.281(1));
- the rights of any secured creditors to enforce their security (IA 1986, s.281(2));
- the realisation of any bankruptcy debt arising in respect of fraud or fraudulent breach of trust by the bankrupt (IA 1986, s.281(3));
- fines imposed for an offence or liability under a recognisance (including liability for confiscation orders under Parts 2, 3 or 4 of the Proceeds of Crime Act 2002), except a penalty imposed by HMRC, where the Treasury has consented (IA 1986, s.281(4));

- any liability for negligence, nuisance or breach of statutory, contractual or other duty to pay by virtue of Part 1 of the Consumer Protection Act 1987, being in either case damages in respect of personal injury to any person (IA 1986, s.281(5)(a));
- a debt which arises under any order in family proceedings (IA 1986, s.281(5)(b));
- debts which are not provable as prescribed by statute (IA 1986, s.281(6)); or
- any third party liability, where that liability arises as a result of providing surety for the bankrupt (IA 1986, s.281(7)).

6.7.4 Post-discharge restrictions

To placate general concern that the liberalisation of the bankruptcy regime and in particular the reduction in the duration of bankruptcy would allow the unscrupulous and dishonest to abuse the new system, a new bankruptcy restrictions order (BRO) regime has been introduced (IA 1986, s.281A, Sched.4A). This is dealt with in greater detail in **Chapter 10**.

The effect of a BRO is that despite discharge, the individual will remain subject to the restrictions of bankruptcy. As a consequence, the application for a BRO must be made before the expiry of the first year of bankruptcy, although the Secretary of State or Official Receiver acting on direction of the Secretary of State may make an application one year after this with the court's permission. However, the court is unlikely to provide permission to extend the time unless there is good reason.

The one-year limitation period will be automatically extended if, e.g. the court has suspended the time for calculating the period of bankruptcy.

A BRO will come into effect on the date provided by the court and cease to have effect at the end of the period specified within the order. The period of restriction will be between two and 15 years, which amplifies the close correlation between the BRO regime and proceedings under CDDA 1986.

If the BRO application cannot be heard before the bankrupt's discharge, an interim order may be made by the court either on the grounds that it is in the public interest, or where there are *prima facie* grounds to suggest an order will be made.

An interim BRO will have the same effect as the BRO itself, but will cease to have effect:

- on determination of the application for the BRO;
- on the acceptance of a bankruptcy restrictions undertaking (BRU) by the bankrupt; or
- if the court discharges the interim BRO on the application of the bankrupt.

6.7.5 Discharge on Official Receiver's notice

If no investigation is deemed necessary by the Official Receiver, he may file at court and serve on the creditors a notice specifying that in his opinion, an investigation into the conduct and affairs of the bankrupt is unnecessary, or has been concluded, and that it is his intention to file a notice of discharge (IR 1986, rule 6.214A(1)).

Where a creditor or trustee in bankruptcy receives notice, the creditor must object within 28 days and inform the Official Receiver in writing of the nature of its objections and the reasons behind them (IR 1986, rule 6.214A(2)).

If no objection is received from any creditor, the Official Receiver will then proceed to file at court a notice stating that his investigations are concluded. The bankrupt will be discharged when the Form 6.82 notice is filed.

Where an objection is received, the Official Receiver cannot file a notice of discharge unless:

(a)   he has given reasons for rejecting the creditor's objection; and
(b)   he has allowed time for an appeal to have expired; or
(c)   the appeal has been determined by the court (IR 1986, rule 7.50(2)). Any appeal against a decision of the Official Receiver must be sought within 14 days of the date of the decision.

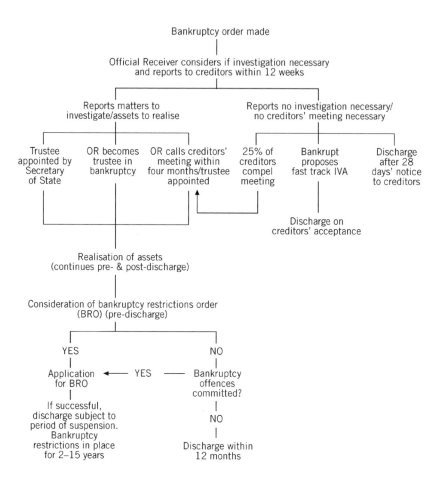

Figure 6.1   The bankruptcy process

CHAPTER 7

The administration process

Irrespective of how the administration commenced (whether by court order or by out-of-court procedure, whether by the debtor company, by a qualifying floating charge holder or on a creditors' application), once the procedure has been commenced, it does not matter who initiated the process; the procedures are the same, with the administrator being appointed for the benefit of the creditors as a whole.

7.1 INITIAL STEPS FOLLOWING APPOINTMENT

The process of administration from appointment to the initial creditors' meeting and thereafter to exit is identical whichever method of appointment was used and whoever appointed the administrator. In this chapter we look at the process of administration following appointment of an administrator, covering publicity, the initial notice to creditors, proposals, the initial creditors' meeting and the requirements for further reporting.

7.1.1 Publicity

While a company is in administration, every business document (meaning invoice, order for goods and services, business letter and order form) issued by and on behalf of the company must state:

(a) the name of the administrator; and
(b) that the affairs, business and property of the company are being managed by the administrator (IA 1986, Sched.B1, para.45(1)).

The requirement for this publicity now also extends to all the company's websites (see Companies (Trading Disclosures) (Insolvency) Regulations 2008, SI 2008/1897).

An administrator, an officer of the company and also, interestingly, the company itself may commit an offence if without reasonable excuse they permit contravention of this section. The penalty for non-compliance on summary conviction is a fine of up to one-fifth of the statutory maximum (IA 1986, Sched.10). (The statutory maximum is £5,000: Criminal Justice Act 1982, s.74, as read with the Magistrates'

Courts Act 1980, s.32(9) (for England and Wales) and the Criminal Procedure (Scotland) Act 1995 s.225(8) (for Scotland), both as amended by the Criminal Justice Act 1991, s.17.)

The importance of publicity is to ensure that those contracting with the company are aware that their rights against the company in administration are limited. It is entirely open for these parties to propose such terms of trading as they think fit. For instance, a supplier may be unwilling to supply goods on credit and instead demand cash on delivery. This has important practical implications for the success of the administration. The administrator must take into account the likely squeeze on cash flow. Sufficient funding must be in place or contingency plans available, such as finding alternative suppliers, if the administration is to have any chance of success.

7.1.2   Advertisement of administrator's appointment

As soon as reasonably practicable, the administrator shall:

(a)   send a notice of his appointment to the company;
(b)   publish a notice of his appointment in the *London Gazette*; and
(c)   advertise his appointment as he thinks appropriate.

The notice of appointment in Form 2.11B will be 'gazetted' and may be advertised in such manner as the administrator thinks appropriate (IR 1986, rule 2.27(1)). Prior to 6 April 2009 (Insolvency (Amendment) Rules 2009, SI 2009/642) the administrator was required to advertise his appointment in such newspaper as he thought appropriate in order to ensure the appointment came to the notice of the company's creditors; this often led to advertisements in both the national and the local press. Now the administrator may in the exercise of his discretion decide whether and how best to advertise his appointment. In response to this change, websites offering to advertise appointments (and other services such as advertising the business and assets for sale) have sprung up.

For Form 2.11B see **www.insolvency.gov.uk/forms/englandwalesforms.htm**.

Within seven days of appointment (meaning the date of order, or date that the administrator receives notice of his appointment if the out-of-court route is followed), notice must be sent to the Registrar of Companies (IA 1986, Sched.B1, para.46(4)).

As soon as reasonably practicable (rather than within 28 days under the old pre-Enterprise Act 2002 regime), the administrator must obtain a list of the company's creditors and send notice in Form 2.12B to each creditor of whose claim and address he is aware (IA 1986, Sched.B1, para.46(3)). In the case of *Re Sporting Options plc* [2005] BCC 88 it was held that the notification of appointment could not be made by email.

Notice must also be sent to:

(a)   any appointed receiver or administrative receiver;

(b)   if there is a pending petition for the winding up of the company, to the petitioner;

(c)   a provisional liquidator, if one has been appointed;

(d)   any High Court enforcement officer (sheriff) who to the administrator's knowledge has been charged with execution or other legal process against the company;

(e)   any person who to the administrator's knowledge has distrained against the company or its property; and

(f)   the supervisor of any CVA which is in place.

This notice should also be in Form 2.12B (IA 1986, Sched.B1, para.46(5) and IR 1986, rule 2.27(3)).

For Form 2.12B see **www.insolvency.gov.uk/forms/englandwalesforms.htm**.

While the phrase 'as soon as reasonably practicable' is used to denote the time in which certain announcements should be made and, as such, specific time limits for service/advertisement are no longer prescribed, it would be prudent for the administrator to take all steps that must be taken as swiftly as possible and, in any event, within the previous time limits. Accordingly, it would be advisable for the advertisement to be within a day or two of appointment and for notice to creditors and other prescribed parties to be sent within a week or two. However, it is possible for the court to direct that notice may be dispensed with altogether or a different time period may apply (IA 1986, Sched.B1, para.46(7)). This should only be considered in exceptional circumstances where an administrator considers it unlikely that he will be able to comply with the usual practice and procedures.

An administrator commits an offence if he fails to comply without a reasonable excuse with any of the requirements of this paragraph (IA 1986, Sched.B1, para.46(9)). A fine of one-fifth of the statutory maximum and a daily fine of one-fiftieth of the statutory maximum can be imposed (currently £1,000 and £100 respectively) (IA 1986, Sched.B1, para.46(9), Sched.10).

7.1.3   Statement of company's affairs

As soon as reasonably practicable after appointment, the administrator must send notice to one or more relevant persons to provide a statement of affairs of the company (IA 1986, Sched.B1, para.47(1)). However, this seemingly mandatory requirement must be reviewed in light of IA 1986, Sched.B1, para.48(2)(a), which provides that an administrator may revoke a requirement under IA 1986, Sched.B1, para.47(1) (see also IR 1986, rule 2.31(1) making it clear that this is an issue to be exercised in the discretion of the administrator).

A 'relevant person', as defined by IA 1986, Sched.B1, para.47(3), is a person who:

(a)   is or was an officer of the company;

(b)   took part in the formation of the company during the period of one year ending with the date on which the company entered into administration;

(c)   was employed by the company (through either a contract of employment or a contract for services) during that period; or

(d)   is or was during that period an officer or employee of a company which is or has been during that year been an officer of the company.

Notice to the relevant person must be in Form 2.13B and the administrator must provide each recipient with the requisite forms for the preparation of the statement of affairs (IR 1986, rule 2.28(4)).

For Form 2.13B see **www.insolvency.gov.uk/forms/englandwalesforms.htm**.

Under IR 1986, rule 2.28(3), the notice to the relevant person must inform each person of:

(a)   the names and addresses of others (if any) to whom the notice has been sent;

(b)   the time within which the statement must be delivered;

(c)   the effect of non-compliance with the notice and the penalty arising; and

(d)   the duties under IA 1986, s.235 to provide information and to attend the administrator if required.

The person upon whom notice is served must provide a statement of affairs within 11 days unless the administrator agrees otherwise or, where the person applies to be released from the obligation, the court otherwise orders (IA 1986, Sched.B1, para.48(1), (2) and (3); IR 1986, rule 2.31). Any person failing to comply with the notice is liable on summary conviction for a fine of up to the statutory maximum (at present £5,000) or on indictment to an unlimited fine (IA 1986, Sched.B1, para.48(4)).

The statement of affairs must be provided in Form 2.14B and must be verified by a statement of truth (IR 1986, rule 2.29(1)). A person providing a statement of truth in which he has no reasonable belief commits an offence. The statement of affairs must:

(a)   give particulars of the company's assets, debts and liabilities;

(b)   give the names and addresses of the company's creditors;

(c)   specify the security held by each and every creditor; and

(d)   state the date upon which any security was granted.

See IA 1986, Sched.B1, para.47(2).

For Form 2.14B see **www.insolvency.gov.uk/forms/englandwalesforms.htm**.

The administrator may also require any other relevant person to submit a statement of concurrence (in Form 2.15B – see IR 1986, rule 2.29(2)) verified by a statement of truth. That person is required to do so within five business days unless agreement to extend has been obtained from the administrator (IR 1986, rule 2.29(4)).

Any statement of concurrence shall be filed together with the statement of affairs with the court (in Form 2.16B) and must also delivered to the Registrar of Companies (IR 1986, rule 2.29(7)).

For Forms 2.15B and 2.16B see **www.insolvency.gov.uk/forms/ englandwalesforms.htm**.

A person preparing a statement of affairs or making a statement of concurrence may be paid such expenses as the administrator considers reasonable out of receipts (IR 1986, rule 2.32). Although any decision on this issue is subject to appeal to the court, it is clear that the obligation to provide the statement of affairs is not removed or limited by any dispute over payment of fees (IR 1986, rule 2.32(3)). It must also be remembered that the obligation to provide a statement of affairs applies irrespective of the size and complexity of the business. It may therefore be the case that a director will require the support of the company's former internal accounts department, or even external accountants, to provide a meaningful statement. In such circumstances the issue of expenses is clearly much more relevant.

Where the administrator thinks it will prejudice the conduct of the administration if either the whole or a part of the statement of the company's affairs were to be disclosed, the administrator may apply to court for an order limiting disclosure (IR 1986, rule 2.30(1)). On application, the court may order that the statement of affairs, or part of it, shall not be filed with the Registrar of Companies (IR 1986, rule 2.30(2)). As soon as the order is made, the administrator will file Form 2.16B together with the order and the statement of affairs (limited to the extent provided by the order) with the Registrar of Companies, together with copies (IR 1986, rule 2.30(3)). A creditor may apply to court for disclosure of the statement of affairs, or part of it where an order of limited disclosure has previously been granted (IR 1986, rule 2.30(4)).

7.1.4 Administrator's proposals

Having taken control of the management of the company, considered the statement of affairs and conducted his own investigations, the administrator must make a statement setting out his proposals for achieving the purpose of the administration (IA 1986, Sched.B1, para.49(1)). This must be as soon as reasonably practicable and in any event no later than eight weeks after the company has entered into administration (IA 1986, Sched.B1, para.49(5)).

The eight-week time limit may only be extended by permission of the court or creditors' agreement obtained in writing or at a creditors' meeting (IA 1986, Sched.B1, para.49(8)). Creditors' consent is obtained by a majority of unsecured creditors in value who respond and from every secured creditor. If the administrator considers the distribution will only be made to secured and preferential creditors and IA 1986, s.176A does not apply, it is only the consent of each secured creditor and of at least 50 per cent (in terms of value) of the preferential creditors who respond that must be obtained (IA 1986, Sched.B1, paras.107, 108).

An extension obtained by creditors' consent:

(a) can be agreed only once;

(b) may not be for more than 28 days;

(c)   cannot be used to extend any court deadline; and

(d)   may not be used to extend the period after expiry (IA 1986, Sched.B1, para.108(5)).

On application to the court, an extension can be obtained and may be granted more than once and/or after expiry (IA 1986, Sched.B1, para.107(2)). Where the court orders an extension of time, the administrator must send notice (in Form 2.18B) to:

(a)   the Registrar of Companies;

(b)   each and every creditor of the company who is claiming a debt and of whom the administrator is aware; and

(c)   every member of the company of whose address he is aware (IR 1986, rule 2.33(4)).

For Form 2.18B see **www.insolvency.gov.uk/forms/englandwalesforms.htm**.

The primary purpose of the proposals is to inform the creditors how the administrator intends to achieve the purpose of administration. The proposals should therefore contain a statement dealing with why administration is considered appropriate (i.e. the purpose of administration) and explain, as appropriate to the circumstances, why the administrator does not consider it reasonable and practicable for the company to be rescued and/or, if appropriate, why it is not reasonably practicable for the company's creditors as a whole to achieve a better result than would be applicable if the company were to be wound up (IA 1986, Sched.B1, para.49(2)(b)).

These provisions ensure that the administrator must not only have regard to company rescue as the pre-eminent objective in fulfilling the purpose of administration, but also highlight to the creditors the reasoning and justification as to why the administrator considers company rescue cannot be achieved, if that is the case.

The statement of administrator's proposals must be sent to the Registrar of Companies in Form 2.17B (IR 1986, rule 2.33(1)) and to the company's creditors and members (so far as the administrator is aware of these). Although notification of appointment cannot be sent by email, in certain circumstances the administrator may be permitted to provide copies of his proposals by email or provide the creditors with reference to a website (*Re Sporting Options plc* [2005] BCC 88). The administrator may also dispense with the need to send proposals to the members if he publishes a notice (advertised as he thinks fit: see IR 1986, rule 2.33(7)) undertaking to provide a copy of the statement of proposals free of charge to any member who applies in writing to a specified address (IA 1986, Sched.B1, para.49(6)).

In accordance with the provisions of IR 1986, rule 2.33(2), the statement of proposals must also include:

(a)   details of the court where the proceedings were initiated and the relevant court reference number;

(b)   the full name, registered address, registered number and any other trading names of the company;

(c) details relating to the appointment, including the date of appointment and manner of appointment;

(d) the names of the directors and secretary of the company and details of any shareholdings that they may have;

(e) an account of the circumstances giving rise to the appointment of the administrator;

(f) a copy of the company's statement of affairs (or summary) with administrator's comments;

(g) if any order limiting disclosure of the statement of affairs has been made, a statement dealing with this;

(h) in the circumstances where a statement of affairs has not been provided, the names and addresses of creditors, including details of any security held;

(i) if no statement of affairs has been provided, details of the financial position of the company at the latest practical date, including a list of the company's creditors, names and addresses and details of debts and an explanation as to why no statement of affairs has been provided;

(j) the basis upon which it is proposed that the administrator's remuneration should be fixed under IR 1986, rule 2.106;

(k) a statement of any pre-administration costs charged or incurred by the administrator or by any other person qualified to act as an insolvency practitioner;

(l) to the best of the administrator's knowledge and belief, an estimate of the value of the prescribed part (i.e. the sum derived from floating charge realisations under IA 1986, s.176A) and an estimate of the value of the company's net property; and if it is not proposed to make any distribution to secured creditors under IA 1986, s.176A(5) (i.e. if the company's net property is less than the prescribed minimum and the administrator thinks the cost of making a distribution to unsecured creditors would be disproportionate to the benefit or, alternatively, where the administrator is to seek a court order for the same), this must be stated;

(m) how it is envisaged the purpose of the administration will be achieved and how it is proposed the administration shall end. If a creditors' voluntary liquidation is proposed, details of the proposed liquidator must be provided together with a statement that the creditors may nominate a different person as the proposed liquidator;

(n) where the administrator has decided not to call a meeting of creditors, the administrator must set out his reasons;

(o) the manner in which the affairs and business of the company have since the date of appointment been managed and financed, including details of any disposals and the terms of such disposals and the manner in which the business affairs of the company will be continued to be managed, if the administration proposals are approved and how they will be financed;

(p) whether the EC Regulation on Insolvency Proceedings (Council Regulation

1346/2000/EC) applies and, if so, whether they are main proceedings or territorial proceedings; and

(q) such other information as the administrator thinks necessary to enable the creditors to decide whether or not to vote on the proposals.

See also IR 1986, rule 2.33(2A) dealing with pre-administration costs and the obligations of disclosure and IR 1986, rule 2.33(2C) dealing with the statement required where it is proposed that the administration will end by the company moving into creditor's voluntary liquidation.

The administrator may propose either a CVA or a scheme of arrangement (one of the two previous pre-Enterprise Act 2002 purposes of the administration) as a means of achieving the purpose of the administration (IA 1986, Sched.B1, para.49(3)). This is logical, as both are methods of achieving the purpose of the administration (rather than purposes in their own right). Both also offer the opportunity for the unsecured creditors to achieve a higher return and/or the opportunity that the company may be rescued.

The administrator's proposals may not include any action which would:

(a) affect the rights of the secured creditors to be paid their full security;

(b) result in a preferential debt being paid otherwise than in priority to non-preferential debts; or

(c) result in one preferential creditor being paid a smaller proportion of the debt than another.

The proposals may, however, provide for such eventualities if the relevant creditors' approval is first obtained, or the proposal involves the company entering into either a CVA or a scheme of arrangement.

7.1.5   Meeting to consider the administrator's proposals

In all cases (except where IA 1986, Sched.B1, para.52(1) applies, i.e. the statement of proposals provides that unsecured creditors will be paid in full or not at all), the administrator's statement of proposals will be accompanied by an invitation to an initial creditors' meeting (IA 1986, Sched.B1, para.51(1)). At least 14 days' notice of the meeting should be given to the creditors (IR 1986, rule 2.35(4)), notice of the meeting being in Form 2.20B (IR 1986, rule 2.35(2)).

For Form 2.20B see **www.insolvency.gov.uk/forms/englandwalesforms.htm**.

The initial creditors' meeting should be held as soon as reasonably practicable and in any event within 10 weeks beginning on the date on which the company enters into administration (IA 1986, Sched.B1, para.51(2)). This provision may only be varied by court order or with the consent of the creditors (see above) (IA 1986, Sched.B1, paras.51(4), 107). Where the court orders an extension, notice in Form 2.18B shall be sent to every person entitled to notice of the meeting (IR 1986, rule 2.34(3)).

For Form 2.18B see **www.insolvency.gov.uk/forms/englandwalesforms.htm**.

Notice of the meeting must also be sent to those past and present directors of the company and such other officers of the company whose presence the administrator thinks is required, using Form 2.19B (IR 1986, rule 2.34(2)). It should be remembered that at least one director wishing to place a company into liquidation needs to be present at a creditors' meeting; this is not the case in administration. However, often the administrator will find the presence of the directors of assistance in answering questions posed by creditors from the floor, although it should be remembered that the initial creditors' meeting is convened to consider the proposals and not to conduct an analysis of the prior conduct of the directors and assessment of why the company failed.

For Form 2.19B see **www.insolvency.gov.uk/forms/englandwalesforms.htm**.

In fixing the venue for the meeting, the administrator is to have regard to the convenience to the creditors and the meeting must be held between 10 am and 4 pm on a business day unless the court directs otherwise (IR 1986, rule 2.35(3)).

Notice of the initial creditors' meeting must be published in the *Gazette* and may be advertised in such manner as the administrator thinks fit (IR 1986, rule 2.34(1)).

The meeting may be adjourned once, for no more than 14 days, by the chairman and must be adjourned in circumstances where there is no requisite majority for approval of the proposals (IR 1986, rule 2.34(4)).

7.1.6 Business and result of creditors' meeting

At the initial creditors' meeting, the creditors must consider the administrator's proposals and may approve them with or without modification (IA 1986, Sched.B1, para.53(1)).

The meeting is chaired by the administrator or, in his place, some other insolvency practitioner or sufficiently experienced employee of the administrator's firm (IR 1986, rule 2.36).

If a modification is proposed and approved by the creditors, the administrator must also consent to the modification (IA 1986, Sched.B1, para.53(1)(b)). This is important as the administrator must act in accordance with the proposals save where any revision to those proposals is not considered substantial (IA 1986, Sched.B1, para.68(1)). As a result, if the modification is one that the administrator thinks is unworkable, he is not required to accept it. If this means that the proposals are not accepted, the administrator will report to the court, which may make such order as it thinks appropriate (IA 1986, Sched.B1, para.55) (whether this means that the court could in theory impose a set of proposals on the creditors is a moot point, although see *DKLL Solicitors* v. *Revenue and Customs Commissioners* [2007] BCC 908 and the *obiter* comment made with regard to steps that an administrator could take in the face of a dissenting majority creditor).

In the case of opposition, the administrator may well adjourn the meeting and put forward revised proposals or perhaps defer the more contentious decisions to a creditors' committee, which may be formed at any creditors' meeting (IA 1986, Sched.B1, para.57). In practice, however, by the time of the creditors' meeting, even though held much sooner than previously, the 'heat' from creditors may have dissipated and the proposals are often uncontentious and drafted in a very general manner to provide the administrator with wide powers of management, control and decision making, to be exercised at his discretion. In addition, one sometimes sees a 'take it or leave it' set of proposals, with one proposed resolution for acceptance or rejection of the proposals as a whole, as opposed to a preferred list of steps to be voted on and approved as separate resolutions by the creditors. Such a practice has been discouraged by insolvency practitioner regulatory bodies in their reports and guidance to members.

A resolution is passed when a majority (in value) of those present and voting in person or by proxy vote in favour of it (IR 1986, rule 2.43(1)). A resolution is invalid if those voting against it include more than half the value of creditors to whom notice of the meeting was sent and who are not to the best of the chairman's belief connected with the company (IR 1986, rule 2.43(2)).

A creditor is entitled to vote if he has lodged with the administrator (not later than 12 pm on the day before the meeting) written details of the debt claimed, or as otherwise permitted by the administrator, and the claim has been duly admitted by the administrator (IR 1986, rule 2.38(1)). The administrator is entitled to call for documents and other evidence to substantiate a claim (IR 1986, rule 2.38(3)). The votes are calculated according to the claims as at the date of administration (less any subsequent payment or adjustment for set-off in accordance with IR 1986, rule 2.85).

A creditor possessing an unliquidated claim is not entitled to vote unless the administrator agrees to puts a value on the claim and, unlike in liquidation (IR 1986, rule 1.17(3)), there is no requirement to fix such a claim with a minimum sum of £1 (IR 1986, rule 2.38(5)).

The chairman has a power to admit or reject creditor claims for the purposes of voting at the meeting. He may mark claims as objected to but allow the creditor to vote subject to a final later determination. Any decision in regard to the admission or rejection of claims is subject to appeal, which must be made not later than 21 days after the date of receipt of the administrator's report (IR 1986, rule 2.39). In practice, the effect of these provisions is likely to have most impact where a creditor purporting to have a majority claim is rejected and the proposals as approved set out a course of action opposed by that creditor. In these circumstances, injunctive relief may be brought to restrain the administrator from acting in a prejudicial manner (perhaps selling the business and assets of the company) pending a determination on the administrator's decision.

Secured creditors are not entitled to vote save where they have valued their security and an estimated unsecured balance remains (IR 1986, rule 2.40). However, if the administrator has given notice that he does not think that any distribution will be made to unsecured creditors apart from the prescribed part payment (i.e. pursuant to IA 1986, Sched.B1, para.52(1)(b)) but a meeting has still been requisitioned by creditors, the secured creditor is entitled to vote in respect of the full value of the debt without deduction of the value of his security (IR 1986, rule 2.40(2)).

A creditor with a debt on, or secured by, a current bill of exchange or promissory note is not entitled to vote, unless he treats as secured the liability to him on that bill or note of every person who is liable on it antecedently to the company, estimates the value of the security and, for the purpose of his entitlement to vote, deducts it from his claim; in such instances the creditor may be entitled to vote for the estimated unsecured balance (IR 1986, rule 2.41).

An owner of goods under a hire purchase or chattel leasing agreement, or a seller of goods under a conditional sale agreement, is entitled to vote in respect of the debt due and payable on the date the company entered into administration (IR 1986, rule 2.42).

At the conclusion of the meeting, the administrator must as soon as practicable report the decision of the meeting to the court, the Registrar of Companies and the creditors (IA 1986, Sched.B1, para.53(2)).

Under IA 1986, Sched.B1, para.52, the administrator is not obliged to call an initial meeting of creditors if he states in his proposals that:

(a)   the company has sufficient property to enable creditors to be paid in full;
(b)   the only distribution to unsecured creditors will be pursuant to IA 1986, s.176A(2)(a) (i.e. the prescribed part); or
(c)   the company cannot be rescued, nor a greater realisation than on winding up achieved (i.e. the appointment of the administrator is being made solely in order to realise property in order to make a distribution to one or more secured or preferential creditors).

Despite the administrator determining that a meeting should not be held, he may be required to summon an initial creditors' meeting if requested to do so by the creditors of the company whose debts exceed 10 per cent of the total debt of the company (IA 1986, Sched.B1, para.52(2)). The request for the meeting must be in Form 2.21B and made within eight business days of the proposals being sent out. A meeting so requisitioned will be held within 28 days and security for the cost of summoning and holding the meeting must be deposited by the requisitioner. This deposit may be repaid if the meeting resolves that the expenses of summoning it should be payable as an expense of the administration (see IR 1986, rule 2.37). This is a high risk-strategy for an unsecured creditor not otherwise financially interested in the outcome of the administration.

For Form 2.21B see **www.insolvency.gov.uk/forms/englandwalesforms.htm**.

The requirement to hold any creditors' meeting may be satisfied by a course of correspondence (IR 1986, rule 2.48). Correspondence can be by telephonic and/or other electronic means and notice must be sent in Form 2.25B to every creditor who is entitled to receive it.

For Form 2.25B see **www.insolvency.gov.uk/forms/englandwalesforms.htm**.

For votes to be counted, the administrator must receive the vote by 12 pm on the closing date specified in Form 2.25B, which must be accompanied by a statement in writing on the creditor's entitlement to vote (IR 1986, rule 2.48(2)).

The closing date set by the administrator is at his discretion, but must not be less than 14 days from the date of issue of notice (IR 1986, rule 2.48(4)).

For the business to be transacted by correspondence, at least one valid form must be returned by a creditor by the time of the closing date (IR 1986, rule 2.48(5)).

At the conclusion of the meeting of creditors and, as soon as reasonably practicable, notice of the result of the meeting in Form 2.23B and a copy of the proposals must be sent to:

(a)   each creditor who received notice of the meeting and any person who received a copy of the original proposals;

(b)   the court;

(c)   the Registrar of Companies; and

(d)   any creditor who did not receive notice of the meeting (IA 1986, Sched.B1, para.53; IR 1986, rule 2.46).

For Form 2.23B see **www.insolvency.gov.uk/forms/englandwalesforms.htm**.

7.1.7   Revision of administrator's proposals, further meetings and creditors' committee

Once the proposals have been agreed, the administrator cannot make any substantial amendment to the proposals without first obtaining the creditors' consent obtained at a further creditors' meeting (IA 1986, Sched.B1, para.54(1)).

What amounts to a 'substantial' amendment may be questionable and hence directions of the court could first be sought by the administrator before going to the cost and expense of calling another meeting (IA 1986, Sched.B1, para.63).

The administrator's statement of revised proposals must be in Form 2.22B and contain information broadly in line with that required in the original proposals (see IR 1986, rule 2.45(2)). These revised proposals must be sent to the creditors and may be advertised as the administrator thinks fit (IR 1986, rule 2.45(4)).

The administrator may act in accordance with any revision to proposals not considered substantial (IA 1986, Sched.B1, para.68(1)(b)). If a creditor is unhappy with any changes to the proposals being undertaken by the administrator without approval, he can use the procedures contained in IA 1986, Sched.B1, para.74 (unfair harm) or para.75 (misfeasance).

After the approval of the proposals, the administrator may summon further meetings of creditors (IA 1986, Sched.B1, para.62) and must do so if required by requisition from creditors holding at least 10 per cent of the total debt or where directed to do so by the court (IA 1986, Sched.B1, para.56). The requisitioning of a meeting is subject to the same rules as apply where a meeting is requisitioned following the administrator's determination not to call an initial creditors' meeting (see IR 1986, rule 2.37).

As opposed to the calling of a number of creditors' meetings during the course of the administration, it may be more expedient to propose to the creditors that a creditors' committee is formed (IA 1986, Sched.B1, para.57). The powers and functions of a creditors' committee are of less importance in the UK than in other jurisdictions (particularly in contrast to the US Chapter 11 procedures), but such committees are often used to sanction company proceedings, the sales processes and the remuneration of the administrators, so their role should not be underestimated.

7.1.8　Progress report

A progress report (as defined in IR 1986, rule 2.47) must be sent to the creditors, the court and Registrar of Companies covering the six-month period commencing on the date the company entered into administration and every subsequent period of six months. The report is to be in Form 2.24B and must be made within one month of the end of the period covered by the report. An extension of time in which to file the report can only be obtained on court application (IR 1986, rule 2.47(5)).

For Form 2.24B see **www.insolvency.gov.uk/forms/englandwalesforms.htm**. The progress report must include:

(a)　details of the court where the proceedings are and the relevant court reference number;

(b)　details of the company's name, address and registered office and registered number;

(c)　the administrator's name and address, date of appointment and circumstances of the appointment;

(d)　details of any extension to the initial period of appointment;

(e)　details of progress made during the period of the report, including a receipts of payments account;

(f)　details of any assets that remain to be realised; and

(g)　any other relevant information to be provided to creditors.

Commercially sensitive information can be excluded, but only if a limited disclosure order is first obtained (IR 1986, rule 2.30).

The receipts and payments account must state the assets that have been realised, for what value and what payments have been made to creditors. The account is to be in the form of an abstract showing receipts and payments during the period of the report (IR 1986, rule 2.47(2)).

Summary: guide to administration procedure

1.　Administrator's appointment (Form 2.11B) advertised 'as soon as reasonably practicable'.

2.　Notice of administrator's appointment served 'as soon as reasonably practicable' on:

- company;
- petitioning creditor; and
- creditors (Form 2.12B).

3. Notice of appointment filed with the Registrar of Companies (within seven days).
4. Administrator sends notice to 'relevant person' to complete a statement of affairs (Form 2.13B).
5. 'Relevant person' to complete and return statement of affairs (within 11 days).
6. Administrator files statement of affairs (Form 2.14B) with Registrar of Companies and court (Form 2.16B).
7. Administrator to prepare statement of proposals.
8. Statement of proposals to be sent by administrator to company's creditors and members (within eight weeks of appointment) (with notice of meeting).
9. File statement of proposals with Registrar of Companies (within eight weeks of appointment) (Form 2.17B attaching proposal).
10. Provide at least 14 days' notice of initial creditors' meeting (to be held within 10 weeks of appointment) (Form 2.20B).
11. Send notice to directors/officers – whose attendance is required (Form 2.19B).
12. If meeting is by correspondence instead of actual meeting send notice (in Form 2.25B).
13. Following meeting send notice of result to company's creditors and members, file with Registrar of Companies (Form 2.23B).
14. Provide progress report within six months and every subsequent period of six months (Form 2.24B).
15. Administration ends on expiry of 12 months unless extended by court order or creditor consent.

7.2   THE EFFECT OF ADMINISTRATION

Checklist

The effect of administration

- Any outstanding winding-up petition must be dismissed (unless the appointment of the administrator was by the floating charge holder by out-of-court route).
- Any administrative receiver must vacate office.
- Any receiver of part of the company's property must vacate office on the administrator's request.
- No resolution may be passed for the winding up of the company (voluntary liquidation).
- No order may be made for the winding up of the company (compulsory liquidation).
- No step may be taken to enforce security over the company's property except with the consent of the administrator or permission of the court.
- No step may be taken to repossess goods in the company's possession under any hire purchase agreement except with consent of the administrator or permission of the court.
- The landlord may not exercise any rights of forfeiture by peaceable re-entry in relation to premises occupied by the company except with consent of the administrator or permission of the court.
- No legal process (including legal proceedings, execution, distress and diligence) may be instituted or continued against the company or the company's property except with the consent of the administrator or permission of the court.

- No administrative receiver can be appointed (IA 1986, Sched.B1, paras.40, 41(1)–(2), 42(2)–(3), 43(2)–(3), 43(4), (6), (6A)).

7.2.1 Introduction of a statutory moratorium

The central feature of the administration process is the commencement of a statutory moratorium preventing certain prescribed creditor actions. This moratorium provides the administrator with a window of opportunity in which to assess the viability of the business and make proposals to the company's creditors. During this time, the administrator is provided breathing space, free from attempts by creditors to enforce claims against the company. An individual creditor's rights are thus necessarily prejudiced in the cause of the collective good of the creditors as a whole. As we shall see, there are checks and balances to ensure that an individual creditor is not unfairly prejudiced, although, as discussed in **7.2.6**, the moratorium has very different implications for a creditor where the administrator has conducted a pre-pack sale of the business and assets on or soon after appointment.

It is important to remember that the moratorium does no more than suspend the enforcement of a creditor's rights against the debtor company; it does not destroy the creditor's rights. Unless otherwise provided for within the contract, a contractual obligation on the part of the company in administration is not revoked by the commencement of the administration; it is only the ability of the contracting party to enforce any rights that might derive from a breach of contract by the insolvent company that is affected.

The effect of the moratorium can also be relaxed with the consent of the administrator, or permission of the court, as a means to avoid potentially unfair treatment to specific creditors/contractual parties. The moratorium is also limited to provide protection only in regard to the debtor company and its property, not guarantors and other third parties.

The fact that there is a suspension (rather than destruction or crystallisation) of rights also has an important consequence for a creditor. In theory, it is entirely possible that the company could enter administration and, with the advantages afforded by the moratorium period, restructure its affairs, return to profitability and exit administration by a return of control and management to the owners of the company. As the moratorium comes to an end, so the creditors' rights to take proceedings are then re-established. It should be noted, however, that despite the existence of the moratorium any relevant Limitation Act 1980 provisions continue to apply to creditor claims against the company (see *Re Cosslett (Contractors) Ltd* [2004] EWHC 658 (Ch)). As a result, if a creditor is approaching the expiry of a Limitation Act period for a claim (not established as a payable debt), consent of the administrator or permission of the court to commence proceedings should be obtained as a means of safeguarding the creditor's position. It is often the case that the proceedings can be issued and then stayed by consent, acting as a protective claim pending determination of the administration.

Ultimately, if the administration has been completed the claimant can continue with the litigation. In the more likely circumstances where another insolvency procedure follows (e.g. liquidation), it is the nature of the subsequent insolvency procedure which will determine the ability and worth of the claimant continuing with those proceedings. It should be noted that a creditor cannot prove for a debt (perhaps in a subsequent liquidation following administration) which is statute-barred.

While the most significant effect of administration is the statutory moratorium that comes into force, other important consequences arise.

7.2.2   The effect of administration on any winding-up petition

A petition for the winding up of a company will be dismissed if an administration order is made (IA 1986, Sched.B1, para.40(1)). Unlike receivership, save for the limited exemption detailed below, administration cannot run concurrently with liquidation, as both are collective processes that deal with the company and its assets, not solely the assets.

Where an administration application is issued (IR 1986, rule 2.6(3)(b)), the application needs to be served on any creditor petitioning for the winding up of the company who may make representations at the hearing (see *DKLL Solicitors* v. *Revenue and Customs Commissioners* [2007] EWHC 2067 (Ch) for an example of a case concerning a contested administration application and how the court may have regard to all the circumstances and not just the wishes of the majority creditor). As a result, it would be advisable for any applicant seeking an administration order to ensure that any court application is heard before, or perhaps listed with, the hearing of the winding-up petition. If the winding-up petition is to be heard first, it would be prudent for the applicant to attend the hearing of the winding-up petition to ensure the court is made aware of the administration application and therefore adjourns or stays the winding-up petition. The costs incurred by the petitioning creditor in seeking a winding-up order will generally be ordered to be an expense of the administration.

Where the administrator has been appointed by a floating charge holder by an out-of-court route, the winding-up petition will be suspended during the course of the appointment (IA 1986, Sched.B1, para.14). Where there is an outstanding winding-up petition and the administrator's proposals are accepted by the creditors, the administrator may apply for directions (IA 1986, Sched.B1, para.63) and/or seek dismissal of the petition. It may not be advisable to leave the petition suspended, as on discharge of the administration it could be revived, which may prejudice the restructured company or the consequent proposals to put the company into voluntary liquidation or seek its dissolution.

Where a winding-up petition is presented under IA 1986, s.124A (public interest grounds), IA 1986, s.124B (petition for winding up of a *Societas Europaea* – see European Public Limited-Liability Company Regulations 2004, SI 2004/2326) or the Financial Services and Market Act 2000, s.367 (i.e. a petition by the FCA), it is possible for the company to be concurrently in administration and liquidation. As a result, in these circumstances IA 1986, Sched.B1, paras.40(1)(a) and 42(3) will not have effect.

7.2.3   The effect of administration on receivers/secured creditors

When an administration order is made, any administrative receiver of the company must vacate office (IA 1986, Sched.B1, para.41(1)); in addition, an administrative receiver of the company cannot be appointed once the company is in administration (IA 1986, Sched.B1, para.43(6A)). An administrator and administrative receiver fulfil the same role of control and management of the company and therefore cannot both be in office at the same time.

However, it should be remembered that an administration application will be dismissed unless:

(a)   the floating charge holder consents to the administration appointment; or

(b)   the court thinks the security under which the appointment of the administrative receiver has been made may be released or discharged under IA 1986, s.238, 240 or 245.

Furthermore, the out-of-court routes of appointment are unavailable where there is an administrative receiver in office.

As a consequence, administration cannot be used as a means to take control and management of the company away from an administrative receiver, save where the validity of the security is in doubt.

Where a secured creditor has appointed a receiver over part of the company's property, the administrator may require that the receiver vacates office (IA 1986, Sched.B1, para.41(2)).

It should also be borne in mind that any step to enforce security (including the appointment of a receiver) over the company's property requires the consent of the administrator, or permission of the court (IA 1986, Sched.B1, para.43(2)). As a result, in theory at least, the power of the secured creditor and any receiver remaining in office will be severely curtailed. In practice, however, the position and the balance of power may be very different, with the administrator recognising that to deal with the assets subject to the fixed charge, the rights of that secured creditor cannot be prejudiced and to realise the secured asset, a release will be required from the secured creditor. In those circumstances the proposed administrator is likely to work closely with the secured creditor and is likely to accede to a request to leave the asset in the hands of the receiver, or where the secured creditor agrees that the administrator takes over control and management of the secured asset it will only be on the basis that this offers a realistic chance of better realisation of their security. In addition, it should be remembered that where a secured creditor has already taken control of the company's principal asset (e.g. the company's business premises), it may have the practical effect of making the purpose of administration unachievable.

Where a receiver or an administrative receiver vacates office, the receiver's right to remuneration is charged and paid (ahead of any claim by the security holder appointing him) from any property in his custody and control immediately before he vacates office (IA 1986, Sched.B1, para.41(3)(a)). This right is, however, tempered by the effects of the statutory moratorium (see IA 1986, Sched.B1, para.41(4)(c)) so cannot be enforced except with consent of the administrator.

As outlined above, the secured creditor cannot take steps to enforce security over the company's property except with the consent of the administrator or the permission of the court (IA 1986, Sched.B1, para.43(2)). IA 1986, s.248 widely defines 'security' to include any mortgage, charge, lien or other security. 'Other security' has been held to include:

- security arising from operation of law (*Re Euro Commercial Leasing Ltd* v. *Cartwright & Lewis* [1995] BCC 830);
- a contractual provision, where there was a right to look to the debtor's property by detention in settlement of a debt (*Bristol Airport plc* v. *Powdrill* [1990] Ch 744);
- commercial arrangements having an effect equivalent to security (see *March Estates plc* v. *Gunmark Ltd* [1996] 2 BCLC 1, although subsequent cases which followed this stressed the need for the security (whether consensual or non-consensual) to be 'security' in a stricter legal sense; see *Razzaq* v. *Pala* [1997] 1 WLR 1336 and *Clarence Café Ltd* v. *Comchester Finance* [1999] L&TR 303); and
- a repairer's lien regardless of any demand for delivery up by the administrator (see *London Flight Centre (Stansted) Ltd* v. *Osprey Aviation Ltd* [2002] BPIR 1115).

It remains unclear whether a demand for payment is deemed to be the 'taking of steps' to enforce security (in *Re Olympia & York Canary Wharf Ltd (No.1)* [1993] BCLC 453 it is noted that this question was specifically not being dealt with). It is proffered that as the moratorium is concerned with enforcement of rights against the company and more importantly its property (not the destruction of rights), the issue of a demand, which might be a necessary prelude to the enforcement of security, would not in any way hamper the ability of the administrator to carry out his functions. Indeed, in many cases it is the commencement of the administration as an insolvency proceeding that triggers the secured creditor's enforcement rights in any event. This trigger does not mean, however, that the secured creditor can exercise those rights and it is contended that a demand for payment should be regarded in the same vein. In practice, the issue may not have reached court because an administrator faced with a demand (against the company) by a secured creditor will almost certainly negotiate with them and ascertain their intention as regards their security.

It should also be noted that where the secured creditor holds a floating charge the creditor will have been given notice of the intended appointment and therefore will have had an opportunity to appoint an administrative receiver or a receiver prior to the commencement of the administration. In regard to a secured creditor holding a fixed charge over a significant asset of the company, it would also not be unusual to find that the proposed administrator has conducted initial negotiations with the secured creditor, so avoiding conflict once the administration has commenced.

7.2.4 Moratorium on insolvency proceedings

While the company is in administration the company cannot enter into voluntary or compulsory liquidation; as a result no resolution may be passed by the members or order made by the court to commence the liquidation (IA 1986, Sched.B1, para.42(2), (3)).

This prohibition does not apply to a winding-up order sought under IA 1986, s.124A (public interest grounds), IA 1986, s.124B (petition for winding up of a *Societas Europaea* – see European Public Limited-Liability Company Regulations 2004, SI 2004/2326) or the Financial Services and Market Act 2000, s.367 (i.e. a petition by the FCA).

If the administrator becomes aware that a public interest winding-up petition has been presented during the course of the administration, he must apply for directions under IA 1986, Sched.B1, para.63 (see IA 1986, Sched.B1, para.42(5)). The court will consider whether both the liquidator and the administrator should remain in office, perhaps because the former is undertaking investigations leading to possible proceedings against former owners/management, while the latter is seeking to realise the business and assets of the company on a going concern basis.

Moratorium on legal processes

Once the company is in administration, the following steps cannot be taken without the consent of the administrator or permission of the court:

- Enforcement of security over the company's property.
- Repossession of goods in the company's possession held under a hire purchase agreement.
- Forfeiture on peaceable re-entry by the landlord.
- Commencement or continuation of any legal process (IA 1986, Sched.B1, para.43).

7.2.5 Moratorium on other legal processes

Enforcement of security

As discussed in **7.2.3**, IA 1986, s.248 widely defines 'security' to include any mortgage, charge, lien or other security. As a result of the moratorium, a secured creditor cannot take any step to enforce security except with consent of the administrator or permission of the court (IA 1986, Sched.B1, para.43(2)). In granting permission to allow the secured creditor to take steps, the court may also impose a condition on, or a requirement in connection with, the transaction (IA 1986, Sched.B1, para.43(7)).

Repossession of goods under a hire purchase agreement

No step can be taken by a lessor exercising rights under a hire purchase agreement (such as repossession in event of insolvency and/or non-payment) without the consent of the administrator or permission of the court (IA 1986, Sched.B1, para.43(3)).

In addition, 'any hire purchase agreement' also includes conditional sales agreements and chattel leasing agreements. Where goods remain in the possession of the debtor company, the 'owner' of the goods is prevented from recovering them even where the agreement to hire/lease, etc. has been terminated prior to the commencement of the administration (*Re David Meek Plant Ltd* [1993] BCC 175).

Importantly, a creditor possessing a retention of title over goods supplied to the debtor is also prevented from exercising rights that may have been retained under the contract of supply, such as the right to go on to the debtor's premises and take back unpaid-for stock.

As we shall see, in practice it will be incumbent on the administrator to quickly to come to some agreement with lessors of equipment under hire purchase agreements or suppliers with the benefit of possible retention of title, as such creditors should not be unfairly harmed and/or the administration process should not be used simply to hamper their rights. Particularly in regard to goods subject to retention of title, a not uncommon arrangement is for an agreement to be reached which allows the administrator to sell to a third party and to hold the proceeds in escrow to be paid to the supplier if the retention of title clause is ultimately found to be effective. In other cases the administrator selling to a third party will do so without representation or warranty as to title and will require that the third party purchaser retains and holds goods subject to possible retention of title and/or indemnifies the administrator against loss and damage suffered by claims from the supplier.

Landlord's right to forfeit

A landlord cannot take any steps to forfeit a lease by peaceable re-entry for non-payment of rent once a tenant company is administration except with consent of the administrator or leave of the court (IA 1986, Sched.B1, para.43(4)). The landlord also cannot distrain for rent or sue for non-payment, although both actions are covered by 'other legal process', discussed below.

In recent years, nowhere has the tension between the individual right of an individual creditor (in this case the landlord) and the collective best interests of the creditors as a whole been more evident than in the interplay between the tenant company, the administrator and the landlord.

While it is often the case that the insolvent company's problems mean that it cannot continue to meet its leasehold obligations, during the recession and fall in property market from mid-2007 onwards, many tenants have found that they are paying rent way in excess of market rate and there is a perception that administration (or at least the threat of administration) has been used as a process to negotiate more favourable terms. The reason for this is that rent is not necessarily payable as a cost and expense of the administration process, much depending on the particular circumstances of the case (see *Innovate Logistics Ltd* v. *Sunberry Properties Ltd* [2009] BCC 164). As a result, during the period of administration, the landlord may find that rent is not paid on an ongoing basis. To compound the situation, the administrator may well find it expedient to grant an unlawful licence to occupy (as far as the tenant company's leasehold obligations are concerned) to a third party/buyer of the tenant company's business and assets. This is almost certainly the case where a pre-pack administration sale is contemplated and there is a fear that prior notice of the proposal to the landlord would cause the landlord to take action. The landlord in such circumstances faces a *fait accompli*, with no immediate ability to enforce rights against the tenant company in administration and an unlawful occupier who perhaps will wish to renegotiate terms as opposed to negotiating an assignment of the existing lease. Where the occupier is a new corporate vehicle controlled and managed by the previous owner-managers of the tenant company, feelings of injustice on the part of the landlord may be magnified.

Each case will of course be fact sensitive and it may be the case that the administrator will seek to negotiate with the landlord over the terms of occupation during the course of the administration, perhaps paying rent on a reduced basis, perhaps weekly in arrears as opposed to quarterly in advance. With such breathing space the administrator may be able to restructure the company and/or introduce the landlord to a potential new tenant company that would be willing to take an assignment of the lease. In such circumstances it might be to the advantage of the landlord if the administrator remains in occupation, particularly in a case where the premises might be unoccupied, where no new tenant can be found and the local authority's demand for business rates (which would fall upon the landlord if the property were taken back) will remain a liability of the tenant company in administration.

We shall explore further the circumstances where the landlord may wish to forfeit and to seek to obtain the court's permission to enforce rights below.

Commencement or continuation of any legal process

No legal process (including legal proceedings, execution, distress and diligence) may be instituted or continued against the company or property of the company except with consent of the administrator or permission of the court (IA 1986, Sched.B1, para.43(6)).

Originally restricted to the enforcement of debt and not quasi-judicial proceedings (see *Air Ecosse Ltd* v. *Civil Aviation Authority* (1987) 3 BCC 492), in recent years this provision has been very widely interpreted to include:

- employment tribunal claims (*Re Divine Solutions (UK) Ltd* [2004] BCC 325);
- a tenant's application for a new lease under the Landlord and Tenant Act 1954, Part II (*Somerfield Stores Ltd* v. *Spring (Sutton Coldfield) Ltd* [2009] EWHC 2384 (Ch));
- revocation of a patent (*Biosource Technologies Inc* v. *Axis Genetics plc* [2000] 1 BCLC 286);
- advertisement of a winding-up petition (*Re a Company (No.001992 of 1988)* [1989] BCLC 9);
- reference of a building contract dispute to a statutory arbitration procedure (*A Straume (UK) Ltd* v. *Bradlor Developments Ltd* [2000] BCC 333); and
- criminal proceedings (*Re Rhondda Waste Disposal Ltd* [2001] Ch 57).

7.2.6 Court's permission to take legal proceedings

As discussed above, if the court is willing to grant permission for a creditor to take any of the above steps, it may impose a condition on, or a requirement in connection with, the proceeding/transaction (IA 1986, Sched.B1, para.43(7)).

The court exercises a discretionary power in considering whether to give a creditor permission to take proceedings. Each case is therefore entirely fact sensitive and the court will carefully balance the interests of the individual creditor, who will necessarily be prejudiced (i.e. it cannot exercise its rights) against the interests of the creditors as a whole. See *Somerfield Stores Ltd* v. *Spring (Sutton Coldfield) Ltd* [2009] EWHC 2384 (Ch) for discussion on the harm caused to the applicant outweighing the benefit to the administrator and the creditors as a whole.

The court will in particular take account of the administrator's proposals and whether there is a reasonable prospect of achieving the purpose of the administration if permission is granted to a particular creditor (see *Royal Trust Bank* v. *Buchler* [1989] BCLC 130). Clearly, the more likely it is that the purpose of administration will be prejudiced if a creditor is granted permission to exercise a right (e.g. if a landlord is permitted to forfeit the company's lease the company will be deprived of a property in which to continue business), the more likely it is that permission will be refused.

The leading authority in this area remains the case of *Re Atlantic Computer Systems plc* [1990] BCC 859. The Court of Appeal made it clear that the court should retain flexibility and should not stick too rigidly to precedent and automatic rules of application. However, the court provided some guidance as to the type of factors it would take into account when considering the question of whether to grant permission:

- In every case, it is for the person seeking permission to make out a case; the burden of proof is on the applicant.
- If granting permission to an owner of land or goods to exercise proprietorial rights to repossess their land or goods is unlikely to impede the purpose of the administration, permission should normally be granted.

- In any other case, the court should balance the interests of the applicant against those of the company's other creditors and consider whether the refusal to grant permission would be inequitable.
- In carrying out the balancing exercise, great weight should be given to the applicant's proprietorial or secured interests.
- The administration procedure should not be used unfairly to prejudice the rights of secured creditors.
- The adequacy of the security and the prejudicial effect of delay may be relevant.
- The benefits obtained by the unsecured creditors should not be at the expense of the secured creditors, except where it is limited and unavoidable.
- If significant loss would result to the applicant, it would normally be appropriate to grant permission; conversely where little to no loss would result to the applicant, permission may be inappropriate.
- Permission may, however, be granted in the case where the loss caused to other creditors is substantially outweighed by the loss caused to the lessor.
- In considering the likely loss to both the applicant and other creditors, the court should have regard to, *inter alia*:

  - the financial position of the company in administration;
  - the company's ability to pay interest, charges and arrears to the applicant;
  - the administrator's proposal and prospect of success for the administration;
  - the period during which the administration has already run and what period is left;
  - the conduct of the parties; and
  - the effect on all parties should permission be granted.

After considering all of the above, the court may impose such terms and conditions upon the exercise of the lessor's rights as it thinks fit. The court may impose conditions on the administrator if permission is refused to the creditor. The court will not seek to adjudicate any dispute regarding security unless it is a short point of law and it is convenient to do so.

In conclusion, the burden of proof in obtaining permission is therefore upon the applicant, who must show that the granting of permission would not defeat the purpose of the administration (*Royal Trust Bank* v. *Buchler* [1989] BCLC 130) and that on balance it is right that the proprietary right of the creditor is allowed to be exercised (e.g. where significant loss will be incurred by the creditor: *Scottish Exhibition Centre Ltd* v. *Mirestop Ltd* [1993] BCC 529). The court will not grant permission if the effect is to prefer one unsecured creditor over another (*Re TBL Realisations plc* [2004] BCC 81).

In practice, to avoid an application for permission, or even an application brought by a creditor alleging unfair harm (IA 1988, Sched.B1, para.74), the administrator should quickly assess the affairs of the company paying particular regard to the interests of any landlord, secured creditor or owner of property/goods in the possession of the company. The administrator should assess whether the equipment, goods and/or the premises occupied or held by the company are essential for the continuation of the company's business and/or whether their continued retention is uneconomic. If it is uneconomic (i.e. the costs of retention, such as rent, mean that the administrator cannot continue the business of the company without loss), the equipment or property should be returned to the lessor immediately.

Often the administrator will be proposing a sale of the company's business and/or its assets and consequently may need to consider whether any leasehold interest of the company could be assigned for value. Careful negotiation with the landlord of the premises or lessor of the equipment is essential once a potential purchaser has been identified. The landlord and lessor will also be likely to wait for proposals to be put forward before considering whether to exercise their rights and/or consent to any assignment. It should, however, be remembered that while the moratorium has the effect of preventing proceedings being commenced by the landlord, the terms of the lease will almost certainly provide that the administrator cannot force a new tenant upon the landlord.

Before commencing the administration, therefore, the administrator should have properly assessed the probable costs and expenses of the company's continued operation and consequently assessed the possibility of whether the purpose of administration is reasonably likely to be achieved. If a sale is likely and a possible premium obtained for the company's leasehold interests, the insolvency practitioner is likely to have accounted for the costs of rental, etc. and will be assured that on appointment ongoing rent will be paid. In a normal case if the rent is to be paid on an ongoing basis then it is unlikely, even taking into account other breaches of leasehold covenant that may have resulted (indeed the fact of tenant administration may give rise to a right of forfeiture), that the landlord would be granted permission to forfeit in the short to medium term.

However, the uncertainty as to the payment of costs such as rent and the possible reaction of creditors is one of the factors behind the increase in use of pre-pack administrations. In such cases, it may well be the case that the individual creditor's rights are very significantly prejudiced, i.e. the injury has been caused and the creditor's ability to negotiate and bargain with the administrator has been removed. For example, the grant to a third party of an unlawful licence to occupy the company leasehold premises or the sale to a third party of goods subject to potential claims may have deprived the creditor of an effective remedy.

The greater preponderance of pre-pack administrations has therefore altered the balance of power between creditors, as an individual creditor may well be excluded from the planning process of the administration and the first they may know of the change in situation is some time later (change in business ownership in the occupier of the premises). The landlord creditor may well find it is then negotiating with a well-funded third party that has acquired the business and assets of the former contracting party and that is willing to drive a hard bargain regarding continued occupation/retention of property.

Checklist

Factors the court may consider on granting creditors leave

- In every case, it is for the person seeking permission to make out his case.
- If granting permission to a lessor of land or hirer of goods to exercise its proprietorial rights to repossess its property is likely to impede the purpose of the administration, permission should not normally be granted.
- In any other case, the court should balance the interests of the lessor against the interests of the company's other creditors and consider whether the refusal to grant permission would be inequitable.
- In carrying out the balancing exercise, greater weight should be given to the lessor's proprietorial or secured interest.
- The administration procedure should not be used to prejudice the rights of secured creditors. The benefits to unsecured creditors should not be obtained at the expense of the secured creditors, except where this is limited and unavoidable.
- If significant loss would result to the lessor, it would normally be appropriate to grant permission.
- Permission may, however, be granted in the case where the loss caused to other creditors is substantially outweighed by the loss caused to the lessor.
- In considering the likely loss to both the lessor and other creditors, the court should have regard to, *inter alia*:
    - the financial position of the company;
    - the company's ability to pay interest, charges and arrears to the lessor;
    - the administrator's proposal and prospect of success for the administration;
    - the period during which the administration has already run and what period is left;
    - the conduct of the parties; and
    - the effect on all parties should permission be granted.
- After considering all of the above, the court may impose such terms and conditions upon the exercise of the lessor's rights as it thinks fit.
- The court may impose conditions on the administrator if permission is refused to the creditor.
- The court will not seek to adjudicate any dispute regarding security unless it is a short point of law and it is convenient to do so.

7.2.7   Powers of directors

The making of an administration order also has the effect of suspending the directors' powers of management over the company (IA 1986, Sched.B1, para.64). The directors may, however, exercise management power with the consent of the administrator, which may be given generally or in relation to specific matters (*Re P&C and R&T (Stockport) Ltd* [1991] BCLC 366).

Irrespective of any loss of management power, the directors are still liable to perform their statutory duties in relation to the company, fulfilling any required obligations under law, such as the filing of annual returns.

The administrator also has the power to remove the directors from office (IA 1986, Sched.B1, para.61) and may appoint a director, whether to fill a vacancy or not. A director removed from office in this manner has no rights other than those that may exist under any service contract for loss of office (*Newtherapeutics Ltd* v. *Katz* [1991] Ch 226).

Often, the administrator may find that the continued involvement of the directors is essential to ensure the smooth running of the company during the administration process. The directors may therefore be called upon by the administrator to deal with suppliers, creditors and employees and many of the day-to-day issues of management, leaving the administrator free to deal with strategy, restructuring and/or sale of the business. In some instances, the situation may require the administrator to compel the directors to assist and co-operate.

The directors may also remain in operational control of the business, where they wish to bid to buy the business and/or assets of the company from the administrator. In such circumstances, one practice that has grown up is for the administrator to enter into a business management/operating licence with the directors/proposed purchasers, who will carry on the business for and on behalf of the administrator, while the business and assets are marketed or perhaps restructured to make the business more attractive to a potential purchaser. The management fee for this service may be any operating profit obtained, but the administrator will be sure to have retained appropriate controls over the management of the business and obtained indemnities for any loss or damage that may result from the period of business operation.

7.2.8 Interim moratorium

An interim moratorium will come into effect where:

(a)   the administration application has been issued, but not heard;
(b)   an administration application has been granted, but the administration order has yet to take effect; or
(c)   notice of intention to appoint an administrator has been filed at court (IA 1986, Sched.B1, para.44).

An interim moratorium will not take effect if there is an administrative receiver in office, unless the administrative receiver and appointor of the administrative receiver have consented to the making of an administration order (IA 1986, Sched.B1, para.44(6)). This provision is necessary as the holder of a floating charge has an effective veto over any attempt to appoint an administrator by court order (IA 1986, Sched.B1, para.39(1)(a) unless the security is liable to be set aside as a transaction at an undervalue, preference or avoided under IA 1986, s.245).

The interim moratorium has the same consequences as the statutory moratorium coming into effect on the commencement of the administration and which is outlined above. However, for obvious reasons, until the appointment is made, the consent of the administrator cannot be obtained to exercise rights that are otherwise prohibited by the statutory moratorium (IA 1986, Sched.B1, para.44(6)).

The effect of the interim moratorium and its continuation for a period of up to 10 business days (IA 1986, Sched.B1, para.44(2)) does mean that it can be used by the company/its directors to halt possible enforcement action by creditors. Indeed, there is nothing in the legislation that expressly prohibits the filing of successive notices of intention to appoint, which could have the effect of extending this 10-day period. Where there is a legitimate reason for the filing of successive notices, such as change in circumstances and the need for final planning/calculation by the proposed administrator prior to commencement of the administration proper, this might be seen as excusable. However, improper use and/or the filing of multiple notices could well be seen as an abuse of process.

For the duration of the interim moratorium, permission of the court is not required for:

(a)   the presentation of certain petitions for the winding up of the company (IA 1986, s.124A (public interest petition) and the Financial Services and Markets Act (FSMA) 2000, s.367 (FCA petition));
(b)   an appointment of an administrator by the floating charge holder;
(c)   an appointment of an administrative receiver by the floating charge holder; or
(d)   the carrying out by an administrative receiver (whenever appointed) of his functions.

Once the permanent statutory moratorium has come into effect, as we have seen, save for the special exemption winding-up petitions, the actions listed (b) to (d) cannot be taken. This presents the floating charge holder with a short window of opportunity on being served the notice of intention or notice of application in which to act and make its own appointment, if it deems it appropriate and in its interests to do so.

Checklist

Powers of the administrator as defined by IA 1986, Sched.1

- To take possession of, collect and get in property of the company and, for that purpose, to take such proceedings as may seem to be expedient.
- To sell or otherwise dispose of the property of the company by public auction, private auction or private contract.
- To raise or borrow money, or grant security therefor over the property of the company.
- To appoint a solicitor, accountant or professionally qualified person to assist him in the performance of his functions.
- To bring or defend any action or other legal proceedings in the name and on behalf of the company.
- To refer to arbitration any question affecting the company.
- To effect and maintain insurances in respect of the business and property of the company.
- To use the company's seal.

- To do all acts and execute in the name of and on behalf of the company any deed, receipt or other document.
- To draw, accept, make and endorse any bills of exchange or promissory notes in the name of and on behalf of the company.
- To appoint any agent to do any business which he is unable to do himself and which may more conveniently be done by an agent.
- To employ and dismiss employees.
- To do all such things (including the carrying out of works) as may be necessary for the realisation of the property of the company.
- To make any payment which is necessary or incidental to the performance of his functions.
- To carry on business of the company.
- To establish subsidiaries of the company.
- To transfer to subsidiaries of the company the whole or any part of the business and property of the company.
- To grant or accept surrender of a lease or tenancy of any of the property of the company and to take a lease or tenancy of any property required or convenient for the business of the company.
- To make any arrangement or compromise on behalf of the company.
- To call up any uncalled capital of the company.
- To rank and claim in the bankruptcy, insolvency, sequestration or liquidation of any person indebted to the company and to receive dividends and to accede to trust deeds for the creditors of any such person.
- To present or defend a petition for the winding up of the company.
- To change the location of the company's registered office.
- To do all such other things as are incidental to the exercise of the foregoing powers.

7.3   ENDING ADMINISTRATION

7.3.1   Introduction

Prior to the Enterprise Act 2002 reforms, administration was often criticised for the length of time taken to complete the process and the procedural difficulties caused in making distributions to creditors. This area of the administration process was therefore substantially reformed, ensuring that the process was one which should be conducted as quickly and efficiently as reasonably practicable (IA 1986, Sched.B1, para.4) and where the exit from administration must be at the forefront of the insolvency practitioner's mind on commencement of the process (indeed forming part of the proposals put to creditors: IR 1986, rule 2.33(2)(m)).

The reforms have left a number of ways in which administration can come to an end:

- Automatically after 12 months.
- On application to court by the administrator (which may be allied to a winding-up petition).
- On filing of notice that the purpose of administration has been achieved (out-of-court appointment application only).

- Following court order (e.g. appointment of administrator was for an improper purpose or on challenge to administrator's conduct).
- Where a winding-up order is made on a public interest petition (IA 1986, ss.124A, 124B, or FSMA 2000, s.367).
- On the commencement of a creditors' voluntary liquidation following administration by notice.
- On the dissolution of the company.

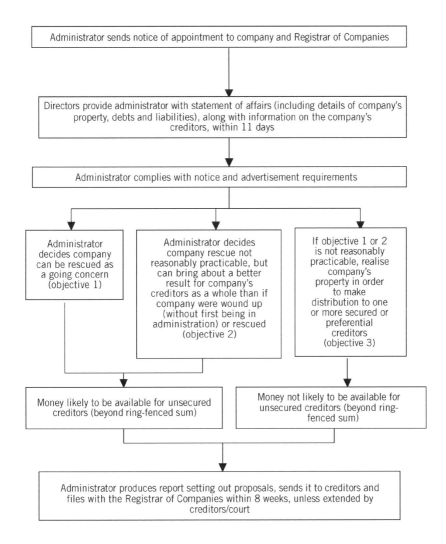

Figure 7.1 The process of administration from appointment to proposal

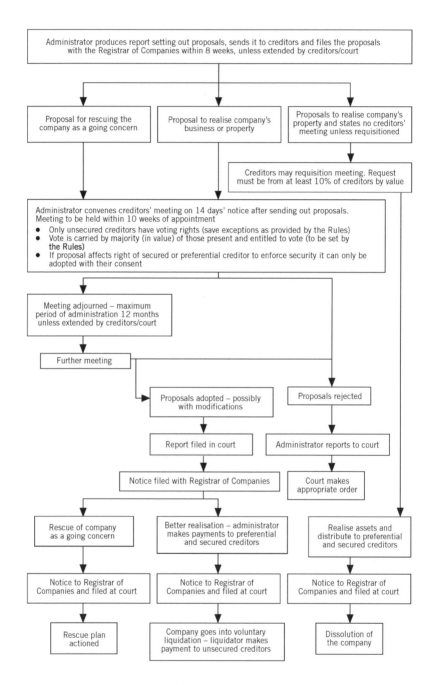

Figure 7.2 The process of administration from proposal to exit

An administrator's appointment will generally cease as a result of either the success or the failure of the administration (i.e. the purposes of the administration have been achieved or are no longer capable of being achieved).

In theory, the company could have been stabilised during the period of moratorium and returned to profitability. The control and management of the company could then be passed back to the directors and shareholders. However, unfortunately this is not a common occurrence. More likely than not, the business and assets of the company will have been realised by the administrator, by selling the business as a going concern, or as part of a restructuring of the business. The realisation of assets may enable the creditors of the company to be satisfied in full or, more likely, to be paid a proportion of their debts. As a consequence, there needs to be some thought as to what insolvency procedures should follow: liquidation, CVA or scheme of arrangement?

The most likely consequence of administration is therefore the liquidation of the original company. While an administrator can make distributions to secured and preferential creditors during the course of the administration (and, with permission of the court, to unsecured creditors), such payments may only be made if they are likely to achieve the purpose of the administration (see *GHE Realisations Ltd* [2006] BCC 139 where it was held that distributions to unsecured creditors could be made if it were in the interests of the creditors as a whole).

In general, a distribution to unsecured creditors after the purpose of the administration has been achieved is unlikely to be viewed as permissible. As previously explained, it appears to be the intention of Parliament that distributions to unsecured creditors should remain within the remit of a liquidator. As a result, while an administrator could propose a CVA or petition for the compulsory winding up of the company, a more common route may be to use the new procedures to move straight into voluntary liquidation.

Checklist

Ending of administration

- Automatically by effluxion of time.
- On application to court by the administrator (which may be allied to a winding-up petition).
- On the filing of a notice that the purpose of administration has been achieved (out-of-court appointment application only).
- Court order (e.g. appointment of administrator was for an improper purpose or on challenge to administrator's conduct).
- Public interest winding-up petition (IA 1986, s.124A; or FSMA 2000, s.367).
- Creditors' voluntary liquidation following administration by notice.

7.3.2 Automatic end of administration

The appointment of an administrator ceases to have effect at the end of one year beginning on the date on which the appointment took effect (IA 1986, Sched.B1, para.76(1)). As a result, simply through elapse of time the company will cease to be in administration (IA 1986, Sched.B1, para.1(2)(c)) by whatever method the administrator was appointed. This is one of the key Enterprise Act 2002 reforms of the administration process and, although calls for the automatic vacation of office as little as three months after the date of commencement (following the Australian model) were rejected, it is a strict measure ensuring that administration is not unnecessarily prolonged without some form of creditor and/or judicial scrutiny.

The one-year period can be extended by court order (for as long as the court thinks necessary) or with consent from the appropriate creditors (for a period not exceeding six months) (IA 1986, Sched.B1, para.76(2)). It should be noted, however, that after the automatic end of the administration the creditors cannot consent to an extension (IA 1986, Sched.B1, para.78(4)(c)), nor can the court order an extension (IA 1986, Sched.B1, para.77(1)(b)). Failure to extend the period during the course of administration cannot be rectified by use of the slip rule in IR 1986, rule 7.55 (for further limitations on use of the slip rule provision in regard to out-of-court appointments of administrators see *Re G-Tech Construction Ltd* [2007] BPIR 1275). However, in *Re TT Industries Ltd* [2006] BCC 372 exceptional circumstances (i.e. error by the court staff in listing the matter) were held to merit an order being granted to extend the administration period after the end of the 12-month period.

If the administration were to come to an end as a result of an oversight, the consequences are severe. The matter cannot be rectified by an out-of-court appointment by the company/directors owing to the prohibition on successive administrations in a 12-month period (see IA 1986, Sched.B1, para.23). The insolvent company would thus be passed back to its directors/shareholders and open to creditor action, leading to potential claims against the former administrator for breach of duty and loss and damage to the company/creditors (see IA 1986, Sched.B1, para.75). While an application to court for a 'new' administration could be made, the possibility of damage to the company in the interim period remains and in any event it could be the case that the court refuses to make an order.

In order to avoid the effects of this provision, it was a relatively common practice after the new provisions came into effect for administrators to seek creditor consent to an extension within the initial proposals, i.e. at the beginning of administration. In guidance issued by the Insolvency Service (*Dear IP*, No.37, October 2008) the efficacy of this practice was questioned and a view expressed that such a provision in the initial proposal should be included only where absolutely necessary.

Extension by creditors' consent

The period of administration can be extended by obtaining creditors' consent (in writing, which includes email (IA 1986, Sched.B1, para.111), or at a meeting) at any time prior to the expiry of the initial term. The term of administration may, however, be extended only once in this manner, it cannot follow an extension granted by the court and can be for no greater period than six months (see IA 1986, Sched.B1, para.78).

Consent is required from:

(a) all secured creditors; and
(b) creditors holding 50 per cent of the total unsecured debt disregarding debts of any creditor who abstains or does not respond (IA 1986, Sched.B1, para.78(1)).

However, if the administrator has provided a statement (under IA 1986, Sched.B1, para.52(1)(b)) that:

(a) the company had insufficient property to pay all creditors;
(b) unsecured creditors will receive no payment other than the prescribed part (IA 1986, s.176A(2)(a)); and
(c) the only possible objective that the administration is capable of achieving is distribution to secured creditors,

consent may be obtained from all secured creditors and, if appropriate, where distribution to preferential creditors is to be made, the consent of the preferential creditors holding at least 50 per cent of the total debts.

As soon as reasonably practicable after the administrator's appointment is extended by consent, the administrator must file notice of extension with the court and notify the Registrar of Companies (IA 1986, Sched.B1, para.78(5)). An administrator who fails to comply with this section without reasonable excuse commits an offence (IA 1986, Sched.10). The penalty is a fine of one-fifth of the statutory maximum and a daily rate fine of one/fiftieth of the statutory maximum.

Extension by court order

An order extending the administration period can be sought from the court at any time before the expiry of the initial period and for any period thought necessary (see IA 1986, Sched.B1, paras.76(2)(a) and 77(1)).

The application must be accompanied by a progress report (IR 1986, rule 2.112)(1)) which details the progress made towards achieving the purpose of administration, including a receipts and payments account (IR 1986, rule 2.47). The court will have regard to the statutory responsibility of the administrator to act as quickly and efficiently as possible and will seek to assess whether the proposals being put forward by the administrator will be successful and for the general benefit of the creditors as a whole. The courts are at the very least likely to require assurances and evidence from the administrator that the purpose of the administration remains reasonably likely to be achieved, and that no unfair prejudice to creditors would result from an extension of the administration period. In exercising its discretion, the court is likely to have regard to the same sort of factors as when making an initial administration order.

7.3.3 Determination of administration on application to court by an administrator

The administrator may make an application to court for his appointment to cease to have effect from a specified time (IA 1986, Sched.B1, para.79(1)) and shall apply to court if:

(a) he thinks the purpose of the administration cannot be achieved in relation to the company;
(b) he thinks the company should not have entered into administration; or
(c) a resolution is passed at a creditors' meeting requiring him to make an application (IA 1986, Sched.B1, para.79(2)).

The use of the word 'shall' imposes a mandatory requirement (see discussion of the use of 'shall' in regard to an application under IA 1986, Sched.B1, para.68(2) in *Re Transbus International Ltd* [2004] 1 WLR 2654). There may also be other circumstances requiring the administrator to make an application to court (e.g. where a compulsory winding-up order is to be made: *Re J Smiths Haulage Ltd* [2007] BCC 135; see also *Re TM Kingdom Ltd* [2007] BCC 480).

On application, the court may:

(a) adjourn the hearing conditionally or unconditionally;
(b) dismiss the application;
(c) make an interim order; or
(d) make any order it thinks appropriate.

The orders that may be made include a direction dealing with the treatment of creditor claims, such as by means of a liquidation where it would be usual for the administrator to petition for compulsory winding up where the administration has failed (see *Oakley Smith* v. *Greenberg* [2003] BPIR 709). There is, however, no requirement that administration should be followed by another insolvency process and the control and management of the company could be returned to the directors, perhaps where the company has been rescued and is no longer insolvent or where a CVA or scheme of arrangement has been put in place compromising creditor claims.

Where the administration has commenced by the making of an administration order, the administrator must apply to court if he thinks the purpose of the administration has been sufficiently achieved in relation to the company (IA 1986, Sched.B1, para.79(3)).

Alternatively, if a court-appointed administrator considers that it is appropriate to move from administration to creditors' voluntary liquidation (IA 1986, Sched.B1, para.83) or to seek the dissolution of the company (IA 1986, Sched.B1, para.84), it has been confirmed by the court that the administrator does not need to apply to court for the administration to come to an end (*Re Ballast plc* [2005] BCC 96 and *Re GHE Realisations Ltd* [2005] EWHC 2400 (Ch)).

Where an administrator reports to court that the creditors have failed to approve the proposals put forward or have proposed a revision which is unacceptable to the administrator, the court may order that the appointment ceases to have effect (IA 1986, Sched.B1, para.55). It remains a moot point as to whether the court could order the administration should continue in light of majority creditor objection, but the case of *DKLL Solicitors* v. *Revenue and Customs Commissioners* [2007] BCC 908 indicates that this is a possibility.

Where the court decides the appointment should come to an end, the court will discharge the administration order and the administrator must send a copy of the order to the Registrar of Companies within 14 days, beginning with the date of the order (IA 1986, Sched.B1, para.86). He commits an offence if he fails to comply with this section.

7.3.4 Termination of administration where objective achieved

If the administrator thinks that the purpose of the administration has been sufficiently achieved, and where the appointment has been made by the floating charge holder, or by the company or its directors by the out-of-court route (IA 1986, Sched.B1, paras.14 or 22), he may file a notice in prescribed Form 2.32B with the court and the Registrar of Companies together with a copy of the final progress report (IA 1986, Sched.B1, para.80; IR 1986, rule 2.113(1)).

For Form 2.32B see **www.insolvency.gov.uk/forms/englandwalesforms.htm**.

The word 'sufficiently' is not defined, but whether the purpose of the administration has been 'sufficiently achieved' would seem to rest on the administrator's assessment of whether the steps outlined in the proposal have generally been achieved. In the majority of cases, the administration is followed by another insolvency procedure or dissolution of the company. In such circumstances, rather than use this procedure the administrator may think it appropriate to apply to court under IA 1986, Sched.B1, para.79 as described above for directions. As a result, the procedure is probably best limited to circumstances where the company has been rescued.

Two copies of the notice must be filed at court and a copy of the notice sent to the Registrar of Companies. The court shall endorse each copy with a date and time of filing and the administrator's appointment shall cease to have effect on that date and time (IR 1986, rule 2.113(3)).

The administrator's discharge takes effect at a time appointed by resolution of the creditors' committee or, if none, by the creditors. An administrator can avoid the need to call a creditors' meeting for this purpose if there is not going to be a distribution to unsecured creditors (except for the prescribed part under IA 1986, s.176A) and the consent of the secured creditors (and if applicable the preferential creditors) is obtained.

An administrator may also seek his discharge from liability under IA 1986, Sched.B1, para.98(2)(c) from the court on application for termination of the administration. If taking this step, the administrator should inform the creditors of this intention in the final progress report (IR 1986, rule 2.114).

The administrator shall, as soon as reasonably practicable and within five business days, send a notice of the end of the administration and accompanying reports to every creditor of the company of whose claim he is aware and every person who was notified of the appointment and also to the company (IR 1986, rule 2.113(5)). The administrator shall, however, be taken to have complied with this requirement if within five business days of filing the notice, he publishes a notice in the *London Gazette* undertaking to provide a copy of the notice of the end of the administration to any creditor who applies for the same; such notice may also be advertised as the administrator sees fit (IR 1986, rule 2.113(6A)).

7.3.5 Court ending administration on application of creditor

On the application of a creditor of the company, the court may provide for the appointment of the administrator to cease to have effect at a specified time (IA 1986, Sched.B1, para.81(1)).

An application under this section must allege that the appointment was by reason of an improper motive on the part of the applicant for the administration order or the appointor by an out-of-court route (IA 1986, Sched.B1, para.81(2)).

This provision should be contrasted with a creditor's right to have the conduct of the administrator examined on the basis of unfair harm (IA 1986, Sched.B1, para.74). Instead, the provisions contained in, para.81 attack the motive behind the appointment, not the conduct of the administrator and, as a consequence, it is necessary to show that the creditor has actually suffered loss or harm as a result of the appointment.

The appointor, the holder of a floating charge, the administrator and the applicant can all be represented at the hearing, of which five days' notice must be given. In practice, the application may also be preceded by injunctive relief seeking to restrain the administrator from acting (and in particular disposing of the business and assets of the company by a pre-pack sale).

There is no statutory guidance given to the meaning of 'improper motive' and the section itself is a new one following the Enterprise Act 2002 reforms; as a result case law is needed to provide further guidance.

In the case of *Doltable Ltd* v. *Lexi Holdings plc* [2006] 1 BCLC 384 it was held that an improper purpose was shown where the appointment of an administrator by the directors of an insolvent company was to prevent a secured creditor taking action, even though they argued that this action was taken in the best interests of the creditors as a whole by seeking to ensure that a higher price for the business was obtained than would have been the case if the bank's nominated administrator took control of the sale.

In contrast, in *Re British American Racing (Holdings) Ltd* [2005] BCC 110 it was held that it was not an abuse and improper purpose for a creditor and 89 per cent shareholder to appoint an administrator, thereby excluding the minority creditors that opposed a sale of the business, as the sale of the business was of benefit to the creditors as a whole.

For an administrator's appointment to be successfully challenged, almost certainly some element of bad faith on the part of the appointor will need to be established. For example, this could be where the directors are clearly using the administration process to avoid the payment of creditors by setting up a phoenix company, stripping the original company of its assets and transferring them to the new company solely in order to avoid creditor claims. The provision might also be used if the directors are seeking to avoid the attention of creditors at a s.98 meeting (i.e. a meeting of creditors on the winding up of a company).

Upon application under this provision, the court may make such order as it thinks appropriate, whether in addition to, in consequence of, or instead of the order applied for (IA 1986, Sched.B1, para.81(3)).

7.3.6 Cessation of appointment on public interest winding-up petition

An administrator's appointment will cease to have effect upon the winding-up order being made by the court on a petition presented in the public interest (IA 1986, s.124A), or on application of the Secretary of State in accordance with Council Regulation 2157/2001/EC of 8 October 2001 on the statute for a European company (location of head office and registered office), introduced by the European Public Limited-Liability Company Regulations 2004, SI 2004/2326 and otherwise known as a *Societas Europaea* (SE) petition (IA 1986, s.124B), or by the FCA under FSMA 2000, s.367. The same effect occurs where a provisional liquidator is appointed in such circumstances.

It is, however, possible for the administrator's powers to be varied and/or limited on direction by the court, which thus provides the only means whereby an administrator could hold office concurrently with a liquidator or provisional liquidator (IA 1986, Sched.B1, para.82).

7.3.7 Moving from administration to creditors' voluntary liquidation

While it is possible that the company could have been stabilised during the period of moratorium and returned to profitability and thereby rescued, in practice this is rare (estimated to occur in fewer than 5 per cent of cases and even in such cases a process such as a CVA or scheme of arrangement is likely to have been the cause of the rescue).

A more likely result of administration is that the business and assets of the company will have been realised by the administrator, by selling the business as a going concern or by selling its assets, which may result in the restructuring of the business, but not the company. The realisation of assets will hopefully result in a return to creditors and indeed the appropriate process for effecting distribution to creditors is something that the administrator should have had in mind in making the original proposals to the creditors.

While an administrator can make distributions to secured and preferential creditors during the course of the administration (and with permission of the court to unsecured creditors), such payments may only be made if they are likely to achieve the purpose of the administration (see *Re GHE Realisations Ltd* [2006] BCC 139 where it was held that distributions to unsecured creditors could be made if it were in the interests of the creditors as a whole).

As a result, a distribution by an administrator to unsecured creditors, to be made after the purpose of the administration has been achieved, is unlikely to be permitted by a court. Accordingly, an administrator could propose a Companies Act scheme of arrangement, a CVA or petition for the compulsory winding up of the company in order to effect the distribution. A more common means of exit and thereby distribution is the use of the procedures introduced in the Enterprise Act 2002 reforms to move the company straight from administration into voluntary liquidation (IA 1986, Sched.B1, para.83).

Where an administrator of the company thinks that the total amount that each secured creditor of the company is likely to receive has been paid or set aside and that a distribution will be made to unsecured creditors, notice should be sent to the Registrar of Companies in Form 2.34B, attaching a final progress report, which must include details of the assets to be dealt with in the liquidation (IR 1986, rule 2.117A(1)).

In practice, a situation can arise whereby further realisations (such as book debt realisations) can equally be made in liquidation and as a consequence the administrator must consider the cessation of the appointment. However, it could be the case that at the time the administrator will not be able to pass over funds to the liquidator, thereby guaranteeing that funds are to be distributed to unsecured creditors and that returns will instead be dependent on the liquidator's realisations. Can the administrator use the process to move from administration to liquidation?

In the case of *Unidare plc* v. *Cohen* [2006] 2 WLR 974 consideration was given to the use of the word 'thinks' in the context of the administrator's decision. It was held that, provided the administrator's decision had been reached through a rational thought process, it was not open to the applicant to challenge the decision on objective grounds. The case supports the wider proposition that the courts will be highly reluctant to intervene in cases of professional/commercial judgment exercised by an administrator rationally and in good faith. Consequently, it is proffered that where the administrator thinks that a return will be made as a result of the further work to be undertaken by the liquidation, he could use this method.

As soon as reasonably practicable, the administrator must send a copy of the notice and documents to those who received notice of his appointment, to the court and the Registrar of Companies. On registration of the notice, the appointment of the administrator shall cease to have effect and the company shall be wound up as if a resolution for voluntary winding up had been passed on that day (IA 1986, Sched.B1, para.83), meaning the winding up will be deemed to have commenced as from the preceding midnight.

This procedure is available whether the administration was commenced by an out-of-court route or following court order (*Re Ballast plc* [2005] BCC 96) and offers a seamless transition from one procedure to another (see *Re E-Squared Ltd* [2006] BCC 379 where notices were not registered until after expiry of the administrator's term of office (i.e. the 12-month automatic cessation) but the court held that the company had been wound up on the date of registration and that as at that date the former administrator would be viewed as its liquidator).

The liquidator will generally be the former administrator, although the creditors may nominate a different person to be the liquidator (IA 1986, Sched.B1, s.83(7)).

Alternatively (and commonly), the company can enter liquidation where it forms part of the administrator's original or revised proposals. The proposals must give the details of the proposed liquidator (generally being the same as the administrator) and inform the creditors that they are free to nominate a different person to act as liquidator. The appointment takes effect by the creditors approving the proposed administrator's proposals or revised proposals (IR 1986, rule 2.117A(2)).

If the administration moves to voluntary winding up without any intervening period, the company is deemed to enter into creditors' voluntary liquidation as if an appropriate resolution has been passed on that date. This means that a meeting of creditors pursuant to IA 1986, s.98 is not required to initiate the process and as a result the relevant date of insolvency (which may be important for the calculation of certain claims, e.g. those of preferential creditors) remains the date of the commencement of the administration.

7.3.8 Moving from administration to dissolution

Where the administrator thinks that the company has no property that might permit a distribution to its creditors, notice of that fact should be sent to the Registrar of Companies (IA 1986, Sched.B1, para.84). Unless the court orders otherwise, the company will be dissolved and struck off the register three months later (IA 1986, Sched.B1, para.84(6)).

In the case of *GHE Realisations Ltd* [2006] BCC 139 it was confirmed that despite the literal wording of the statute, such notice may also be provided under this provision where there has already been a distribution of all the company's property during administration. This generally arises where there has been a payment to secured and preferential creditors and after the costs and expenses of administration are taken into account there will be no further distribution to creditors. As we have seen, where the only payment to be made to unsecured creditors is the prescribed part (IA 1986, s.176A), in order to avoid the need to move into creditors' voluntary liquidation, an application by the administrator to make this payment will be required. Following such payment, the administrator could then use this route as the appropriate exit route from administration.

The notice must also be served as soon as reasonably practicable upon the court and on each creditor, accompanied by a final progress report in Form 2.35B.

For Form 2.35B see **www.insolvency.gov.uk/forms/englandwalesforms.htm**.

The administrator or any interested party can apply to court to extend or suspend the three-month period to dissolution or apply for an order that the dissolution should not take effect (IA 1986, Sched.B1, para.84(7)). Where an order is made to extend, suspend or disapply the period before dissolution, the administrator shall as soon as reasonably practicable notify the Registrar of Companies in Form 2.36B.

For Form 2.36B see **www.insolvency.gov.uk/forms/englandwalesforms.htm**.

This provision may be relied on where the administrator or creditor(s) consider that despite there being no assets, further investigation is required, for instance into the conduct of the directors or into antecedent transactions entered into by the company. The company could therefore move from administration to liquidation, although thought would need to be given as to how the liquidator would be funded or, alternatively, whether the proposed liquidator (and potentially the legal team that may be required) would act on the basis of some form of conditional fee arrangement, recovering fees from realisations. Such arrangements are not uncommon.

In general, however, the provisions of IA 1986, Sched.B1, para.84 offer a swift and easy exit route from administration (by whatever means the company entered into administration: see *Ballast plc* [2005] BCC 96) in circumstances where there are no assets or further assets to distribute, there is no future for the insolvent corporate shell and/or where the expenses and costs of liquidation cannot be justified.

It should be noted that should it later transpire that, e.g. the company had realisable assets, an application to restore the company to the register will be required. As there is no power to restore the administration (IA 1986, Sched.B1, para.84(4)), a petition to wind up the company in parallel to its restoration would be required (CA 2006, s.1029). It is, however, difficult to envisage circumstances where after dissolution and then restoration, administration would result in a more favourable outcome than liquidation.

7.3.9 Resignation of an administrator

The administrator may resign from office in limited prescribed circumstances (IA 1986, Sched.B1, para.87). These are set in IR 1986, rule 2.119, namely:

(a) ill health;

(b) the intention to cease being in practice as an insolvency practitioner;

(c) a conflict of interest or change in personal circumstances, which precludes or makes impracticable the discharge of his duties; or

(d)   other grounds where permitted by the court.

The administrator must provide at least five business days' written notice in Form 2.37B of his intention to resign or to apply to court for permission to resign, such notice being sent to:

- the court, if administrator appointed by the court;
- the floating charge holder, if administrator appointed pursuant to the out-of-court route provided in IA 1986, Sched.B1, para.14;
- the company, if administrator appointed pursuant to the out-of-court route provided in IA 1986, Sched.B1, para.22(1);
- the directors, if administrator appointed pursuant to the out-of-court route provided in IA 1986, Sched.B1, para.22(2).

For Form 2.37B see **www.insolvency.gov.uk/forms/englandwalesforms.htm**.

The notice of resignation must be in Form 2.38B; this must be filed at court and a copy sent to the Registrar of Companies within five business days of filing at court (IR 1986, rule 2.121).

It must also be served on any prescribed party as set out above.

For Form 2.38B see **www.insolvency.gov.uk/forms/englandwalesforms.htm**.

On ceasing to be qualified to act as an insolvency practitioner (IA 1986, Sched.B1, para.89), the insolvency practitioner must give notice to the court and the holder of a floating charge, or the company or directors, depending on his mode of appointment, in Form 2.39B.

For Form 2.39B see **www.insolvency.gov.uk/forms/englandwalesforms.htm**.

7.3.10   Replacement of an administrator

Where an administrator dies, resigns, is removed from office by court order or vacates office on ceasing to be qualified to act as an insolvency practitioner in relation to the company, he may be replaced (IA 1986, Sched.B1, paras.91–95). Such application must be accompanied by a written statement in Form 2.2B by the person proposed to be the replacement (IR 1986, rule 2.125(1)).

In practice, such replacements are often done in a single block transfer application (see *Re Equity Nominees Ltd* [2000] BCC 84 and *Donaldson* v. *O'Sullivan* [2009] BCC 99 in regard to an unsuccessful challenge as to the lawfulness of the procedure).

Where the administrator was appointed by court order, the administrator may only be replaced on application to court by:

- the creditors' committee;
- the company;
- the directors of the company;
- one or more creditors of the company; or
- the remaining administrator(s) still in office.

An application will also be granted if the court is satisfied that the creditors' committee or any remaining administrator in office is not taking reasonable steps to find a replacement, or the court is satisfied for another reason that it is right for a replacement application to be made (IA 1986, Sched.B1, para.91(2)).

Where the administrator was appointed by the floating charge holder, the appointor retains the power to replace the administrator (IA 1986, Sched.B1, para.92). The holder of a prior qualifying floating charge in respect of the company's property may apply to the court for the administrator to be replaced by an administrator nominated by the holder (IA 1986, Sched.B1, para.96(2)). It should be noted, however, that there does not necessarily need to be a vacancy in office for the prior floating charge holder to apply to court.

Where the administrator was appointed by the company or its directors and notice of intention has been served on the holder of a floating charge, the administrator can only be replaced if:

(a) the holder of the qualifying floating charge consents; or
(b) if the consent is withheld, the court grants permission (IA 1986, Sched.B1, para.94).

If there is no qualifying floating charge holder and the administrator has been appointed by the company and its directors, the administrator may be replaced by requisite resolution at a duly convened creditors' meeting (IA 1986, Sched.B1, para.97). The unsecured creditors can also ensure, by application to the court, that any administrator chosen by the company or directors is removed from office if they consider the administrator is not acting in their best interests, or perhaps not acting as quickly and efficiently as reasonably practicable (for an example of IA 1986, Sched.B1, para.88 allied to an application under IA 1986, Sched.B1, para.74(2) see *Sisu Capital Fund Ltd* v. *Tucker* [2006] BPIR 154).

7.3.11 The effect of vacation of office

Where a person ceases to be in office and/or where he is replaced, he is under a duty to deliver up the assets of the company (after deduction of properly incurred expenses), its books and records as soon as reasonably practicable, default leading to possible fine (IR 1986, rule 2.129).

The administrator removed from office is discharged from liability in respect of any action taken as administrator (IA 1986, Sched.B1, para.98(1)).

The discharge takes effect as follows:

1. In the case of an appointment by the company/directors, discharge is effected on the passing of a resolution by the creditors' committee or by resolution of the creditors.
2. Where an administrator has died, discharge takes effect on the filing at court of notice of his death.
3. If an administrator thinks the company has insufficient property to make a

distribution to the unsecured creditors, except for the payment of the pre-scribed part (IA 1986, s.176A), and makes a statement to that effect (IA 1986, Sched.B1, para.52(1)(b)), a resolution approving his discharge can then be passed by the secured creditors and, if appropriate, the majority of the preferential creditors so voting.

4. In the case of appointment by court order, the court will sanction discharge (IA 1986, Sched.B1, para.98(2)(c)).

Although the administrator is discharged from any liability accrued before the discharge takes effect, it does not prevent the court from exercising the right to examine the administrator's conduct in respect of any potential misfeasance, although any claim of this nature can only be after permission of the court is obtained (IA 1986, Sched.B1, para.75(6)). The discharge may also be postponed if the court thinks that investigation into the administrator's conduct is necessary (see *Re Sibec Developments Ltd* [1993] BCC 148 and *Re Newscreen Media Group plc* [2009] 2 BCLC 353, where it was confirmed that while the court had jurisdiction to set aside the administrator's release it would do so rarely, such as in cases of the release being obtained by fraud; if a creditor felt there were irregularities in the conduct of the administration the appropriate remedy was the use of 1A 1986, Sched.B1, para.75).

7.3.12 Administrator's remuneration

The former administrator's remuneration and expenses and any sum payable in respect of a debt or liability arising out of any contract entered into by him in connection with the appointment will be:

(a) charged on and payable out of the property of the company of which the former administrator had custody and control immediately prior to the time he ceased to be the company's administrator; and

(b) payable in priority to any debts secured by the floating charge (IA 1986, Sched.B1, para.99).

The administrator is entitled to receive remuneration for his services (IR 1986, rule 2.106(1)), fixed either as a percentage of the total of the property or on a time costs basis. This is determined by the creditors' committee or, where there is none, by the meeting of creditors. In the absence of creditor agreement, it is to be fixed by application to court. The Insolvency (Amendment) Rules 2010, SI 2010/686, which came into force on 6 April 2010, also allow for remuneration for insolvency practitioners to be on a fixed-fee basis.

Where there are insufficient monies to pay unsecured creditors anything other than payment under IA 1986, s.176A (the prescribed part), agreement regarding remuneration is required from each secured creditor. If distribution is to be made to preferential creditors, the consent of those preferential creditors with debts exceeding more than 50 per cent of the preferential debts of the company is required.

The basis of the remuneration is often dealt with in the initial proposals sent to creditors at the outset of the administration, allowing the administrator to draw down fees on an interim basis.

If the administrator considers that the remuneration fixed by the creditors/ creditors' committee is insufficient, he may request that it be increased by resolution of the creditors (IR 1986, rule 2.107) or by application to the court (IR 1986, rule 2.108).

Any creditor of the company with the concurrence of at least 10 per cent of the value of the creditors may apply to court for an order that the administrator's remuneration be reduced on the grounds that it is in normal circumstances excessive (IR 1986, rule 2.109). If the court considers the application to be well founded, it may make an order fixing the remuneration at a reduced amount or rate.

In assessing office holders' remuneration (see *Re Cabletel Installations Ltd* [2005] BPIR 28) the court will have regard to:

(a) the main categories of work undertaken and whether the time spent was justified;
(b) the level at which the work was done;
(c) the benefit of the work done and whether it was necessary; and
(d) the proportionate value of the work.

See also the guiding principles to be considered by the court as set out in *Practice Statement (Ch D: Fixing and Approval of Remuneration of Appointees)* [2004] BPIR 953. Both the *Cabletel* decision and the Practice Statement indicate that the courts will subject office holders' remuneration to the degree of scrutiny associated with a solicitors' *inter-partes* costs assessment, although regard will be had to the administrator's role as an officer of the court and the public collective function being fulfilled by the office holder.

CHAPTER 8

The receivership process

In **1.5** the nature and purpose of receivership were briefly outlined, while in **5.4** the reasoning behind, the restrictions on and the procedure for appointment were explored. As we have seen, therefore, receivership is not per se an insolvency process, it is not a collective remedy for the benefit of the creditors of the insolvent company; rather, it is an enforcement remedy pursued solely at the behest of a secured creditor as a means of securing repayment of a debt. Indeed, as we shall see, there is no requirement that the company is insolvent. A receivership will, however, in all likelihood dovetail with a form of insolvency process and it also should be remembered that one type of receiver, namely an administrative receiver, is an insolvency office holder pursuant to statute and has certain statutory powers and responsibilities (IA 1986, ss.233–236). This form of the receivership is now increasingly uncommon but is considered in **8.2**. We turn first, however, to consider a receiver appointed pursuant to a mortgage or charge, whether or not pursuant to the powers contained in the Law of Property Act 1925. Such a receiver is thus referred to generically as a non-administrative receiver.

8.1 NON-ADMINISTRATIVE RECEIVERSHIP

8.1.1 Duty of care

A security instrument will set out the terms on which a borrower provides a lender with collateral as security for a debt and the lender's rights and powers over that collateral to achieve repayment of the debt. As a mortgage involves the transfer of title to the collateral from the debtor to the creditor, no duty is owed under common law by the mortgagee exercising a power of sale, as the mortgagee is deemed to be the legal owner and is thereby selling his own property. The position differs where the lender is granted a charge over the collateral; here title to the collateral remains vested in the debtor. However, in both instances, the beneficial ownership to the collateral remains vested in a debtor, represented in the case of the charge by the title and in the case of the mortgagor by his equity redemption (including the right to reclaim title to the collateral). Therefore, by virtue of the fact that the mortgagor has a beneficial interest in property, a mortgagee (and receiver) owes a duty of care in equity to protect and/or act reasonably in regard to the mortgagor's property, this duty being one of acting in good faith and acting for a proper purpose. As we have seen in **5.4**, this duty extends to one of reasonable care (*Medforth* v. *Blake* [2000] Ch 86).

Mortgagee in possession

Unless otherwise agreed, a mortgagee is entitled to take possession of secured property for the purposes of protecting or realising his security. This right arises as soon as the mortgage is created and continues irrespective of whether the borrower is in default or has a claim against the lender. In exercising such rights, the mortgagee need only take account of his own interests. In practice, however, a mainstream lender will act in accordance with a banking code of conduct and will not seek to depart from the terms and conditions of an agreed facility before taking steps to exercise rights such as taking possession.

Where a mortgagee takes possession of a charged property, the mortgagee becomes accountable to the mortgagor, keeping the property in repair and liable to account for rents collected and that which should have been collected if the property was managed with due diligence (*Sherwin* v. *Shakspear* (1854) 5 DM&G 517). The mortgagee is not, however, under a duty to take steps to increase the value of the property (*Silven Properties Ltd* v. *Royal Bank of Scotland* [2004] 1 WLR 997).

A receiver

Save for the statutory power to appoint a receiver conferred on a mortgagee when the mortgage debt becomes due and payable (see Law of Property Act 1925, s.101 and **8.1.2**), a receiver will most commonly be appointed by a lender where the circumstances set out in the security instrument, be that legal charge or mortgage deed, have arisen. It is unusual to see an ability to appoint a receiver without a form of default as defined within the security instrument. Where appointed, a receiver must act reasonably in a respectable, responsible and logical manner (*Bolitho* v. *Hackney HA* [1997] 3 WLR 1151).

A receiver may in appropriate circumstances seek necessary expert advice on any specialist property in which he is dealing (*American Express Banking Corp* v. *Hurley* [1985] 3 All ER 564). However, a receiver cannot delegate his responsibility, e.g. to obtain best price by simply relying on an expert's (valuer's) report. In practice, where a receiver has incurred liability to the company in this manner, it may form the subject of a claim by a receiver for professional negligence against the valuer. It also avoids the necessity of the mortgagor having to apportion blame between a receiver and a valuer.

A mortgagee and a receiver are not entitled to enter into transactions in a personal capacity where this will conflict with the duties owed to the mortgagor, unless the formal consent of all parties is obtained or with leave of the court (*Tito* v. *Waddell (No.2)* [1977] Ch 106). It is a long-established rule that the mortgagee may not sell to himself, but there is nothing to prevent a sale to a company in which the mortgagee has an interest (*Applefields Ltd* v. *Dames Holdings Ltd* [2004] NZLR 721). Indeed, for a time this practice became increasingly attractive to mortgagees who might have wished to take back a property to improve and develop its potential before sale to a third party. By taking possession and then transferring the property into a special purpose vehicle in which the lender had an interest, the lender could enjoy the profits of any speculative investment as opposed to simply accounting back to the mortgagor.

Where a receiver is invalidly appointed, the debenture holder and receiver will be liable for damages for wrongful interference in the company and its property (*OBG Ltd* v. *Allan* [2007] UKHL 21).

In contrast, IA 1986, s.234 provides that, as with any other insolvency office holder, an administrative receiver will not be liable if he seizes or disposes of a property that is not the property of the company and at the time of seizure or disposal he has reasonable grounds for believing that he was entitled to deal, provided that he was not negligent in dealing. The office holder has a lien on the property and its proceeds of sale for such expenses that were incurred in connection with a seizure or disposal. This exemption does not, however, prevent a claim for wrongful interference and only extends to the disposal of tangible property; it does not include choses in action (*Welsh Development Agency Ltd* v. *Export Finance Co.* [1992] BCC 270).

A non-administrative receiver is under:

- a statutory duty to deliver to Companies House a receipts and payments account within one month of the anniversary of his appointment and thereafter every six months (IA 1986, s.38);
- a duty to account at the end of a receivership (*Smiths Ltd* v. *Middleton* [1979] 3 All ER 842).
- a duty to supply to a director or liquidator necessary information or documentation to enable that party to perform their functions, e.g. file accounts (*Gomba Holdings (UK) Ltd* v. *Homan* [1986] 3 All ER 94).

An appointor is under a duty within seven days of the initial appointment to give notice of the receiver's appointment to the Companies Registrar (CA 2006, s.871(1)). Save for these limited duties, the process and procedure in regard to a receivership is one dictated by the terms of the security instrument and the particular circumstances arising from the enforcement of the security; it is not a court-driven process, nor is it governed by statute.

8.1.2   The function and powers of a receiver

A receiver appointed under a statutory power is often referred to as an 'LPA receiver,' their powers being contained in the Law of Property Act 1925. Indeed a security instrument will often adopt (and extend) the statutory powers contained in the Law of Property Act 1925 allowing a lender to appoint a receiver in certain circumstances to enforce the security. Where there is no express provision, a power of appointment is contained in Law of Property Act 1925, s.101(1)(ii) in any case where there is a mortgage by deed.

However, the statutory powers of an LPA receiver are very limited (to collect rent and to insure the property: see Law of Property Act 1925, s.109) and do not extend to the power to manage (a business) and even to sell the mortgaged property (which is the statutory right of the mortgagee alone). As a result, the security instrument will contain a large and wide-ranging number of powers, giving express powers of management, control, trade and sale, which are often equivalent to those of an administrator (IA 1986, Sched.1).

A receiver's powers are exercisable only over property covered by the charge, but it should be remembered that a floating charge will generally provide for security over 'all other property of the company' and/or the power will be conferred on the receiver to carry on the company's business and to do so as agent for the company. This will generally give the receiver wider powers to deal with company property.

The powers of a receiver are not, however, exercisable over property subject to any prior fixed charge. This contrasts with the position of an administrative receiver, which is explored in **8.2.1**.

Application to court for directions

The receiver or the appointor may apply to court for directions in relation to a particular matter arising in connection with the performance of the functions of the receiver or manager (IA 1986, s.35(1)).

A court may make such direction, order or declaration as it thinks just in the exercise of its discretion. The assistance of the courts may be sought in a wide variety of scenarios (see *Re Beam Tube Products Ltd* [2006] BCC 615), including issues of remuneration (*Munns* v. *Perkins* [2002] BPIR 120) and resolving questions regarding the order of priorities for payment. Directions should not be sought, however, where the issues should be resolved in the ordinary course of litigation (*Re Stetzel Thomson & Co. Ltd* (1988) 4 BCC 74) or where the matter is one of commercial judgment (*Re T&D Automative plc* [2000] 1 BCLC 471).

8.1.3　Agency and liability for contracts

Where a receiver has the power to carry on the business of the company, it will be almost universally provided in the security instrument that the receiver will be deemed to be the company's agent unless or until the company goes into liquidation (*Thomas* v. *Todd* [1926] 2 KB 511).

As agent of the company, a receiver is not personally liable for the acts of the company during his period in office, save in two circumstances:

(a)　Any contract entered into by him in the carrying out of his functions (except in so far as the contract otherwise provides and this will generally be provided on all letters, orders, etc. sent out by the receiver) (see *Hill Samuel & Co. Ltd* v. *Laing* [1991] BCC 665).

(b) To the extent of any qualifying liabilities on any contract of employment adopted by him in carrying out his functions.

In both instances, however, the receiver is entitled to an indemnity out of the assets under his custody or control in respect of any liability so incurred (IA 1986, s.37(1)(b)). Likewise, where an administrative receiver is deemed to have personal liability for contracts, he is entitled to an indemnity from the assets of the company in respect of that liability (IA 1986, s.44(1)(c)).

A receiver is not, however, taken to have adopted a contract of employment by reason of having done or omitted to do anything within 14 days of appointment (IA 1986, s.37(2) and in the case of an administrative receiver s.44(2)). The issue of adoption of employment contracts was one which exercised the courts through the late 1980s and early 1990s (see *Nicoll* v. *Cutts* [1985] BCLC 322 (CA); *Powdrill* v. *Watson*: *Re Paramount Airways Ltd (No.3)* [1994] 2 All ER 513 (CA); *Re Leyland DAF Ltd*; *Re Ferranti International plc* [1994] BCC 658).

The outcome of case law in this area was to prohibit a practice that had grown up, whereby a receiver would retain employees to assist in the running of the company, while obtaining their agreement that in doing so he had not personally adopted their contracts of employment. However, the decisions of the court posed a threat to corporate rescue and the efficient running of administrative receiverships. As a result, the Insolvency Act 1994 was quickly introduced and inserted new provisions into the relevant legislation, limiting the liability of an administrative receiver (although *not* non-administrative receivers) to 'qualifying liabilities' falling due under a contract of employment (IA 1986, s.44(2A), (2D)).

A qualifying liability is defined as a liability that is:

- to pay by way of wages or salary or contribution to an occupational scheme;
- incurred while the administrative receiver is in office; and
- in respect of services rendered wholly or partly after the adoption of the contract.

The legislation applies to all contracts of employment adopted on or after 15 March 1994 and also has application (more generally of application) to administrators.

In contrast to an administrator (see *Exeter City Council* v. *Bairstow* [2007] EWHC 400 (Ch)), a receiver is not liable for business rates, which remain a company liability (*Brown* v. *City of London Corporation* [1996] 1 WLR 1070) even in the event of liquidation of the company and termination of the receiver's agency (*Re Beck Foods Ltd* [2001] 2 BCLC 663). Likewise, tax liability (e.g. capital gains tax) incurred on sale of property will be a liability of the company and will not be treated as a cost and expense of the receivership. This is to be contrasted with administration, where such tax liability will be a cost and expense.

A receiver will also (save in exceptional circumstances) not be personally liable for the costs of unsuccessful litigation brought in the company's name (*Mills* v.

Birchall [2008] BPIR 607, although contrast with the case of *Re Dairy Farmers of Britain Ltd* [2010] BCC 637).

A person paying money to the receiver has certain protection afforded by statute in that the person 'shall not be concerned to inquire whether any case has happened to authorise the receiver to act' (Law of Property Act 1925, s.109(4)), i.e. he does not need to concern himself as to the circumstances of the appointment.

8.2 ADMINISTRATIVE RECEIVERSHIP

Post the Enterprise Act 2002 reforms, save in a number of exempted circumstances, the holder of a qualifying floating charge may no longer appoint an administrative receiver, the most significant exemption being where the floating charge was created before 15 September 2003. By effluxion of time, therefore, the use of administrative receivership is dwindling and soon will have a place only in specialist works.

This section therefore looks briefly at the process and procedure post appointment, the powers and duties of an administrative receiver and the likely outcome of the administrative receivership.

8.2.1 Duties and powers of an administrative receiver

A person dealing in good faith with the administrative receiver for value is not concerned to enquire as to whether the administrative receiver is acting within his powers (IA 1986, s.42(3)). In the exercise of his powers, the administrative receiver is under a duty to act in good faith and take reasonable care in realising the assets for the benefit of the chargee (*Downsview Nominees Ltd* v. *First City Corporation Ltd* [1993] AC 295). This equitable duty extends only to those interested in the equity of redemption, such as the company, guarantors or subsequent chargees.

The powers of an administrative receiver are deemed to include, except where they are inconsistent with the terms of the debenture, the same powers as an administrator specified in IA 1986, Sched.1. This non-exhaustive list of 23 different powers is applicable to all administrators, whether appointed by court order or by out-of-court route, as well as to administrative receivers.

These powers include the right to:

- take possession and collect in the company's property;
- sell, auction, hire or otherwise dispose of company property;
- borrow;
- appoint solicitors, agents or accountants to assist;
- carry on the business of the company;
- make arrangements and compromises on behalf of the company; and
- prevent a winding-up petition.

The administrative receiver also has certain investigatory powers (IA 1986, s.235 (power to obtain co-operation), s.236 (power to compel attendance at court): see discussion of these sections below) and powers to get in and deal with company property (IA 1986, s.234). This is to be contrasted with a receiver, who has no such insolvency office holder powers. In practice, however, as we have seen above, the terms of the facility and/or security instrument may impose on the borrower certain contractual obligations to hand over documentation and assist the receiver in his duties and it may often be to the borrowers' advantage to ensure that the debt owed to the secured creditor is minimised.

However, an administrative receiver (like an administrator) has a power to apply to court to dispose of assets subject to security if it would promote a more advantageous realisation of the company's assets (IA 1986, s.43(1)) (see the court's approach in *Re Harris Simons Construction Ltd* [1989] 1 WLR 368). In practice, an order will be sought where the prior charge holder has refused consent (*Re ARV Aviation Ltd* (1988) 4 BCC 708). The ability of the administrative receiver to apply to court for an order for sale does not, however, apply to security possessed by the appointor. This highlights the fact that the administrative receiver's principal duty is to the appointor and that administrative receivership remains a proprietorial remedy. The administrative receiver will not dispose of such secured property without the consent of the appointor.

The circumstance where this provision may be used is where there is a prior existing charge (normally a fixed charge). If the administrative receiver obtains an order permitting sale, it will be on a condition that:

- the net proceeds of the disposal; and
- where those proceeds are less than an amount determined by the court, which is considered to be the realisable sale value of the property on the open market, a sum to make good the deficiency,

are provided towards discharging the sum secured by the security (IA 1986, s.43(3)).

As a consequence, the court needs to consider whether there might be a potential for the sale of the secured asset to be less than market value and, if a sale is so ordered, the deficiency will be made good. Expert evidence adduced by the charge holder will be necessary. A copy of the order must be registered at Companies House within 14 days (IA 1986, s.43(5)).

In performing his duties, the administrative receiver is assisted by the powers contained in IA 1986, ss.234–237, which are common to all office holders.

Briefly, the powers are as follows.

Section 234

The court may direct a person who has possession or control of any property, books, papers or records of the company, to deliver those to the administrative receiver.

With respect to any property seized by the administrative receiver which he has reasonable grounds for believing was company property, he is not liable for any loss or damage, in so far as it was not caused by his own negligence. As a consequence, property which may be subject to a retention of title clause could be sold by the administrative receiver without fear of a claim for damages (although an action for the tracing of proceeds could be commenced). However, the administrative receiver must act reasonably and will seek to establish from creditors whether such claims exist and/or, if claims are made, he will need to investigate fully. Importantly, the administrative receiver will be liable if, after receiving notice of the claim, he has without good reason disposed of the property to a third party.

Information obtained under IA 1986, s.234 cannot be passed to the appointor to assist it in claims against third parties (*Sutton* v. *GE Capital Commercial Finance Ltd* [2004] 2 BCLC 662).

Section 235

Officers, employees or those who within one year have been involved in formation of the company may be required to provide the administrative receiver with such information concerning the company's promotion, formation, business dealings and affairs as may be reasonably required and attend upon the office holder as and when reasonably required. Any person who fails to comply with this section may be liable to a fine (IA 1986, Sched.10: the fine is up to the statutory maximum (£5,000 as at 30 April 2007) and daily default of one-tenth of the statutory maximum).

Any statements obtained can be used in director disqualification proceedings (*Re Westminster Property Management Ltd* [2000] 1 WLR 2230) and, if in the public interest, disclosed to regulatory authorities (*R.* v. *Brady* [2005] BCC 357).

Section 236

The court may on the administrative receiver's application summon to appear before it any:

- officer of the company;
- person known or suspected of being in possession of company property;
- person indebted to the company; or
- person who the court thinks could give information concerning the promotion, formation, business, dealings or affairs of the company.

The person ordered to appear before the court may also be required to submit an affidavit containing an account of his dealings with the company and/or produce books, papers or records in his possession or control relating to the company. Any person failing to appear before the court without reasonable excuse may be liable to arrest and/or subject to an order for seizure of books, papers, records and goods.

It is to be remembered that the court will only order an examination of an individual if it is necessary to further the insolvency process and if it is not oppressive or unduly unfair to the respondents (see *Re Embassy Art Products Ltd* (1987) 3 BCC 292). As a result, the power is generally exercised where the administrative receiver is seeking to investigate and not to obtain any special information which would otherwise be disclosed in litigation (see *Re Atlantic Computers plc* [1998] BCC 200). An order can, however, be made where the sole purpose of the examination is to obtain information to support director disqualification proceedings (*Re Pantmaenog Timber Co. Ltd* [2004] 1 AC 158).

The administrative receiver will generally seek to obtain the information voluntarily and/or will seek the attendance of the individual in interview, prior to making any application to court.

Section 237

If it appears to the court, on consideration of any evidence obtained under a s.236 examination, that a person has in his possession any property of the company, the court may on application of the administrative receiver order the person to deliver the whole or part of the property to the administrative receiver on such terms as the court thinks fit. A solicitor cannot claim legal professional privilege where the papers belong to the company in question (*Re Brook Martin & Co. (Nominees) Ltd* [1993] BCLC 328).

If a debt has been established to be payable from the person, the court can order that this be paid to the administrative receiver. An example of this could include where the director has admitted on examination that he has received unauthorised loan payments from the company.

8.2.2   Administrative receivership process and procedure

Guide to procedure

The administrative receivership process

1.   Administrative receiver serves notice of appointment on company.
2.   Appointment advertised in *Gazette* and newspaper.
3.   Within seven days, notice sent to Registrar of Companies and registered.
4.   Within 28 days, notice sent to creditors.
5.   Statement of affairs completed by officer/employee of company.
6.   Within three months, administrative receiver reports on progress, etc.
7.   Meeting of creditors held on 14 days' notice.
8.   Administrative receiver realises secured assets of the appointor.

On appointment, the company will receive notice from the administrative receiver of his appointment (IA 1986, s.46(1)(a)). This notice will state:

(a)   the registered name of the company as at the date of appointment and its registered number;

(b)   any name with which the company has been registered in the previous 12 months;

(c)   any name under which the company has traded in the previous 12 months, if substantially different from the registered name;

(d)   the name(s) and address(es) of the administrative receiver(s) and date of appointment;

(e)   the name of the appointor;

(f)   the date of the instrument of appointment and brief details of the instrument; and

(g)   a brief description of the assets of the company in respect of which the person appointed is not made receiver (IR 1986, rule 3.2(2)).

The administrative receiver will advertise his appointment in the *Gazette* and in any such other manner as he thinks appropriate (IR 1986, rule 3.2(3) in Form 3.1A). Thereafter every invoice, order or business letter issued must contain a statement that a receiver has been appointed (IA 1986, s.39(1)).

Within seven days, the appointor must give notice of the appointment to the Registrar of Companies (CA 2006, s.871(1)).

Within 28 days of appointment, the administrative receiver must send notice of appointment to the creditors of the company, as far as he is aware of their addresses, unless the court otherwise directs (IR 1986, rule 4.6(1)(b)).

Statement of affairs

The administrative receiver will require a statement of affairs to be provided by any or all of (IA 1986, s.47):

- an officer or former officer of the company;
- those taking part in the formation of the company at any time within one year of appointment;
- an employee or former employee of the company at any time within one year of appointment; and/or
- those individuals who were or have been officers or employees of a company which is or was within one year of appointment an officer of the company.

Notice must be served by the administrative receiver upon the individual in a prescribed form (IR 1986, rule 3.3(1) in Form 3.1B). The person served with the notice must provide a statement of affairs within 21 days (IA 1986, s.47(4)). The period for complying with the notice to provide a statement of affairs may be extended by agreement with the administrative receiver in the exercise of his discretion (IR 1986, rule 3.6(1)) or on application to the court (IR 1986, rule 3.6(2)). Failure to comply with a notice without a reasonable excuse can lead to a fine (IA

1986, Sched.10). The fine is up to the statutory maximum penalty (which is at present £5,000) and a daily default fine of up to one-tenth of the statutory maximum.

The statement of affairs must be provided in Form 3.2 and the administrative receiver may require the statement of affairs to be accompanied by an affidavit of concurrence (i.e. agreement by some officer(s) of the company to the truth and accuracy of the statement of affairs). While there is some flexibility as to who should provide the statement of affairs and when, the provision of a statement of affairs by someone is a mandatory requirement.

Where the administrative receiver is of the belief that disclosure of whole or part of the statement of affairs would prejudice the conduct of the receivership, the administrative receiver may apply to court for an order limiting disclosure (IR 1986, rule 3.5). Although in providing a report to creditors (see below), the administrative receiver need not disclose information which would prejudice the carrying out of his functions (IA 1986, s.48(6)), covering, e.g. the non-disclosure of confidential offers for the business; it is not intended to cover the non-disclosure of the statement of affairs, where specific permission of the court will be required.

A person making the statement of affairs is entitled to reasonable expenses incurred in producing a statement of affairs payable from the company's assets (IR 1986, rule 3.7).

Meeting of creditors

Within three months (or such longer period as the court may allow), the administrative receiver should send a report (known as the 'section 48 report') to:

- the Registrar of Companies;
- the secured creditors of the company; and
- all other creditors.

The report should deal with:

- the events leading up to the administrative receiver's appointment;
- any disposals made by the administrative receiver of company property;
- the amounts payable to any debenture holders and preferential creditors; and
- the amount likely to be payable to other creditors.

The report should contain a summary of the statement of affairs and any comments made by the administrative receiver on it (IA 1986, s.48(5)). A meeting of creditors should then take place, with not less than 14 days' notice being provided.

It should be remembered that an administrative receiver is not responsible for dealing with claims of unsecured creditors, or for making any distribution to them. However, a report must be submitted to unsecured creditors and a meeting of creditors will be held unless the court otherwise directs. In his report and at the meeting, the administrative receiver will outline his plans for the company. The importance of a meeting for the unsecured creditors is for them to assess the rights of action that they may possess against the company and/or whether further insolvency procedures are likely to follow, e.g. a liquidation. The receiver may apply to court to dispense with the holding of such a meeting (IA 1986, s.48(2)). The court will not, however, dispense with the meeting unless the administrative receiver gives notice in his report of his intention to apply to the court for directions (IA 1986, s.48(3)).

At the meeting, it may be determined that it is appropriate for a creditors' committee to be established (IA 1986, s.49). If it is formed, the committee can request information from the receiver and assist the administrative receiver in discharging his function and act in a manner as agreed from time to time (IR 1986, rule 3.18). The power of the creditors' committee in an administrative receivership is limited in comparison with the role and powers of a creditors' committee in a liquidation or administration. The creditors' committee in administrative receivership has no formal powers and the role is as defined by agreement with the administrative receiver; it can, however, on giving seven days' notice require the receiver to attend before it at any reasonable time and place and provide it with such information 'as it may reasonably require' (IA 1986, s.49(2)).

In practice, given the limited role performed by the committee, it is usually found only in situations of multi-secured creditor insolvencies, when the interests of differing secured creditors with varying degrees of priority overlap.

An administrative receiver appointed by a debenture holder has his remuneration fixed by agreement with the debenture holder, not the creditors generally or the creditors' committee. This does not, however, prevent a subsequently appointed liquidator from applying to court to fix the receiver's remuneration, although such applications are rare.

8.3   DISTRIBUTION TO CREDITORS

As described above, the receiver's overriding duty is to realise the secured assets of the appointor. Receivership is an individual secured creditor's means of enforcement; it is not a collective insolvency process. The receiver is therefore not concerned with making returns to unsecured creditors save for the obligations that may arise under IA 1986, s.176A (prescribed part payment from floating charge).

The receiver is, however, under a statutory obligation to discharge claims of preferential creditors in respect of any monies received upon floating charge realisations (IA 1986, s.40). This is a personal duty (*IRC* v. *Goldblatt* [1972] Ch 498) and failure can lead to personal liability (*Woods* v. *Winskill* [1913] 2 Ch 303).

Any payments made from floating charge realisations should be recouped as far as possible out of the assets of the company, which are otherwise available for unsecured creditors. This is a continuing responsibility which is not discharged merely because the claims of the debenture holder have been satisfied (see *Re Pearl Maintenance Services Ltd* [1995] BCC 657) or where the charge has crystallised at or prior to appointment (*H & K Medway Ltd* [1997] 1 BCLC 545). The obligation to pay preferential creditors out of the floating charge realisations also continues despite the fact that the company may have gone into liquidation (see *Re EISC Teo Ltd* (1991) ILRM 760).

As we have previously seen, the issue of whether the debenture holder possesses security under a fixed and floating charge is important in determining priorities of payment and the likely return to the creditor (see *Re Spectrum Plus Ltd* [2005] UKHL 41). The importance of this issue has, however, been somewhat diminished by the Enterprise Act 2002 reforms, which provide that for all administrations or administrative receiverships commencing after 15 September 2003, the Crown will not enjoy preferential creditor status (IA 1986, s.386). IA 1986, s.386 provides that 'a reference in this Act to the preferential debts of a company or an individual is to the debts listed in Schedule 6 to this Act (contributions to occupational pension schemes; remuneration, etc. of employees; levies on coal and steel production); and references to preferential creditors are to be read accordingly'.

Of these remaining preferential creditors, employee claims remain an important liability, with arrears of wages and salary within the last four months, holiday pay and pensions contributions being afforded preferential status. However, redundancy pay and compensation for unfair dismissal are not wages and salary and are not preferential claims (*Re Allders Department Stores Ltd* [2005] 2 All ER 122) and the amount available to employees in respect of unpaid remuneration is subject to a maximum amount prescribed by the Secretary of State (this is a limited amount at present £800 – Insolvency Proceedings (Monetary Limits) Order 1986, SI 1986/1996, art.4).

In respect of security created after 15 September 2003, the ring-fenced sum provisions contained in IA 1986, s.176A ensure that receivers will still have to take into account the distinction between fixed and floating charge assets, as the prescribed amount is deducted from floating charge realisations.

As a result of these reforms, a windfall has occurred to those secured creditors whose floating charge was created prior to 15 September 2003.

Example
Amount due under fixed charge – £250,000
Amount due under floating charge – £300,000
Amount due to Crown creditors – £50,000
Net available property – £500,000

1. Administrative receiver appointed prior to 15 September 2003

   Distribution:

   - Fixed charge holder £250,000
   - Crown creditors £50,000
   - Floating charge holder £200,000

2. Administrative receiver or administrator appointed after 15 September 2003, security created before 15 September 2003

   Distribution:

- Fixed charge holder £250,000
- Floating charge holder £250,000

3. Administrator appointed after 15 September 2003, security created after 15 September 2003 (IA 1986, s.72A prohibits the appointment of an administrative receiver in respect of security created after 15 September 2003)

Distribution:

- Fixed charge holder £250,000
- Unsecured creditors £53,000*
- Floating charge holder £197,000

*IA 1986, s.176A, prescribed amount is 50 per cent on first £10,000 plus 20 per cent thereafter, on maximum net available sum of £600,000.

If the administrative receiver is able to discharge the company's secured and preferential claims in full, the surplus is likely to be distributed to the creditors via a liquidation process. If this is initiated by the company/directors, it is likely to be a creditors' voluntary liquidation. If it is initiated by the creditors or the administrative receiver himself, it will be a compulsory liquidation. In contrast, where a secured creditor's debt remains partially unpaid after realisation of the secured assets (fixed or floating), the secured creditor cannot claim any part of the prescribed part (*Re Permacell FinesseLtd* [2008] BCC 208 and *Re Airbase Services (UK) Ltd* [2008] BCC 213), although it will be able to claim a dividend as an ordinary unsecured creditor. As previously discussed, a secured creditor may surrender its security and will then be entitled to a share of the prescribed part (*Re PAL SC Realisations 2007 Ltd* [2011] BCC 93).

It is of course possible that despite the appointment of an administrative receiver the company is solvent; in this case the surplus will be returned to the company, and control and management passed back to the directors and the company, who can thereafter resume trading. This, it has to be said, is very rare.

As an alternative to liquidation, a CVA could be put forward to creditors. It is not, however, the role of the administrative receiver to deal with creditor claims generally, nor is he concerned to save the company or its business.

8.4 ENDING THE RECEIVERSHIP

A receivership will end on the realisation of the secured asset or where the appointor removes the receiver from office. This right to remove needs to be exercised in accordance with any formality as per the security instrument, although in practice if there is an express provision it will state that removal needs to be made in writing. Where removed from office, the former receiver is entitled to an indemnity out of the assets of the company in respect of fees and expenses and this is charged on and paid out of property which is in his custody or control at the time that the receivership comes to an end (IA 1986, s.37(4); see *Choudhri* v. *Palta* [1992] BCC 787 which confirms that this right to an indemnity does not extend to assets covered by a prior security).

An administrative receiver of the company may at any time be removed from office by order of the court (there is no restriction on who may apply for removal: see *Sheppard & Cooper Ltd* v. *TSB Bank plc* [1997] 2 BCLC 222), or may resign office upon giving at least five business days' notice to:

- the appointor;
- the company;
- if the company is in liquidation, to the liquidator; and
- if appropriate to the creditors' committee (IR 1986, rule 3.33).

No notice of resignation is required if the receiver resigns as a consequence of an administration order having been made.

The power of replacement lies with the appointor. It should be noted, however, that once the administrative receiver has been appointed a debenture holder cannot simply remove that administrative receiver and would need to go to court for an order to remove him unless he resigned. The court has no power to appoint a replacement (*Re A & C Supplies Ltd* [1998] 1 BCLC 603).

When the administrative receiver vacates office otherwise than by death, he must inform the Registrar of Companies within 14 days (IA 1986, s.45(4)).

Upon vacation of office, the administrative receiver is entitled to be indemnified in respect of any remuneration and any expenses to which he is entitled, from any property in his possession, custody or control, and this is payable in priority to any security held by the appointor (IA 1986, s.45(3)).

An agreement as to fees payable is a matter between the receiver and his appointor. The court may on application of a liquidator fix an amount to be paid by way of remuneration to a receiver (IA 1986, s.36(1)) (see *Re Potters Oils Ltd (No.2)* [1986] 1 WLR 201).

CHAPTER 9

The liquidation process

The steps leading to the commencement of voluntary liquidation, generally a debtor-led process, were considered in **3.11**, while the commencement of compulsory liquidation, generally a creditor-led process, was considered in **5.5**.

Once the procedure has commenced, however, the key purpose of winding up, i.e. the realisation of available company assets for distribution to creditors, is common to both the voluntary and compulsory liquidation processes. However, there are important differences in practice and procedure post commencement, which are explored in this chapter.

9.1 FROM LIQUIDATOR'S APPOINTMENT TO CREDITOR'S MEETING

Guide to procedure

Creditors' voluntary liquidation

1. Five days' notice of proposed resolution to wind up company is given to qualifying floating charge holders who possess security created after 15 September 2003 (IA 1986, s.84 (2A)).
2. Members' meeting is held to consider the passing of a special resolution that the company should go into liquidation (IA 1986, s.84(1)); thereafter the members will nominate a liquidator.
3. Notice of company resolution must be placed in the *London Gazette* within 14 days of resolution (IA 1986, s.85(1)) (NB step (10)).
4. A creditors' meeting is held within 14 days of the company members' resolution (IA 1986, s.98(1A)(a)).
5. Seven days' notice of meeting given to creditors (IA 1986, s.98(1A)(b)).
6. Commonly, the members' and creditors' meetings are held on the same day. Creditors will vote on whether to appoint the liquidator proposed by the members (IA 1986, s.100).
7. Chairman of meeting certifies liquidator's appointment in Form 4.27 (or Form 4.28 in case of joint appointment).
8. Certificate of appointment is proof of appointment and authority to act.
9. Liquidation committee of up to five members can be formed.
10. Notice of appointment must be placed in the *London Gazette* within 14 days of appointment (IA 1986, s.109(1)).

11.   Liquidator proceeds to realise assets of company and make distributions to creditors, leading to dissolution of company.

Compulsory liquidation

1.   Winding-up order made by court in Form 4.11.
2.   Court gives notice to Official Receiver, petitioner and other persons who appeared at the hearing no later than the day following the order.
3.   Official Receiver sends copy of order to company and Registrar of Companies.
4.   Official Receiver advertises order in *London Gazette* and may advertise in such other manner as thought appropriate (IR 1986, rule 4.106A).
5.   Official Receiver sends notice to appropriate person to complete statement of affairs.
6.   Statement of affairs must be submitted in Form 4.17 within 21 days.
7.   At least once after the order, the Official Receiver must report to the creditors and contributories of the company.
8.   Official Receiver acts as liquidator in the absence of any other appointee. He may at any time call a meeting of creditors to appoint any person in his place.
9.   If the Official Receiver does not intend to call a meeting of creditors, he must give notice of this to the creditors within two weeks.
10.   If it appears that there are insufficient assets to meet the costs of the liquidation and further investigation is not necessary, the Official Receiver may apply to the Registrar of Companies for early dissolution, giving 28 days' notice beforehand to the creditors, contributories and any administrative receiver. The company will normally be dissolved three months after notice.
11.   Alternatively, a liquidator may be appointed in place of the Official Receiver by the court (where a winding-up order is made on the application of an administrator or a supervisor of the company). The liquidator notifies the Registrar of Companies in Form 4.31.
12.   Alternatively, the Official Receiver may apply to the Secretary of State for the appointment of an insolvency practitioner to act as liquidator in his place, who will issue a certificate of appointment. The liquidator notifies the Registrar of Companies in Form 4.31.
13.   Alternatively, the Official Receiver may call a first meeting of creditors. Beforehand, forms of proof in Form 4.25 must be sent to the creditors and proxy forms provided. The court may order notice to be given by advertisement rather than individually to creditors.
14.   At the meeting, a liquidator may be appointed by majority vote.
15.   Liquidation committee of up to five members can be formed.
16.   Chairman of meeting certifies liquidator's appointment in Form 4.27 (or Form 4.28 in case of joint appointment).
17.   On receipt of certificate of appointment, liquidator must give notice of appointment by advertisement in the *London Gazette* and in such other manner as thought appropriate.
18.   Liquidator proceeds to realise assets of the company and make distributions to creditors, leading to eventual dissolution of the company.

9.1.1   Creditors' meeting and creditors' voluntary liquidation

In the case of a creditors' voluntary liquidation, the power to appoint the liquidator is vested in the company by its members at a general meeting and by its creditors (IA 1986, s.100(1)). This calls for the need for two separate meetings, with the

383

requirement that the creditors' meeting must be called no later than 14 days after the date of the company's general meeting at which the resolution for voluntary winding up is proposed (IA 1986, s.98 (1A)).

The liquidator will be the person nominated by the creditors or, if no person has been so nominated, the person nominated by the company (IA 1986, s.100(2)). A liquidator nominated by the company and/or appointed by the creditors is not an officer of the court (*Re T H Knitwear (Wholesale) Ltd* (1988) 4 BCC 102).

If there is a conflict in the choice of liquidator between the company and the creditors, it is open to any director, member or creditor to apply to court within seven days from the date of the creditors' meeting for an order directing that the company's nominated liquidator acts in place of the creditors' nominated liquidator, or the two nominated liquidators act jointly, or another person be appointed liquidator (IA 1986, s.100(3)). The members or directors may feel this is appropriate if they have used the services of an insolvency practitioner to advise the company and assist in the calling of the meeting and feel that the creditors' alternative choice will lead to duplication and additional costs and expense. By contrast, it should be remembered that the creditors may feel that the insolvency practitioner's involvement and previous association with the management of the company is a reason to fear that proper investigation of directors' conduct will not take place. It should be noted, however, that the creditors' decision and choice of liquidator will, save in the most extraordinary circumstances, prevail.

The creditors' meeting is generally known as a 'Section 98 meeting', taking its name (unsurprisingly) from the statutory section which governs the calling of the meeting of creditors. Notice must be sent to all creditors not less than seven days before the date of the meeting (IA 1986, s.98(1A)(b)); it must be advertised in the *Gazette* (IA 1986, s.98(1A)(c)) and may be advertised in any such other manner as the directors think fit, e.g. newspaper advertisement (IA 1986, s.98(1A)(d)). The notice must state the name and registered number of the company, specify the venue of the meeting and the time (not earlier than 12 pm on the business day before the day fixed for hearing) and the place at which creditors must submit proofs and proxies necessary to entitle them to vote at the meeting (IR 1986, rule 4.51(2)).

The venue of the meeting must be a place which is convenient for the attendees (other than the chairman: IR 1986, rule 4.60(1)) and the time set for the meeting must be between 10 am and 4 pm on any business day unless the court allows and orders otherwise (IR 1986, rule 4.60(2)).

In order to assist the creditors, the directors of the company are obliged to provide financial information regarding the company in the form of a statement of affairs (IA 1986, s.99), which has to be in a prescribed form (Forms 4.18, 4.19) setting out the assets, debts, liabilities of the company, the names and addresses of the company's creditors and details of any securities held by any creditor. The statement of affairs must be verified by some or all of the directors providing a statement of truth (IA 1986, s.99(2A)). Directors who fail to comply with these requirements are guilty of an offence and liable to a fine (IA 1986, s.99(3)).

The directors are also required to appoint one of their number to preside over the Section 98 meeting and any director who then fails to attend without reasonable excuse is similarly guilty of an offence and liable to a fine (IA 1986, s.99(1)(c), (3)(b)). If the appointed director fails to attend it will not, however, invalidate the meeting, as it remains open to the creditors to appoint another person to preside over the meeting (*Re Salcombe Hotel Development Co. Ltd* (1989) 5 BCC 807).

9.1.2   Creditors' meeting and compulsory liquidation

In compulsory liquidation, on the making of a winding-up order the Official Receiver will become liquidator and will remain in office until another person becomes liquidator (such as an insolvency practitioner from private practice) is appointed (IA 1986, s.136(2)). In any case (whether the Official Receiver remains liquidator or is replaced), the Official Receiver is under a statutory duty to investigate the causes of the company's failure and generally its promotion, formation, business and dealings (IA 1986, s.132(1)). This can lead, in the exercise of the Official Receiver's discretion, to a report to the court (IA 1986, s.132(1)) or referral to the Directors' Disqualification Unit of the DBIS.

The liquidator is under a duty to protect the company's assets and, where appropriate, take into custody the company's property, to realise it and then to distribute it (IA 1986, ss.143(1), 144(1)). However, where there are significant assets and/or issues of complexity, the Official Receiver, rather than continuing to act as the liquidator, is likely to conclude that a liquidator from private practice should be appointed. This could follow the Official Receiver calling a meeting of creditors to appoint a liquidator, or the nomination of a liquidator following a 'Secretary of State's appointment'. The process of appointment is driven by the Official Receiver's office acting for and on behalf of the Secretary of State. In theory, the appointment is rota driven, with a 'cab rank' rule applying; however, an appointment may follow representation from any majority creditor.

Where a winding-up order is made following an administration or a CVA, it is possible for the former administrator or supervisor to be appointed as liquidator by court order (IA 1986, s.140(1); see also *Re Exchange Travel (Holdings) Ltd* [1992] BCC 954 confirming that the court does not have power under this section to appoint a liquidator who was not previously the administrator or supervisor).

The Official Receiver has 12 weeks in which to decide whether to summon a first meeting of creditors; and any such meeting must be held within four months of the winding-up order (IA 1986, s.136(5)(a)). Where the Official Receiver does not summon a meeting of creditors, he must give notice of the decision to the creditors accompanied by a report (IA 1986, s.136(5)(b)). In practice, the report is likely to state that there are no assets available, or that further investigations are required before meriting a meeting and/or the appointment of a liquidator other than the Official Receiver can be evaluated. It is, however, still possible for the Official Receiver later to decide to summon a meeting of creditors.

A meeting of creditors will also need to be held where it is requisitioned by the creditors holding 25 per cent in value of the company's debt (see IA 1986, s.136(5)(c) and IR 1986, rule 4.50). The request (in Form 4.21) must set out the debt of the requisitioning creditor and that of any supporting creditor necessary to achieve the requisite 25 per cent, together with a statement that the purpose of the meeting is to appoint a liquidator. The requisitioned meeting must be held within three months of receipt of the request or after payment of the estimated cost (whichever is later).

9.1.3 Statement of the company's affairs

The directors of the company are obliged to provide a statement in a prescribed form (Form 4.19) as to the affairs of the company, to be laid down at the creditor's meeting in the case of voluntary liquidation (IA 1986, s.99(1)(b)) and to the Official Receiver in the case of compulsory liquidation (IA 1986, s.131).

The statement of affairs should set out the company's debts and liabilities, its creditors, securities held by the creditors and dates when security was given. While the directors may appoint one of their number to prepare the statement and preside at the creditors' meeting, the requirement to provide a statement of affairs is one that rests on all the directors. A director who, without reasonable excuse, fails to provide a statement of affairs and/or attend the creditors' meeting as outlined above is guilty of an offence and liable to a fine (IA 1986, s.99(3)).

The statement of affairs must be verified by two or more directors (IA 1986, s.99(2A)) and be made up to a date not more than 14 days before the date of the company's resolution to wind up the company is passed (IR 1986, rule 4.34(4)).

At the Section 98 meeting, if the statement of affairs laid before the creditors does not accurately reflect the true state of the company's affairs as at the date of the meeting, the directors must cause a report to be presented to the meeting by the director presiding over the meeting as chairman, or by a person with knowledge of relevant matters. The report, which can be presented orally or in writing, must deal with any material transactions that have occurred between the date of the making of the statement of affairs and the date of the meeting (IR 1986, rule 4.53B(1)) and the report must be recorded in the minutes of the meeting (IR 1986, rule 4.53B(2)).

After the Section 98 meeting, the statement of affairs must be delivered by the directors to the appointed liquidator and the liquidator must within five business days deliver the same to the Registrar of Companies (IR 1986, rule 4.34(3)). Where a liquidator is nominated by the company at a meeting on a day before the Section 98 meeting, the directors must at that stage deliver the statement of affairs to the nominated liquidator (IR 1986, rule 4.34A).

In practice, where the directors plan to put the company into liquidation, they will liaise with a proposed liquidator who will assist in the calling of both the company and creditors' meetings and advise as to the format and content of the statement of affairs. The statement of affairs will, however, be that of the directors and while this may be the starting point for any liquidator in his investigations of the assets and liabilities of the company, at the time of its production to the creditors it is no more than a guide from which the liquidator is entitled to depart (e.g. the directors may regard a creditor as possessing valid security and provide a statement to that effect; however if, on investigation, the liquidator deduces that the security is defective he will in his report to creditors advise of the same).

The cost and expense of preparing the statement of affairs may be met out of the company's assets as an expense of the liquidation either before or after the commencement of the winding up (IR 1986, rule 4.38). If payment is made before commencement, the chairman of the meeting must inform the creditors as to the amount and the recipient of the payment. If the payment is made post commencement by the liquidator, he cannot pay himself or an associate of his, although where a creditors' committee is formed the liquidator must give five business days' notice of his intention to make the payment. It is not uncommon to find that the company's accountant/bookkeeper can in this way receive a fee for providing the statement of affairs.

Where a court has made a winding-up order or appointed a provisional liquidator, the Official Receiver may request that any director or former director (or other person considered responsible such as employees/officers of the company: see IA 1986, s.131(3)) provide a statement of affairs. A person so required then has 21 days from the date of notice to comply (IA 1986, s.131(4); IR 1986, rule 4.32), unless released from the obligation by the Official Receiver or given an extension of time from the Official Receiver or by court order (IA 1986, s.131(5); IR 1986, rule 4.36).

The statement of affairs (in Form 4.17) must be sworn and verified by the deponents (a deponent being a person who makes a deposition or affidavit under oath); and the Official Receiver can require any person considered responsible (see IA 1986, s.131(3)) to submit an affidavit of concurrence, stating that he concurs with the statement of affairs (IR 1986, rule 4.33(2)(3)). The maker of the affidavit may qualify his agreement by making reference to anything he considers is erroneous or misleading, or in respect of which he does not have direct knowledge (IR 1986, rule 4.33(3)). The Official Receiver will file at Companies House the statement of affairs and any affidavit of concurrence (IR 1986, rule 4.33(6)).

A person who without reasonable excuse fails to comply with the requirements of any of the office holders to provide a statement of affairs commits an offence (IA 1986, Sched.10), punishable on indictment with an unlimited fine; on summary conviction, a maximum £5,000 fine and default rate of £500 per day.

Where the Official Receiver thinks that it may prejudice the conduct of the liquidation for the whole or part of the statement of affairs to be disclosed, he may apply to court for an order limiting disclosure in respect of the statement or any specified part of it (IR 1986, rule 4.35(1); see also Practice Direction: Insolvency Proceedings [2012] BCC 265). An order may be made that the statement or part of it may not be filed, may be filed separately or may not be open to inspection without leave of the court (IR 1986, rule 4.32(2)).

9.1.4 Resolutions to be passed at first creditors' meeting

At the first meeting of creditors, the only resolutions that can be taken concern the appointment of the liquidator(s), the establishment of a creditors' committee and, if no committee is established, the terms on which the liquidator is to be remunerated and/or the possibility of an adjournment of the meeting for no more than 14 days (IR 1986, rule 4.52(3A)). This rule is, however, capable of variation if the chairman of the meeting thinks there are special reasons why any other resolution should be allowed to be put to the creditors.

All creditors are entitled to attend the meeting (including prospective, future and contingent creditors), although as we shall see below, entitlement to vote at the meeting is subject to certain requirements. The meeting may be held where a quorum is present, which in the case of a creditors' meeting means the 'attendance' (whether actual, remotely (see below) or by proxy) of at least one creditor entitled to vote (IR 1986, rule 12A.21(2)).

While a director nominated to preside over the meeting will act as chairman, in practice the insolvency practitioner who has assisted in the calling of the meeting and who has been nominated by the company at the prior general meeting will conduct the meeting. He will explain to the attendees who he is and his role, introduce anyone else sitting 'on the top table', detail the purpose of the meeting and then report to the creditors on the reasons for the liquidation (which are usually set out in the report which accompanied the notice to creditors).

He will then report on and explain the details contained within the statement of affairs that is laid before the meeting. At this stage of the meeting, the insolvency practitioner will invite the attendees to ask questions of him or the directors. This can lead to boisterous exchanges, where possible allegations of directors' misconduct are aired and/or where a creditor may propose an alternative nomination as liquidator. The creditors, possibly with the assistance of an alternative insolvency practitioner, or by virtue of appointing the alternative insolvency practitioner as their proxy at the meeting, may through careful questioning of the directors imply that they are better placed to investigate the affairs of the company than the insolvency practitioner nominated by the company, and this may sway the meeting to make a different appointment. 'Taking an appointment from the floor' has become much less common, as creditors commonly appearing at meetings (such as HMRC) will be contacted beforehand and they will either have accepted the nomination or proposed an insolvency practitioner from their panel, prior to the meeting. As a result, in the majority of cases creditors' meetings are prosaic and lacking in incident, with little or no attendance by creditors, with the meeting swiftly moving on to its 'formal part', where the resolutions are put to the meeting.

9.1.5 Voting at first meeting of creditors

A creditor may vote at the meeting where:

(a)   it has lodged a proof of debt;

(b)   the chairman of the meeting has admitted the creditor's claim set out in the proof of debt for the purposes of entitlement to vote; and

(c)   a proxy has been lodged by the time and date stated in the notice of the meeting.

In the circumstances that the creditor's claim is unliquidated or unascertained, the chairman may agree to 'put upon the debt an estimated minimum value for the purposes of entitlement to vote' (see IR 1986, rule 4.67(3) and *Re Newlands (Seaford) Educational Trust* [2006] BPIR 1230, a case concerning creditor's claims within a proposed CVA). This does not mean that the chairman needs to obtain the creditors' consent to the estimated valuation, only that the claim is estimated at that time for a minimum sum which stands true for a particular sum. While the chairman may commonly agree a value of £1, this is not good practice where sufficient evidence is available to make a more appropriate valuation by means of legal/accounting advice (see *Doorbar* v. *Alltime Securities Ltd* [1995] BCC 1149).

A secured creditor is not entitled to vote at the creditors' meeting unless, after deducting the estimated value of its security from its debt, a balance is still due (IR 1986, rule 4.67(4)). The creditor may therefore be admitted for voting purposes in respect of its unsecured balance.

In the case of voluntary liquidation, the chairman has discretion as to whether to allow a creditor to vote even if it has failed to submit a proof, if he is satisfied that the failure was due to circumstances beyond the creditor's control (IR 1986, rule 4.68). The proof may also be in any form (IR 1986, rule 4.73(4)). Further details of the debt submitted on the proof may be requested (IR 1986, rule 4.75(3)).

At the meeting, the chairman also has the power to admit or reject (in whole or in part) the creditor's proof (IR 1986, rule 4.70(1)). If in doubt as to whether to admit the claim for voting purposes or not, the chairman may mark it as objected to but permit the creditor to vote, seeing whether this makes any difference to the passing of the resolution being proposed. Any decision made is only in regard to the creditor's ability to vote and is not binding for other purposes (such as the right to a distribution: see *Re Assico Engineering Ltd* [2002] BCC 481).

The decision of the chairman is subject to a right of appeal to a court within 21 days of the date of the meeting (IR 1986, rule 4.70(4A)). The court, on hearing the appeal, is not precluded from considering information that was not available to the chairman (*Re a Company (No.004539 of 1993)* [1995] BCC 116).

An aggrieved creditor (on this issue or indeed any other regarding the conduct of the liquidator) could also consider petitioning for the compulsory winding up of the company, although a court will give significant weight to the views of the majority creditors. In extreme cases, where the conduct of the appointed liquidator at the meeting is called into question, the creditor could apply to remove the liquidator by court order (IA 1986, s.171; see *Re Inside Sport Ltd* [2000] 1 BCLC 302). Alternatively, the creditor could apply to court for direction upon any issue arising in the winding up (IA 1986, s.112), although the court will always be reluctant to intervene on issues of commercial judgment or the exercise of any discretion by a professional, save in case of unfairness or injustice (*Re Palmer Marine Surveys Ltd* [1986] BCLC 106).

At the meeting of creditors, a resolution is passed when a majority (in value only) of those present and voting in person or by proxy have voted in favour (IR 1986, rule 4.63(1)). In the case of a resolution for the appointment of a liquidator where two nominees have been put forward, the insolvency practitioner with the majority of votes is appointed. Where three or more nominees are put forward, the insolvency practitioner with the clear majority over both, or all, is appointed, and in other cases the chairman of the meeting will continue to take votes (disregarding nominees who have withdrawn/obtained least support) until a clear majority is obtained for one nominee (IR 1986, rule 4.63(2)). It is possible, and indeed not uncommon, to put forward to the meeting a resolution for the joint appointment of two or more nominees (IR 1986, rule 4.62(3)). In such a case, whether by formal agreement or compromise after the meeting, the two liquidators may each take primary responsibility for one particular aspect of the liquidation, e.g. one may agree to realise the assets and make distributions to creditors, the other to investigate the affairs and take conduct of any antecedent transaction litigation.

At the meeting, the chairman may in his discretion suspend the meeting for up to one hour (IR 1986, rule 4.65). This power may be exercised where a meeting is threatening to be unhelpfully acrimonious, or where instructions need to be taken/advice received on any matters arising. If no quorum is present within 30 minutes of the appointed time of the meeting, the chairman may in his discretion adjourn the meeting to such time and place as he may appoint (IR 1986, rule 4.65(4); see also *Re Altitude Scaffolding Ltd* [2006] BCC 904 where it was held that the attendance of just one creditor was sufficient). This necessity can be avoided if, prior to the meeting, the chairman has received proxies for one or more creditors, appointing the chairman of the meeting. This proxy may be general, allowing the chairman to vote in accordance with the exercise of his discretion, or specific, nominating that the chairman votes in a particular way on any proposed resolutions. In such circumstances, the proxy holder/chairman can move to pass the requisite resolutions. The naming of an individual as proxy holder is not of significance and if another person attends in place of the named proxy holder and no objection is taken, the requirement to name the proxy holder by 12 pm the day before the meeting may be deemed waived (*Re Shruth* [2007] BCC 960). It is common to find that a corporate creditor may appoint as proxy a director/officer of the company, and in his absence the company's lawyer/accountant/an insolvency practitioner (who may even be willing to attend without a fee, if there is a chance to sway the meeting as outlined above), or if none of the above attend, the chairman.

Any adjournment of the meeting must be for no longer than 14 days unless the court orders otherwise (IR 1986, rule 4.52(3A)–(3C)).

At the first meeting and on any subsequent meeting, the chairman (and then liquidator) will cause minutes to be kept, along with a list of attending creditors and a record of any resolutions passed (IR 1986, rule 4.71).

Since 6 April 2010 (see the Legislative Reform (Insolvency) (Miscellaneous Provisions) Order 2010, SI 2010/18 and IA 1986, s.246A), it was made clear that, with retrospective effect, a meeting (other than a meeting of members of a company in respect of a solvent members' voluntary liquidation) may be held without the need for the physical presence of its participants.

The convener of the meeting may conduct the meeting in such a way that persons who are not present together at the same place may attend it (IA1986, s.246A(3)), allowing therefore the use of, *inter alia*, video-link, web-cam or telephone conferencing. The participants must be allowed the right to speak, communicate and vote, with the convener of the meeting needing to ensure that the mode of communication is appropriate, enables identification of the participants and is secure (IA 1986, s.246A(6)). The holding of a meeting in such a manner may only take place after due consideration of the legitimate interests of the creditors, members or contributories and others attending the meeting and in the efficient dispatch of the business of the meeting (IA 1986, s.246A(8)). Where the convener of the meeting decides not to specify a location for the meeting (i.e. where it is intended that every participant will take part in the meeting remotely), creditors holding at least 10 per cent in value of the company's debt can within seven business days of the date of notice require the convener to specify a place for the meeting (see also IR 1986, rule 12A.22). Members of a company have an equivalent right with regard to any meeting of members, although, as noted above, the ability to dispense with a physical meeting is not permitted in the case of a members' meeting in a members' voluntary liquidation (IA 1986, s.246A(1)(b)).

If during the course of the remote meeting a person becomes excluded (e.g. the video-link fails), the chairman of the meeting may continue, declare the meeting void, declare the meeting valid to that point and then adjourn the meeting. Where the meeting is continued, it is deemed valid unless there is a complaint from the excluded participant or someone is adversely affected by the exclusion (IR 1986, rule 12A.25), which the chairman decides invalidates the meeting, or where the court otherwise directs. The new rules thus allow the chairman to exercise discretion and consider whether prejudice has been caused and/or whether an appropriate remedy is available.

9.1.6 Liquidation committee and subsequent creditors' meetings

Following the initial creditors' meeting, the liquidator may seek to obtain the passing of further resolutions by the creditors. While further meetings of creditors can be held and/or conducted remotely as explained above, it is also possible to obtain any necessary further resolutions by correspondence without the need for a meeting.

Notice must be sent to every creditor and contributory entitled to vote. In order for votes to be counted, the vote must be lodged in writing by 12 pm on the closing day specified in the notice, and where a creditor has not already lodged a proof of debt it must do so at this time (IR 1986, rule 4.63A). The time for voting must be set not less than 14 days from the giving of notice (IR 1986, rule 4.63A(4)). At least one vote must be received in order for the resolution to be passed, and if none is received or 10 per cent of the creditors in value of the company's debt require (and give notice within five days of the notice for the resolution by correspondence), a meeting must be summoned.

Alternatively, either at the initial meeting or at any subsequent meeting, a creditors' committee may be established (IA 1986, s.101(1)), and it is to the committee that the liquidator may turn for guidance/to pass appropriate resolutions. The committee may consist of between three and five members. Any unsecured creditor of the company (which can be a body corporate) may be eligible to be a member of the committee, provided that they have lodged a proof and this has not been disallowed for voting purposes or wholly rejected for the purposes of distribution/dividend (IR 1986, rule 4.152(3)). The committee comes into being when the liquidator has issued a certificate of its due constitution (IR 1986, rule 4.153, Form 4.47).

It is common practice where a committee has been formed at the initial creditors' meeting for the first creditors' committee meeting to be held immediately afterwards. At this first meeting, the terms of engagement are established (the purpose of the committee, when it should meet, what it should determine, the treatment and use of confidential information coming into the hands of committee members). The liquidator will then report to the committee on all matters of concern to the creditors and advise the committee that it will have the right to request a report on matters arising in the winding up (unless the request is frivolous or unreasonable, the cost of compliance with the request is unreasonable or there are insufficient assets to enable the company to comply: IR 1986, rule 4.155). The first meeting must be held within six weeks of the committee being established (IR 1986, rule 4.156) and will then meet as agreed at a meeting, or on the request of a committee member (and be held within 21 days of such request).

A vacancy on the committee may be filled by the liquidator nominating a creditor prepared to act and agreed by the other members of the committee, or by a resolution at a subsequent meeting of creditors. A vacancy can arise after resignation by notice in writing (IR 1986, rule 4.160), or if the member becomes bankrupt, does not attend three consecutive meetings, ceases to be or is found never to have been a creditor, or is removed by resolution at a creditors' meeting (IR 1986, rule 4.162).

At a creditors' committee meeting, each member has one vote and resolutions are passed by simple majority. Copies of any resolutions passed must be retained. Resolutions that are commonly proposed may include those related to the powers of directors (IA 1986, s.103), the remuneration of the liquidator or the approval of certain litigation to be commenced by the liquidator (IA 1986, Sched.4, Part I, para.3A).

A member of the committee may not be involved in any transaction involving company assets without leave of the court and/or with permission of the remaining committee members (who are satisfied that due disclosure has been made: IR 1986, rule 4.170).

Creditors' committee meetings may also now be held remotely (see IA 1986, s.246A).

9.1.7 Liquidator's progress report

Until 6 April 2010 (see the Legislative Reform (Insolvency) (Miscellaneous Provisions) Order 2010, SI 2010/18), the liquidator was required to hold an annual creditors' meeting. This requirement has been replaced by an obligation to report to the creditors on an annual basis (IA 1986, s.104A). Included in the report are details regarding remuneration, expenses incurred, progress made and assets that remain to be realised, and a receipts and payments account (IR 1986, rules 4.49B, 4.49C(5)).

9.2 THE EFFECT OF LIQUIDATION

9.2.1 The status of the liquidator

On appointment of the liquidator, the powers of the directors, except so far as they are necessary for the holding of a general meeting, or where the liquidator consents, will cease. The company as a corporate entity continues until dissolution; consequently, the legal title to the property remains vested in the company and does not vest in the liquidator (this contrasts with the situation of a trustee in bankruptcy, where the bankrupt's property automatically vests in the trustee).

In compulsory winding up, the liquidator is an officer of the court and is therefore under a special duty to act fairly and honourably in dealing with persons who have adverse claims and must not merely stand on his rights at law or in equity (see *Ex p. James* (1873–74) LR 9 Ch App 609 (CA)). Irrespective of whether the winding up is voluntary or compulsory, every appointed liquidator must act in accordance with the purposes of the liquidation with impartiality and without any personal conflict of interest (see *Re Silver Valley Mines* (1882) LR 21 Ch D 381).

9.2.2 Effect upon the company's business

The liquidation process leads to the orderly and controlled determination of the company's life. Accordingly, the company will cease to carry on business except, in the case of voluntary liquidation, 'so far as may be required for its beneficial winding up' (IA 1986, s.87(1)); and in the case of compulsory liquidation, except 'so far as may be necessary for its beneficial winding up' (IA 1986, s.167(1)(a) and Sched.4, Part II, para.5) and only then with sanction of the court or the creditors' committee.

While little may turn on the different wording used in respect of voluntary and compulsory liquidation, it is perhaps recognition that in practice it is highly unlikely that on the making of a winding-up order, an Official Receiver will be ready and able to carry on the business of a company. Instead, where a creditor thinks that the extraction of some value from the trading business of the debtor company is possible, it is best advised to seek either the making of an administration order, or alternatively the appointment of a provisional liquidator.

In contrast, on appointment a voluntary liquidator might be better placed (and qualified) to continue running the business of the company, at least in the short term; this is recognised by the fact that 'the corporate state and corporate powers of the company, notwithstanding anything to the contrary in its articles, continue until the company is dissolved' (IA 1986, s.87(2)).

A liquidator may therefore keep a business running, e.g. in a retail business, shop premises may be kept open for a day or two to allow stock to be run down. However, often in practice the risks of bearing unconscionable costs/expenses by virtue of the operation of the 'salvage principle' (see *Lundy Granite Co.* (1870–71) LR 6 Ch App 462) are often considered by the liquidator as too high. As a result, where this is the case and/or where a sale of the company's business as a going concern is possible, the company would be better advised to seek the appointment of an administrator (IA 1986, Sched.B1, para.38).

It is beyond the power of a liquidator to carry on business with a view to restructuring and rescuing the company, and the liquidator may be restrained from doing so (*Re Wreck Recovery and Salvage Co.* (1880) LR 15 Ch D 353 (CA)).

As we shall see, however, the sometimes subtle differences between voluntary and compulsory liquidation continue in areas such as the status of employment contracts, the treatment of landlords and other legal proceedings (see **Chapter 13**), e.g. in voluntary liquidation, the liquidator generally has a discretion and has to take positive steps to determine legal relations; in contrast, in compulsory liquidation there is more likely to be an automatic cessation. These factors all have impact as to whether it is possible (and advisable) to keep the business trading after liquidation.

Despite the fact that a contract may be entered into after the date of liquidation, the liquidator enters such a contract for and on behalf of the company, and the liquidator will not be deemed personally liable unless he has (unusually) personally adopted the contract (*Re S Davis & Co. Ltd* [1945] Ch 402).

If a liquidator has a reasonable and genuine belief that the continuation of the company's business will be in the interests of its creditors, but ultimately he is mistaken in this belief and loss is caused, he will not incur liability (*Re Great Eastern Electric Co. Ltd* [1941] 1 All ER 409). This general rule, however, should be contrasted with *Re Centralcrest Engineering Ltd* [2000] BCC 727, where a liquidator carried on business without sanction of the court or creditor agreement and incurred liability for Crown debts after appointment that he was unable to discharge. In this case, the liquidator was found guilty of misfeasance.

It must also be remembered that the liabilities incurred by the liquidator for and on behalf of the company will be treated as necessary disbursements and therefore paid as costs and expenses of the liquidation (see IR 1986, rule 4.218(3)(b), (m)) and treated in priority to the liquidator's own remuneration. A liquidator will therefore undoubtedly be very cautious in determining whether to continue to trade during the liquidation.

9.2.3 Effect upon the management and control of the company

During the liquidation process, the liquidator exercises powers of management and control in respect of the company as set out in IA 1986, Sched.4 (see IA 1986, s.165(2)) and the additional powers in IA 1986, ss.165, 166 (IA 1986, s.167(1) regarding voluntary liquidation and s.168 regarding compulsory liquidation).

It is important to note that some powers may be exercised only with the sanction of the court or of a creditors' committee.

On the appointment of the liquidator in voluntary liquidation, all powers of the directors cease except so far as the liquidation committee, or the creditors (if no committee is formed), allow (IA 1986, s.103). This provision should be contrasted with the dicta that in compulsory liquidation directors are removed automatically from office (*Measures Brothers Ltd* v. *Measures* [1910] 2 Ch 248). Drawing the statutory provision and this dicta together, one can therefore conclude that in voluntary liquidation a director remains in office, but without power of control and management (see also IA 1986, s.91 and *Madrid Bank Ltd* v. *Bayley* (1866–67) LR 2 QB 37). In the case of administration, this issue can cause difficulty as statutory obligations continue for the directors. In voluntary liquidation there is less practical difficulty, as the insolvent company's/directors' duties are superseded by the liquidation, e.g. any requirement to report to Companies House is an obligation of the liquidator, etc. The effect of liquidation on the director as employee is considered in **13.4.3**.

9.2.4 Effect upon property of the company

As described above, despite the commencement of the liquidation process, the company as a distinct legal corporate entity does not cease to exist until dissolution. Dissolution of the company follows the liquidator concluding the winding up and sending notice of the same to Companies House. As a result, during the liquidation process the company continues to hold legal title to property; the property of the company does not vest in the liquidator (contrast this with individual insolvency and the vesting of a bankrupt's property in the trustee in bankruptcy: IA 1986, s.306).

A consequence of this is that the liquidator will realise the company's property for and on behalf of the company; the company (in liquidation) is regarded as the seller, not the liquidator. From a practical point of view, however, a liquidator may be a party to the sale and purchase agreement in a personal capacity solely to receive the benefit of covenants that he will not be treated as personally liable, etc.

It is possible for the liquidator of a company in voluntary liquidation, a contributory or creditor to apply to court for the vesting of assets in the liquidator's name (pursuant to IA 1986, s.112(1) being the provision which enables the liquidator to refer questions/seek directions from the court). This step might be taken so that the liquidator can bring or defend proceedings in his own name in respect of any particular asset. The reason for this is that security for costs could be ordered against the insolvent company but not the liquidator (*Re Strand Wood Co. Ltd* [1904] 2 Ch 1), although a liquidator would bear a risk of personal liability for costs of unsuccessful proceedings in such circumstances (*RBG Resources plc* v. *Rastogi* [2005] 2 BCLC 592).

The company's assets will be realised and the proceeds distributed to the creditors in a prescribed order of priority, and any surplus distributed to members (IA 1986, ss.107, 143). It is possible for the liquidator to transfer assets (*in specie*) to creditors should realisation be impractical or not cost-effective. However, until the assets are realised, distributed or abandoned the creditors have no right to the assets (legally or beneficially); the creditors' right is limited solely to having the assets administered by the liquidator in accordance with his statutory duty (*Banque Nationale de Paris plc* v. *Montman Ltd* [2000] 1 BCLC 576).

The resolution or order for winding up does, however, divest the company of its beneficial interest in its assets. They 'become a fund which the company thereafter holds on trust to discharge its liabilities' (per Lord Hoffmann in *Buchler* v. *Talbot; Re Leyland DAF Ltd* [2004] UKHL 9). The relationship between the company, acting through its liquidator, and its creditors has thus been described as a form of quasi-trust (*Lyall (P) and Sons Construction Co. Ltd* v. *Baker* [1933] OR 286).

The liquidator may, of course, also acquire control of third party assets, either assets held on trust by the company for third parties or, commonly, goods subject to retention of title. The liquidator takes no better title to assets than that held by the company; as a result, such assets are not available to be realised for the benefit of the creditors.

9.2.5 Effect on creditors

Liquidation is a collective insolvency process binding on all unsecured creditors, ensuring, subject to specific exemptions, that creditors of a particular class are treated on a *pari passu* basis and that the interests of the creditors as a whole are protected (*Re Aro Co. Ltd* [1980] 2 WLR 453). As we shall see, there are a host of statutory provisions to ensure that individual creditors do not 'steal a march' or unfairly benefit once the winding-up process has commenced.

In addition, as we shall see in **Chapter 13**, there are also statutory provisions that guard against certain transactions entered into prior to the commencement of the liquidation that have the effect of preferring one creditor over other creditors as a whole, which can lead to the setting aside of such transactions (IA 1986, s.239).

Proceedings against the company by creditors are not automatically stayed in a creditors' voluntary liquidation and the creditor may proceed to judgment. It is, however, open for the liquidator, member or creditor to apply to restrain the continuation of proceedings (IA 1986, s.112) after satisfying the court that there is good reason for the stay (*Anglo-Baltic and Mediterranean Bank* v. *Barber & Co.* [1924] 2 KB 410). It is usual practice for the court to stay any enforcement action (see *Anglo-Baltic and Mediterranean Bank*), but the court will guard against any stay which has the purpose of stifling claims against the directors of the company (*Re J Burrows (Leeds) Ltd* [1982] 2 All ER 882).

In the case of a compulsory winding up, or where a provisional liquidator is appointed, no action or proceeding may be proceeded with or commenced against the company or its property except by leave of the court and thereafter subject to such terms that the court may impose (IA 1986, s.130(2)).

The phrase 'action or proceeding' is widely interpreted by the courts and has included counterclaims (*Langley Constructions (Brixham) Ltd* v. *Wells* [1969] 1 WLR 503), distress and other forms of execution, and even criminal prosecutions (*R.* v. *Dickson* [1991] BCC 719).

Where proceedings have erroneously continued after commencement, permission can be obtained retrospectively (*Re Linkrealm Ltd* [1998] BCC 478).

The court in exercise of its discretion (see Jonathan Parker LJ in *New Cap Reinsurance Corp.* v. *HIH Casualty & General Insurance Ltd* [2002] 2 BCLC 228) has great freedom to consider what is right and fair in all the circumstances of the case. The court will thus generally weigh up whether the matter can best be resolved in the liquidation process, such as by submission of proof of debt and determination of the claim by the liquidator (*Re Exchange Securities and Commodities Ltd* [1983] BCLC 186), although it will not look into the merits of the claim in carrying out this exercise (*Re BCCI (No.4)* [1994] 1 BCLC 419). As a result, most claims are dealt with by the proof of debt procedure, negotiation and, if necessary, challenge to the liquidator's determination, rather than the more costly commencement or continuation of existing legal processes. The applicant will thus generally need to show that the usual process of proving in the liquidation is not an adequate remedy (e.g. alleged trespass by the company: see *Re Wyley* v. *Exhall Coal Mining Co. Ltd* (1864) 33 Beav 538, 55 ER 478). In granting leave, the court may impose such conditions as it thinks fit (*Re Marine Investment Co. Ltd* (1868) 17 LT 535).

As we shall see below, the position of a secured creditor on liquidation of a debtor company is radically different from that of an unsecured creditor. Accordingly, if the secured creditor wishes to take proceedings to realise its security then, save for good reason, leave will be granted (*Lloyd* v. *David Lloyd & Co.* (1877) LR 6 Ch D 339; *Re Swissair* v. *Edwards* [2003] BCC 361; and *Tradegro (UK) Ltd* v. *Wigmore Street Investments Ltd* [2011] 2 BCLC 616, the latter two cases turning on whether the creditor possessed a secured interest).

After the presentation of any winding-up petition, but before the winding-up order is made, the company or creditor or contributory may apply to the court for a stay of any action or proceeding (IA 1986, s.126). This is an important power which can prevent creditors attempting to engineer a better position for themselves than would otherwise be the case in the winding up and covers existing litigation and enforcement procedures, including steps to distrain (*Re Memco Engineering Ltd* [1985] 3 WLR 875).

9.2.6 Effect upon secured creditors' interests

A 'secured creditor' is defined as one who holds, in respect of his debt, a security over property of the company (IA 1986, s.248(a); and see *Re Hallett & Co., ex p. Cocks, Biddulph & Co.* [1894] 2 QB 256 which confirmed that the security must be over property of the company and not over a third party's assets). 'Security' is defined as any 'mortgage, charge, lien or other security' (IA 1986, s.248(b)).

The following are examples of an interest possessed by a 'creditor' which is not to be regarded as a secured interest:

- A guarantee of a company's debt by a third party, whether or not secured over that third party's assets, is not security over the company's property (*Pearce* v. *Bullard, King & Co.* [1908] 1 Ch 780).
- An interest in a payment made into a fund pending the outcome of litigation unless expressly provided (see *Re Swissair* v. *Edwards* [2003] BCC 361 regarding a payment made into a joint account of the litigants to discharge a freezing injunction and *Tradegro (UK) Ltd* v. *Wigmore Street Investments Ltd* [2011] 2 BCLC 616 regarding money paid as so-called 'security for costs').
- A creditor owed monies under a hire purchase agreement or leasing agreement.
- A creditor holding a valid retention of title, as such a party, remains the owner of the property in the hands of the company.
- A landlord's right to distrain for rent/right to re-enter, etc. (*Re Park Air Services* [2000] 2 AC 172).

See **13.4.1** for further details of how such creditors exercise rights over the company.

Where a creditor is a secured creditor, the creditor is effectively treated as being outside the winding-up process and can exercise such rights and interests (e.g. enforcement) as provided for within the security. It is for this reason that the company may consider administration to be a more effective remedy, as it stays a secured creditor's rights of enforcement while allowing a plan of reconstruction to be drawn up and agreed. It should, however, be remembered that the administrator cannot overreach the security, without consent or court order.

Where a company is in compulsory liquidation, enforcement proceedings still require permission of the court (IA 1986, s.130(2)) and it is questionable whether leave can be granted retrospectively (see *Re Saunders; Bristol and West Building Society* v. *Saunders* [1997] Ch 60 where retrospective leave was granted but the rationale for it was subsequently questioned by the majority of the House of Lords in *Seal* v. *Chief Constable of South Wales Police* [2007] 1 WLR 1910).

Where a secured creditor holds a floating charge, the commencement of liquidation will cause a crystallisation of the charge, although an earlier event such as ceasing to carry on business may have the same effect (*Re Woodroffes (Musical Instruments) Ltd* [1986] Ch 366). However, this does not give the floating charge holder priority over preferential creditors and/or avoid the relevant insolvency provisions (IA 1986, s.172A), as a floating charge is defined as one which 'as created' was a floating charge (IA 1986, s.251). It should also be remembered that a floating charge created within 12 months (in the case of an unconnected party) or 24 months (in the case of a connected party) of the onset of insolvency may be held to be invalid, except to the extent that 'fresh' consideration was provided to the company at the time of or after creation of the charge (IA 1986, s.245) (see **5.3.3** for full details).

A secured creditor is entitled to prove for his debt in the liquidation but is not obliged to. The secured creditor may, however, realise the value of his security and prove for the balance of his debt, or alternatively surrender his security for the benefit of all of the creditors and prove for his entire debt (IR 1986, rule 4.88).

Where, after valuation, the secured creditor goes on to realise his security, he must substitute the value obtained and prove for the balance (IR 1986, rule 4.99); until such time, the valuation can be altered by agreement of the liquidator or permission of the court (IR 1986, rule 4.84). In compulsory liquidation, permission of the court is required for revaluation where the secured creditor is the petitioning creditor for the winding up or where the creditor has voted in respect of the unsecured balance (IR 1986, rule 4.95).

Importantly however, a secured creditor who proves for the debt but fails to disclose his security is deemed to have surrendered his security, save where the creditor satisfies the court that the failure was an inadvertent (accidental) or honest mistake (see IR 1986, rule 4.96 and *Re Henry Lister & Co. Ltd* [1892] 2 Ch 417; see also *LCP Retail Ltd* v. *Segal* [2007] BCC 584 where the failure to disclose the 'quasi-security' of a walking possession agreement under a landlord's distraint notice was fatal).

The liquidator may at any time give 28 days' notice to the secured creditor that he intends to redeem the security at the value provided for in the proof (IR1986, rule 4.97). The creditor then has 21 days to revalue the security, if necessary with court permission. Conversely, a secured creditor can serve notice of election on the liquidator, requiring the liquidator to elect whether or not he will redeem the security at the value placed upon it within three months (IR 1986, rule 4.97(4)).

Where the liquidator is dissatisfied with the valuation placed upon the security, the liquidator may require the property to be offered for sale, on terms to be agreed between liquidator and creditor or as the court directs, and if the sale is by auction both liquidator and creditor may bid (IR 1986, rule 4.98).

As can been seen from the interplay between IA 1986 and IR 1986, a secured creditor must therefore think carefully about any position it wishes to take in the winding up. For a secured creditor with subservient ranking security and little prospect of realisation, the election to surrender may be appropriate in order to receive a potential dividend in the liquidation, possibly to share in the spoils of claims brought by the liquidator as office holder (see e.g. IA 1986, ss.213, 214, 238,

239), which should be contrasted with 'company' claims, which are capable of being secured assets (see *Oasis Merchandising Services Ltd* [1997] 2 WLR 764).

It should be noted, however, that in practice a liquidator's power to challenge the value placed on the security and/or to take control of secured assets is one rarely exercised. The reasons for this may be pragmatic, e.g. in recent times companies have tended to be highly geared, meaning that there are few assets not subject to security and those assets that are charged are fully leveraged with no available equity for the unsecured creditors (and liquidator); and/or falling valuations mean a reduction in possible returns. Also, the insolvency profession works closely and almost continually with the banking industry, meaning that the fostering of a long-term working relationship militates against regular disputes and challenges.

In the case of an ongoing liquidation, a secured creditor with security created before 15 September 2003 retains a right to appoint an administrative receiver. Although administrative receivership is not a collective insolvency process, it is very often the beginning of the process which will lead to the winding up of the company. As a result, after an administrative receiver has completed his duties, it is likely that the company will enter into liquidation.

As the appointment of a receiver over property subject to a fixed charge is an enforcement remedy against the secured property and not against the debtor company, it is possible for a liquidator and receiver to be in office at the same time.

It should be noted, however, that where the security is created post-15 September 2003, there is no ability to appoint an administrator (who of course takes over the control and management of the company) by an out-of-court route, where the company is already in liquidation. As a consequence, notice of intended voluntary winding up must be provided to secured creditors, who may exercise their right to appoint an administrator (IA 1986, s.84(2A)). Should they fail to appoint an administrator within five days of notice and the company passes into liquidation, the secured creditor may only place the company into administration by application to the court.

9.2.7 Effect upon company's contractual agreements

As set out in **9.2.1** in regard to the company's ability to trade post liquidation, contracts entered into by the company prior to liquidation are not automatically terminated by reason of the company's liquidation. The termination of the contract will entirely depend upon the terms of the agreement, i.e. the contract may provide that in the event of insolvency the contract automatically determines, or it may give the innocent party the right to terminate (e.g. a lease will often give the landlord a right to forfeit the lease on the tenant's liquidation). However, it should be remembered that a company in liquidation is unlikely to be able to perform its contractual obligations and, consequently, the contracting party may well be able to show that the insolvent company is in breach of contract and seek to terminate/rescind the agreement. In certain circumstances, a contracting party may argue that by commencing a winding-up process the company is in anticipatory breach of contract

(*Sale Continuation Ltd* v. *Austin Taylor & Co. Ltd* [1967] 2 All ER 1092). Each case must be assessed on its own merits by reference to the terms of the contract.

It should, however, be borne in mind that a liquidator possesses the power to disclaim the company's interest in an unprofitable contract (IA 1986, s.178(3)) as being 'onerous property' (see **9.3.4** for full details).

The right to disclaim is exercised by the giving of notice in the prescribed form, and the liquidator may do so notwithstanding having taken possession of the property, endeavoured to sell it or otherwise exercised rights of ownership in relation to it (IR 1986, rule 4.187, Form 4.53A). The liquidator is not, however, entitled to disclaim a contract merely because it is disadvantageous, or because a better bargain could have been made (see *Re Bastable, ex p. Trustee* [1901] 2 KB 518; and the Australian authority *Transmetro Corporation Ltd* v. *Real Investments Pty Ltd* [1999] 17 ACLC 1314, cited with approval by Chadwick LJ in *Re SSSL Realisations Ltd; Squires* v. *AIG Europe UK Ltd* [2006] BCC 233). The purpose of the statutory power of disclaimer is to enable swift and efficient realisation of property in order to effect the winding up of the company, and while the ability to disclaim is now exercised outside the court and is in the exercise of the discretion of the liquidator, in the event of challenge the court will weigh up whether the performance of future obligations under the contract would be detrimental to the creditors and prejudicial in realising assets (*Re SSSL Realisations Ltd*).

9.2.8 Effect on directors

During the course of the winding up, the liquidator is under a duty to investigate the cause of the company's failure and whether the conduct of the directors has contributed to its failure and caused loss. Despite limited liability status afforded to the majority of companies, in the event of liquidation there are various statutory and common law remedies available to the company and the liquidator which can lead to the imposition of personal liability on individuals to compensate the company and/or its creditors. As a consequence, in addition to the public policy considerations which attach to this duty (e.g. the need to report to the Official Receiver *vis-à-vis* possible CDDA 1986 proceedings), the liquidator will have regard to whether causes of action against the directors and/or third parties may have the effect of swelling the available assets for the creditors of the company. See **Chapter 13** for full details.

As discussed in **9.2.3**, the powers and duties of the directors will cease on liquidation unless there is express delegation by the liquidator back to the directors. The contract of employment of an executive director is not automatically terminated on a voluntary liquidation, although this may be the practical effect of cessation of business, giving rise to a claim for wrongful dismissal (breach of contract, failure to provide notice, etc.). In the case of compulsory liquidation, the executive directors, like all employees, are deemed dismissed, although in the case of creditors' voluntary liquidation, dismissal (deemed or otherwise) will depend on the circumstances (see as to the effect upon employees, below).

The liquidator's powers of investigation are considered in **9.4.3**, while actions that could be commenced against directors and third parties are considered in **11.5**.

9.2.9 Effect on employees

In the case of compulsory liquidation, the contracts of employees are automatically terminated. As a result, on liquidation an employee is likely to have a claim against the company for unfair dismissal and/or wrongful dismissal and/or arrears of wages/other benefits. The position of employees is considered in detail in **13.4.3**.

A brief summary of their position is as follows.

- Where a compulsory winding-up order is made, this is deemed to constitute notice of termination of the employee's contract of employment (see *Gosling* v. *Gaskell* [1897] AC 575). The employee is entitled to claim for wrongful dismissal (breach of contract) as against the company as an unsecured creditor. Certain claims are treated as preferential and where the employer is insolvent and unable to meet certain claims, payment can be sought from the National Insurance Fund.

- Where the company enters into creditors' voluntary liquidation, it is not necessarily the case that contracts of employment are terminated (see *Fowler* v. *Commercial Timber Co. Ltd* [1930] 2 KB 1). However, it could be the case that the employee's contract expressly provides that a resolution to wind up the company or a likely cessation of business would amount to a repudiatory breach. Even if the contract survives, on cessation of business there will be a wrongful termination of all contracts of employment still in force.

As we have seen, it is possible for the liquidator to continue the business (IA 1986, s.87(1)) for its beneficial winding up and in doing so he may offer the employees continued employment. However, this is better viewed as the cessation of employment followed by a new offer from the liquidator (which can be rejected or accepted) for an agreed period on whatever terms are agreed. Such liabilities as arise under these agreed terms and conditions will be treated as costs and expenses of the liquidation (see *Golding and Howard* v. *Fire, Auto and Marine Insurance Co. Ltd* [1968] 3 ITR 372).

9.3 THE FUNCTIONS AND POWERS OF A LIQUIDATOR

The liquidator's role is to wind up the affairs of the company in an orderly and fair manner in accordance with the statutory provisions as set out in IA 1986 and the accompanying Rules (see IA 1986, s.143(1) which sets out the function of a liquidator in compulsory liquidation and IA 1986, s.107 in respect of voluntary liquidation).

The powers granted to a liquidator to enable him to fulfil his function to collect in and realise the company's available assets and make distributions to creditors are listed in IA 1986, Sched.4 and are divided between those exercisable with or without sanction of the creditors; the numbering of each of the powers as set out in IA 1986, Sched.4 is adopted in the discussion below.

9.3.1 Powers exercisable with sanction in any winding up

In a creditors' voluntary winding up, sanction is required from the court or the creditors' committee, or, if no committee is formed, consent is required from the creditors in general meeting (by simple majority); in a members' voluntary winding up, sanction by the members is obtained by special resolution (IA 1986, s.165(2)).

In the case of compulsory liquidation, sanction is required from the court or the creditors' committee. If no committee is formed, and where the liquidator is not the Official Receiver, consent of the Secretary of State is required (IA 1986, ss.167(1), 141(5)). In practice, this power is exercised by the Official Receiver/Insolvency Service and is a reminder of the greater intervention and supervision imposed on a court-led compulsory liquidation process.

The following powers (numbered as per IA 1986, Sched.4) are exercisable with sanction:

1. *Power to pay any class of creditors in full.*

    It should, however, be noted that the liquidator has a duty to pay the preferential creditors pursuant to IA 1986, s.175. As a result, it is the view of the Insolvency Service (see *Dear IP*, ch.17(2), available at **http:// www.insolvencydirect.bis.gov.uk/insolvencyprofessionandlegislation/ dearip/dearipindex.htm**) that court sanction is not required in order to pay the preferential creditors ahead of other creditors.

2. *Power to make any compromise, or arrangement with creditors or persons claiming to be creditors, or having or alleging to have any claim (present or future, certain or contingent, ascertained or sounding only in damages) against the company, or whereby the company may be rendered liable.*

    This power allows a liquidator to depart from the usual priority of distribution or *pari passu* basis by scheme or compromise, if it is something the company could have done itself (*Re BCCI (No.3)* [1993] BCLC 1490). This compromise may be with a group of creditors or with one individual creditor.

3A. *Power to bring legal proceedings under IA 1986, ss.213, 214, 238, 239, 242, 243 or 423.*

    It should be noted that as the corporate status of the company continues despite liquidation (IA 1986, s.87(2)), the liquidator will bring legal actions for and on behalf of the company, in the name of the company, e.g. 'X Ltd (in Liquidation)'. However, where the action is brought by the liquidator (or office holder) pursuant to powers devolved upon the office holder by the terms of the statute, then the claim should be in the office holder's own name, e.g. 'A

Smith (Liquidator of X Ltd (in Liquidation))' (see *Re Cosslett Contractors Ltd (No. 2); Smith* v. *Bridgend Borough Council* [2001] BCC 740).

9.3.2 Powers exercisable without sanction in voluntary winding up, with sanction in compulsory winding up

The following powers are exercisable without sanction in a voluntary winding up, with sanction in a compulsory winding up:

4. *Power to bring or defend any action or other legal proceedings in the name and on behalf of the company.*

   Although acting for and on behalf of the company, where a liquidator takes proceedings in the name of the company it is possible that he may incur personal liability (see *Walker* v. *Walker* [2005] BPIR 454 regarding the discontinuance of proceedings) or be subject to a non-party costs order (*Aiden Shipping Co. Ltd* v. *Interbulk Ltd* [1986] AC 965). As a result, the liquidator will need to think very carefully about the commencement or continuation of any legal proceedings. While in voluntary liquidation legal proceedings are not stayed (contrasting with the situation in compulsory liquidation), it is often the case that the liquidator will seek to negotiate with the potential creditor or debtor rather than proceed with litigation.

   It is also open to the liquidator to seek to realise value from causes of action vesting in the company, although, it should be noted, not from those vesting in the liquidator, see e.g. IA 1986, ss.214, 238 and 239 (*Re Oasis Merchandising Services Ltd* [1997] 2 WLR 764). This ability is viewed as an extension of the liquidator's statutory power to sell company property and the usual fetters on the dealing in causes of action (public policy reasons meaning that such arrangements are viewed as champertous) do not apply. The liquidator must, however, exercise this power cautiously, taking proper expert (legal) opinion on value. The liquidator as an officer of court also has a duty to act fairly and reasonably and not simply rely on the letter of the law (the so-called 'rule in *Ex parte James*' (1873–74) LR 9 Ch App 609 (CA)). Accordingly, he must also guard against assigning an unmeritorious cause of action for little or no payment, where the likelihood is that the claimant (perhaps a former director) is impecunious and will cause significant nuisance value to the defendant, particularly in circumstances where an assignment of the cause of action has not been offered to the defendant (see *Hopkins* v. *TL Dallas Group Ltd* [2005] 1 BCLC 543).

5. *Power to carry on the business of the company, so far as may be necessary for its beneficial winding up.*

   On the commencement of the winding up, the company in the case of voluntary liquidation will cease to carry on business, except so far as may be required for its beneficial winding up (IA 1986, s.87(1)); or as far as may be necessary for its beneficial winding up in the case of compulsory liquidation (IA 1986, s.167(1)(a)). It should be noted, therefore, that the liquidator thus has the 'power' to carry on business. However, the power should not be exercised simply because it is of benefit to the company, i.e. simply to make a profit or to wait and see if a valuable permission is obtained (*Re Wreck Recovery and Salvage Co.* (1880) LR 15 Ch D 353). It must be to assist in the winding up, e.g. to allow for the better realisation of the company's assets. However, if the liquidator in good faith takes the view that it is beneficial for the winding up for the company to continue to trade, the court will not interfere, even if subsequently this view is shown to be mistaken (*Re Great Eastern Electric Co. Ltd* [1941] Ch 241).

This decision is therefore a matter for the liquidator's judgment, but in practice seldom leads to 'trading' liquidations. It should be remembered that if it is anticipated that the assets and business of the company can be disposed of on a going concern basis, then it is almost certain that administration will be the better process to pursue.

9.3.3 Powers exercisable without sanction in any winding up

The following powers are exercisable without sanction in any winding up:

6. *Power to sell any of the company's property by public auction or private contract, with power to transfer the whole of it to any person or to sell the same in parcels.*

    The liquidator has a wide power to sell or transfer company property in such manner as he thinks fit. In practice, the liquidator is likely to appoint agents to value the property and they will then market the assets on his behalf.

    The court will not interfere with a sale by a liquidator provided he acts in good faith, with no possible fraud and in a not wholly unreasonable manner (see *Leon* v. *York-o-Matic Ltd* [1966] 1 WLR 1450 and *Harold M. Pitman & Co.* v. *Top Business Systems (Nottingham) Ltd* (1985) 1 BCC 99 for two unsuccessful challenges to proposed sales). This follows the consistent approach of the court not to interfere readily in the exercise of a liquidator's reasonable commercial judgment.

    As commented on above, the express power to sell company property gives rise to an exemption from the rules of champerty (*Empire Resolution Ltd* v. *MPW Insurance Brokers Ltd* [1999] BPIR 486) and provides an ability to sell and assign causes of action vesting in the company.

6A. *Power to compromise on such terms as agreed (a) all calls and liabilities to calls, all debts and liabilities capable of resulting in debts and all claims (present or future, certain or contingent, ascertained or sounding only in damages) subsisting or supposed to subsist between the company and a contributory or alleged contributory or other debtor or person apprehending liability to the company; and (b) subject to IA 1986, Sched.4, Part I, para.2 (listed as 2 above), all questions in any way relating to or affecting the assets or the winding up of the company, and to take any security for the discharge of any such call, debt, liability or claim and give a complete discharge in respect of it.*

This power was inserted by virtue of the Legislative Reform (Insolvency) (Miscellaneous Provisions) Order 2010, SI 2010/18 as from 6 April 2010. Prior to this date, the power to compromise debts and liabilities was one exercisable only with sanction.

7. *Power to do all acts and execute, in the name and on behalf of the company, all deeds, receipts and other documents and for that purpose to use, when necessary, the company's seal.*

In most instances, the liquidator will act in the name of the company, by reason of the fact that it is the company's property being dealt with and such property is not vested in the liquidator. In addition, a liquidator will not become personally liable for any contracts provided that he makes it clear that he is entering into the contract as agent of the company (*Stead, Hazel & Co.* v. *Cooper* [1933] 1 KB 840).

8. *Power to prove, rank and claim in the bankruptcy, insolvency or sequestration of any contributory for any balance against his estate, and to receive dividends in the bankruptcy, insolvency or sequestration in respect of that balance, as a separate debt due from the bankrupt or insolvent, and rateably with the other separate creditors.*

9. *Power to draw, accept, make and endorse any bill of exchange or promissory note in the name and on behalf of the company, with the same effect with respect to the company's liability as if the bill or note had been drawn, accepted, made or endorsed by or on behalf of the company in the course of its business.*

10. *Power to raise on the security of the assets of the company any money requisite.*

While it is possible for the liquidator to borrow money, secured against the assets of the liquidation estate, it would be an unusual step, affording the lender 'super' priority over other creditors by virtue of the fact that the cost of borrowing will be viewed as a cost and expense of the liquidation. It could, however, be used to unlock equity in company property that might discharge creditor claims (where the company was insolvent on a cash flow test but not a balance sheet test), but it is more likely that in such circumstances administration and/or a CVA may offer a better procedure to effect such a rescue. In creating security, a liquidator cannot overreach or grant priority over an existing secured creditor (*Re Regent's Canal Ironworks Co.* (1876) LR 3 Ch D 411).

11. *Power to take out in his official name letters of administration to any deceased contributory, and to do in his official name any other act necessary for obtaining payment of any money due from a contributory or his estate which cannot conveniently be done in the name of the company.*

In all such cases the money due is deemed, for the purpose of enabling the liquidator to take out the letters of administration or recover the money, to be due to the liquidator himself.

12. *Power to appoint an agent to do any business which the liquidator is unable to do himself.*

In addition to legal representation, a liquidator may find it necessary to appoint valuers, surveyors and marketing agents. It is also possible that the liquidator of a trading business may employ managing agents to assist in the running and winding down of the business. This may also be needed where the winding up of the business requires specialist skills or the liquidator finds it more efficient to outsource. Specialist firms have grown up to assist insolvency practitioners dealing in areas such as the retail trade, licensed trade, hotels and care homes.

13. *Power to do all such other things as may be necessary for winding up the company's affairs and distributing its assets.*

As can be seen, the powers that a liquidator possesses are extremely widely drawn but this last provision acts as a 'catch all'. However, if there is any doubt whether an act is or is not within the liquidator's powers, an application for court direction should be considered (*Re Banque des Marchands de Moscou* [1953] 1 All ER 278).

9.3.4 Power to disclaim onerous property

The liquidator may, on the giving of prescribed notice (see IR 1986, rule 4.187, Form 4.53A), disclaim onerous property (IA 1986, s.178). This is an important power which enables the liquidator to wind up the affairs of the company more quickly and efficiently, in the interests of the creditors as a whole. It is a power unique to the liquidator and is not available to an administrator, a receiver or a supervisor of a voluntary arrangement.

The power to disclaim may be exercised notwithstanding any steps taken by the liquidator to take possession of the property, sell it or otherwise exercise rights of ownership in relation to it (IA 1986, s.178(2)).

Onerous property for the purposes of the section (IA 1986, s.178(3)) means:

(a) any unprofitable contract;
(b) any other property of the company which is unsaleable;
(c) any property not readily saleable; or
(d) any property that may give rise to a liability to pay money or perform any other onerous act.

While 'property' in the context of insolvency is widely defined (IA 1986, s.436), the issue as to whether property is 'onerous' requires a subjective assessment on the part of the liquidator, as does the question as to whether a contract is deemed unprofitable. It should be noted, however, that this power of disclaimer is not unfettered and property may not be disclaimed simply because such disclaimer is more beneficial to the insolvent estate (*Re Bastable, ex p. Trustee* [1901] 2 KB 518), nor may a contract be disclaimed simply because it represents a poor bargain or is financially disadvantageous to the company. Instead, it must be of a nature which prevents the realisation of assets and the payment of a dividend to creditors within a reasonable period (*Re SSSL Realisations Ltd; Squires* v. *AIG Europe UK Ltd* [2006] BCC 233). The most common example of the continuation of a contractual obligation preventing ready winding up of the company's affairs is continuing a (possibly long-term) lease of property that is incapable of assignment (and realisation) by the liquidator.

The disclaimer must contain such particulars of the property as to enable it to be easily identified and must be authenticated and dated by the liquidator (IR 1986, rule 4.187(1) and (2)).

The disclaimer operates so as to determine from the date of disclaimer the rights, interests and liabilities of the company in or in respect of the property disclaimed, but does not, except so far as is necessary for the purposes of releasing the company from any liability, affect the rights or liabilities of any other person (IA 1986, s.178(4)). The effect of this is that, save where a vesting order is made (see below), the disclaimed property will vest in the Crown *bona vacantia*. As a result, the property interest itself and rights flowing from that do not cease to exist, so e.g. a charge over disclaimed freehold property or leases created out of disclaimed freehold property continue to be effective (*Scmlla Properties Ltd* v. *Gesso Properties (BVI) Ltd* [1995] BCC 793). The disclaimer will also, as far as possible, not affect third party rights; the liability of a guarantor or a surety for future liabilities under a lease will continue despite disclaimer (*Hindcastle Ltd* v. *Barbara Attenborough Associates Ltd* [1997] AC 70; *Shaw* v. *Doleman* [2009] BCC 730).

There is no time limit on when a liquidator may in the exercise of his discretion disclaim onerous property, save where an interested party has served a notice of election upon the liquidator requiring the liquidator to state whether he will or will not disclaim; in such a case the liquidator has 28 days in which to disclaim (or such longer period as the court may allow), otherwise the power to disclaim is lost (IA 1986, s.178(5)). This notice may be delivered personally, electronically or by a means which enables proof of receipt (IR 1986, rule 4.191A).

On signing and dating the notice of disclaimer, the liquidator must send a copy to the Registrar of Companies and in the case of registered land to HM Land Registry (IR 1986, rule 4.187(3A)).

Within seven business days, the liquidator must send or give copies of the notice:

(a) in the case of leasehold property, to every underlessee or mortgagee of whom the liquidator is aware;

(b) to any person claiming an interest in the disclaimed property;

(c) to any person under a liability in respect of the property which is not being discharged by the disclaimer;

(d) in the case of an unprofitable contract, to every party to the contract or party who may have an interest under it (IR 1986, rule 4.188); and

(e) to any person who in the liquidator's opinion, as a matter of public interest or otherwise, should be informed (IR 1986, rule 4.189).

Where the liquidator is unsure as to whether a party has an interest in the property, he may serve notice on that person calling him to declare within 14 days whether he claims an interest. Failure to respond will entitle the liquidator to assume that the person has no interest (IR 1986, rule 4.192).

Since 6 April 2010 (see the Legislative Reform (Insolvency) (Miscellaneous Provisions) Order 2010, SI 2010/18), the liquidator no longer needs to file notice of disclaimer at court and then serve an endorsed copy of the disclaimer on interested parties. Instead, the liquidator must, as stated above, file notice at Companies House (and HM Land Registry if appropriate) and must keep records on whom he has served and the dates on which he has served notice (IR 1986, rule 4.190A).

Any person who by operation of the disclaimer suffers loss and damage is entitled to prove in the winding up as a creditor for that loss (IA 1986, s.178(6)). The method of calculating loss and damage was examined in the context of the disclaimer of a long lease by a liquidator in a solvent members' voluntary liquidation (*Re Park Air Services plc* [2000] 2 AC 172). In this case, the House of Lords held that in place of the right under the lease for future rent, on disclaimer the landlord/claimant instead had a statutory right of compensation calculated on the same basis as if there had been a wrongful termination of the contract, i.e. damages. Accordingly, a careful and detailed consideration was required as to whether the premises could be re-let and at what rate, whether repairs were necessary, what costs were associated with re-letting, the benefit of accelerated receipt and indeed whether a vesting order should be made.

Leasehold property and vesting orders

A disclaimer of leasehold property will not take effect until 14 days after the last notice was served upon any every person claiming to be an underlessee or mortgagee of the property (IA 1986, s.179).

This is important, as unlike a lease created out of a freehold which continues to exist post disclaimer, an underlease is destroyed on disclaimer of the lease. As a result, the underlessee has a right of continuing occupation for the duration of the sublease only if he is willing to pay the rent reserved and perform the covenants in the disclaimed head lease (*Re AE Realisations (1985) Ltd* [1988] 1 WLR 200). In such an instance, the underlessee has 14 days in which to apply for a vesting order to be made in his favour or such other relief as the court thinks fit (IA 1986, ss.179, 181, 182).

A vesting order cannot be made which makes the landlord subject to or having the benefit of existing underleases; the interests of all parties who could obtain an interest in the property must be cleared away before a vesting order can be made (*Re ITM Corp. Ltd (in Liquidation)* [1997] BCC 554).

Where a mortgagee has failed to apply for a vesting order, on disclaimer the leasehold interest becomes effectively ownerless and it is at risk that the landlord of the property will have taken possession and will prevent any enforcement of security by appointment of a receiver. Accordingly, where the mortgagee considers that the leasehold property has some realisable value to the mortgagee (if not to the liquidator/original tenant company), it is usual to come to some arrangement with the landlord (to pay the rent, etc.) while marketing the property.

The vesting of the lease will be on the same terms and be subject to the same liabilities and obligations as applied to the original tenant, meaning that, unless the court orders otherwise, the applicant will be liable to the landlord for the tenant's breaches/defaults prior to winding up. In every case, the applicant will bear the liability for defaults between the date of liquidation and the date of the vesting order (*Re Walker, ex p. Mills* (1895) 64 LJQB 783).

In the past, a landlord on tenant insolvency would generally want the property back as soon as possible in order to re-let. In practice, the process of disclaimer and then application for a vesting order brings with it uncertainty, and, particularly due to the current depressed commercial property market, it is not uncommon for informal arrangements to be agreed and made between the landlord, liquidator, mortgagee, sub-tenants and guarantors as to occupation, payment of rent and the future occupation. The effect of liquidation upon landlords generally is considered at **12.4.2**.

9.4 LIQUIDATOR'S DUTIES

9.4.1 Duty to keep proper records

Under the Insolvency Regulations 1994, SI 1994/2507, the liquidator is under a duty to keep proper books of account and minute books. A creditor, contributory or director may, subject to control of the court, inspect them.

In the case of a creditors' voluntary winding up, the liquidator must keep such books and records as directed by the liquidation committee and must submit them for inspection on request (Insolvency Practitioners Regulations 2005, SI 2005/524, Part 4). The records must be retained for six years following release from office (Insolvency Practitioners Regulations 2005, reg.13(5)).

The liquidator also has the following express duties:

- When the winding up is completed, to make up a final account for the final meeting of members and creditors (IA 1986, ss.105, 146).
- In the case of a creditors' voluntary liquidation, if the winding up is not completed, within 12 months to produce a progress report to be sent to the

members and creditors with interim accounts (IA 1986, s.104A for liquidations commencing after 6 April 2010; for liquidations commencing prior to this date, a meeting had to be called).

- To make a statement (in Form 4.68) at the end of the first year and at half-yearly intervals thereafter, to be filed with the Registrar of Companies (IA 1986, s.192).

9.4.2 Duty to take possession of company property

Although the company's property does not automatically vest in the liquidator (as contrasted with a trustee in bankruptcy: see IA 1986, s.306), the liquidator is under a duty to take into his custody all property of the company, including books, papers and records.

Where any person has in his possession or control any property, books, papers or records to which the company appears to be entitled, the court may on application of the liquidator require that person forthwith to deliver, surrender or transfer the property, books or records to the liquidator (IA 1986, s.234(2)).

In considering whether to make an order, the court will look to see if it is property to which the company was entitled. In making this assessment the liquidator is in no better position than the company (see *Re Leyland DAF Ltd (No.1)* [1994] BCC 166 for the need to identify whether the papers were 'company' property). Hence, if the party in possession of the property claims a lien then permission may be refused (*Re Cosslett (Contractors) Ltd* [2001] BCC 740).

However, conversely the liquidator is in no worse position than the company (see *Walker Morris* v. *Khalastchi* [2001] 1 BCLC 1 where a third party attempted unsuccessfully to impose conditions on the release of company records to the liquidator).

Generally, the liquidator should not proceed to seek recovery of property on an *ex parte* basis (*Re First Express Ltd* [1991] BCC 782) and is required to bring the application in his name rather than in the name of the company (*Re Cosslett (Contractors) Ltd* [2001] BCC 740).

9.4.3 Duty of investigation

The liquidator has a limited duty to investigate the affairs of the company to see whether the conduct of the directors is such that they may have been guilty of a civil or criminal offence (see Statement of Insolvency Practice No.2, 2010 and a new obligation to act in the public interest). In a compulsory liquidation, the Official Receiver is under a concurrent duty to investigate the causes of the company's failure and generally its affairs and dealings (IA 1986, s.132(1)). In carrying out his functions the liquidator can exercise the powers open to any insolvency office holder contained in IA 1986, ss.234–237 (set out below).

The issue of liquidator's investigation is one that often causes some agitation among creditors, as many believe that some form of punishment should be meted out to the directors of the failed company. However, as liquidators are generally under a duty to investigate the affairs of the company only to the extent that it will assist in the realisation of company assets (including causes of action), the steps they take in accordance with this function are limited by the resources they have available to them. If there are no assets in the insolvent company to fund extensive investigations, alternative funding must be obtained, possibly from the creditors themselves or via some form of conditional fee arrangement. In reality, few unsecured creditors that are asked to provide funding are willing to do so, fearing it will be throwing good money after bad.

In carrying out this duty of investigation, the liquidator is assisted by a variety of powers. As described above, where the company is in liquidation or a provisional liquidator is appointed, a person who has in his possession or control any property, books, papers or records to which the company appears to be entitled may be ordered by the court forthwith to pay, deliver, convey or surrender books, property or records to the liquidator (IA 1986, s.234).

Where the party so requested neglects or refuses to agree to deliver up the company's property, the liquidator may make an application in his own name, but if suing a party for the unlawful retention of company property (i.e. the tort of conversion), the claim would be in the name of the company in liquidation (*Smith* v. *Bridgend Borough Council* [2002] 1 AC 336). It should be noted that the liquidator can take proceedings in respect of property to which the company 'appears to be entitled'; he does not need to first 'prove' ownership (*Euro Commercial Leasing Ltd* v. *Cartwright & Lewis* [1995] BCC 830).

Any officer, director, employee or former director of the company is under a clear and specific duty to give to the liquidator such information concerning the company and its promotion, formation or business dealings, affairs or property as the liquidator may at any time require (IA 1986, s.235(2)(a)).

This duty applies to any person who has been an officer of the company, those persons who have taken part in the formation of the company, been employed, or who were officers/employees of another company which was a corporate director, within one year of the company being wound up (IA 1986, s.235(3)).

Such individuals are also under a duty to attend the liquidator at such time as may be reasonably required (IA 1986, s.235(2)(b)). This is often an informal meeting, but the director should be aware that the meeting may be recorded or a note made and that statements made in such meetings may be used in director disqualification proceedings (*Re Polly Peck International plc* [1994] BCC 15) or disclosed to relevant authorities (*R.* v. *Brady* [2004] BPIR 962).

A person who without reasonable excuse fails to comply with any request or obligation under this section commits a criminal offence and will be liable to a fine (IA 1986, Sched.10, on indictment, an unlimited fine; on summary conviction, a maximum £5,000 fine and a default rate of £500 per day).

A more formal means of obtaining the co-operation of a director or former director of the company to assist in the liquidator's enquiries is the use of the private examination procedure outlined in IA 1986, s.236 (to be contrasted with the public examination procedure open solely to the Official Receiver, IA 1986, s.133), where a liquidator or creditor can be represented and seek to examine an officer of the company.

IA 1986, s.236 provides that the court may, on application of the liquidator (or Official Receiver where the company is being wound up compulsorily), summon before it any officer of the company or any person known or suspected to have in his possession any property of the company, or who is or is supposed to be indebted to the company, or any person whom the court thinks capable of giving information concerning the promotion, formation or business dealings and affairs and property of the company.

An application under this section is sought where the informal approaches under IA 1986, s.235 have been unsuccessful in obtaining co-operation, perhaps because the individual has failed to attend the liquidator (or Official Receiver) before and/or where the liquidator (or Official Receiver) determines that a more formal method of compulsion is necessary.

A person so ordered may be required to submit an affidavit to account for his dealings with the company and/or produce any books or records in his custody or control relating to the company (IA 1986, s.236(3)).

If a person without reasonable excuse fails to appear before the court, or there are reasonable grounds for believing they have absconded, the court has a power of arrest that includes seizure of any books, papers, records, money or goods in that person's possession (IA 1986, s.236(5)).

In weighing up whether to exercise its discretion, the court will not act in a way which is oppressive or unfair to the respondent, although this does not mean that the liquidator is first obliged to provide the respondent with a list of questions or topics that will be dealt with (see *Re Embassy Art Products Ltd* (1987) 3 BCC 292).

The liquidator cannot use this procedure simply to obtain evidence which might be useful during the course of litigation (see *Re Sasea Finance Ltd* [1999] BCC 103), or to determine a proof of debt (*Bellmex International Ltd* v. *Green* [2001] BCC 253), but the court may order an examination even if the purpose is only to support the issue of disqualification proceedings (*Re Pantmaenog Timber Co. Ltd* [2004] 1 AC 158) and may do so even if legal proceedings alleging fraud have already been commenced (*Shierson* v. *Rastogi* [2003] BPIR 148).

The court will not make an order where the request is opportunistic, i.e. such as where the liquidator is fishing for evidence or where the liquidator has already settled upon a course of action (see *Re RBG Resources plc* [2002] BCC 1005). The court will also refuse to make an order if it considers the examination unnecessary, unreasonable or otherwise oppressive (*Long* v. *Farrer & Co.* [2004] BPIR 1218). While the making of an order may in itself be inconvenient to the respondent, the difficulties and costs which would be incurred by the respondent in dealing with the request are not regarded as unreasonable (see *British and Commonwealth Holdings plc (Joint Administrators)* v. *Spicer & Oppenheim (No.2)* [1992] BCC 977).

In view of these factors, it is very often advisable for the liquidator first to set out the information that he would wish to obtain on examination, seeking co-operation under IA 1986, s.235 (*Re Barlow Clowes Gilt Managers Ltd* [1992] Ch 208). On refusal and/or failure to reply, an application to court should then be considered.

A person who without reasonable excuse fails to comply with the obligations under IA 1986, s.236 is liable to a fine (IA 1986, Sched.10, on indictment, an unlimited fine; on summary conviction, a £5,000 fine).

If in the course of the private examination it appears to the court that any person has in his possession any company property, on application by the liquidator the court can order that person to deliver up the property on such terms as it sees fit (IA 1986, s.237(1)).

If in the course of the private examination it appears to the court that any person is indebted to the company, on application by the liquidator the court may order that person to make payment to the liquidator on such terms as it thinks fit (IA 1986, s.237(2)).

These two provisions are a useful means of summary determination of issues that would otherwise require separate proceedings.

9.4.4 Duty to report on directors' conduct

After conducting an investigation, a liquidator is under a duty to report to the Secretary of State on the conduct of the directors of the company in liquidation. The report to the Secretary of State (the so-called 'D-Report') outlines any concerns that the liquidator has as to whether the directors' conduct is such as to deem them unfit to be concerned in the management of a company (CDDA 1986, s.7(3)). The Secretary of State (administered by the Directors Disqualification Unit of the DBIS) will look at the report and decide whether it is in the public interest to take proceedings under CDDA 1986. If proceedings are taken, the liquidator is generally called upon to provide evidence at the hearing and any subsequent hearing. If there is little or no dispute as to the facts of the case, a hearing can be dispensed with and an undertaking provided by the directors. This is dealt with more fully in **Chapter 13**.

If the liquidator considers that criminal offences have been committed by the past or present directors of the company or any member, he must report the matter to the Director of Public Prosecutions and provide such information and give such access to documents, etc. as may be required (IA 1986, s.218).

If the liquidator considers the company has disposed of the property at an undervalue (IA 1986, s.238) or has given a preference to a creditor (IA 1986, s.239), the liquidator may apply to court for an order setting aside the same. A remedy is also available for transactions which the company has made with the intention of putting assets beyond the reach of a creditor (IA 1986, s.423). These provisions are dealt with in more detail in **Chapter 13**.

The liquidator can only take such proceedings after sanction from the creditors or permission of the court. The problem in taking such proceedings, however, remains one of funding. Creditors need to consider very carefully whether to allow the liquidator to expend funds that would otherwise be returned as dividends, against the possibility of them recovering a greater sum through successful proceedings. Unfortunately, unlawful conduct by the company and its directors prior to insolvency often goes unpunished due to the lack of funds in the insolvent company.

9.4.5 Duty to realise assets

The company's property does not vest in the liquidator (save by court order in compulsory liquidation under IA 1986, s.145(1) and in voluntary liquidation under IA 1986, s.112(1)); and through examination of the books and records, meetings with the company's former directors, officers and professional advisers, the liquidator will seek to establish, get in and receive all tangible and intangible assets of the company, including causes of action vesting in the company.

If the liquidator seizes or disposes of property that is not in fact property of the company, provided the liquidator has reasonable grounds for his belief in his entitlement, he will not be liable for loss or damage provided that loss or damage was not caused by the liquidator's own negligence. With regard to such property, the liquidator also has a charge on the property or its proceeds of sale for expenses incurred in dealing with it (IA 1986, s.234(3), (4)). This statutory protection does not, however, extend to any dealings with intangible property, such as a cause of action (*Welsh Development Agency Ltd* v. *Export Finance Co.* [1992] BCC 270).

This protection does not prevent the owner of the property from asserting rights of ownership and seeking recovery of the goods or the proceeds of sale. If the liquidator was put on notice of the owner's claim but nevertheless went on to dispose of the property, he would be liable for the tort of conversion.

A common issue that arises in corporate insolvencies is where a supplier claims to have retained title to goods supplied but as yet unpaid for; if the liquidator has notice of the retention of title claim (or should have had notice by reason of the surrounding facts, i.e. constructive notice) he may well be held negligent if he disposes of those goods and liable to the supplier for damages (i.e. payment of the full price of the goods despite possible sale at a lesser value). As a result, the liquidator is better advised to seek agreement with those claiming retention of title (perhaps agreeing to hold the proceeds of sale in a separate escrow account pending determination of the claim) or seeking directions of the court in cases of dispute.

As we shall see, once assets are realised the liquidator is under a duty to ensure that they are only used to pay creditors in the prescribed statutory order and then to distribute any surplus to members (IA 1986, ss.107, 143).

Underpinning the collective nature of the liquidation regime is the principle of *pari passu* distribution, namely that creditors of the same nature, type or class are dealt with equally, and that any distributions made to creditors of the same class are made on a rateable basis.

Creditors will thus claim in the liquidation and will be entitled to a dividend payment in proportion to the value of their claim. At the commencement of the winding up there is a theoretical determination of the creditors' claims against the company and a calculation of what is owing to them as at that date. As previously noted, a secured creditor is more or less unaffected by the winding up of the company and can rely upon and enforce its security outside the winding-up process. A secured creditor can, however, seek to claim for a dividend where there is an unsecured balance of their claim. The class of preferential creditors has, since the Enterprise Act 2002 reforms came into force on 15 September 2003, been significantly limited, with the Crown losing its preference in respect of tax liability owed by the company. As a result, preferential debts are generally limited to certain specific claims of employees. Accordingly, the liquidator is primarily concerned with the claims of unsecured creditors.

On appointment, the liquidator will seek to establish who is, or potentially is, a creditor of the company. He will do this by:

- reviewing the company's statement of affairs;
- considering any representations made by creditors at the initial meeting;
- investigating the company's books, records and accounting records;
- questioning the directors, senior management and employees;
- reviewing correspondence of the company to assess whether there are any potential claims from suppliers and customers; and
- contacting the company's accountants and solicitors to see if there is any current litigation or other potential claims that could fall upon the company.

Armed with the information gathered from this exercise, the liquidator will write to all known creditors and all potential creditors informing them of his appointment.

When the liquidator sends notice of his appointment, he may at this particular stage also invite the creditors to submit claims. It should be remembered, however, that some, if not most, of the creditors may already have submitted claims for the purposes of attending and voting at the initial creditors' meeting.

In compulsory winding up, a creditor cannot vote unless it has lodged a claim in a formal proof of debt by the time and date given on the notice (IR 1986, rules 4.74, 4.67(1)). It is also the case that a creditor in compulsory liquidation may not be paid a dividend, unless it has submitted a proof of debt. In voluntary liquidation, there is less formality, although the liquidator may still require a person claiming to be a creditor to submit a written claim. In practice, a liquidator is almost certain to provide creditors with a blank Form 4.25 (proof of debt form), which will be used to set out the claim with all of the necessary information required for the liquidator to consider and then admit or reject the claim.

Whether or not the liquidator has received a proof of debt, lodged prior to the meeting or following notice of his appointment, he is unlikely to move on to the formal process of assessment of the proof of debt until he is in a position to confirm that distribution to creditors is likely to be made. At that stage, the liquidator is likely once again to ask the creditors to submit a proof of debt or, where they have already done so, any revision to their proof of debt; he may also advertise for creditors to come forward to prove as and when a likely distribution is to be made.

The liquidator may require a claim for a debt to be verified by affidavit and may call upon the creditor to provide proof by means of documentary evidence. The rejection of any proof of debt must be accompanied by a statement as to the grounds for rejection (IR 1986, rule 4.82). There is no specific time limit for admission or rejection of claims; any creditor dissatisfied with the liquidator's decision may apply to the court for review of the decision.

Before declaring a dividend, the liquidator must give notice of his intention to do so to all known creditors (IR 1986, rule 11.2(1)); he must also advertise notice in the *London Gazette* and may advertise in such other manner as he thinks fit (IR 1986, rule 11.2(1A)). This requirement will not be necessary if prior to this date the liquidator has by notice invited creditors to prove for their debts (IR 1986, rule 11.2(1B)). As set out above, the liquidator is quite likely to have previously asked the creditors to submit a proof of debt, prior to the initial meeting or after notice of appointment, even where the liquidation was preceded by administration and a proof of debt was requested during that process. While a proof may thus have been requested and considered for the purposes of admission for voting only, the liquidator would be negligent in failing to take account of a claim, if at a later date despite a request (e.g. for dividend purposes) the creditor failed to submit a further proof. Despite this, it is not unknown in practice for multiple proof of debt forms to be required from creditors.

The notice of dividend will provide a date on which proofs of debts must be lodged (allowing at least 21 days from the notice). The liquidator will within seven days of the last date of proving then deal with the proofs, where he has not already done so, admitting or rejecting the claims in whole or in part. The liquidator has a discretion to admit late submitted proofs (IR 1986, rule 11.3; see also *Painter* v. *Hutchison* [2008] BPIR 170).

Within four months of the last date of proving, unless the liquidator has postponed or cancelled the dividend, he will declare the dividend (IR 1986, rule 11.5(1)) (e.g. *x*p in the £). Where a creditor has proved, he will then receive payment in accordance with the value of the admitted claim.

As stated above, in calculating the dividend the liquidator cannot disregard claims of which he is aware simply because the creditor has failed to follow the set procedure. As has been seen, a creditor may have submitted a proof of debt at many different times during the insolvency process. Consequently, the debt would have come to the attention of the liquidator, who bears a risk if he disregards such claims (see *Re Armstrong Whitworth Securities Co. Ltd* [1947] Ch 673).

9.4.6 Duty to distribute assets

After ascertaining and determining the liabilities of the company by the proof of debt process outlined above, the liquidator is under a duty to pay the debts of the company out of realised assets, which will be applied *pari passu* (i.e. by rateable value equally among members of the same class of creditors). After the payment of all debts and other claims, any surplus will be distributed among the members (unless the articles provide otherwise) according to their rights and interests in the company (IA 1986, s.107).

Checklist

Priority of distribution of assets available to liquidators

- The expenses of preserving and realising assets.
- Liquidator's remuneration and proper costs and expenses of the winding up.
- Preferential debts.
- Sums due to any floating charge holder to the extent that preferential debts have been paid out of assets subject to the floating charge.
- Unsecured debts.
- Post-insolvency interest on debts.
- Deferred debts.
- Balance if any to contributories.

Buchler v. *Talbot*; *Re Leyland DAF* [2004] UKHL 9 overturned *Re Barleycorn Enterprises Ltd* [1970] 2 WLR 898 by holding that two distinct funds are created on the crystallisation of a floating charge. First, those assets caught by the charge, and second, those assets free from security (if any), which belong to the company that the liquidator may realise and upon which the expenses of the liquidation are a first charge (see, however, IA 1986, s.176ZA on the issue of liquidation expense detailed in **9.5.8**).

Definition

Deferred debt

A debt which by virtue of one of the following statutory provisions is deferred for payment until all other liabilities have been discharged:

- Loans made where the rate of interest depends upon the level of company profit (Partnership Act 1890, ss.2 and 3).
- Payments due from the company to redeem or purchase back its own shares (CA 1985, s.178(3)).
- Sums due to a member of the company by way of dividend, profit or otherwise (IA 1986, s.74(2)(f)).
- Sums due to a party from the company, where that party has been found guilty of fraudulent or wrongful trading and the court so orders (IA 1986, s.215(4)).

9.5 THE ENDING OF THE WINDING UP

9.5.1 Removal from office

The liquidator of a voluntary winding up may be removed from office by:

- order of the court;

- the company general meeting in members' voluntary liquidation; or
- the creditors in general meeting in creditors' voluntary liquidation.

Order of the court

Under IA 1986, s.108(2): 'The court may, on cause shown, remove a liquidator and appoint another.'

An application can be made by any person the court considers proper. However, the court will not remove a liquidator of an insolvent company on the application of a contributory (*Deloitte & Touche AG* v. *Johnson* [1999] BCC 992).

The applicant may apply either for the court to remove the liquidator by order or for the court to order that the liquidator summons a meeting of creditors for the purposes of his removal (IR 1986, rule 4.120(1); see Form 4.39).

The court will exercise its powers sparingly (see *Re Keypak Homecare Ltd (No.1)* (1987) 3 BCC 558 and *AMP Music Box Enterprises Ltd* v. *Hoffman* [2002] BCC 996) and may summarily dismiss the application if there is insufficient cause shown. In such instances, however, the applicant must first have the opportunity of a hearing before the court to show due cause on an *ex parte* basis, on being given seven days' notice. The court also has power to order that, as a condition of proceeding with the application, the applicant provides security for costs or pays a deposit.

Where the court considers that there is sufficient cause, a hearing date will be fixed, the applicant providing at least 14 days' notice of the same to the liquidator. The applicant is required to serve a copy of the application and evidence in support upon the liquidator (IR 1986, rule 4.120(4)).

At the hearing, the court makes such order as it thinks fit having regard to all the circumstances of the case. A liquidator will not be removed simply because his conduct has in one or more respects fallen short of the ideal (*AMP Music Box Enterprises Ltd* v. *Hoffman* [2002] BCC 996). A liquidator may, however, be removed if there is sufficient conflict of interest (see *Re Charterland Goldfields* (1909) 26 TLR 132); where there has been a wilful and flagrant disregard of the creditors' wishes (see *Re Rubber and Produce Investment Trust* [1915] 1 Ch 382); or where there has been a significant default in the exercise of the liquidator's duties (see *Re Ryder Installations* [1966] 1 WLR 524).

Where the court has ordered the removal of the liquidator, two copies of the order must be sent to the liquidator and the liquidator must send a copy of the order with a notice of the cessation of acting to the Registrar of Companies.

The court may, on application to remove the existing liquidator, appoint a new liquidator (IA 1986, s.108(2)). The new appointment takes effect upon the liquidator confirming his qualification to act and agreeing to the appointment (IR 1986, rule 4.103(2)). Within 28 days of appointment, the liquidator must give notice to all creditors of the company of which he is aware and cause advertisement of his appointment in accordance with any directions given by the court (IR 1986, rule 4.103(4)).

Removal by meeting

A liquidator may be removed by a meeting of the company (in the case of a members' voluntary liquidation (MVL)) or the company's creditors (in the case of a creditors' voluntary liquidation (CVL)), but in either case the meeting must be specifically summoned for the purposes of removing the liquidator (IA 1986, s.171(2) and see IR 1986, rule 4.143 (MVL) and rule 4.120 (CVL)).

In the case of an MVL, the liquidator may be removed by the company in a general meeting of its members (IA 1986, s.171(2)(a)). It may be necessary for a member to apply to court seeking an order which compels the liquidator to call such a meeting, as there is no specific procedure set out in the statute for a member to call and summon a general meeting.

In a CVL, the creditors have a right to call a meeting for the purposes of removing the liquidator (IA 1986, s.171(2)(b)) and a liquidator is obliged to summon a meeting, if requested to do so by 25 per cent or more in value of the company's creditors, excluding connected creditors (see IA 1986, s.249, 'connected' meaning a director or shadow director of a company or associate as defined in IA 1986, s.435).

Any request by the creditors to summon a meeting of creditors for the purposes of removing the liquidator must be accompanied by:

(a)   a list of the creditors concurring with the request and the amount of their respective claims in the winding up;
(b)   written confirmation of concurrence from each creditor; and
(c)   a statement of the purpose of the proposed meeting (i.e. removal of the liquidator; see Form 4.21 and IR 1986, rule 4.57).

If the request has been properly made, the liquidator is required to fix a venue for the meeting not less than 28 days from receipt of the request (IR 1986, rule 4.57(2)). The meeting should be held on at least 14 days' notice and the creditors' attention drawn to the potential effects of the liquidator's release. At the meeting, a chairman may be elected, who cannot be the liquidator. The requisite resolutions are passed by the majority in value of those present and voting in person or by proxy being in favour of the resolution (IR 1986, rule 4.63(1)).

In a compulsory winding up, the liquidator may be removed by court order or by a general meeting of the company's creditors specifically called for the purposes of a liquidator's removal (IR 1986, rule 4.113).

The additional requirements in the case of compulsory liquidation are that notice of the meeting must also be sent to the Official Receiver, and where a resolution is passed to remove the liquidator a copy must be sent to the Official Receiver.

Where a liquidator has been appointed by the Secretary of State, he may only be removed at the direction of the Secretary of State (IA 1986, s.172(4)).

9.5.2 Vacation from office

In addition to being removed from office by court order or at a meeting, the liquidator may vacate office through:

- death (see IR 1986, rule 4.145 (MVL) and IR 1986, rule 4.113 (CVL)); or
- resignation, in the circumstances set out below.

A liquidator may resign:

(a) on grounds of ill health;
(b) where he intends to cease practising as an insolvency practitioner;
(c) where there arises a conflict of interest or a change in the personal circumstances of the liquidator which make it impractical for him to be able to discharge his duties;
(d) where there are two or more joint liquidators appointed, and they have reached the opinion that it is no longer expedient to retain the present number of liquidators and one or more should be removed.

Before resigning, the liquidator must call a meeting of the company's members or creditors, as is appropriate. The notice of the meeting must state the purpose of the meeting (i.e. his resignation) and the consequences of the liquidator's release. Together with the notice, the liquidator must provide a report detailing his administration of the liquidation and a receipts and payments account.

At the meeting, resolutions can be passed as to the release of the liquidator and his remuneration.

In the event that the creditors refuse to accept the resignation, the liquidator can apply to court for direction (IR 1986, rule 4.111).

It is common for an insolvency practitioner on leaving one firm of accountants to transfer appointments to one or more of his ex-partners. In such circumstances, the court will consider and hear block transfer applications to avoid the cost and expense of holding separate creditors' meetings (see *Clements* v. *Udal* [2001] BCC 658).

9.5.3 Liquidator's release

The release of a liquidator operates as a discharge of all liabilities for any acts or omissions in the winding up and otherwise in relation to his conduct as a liquidator (see IA 1986, s.173(4) (voluntary liquidation) and IA 1986, s.174(6) (compulsory liquidation)).

The release is effective from the 'relevant time', which means on death, removal or resignation of office:

(a) where a resolution has been passed for release at a meeting of creditors, the date of the resolution;
(b) where a resolution has not been passed to release or there has been a failure to

pass such a resolution (perhaps because no creditor has attended the final meeting), at the time of notification by the liquidator to Companies House;

(c) where a resolution has been passed not to release the liquidator, the date the Secretary of State has provided in a certificate of release after application by the liquidator, the date of release being determined by the Secretary of State;

(d) on an MVL, on vacation of office after the final meeting of the company.

Where a liquidator is removed from office by court order, the liquidator must apply to the Secretary of State for his release (see IR 1986, rule 4.144(3)).

It is important to note that the liquidator, despite the release, may be subject to any action under IA 1986, s.212 (i.e. the summary remedy for misfeasance in office, a breach of duty causing loss and damage to the company: see *Re VGM Holdings* [1942] Ch 235), but only where the court first grants permission. If the creditors have resolved against releasing the liquidator, as stated above, the liquidator may be released on the determination of the Secretary of State upon application by the liquidator (IA 1986, s.173(2) (voluntary liquidation) and s.174(4)(d) (compulsory liquidation)). This is an important provision; where the liquidator has not been released, a creditor may sue the liquidator in his personal capacity for loss and damage caused by any act or omission, irrespective of whether the company has been subsequently dissolved (see *Pulsford* v. *Devenish* [1903] 2 Ch 625).

In the case of a voluntary liquidation, three months after the registration of the liquidator's final account and return, the company is dissolved (IA 1986, s.201). In compulsory liquidation, three months after receipt and registration of the liquidator's, or Official Receiver's, notice of final meeting of creditors, the company is dissolved (IA 1986, s.205).

9.5.4   Conversion of members' voluntary liquidation into creditors' voluntary liquidation

If, during the course of an MVL, the liquidator forms the view that the company is unable to pay its debts in full together with interest (remembering that the directors' declaration at the commencement of the liquidation was that debts would be paid within 12 months), he is required to:

* summon a creditors' meeting within 28 days;
* send notice of the meeting to the creditors, giving not less than seven days' notice of the meeting;
* advertise the meeting in the *London Gazette* and as otherwise thought appropriate; and
* prepare a report setting out a statement of the company's affairs to be laid before the creditors at the meeting.

The MVL is converted into a CVL on the day of the creditors' meeting (IA 1986, s.96). The liquidation then proceeds as if the directors' statutory declaration of solvency had not been made and the resolution by its members and creditors to put the company into liquidation had been passed at that meeting (see IA 1986, s.97). The creditors are free to appoint a liquidator of their choosing and appoint a liquidation committee.

9.5.5 Liquidation and alternative insolvency processes

It is possible for an administrative receiver, an administrator or a supervisor of a CVA to apply to court for the compulsory winding up of the company. Each will do so in the name of the company.

In the case of a CVA, the funds collected by the supervisor before the commencement of the liquidation will generally be regarded as held on quasi-trust for the creditors previously bound by terms of the CVA (see *Re Kudos Glass* [2001] 1 BCLC 390; *Re NT Gallagher & Sons Ltd* [2002] 1 WLR 2380; and *Leisure Study Group Ltd* [1994] 2 BCLC 65). This general principle, however, depends upon the form of wording of the CVA and/or irrespective of the intention/absence of such wording, if in practice the funds were held on trust exclusively for the CVA creditors. Creditors not obtaining full payment under the terms of the CVA are entitled to prove for the balance in the liquidation.

In addition to the power to seek the compulsory winding up of a company (IA 1986, Sched.B1, para.60), an administrator is also able to move the company from administration into CVL (IA 1986, Sched.B1, para.83). This convenient route of exit from an administration may be taken when the purpose of the administration has been achieved and a distribution to unsecured creditors will be made. Although an administrator may seek leave of the court to make a distribution to unsecured creditors, it is more usual practice for the assessment of claims and distribution to unsecured creditors to be undertaken while the company is in liquidation.

The administrator must provide notice of intention to convert the administration into company voluntary liquidation to the Registrar of Companies, and send notices to creditors. On registration of the notice, the company will be wound up as if a resolution for voluntary winding up under IA 1986, s.84 had been passed on that day (IA 1986, Sched.B1, para.83(6)(b)). The creditors are given an opportunity of calling a meeting to choose an alternative insolvency practitioner to act as liquidator.

While the company is in administration, it cannot otherwise be placed into liquidation without leave of the court (IA 1986, Sched.B1, para.42, save for a public interest petition). Where a winding-up petition has been presented and then an administration order is made, the petition will be dismissed. Where the appointment of the administrator is made out of court by a qualifying floating charge holder, the petition is suspended and may be revived when the administrator leaves office (IA 1986, Sched.B1, para.40(1)(b)). The company and/or its directors cannot appoint an administrator by the out-of-court process where a winding-up petition remains pending (IA 1986, Sched.B1, para.25(a)).

In contrast, where assets of the company have been placed in any form of receivership, there is nothing to prevent the winding up of the company by voluntary or compulsory winding up.

9.5.6 Liquidator's remuneration

In a creditors' voluntary winding up the liquidator's remuneration must be approved by the liquidation committee or if there is no committee, approval rests with the creditors. A liquidator cannot set his own basis of remuneration (*Re Salters Hall School Ltd* [1998] BCC 503).

The basis of the remuneration is a percentage of the assets realised and distributed, or on a time cost basis, or as a fixed fee (IR 1986, rule 4.127). In practice, the basis of remuneration is usually determined at the beginning of the liquidation (at the Section 98 meeting) rather than at the end, and will generally be on a time cost basis, sometimes on a fixed basis, but rarely on a percentage basis. As we have seen, however, the liquidator will in reports to creditors (or the creditors' committee) advise upon how remuneration is proposed to be drawn and seek resolutions approving the same. While the basis of remuneration is fixed, the issue of the actual amount of the remuneration to be drawn is often left to the final meeting.

If the basis of remuneration has not been settled by approval of the creditors' committee or the creditors at a general meeting, the liquidator may within 18 months apply to court for the basis of the remuneration to be fixed by the court (IR 1986, rule 4.127(7)).

If the liquidator's remuneration is not fixed within 18 months after appointment in accordance with these procedures, he is entitled to remuneration in accordance with the provisions of IR 1986, rule 4.127A (IR 1986, rule 4.127(6)).

IR 1986, rule 4.127A applies where a liquidator who is not the Official Receiver has not had his remuneration fixed or treated as fixed as above. The liquidator is entitled to remuneration in accordance with the Official Receiver's scale rates as set out in IR 1986, Sched.6, being an application of both:

- the realisation scale:

    (i)   on the first £5,000 or fraction thereof, 20 per cent;
    (ii)   on the next £5,000 or fraction thereof, 15 per cent;
    (iii) on the next £90,000 or fraction thereof, 10 per cent;
    (iv)   on all further sums realised, 5 per cent;

- and the distribution scale:

    (i)   on the first £5,000 or fraction thereof, 10 per cent;
    (ii)   on the next £5,000 or fraction thereof, 7.5 per cent;
    (iii) on the next £90,000 or fraction thereof, 5 per cent;
    (iv)   on all further sums realised, 2.5 per cent.

The realisation scale is applied to monies received from realisations of the assets of the company (including VAT but excluding sums paid to secured creditors and sums spent on carrying on the business of the company). The distribution scale is applied to the value of assets distributed to creditors of the company (including payments made in respect of preferential debts) and to contributories.

In cases where the liquidator considers that the basis of remuneration fixed by any committee, or by resolution of the creditors, is insufficient or inappropriate, or where creditors holding at least 10 per cent of the value of the company's debt consider it excessive, application can be made to court (IR 1986, rules 4.130 and 4.131). The court will have regard to the guiding principles laid down in Practice Statement on Fixing and Approval of Remuneration of Appointees [2004] BPIR 953 (see also *Re Cabletel Installations Ltd* [2005] BPIR 28).

In compulsory liquidation, the court may review the liquidator's remuneration at any stage, but generally the issue of remuneration will again be resolved by the creditors.

Where the liquidator sells assets on behalf of a secured creditor, the liquidator is entitled to charge the costs and expenses incurred in the sale against the sums realised (see *Buchler* v. *Talbot; Re Leyland DAF* [2004] UKHL 9). The level of those expenses, if not agreed, will be on the Official Receiver's scale (IR 1986, rule 4.127B).

9.5.7 Voluntary liquidation: final creditors' meeting and report

The process and procedure for the holding of creditors' meetings has been dealt with in **9.1** above. However, as soon as the company's affairs are fully wound up, a final meeting will be held.

The affairs of the company are deemed to have been fully wound up by the liquidator when he has realised assets as far as he can realise them, and made distributions as far as can be made. This may mean that the company still holds property. As we have seen, the liquidator has a power to make a distribution *in specie*, but if he does not and the company is dissolved any property which remained vested in the company until dissolution will vest as *bona vacantia* (*Re Wilmott Trading Ltd (No.2)* [2000] BCC 321). Any creditor or party wishing to claim such property (or perhaps where they have found further property which was not dealt with or known to the liquidator) will then need to apply to restore the company to the register or liaise with the Treasury solicitor acting on behalf of the Crown in order to deal with the property (see CA 2006, ss.1029–1034).

The liquidator is required to prepare an account of the winding up, showing how it was conducted and how the company's property has been disposed of. The report must include, *inter alia*, a summary of receipts and payments, including separate identification of trading receipts and payments, sources of other receipts, payments to redeem securities, legal costs, property management, auctioneer's/valuer's costs and the liquidator's remuneration. The account will also deal with the distributions and interest paid to secured, preferential and unsecured creditors (IR 1986, rule 4.126(1E)).

A draft of this final report must first be sent to the creditors at least eight weeks prior to the final meeting. The report itself may not be sent until the liquidator has first sent notice of intention to declare a final dividend, or notice that he intends to make no further dividend (IR 1986, rule 4.49D).

This period of time allows the creditors to come forward with any further information as to potential investigation and/or asset realisation, as well as questions which might be resolved on issues of costs, expenses and remuneration, prior to the final meeting.

The liquidator will then call a general meeting of the company and meeting of creditors for the purpose of laying the account before the meeting and giving an explanation of it (IA 1986, s.106(1)).

The meeting must be advertised in the *London Gazette* giving at least one month's prior notice. Within one week after the date of the meeting, the liquidator must send the Registrar of Companies a copy of the account and make a return of the holding of the meeting and its date (IA 1986, s.106(3); Forms 4.71 and 4.72). The meeting may also be advertised in such other manner as the liquidator thinks fit (IR 1986, rule 4.126(1B)).

At the final meeting, the creditors may question the liquidator and may resolve against the liquidator's release (IR 1986, rule 4.126(2)).

The liquidator is released from making the return to the Registrar of Companies if no quorum (i.e. no one) was present at either the creditors' or members' meeting, although the liquidator must file a return to that effect with the Registrar of Companies (IA 1986, s.106(5)).

If the liquidator fails to comply with these provisions, he may be punished by a fine.

9.5.8 Compulsory liquidation: final creditors' meeting and report

If the liquidator is not the Official Receiver and if it appears to the liquidator that for practical purposes the winding up of the company is complete (see above), the liquidator must summon a final meeting of creditors to receive the liquidator's report of the winding up and determine whether the liquidator should be released (IA 1986, s.146).

As is the case in a voluntary winding up, the final meeting of creditors may not be called until a draft of the final report, to be laid before the creditors at the final meeting, has first been sent to the creditors. This draft report must be sent at least eight weeks prior to the final meeting. The report itself may not be sent until the liquidator has first sent notice of intention to declare a final dividend or make no further dividend (IR 1986, rule 4.49D(3)).

In compulsory liquidation, the liquidator is also required to give at least 21 days' notice of the meeting and details of any unrealised property to the Official Receiver

(IR 1986, rule 4.137). Where there remains unrealised property or undistributed funds the liquidator should also supply any proofs of debt to the Official Receiver.

The final meeting is to be held after first giving 28 days' notice to all creditors of whom the liquidator is aware. Notice of the meeting must be advertised in the *London Gazette* and may be advertised in such other manner as the liquidator sees fit. The liquidator's final report must contain a statement of account reconciling the summary of receipts and payments of the account held by the Secretary of State (i.e. the Insolvency Service account).

After the final meeting has been held, the liquidator will give notice to the court and to the Registrar of Companies that the meeting has been held and will include a statement as to whether or not he has obtained a release (IA 1986, s.172(8)). On vacation of office, the liquidator must deliver up the company's books and records to the Official Receiver (IR 1986, rule 4.138(3)).

Where there are joint liquidators, it is for them to agree how as between themselves they are to be remunerated and how the remuneration is to be apportioned between them both. Any dispute between them shall be referred to the court, the liquidation committee or a meeting of creditors (IR 1986, rule 4.128(2)).

Property subject to a floating charge

Where the realised unsecured assets of the company are insufficient to cover the costs and expenses of the liquidation, such costs and expenses may be deducted from the floating charge realisations (IA 1986, s.176ZA(1)).

IA 1986, s.176ZA was inserted by CA 2006, s.1282, with effect from 6 April 2008. This section overcame the difficulties presented by the House of Lords' decision in *Re Leyland Daf Ltd; Buchler* v. *Talbot* [2004] UKHL 9, which had overturned established practice and held that a liquidator was not entitled to the expenses of the liquidation from assets subject to a floating charge. This decision had significant impact, as under many modern corporate financing arrangements, companies have few if any unsecured free assets and with high gearing ratios it is less likely that the secured creditor would be paid in full. As there are few unencumbered assets available for realisation, the interests of the unsecured creditors in ensuring full and proper investigation by a liquidator and taking proceedings against delinquent directors were potentially prejudiced by the decision.

IA 1986, s.176ZA attempts to redress the balance between secured and unsecured creditors and provides that the expenses of a winding up shall, where the unencumbered assets are insufficient to meet those expenses, be paid in priority to unsecured creditors, preferential creditors and the claims of floating charge holders.

However, the provisions of the section are subject to detailed rules (IR 1986, rules 4.218A–4.218E) which restrict the application of the section, requiring that certain expenses are authorised or approved by the holder of a floating charge, preferential creditors or the court. The restrictions contained within IR 1986 generally relate to the initiation of certain categories of litigation, but the court can sanction the proceedings (and recovery of the expenses therein) where the creditor concerned is the defendant (e.g. a challenge as to the validity of security under IA 1986, s.239 or s.245). The rules and restrictions do not apply to litigation expenses which do not exceed £5,000 (IR 1986, rule 4.218A(1)(d)(ii)).

9.5.9 Dissolution of the company

On dissolution, the company as a distinct legal entity ceases to exist. Any property of whatever nature or any right of action which remains vested in the company as at the date of dissolution will vest in the Crown as *bona vacantia* (CA 2006, s.1012).

Where a company has been wound up voluntarily and the final account and return sent to the Registrar of Companies, three months after registration of the same the company is deemed to be dissolved (IA 1986, s.201(2)). Dissolution may be deferred by order of the court on application by the liquidator or other interested person (IA 1986, s.201(3)).

In a compulsory winding up, the Official Receiver (where he is liquidator) may seek the early dissolution of the company in circumstances where there are no available assets. Statistically, up to one-third of compulsory winding-up cases involve companies with no realisable assets. If the Official Receiver discovers the realisable assets of the company are insufficient to cover the expenses of the winding up, he may apply to the Registrar of Companies for early dissolution (IA 1986, s.202). The Official Receiver must also be of the opinion that the affairs of the company do not require further investigation. Twenty-eight days' notice must be given of this intention to the company's creditors, contributories and, if applicable, administrative receiver.

The recipients of the notice may apply to court for directions on the grounds that there are realisable assets to cover the expenses of winding up or the affairs of the company require further investigation, or for any other reason early dissolution of the company is inappropriate (IA 1986, s.203).

In other cases where the liquidator has served notice of the final meeting and vacation of office, or where the Official Receiver has given notice that the winding up is complete, the Registrar of Companies must register the same and after three months, the company will be deemed dissolved (IA 1986, s.205). This is subject to the right of the Secretary of State to defer the dissolution on application by the Official Receiver or another interested party (IA 1986, s.205(3)).

As set out above, in cases of compulsory liquidation, where the Official Receiver as liquidator of the company is satisfied that there are no available assets, or that any realisable assets are insufficient to cover the expenses of winding up and that the affairs of the company do not require investigation, an application for early dissolution may be made (IA 1986, s.202(2)). Notice of the application must be provided to creditors, who have 28 days in which to make representations. In the absence of objection, the Official Receiver's application for early dissolution is lodged with the Registrar of Companies and, unless directed by the Secretary of State, the company will be dissolved at the end of three months.

PART III

Post-commencement considerations

CHAPTER 10

The debtor's position during the personal insolvency process

10.1 THE BANKRUPT'S PROPERTY

10.1.1 Introduction

As we have seen in **Chapter 6**, the treatment of a bankrupt during the bankruptcy process is identical whether the procedure was initiated on a creditor's or debtor's petition. The bankruptcy order takes effect on the day the order is made by the court and continues until the individual is discharged (IA 1986, s.278). Discharge may be suspended until the end of a specified period, or until fulfilment of a specified condition (IA 1986, s.279(3) on application by the Official Receiver or trustee).

During the period of bankruptcy, the bankrupt is under a number of restrictions and has obligations to the Official Receiver/trustee in bankruptcy; default can lead to criminal liability and ultimately imprisonment. Furthermore, where the bankrupt fails to comply with any obligation imposed by IA 1986 (such as co-operating with the Official Receiver or trustee), the court may order that the discharge from bankruptcy is suspended (IA 1986, s.279(1)).

Legal title to the bankrupt's property does not automatically transfer from the bankrupt on the making of bankruptcy order. Until the appointment of the trustee in bankruptcy, the Official Receiver effectively acts as a caretaker, being the receiver and manager of the bankrupt's property/estate (IA 1986, s.287(1)). While acting in this manner the Official Receiver is under a duty to protect the estate. A receiver/manager is entitled to sell or dispose of any perishable goods comprised in the estate and any other goods which are likely to diminish in value if not otherwise disposed of.

The bankrupt's estate does, however, vest upon the trustee immediately on his appointment, or in the Official Receiver on him becoming a trustee (IA 1986, s.306(1)), without the need for any conveyance, assignment or transfer and wherever it is located (see *Pollard* v. *Ashurst* [2001] BPIR 131 and *Singh* v. *Official Receiver* [1997] BPIR 530, confirming that the automatic vesting provisions apply equally to assets located abroad).

Prior to the appointment of the trustee, the bankrupt therefore retains title to his property, but has no capacity to deal with it. The bankrupt thus remains liable for the charges of utility suppliers made to his private premises (see *Re Smith* (1893) 1 QB 323 and *Dadourian Group International* v. *Simms* [2008] BPIR 508), although any disposition by the bankrupt post commencement of the bankruptcy is void (IA 1986, s.284, see below).

The bankruptcy estate will thus remain vested in the trustee; it will not revert to the bankrupt, who loses all right to deal with those assets, including, e.g. choses in action. The one major exemption to this rule is in respect of the realisation of the bankrupt's interest in the family home (IA 1986, s.283A). Since 1 April 2004, in respect of any individual made bankrupt, the bankrupt's family's home will vest back in the bankrupt, unless the trustee has within three years taken any step to realise his interest (see **10.8**). Furthermore, until such time as a surplus is declared (meaning that payment can be effected to all creditors in full), the bankrupt has no immediate (beneficial) interest in the assets in the bankruptcy estate (*Ram* v. *Ram (No.2)* [2005] BPIR 628), merely a contingent right to the benefit of any surplus (*James* v. *Rutherford-Hodge* [2006] BPIR 973).

The trustee will not acquire any better title to the assets than the bankrupt, and will take subject to any third party rights and interests that may fetter the ability to release the assets. In this regard, the key consideration may be whether the asset is subject to any secured interest or equitable interest (see *Avis* v. *Turner* [2007] BPIR 663).

As we shall see, creditor claims are assessed as at the date of commencement of the bankruptcy, i.e. the debtor's liabilities are crystallised as at that date; the debtor's assets are those vesting in the bankruptcy estate as at the date of commencement (subject also to the possible addition of after-acquired property vesting during the duration of the bankruptcy: IA 1986, s.307). At **10.1.2**, we shall consider the effect of disposal of assets after the presentation of a petition but before the making of a bankruptcy order.

The effect of this crystallisation of debts/liabilities and assets as at the date of the presentation of the petition means that a debtor can be made bankrupt subsequently for debts that are incurred post bankruptcy (and even prior to discharge). On the occurrence of a further, second bankruptcy it must be remembered that the creditors in the second bankruptcy will not have any rights to the assets vesting in the first bankruptcy estate.

It should also be remembered that the assets vesting in the bankruptcy estate may rise in value post bankruptcy (e.g. shares); any gain in value will generally be a windfall to the creditors whenever it arises.

The effect of discharge is to release the individual from the restrictions of bankruptcy and release him from possible proceedings by creditors possessing claims as at the date of bankruptcy. Post bankruptcy, a creditor's rights are against the bankruptcy estate not the bankrupt himself. This allows the bankrupt a second chance, free from bankruptcy debt, financial rehabilitation remaining a key component of the bankruptcy system.

10.1.2 Dispositions of property post petition

The central purpose of bankruptcy is the realisation of the bankrupt's estate leading to a rateable distribution among the bankrupt's unsecured creditors.

The bankrupt's estate should be that which is held at commencement of the bankruptcy (i.e. on presentation of a petition). As a result, any disposition of property made by the bankrupt post presentation of the petition, but prior to the vesting of the bankruptcy estate in the trustee in bankruptcy, is void except to the extent that the disposition was with the consent of the court or was subsequently ratified by the court (IA 1986, s.284).

A disposition of property means any 'alienation' of an asset made by the debtor (*Re Mersey Steel & Iron Co.* v. *Naylor, Benzon & Co.* (1884) 9 App Cas 434 (HL)).

The effect of this provision fetters the debtor's ability to settle a petition debt. A petitioning creditor, in accepting payment of the debt from funds belonging to the debtor, risks the possibility that this will be viewed as disposition of property and be declared void, should the debtor subsequently become bankrupt on the hearing of the petition, or following substitution of the petitioning creditor by another, or on change of carriage of the original petition. In those circumstances the only remedy for the petitioning creditor receiving the payment is to seek approval of the court before or after the hearing of a petition. This also has the strange but understandable consequence that a petitioning creditor is not under any obligation to accept payment of the petition debt tendered by the debtor (*Smith (a Bankrupt)* v. *Ian Simpson & Co.* [2000] 3 All ER 434 (CA)).

Where a payment or transfer is declared void, the recipient of the payment holds the sum paid or the property transferred by the bankrupt as part of the bankrupt's estate. The trustee, therefore, is at liberty to claim the property or money transferred, unless the recipient was a person who acted in good faith for value and without notice of the petition (IA 1986, s.284(4)(a)).

A further defence for the recipient is that they may have acted to their detriment on reliance that the transfer was made bona fides by the debtor (the so-called change of position defence; see *Re Tain Construction Ltd* [2003] 1 WLR 2791).

In determining whether to approve or ratify any disposition of property of the debtor, the court will seek to ensure that the interests of the creditors are not unduly prejudiced (see *Re Gray's Inn Construction Co. Ltd* [1980] 1 All ER 814 and *Re Fairway Graphics Ltd* [1991] BCLC 468). Indeed, it may be the case that the transfer/disposition may be seen to be a benefit to the creditors as a whole, i.e. effecting the realisation of the debtor's property.

The application should be supported by witness statements and served on the debtor, a petitioning creditor (or creditor substituted with carriage of the petition) and any creditor who has given notice of intention to appear at the bankruptcy petition hearing (see Practice Note: Validation Orders (Sections 127 and 284 of the Insolvency Act 1986) [2007] BPIR 94).

10.1.3 After-acquired property

Property and assets acquired by the bankrupt after the date of bankruptcy are treated differently from property held by the bankrupt at the commencement of the bankruptcy – such after-acquired property does not automatically vest in the trustee.

Instead, it is open to the trustee to serve notice on the bankrupt in respect of such property (IA 1986, s.307), and on service of the notice that property will be deemed part of the bankruptcy estate. This would include any potential windfall received by the bankrupt, such as an inheritance. It does not cover property that could be regarded as income and to which separate provisions apply (namely IA 1986, s.310 on IPOs; see *Supperstone* v. *Lloyd's Names Working Party* [1999] BPIR 832), nor property acquired after the date of discharge (*Arnold* v. *Williams and HMRC* [2008] BPIR 247). The trustee's notice is not effective as against a person acquiring property in good faith, without notice of the bankruptcy, or where a banker enters into a transaction in good faith without such notice (IA 1986, s.307(4)).

As the trustee is unlikely to become aware of what the bankrupt may have acquired post bankruptcy, there is a positive obligation on the bankrupt to inform the trustee of his acquiring such property (IA 1986, s.333(2)); and the bankrupt must do so within 21 days of becoming aware of the fact (IR 1986, rule 6.200(1)). This very wide obligation of disclosure does not apply to a bankrupt who is carrying on business and who disposes of property in the ordinary course of that business. Instead, such a bankrupt must provide the trustee with information on the goods bought and sold (or services supplied) and the profit of the business when required to do so by the trustee (IR 1986, rule 6.200(5)).

If the bankrupt fails to fulfil his obligation to disclose after-acquired property, he may be found to be in contempt of court (IA 1986, s.333(4)).

Having given notice, the bankrupt must not dispose of the property within 42 days. The trustee therefore has 42 days in which to decide whether to claim the property (under IA 1986, s.307). If no notice is served, the bankrupt is free to dispose of the property, although it is possible for an application to be made out of time by the trustee to claim after-acquired property (*Solomons* v. *Williams* [2001] BPIR 1123; see, however, *Franses* v. *Andre Oomerjee* [2005] BPIR 1320).

If the bankrupt has disposed of such after-acquired property without giving notice to the trustee, he is under an obligation to inform the trustee as soon as reasonably practicable and provide the name and details of the disponee together with such information as may be necessary to enable the trustee to trace the disponee (IR 1986, rule 6.200(3)). The trustee has 28 days from becoming aware of the property, its disposition and the disponee to serve notice on the disponee claiming the property as part of the bankruptcy estate by virtue of IA 1986, s.307(3) (IR 1986, rule 6.201).

10.2   THE BANKRUPT'S DUTIES AND OBLIGATIONS

10.2.1   Duties to Official Receiver/trustee

As we have seen in connection with the getting in and realisation of the bankruptcy estate, in the discussion regarding the trustee's investigations (see **6.4**), the bankrupt is under a number of duties and obligations.

Where a bankruptcy order is made the bankrupt must:

- deliver possession of his estate to the Official Receiver (IA 1986, s.291(1)(a));
- deliver up all books, papers and records in his possession or control and which relate to his estate and affairs (including any which would have been privileged from disclosure in any proceedings) (IA 1986, s.291(1)(b));
- do all such things as are reasonably required by the Official Receiver for the protection of property which cannot be delivered but may be claimed by the trustee of the bankrupt's estate (IA 1986, s.291(2)); and
- provide an inventory of his estate and such other information as required and attend on the Official Receiver at such times as the Official Receiver reasonably requires (this duty applies even after discharge) (IA 1986, s.291(4)).

Where the Official Receiver is not the trustee, the bankrupt is under a duty to give to his trustee in bankruptcy such information as to his affairs, attend on the trustee at such times and do all such other things as the trustee may, for the purpose of carrying out his functions, reasonably require (IA 1986, s.333(1)).

The trustee is given an intentionally wide power that is to be exercised at his discretion and in respect of which the court is unlikely to intervene unless the use of the power is unreasonable in all the circumstances, or unfair or oppressive. If the bankrupt fails to comply with the reasonable request of the Official Receiver and/or trustee, as they are both officers of the court (*Re Condon, ex p. James* (1874) 9 Ch App 609), the bankrupt is guilty of contempt of court and may be punished by fine and/or imprisonment (IA 1986, s.333(4)). The obligations may also be enforced through mandatory injunction, or by the court executing documents on behalf of the bankrupt (*Morris* v. *Murjani* [1996] 1 WLR 848). Failure to comply with the duties to the trustee may also be a ground for suspension of the bankrupt's discharge (*Re Thorogood (No.3)* [2003] BPIR 1476; *Shierson* v. *Rastogi* [2007] BPIR 891).

The Official Receiver or trustee in bankruptcy may at any time apply to the court for a direction requiring the bankrupt to do such things as may be directed for the purpose of his bankruptcy or the administration of his estate (IA 1986, s.363(2)). This provides a wide power to ensure that the bankrupt provides every possible assistance in the administration of the estate, failure to comply with an order of the court being a contempt of court (*Official Receiver* v. *Cummings-John* [2000] BPIR 320; see also *Boydon* v. *Canty (No.2)* [2007] BPIR 299, where a six-month term of imprisonment was imposed).

The court may also order a warrant of arrest and seizure of any books, papers or records, including computer and non-documentary records (IA 1986, s.436) and money or goods in the possession of the person arrested under the warrant (IA 1986, s.364).

These powers may be exercised where:

(a)   there are reasonable grounds for believing that the bankrupt may abscond, or is about to abscond, avoid or delay payment of his debts, or avoid appearing on the hearing of his bankruptcy petition, or avoid, delay or disrupt any proceedings in bankruptcy, or the examination of his affairs;

(b)   the bankrupt is about to remove goods with a view to preventing or delaying possession being taken by the Official Receiver or trustee;

(c)   there are reasonable grounds for believing that the bankrupt has concealed or destroyed or is about to conceal or destroy goods, books or records which may be of use to the creditors in the course of the bankruptcy or in connection with the administration of the estate;

(d)   the bankrupt has without leave of the Official Receiver or trustee removed any goods in his possession which exceed £1,000 in value (Insolvency Proceedings (Monetary Limits) (Amendment) Order 2004, SI 2004/547); or

(e)   the bankrupt has failed without reasonable excuse to attend an examination on order of the court.

The power of arrest and the interplay with Art.5 of the European Convention on Human Rights was considered in *Hickling* v. *Baker* [2007] BPIR 346. In this case, the Court of Appeal held that an application under IA 1986, s.364 could be made without notice to the bankrupt if supported by appropriate evidence showing why such a course was necessary. Once arrested, the bankrupt should be brought before the court at the earliest possible opportunity. The court also made it clear that the power of arrest under this section was to be treated as a means to compel co-operation rather than as a penalty for which conviction under criminal law is more suitable.

Where the bankrupt may have transferred property into the possession of a third party, the Official Receiver or trustee is entitled to obtain a warrant authorising seizure of the property, or books, papers or records. The court can order forced entry into premises and a search warrant may be obtained.

The Official Receiver and trustee in bankruptcy may also apply for redirection of the bankrupt's incoming post for a period not exceeding three months (IA 1986, s.371 and IR 1986, rule 6.235A). This power has been challenged by a number of bankrupts, using arguments as to their right of private life/privacy enshrined in the European Convention on Human Rights (see *Foxley* v. *United Kingdom* [2000] BPIR 1009; *Narinen* v. *Finland* [2004] BPIR 914; and *Smedley* v. *Brittain* [2008] BPIR 219). However, provided that the terms of the redirection order are strictly observed and the power is exercised proportionately, the power can still be used by a trustee.

10.2.2   Bankruptcy offences

As we have seen above, the bankrupt is under a number of duties and obligations during the course of the bankruptcy. Where in connection with such duties and obligations there has been a failure to abide by a reasonable request of the trustee, in order to compel the bankrupt to discharge his duty the trustee may use the civil courts. If the bankrupt thereafter fails to comply with an order this may be regarded as a contempt of court, which may even lead to arrest.

There are also a number of specific bankruptcy offences that may be committed by the bankrupt either before or after the commencement of the bankruptcy, which may lead to criminal prosecution by the Secretary of State (through the Insolvency Service) or the Director of Public Prosecutions (IA 1986, s.350(5)).

A bankrupt may be prosecuted in respect of such offences irrespective of whether the bankruptcy order has been annulled, although proceedings must have commenced before the annulment (IA 1986, s.350(2)). The bankrupt may also be prosecuted after discharge for offences committed prior to discharge, although again the proceedings must have commenced before the discharge (IA 1986, s.350(3)).

Defence of innocent intention

The bankrupt will not be guilty of any offence (as set out in IA 1986, ss.350–360) if he proves that at the time of the conduct that *prima facie* constituted the offence, he had no intent to defraud or conceal the state of his affairs (IA 1986, s.352). This would suggest that the burden of proof rests on the bankrupt, i.e. it will be for the accused to show positive evidence of a lack of fraud or dishonesty, which reverses the usual burden. While this may seem to be incompatible with European Convention on Human Rights, Art.6(2) (the presumption of innocence unless proven guilty), in *R.* v. *Johnstone* [2003] 3 All ER 884, *Sheldrake* v. *DPP, A-G's Reference (No.4 of 2002)* [2005] 1 AC 264 and *R.* v. *Edwards* [2005] 4 All ER 457, it has been confirmed that in appropriate circumstances it is not an infringement of Art.6(2) to reverse the burden.

This defence will not apply to the offences of:

- failure to account for or explain loss of property;
- failure to inform of a false proof;
- accounting for loss by fictitious losses or expenses;
- fraudulently obtaining the creditor's consent to an agreement, or in relation to the bankrupt's affairs;
- obtaining credit without disclosing bankruptcy status; and
- using a business name other than that in which the individual was adjudged bankrupt.

Each of the offences listed above, however, will require proof of dishonest intention.

Types of offences

The punishment for all of the following offences is on indictment up to seven years' imprisonment and/or an unlimited fine; on summary conviction up to six months' imprisonment and/or a £5,000 fine (IA 1986, Sched.10).

NON-DISCLOSURE

The bankrupt is guilty of an offence (IA 1986, s.353) if he does not, to the best of his knowledge and belief, disclose to the Official Receiver or trustee all of the property comprised in his estate, or where he has disposed of such property which would otherwise have been in his bankruptcy estate.

However, the bankrupt has a defence if he has disposed of property in the ordinary course of business carried on by him, or made payments which are ordinary expenses of the bankrupt and his family.

CONCEALMENT OF PROPERTY

Under IA 1986, s.354, the bankrupt is guilty of an offence if:

- he does not deliver up possession to the Official Receiver or trustee such part of his property as is comprised in his estate and which is within his possession and control;
- he conceals any debt due to him, or from him, or conceals any property the value of which is not less than £1,000 (Insolvency Proceedings (Monetary Limits) (Amendment) Order 2004, SI 2004/547);
- within 12 months of the petition, or between the date of the presentation of the petition and the commencement of the bankruptcy, the bankrupt conceals any debt due or conceals any property;
- he removes, between the date of presentation of the petition and commencement of bankruptcy, any property in excess of £1,000 in value which he would otherwise have been required to deliver to the Official Receiver or trustee (this includes payment of a non-provable debt; see *Woodley* v. *Woodley (No.2)* [1994] 1 WLR 1167); or
- without reasonable excuse the bankrupt fails, on being required to do so, to account for the loss of any substantial part of his property in the 12 months prior to bankruptcy and to give an explanation as to the manner in which and why loss had been incurred (this is an offence of strict liability, in respect of which the defence of innocent intention does not apply; see *R.* v. *Salter* [1968] 2 All ER 951 and *R.* v. *Kearns* [2002] 1 WLR 2815, where the court confirmed there is no right against self-incrimination).

CONCEALMENT OF BOOKS AND PAPERS; FALSIFICATION

Under IA 1986, s.355, the bankrupt is guilty of an offence if he:

- does not deliver up to the Official Receiver or trustee all of his books, papers and records which are in his possession or control, and which relate to his estate, or his affairs;
- prevents, or between the date of the petition and the commencement of the bankruptcy prevented, production of any books, papers or records relating to his affairs by any third party;
- destroys, conceals, mutilates or falsifies or causes or permits the concealment, destruction, mutilation or falsification of any books, papers or records relating to his estate or affairs, or did so within 12 months before the date of the petition (two years in the case of any 'trading record', defined in IA 1986, s.355(5)), or between the date of the petition and the commencement of the bankruptcy;
- makes or causes the making of any false entries in any books, documents or records relating to his estate or affairs, or did so within 12 months before the date of the petition (two years in the case of any trading record, defined in IA 1986, s.355(5)), or between the date of the petition and the commencement of the bankruptcy; or
- disposes of, or alters, or makes any omission in, or causes or permits the disposal or alteration of, or omission in, any books, documents or records of his estate, or did so within 12 months before the date of the petition (two years in the case of any trading record, defined in IA 1986, s.355(5)), or between the date of the petition and the commencement of the bankruptcy.

FALSE STATEMENTS

Under IA 1986, s.356, the bankrupt is guilty of an offence if he:

- makes, or has made, any material omission in any statement provided to the Official Receiver or trustee in bankruptcy;
- knowing or believing that a false debt has been proved by any person in the bankruptcy, fails to inform the trustee as soon as practicable or attempts to account for any part of his property by fictitious losses or expenses;
- within 12 months before the commencement of bankruptcy, attempts to account for any part of his property by fictitious losses or expenses; or
- has made a false representation or other fraud for the purpose of obtaining the consent of his creditors or any of them to an agreement with reference to his affairs or to his bankruptcy.

There is a specific provision dealing with falsification in respect of IVA procedures, although this section provides wider relief for creditors in respect of all forms of agreement, formal or informal.

FRAUDULENT DISPOSAL OF PROPERTY

Under IA 1986, s.357, the bankrupt is guilty of an offence if he:

- makes or causes to be made, or in a period of five years ending with the commencement of the bankruptcy has made or caused to be made, any fraudulent gift or transfer of, or any charge on, his property; or
- conceals or removes property, or at any time before the commencement of the bankruptcy has concealed or removed any part of his property within two months of the date upon which an unsatisfied judgment or order for payment of money was obtained against him (see *R.* v. *Mungroo* [1998] BPIR 784).

ABSCONDING WITH PROPERTY

The bankrupt is guilty of an offence if he leaves or attempts to leave England and Wales with any property of a value in excess of £1,000 (Insolvency Proceedings (Monetary Limits) (Amendment) Order 2004, SI 2004/547), possession of which is required to be delivered up to the Official Receiver or trustee, or did so within six months before the date of the petition, or between the date of the presentation of the petition and the date of the bankruptcy order (IA 1986, s.358).

FRAUDULENT DEALING WITH PROPERTY OBTAINED ON CREDIT

The bankrupt is guilty of an offence if within 12 months of the date of the petition, or between the date of the petition and commencement of the bankruptcy, he disposed of property which he had obtained on credit and at the time of disposal it had not been paid for (IA 1986, s.359).

A recipient is also guilty of an offence if he acquired property from the bankrupt knowing or believing the bankrupt owed money in respect of that property and that the bankrupt did not intend or was unlikely to pay the money he owed.

An offence is not committed if the disposal, acquisition or receipt of property was in the ordinary course of business carried on by the bankrupt at the time of disposal, acquisition or receipt.

OBTAINING CREDIT/ENGAGING IN BUSINESS

Under IA 1986, s.360, a bankrupt is guilty of an offence if:

- either alone or jointly with any other person he obtains credit in excess of £500 (Insolvency Proceedings (Monetary Limits) (Amendment) Order 2004, SI 2004/547), either in one transaction or over several transactions (*R.* v. *Hartley* [1972] 2 QB 1), without giving the person for whom he obtains credit relevant information regarding his bankruptcy; or
- he engages in any business under a name other than that under which he was adjudged bankrupt without first disclosing to persons with whom he enters into any business transaction the name under which he was adjudged bankrupt.

These provisions restrict the bankrupt's ability both to obtain credit and to trade in business. It is important to remember, however, that if a creditor is willing to lend money to the bankrupt it can do, although the creditor clearly bears a risk in doing so. The obligation on the bankrupt is simply to disclose the fact of his bankruptcy (see *Fisher* v. *Raven* [1964] AC 210 and *R.* v. *Miller* [1977] 3 All ER 986).

10.2.3 Further restrictions during bankruptcy

An important aim of the Enterprise Act 2002 was to relax the prohibitions and restrictions on bankrupts generally. To counter this liberalisation, a BRO regime was introduced (see **10.3**). For non-culpable bankrupts (who it was estimated by the Insolvency Service represent 85–95 per cent of all bankrupts), it was hoped that significantly less stigma would attach to bankruptcy and that many professional bodies may follow the example set by the legislature in distinguishing between those bankrupts who are subject to a BRO and those who are not. Hundreds of restrictions which arise on bankruptcy remain, although the Secretary of State has wide powers to review the current statutory restrictions on bankrupts.

Examples

- Prior to the Enterprise Act 2002, an MP declared bankrupt could not be elected to sit or vote in the House of Commons. These restrictions now apply only to individual MPs who are subject to a BRO (IA 1986, s.426A).
- An undischarged bankrupt will no longer be automatically disqualified from being a Justice of the Peace.
- An individual is no longer automatically disqualified from holding office in local government while bankrupt.
- An undischarged bankrupt may not act as a director of, or be directly or indirectly concerned in or take part in the promotion, formation, or management of a company except with leave of the court (CDDA 1986, s.11(1)). The prohibition on directorship also applies where the discharged bankrupt is subject to a BRO (CDDA 1986, s.11(1), as amended by the Enterprise Act 2002, Sched.21, para.5).
- An undischarged bankrupt, or a person subject to a BRO, may not be a receiver or manager of a property or company on behalf of a debenture holder (IA 1986, s.31).
- An undischarged bankrupt is not automatically disqualified from acting as a trustee, although the circumstances surrounding bankruptcy may provide cause for his removal (Trustee Act 1925, s.36(1)).
- An undischarged bankrupt is prohibited from acting as a trustee of a charity (Charities Act 1993, s.72(1)(b)).
- An undischarged bankrupt may not be appointed attorney under a lasting power of attorney (Mental Capacity Act 2005, s.10(2)).
- An insolvency practitioner is automatically disqualified from acting while bankrupt, or while subject to a BRO (IA 1986, s.390(4)).

10.3 BANKRUPTCY RESTRICTIONS ORDERS (BROS)

10.3.1 Introduction

The BRO and bankruptcy restrictions undertaking (BRU) procedures were introduced by the Enterprise Act 2002 and came into effect on 1 April 2004.

The procedures act as a safeguard, penalising certain culpable bankrupts whose conduct is such that some form of sanction is considered by the court to be appropriate. These include individuals who are perceived to have abused the bankruptcy system by taking on credit when they had no possibility of paying, or being engaged in other improper or unlawful conduct, or where the bankrupt is otherwise to blame for his own financial misfortune.

The DBIS maintains a searchable database of those subject to a BRO or BRU (under the obligation in IA 1986, Sched.4A, para.12) (see **www.bis.gov.uk/ insolvency**). This seems to show that most restrictions are imposed on debtors who have taken on debt with no reasonable prospect of payment, where gambling and unreasonable extravagance have led to bankruptcy, or where there has been neglect of business affairs.

In the consultation process leading up to the reforms, it was estimated by the Insolvency Service that 7–12 per cent of all bankrupts are in some way culpable. In respect of the numbers of bankrupts since 2004, those being penalised by further restriction represent a mere fraction, although as the procedure has become better established, and the use of the undertaking process increased, numbers are swiftly rising.

The provisions were also introduced to allow lenders and the public to differentiate between the culpable and non-culpable bankrupts and allow better informed decision making, encouraging the financial rehabilitation of debtors who are adjudged to be without blame.

The provisions are also aimed at deterring fraud and misconduct. With BRO numbers representing a small fraction of the numbers entering bankruptcy, it is not clear if the provisions have had any such effect.

10.3.2 Procedure

Guide to procedure

BRO

- The application for a BRO must be supported by the Secretary of State's report, which must set out the conduct which it is alleged justifies the making of a BRO. Any evidence relied upon should be in the form of an affidavit if produced other than by the Secretary of State.
- The Secretary of State must serve the application and evidence upon the bankrupt within 14 days of filing.

- The bankrupt must acknowledge service within 14 days. Where the bankrupt fails to do so, he may only attend or take part in the forthcoming hearing if given permission by the court.
- If the bankrupt wishes to serve evidence in rebuttal, he has 28 days from the date of service of the application to file such evidence.
- The bankrupt has three days after filing evidence to serve a copy upon the Secretary of State.
- The Secretary of State has 14 days thereafter to file further evidence in reply.
- The court may make a BRO whether the bankrupt appears at the hearing or not and whether evidence has been filed in rebuttal or not.
- Where the court makes a BRO, two copies are sent the Secretary of State. Upon receipt, the Secretary of State must send a sealed copy of the order to the bankrupt (IR 1986, rules 6.241(1), 6.241(3), 6.242(4), 6.243(2)).

The BRO may be made by order of the court on application of the Secretary of State (through the office of the Insolvency Service) or the Official Receiver, acting on the directions of the Secretary of State (IA 1986, Sched.4A, para.1).

The court has a wide discretion as to whether to grant an order, having regard to the conduct of the bankrupt both before and after the making of the bankruptcy order. Each case will depend on its own facts. (See *Randhawa* v. *Official Receiver* [2006] BPIR 1435, where it was held that once the court was persuaded that the conduct merited a BRO it was obliged to make an order; *Official Receiver* v. *Doganci* [2007] BPIR 87, where the bankrupt's explanation as to loss of property was implausible but not necessarily untruthful and as a result no BRO was made; *Official Receiver* v. *Southey* [2009] BPIR 89, where the court was not persuaded that the bankrupt had incurred credit with no prospect of repaying it.)

The court must in particular take account of the following kinds of behaviour on the part of the bankrupt (IA 1986, Sched.4A, para.2(2)):

(a) Failing to keep records which account for the loss of property by the bankrupt, or by a business carried on by him, where the loss occurred in the period beginning two years before the petition and ending with the date of the application.

(b) Failing to produce records of that kind when demanded by the Official Receiver or trustee.

(c) Entering into a transaction at an undervalue (IA 1986, s.339).

(d) Giving a preference (IA 1986, s.340).

(e) Making an excessive pension contribution (IA 1986, s.342A).

(f) Failing to supply goods or services that were wholly or partly paid for, which gave rise to a claim provable in the bankruptcy.

(g) Trading at a time before commencement of the bankruptcy when the bankrupt knew or ought to have known that he was going to be unable to pay his debts (note this introduces into personal insolvency law a provision akin to wrongful trading).

(h) Incurring, before the commencement of the bankruptcy, a debt which the bankrupt had no reasonable expectation of being able to pay.

(i) Failing to account satisfactorily to the court, the Official Receiver or trustee for loss of property or for an insufficiency of property to meet his bankruptcy debts.

(j) Carrying on any gambling, rash or hazardous speculation or unreasonable extravagance which may have materially contributed to or materially increased the extent of the bankruptcy debt or which took place between the presentation of the petition and the commencement of the bankruptcy.

(k) Neglect of business affairs of a kind which may have materially contributed to or increased the extent of the bankruptcy debt.

(l) Fraud or fraudulent breach of trust.

(m) Failing to co-operate with the Official Receiver or trustee.

The court must also, in particular, consider whether the bankrupt was an undischarged bankrupt at some time during the six years ending on the date of the bankruptcy to which the application relates (IA 1986, Sched.4A, para.2(3)).

An application for a BRO must be made before the end of the expiry of the first year of bankruptcy, calculated from the date upon which the bankruptcy commences. The one-year limitation period will be automatically extended if the bankrupt's discharge has been suspended (IA 1986, Sched.4A, para.3(2)).

If proceedings are deemed to be appropriate after that date, an application must be made to the court for permission to commence BRO proceedings. The court is unlikely to provide permission to extend the time unless there is good reason for the delay, as Human Rights Act 1998 considerations come into play. An individual has a right to a fair trial, and this includes determination of his civil rights and obligations within a reasonable time.

The BRO comes into effect upon the date the order is made and will continue for a minimum of two years or a maximum of 15 years. Guidance on the appropriate period of the BRO may be obtained by looking at the procedures under CDDA 1986, in particular, the guidance delivered by the Court of Appeal in *Re Sevenoaks Stationers (Retail) Ltd* [1991] 3 All ER 578 (see also *Randhawa* v. *Official Receiver* [2007] 1 All ER 755).

The *Sevenoaks* case laid down a three-tier approach as follows:

(a) The maximum period of disqualification, periods of over 10 years, should be reserved for particularly serious cases, including previous disqualification.

(b) The middle bracket, between six and 10 years, is for the 'serious cases, which do not merit top bracket'.

(c) The minimum bracket of two to five years' disqualification should be applied where 'the disqualification is merited, but the case, relatively, is not very serious'.

In directors' disqualification proceedings, the court has always been left with a broad discretion to weigh up the relative degree of seriousness of each case.

Guidance provided by case law, while of assistance, does not set out specific types of conduct that will automatically justify a particular sentence. The register kept by the DBIS will be a good guide to the current duration of BROs/BRUs.

In *Randhawa* v. *Official Receiver* [2007] 1 All ER 755, a three-year BRO was imposed on a bankrupt who had incurred significant credit card debts on his and his wife's cards when both had just had an IVA proposal rejected and faced near certain bankruptcy. In *Official Receiver* v. *Pyman* [2007] All ER (D) 25 (Mar), on appeal a BRO of seven years was imposed on a debtor who had previously been bankrupt and was found to have transferred the assets of a business to his son for no proper value prior to petitioning for his own bankruptcy. In *Official Receiver* v. *Bathurst* [2008] BPIR 1548, a case which established that there are moral obligations to be considered, a nine-year period of restriction was imposed.

10.3.3   Interim bankruptcy restrictions order (interim BRO)

Guide to procedure

- The Secretary of State applies for an interim BRO. The court fixes a date and venue for a hearing.
- Notice of the application to be given to the bankrupt at least two days before the date set for hearing.
- The Secretary of State must file a report in court as evidence in support of his application. The report must include evidence of the bankrupt's conduct which constitutes *prima facie* justification for making an interim BRO or evidence which shows the public interest in making a BRO.
- Any evidence produced other than by the Secretary of State must be verified by an affidavit.
- The bankrupt may file any evidence at court, which may or may not be taken into consideration.
- The court may make an interim BRO whether or not the bankrupt appears at the hearing or whether he has submitted evidence or not.
- On making of the interim BRO, two copies of the order should be sent to the Secretary of State and thereafter one copy should be served by the Secretary of State on the bankrupt.
- A bankrupt may apply to the court to set aside an interim BRO. The application must be supported by an affidavit.
- Where the bankrupt has applied to set aside the interim BRO, not less than seven days before the date of hearing he must serve upon the Secretary of State the application notice and copy of the affidavit in support.
- The Secretary of State may attend the hearing and call to the attention of the court such matters he considers relevant and may himself give evidence or call witnesses.
- If the court sets aside the interim BRO, two copies must be sent to the Secretary of State and thereafter one copy shall be served upon the bankrupt by the Secretary of State (IR 1986, rules 6.246, 6.247, 6.248).

Where it is unlikely that a substantive hearing of the BRO will take place prior to the discharge of the bankrupt, an application may be made to the court for an interim order by the Secretary of State. This would appear to be particularly useful in a case where it is likely that the BRO will be contested and directions might be required regarding the exchange of evidence.

An interim order is likely to be made where the court is satisfied that it is in the public interest, or there are *prima facie* grounds to suggest that the BRO will be successful.

The interim BRO can only be made after the institution of an application for a BRO (IA 1986, Sched.4A, para.5(1)(a)).

An interim BRO will have the same effect as a BRO and will cease to have effect on:

- the determination of the application for the BRO;
- the acceptance of a BRU made by the bankrupt; or
- discharge by the court.

In the event that the BRO is subsequently made, the commencement date is backdated to the date on which the interim BRO commenced (IA 1986, Sched.4A, para.6(2)).

10.3.4 Bankruptcy restrictions undertaking (BRU)

Guide to procedure

- A BRU signed by the bankrupt is deemed to have been accepted by the Secretary of State when the undertaking is signed by the Secretary of State.
- As soon as the BRU has been accepted, copies will be sent to the bankrupt and filed at court. Copies should be sent to the Official Receiver and not to the applicant.
- An application by the bankrupt to annul the BRU is made to court and supported by an affidavit.
- The bankrupt's application must give the Secretary of State at least 28 days' notice before the date fixed for a hearing.
- The Secretary of State may attend the hearing, calling the court's attention to such matters considered relevant and may himself give evidence or call witnesses.
- The court sends a sealed copy of any order annulling or varying the BRU to the applicant and to the Official Receiver (IR 1986, rules 6.249, 6.251).

IA 2000 introduced reforms to the CDDA 1986 procedure to enable directors to provide undertakings in place of disqualification by court order. Prior to this reform, procedures had developed whereby the Secretary of State (through the DBIS Disqualification Unit) would agree a set of facts to be put before the court and suggest a disqualification tariff. This procedure was known as the *Carecraft* procedure (see *Re Carecraft Construction Co. Ltd* [1994] 1 WLR 172). IA 2000 put this form of procedure on a statutory footing and allowed the summary disposal of applications which were not contested.

In respect of bankruptcy restrictions, a similar procedure has been introduced, namely to avoid the necessity and associated costs of a hearing, the bankrupt may offer a BRU to the Secretary of State. As a result, the majority of bankruptcy restrictions now follow from an undertaking.

The Secretary of State will consider whether accepting a BRU is appropriate, having regard to the behaviour considered by the court when making a BRO (IA 1986, Sched.4A, para.7(2)).

A BRU will come into force on being accepted by the Secretary of State and will cease to have effect upon the date specified in the undertaking. The undertaking must be for a period of between two and 15 years. The bankrupt may apply to court to annul the BRU or provide that the BRU ceases to have effect before the date specified in the undertaking (IA 1986, Sched.4A, para.9(3)).

One possible problem identified during the passage of the Enterprise Bill through Parliament was the interplay between the new BRO regime and post-bankruptcy fast-track voluntary arrangements (FTVAs) (see **10.5**).

The effect of any IVA is to annul the bankruptcy. While this procedure offers clear encouragement for debtor rehabilitation and may ensure a greater return to creditors, it could potentially be exploited by unscrupulous bankrupts to avoid the restrictions of a BRO or BRU.

As a consequence, if the court annuls a bankruptcy order on the ground that at the time of the order grounds existed which meant that the order should not have been made, the BRO/BRU will be annulled (IA 1986, s.282(1)(a), (2)). However, where the bankruptcy debts are purposely paid off in full, or where there has been an annulment on different grounds (IA 1986, ss.261, 263D):

(a) the annulment will not affect any BRO, interim BRO or BRU;

(b) the court may still make a BRU in relation to the bankrupt on application instituted before the annulment; and/or

(c) the Secretary of State may still accept a BRU offered before such an annulment.

In *Jenkins* v. *Official Receiver* [2007] All ER (D) 139 (Apr), despite the fact that the bankrupt had paid off the bankruptcy debts and obtained an annulment, a BRO remained in place as the debtor, while bankrupt, had continued to act as a director of a company and had failed to distinguish between his own money and that of the company.

However, it should be noted that an application for a BRO or an interim BRO has to be instituted before the annulment. Therefore, the Official Receiver must ensure that the application for a BRO has been commenced before an annulment is granted by the court. This means that within the first 28 days of bankruptcy (i.e. before an FTVA can be proposed) the Official Receiver must have completed his investigations, concluded that he is satisfied that the BRO should not be instituted and agreed that an FTVA may be proposed. If this is not the case, the FTVA should not be recommended to the bankrupt's creditors as this would risk allowing a bankrupt to avoid being subject to the new BRO regime. The whole bankruptcy process needs to be quickly and efficiently dealt with by the Official Receiver's office. However, coupled with the fact that there is no mandatory duty on the Official Receiver to investigate, this speed may mean that some unscrupulous bankrupts can abuse the system. Greater creditor participation in the bankruptcy process is necessary to avoid such abuse.

10.4   THE BANKRUPT'S INCOME

10.4.1   Introduction

Save for the bankrupt's basic necessities (tools of the trade, a vehicle, household effects, etc. as defined in IA 1986, s.283(2) and subject to IA 1986, s.308 where they are of substantial value), the majority of assets within the bankrupt's estate vest in the trustee in bankruptcy immediately on the appointment taking effect or, in the case of the Official Receiver, on him becoming trustee (IA 1986, s.306).

As we have seen above (**10.1.3**) property and assets acquired by the bankrupt after the date of bankruptcy are treated differently; they do not automatically vest in the trustee. Income falls into this category. To take into account income earned by the bankrupt during the duration of the bankruptcy, IA 1986 introduced certain statutory provisions, including a system of income payments orders (IPOs), whereby the trustee could claim part of the bankrupt's income for the benefit of his creditors (IA 1986, s.310(1)).

'Income' comprises every payment received or to which the bankrupt is entitled, including payments by way of guaranteed minimum pension and payments giving effect to the bankrupt's protected rights as a member of a pension scheme (IA 1986, s.310(8), introduced by the Pensions Act 1995, Sched.3, para.15). Note that prior to the changes introduced by the Welfare Reform and Pensions Act 1999, pensions (both the policy and the right to receive an annuity) were more likely to form part of the bankrupt's estate vesting in the trustee on appointment; as a result the payments under the annuity were not treated as income (*Re Landau (a Bankrupt)* [1998] Ch 223). Payments of income can be periodic or one-off payments (*Supperstone* v. *Lloyd's Name Association Working Party* [1999] BPIR 832). 'Income' is very widely defined and covers virtually any monies received by an employee or a self-employed person for labour and services (IA 1986, s.310(7)).

Prior to 1 April 2004, when an IPO order had been obtained it ended on the discharge of the bankrupt. As the Enterprise Act 2002 reforms have the effect of generally shortening the duration of the bankruptcy in the majority of cases, there was concern that if the IPO procedure remained unamended, undoubtedly it would have resulted in less income being available to the bankrupt's creditors. While the application can only be made by the trustee before the discharge of the bankrupt (IA

1986, s.310(1A)), the order may be for a period expiring after the discharge of the bankrupt and up to a maximum of three years from the date of the bankruptcy order (IA 1986, s.310(6)).

To save costs and speed up the procedure, settlement can also be effected by means of an income payments agreement (IPA) (i.e. an agreement reached between the bankrupt and his trustee in bankruptcy), which will be enforceable as if it were an IPO (IA 1986, s.310A).

Since the reforms of 1 April 2004, there has been a dramatic rise in the use of IPAs, with only a handful of IPOs now being obtained or indeed needed. The rise in the use of the procedure may be partially ascribed to the rise in the number of individual insolvencies, but anecdotal evidence also suggests that the Official Receiver's office now looks much more closely at the bankrupt's income and seeks to impose some form of income recovery as a matter of course. Recent falls in bankruptcy numbers and possibly cuts within the insolvency service may account for falls in 2011/12.

Table 10.1 IPOs and agreements 1998–2012

Year	Total	IPOs	IPAs
1998	1487	1487	
1999	1799	1799	
2000	1811	1811	
2001	1947	1947	
2002	1893	1893	
2003	2357	2265	92
2004	6254	1254	5000
2005	9102	69	9033
2006	11990	86	11904
2007	13332	77	13255
2008	13265	67	13198
2009	15401	64	15337
2010	12891	Not available	Not available
2011	10643	Not available	Not available
2012	6877	76	6801

Source: Insolvency Service Statistical Directorate

10.4.2   Income payments order

Procedure

Guide to procedure

IPO

- Trustee issues application and serves this on the bankrupt (in Form 6.64), giving at least 28 days' notice.
- The bankrupt can up to seven days before the hearing consent to the application.
- Otherwise, a hearing takes place and, if an order is made (in Form 6.65 or 6.66), it will be served upon the bankrupt.
- If the bankrupt fails to comply with the terms of an agreed IPO, the trustee may apply (in Form 6.67) *ex parte* to vary the agreed order, so as to take effect as if it were an order made by the court.
- At any time the trustee or bankrupt can apply to vary or discharge the IPO.

On application by the trustee and before the discharge of the bankrupt, the court may order that the bankrupt provides to the bankruptcy estate, from his income, such payment as is thought appropriate, a so-called 'income payments order' (IPO) (IA 1986, s.310(1)).

'Income' is very widely defined and covers virtually any monies received by the bankrupt as an employee or a self-employed person for labour and services (IA 1986, s.310(7)). Where the bankrupt is carrying on a business, the income from the business will be treated as estate income (*Papanicola* v. *Humphreys* [2005] 2 All ER 418 concerning the bankrupt's restaurant business).

Income also includes payments made by way of a guaranteed minimum pension, and payments giving effect to the bankrupt's protected rights as a member of a pension scheme (IA 1986, s.310(8), introduced by the Pensions Act 1995, Sched.3, para.15). See comments in section above the treatment of income in the context of pension provision.

The court will not make an IPO if it will reduce the income of the bankrupt to a level below what is necessary to meet the reasonable domestic needs of the bankrupt and his family (IA 1986, s.310(2)). The court needs to weigh up the interests of the creditors against those of the bankrupt and his family. 'Family' means persons who are living with the bankrupt and dependent on him (IA 1986, s.385(1)), although payments made to children living away from the bankrupt may also be considered (*Re X (a Bankrupt)* [1996] BPIR 494).

The amount that a bankrupt may be able to retain from his income, either in terms of an amount or as a percentage, is adjudged according to the bankrupt family's particular needs. The test is therefore subjective rather than objective. See *Re Rayatt (a Bankrupt)* [1998] 2 FLR 264, where the court decided that expenditure by the bankrupt on the private schooling of his children was reasonable. See also *Malcolm*

v. *Official Receiver* [1999] BPIR 97, where it was held it was unreasonable for a bankrupt to live in a home which required mortgage payments of £820 per month out of a monthly income of £1,100. In *Scott* v. *Davis* [2003] BPIR 1009, the court stressed the importance of viewing each particular case in relation to its own facts, e.g. would there be a detrimental effect on the children in removing them from private school? The court will not, however, make a bankrupt a 'slave to his creditors' (*Re Rayatt (a Bankrupt)* [1998] 2 FLR 264; *Kilvert* v. *Flackett* [1998] BPIR 721) or reduce him and his family to penury (*Re Roberts* [1900] 1 QB 122 and *Boyden* v. *Watson* [2004] BPIR 1131).

It should be noted that, provided there is surplus income and the amount of the income payment will exceed £20, it is anticipated that an IPO will be made, or more likely an IPA will be agreed.

The Insolvency Services technical manual (**www.insolvency.gov.uk**) at 31.7, Part 2 provides some useful guidance to the Official Receiver/trustee on what may be regarded as a reasonable domestic need. It includes payments for a TV licence, reasonable mobile phone costs, modest holiday requirements and one extra-curricular class per child. In contrast, payments for gym membership, private healthcare or additional pension contributions would not generally be regarded as reasonable, unless there were extenuating circumstances.

While the application for an IPO can only be made by the trustee before the discharge of the bankrupt (IA 1986, s.310(1A)), the order may be for a period expiring after the discharge of the bankrupt and up to a maximum of three years from the date of the bankruptcy order (IA 1986, s.310(6)).

To save costs and to speed up the procedure, settlement can also be effected by means of an IPA (i.e. an agreement reached between the bankrupt and his trustee in bankruptcy), which will be enforceable as if it were an IPO (IA 1986, s.310A). This is by far the most relied-upon procedure, with anecdotal evidence suggesting that the Official Receiver's office now looks much more closely at the bankrupt's income and seeks to impose some form of income recovery as a matter of course.

An application for an IPO may only be made by the trustee prior to the bankrupt's discharge and will be made to the court that is dealing with the bankruptcy (IA 1986, s.310(1A)). The court will fix a venue and date for the hearing and the bankrupt should be given not less than 28 days' notice (IR 1986, rule 6.189, application in Form 6.64).

The notice provides that not less than five business days before the hearing, the bankrupt should set out whether he will consent to the order: if he does not consent, he is obliged to attend the hearing and will be given the opportunity to show cause as to why the order should not be made, or why an order other than that being sought by the trustee should be made.

Where an order is made by the court (in Form 6.65), it should be served on the bankrupt by the trustee as soon as reasonably practicable.

An IPO may be made to require the bankrupt to pay a sum to his trustee or it may require a third party to pay monies otherwise due to the bankrupt to the trustee. A common example of this would be an order on the bankrupt's employer (IA 1986, s.310(3)). If the third party is no longer liable to pay the bankrupt any income or has complied with the order of the court, the third party is no longer liable; it is however the third party's duty to give immediate notice of the fact to the trustee (IR 1986, rule 6.192(3)).

The amount ordered to be paid may be staggered and incrementally increased, allowing for the bankrupt to change spending patterns and make alternative arrangements (e.g. to reduce what may be considered excessive mortgage payment contributions).

At any time during the duration of the IPO, the trustee or the bankrupt may apply to discharge or vary the order (IA 1986, s.310(6A)). An application to review the order should be accompanied by a short statement from the applicant setting out the grounds upon which it is made (IR 1986, rule 6.193(3)). The court may dismiss the application, but will not do so unless the applicant has been given the opportunity of obtaining an *ex parte* hearing before the court, with at least five business days' notice provided of that hearing (IR 1986, rule 6.193(4)). In the case that the court is prepared to review the order, 28 days' notice will be given to the trustee of the hearing (IR 1986, rule 6.193(5)).

The trustee may appear at the hearing and in any event not less than five business days before the date of the hearing may file a written report of any matters he considers ought to be drawn to the court's attention. This report will be sent by the trustee to the bankrupt (IR 1986, rule 6.193(6)).

10.4.3   Income payments agreement

Guide to procedure

IPA

- Prior to discharge, the trustee in bankruptcy may agree the terms of an IPA.
- Within 14 days of receiving a draft IPA, the bankrupt has to sign or give reasons for refusal.
- On receipt, the trustee shall sign and date the IPA and at that point the IPA comes into force.
- The trustee sends a copy of the IPA to the bankrupt and to any third party (if appropriate).
- An application to vary the terms of the IPA may be made to court by either the trustee or the bankrupt, giving at least 28 days' notice of hearing.
- The court may order a variation of the IPA (in Form 6.81).

An IPA must be made in writing, between the bankrupt and the trustee or between the bankrupt and the Official Receiver (IA 1986, s.310A(1)).

When the trustee and the bankrupt have reached agreement in principle, the trustee will send to the bankrupt a draft IPA giving at least 14 days for the bankrupt to decide whether to accept the terms of the agreement, sign it and return it, or notify the trustee in writing of his decision not to approve the terms of the agreement (IR 1986, rule 6.193A(3)). On refusal by the bankrupt, the trustee may seek to renegotiate the terms of the IPA or apply to court for an IPO.

Once the IPA has been signed by the bankrupt and returned to the trustee, on authentication and dating by the trustee it will become enforceable as if it were created by order of the court (IA 1986, s.310A(2) and IR 1986, rule 6.193B).

Where the agreement provides for payment from a third party (e.g. an employer), the trustee must send notice of the agreement to the payor (IR 1986, rule 6.193B(4)), who is entitled to deduct an administrative charge for dealing with the notice requirements (IR 1986, rule 13.11; as at September 2011, 50 pence).

An IPA may be varied at any time by written agreement between the parties, or on application to the court. When an application to the court is made, the application must contain a copy of the agreement (IR 1986, rule 6.193C(1)). Notice of the hearing must be served by the bankrupt upon the trustee or vice versa, giving at least 28 days' notice of the hearing (IR 1986, rule 6.193C(2), (3)). The court may not vary the IPA to include a provision which could not have been included in an IPO (IA 1986, s.310A(7)). This brings into play considerations of the reasonable domestic needs of the bankrupt and his family, which would not otherwise be directly considered on the making of an IPA. However, it is unlikely that a trustee would seek to impose unreasonable or harsh terms on the bankrupt if satisfactory evidence were provided by the bankrupt of his reasonable domestic needs.

An IPO (IA 1986, s.310(6)) or IPA (IA 1986, s.310A(5)) may not exceed a term of three years from the date of the bankruptcy order.

10.5 FAST TRACK VOLUNTARY ARRANGEMENT (FTVA)

10.5.1 Introduction

One option which is now available to any bankrupt prior to discharge is to put forward a voluntary arrangement to his creditors under IA 1986, s.263B (a 'fast track voluntary arrangement' (FTVA)). This provision was introduced by the Enterprise Act 2002 and came into force on 1 April 2004. It provides the Official Receiver with an ability to act as nominee and supervisor of an FTVA (IA 1986, s.389B).

It was the hope of the government that post-bankruptcy FTVAs would be one of the measures which encouraged greater debtor rehabilitation, greater return to creditors and economies of scale in cost of the operation resulting from the process being centrally managed by the Official Receiver's office. Despite the fact that there has been a very large rise in IVAs since 2004, the FTVA procedure has been little used. Whether this is as a result of the administrative burden imposed on the Insolvency Service and therefore a failure to set up the systems necessary to run large numbers of FTVAs, a lack of suitable debtors, or an unwillingness of debtors to enter into IVAs post bankruptcy is unclear.

Table 10.2 Advantages and disadvantages to debtor of FTVA

Advantages	Disadvantages
• Avoids disability/restrictions of a bankruptcy	• On failure of IVA, bankrupt deemed bankrupt a second time and therefore possible BRO
• Certainty	• Terms may be potentially more harsh than bankruptcy
• Inexpensive	• Long-term effect
	• Unsuitable for complex IVA provisions (trader or professional)

The advantage of the procedure is that the FTVA will annul the bankruptcy order so that the debtor avoids the disabilities and restrictions of bankruptcy. The debtor will also have the certainty of knowing exactly how much he will need to contribute to the FTVA and when. Creditors may also have an advantage in this procedure, as the FTVA may be subject to contributions from a third party which would not otherwise be available in bankruptcy. A greater return may therefore result. It is also likely to be an inexpensive and quick procedure, as we shall see below.

The significant disadvantages to the bankrupt, however, are that if the FTVA fails the consequential bankruptcy of the individual will result in a second bankruptcy, in which case the bankrupt may be subject to a BRO (IA 1986, Sched.4A, para.2(3)). In considering whether to impose a BRO, the court will consider whether the bankrupt was an undischarged bankrupt at some time during the last six years. The terms the creditors also seek to impose may be considerably harsher than those a debtor would bear during bankruptcy. The debtor may also be subject to the FTVA for a considerably longer term than under bankruptcy.

The guidance leaflet introduced by the Insolvency Service makes it clear that FTVAs will be unsuitable where the bankrupt has a number of assets to sell or the proposal is otherwise complicated. The procedure is designed to deal only with straightforward sales, or disposal of assets or simple regular repayment programmes. As a result, the procedure is unlikely to appeal to traders and professionals, who will continue to use the services of private sector insolvency professionals to draw up more complex proposals. The large growth in consumer debtors has, however, seen an explosion in simple pre-bankruptcy IVAs proposed by specialist firms that heavily advertise their services; this means that those debtors with some assets (say a house) or a regular income have been attracted in unprecedented numbers to enter into IVAs prior to bankruptcy. As a result, it could be the case that those now entering bankruptcy may have less to offer creditors (in terms of either assets available for sale or income to make payments); this therefore reduces the numbers of those suitable for an FTVA and may partially explain its low take-up rate.

10.5.2 Procedure

Guide to procedure

- Debtor puts forward proposal accompanied by a £300 fee to cover the Official Receiver's costs and a £35 registration fee.
- The Official Receiver has 28 days to agree/decline to accept a nominee in relation to the proposal. The Official Receiver may, however, ask for more information.
- As soon as reasonably practicable, after agreeing to the proposal, the Official Receiver will send notice of the proposal to creditors and give between 14 and 28 days for the creditors to reply.
- Creditors either accept or reject proposals (in Form 5.6).
- The proposal requires a majority in excess of three-quarters in value of those voting.
- On a result being obtained, the Official Receiver reports to the court and sends notice to the Secretary of State and creditors.
- Not less often than every 12 months thereafter, the supervisor should report on the progress of the IVA.
- Not more than 28 days after completion of the IVA, the supervisor will send notice to all creditors of the debtor bound by the voluntary arrangement, and to the debtor, a report summarising all receipts and payments made. Copies should also be sent to the Secretary of State upon which date the supervisor vacates office.

At the initial interview with the debtor, the Official Receiver may discuss the possibility of the debtor putting forward an FTVA. If appropriate, the debtor, in submitting a statement of affairs, will put forward a document setting out the terms of the proposal (IA 1986, s.263(B)) together with the appropriate fee (Insolvency Proceedings (Fees) Order 2004, SI 2004/593). In addition to these fees, if approved, the Official Receiver as supervisor of the FTVA will charge a fee equal to 15 per cent of realisations.

If the Official Receiver thinks that the voluntary arrangement has a reasonable prospect of being approved by the creditors, he must send to every creditor a copy of the proposed FTVA and ask them to approve or reject it. The Official Receiver retains a discretion as to whether to accept the proposal and act as nominee; he may reject it if he thinks that it is too complicated and more suitable for presentation by a private practice insolvency practitioner.

There is no provision for modification of the proposal (IA 1986, s.263(B)(4)). The FTVA proposal is therefore a 'take it or leave it' option for the creditors.

The debtor may not apply to court for an interim order (IA 1986, s.253) until the Official Receiver has completed the notice provisions to the creditors and where the creditors have failed to consent, or where the Official Receiver informs the debtor that he does not intend to put forward the proposals.

After implementation of the FTVA the Official Receiver must report to the court as soon as reasonably practicable on the approval or rejection of the proposal (IA 1986, s.263C).

In the same way as any other IVA, the FTVA takes effect and binds every creditor entitled to participate in the arrangement (IA 1986, s.263D(2)). This includes creditors who were informed of the proposal or would have been entitled to be informed.

10.5.3 Debtor's proposal

Under IR 1986, rule 5.37, the debtor's proposal must contain:

(a) the debtor's eligibility to propose a voluntary arrangement;

(b) an explanation of why in the debtor's opinion an FTVA is desirable and the reasons why the creditors might be expected to concur with such an arrangement;

(c) a statement that the debtor is aware that he will commit an offence if he makes a false representation or fraudulently does or omits to do anything in connection with the proposal (IA 1986, s.262A);

(d) the purposes of obtaining the approval of his creditors to the proposal;

(e) the debtor's assets with estimated values;

(f) the extent to which any assets are charged in favour of any creditors;

(g) the extent to which any particular assets are to be excluded from the FTVA;

(h) particulars of any third party property which has been included in the FTVA, the source of such property and the terms upon which it is available for inclusion;

(i) the nature of the debtor's liabilities, in particular, how it is proposed to deal with the preferential creditors, secured creditors and associates of the debtor;

(j) whether to the debtor's knowledge any claims have been made under IA 1986, s.339 (transaction at an undervalue), s.340 (preferences), s.343 (extortionate credit transactions) and/or whether there are any circumstances giving rights to the possibility of such claims;

(k) whether any guarantees have been given in respect of the debtor's debts;

(l) the proposed duration of the FTVA;

(m) the proposed date of distributions with estimates and amounts;

(n) how it is proposed to deal with the claims of persons who have not been given notice of the FTVA, but may nevertheless be bound to it;

(o) an estimate of the fees and expenses likely to be incurred in connection with the approval and implementation of the FTVA;

(p) whether any guarantees are to be offered by any other third party or security given;

(q) the manner in which funds are to be held and, if not for the purpose of the creditors, how they would be dealt with if the FTVA terminated;

(r) functions to be undertaken by the supervisor;

(s) the address of the Official Receiver to which correspondence should be sent;

(t) the names and addresses of all the debtor's creditors so far as they are within his knowledge and belief; and

(u)   whether the EC Regulation on Insolvency Proceedings will apply and whether the proceedings will be main or territorial proceedings.

10.5.4   Creditors' response

A creditor who wishes to vote on the proposal must give notice of his acceptance or rejection in Form 5.6. There is no provision for modifying the proposal, which is intended to make the procedure streamlined and cost-effective.

The creditor is entitled to vote and send notice to the Official Receiver of the values of the vote, calculated by reference to the amount of the creditor's debt at the date of the bankruptcy order (IR 1986, rule 5.41(2)). If the creditor has an unliquidated debt or the value is unascertained, it should be valued at £1 unless the Official Receiver puts a higher value on it. The Official Receiver may admit or reject the claims for the purposes of voting. This decision is subject to appeal to the court by the creditor or the debtor (IR 1986, rule 5.42(2)). An application to court by way of appeal must be within 28 days of the date when the result of the IVA is filed at court. The Official Receiver is not personally liable for any costs incurred by a person in respect of any appeal.

The court may make an order revoking the IVA on the grounds that it unfairly prejudices the interests of a creditor or there is material irregularity in respect of the arrangements (IA 1986, s.263F). An application must be made within 28 days of the date that the report was made to court regarding the result of the IVA proposal. If a creditor was not aware of the arrangement, he has 28 days to apply from the date he becomes aware of the IVA (IA 1986, s. 263F(4)).

The court may make an order revoking the FTVA and the applicant must serve the debtor, supervisor, trustee or Official Receiver as appropriate. The supervisor must, as soon as reasonably practicable after receiving a copy of the court order, give notice of it to all persons who were given a copy of the proposal (IR 1986, rule 5.46(3)). Within seven days of the date of the order, the applicant must give notice to the Secretary of State.

10.6   ADJUSTMENTS OF PRIOR TRANSACTIONS

10.6.1   Introduction

As we have examined in **Chapter 6**, the trustee, in seeking to effect better realisations for creditors, will investigate the bankrupt's affairs. In particular, the trustee will look closely at the circumstances of transactions conducted prior to bankruptcy in order to see whether, in accordance with the provisions contained in IA 1986, any of these transactions could be open to challenge and adjusted so as to enhance any possible distribution to creditors.

In addition to his attempts to maximise realisations, the trustee's investigation may reveal that the bankrupt has committed any one of a number of offences as set out in the insolvency legislation, and indeed his review of such unlawful conduct may overlap with his attempts at recovery of property (e.g. where the bankrupt has entered into a transaction at an undervalue). The trustee will report such matters to the Official Receiver, which may ultimately lead to the imposition of a BRO. This issue is looked at more closely at **10.3**.

In this section we will look at the potential areas of recovery of property available to the trustee. The provisions of IA 1986, ss.339–343 closely mirror the corporate law provisions found in IA 1986, ss.238–244 and thus much of the case law overlaps and can provide assistance in the consideration of the liabilities of the bankrupt and third parties who have entered into relevant transactions.

The trustee may apply to the court for an order in respect of:

- transaction at an undervalue (IA 1986, s.339);
- preference (IA 1986, s.340);
- recovery of excessive pension contributions (IA 1986, s.342A);
- extortionate credit transactions (IA 1986, s.343);
- avoidance of assignment of book debts (IA 1986, s.344); and
- transaction defrauding creditors (IA 1986, s.423).

When a trustee in bankruptcy is appointed, part of his role will be to look at transactions.

Table 10.3 Transactions in respect of which trustee may apply to court for an order

Type of transaction	Period in which transaction took place	Insolvency of individual at time of transaction	Presumption of insolvency	Intention of individual in making transaction	Presumption of intention
Transaction at an undervalue to an associate of the bankrupt	In last 5 years	✔*	✔	✗	✗
Transaction at an undervalue to unconnected person	In last 5 years	✔*	✗	✗	✗

Type of transaction	Period in which transaction took place	Insolvency of individual at time of transaction	Presumption of insolvency	Intention of individual in making transaction	Presumption of intention
Transaction at an undervalue to put assets beyond reach of creditor(s)	At any time	✗	✗	✔	✗
Preference to an associate of the bankrupt	In last 2 years	✔	✗	✔	✔
Preference to unconnected person	In last 6 months	✔	✗	✔	✗

* Unless entered into within two years of bankruptcy.

10.6.2 Transaction at an undervalue

Where an individual is adjudged bankrupt and has, within five years prior to the commencement of the bankruptcy, entered into a transaction with any person at an undervalue, the trustee may apply to the court for an order under IA 1986, s.339.

Before embarking on any application, the trustee must first obtain the consent of the creditors' committee or the court (IA 1986, s.314, Sched.5, para.2A). The right to bring the action under IA 1986, s.339 is only available to the trustee, as it is a right of action that accrues on the making of a bankruptcy order. As a result, an action under IA 1986, s.339 is incapable of assignment (*Re Oasis Merchandising Services Ltd* [1998] Ch 170).

The court may, on the application of the trustee, make such order as it thinks fit and may, so far as is practicable, restore the position to what it would have been had the individual not entered into the transaction (IA 1986, s.339(2); see also *Chohan v. Saggar* [1994] 1 BCLC 706, which dealt with the situation where there was no longer an ability to fully restore the position, but confirmed that this would not prevent the court from ordering what it considered to be right and just). The court's approach to transactions found to have been entered into at an undervalue is, however, to attempt if at all possible to have them set aside, rather than allowing the parties to the transaction to compensate the bankruptcy estate by paying the difference between the consideration provided and the true value. This is very much a matter of public policy, ensuring that parties are not encouraged to enter into transactions at an undervalue, safe in the knowledge that if they are found out they can simply pay the shortfall.

An individual enters into a transaction at an undervalue if he:

(a)   makes a gift to a person or otherwise enters into a transaction for no consideration;

(b)   enters into a transaction in consideration of marriage or formation of a civil partnership; or

(c)   enters into a transaction with a person for consideration the value of which, in money or money's worth, is significantly less than the value, in money or money's worth, of the consideration provided by the individual.

In order to succeed in establishing that a transaction was at an undervalue, it has generally been thought that the trustee must establish that there was a transfer between the bankrupt and another party of the bankrupt's property, resulting in a depletion of the bankrupt's assets (see *Mears* v. *Naema Latif* [2006] BPIR 80, where the trustee failed to establish that the bankrupt was the owner of the property at the date of transfer; and *Re Brabon* [2000] BPIR 537, in which it was held that the transaction must have been carried out by the debtor). In *Official Receiver for Northern Ireland* v. *Stranaghan* [2010] BPIR 928, it was held that the granting of security in respect of a loan that had been made some time previously could be regarded as a transaction at an undervalue (see in contrast *Re Mistral Finance Ltd (in liquidation)* [2001] BCC 27 for discussion as to whether a transaction of this nature is in reality a preference as it does not result in a diminution in assets; rather it results in different creditors being preferred).

The consideration provided for the transaction must be at a value which is 'significantly' less than the true worth to be viewed as potentially vulnerable (*Doyle* v. *Saville* [2002] BPIR 947). As a rule of thumb, any value 7.5 per cent or more below market value may be seen as a significant undervalue, although it should always be remembered that what is significant will depend on the facts of the case (see *Re Kumar* [1993] BCLC 548; *Re Marini Ltd* [2004] BCC 172; *Re Marsh* [2009] BPIR 834).

The issue of what could constitute valid consideration was considered in the case of *Haines* v. *Hill* [2007] EWHC 1012 (Ch), where it was held at first instance that a property adjustment order made in matrimonial proceedings could constitute a transaction at an undervalue and therefore be set aside. This determination was overturned in the Court of Appeal ([2007] BPIR 1280) on the grounds that the wife had given some consideration in compromising her rights to seek ancillary relief, although the judgment left open the possibility that where an order had been made by consent, with some element of collusion between the husband and wife, it could still be capable of challenge (see, however, *Re Jones* [2008] BPIR 1051 where the court refused to make such an order).

The transaction must have been entered into within five years of the commencement of bankruptcy and the individual must have been insolvent, or have been made insolvent as a consequence of the transaction, unless the transaction was within two years of the date of the bankruptcy (IA 1986, s.341(2)). In *Papanicola* v. *Fagan* [2009] BPIR 320, the trustee failed to establish that the bankrupt was insolvent at the time he transferred his interest in the matrimonial home to his wife; in this case the court was also satisfied that the wife had given due consideration for the transfer by her agreement not to pursue a divorce.

The court also retains an overriding discretion under this section and even where it has found that a transaction at an undervalue has occurred, it may in exceptional circumstances decide to make no order (*Singla* v. *Brown* [2007] BPIR 424).

The cause of action was generally seen to accrue from the date of the bankruptcy order (see *Re Nurkowski* [2006] BPIR 789 concerning Limitation Act periods and IA 1986, s.423). However, in the more recent case of *Stoneham* v. *Ramrattan* [2011] EWCA Civ 119 it was stated (*obiter*) by Lloyd LJ that the 12-year Limitation Act period applicable to IA 1986, s.339 (see *Segal* v. *Pasram* [2007] BPIR 881) ran from the date of appointment of the first trustee. It is, however, then necessary to look before the date of bankruptcy to the date when the transaction occurred to see if an application can be made. Furthermore, inexcusable delay in bringing proceedings may result in the claim being struck out (*Hamblin* v. *Field* [2000] BPIR 621).

The court may only make an order if at the time of the transaction the bankrupt was insolvent or if he became insolvent as a result of the transaction, unless the transaction took place within two years of the commencement of the bankruptcy, in which case the solvency of the bankrupt at the time of the transaction is irrelevant (IA 1986, s.341).

There is in any event a presumption that, in the case of a transaction with an associate of the individual, the individual was insolvent, i.e. unable to pay his debts as they fall due; or the value of the individual's assets was less than the amount of his liabilities, taking into account contingent and prospective liabilities (IA 1986, s.341(3)).

An associate of the bankrupt is defined as:

(a) the individual's husband, wife or civil partner;
(b) a relative;
(c) the husband, wife or civil partner of a relative;
(d) a relative of the individual's husband, wife or civil partner (IA 1986, s.435(2));
(e) a person with whom he is in partnership and/or the husband or wife or civil partner or relative of any individual with whom he is in partnership (IA 1986, s.435(3));
(f) a person whom he employs or by whom he is employed (IA 1986, s.435(4));
(g) a trustee, where the beneficiary of the trust is an associate of the individual, or the terms of the trust confer a power that may be exercised for the benefit of that other person or an associate of that other person (IA 1986, s.435(5));
(h) a company, whereby the individual has control of it or that person and persons who are his associates together have control of it, meaning that the company is accustomed to act in accordance with the directions of the person or that

person is entitled to exercise one-third or more of the voting power of the company at any general meeting.

A relative is the individual's brother; sister; uncle; aunt; nephew; niece; lineal ancestor; or lineal descendant. Any relationship of the half blood is treated as a relationship of the whole and any stepchild, adopted child or illegitimate child of the person is treated as a relative for these purposes. Reference to husband and wife includes former husband and wife or 'reputed' husband or wife, which covers so-called 'common law' spouses. Despite the addition of civil partners and former civil partners from 5 December 2005 (Civil Partnership Act 2004, s.261(1), Sched.27, para.122), there is no extension of the definition of associate to 'reputed' civil partners.

In other cases, where the transaction took place no more than five years but not less than two years from the bankruptcy, and the transaction was not to an associate of the bankrupt, the trustee is obliged to prove to the satisfaction of the court that the bankrupt was or became insolvent as a result of the transaction. The proof of insolvency may be either on a cash flow basis (i.e. inability to pay debts as they fall due) or on a balance sheet basis (liabilities exceeding assets).

In assessing the solvency of the individual, the court can take a broad commercial view of all the facts of the case and may infer insolvency from the surrounding circumstances (see *DKG Contractors Ltd* [1990] BCC 903 and contrast this case with *Re Taylor Sinclair (Capital) Ltd* [2001] 2 BCLC 176 and the weight that could be given to the failure to pay invoices).

On the issue of balance sheet insolvency, contingent, prospective and future liabilities are to be taken into account (see *Re a Company (No.6794 of 1983)* [1986] BCLC 261; *Byblos Bank* v. *Al-Khudhairy* [1987] BCLC 232) unless the court determines that the prospective assets should not be taken into account.

Effect on third parties

An order will not be made affecting the rights of third parties who have acquired the bankrupt's assets from a person other than the individual who is subsequently adjudged bankrupt in good faith and for value (IA 1986, s.342(2)).

A person is deemed to act in good faith unless:

(a) he had notice of the relevant surrounding circumstances and of the relevant proceedings; or

(b) he was an associate of, or connected with either the individual in question (i.e. the bankrupt) or the person with whom that individual entered into the transaction (IA 1986, s.342(2A)).

A person shall be deemed to have notice of 'relevant surrounding circumstances' if he was aware that the individual transferor in question entered into the transaction at an undervalue. A person will have notice of the 'relevant proceedings' if he had notice of the fact that a bankruptcy petition had been presented against the transferor, or the fact that the transferor had been adjudged bankrupt (IA 1986, s.342(4), (5)).

Also, an order will not be made which would require a person who has received benefit from the transaction in good faith for value to pay a sum to the trustee, except where he was a party to the transaction at an undervalue (IA 1986, s.342(2)(b)).

Under IA 1986, s.342, when the conditions of the legislation are fulfilled, the court may make any of the following orders:

(a)   Requiring any property transferred as part of the transaction to be vested in the trustee as part of the estate.
(b)   Requiring any property to be so vested in the trustee if it represents in a person's hands the application of either the proceeds of sale of the property so transferred, or money so transferred.
(c)   Release or discharge (in whole or in part) of any security given by the individual;
(d)   Requiring any person to pay in respect of benefits received by him from the individual, such sums to the trustee of his estate as the court may direct.
(e)   Providing for any surety or guarantor whose obligations to any person were released or discharged (in whole or in part) under the transaction, to be under such new security obligations as the court thinks appropriate.
(f)   Providing for security to be provided for the discharge of any obligation imposed by or arising under the order, for such an obligation to be charged on any property and for the security or charge to have the same priority as the security or charge released or discharged (in whole or in part) under the transaction.
(g)   Providing for the extent to which any person whose property is vested by the order in the trustee, or on whom obligations are imposed by the order, is able to prove in the bankruptcy for debts or other liabilities which arose from, or were released or discharged (in whole or in part) under or by, the transaction.

This is not an exhaustive list and the court, subject to affording protection to innocent third parties, as previously stated, will endeavour to restore the position to what it was before the transaction took place (*Chohan* v. *Saggar* [1994] BCC 134).

10.6.3   Preference

An individual gives a preference to a person if:

(a)   that person is one of the individual's creditors or a surety or guarantor for any of his debts or liabilities; and
(b)   the individual does anything or suffers anything to be done which (in either case) has the effect of putting that person into a position which, in the event of the individual's bankruptcy, will be a better position than he would have been in if that thing had not been done (IA 1986, s.340(3)).

The preference must have been given at a time when the individual was insolvent or the individual must have become insolvent as a result of the transaction and the transaction must have occurred within two years of the date of bankruptcy, in the case of a preference to an associate, or six months, in the case of a non-connected person. See commentary above regarding transactions at an undervalue and associates of the bankrupt.

In *Re MC Bacon Ltd* [1990] BCC 78, it was held that the two-year or six-month period begins to run when the decision to prefer the other party was taken, which is not necessarily at the same time as when the transaction is completed (e.g. execution of a debenture).

As is the case of proceedings in respect of a transaction at an undervalue, a trustee needs permission of the creditors' committee or the court in order to make an application (IA 1986, Sched.5, para.2A), the action is one that accrues post bankruptcy, is one that can be pursued only by the trustee, and is not assignable (*Re Oasis Merchandising Services Ltd* [1998] Ch 170).

An essential consideration on examining the treatment of a party is to look at why the individual preferred one creditor over another. An order will not be made unless the individual who gave the preference was influenced in deciding to give it by a desire to produce the effect of the preference (IA 1986, s.340(4)). It should be noted, however, that an individual is deemed to have been influenced by a desire to put an individual in a better position where the transaction was with an associate.

The necessary motive (i.e. the debtor was influenced by a desire to produce the effect of the preference) is often difficult to prove. See *Re MC Bacon Ltd* [1990] BCC 78, the leading authority dealing with the meaning of 'influenced by a desire to prefer' in the context of payments made in a corporate insolvency; see also *Re Ledingham-Smith* [1993] BCLC 635, for a case of preferential payments made by an individual. If the debtor was simply paying in response to commercial pressure, e.g. to continue trading or to obtain essential professional services (such as in *Re Ledingham-Smith* [1993] BCLC 635 and *Re Fairway Magazines Ltd* [1992] BCC 924), this is likely to be seen as a good defence to any action.

The fact that an action which has the effect of preferring one party was pursuant to a court order does not without more prevent that from constituting a preference (IA 1986, s.340(6)). This can arise in the context of matrimonial proceedings and there can be a conflict between orders of the insolvency court and orders of the family court (see *Haines* v. *Hill* [2007] BPIR 1280, where the Court of Appeal determined that the transfer of property made pursuant to a property adjustment order was made for good consideration, namely the wife giving up a claim for ancillary relief). The trustee will, however, remain alive to the possibility that an individual may have allowed a judgment or an order to be obtained, or given consent to an order where he would reasonably have been expected to oppose the creditor's action.

Where the court is satisfied that a preferential payment has been made, the court will make such order as it thinks fit, restoring the position to that which it would have been if the individual had not given the preference (IA 1986, s.340(2)). The court can also make such an order as set out in the non-exhaustive list provided by IA 1986, s.342(1) outlined in the previous section.

An order will not be made which affects any interest in property acquired by the person to whom the preference was given, where that person acquired the benefit in good faith and for value. Furthermore, any such person who has received benefit from the preference in good faith for value will not be required to pay any sum to the trustee, except where the preference was given to that person at the time that he was a creditor of the individual (IA 1986, s.342(2)).

A person who has received benefit from the preference is deemed to have acted in good faith unless:

(a)   he has notice of the relevant surrounding circumstances and of the relevant proceedings; or

(b)   he was an associate of, or was connected with, either the individual in question or with the person to whom the individual gave the preference (IA 1986, s.342(2A)).

10.6.4   Recovery of excessive pension contributions

The trustee in bankruptcy may apply to the court where he considers that an individual has made an excessive contribution to his pension which has unfairly prejudiced the individual's creditors and has resulted in direct or indirect benefits to the bankrupt which are the fruits of the relevant contributions (IA 1986, s.342A(2)).

The treatment of pensions and the trustee's right of recovery of excessive pension contributions are dealt with in greater detail at **10.7**.

10.6.5   Extortionate credit transactions

An application by a trustee in bankruptcy may be made in respect of a credit transaction which is deemed extortionate and was made within three years of the date of bankruptcy (IA 1986, s.343).

A transaction is deemed extortionate if, having regard to the risks accepted by the person providing credit, the terms require grossly exorbitant payments, whether conditionally or on certain contingencies arising, or otherwise grossly contravene ordinary principles of fair dealing. There is no requirement that the bankrupt was insolvent at the time or was made insolvent as a result of the credit transaction and it is for the provider of credit to show that the transaction was not extortionate. However, examples of challenge are rare and in the case law arising under the Consumer Credit Act 1974 the courts have generally not intervened, even where there were very high interest rates, as long as the borrower acted freely and was properly informed at the beginning of the transaction (see *Ketley Ltd* v. *Scott* [1981] ICR 241 and the more recent case of *Finnerty* v. *Clark* [2011] EWCA Civ 858, which concerned an administrator's refusal to commence proceedings under parallel corporate insolvency provisions).

If the court is satisfied that the transaction entered into was extortionate, it may make such orders as it thinks fit, including:

(a) setting aside the whole or part of the obligations created by the transaction;
(b) varying the terms of the transaction, or varying the terms upon which any security for the purposes of the transaction is held;
(c) requiring any person who is, or was, party to the transaction to pay the trustee any sums paid by the bankrupt to that person by virtue of the transaction;
(d) requiring any person to surrender to the trustee any property held by him as security for the purposes of that transaction; or
(e) directing that an account be taken of the dealings between the parties to the transaction.

10.6.6   Avoidance of general assignment of book debts

A general assignment by a person engaged in business of existing or future book debts, or any class of them, is void against the trustee in bankruptcy, to the extent that any book debts have not been paid before the presentation of the bankruptcy petition, unless the assignment has been registered under the Bills of Sale Act 1878 (IA 1986, s.344).

This provision applies only to 'general assignments' of book debts (IA 1986, s.344(3)) and does not include an assignment by way of security or charge, or assignment of book debts due at the time of assignment from specified debtors, or of debts becoming due under specific contracts, or assignment of book debts included in a transfer of a business in good faith and for value. It is therefore of limited application.

10.6.7   Enforceability of liens on books, records, etc.

A creditor exercising a lien or other right to retain possession of any books, papers or records of the bankrupt cannot exercise such rights against the Official Receiver or trustee in bankruptcy to the extent that the enforcement will deny possession of any books, papers or records to the office holder (IA 1986, s.349).

This provision does not apply to documents that give title to property and are held as such. (See *Re SEIL Trade Finance Ltd* [1992] BCC 538, where it was held that the party with possession of the documents need not enjoy a proprietary interest but rather the documents are held as quasi-security, allowing, e.g. a solicitor to exercise a lien over title deeds.)

10.6.8   Transactions defrauding creditors

Where an individual enters into a transaction which (IA 1986, s.423):

(a) is a gift to another person or is otherwise a transaction on terms that provide for no consideration;

(b)   is in consideration of marriage; or

(c)   is entered into for consideration the value of which, in money or money's worth, is less than the value in money or money's worth of the consideration provided by the individual,

and the court is satisfied that this transaction was entered into for the purposes of putting assets beyond the reach of a person who is making, or may make, a claim, or otherwise prejudices the position of creditors, the court may restore the position to what it would have been had the transaction not been entered into.

The provisions contained in IA 1986, s.423 have long historical antecedents and provisions which enable the setting aside of dishonest transactions that have the effect of defrauding creditors can be traced back to the Bankruptcy Act 1571.

Although there is a considerable degree of overlap between IA 1986, s.339 and s.423, an action under IA 1986, s.423 is not in fact an 'insolvency proceeding' as the solvency of the individual at the time of the transaction, and indeed at the time of the proceedings is in fact irrelevant (*Trowbridge* v. *Trowbridge* [2003] BPIR 258; *Byers* v. *Yacht Bull Corp.* [2010] BPIR 535). Furthermore, an application under s.423 may be made not only by the Official Receiver or trustee in bankruptcy, but also by a victim of the transaction (see *Moon* v. *Franklin* [1996] BPIR 196; *Clydesdale* v. *Smailes* [2010] BPIR 77, cases which confirm that 'victim' has a wider meaning than 'creditor').

The court must be satisfied that the 'real substantial' purpose of the transaction was to put assets beyond the reach of creditors (*IRC* v. *Hashmi* [2002] BPIR 974, where the Court of Appeal held that the 'dominant' purpose test as set out in *Chohan* v. *Saggar* [1992] BCC 306 was no longer appropriate). It is, however, notoriously difficult to prove the requisite degree of dishonest intention, and unlike under IA 1986, s.339, there are no statutory presumptions to assist the applicant.

The burden of proof is on the applicant (*Habib Bank Ltd* v. *Ahmed* [2004] BPIR 35), although the applicant does not need to prove that the transaction was risky or hazardous (*Sands* v. *Clitheroe* [2006] BPIR 1000). The applicant must show evidence which is specific and not speculative (*Law Society* v. *Southall* [2002] BPIR 336).

The claim must be brought within six years if the claim is for money, and 12 years if it is a claim that would see the return of property (a claim for a specialty). The cause of action accrues in respect of a trustee on the date of appointment, but for a normal creditor on the date of the transaction, which could result in certain cases in very different outcomes (*Re Nurkowski* [2006] BPIR 789, where the Court of Appeal, by majority, held that separate Limitation Act periods for different applicants could exist).

An application brought by a trustee under IA 1986, s.423 is made on behalf of every victim of the transaction.

On being satisfied that the individual has entered into a transaction to defraud creditors, the court may make such order as it thinks fit, including restoring the position to what it would have been had the transaction not been made and/or protecting the interests of the victims of the transaction (IA 1986, s.423(2)). As a consequence, this may lead to a payment to the bankruptcy estate or potentially to a specific victim who is being defrauded, although the applicant cannot be put in a better position than they would have been in had the transaction not occurred (see *Ram* v. *Ram (No.1)* [2005] BPIR 616).

Where a person is a bona fide purchaser for value without notice of the relevant circumstances, their interest cannot be prejudiced (IA 1986, s.425(2)).

Examples of transactions to defraud creditors include the creation of a sham family trust to protect the debtor's assets in the event of business failure (*Midland Bank* v. *Wyatt* [1996] BPIR 288) and where the debtor created an agricultural tenancy in order to defeat the claim by a mortgagee (see *Agricultural Mortgage Corporation plc* v. *Woodward* [1994] BCC 688).

10.7   THE BANKRUPT'S PENSION

Following the introduction of the Welfare Reform and Pensions Act 1999 (which came into force on 29 May 2000), the answer to the question as to whether the bankrupt will retain pension rights depends upon whether a pension is approved or unapproved (Welfare Reform and Pensions Act 1999, ss.11 and 12).

'Approved pension arrangements' (the majority of pensions) are now excluded from the bankrupt's estate and will include most personal pension schemes, occupational pension schemes and retirement annuity plans (see Finance Act 2004, s.153, Welfare Reform and Pensions Act 1999, s.11(11)(a) and Finance Act 2004, Part 14 for the definition of what is, or is not, approved).

As a result, since 29 May 2000, it can generally be said that pension benefits are excluded from the bankruptcy estate, although where the bankrupt is entitled to an annuity or a lump sum payment, the trustee may claim either under the provisions related to an IPO (see **10.4**) or as after-acquired property (see **10.1.3**). (See *Jones* v. *Patel* [1999] BPIR 509 and *Raithatha* v. *Williamson* [2012] EWHC 909 (Ch) where it was held that the trustee was also entitled to an IPO in regards to undrawn pension entitlements.)

'Unapproved pension arrangements' will rarely be encountered, although it should be noted that they are not simply pension arrangements that are not approved (see Occupational and Personal Pension Schemes (Bankruptcy) (No.2) Regulations 2002, SI 2002/836 for further details). Even then, certain unapproved pension schemes, in limited circumstances, may also be excluded from the bankrupt's estate as long as the scheme is the bankrupt's sole or main pension arrangement, and the exclusion from the bankrupt's estate is effected by either:

(a)   the bankrupt's application to the court for an exclusion order; or

(b)   a qualifying agreement being reached between the bankrupt and his trustee in bankruptcy.

Exclusions are subject to strict time limits, with the obligation on the bankrupt to commence a court application within 13 weeks and to conclude a qualifying agreement with the trustee within nine weeks. The court will take into account the likely needs of the bankrupt and his family, and decide whether they will be adequately met by other pension benefits, and weigh this up against the interests of the bankrupt's creditors.

For bankruptcies commenced between 29 December 1986 and 29 May 2000, personal pension rights automatically vested in the trustee in bankruptcy. See the Welfare Reform and Pensions Act 1999 which, when read in conjunction with the Occupational and Personal Pension Schemes (Bankruptcy) (No. 2) Regulations 2002, SI 2002/836, confirms that neither the 1999 Act nor the Regulations have retrospective effect and bankruptcies are therefore subject to the case law which followed the implementation of IA 1986 (see *Re Landau (a Bankrupt)* [1998] Ch 223, upheld by the Court of Appeal in *Krasner* v. *Dennison*, sub nom. *Lesser* v. *Lawrence*; *Dennison* v. *Krasner* [2000] 3 WLR 720; and *Malcolm* v. *Mackenzie* [2005] BPIR 176 for an unsuccessful Human Rights Act 1998 challenge by the bankrupt to the vesting of contractual pension rights).

Where the bankruptcy was commenced between 29 December 1986 and 29 May 2000 and the bankrupt was a member of an occupational pension scheme that provided that payments are made only to the member on exercise of the discretion of the trustees, the pension is likely to have been excluded from the bankrupt's estate. Unlike similar provisions in personal pension schemes, such clauses are not necessarily unenforceable. This differing treatment is because the occupational pension scheme employees have a future interest in pension benefits which does not automatically accrue, while a personal pension plan provides for an unqualified right to the pension benefit.

Table 10.4 Bankruptcy and pension rights

Date bankruptcy commenced	State retirement pension*	Personal pension	Occupational pension
To 28 December 1986	×	×**	×
29 December 1986 to 28 May 2000	×	✔	×
29 May 2000 to date	×	×***	×

* Income, or right to income, needs to be disclosed and could be claimed as part of an IPO.

** See *Ex p. Huggins* (1882) 21 ChD 85.

*** Provided schemes are approved or excluded by court order.

Excessive contributions

In all cases, the trustee may apply to the court for an excessive pension contributions order (IA 1986, s.342A).

If the court is satisfied that the bankrupt has made excessive contributions to a pension scheme, which has unfairly prejudiced the individual creditors, the court may make such order as it thinks fit, including restoring the position to that which it would have been had the excessive contributions not been made (IA 1986, s.342A(2)).

The court may only make such an order if it considers that:

(a)   any contribution was made for the purpose of putting assets beyond the reach of the bankrupt's creditors or any one of them; and

(b)   the total amount of contributions is excessive in view of the individual circumstances when the contributions were made.

The evidential burden is therefore placed upon the trustee to show that on the balance of probabilities the bankrupt was attempting to defraud his creditors by making excessive pension contributions. Each case will obviously depend upon its own merits. The wording of this section obviously has similarities to the provisions contained in IA 1986, s.423 (see **10.6.8** for further details).

Any person responsible (be that the trustee, manager or the provider of an approved pension scheme or unapproved pension arrangement under which the bankrupt has any rights) must on the trustee in bankruptcy's request provide such information as is reasonably required (IA 1986, s.342C).

The changes brought in by the Welfare Reform and Pensions Act 1999 were certainly politically motivated, as pension provisions have increasingly moved away from state to private pension arrangements. As a result, it is politically expedient to encourage private pension provision by ensuring that pensions are generally free and safe from creditor challenge.

10.8   THE BANKRUPT AND THE FAMILY HOME

10.8.1   Vesting and realisation

As we have seen in **Chapter 6**, the bankrupt's estate comprises all property belonging to and vested in the bankrupt at the commencement of the bankruptcy (IA 1986, s.283(1)). The bankrupt's estate will thereafter vest in the trustee (IA 1986, s.306), who will realise the bankrupt's interest in the property for the benefit of his creditors. This process of realisation continues after the bankrupt's discharge, save for one important exception – the family home, which is the topic of this section.

Against a background of almost continually rising house prices, generally the most important asset in the bankrupt's estate was the interest he possessed in the family home. As we have seen, secured creditor rights continue post bankruptcy, so for the majority of home-owning bankrupts the trustee would be seeking to realise the value of the equity (i.e. the value of the home net of the mortgage) that the bankrupt possessed.

In practice, in most cases the bankrupt's spouse was first given the opportunity of buying out the bankrupt's equitable interest; if this opportunity was not taken up the trustee would then proceed to realise the interest that remained vested in the estate. Even if it was the case that during the duration of the bankruptcy the equitable interest was of low value, due to house price inflation it was likely that, at some future date, the equitable interest would rise in value. This made the (eventual) realisation of the bankrupt's interest in the family home a central feature of overall asset realisation.

In more recent years a slowing (and even falling) of house prices has caused a consequently higher loan to asset value ratio, and that means in all likelihood the bankrupt's equitable interest will be much smaller. As we shall see, this has been coupled with a change in the law after 1 April 2004 (IA 1986, s.283A), which provides for the automatic re-vesting of the bankrupt's interest in the bankrupt's principal residence after a period of three years. All of these factors have meant that realisations of a bankrupt's interest in the family home have decreased in value and volume. However, that ability to realise the bankrupt's interest in the family home still remains an important feature of bankruptcy law and practice, and provides a good illustration of the balancing act performed by the court between the interests of the bankrupt (and his family) and the interests of the creditors. As we shall see, there are various statutory safeguards that also limit the power of the trustee to realise and sell the family home.

10.8.2   Establishing the bankrupt's beneficial interest

Sole ownership

Where a dwelling house is registered in the sole name of the bankrupt, the trustee is entitled to be registered as the sole proprietor (Land Registration Act 1925, s.42(1)). Assuming the registration is completed correctly, as the registered legal owner the trustee in bankruptcy is entitled to sell the dwelling house. Where the bankrupt is sole legal owner and sole occupier of the property, if necessary, the trustee may apply to court for an order for possession against the bankrupt in order to sell with vacant possession and increase the potential realisation.

It should be remembered, however, that even where the bankrupt is sole legal owner of the property, he may be holding the property in whole or in part on trust for himself and his spouse or any other third party. If the property is held under the terms of a properly constituted trust, then in the absence of fraud or misfeasance, the bankrupt's beneficial entitlement is determined in accordance with the terms of the trust (*Goodman* v. *Gallant* [1986] 1 All ER 311). As a starting point, therefore, the trustee in bankruptcy will determine whether the parties entered into an express declaration of trust. It is often the case, however, that co-ownership is determined by informal arrangements between the occupiers and in many cases the parties involved have never given any thought as to how the property is held.

The trustee is therefore required to undertake a careful review of the factual situation, assessing whether property is held on a constructive or resulting trust (see *Pettitt* v. *Pettitt* [1970] AC 777 and *Gissing* v. *Gissing* [1971] AC 886) and must apply the same critical analysis of property ownership that arises on marital breakdown or in cases where cohabitees are in dispute.

Co-ownership

Where there are two or more registered proprietors, the trustee in bankruptcy cannot register his interest on the legal title. The co-owners will share legal ownership as joint legal tenants and despite the bankruptcy of one co-owner there is no change to ownership of the legal estate. The legal title remains vested in the joint proprietors (including the bankrupt), but will be held upon trust for the benefit of the spouse and the bankrupt's estate. This stresses once again that the trustee in bankruptcy is concerned only with the realisation of the bankrupt's beneficial interest in the property.

The trustee will, however, apply to register a restriction at HM Land Registry, which requires prior notice of any disposition to be given to the trustee. A restriction on the register of title will generally be sufficient to protect the trustee's interest, as any party dealing with the bankrupt will therefore have notice of the trustee's (beneficial) interest.

Dispute may well arise on the bankruptcy of one co-owner as to the parties' respective beneficial rights and interests. As referred to above, the parties may hold the property under an express declaration of trust. If there is no express declaration, the rebuttable presumption is that the co-owners hold the beneficial interest as tenants in common in equal shares (*Stack* v. *Dowden* [2007] 2 All ER 929).

In determining the respective beneficial interests (whether legal title is held by one party and another party claims that they possess a beneficial interest in the property, or where legal title is jointly held and one party is claiming a greater than 50 per cent share of the beneficial interest):

1. The court will look for an express agreement, arrangement or a common understanding as to how the property is to be shared. On establishing this factual background, the court will need to be persuaded that the party who does not hold the legal title acted to her detriment, or significantly altered her position in reliance on the agreement, giving rise to a finding that the property was held by the party with legal title on constructive trust for them both. A beneficial interest has been found to have arisen where a party made substantial contributions towards the household expenditure (*Grant* v. *Edwards* [1986] Ch 638) and where physical assistance was provided in improving the property (the so-called 'muscular mistress' cases, see *Eves* v. *Eves* [1975] 1 WLR 1338).

472

2.   In the absence of an express agreement, arrangement or a common under-
     standing, the court will need to be persuaded that some subsisting property
     right exists for the party not holding any legal title. For instance, a direct
     payment to fund the purchase price, or payments of mortgage instalments
     may be sufficient to give rise to an inference that a constructive trust has arisen
     (*Lloyds Bank* v. *Rosset* [1990] 1 All ER 1111). The court, however, has not
     defined what is necessary to infer the existence of a constructive trust and
     cases will thus need to be examined on their own facts (see *Stack* v. *Dowden*
     [2007] 2 WLR 831).

Once the court has established that a party has a beneficial interest, it will go on to
consider the equally vexing question of quantifying that interest. Clearly, an express
agreement as to the respective interests would resolve this issue; however, in most
cases the parties are likely never to have discussed the exact terms of their
co-ownership. As a result, all the parties' dealings and conduct will need to be
examined (e.g. who contributed what to the purchase price and to the household
expenditure) in order to assess what was intended (*Oxley* v. *Hiscock* [2004] 3 All ER
703). The former jurisprudence relating to the existence of a resulting trust, which in
turn led to a presumption that the value of each contribution determined the
respective beneficial interests, is doubtful following the majority opinion of the
House of Lords in *Stack* v. *Dowden* [2007] 2 WLR 831.

Other factors influencing beneficial entitlement

Under the Matrimonial Proceedings and Property Act 1970, s.37, where a spouse
has made a substantial contribution in money or money's worth to improve the
property, this contribution can be reflected in the respective beneficial entitlements.
This brings into play indirect contributions (e.g. bringing up the family), but it must
be remembered that this only applies where it is first established that both spouses
have a beneficial entitlement to the property (a matter determined by property
rights, not rights of equity or fairness).

   Where one party has contributed more or, conversely, one party has burdened the
property with more debt, regard is had to the sums that one party ought to give credit
to the other for (the equity of redemption). This exercise of equitable accounting
may occur where one party has made a disproportionate contribution towards
expenditure to improve the property, or has paid down the capital sum due under the
mortgage (*Re Pavlou* [1993] 3 All ER 955). Where one party, typically the husband,
has borrowed money for his own purposes but secured it against the co-owned
property, the wife is entitled to claim (pursuant to the right of the equity of
exoneration) that on the sale of the property the loan should be deducted from the
husband's share of the beneficial interest, and only if that share is insufficient to
discharge the entirety of the loan should it be deducted from her share (*Re Pittortou*
[1985] 1 WLR 58). The fact that a loan has been taken for the purposes of only one
co-owner does not, however, affect the parties' proprietary interests (*Re a Debtor*

(No.24 of 1971), ex p. Marley v. Trustee [1976] 2 All ER 1010). Furthermore, before the equity of exoneration can be relied upon, the circumstances of the loan will be carefully reviewed, e.g. as to whether the wife received direct or indirect benefit from the loan (e.g. did it fund an extravagant lifestyle, *Paget* v. *Paget* [1898] 1 Ch 470).

With regard to mortgage payments, where one party agrees to pay the mortgage interest payments while the other is excluded from the property (e.g. typically on a marital breakdown, where only one party maintains the mortgage) this will not automatically increase the quantification of the beneficial interest of the remaining mortgage paying party. It is worth noting also the provisions of IA 1986, s.338, which provides that a bankrupt who occupies premises on condition that he discharges the mortgage or other outgoings does not by virtue of such payments acquire an interest in those premises. Instead, in both cases the mortgage payments are treated akin to rent to secure occupation.

In the context of matrimonial breakdown (see **10.9**), it is not uncommon to find the court making an order that will affect property rights (Matrimonial Causes Act 1973; Children Act 1989; Civil Partnership Act 2004). Such orders often provide for the transfer of a person's interest, which is treated as being a disposal of property (*Treharne* v. *Forrester* [2004] 1 FLR 1173). As it is a deemed disposal, it remains subject to potential challenge under the antecedent transactions provisions (IA 1986, ss.339 and 340; although see *Hill* v. *Haines* [2007] BPIR 1280, where the Court of Appeal determined that a wife had given appropriate consideration, namely the abandonment of her claim for ancillary relief, where an order pre-bankruptcy had transferred her ex-husband's interest in the former family home to her). This is an area of law that remains open to further development, with the possibility remaining that where a property adjustment order was made under a consent order and where the husband and wife colluded in a sham divorce settlement, it could be set aside (see, however, *Re Jones* [2008] BPIR 1051, where such an argument was rejected).

10.8.3   Realisation of bankrupt's interest

Third party proprietary rights

In seeking to realise the bankrupt's interest, as has been explored above, the trustee may need to consider (and quantify) the beneficial interest of another party in the property. This exercise may arise whether the legal title is held solely or jointly by the bankrupt. Once the respective interests are established, unless the parties are willing to co-operate voluntarily, the trustee may be required to obtain a court order in order to sell with vacant possession. It should be remembered that although similar issues are considered by the court, the determination of what, if any, beneficial interest a party has, and what right of occupation a party has, are distinct questions determined by separate statutory provisions.

In the case of a jointly owned property, the legal title is held on a trust of land, and it is for the trustees of the land to decide whether to sell. However, where any party who has an interest in land held on trust wishes to sell and the trustees refuse, that party may apply to the court for an order directing sale under the Trusts of Land and Appointment of Trustees Act 1996, s.14. As a result, a trustee in bankruptcy who has vested in him the bankrupt's beneficial interest in the property may apply to the court that has jurisdiction in relation to the bankruptcy under this section for an order for sale (IA 1986, s.335A(1)).

On application by a trustee for the sale of the property, the court will weigh up a number of factors in making such an order as it thinks just and reasonable under IA 1986, s.335A(2), namely:

(a)   the interests of the bankrupt's creditors;
(b)   where the application is in respect of a dwelling house, which has been the home of the bankrupt or the bankrupt's spouse, civil partner or former spouse or former civil partner:

    (i)   the conduct of the (former) spouse/civil partner so far as contributing to the bankruptcy;
    (ii)   the needs and financial resources of the (former) spouse/civil partner; and
    (iii) the needs of any children; and

(c)   all the circumstances of the case, other than the needs of the bankrupt.

The careful balancing exercise carried out by the court in determining what is just and reasonable as regards the interests in the family home is carried out during the first year following the vesting of the estate in the trustee. After one year, the court will assume, save in exceptional circumstances, that the interests of the creditors prevail (IA 1986, s.335A(3)) over all other considerations. This 'one year' provision applies only to the case of a dwelling house occupied by the bankrupt or the bankrupt's (former) spouse/civil partner and not other land or property; it also does not apply to cohabiting couples, although the court in considering what is just and reasonable is likely to give similar regard to the rights of unmarried cohabitees.

As a result, in practice, the trustee will seldom seek to realise the bankrupt's interest in the first year of bankruptcy. During this period, he is likely to investigate the beneficial ownership of the property and the claims of the spouse/co-owner, as well as valuing the property and liaising with the mortgagee. As stated above, he may well make enquiries of the spouse/co-owner to see if they have an ability to buy out the bankrupt's interest. Often this can be obtained at a discount to market value, as the trustee will take into account the costs and expenses of realising the property by forced sale.

The effect of IA 1986, s.335A(3) and the 'sunset provision' contained in IA 1986, s.283A (see **10.8.4**) continue to provide a practical challenge to any trustee seeking to realise the bankrupt's interest. The trustee will need to take proceedings within what is effectively a two-year window. While this may seem sufficient time, some practical difficulties arise. Often, there is a delay in the appointment of the trustee and initial investigations can take time; secondly, by the time that proceedings are contemplated the bankrupt may have been discharged and assistance more difficult to obtain. Increased levels of personal borrowings and the growth of the sub-prime mortgage market also mean that there is likely to be less equity in the home; as a result, taking proceedings may not be worthwhile in the first three years of the bankruptcy.

Where a trustee seeks to realise the interest after one year, *prima facie* he will be entitled to an order for sale and possession unless 'exceptional circumstances' are shown. These exceptional circumstances are unsurprisingly undefined – each case will depend upon its own facts. It should, however, be noted that even if an exceptional circumstance is found to exist, the court will still carry out the same balancing exercise that it would have done if the trustee had brought the application for sale in the first year of bankruptcy (*Nicholls* v. *Lan* [2007] 1 FLR 744). Case law provides certain guidance as to what does and does not amount to an exceptional circumstance:

- The illness of the bankrupt's wife or other dependant can prevent an order being made (see *Judd* v. *Brown* [1997] BPIR 470, where the spouse had terminal cancer and evidence was adduced as to the possibility that even a suspended order for possession might damage her health; *Re Raval* [1998] 2 FLR 718, where similar exceptional circumstances were said to merit suspension of an order for sale; *Claughton* v. *Charalamabous* [1999] 1 FLR 740, where a spouse's renal failure and osteoarthritis caused a chronic lack of mobility and reason for the court to postpone a sale indefinitely; *Re Mott* [1987] CLY 212, where sale was postponed until the death of the bankrupt's mother, who was in ill health and who had lived at the property for 40 years).
- The illness itself need not be sudden or arising post bankruptcy to amount to an exceptional circumstance (*Re Raval* [1998] 2 FLR 718, where the wife had for many years suffered from paranoid schizophrenia).
- The hardship and 'melancholy consequences of debt' caused to the bankrupt's wife and young children by a possession order are not exceptional circumstances such as to prevent an order for possession and sale, although the postponement of the sale might be ordered if it was unlikely to harm creditors (see *Re Citro* [1990] 3 All ER 952; *Dean* v. *Stout* [2005] BPIR 1113; and *Donohoe* v. *Ingram* [2006] BPIR 417).
- The fact that the sale of the family home might not immediately benefit creditors is not sufficient reason to prevent the sale of the family home (see *Trustees of the Estate of Bowe (a Bankrupt)* v. *Bowe* [1997] BPIR 747), nor is the fact that the sale will simply defray the costs and expenses of bankruptcy (*Re Karia* [2006] BPIR 1226).
- Protecting a child's educational needs will not necessarily amount to exceptional circumstances, if the family could move to a different property within the school's catchment area (see *Re Bailey* [1977] 2 All ER 26).

- The needs of the children to live in a particular area may, however, be exceptional (*Martin-Sklan* v. *White* [2006] All ER (D) 77 (Nov), where the alcoholic mother of the bankrupt's children frequently left home for several days at time, meaning the children relied on a substantial support network in the local area. In this case the court was willing to postpone sale until the children were adult).
- The 'needs' of a spouse may include evaluation of financial, medical, emotional and mental needs (*Everitt* v. *Budhram* [2010] BPIR 567, where both husband and wife were made bankrupt for failure to pay council tax and both suffered chronic medical conditions. The husband lacked legal capacity and, as a result, while the wife's needs were disregarded, an order for possession was postponed due to the husband's medical and mental health needs).

The statutory provisions have received consideration in light of the Human Rights Act 1998 and, in particular, the European Convention on Human Rights, Art.8, which provides for the right to respect for private family life and home (see *Barca* v. *Mears* [2004] All ER D 153; *Nicholls* v. *Lan* [2006] EWHC 1255 (Ch); and *Foenander* v. *Allan* [2006] BPIR 1392). However, the courts have consistently found that the bankruptcy provisions, in providing a balance between the interests of the bankrupt (and his family) and the interests of the creditors, are compatible with Art.8.

Third party rights of occupation

As we have seen with regard to the quantification of the bankrupt's interest, where the bankrupt is the sole registered proprietor, a spouse or civil partner may well claim a beneficial interest in the property. Where this is the case, the spouse/civil partner has a statutory right to occupy (Family Law Act 1996, s.30(9)), which is something not enjoyed by the spouse with both a legal and beneficial interest in the property. This statutory right of occupation is capable of protection by registration at HM Land Registry. However, family home rights cannot be registered after the presentation of a bankruptcy petition and the vesting of the bankrupt's estate in the trustee in bankruptcy (IA 1986, s.336(1)).

The effect of the registration is that, if in occupation, the spouse cannot be excluded from the family home without a court order and, if not in occupation, the spouse may seek the court's permission to enter and occupy the home (see *Re Gorman (a Bankrupt)* [1990] 1 WLR 616 and Family Law Act 1996, s.33).

If such rights have been registered, the trustee must apply for an order terminating the spouse's right of occupation in the family home. In considering the application by the trustee under the Family Law Act 1996, s.33, the court must make such order as it thinks just and reasonable having regard to:

(a) the interests of the bankrupt's creditors;
(b) the conduct of the (former) spouse/civil partner so far as contributing to the bankruptcy;

(c)   the needs and financial resources of the (former) spouse/civil partner;
(d)   the needs of any children; and
(e)   all the circumstances of the case, other than the needs of the bankrupt.

If an application for possession is commenced after the first year in which the estate vested in the trustee in bankruptcy, the court will assume, unless there are exceptional circumstances, that the interests of the creditors outweigh all other factors (IA 1986, s.336(5)). In *Hoskings* v. *Michaelides* [2004] All ER (D) 147 (May), 'exceptional' was held to mean outside the ordinary course, or unusual, or special, or uncommon.

We have looked at the issue of exceptional circumstances when considering the realisation of the bankrupt's interest where the bankrupt is a co-owner. In the context of rights of occupation, an order for sale was postponed in *Re Holliday* [1981] Ch 405 for several years to allow the children to finish their education; in *Re Mott* [1987] CLY 212, to allow the bankrupt's mother to die in her own home; and in *Re Haghighat* [2009] BPIR 268, because of the disability of a child. It should be noted that in these cases, the right to sale was postponed due to the rights/interests of a party other than the bankrupt.

If the trustee is unsuccessful in his application under the Family Law Act 1996, s.33, he is still entitled to apply for a further order to protect his interest in the home, which could compel the spouse to:

(a)   ensure the repair and maintenance of the family home; and/or
(b)   make mortgage payments and meet other outgoings (Family Law Act 1986, s.40).

Where a bankrupt has dependent children living with him, the trustee cannot obtain possession of the home without a court order (IA 1986, s.337). The factors the court will consider are similar to those in IA 1986, s.336(4) as set out above.

To prevent abuse, such as the bankrupt simply asserting the existence of a trust relationship resulting in a third party acquiring an interest in the home, which in turn could thwart the creditors' rights, there are a variety of statutory safeguards. These antecedent transaction provisions are looked at more closely at **10.6.** Briefly, a third party's rights may be set aside on the following grounds:

- Transaction at an undervalue (IA 1986, s.339).
- Preference (IA 1986, s.340).
- Transaction defrauding creditors (IA 1986, s.423).
- Failure to ratify a family proceedings property transfer order by the bankruptcy court (IA 1986, s.284(1)).

In the event that court proceedings are necessary to ensure the bankrupt and the co-occupiers vacate the property, the trustee in bankruptcy should consider applying for:

(a)   an order compelling that third party to join the trustee in bankruptcy in selling the family home (in vacant possession);

(b)   an order providing that the conduct of the sale is given to the trustee in bankruptcy and/or the solicitor;

(c)   a declaration as to the value of the respective beneficial interests of the trustee in bankruptcy and any third party;

(d)   an order that the proceeds of sale be distributed between the trustee in bankruptcy and the third party in accordance with the respective beneficial interests, once appropriate deduction has been made for all necessary expenses of sale and any valid secured charges have been redeemed;

(e)   an order under the Family Law Act 1996 determining any matrimonial home rights or rights of occupation; or

(f)   an order for possession.

10.8.4 The re-vesting provision

Following criticism of the perceived injustice that allowed a trustee to return many years after the bankrupt's discharge and seek to realise the (increased) equitable interest in the family home, the law was amended. As a result, in the case of any bankruptcy commencing after 1 April 2004, where the bankrupt's estate consists of an interest in a dwelling house which, at the date of bankruptcy, was the sole or principal residence of the bankrupt, or the bankrupt's spouse/civil partner or a former spouse/civil partner of the bankrupt, the trustee has three years beginning at the date of bankruptcy in which to realise the bankrupt's interest in the property, or apply for an order for sale, and/or a possession order, in respect of that interest or agree with the bankrupt a specified liability in respect of the interest.

Sometimes referred to as 'the sunset provision' or the 're-vesting provision', this does not have retrospective effect and has no application to bankruptcies commenced before 1 April 2004 (*Vidyarthi* v. *Clifford* [2005] BPIR 233).

If the trustee fails to carry out any of the above within the three-year period, the dwelling house will cease to be part of the bankrupt's estate and vest in the bankrupt without conveyance, assignment or transfer (IA 1986, s.283A(2)).

If the bankrupt fails to inform the trustee or the Official Receiver within three months of the date of bankruptcy that he has an interest in the dwelling house, the three-year re-vesting provision does not begin to apply until the trustee or the Official Receiver has become aware of the bankrupt's interest (IA 1986, s.283A(5)).

The three-year period may, however, be extended by the court as it thinks just and reasonable in the circumstances of the case (IR 1986, rule 6.237C; see *Vidyarthi* v. *Clifford* [2005] BPIR 233).

10.8.5 Low value home exception

A further reform introduced by the Enterprise Act 2002, which came into effect on 1 April 2004, was the provision that where a dwelling house is at the date of bankruptcy the sole or principal residence of:

- the bankrupt;
- the bankrupt's spouse or civil partner; or
- the former spouse or civil partner of the bankrupt,

and the trustee applies for:

- an order for sale;
- an order for possession; or
- a charge under IA 1986, s.313 or 313A,

the court must dismiss the application if the bankrupt's interest in the property is below a prescribed value (Insolvency Proceedings (Monetary Limits) (Amendment) Order 2004, SI 2004/547). Since its introduction, the prescribed value has remained at £1,000.

The bankrupt's interest is determined after deduction of any secured loans, third party interests and reasonable costs of sale.

This provision was introduced as it was felt there was only limited value to the creditors and disproportionate suffering to the bankrupt where the trustee realised a small interest in the home.

10.8.6 Charge on the bankrupt's home

Where a trustee is unable to realise the bankrupt's interest in a dwelling house occupied by the bankrupt or his (former) spouse/civil partner, the trustee may apply for an order imposing a charge on the property for the benefit of the bankruptcy estate (IA 1986, s.313(1)). This charge will endure after the re-vesting of the property in the bankrupt (IA 1986, s.283A).

The value of the charge on the property is, however, limited to the value as at the date of the charge together with interest (IA 1986, s.313(2A)). This means that any additional rise in the value of the bankrupt's interest due to property inflation after the date of the order will be for the benefit of the former bankrupt.

10.9 THE EFFECT OF BANKRUPTCY ON MATRIMONIAL PROCEEDINGS

10.9.1 Introduction

An unfortunate consequence of financial difficulty is the stress and strain that it will cause to a debtor's personal relationships. Often bankruptcy is accompanied by marriage difficulties and may lead to the institution of divorce proceedings prior to or post bankruptcy. The conflict that can then arise between matrimonial and bankruptcy jurisdictions often poses difficult challenges, with, e.g. the matrimonial courts perhaps being inclined to give primacy to the interests of the children in a marriage (and therefore often the non-bankrupt spouse) against the bankruptcy courts wishing to give primacy to the interests of creditors.

Quite obviously each situation is unique, but for the purposes of this section we will assume that the husband is the debtor and that there has been a transfer of property, perhaps his equity in the matrimonial home to his wife (ex-wife) and/or a lump sum or continuing maintenance being paid.

Prior to his bankruptcy, the husband may have transferred property or made maintenance payments, either pursuant to an order of the court in matrimonial proceedings or having done so in contemplation of marriage breakdown. The creditors may feel that they have been prejudiced by this transfer, that the bankrupt's assets have been put beyond their reach and there may even be suspicion that the divorce is in reality a sham. In other circumstances the wife may feel that the husband is using bankruptcy to avoid the consequences of matrimonial proceedings.

Whether the transfer of the equity in the matrimonial home was pursuant to an order in family proceedings has some relevance, although as we shall see, the fact that the order was made pursuant to family proceedings does not leave the transfer/payments entirely free from the scrutiny of the trustee in bankruptcy.

It should also be noted that after a bankruptcy order is made, the matrimonial court has no jurisdiction to make a subsequent property adjustment order (*McGladdery* v. *McGladdery* [2000] 1 FCR 315); as we have seen, the bankrupt's property will vest in the trustee. The matrimonial court does, however, retain a right to make a lump sum order, which, taking into account any pre-existing IPO, is likely to be of limited financial value, at least for the duration of the bankruptcy/IPO.

10.9.2 Transfer/payments made pre-bankruptcy without court order

If a lump sum payment, a transfer of property or a payment of maintenance was made outside the terms of family proceedings, then at common law this is said to suspend the wife's common law and statutory rights to claim maintenance. On the husband's bankruptcy, the agreement comes to an end and any unpaid arrears can be claimed in the bankruptcy (they are a 'provable' debt) (IR 1986, rule 12.3). The effect of the bankruptcy will determine the agreement and reinstate the wife's right to claim maintenance under statute (under the Matrimonial and Family Proceedings Act 1984). This right, however, is unlikely to be of much value to the wife if the husband is then bankrupt (see *Dewe* v. *Dewe* [1928] P 113).

In respect of any transfer of property pre-bankruptcy outside matrimonial proceedings this can be challenged in the usual way (as a transaction at an undervalue, IA 1986, s.339) (see **10.6.2**).

10.9.3 Transfers/payments made pre-bankruptcy with court order

Wife's position

Before 1 April 2005 a payment due under 'family proceedings', as defined in IA 1986, s.281(8), could not be claimed as a debt in any subsequent bankruptcy as they were classified as 'non-provable' debts (IR 1986, rule 12.3(2)(a)). This was held to include any award of costs which may have been made during the proceedings (*Levy* v. *Legal Services Commission* [2000] BPIR 1065). However, the position was altered by the Insolvency (Amendment) Rules 2005, SI 2005/527 to provide that in respect of any bankruptcy commencing after that date, any obligation to pay a lump sum or a costs order arising under such family proceedings is provable.

Despite this amendment, some family proceedings will result in obligations that are not provable in bankruptcy. This means that the bankruptcy order does not prevent the enforcement of such debt (and committal proceedings for any default in regard to conditions imposed) during bankruptcy. Furthermore the discharge from bankruptcy does not release the husband from the debt (e.g. see IA 1986, s.281(5)(b), as inserted by the Child Support Act 1991). It should, however, be remembered that the husband will most probably seek relief in the family proceedings (based on his bankruptcy) and the court will have regard to the creditors' interests in assessing the case.

Even if a debt being owed pursuant to an order in family proceedings is potentially one which is not provable in bankruptcy, the wife can still petition for the husband's bankruptcy, in regard to any debt arising as, although it is not a provable debt, she is still a creditor. A bankruptcy order is, however, only likely to be made in exceptional circumstances, as the wife will have no legitimate financial interest in the bankruptcy process. An exceptional circumstance might be one, e.g. where the husband is using bankruptcy proceedings as a shield against the wife's claim in family proceedings and/or where the investigations of the Official Receiver's office are deemed appropriate (*Russell* v. *Russell* [1998] 1 FLR 936).

Trustee's position

As we have seen in **10.6.2**, if the husband has within five years of the date of bankruptcy made a transfer to his wife in consideration of the marriage, or where the value of the consideration in money or money's worth is significantly less than the value of transfer, then if at the date of the transfer the husband was insolvent, or made himself insolvent as a result of the transfer, the transfer may be set aside as a transaction at an undervalue (IA 1986, s.339). A presumption of insolvency is deemed in the case of a 'transfer to an associate' (i.e. the wife), but this remains a rebuttable presumption (IA 1986, s.435(2)).

Similarly, as discussed in **10.6.3**, if the bankrupt has within two years of the date of bankruptcy put a creditor (e.g. his wife) in a better position in the event of bankruptcy than she would have been had the event not taken place, and did so being influenced by a desire to produce that result, then the transaction can be set aside as a preference (IA 1986, s.340).

The fact that the payment/transfer is made pursuant to an order of the court in matrimonial proceedings will generally prevent a finding that the transaction could be either a transaction at an undervalue or a preference. However, the law in this area remains unclear.

In *Hill and Bangham* v. *Haines* [2007] EWHC 1012 (Ch) at first instance a property adjustment order made after a fully contested hearing was overturned. Following the reasoning in *Xydhias* v. *Xydhias* [1999] 2 All ER 386, *G* v. *G (Financial Provisions: Equal Division)* [2002] 2 FLR 1143 and *McMinn* v. *McMinn* [2003] 2 FLR 823, the court held in the *Hill* case that 'the position is the same whether the Matrimonial Court makes an order following a contested hearing or following a compromise agreement – in neither case does the receiving party give, nor the paying party receive, consideration' (Pelling J, at [23]). This finding was overturned on appeal, with the Court of Appeal (*Haines* v. *Hill* [2007] BPIR 1280) holding that the wife provided a form of consideration in giving up her claim for ancillary relief in return for the transfer of property. What was left open to question, however, was whether there might be an argument to say that in certain cases proper consideration was not provided, in particular, where there was collusion and/or the court was misled/possibly if the order was by consent. The suspicion may remain for some creditors that the divorce proceedings are a sham (see however *Re Jones* [2008] BPIR 1051 for an unsuccessful attempt to challenge a pre-existing court order on the basis that there was collusion between husband and wife).

On the same basis, the trustee may also wish to consider whether maintenance payments could be viewed as preferential payments (IA 1986, s.340). The key question to determine is whether in making such a payment the husband sought to put his (ex) wife in a better position than other creditors. In the case of an order by consent, the requisite element of desire may be easier to make out than if the order was made to compel payments following a contested hearing.

As a result of the provisions of IA 1986, ss.339 and 340 and the continuing uncertainty on bankruptcy, the trustee in bankruptcy will still look carefully at any transfer of the family home or any other transfer of assets, be it made by agreement or by court order, providing that such a transfer took place within the requisite period.

10.10 ANNULMENT OF BANKRUPTCY

The court has the power to annul a bankruptcy order if it appears that:

(a) grounds existed at the time of the order which meant that the order should not have been made (IA 1986, s.282(1)(a));
(b) to the extent required by the rules, the bankruptcy debts and expenses of the bankruptcy have all, since the making of the order, been paid or secured to the satisfaction of the court (IA 1986, s.282(1)(b)); or
(c) the bankrupt has entered into an IVA with his creditors (IA 1986, s.261(2)(a)).

Annulment of the bankruptcy order can take place whether or not the bankrupt has been, or is being, discharged from the bankruptcy (IA 1986, s.282(3)); there is no prescribed time period within which an application for annulment should be brought.

Annulment is distinguished from discharge in that post annulment, the party is returned to the position he was in before the bankruptcy, meaning the record of bankruptcy is expunged. This also means that the debtor is liable for, and can be pursued for, what were regarded as 'bankruptcy debts'. In contrast, on discharge (see below), the former bankrupt is released from bankruptcy debts.

The court's power to annul is, however, discretionary and, even if it finds that grounds exist that would justify annulment, the court can refuse to make the order (*Gill* v. *Quinn* [2005] BPIR 129; *Society of Lloyd's* v. *Waters* [2001] BPIR 698, which stresses the two-stage process; *Askew* v. *Peter Dominic Ltd* [1997] BPIR 163 on the exercise of the court's discretion; and *Harper* v. *Buchler* [2004] BPIR 724, which held that annulment is a privilege granted within the unfettered discretion of the court). Annulment of the bankruptcy will not be ordered simply because the original petitioning creditor does not object to the annulment of the bankruptcy (*Leicester* v. *Plumtree Farms Ltd* [2004] BPIR 296). Annulment will also not generally be granted conditionally (*Re Hagemeister* [2010] BPIR 1093, although see the earlier authorities of *Engel* v. *Peri* [2002] BPIR 961 and *Hirani* v. *Rendle* [2004] BPIR 274).

Despite annulment, any sale or disposition of property, payment or anything done pursuant to statutory powers by the Official Receiver or trustee in bankruptcy will remain valid, although the court may order that property shall be transferred or revert to the bankrupt or third parties (IA 1986, s.282(4)).

There is no limitation imposed by statute on who may apply to annul the bankruptcy. If the applicant seeking an annulment is not the bankrupt, notice of hearing and the evidence filed must be sent to the bankrupt (see *F* v. *F* [1994] 1 FLR 359, where an application was made by a wife for annulment of her husband's bankruptcy where it was thought bankruptcy was being used to defeat her application for ancillary relief).

The application for an annulment should be supported by a witness statement (IR 1986, rule 6.206(2)). A copy of the application and supporting witness statement should be filed at court, and the court will fix a date for hearing. Notice of the hearing will be served upon the Official Receiver and, as appropriate, the trustee and the bankrupt.

If the grounds for annulment have already been considered at the statutory demand or petition stage, the application for annulment should be dismissed (*Atherton* v. *Ogunlende* [2003] BPIR 21); an application for annulment should not be confused with the rights of appeal and the court's power to rescind and review insolvency proceedings (IA 1986, s.375). Furthermore, it should be remembered that where the bankrupt is seeking to annul on the basis that the order should not have been made, the evidence must relate to matters prior to the order; the bankrupt cannot rely on events that occurred after the date of bankruptcy. Despite this, it may be possible to put matters before the court that were not before the court on the original hearing of the petition (*Hope* v. *Premierpace (Europe) Ltd* [1999] BPIR 695).

In advance of the hearing, on application the court may make an interim order staying the bankruptcy proceedings, if thought appropriate. An application for such a stay may be made *ex parte*, except where the application is made to stay all or part of the proceedings. In such cases, the application must be served upon the trustee giving sufficient time to allow him to be present at the hearing. This provision may be important if a bankruptcy order has only just been made and will prevent the trustee in bankruptcy from advertising and/or the trustee/Official Receiver collecting in and realising assets where an application for annulment is pending.

Where an application is made for an annulment on the basis that the order should not have been made, the Official Receiver and trustee must be given sufficient time to enable them to be present at the hearing. The application must also be served upon the petitioning creditor.

If an annulment order is granted on this ground, there is a strong argument that the creditor should bear the costs of the proceedings (*Butterworth* v. *Soutter* [2000] BPIR 582). Where the bankrupt has delayed bringing the proceedings, it is more reasonable that despite the order granting an annulment he should first pay the costs of the trustee (*Thornhill* v. *Atherton* [2005] BPIR 437).

Where the application is on the basis that all debts and expenses of the bankruptcy have been paid, 28 days' notice must be provided. The applicant must satisfy the court that all bankruptcy debts have been paid in full (IA 1986, s.382; IR 1986, rule 6.211(2)). This therefore includes creditors who may not have proved in the bankruptcy, although as set out below the court may make special provision in order to deal with creditors who cannot be found, etc.

If a debtor has successfully obtained creditors' approval to an IVA, the court must annul the bankruptcy order on the application of the bankrupt or on that of the Official Receiver, if the bankrupt fails to do so (IA 1986, s.261). The court can at that time give directions as to the treatment/administration of the bankruptcy in order to facilitate the implementation of the voluntary arrangement, which may include issues regarding fees.

Where it is known that there are creditors who have not proved in the bankruptcy, the court may direct the trustee or Official Receiver to send notice of the application to all creditors with a view to their proving their debt within 21 days and direct adjournment of the application for annulment for a period of not less than 35 days (IR 1986, rule 6.209).

If at the hearing it is considered by the court that a debt is disputed, or a creditor can no longer be traced, the debtor may be ordered to provide security by paying money into court or providing a bond entered into with sureties, to the extent that the court thinks such security is necessary to cover those creditors' claims. Where security is being provided, the court may direct the applicant to advertise for creditors who cannot otherwise be traced. If an advertisement is ordered and no claim is made within 12 months from the date of the advertisement, the court will grant an application that the security can be released (IR 1986, rule 6.211).

These provisions ensure a careful balance between the interests of the individuals being released from bankruptcy and the interests of those potential creditors that may be unable to be traced. It is often the case that after a period of time has elapsed, creditors cannot easily be located, as in reality in the majority of cases a creditor may well have given up any prospect of receiving any payment and not have kept in contact with the trustee. The court will, however, be wary of any delay by the bankrupt in bringing the application as it may have been with the intention that such creditors are less likely to come forward, and in such circumstances the court may therefore refuse to grant the annulment (*Gill* v. *Quinn* [2005] BPIR 129).

Although statutory interest on debts is not viewed as a debt or an expense (*Harper* v. *Buchler* [2004] BPIR 724), the court will generally expect it to be paid, although in the exercise of its discretion the court may agree that the bankrupt may forgo the payment of statutory interest where the application has been made promptly (see *Harper* v. *Buchler (No.2)* [2005] BPIR 577).

An annulment sought by a bankrupt is often on the basis that a third party has been willing to offer payment of the bankrupt's debts. The payment by a third party avoids the *ad valorem* fees of the DBIS/Insolvency Service account that would otherwise be payable on the realisation of the bankrupt's estate and therefore has some attractions to the debtor (and paying third party), who may be able to obtain a release of the bankruptcy debts for a lower sum. In addition, the court may also be minded to consider that the bankruptcy debts are discharged without payment of interest.

While it is not unusual for the third party to approach creditors directly and agree a payment in return for the creditor agreeing not to prove in the bankruptcy, a creditor should be wary of accepting such an offer as it may be forgoing statutory interest and possibly a better return if it were to wait for a dividend after the trustee has realised the bankruptcy estate. The trustee should, however, seek the views of creditors and report on their responses to assist the court in making its decision (see *Wilcock* v. *Duckworth* [2005] BPIR 682).

Where the application is made on the basis that all the debts have been paid, the trustee (or Official Receiver if no trustee has been appointed) must in any event, and not less than 21 days before the date of hearing, file a report at court in respect of (IR 1986, rule 6.207(2)):

(a) the circumstances leading to the bankruptcy;
(b) a summary of the bankrupt's assets and liabilities as at the date of the bankruptcy order;
(c) a summary of the bankrupt's assets and liabilities as at the date of the application;
(d) details of creditors who are known to have claims but have not proved; and
(e) all other matters considered necessary to be put before the court.

The trustee's report must include particulars of the debts and expenses of the bankruptcy and how they have been paid or secured. A copy of the report should be sent to the applicant 14 days before the date of the hearing. The applicant may file an affidavit in answer to the statements in the report. If the trustee is not the Official Receiver, a copy will be served on the Official Receiver not less than 21 days before the date of the hearing. The Official Receiver may file an additional report, which must be served on the applicant at least seven days before the date of the hearing.

The trustee must attend the application to annul (IR 1986, rule 6.210). On an order for annulment being made, the petition for bankruptcy is deemed dismissed (see IR 1986, rule 6.213; although contrast with *Choudhury* v. *IRC* [2000] BPIR 246), and the bankruptcy order annulled. The court will send copies of the order to the applicant, the Official Receiver and, if different, the trustee (IR 1986, rule 6.208(5)). It will also give notice of the order to the Secretary of State (IR 1986, rule 6.213(2)), who will delete all information concerning the bankruptcy from the Insolvency Register, if the annulment was on the grounds that the order should never have been made (IR 1986, rule 6A.5(a)).

The court will order the vacation of the registration of the bankruptcy petition as a pending action and of the bankruptcy order in the register of writs and orders affecting land (IR 1986, rule 6.213(1)).

If requested by the bankrupt, the Secretary of State will give notice of the annulment in the *London Gazette* or in the newspaper in which the bankruptcy order was advertised, or in both, the costs being borne by the bankrupt (IR 1986, rule 6.213(3)). Where the Official Receiver has given notice of the bankruptcy to creditors, following annulment, he is obliged to give them notice of the same (IR 1986, rule 6.212(1)).

The trustee thereafter prepares and submits a copy of his final account to the Secretary of State and files the same at court (IR 1986, rule 6.214(2)). The final account includes a summary of all receipts and payments. On filing, the trustee may be released from such time as the court determines.

Guide to procedure

- Bankrupt (generally) prepares notice of application (ordinary application), stating ground upon which he relies.
- Bankrupt prepares witness statement in support, providing evidence why bankruptcy order should not have been made, or that debts paid in full.
- Bankrupt files an application and witness statement at court in which bankruptcy order made.
- Court fixes time and venue.
- Bankrupt serves Official Receiver and trustee and, if on grounds that order should not have been made, the petitioning creditor.
- Twenty-eight days' notice must be given where application is on grounds that debts have been paid, otherwise must give sufficient notice for Official Receiver and trustee to be present.
- Trustee/Official Receiver files report at court 21 days prior to hearing, serving a copy on the bankrupt at least 14 days prior to hearing.
- Further statements/reports may be exchanged prior to hearing.
- Court may at any time make an interim order staying the bankruptcy proceedings.
- Court hearing. Trustee must attend; the Official Receiver may attend.
- If annulment is to be ordered on grounds that debts have been paid in full, but some creditors have not proved, or where there are disputed debts or untraced creditors, directions may be provided by the court.

- Court sends order to applicant, Official Receiver, Secretary of State and, if appropriate, the petitioning creditor and trustee.
- Official Receiver gives notice to creditors.
- Trustee submits final account and seeks release.

10.11   A SECOND BANKRUPTCY

If a debtor is made bankrupt while still being undischarged from a former bankruptcy, it is only after-acquired property, the proceeds of sale of that property, or money paid pursuant to an IPO which remains undistributed that will be treated as vesting in the bankrupt's estate of the later second bankruptcy (IA 1986, ss.334, 335). The costs and expenses of the first trustee in dealing with such property will, however, be a first charge on the property realised in the second bankruptcy estate.

A creditor of the first bankruptcy cannot prove in the second bankruptcy, although the first trustee may prove for the unsatisfied debts from the first bankruptcy in addition to unpaid interest and expenses. Such debts are, however, treated as deferred debts (IA 1986, s.335(5), (6)), being payable after all debts and interest in the second bankruptcy are paid. As the right to prove belongs to the first trustee, and not the creditors of the first bankruptcy, the Limitation Act period does not arise until the commencement of the second bankruptcy (*Re Cullwick, ex p. London Senior Official Receiver* [1918] 1 KB 646).

If a bankrupt has been an undischarged bankrupt within six years before the date of the second bankruptcy, the Secretary of State may well apply to court for the granting of a BRO (IA 1986, Sched.4A, para.2(3)). Indeed, among the factors that the court will consider in granting a BRO, particular attention will be given to a second bankruptcy.

CHAPTER 11

The debtor's position during the corporate insolvency process

11.1 INTRODUCTION

Chapters 3, **5**, **7**, **8** and **9** dealt with the corporate insolvency processes and looked at the position of the company. What happens to the corporate entity, who has control and management and what is the likely result of the process? This chapter looks at the position of the directors, shareholders and those closely concerned with management during the insolvency process and those maintaining control of the insolvent company. Despite the limited liability status afforded to the majority of companies, there are various statutory and common law remedies available to the company and the office holder that can lead to the imposition of personal liability on individuals to compensate the company and/or its creditors.

11.2 DIRECTOR'S DUTIES AND RESPONSIBILITIES

Even well-managed and established businesses may find themselves in financial difficulty. In such circumstances, the directors need to have regard to both statutory and common law duties that are owed to the company and its creditors. These duties, obligations and liabilities are brought to the fore on the liquidation of a company, and the failure reasonably to discharge such duties may lead to civil or even criminal sanctions.

The law distinguishes between company directors involved in the management of the company and the company's officers. Directorship entails more serious legal obligations and liabilities than those imposed on officers of the company.

11.2.1 Common law duties

A director owes the company a duty to exercise reasonable skill and care. Former case law led to the conclusion that the degree of skill and care expected of the director is subjectively assessed on that which is reasonable for a director possessed of that individual's particular knowledge and expertise, e.g. the ill-informed, inexperienced director would be judged differently (and, perversely, less harshly) than the fully informed director of many years' standing. However, former authorities on the extent of a director's common law duties should be treated with care; each case will rest on its own facts. Indeed, a more objective assessment (such as that applied in IA 1986, s.214, wrongful trading applications) seems in recent years to have gained more favour with the courts. As a result, the standard expected of a 'reasonable' director may be seen to better reflect the standard of skill, care and diligence that should be shown by all (see *Re D'Jan of London* [1993] BCC 646).

11.2.2 Fiduciary duties

A director has an equitable duty to act in good faith and in the best interests of the company. This may involve additional duties to act independently and not personally profit by competing with the company or allowing personal interests to conflict with those of the company (see *Bhullar* v. *Bhullar* [2003] 2 BCLC 241). Failure to disclose to a company a personal interest which could have been pursued by the company in its own interest may make a director liable to account to the company for any profit made. An example of this arises in cases of 'phoenix trading', where prior to the commencement of the liquidation, the insolvent company's business has been unlawfully diverted to another company connected with the director.

11.2.3 Statutory duties

CA 2006 contains over 250 offences of application to a company director, the majority of which are summary offences which can be brought before, and considered by, magistrates. These include failure to deliver annual accounts, failure to disclose an interest in shares and failure to disclose an interest in contracts made by the company.

Directors may also be liable for a wide variety of offences under statutes such as the Theft Act 1968 (obtaining property by deception), the Trade Descriptions Act 1968 (providing misleading trade descriptions), the Value Added Tax Act 1994 (fraudulent evasion of VAT) and the Health and Safety at Work etc. Act 1974.

CA 2006 received Royal Assent on 8 November 2006. With over 1,300 sections, it is partly a restatement and codification of the law and partly a reforming measure intended to simplify many issues of corporate governance. One of the most contentious areas has been the partial codification for the first time of directors' duties, as well as the introduction of a concept known as 'enlightened shareholder value'. These provisions came into force in October 2007.

Directors' fiduciary and common law duties have evolved through case law, but effectively boil down to a duty to act in good faith and in the best interests of the company. CA 2006 gives statutory effect to many common law rules and equitable principles, and it also contains several new duties.

Duty to promote the success of the company (CA 2006, s.172)

The duty to promote the success of the company has replaced the director's duty to act 'in the best interests of' the company. In fulfilling this duty, the director must act in good faith and in a way which is likely to promote the success of the company for the benefit of its members as a whole. This is a new concept, but what does 'success' mean? It would seem that if the company's constitution includes a purpose other than for the benefit of its members (e.g. a charitable purpose), the director must act in a way that he considers, in good faith, to be most likely to achieve that purpose.

In fulfilling the duty in CA 2006, s.172, the director must have regard to:

- the likely consequence of any decision in the long term;
- the interests of the company's employees;
- the need to forge the company's business relationships with suppliers, customers and others;
- the impact of the company's operations on the community and environment;
- the desirability of the company maintaining a reputation for high standards of business conduct;
- the need to act fairly between members of the company.

This section introduces the principle of so-called 'enlightened shareholder value', i.e. the concept that a shareholder will realise that wider social responsibilities are an important part of any business decision and will not be motivated simply by profit. This replaces the broad concept of acting in the company's best interests.

Duty to exercise independent judgment (CA 2006, s.173)

This section is a codification of an existing common law principle. It should be remembered, however, that a director is entitled to delegate certain decision-making powers if provided for in the company's constitution. This will not absolve a director of liability for decisions made while he was a director, but it may be a mitigating factor in the assessment of any liability owed.

Duty to exercise reasonable care, skill and diligence (CA 2006, s.174)

This section is modelled on IA 1986, s.214, and therefore imposes on a director an objectively assessed standard of care, with recognition of the subjective factors that influenced the performance of his duties as a director. It therefore involves taking into account the particular director's responsibilities, level of knowledge, skills and experience, and comparing this with the standard of skill that can reasonably be expected of a person with the same general knowledge, skill and experience as those possessed by the particular director carrying out those functions.

Duty to avoid conflicts of interest (CA 2006, s.175)

The director must avoid any direct or indirect conflict with the company's interests, including, in particular, the exploitation of the company's property, information and opportunity. This is not infringed where there is no possibility of a situation giving rise to a conflict of interest or where the dealing is authorised by the directors. Such an authorisation by the directors may be given in a private company where its constitution does not invalidate the authorisation, but it will still only be effective if the required board resolution can be passed without the involvement of the director in question. This represents a change, as there was previously a requirement for shareholder approval.

Although directors who are privy to information in the capacity of a director of one company cannot use this information for the benefit of another company, in practice this can often be a complex issue, particularly at times of financial difficulty. Directors of a number of companies in a group structure, and directors of joint venture companies, are often exposed to information when other companies in the group structure are not. This can result in difficulties for the director. The individual should wear 'different hats' as director of the different companies. If the director is privy to information from the parent company which enables him to conclude that the subsidiary is insolvent, his duty as a director of the subsidiary will be significantly changed. This is a clear example of a conflict and the difficulties such directors may encounter, and in such circumstances it may be necessary for the director to resign. In order to avoid such conflict, utmost care must be taken by directors of companies in a group structure and directors involved in joint ventures.

Duty not to accept benefits from third parties (CA 2006, s.176)

A director should not accept a benefit from a third party which is derived because of his being a director or from doing or not doing anything as a director. However, the duty will not be infringed if the benefit is not regarded as a conflict of interest. If such a situation does arise, benefits conferred may be authorised by members of the company (not the board).

Duty to declare interest in proposed transaction or arrangement with the company (CA 2006, s.177)

The director must declare the nature and extent of any interest, direct or indirect, in respect of any proposed transaction. Previously, a director only needed to declare a direct interest; now there is a need to disclose indirect interests, e.g. those of family members. Declarations must have been made before the company enters into the transaction or arrangement. Declarations may be at a board meeting, or by way of notice in writing, or a general notice under CA 2006, ss.184 or 185. The DBIS has suggested that, as the performance of this duty requires disclosure to the other directors of the board, no disclosure is required where the company only has one director.

Breach of duty and shareholder/liquidator claims

Following the codification and changes to directors' duties (in particular, the wider considerations which will arise in giving effect to enlightened shareholder value), coupled with the reform of derivative actions (claims by shareholders for and on behalf of the company: CA 2006, ss.260–264), some commentators were concerned that directors faced an unreasonable increase in the risk of litigation from shareholders alleging loss and damage caused to the company. It should also be remembered that an insolvency practitioner appointed over the insolvent company will always consider whether claims may be commenced by the company against its former directors for any breach of duty and obligations (see IA 1986, s.212). Indeed, it is often only on liquidation of the company that the directors' role in the company's failure (and loss and damage which arose) is fully considered. Such claims by the liquidator will, of course, be for the benefit of the creditors as a whole, as opposed to simply the members.

Infringement of the statutory duties (CA 2006, ss.171–177) other than that of the duty of reasonable care, skill and diligence (s.174) is enforceable in the same way as any breach of fiduciary duty owed to the company, and the consequences of any breach of statutory duty are the same as would apply if the corresponding common law rule or equitable principle applied (e.g. injunctive relief may be sought and/or a claim commenced by the company for loss and damage).

Where a claim rests against a director for negligence, breach of duty or breach of trust, the court has the power to relieve the director of liability if the director has acted honestly and reasonably, having regard to all the circumstances of the case (CA 2006, s.1157). Directors may also have relief from liability where the company has ratified the conduct by a director even though the conduct could amount to negligence, default, breach of duty or breach of trust (CA 2006, s.239). While such loss caused to the company may thus be excused, where loss is caused to the creditors of the company, as we shall see (e.g. IA 1986, s.214 and antecedent transaction legislation), different considerations apply.

11.2.4 Contractual duties

An executive director will owe duties to the company as set out in his contract of employment. A duty of reasonable care and skill is an implied term of the contract, in addition to express contractual provisions. The extent of the director's role, duties and responsibilities as defined by contract will be a factor in determining the standard of care which is expected from that director, e.g. a finance director will have a greater degree of responsibility for the financial affairs of the company than the marketing director.

The importance of these duties is that a breach of duty to the company can lead to a claim by the company against its directors. This is irrespective of insolvency. It is often the case, however, that a company does not commence proceedings against its directors until there is financial difficulty. Furthermore, once a company has entered into liquidation, the liquidator may take action on behalf of the company against the former directors in respect of such a breach.

11.3 DIRECTORS' LIABILITY ON INSOLVENCY

11.3.1 Duty to creditors

If the directors of the company consider that the company may become insolvent (on either a cash flow or balance sheet test), they are obliged to take all reasonable steps to minimise loss to creditors. This overriding duty to act in the best interests of the creditors as a whole arises both from a common law duty and indirectly from IA 1986, s.214(3) (which provides a director with a defence to a claim of wrongful trading) and the DBIS guidance on the performance of the directors' statutory duty to promote the success of the company (CA 2006, s.172).

Importantly, on insolvency, the directors' primary obligation shifts from promoting the success of the company to acting in the best interests of its creditors. This has significant implications and may well cause the directors to consider that the company should cease trading immediately. However, the cessation of a company's business is not always in the best interests of its creditors. The company may consider it appropriate to continue trading, possibly to trade through its difficulties (if it is a cash flow problem) or, alternatively, where it is likely that further funding will be obtained in the not too distant future (to alleviate a balance sheet problem). (See *Re Imperial Board Products Ltd; Official Receiver* v. *Huw Jones* [2004] EWHC 2096 (Ch) for an example of unsuccessful directors' disqualification proceedings where directors continued to trade on the basis that there was a reasonable belief that the company's insolvency was a short-term problem and further funding could be obtained with the prospect of paying creditors' claims.)

The fact that the directors' decision turns out to be wrong, in that the company is unsuccessful in trading through its difficulties or further funding is not obtained, does not necessarily lead to criticism of the directors' actions and personal liability. What is important, however, is that the directors show that at the time their decision making was reasonable, prudent and justifiable. They should therefore keep themselves fully informed of the situation, take professional advice, regularly monitor the situation and meet regularly to discuss and evaluate the same. In doing so, they must clearly and carefully minute their decisions so as to provide contemporaneous evidence as back-up if questions arise. In such cases, it is more likely to be considered that the directors have acted reasonably and have taken a course that a reasonable director in their position would have taken.

Checklist

Issues directors should consider when facing corporate insolvency

1. In any case:

    1.1 Obtain accurate, up-to-date financial information.
    1.2 If possible, identify the cause of financial difficulty.
    1.3 Assess with the board the possibility of resolving that financial difficulty.
    1.4 Meet regularly to discuss the situation.
    1.5 Obtain professional (accounting and legal) advice.
    1.6 Consider whether cessation of trade will minimise loss to creditors.
    1.7 Consider whether to cease trading immediately or after an organised wind-down.
    1.8 Give consideration to seeking an immediate insolvency procedure.

2. Institute regime of good corporate house keeping:

    2.1 Board to meet regularly to justify actions being taken.
    2.2 Carefully minute decisions taken.
    2.3 If director is in a minority on any decision regarding the solvency of the company, have objections to course taken been noted? Consider resignation if cannot influence board's course of action.

3. Seek to resolve financial difficulty:

    3.1 Explore funding/restructuring possibilities.
    3.2 Consider meeting with and discussing the situation with key creditors, if possible obtaining support.
    3.3 Consider and obtain advice upon the feasibility of obtaining a moratorium from creditor action to give time in which to resolve financial difficulties.
    3.4 Review longer term contracts/orders: can they be cancelled/suspended?

4. Manage cash flow carefully:

    4.1 Examine and if it is possible, cut expenditure/cost base.
    4.2 Request rent free period from the landlord and, if it is possible to terminate the lease, consider new premises.
    4.3 Reduce staff overheads, including reducing working hours, voluntary unpaid leave, redundancies and avoid using employment agents.
    4.4 Negotiate longer periods of credit with creditors and, if possible, change supplier to obtain better prices and trading terms.
    4.5 Request time to pay arrangements with creditors.
    4.6 Ensure the taxation affairs are dealt with in the most tax-efficient manner.
    4.7 Consider factoring the book debts.

However, in the event of insolvency, the directors of the company may find themselves subject to the following actions:

- Wrongful trading (IA 1986, s.214).
- Fraudulent trading (IA 1986, s.213).
- Misfeasance (IA 1986, s.212).
- Disqualification (CDDA 1986).

11.3.2 Wrongful trading

In the course of the winding up of the company, the liquidator may apply to court for a declaration that a person who is, or was, a director of the company may make such contribution to the company's assets as the court thinks fit (IA 1986, s.214(1)).

An application can be brought if:

(a) the company has gone into insolvent liquidation;

(b) some time before the commencement of the winding up of the company, that person knew or ought to have concluded that there was no reasonable prospect that the company would avoid going into insolvent liquidation; and

(c) that person was a director of the company at that time.

It should be noted that IA 1986, s.214 applies only if the company is in liquidation. It applies to directors, former directors, shadow directors, *de facto* directors and the estate of a deceased director (see IA 1986, s.214(7); *Re Hydrodam (Corby) Ltd* [1994] BCC 161; *Re Sherborne Associates Ltd* [1995] BCC 40). The Act may also be invoked by the liquidator of a foreign company against foreign directors being wound up in the UK as an unregistered company (*Re Howard Holdings Ltd* [1998] BCC 549).

However, the court will not make an order if, at the time, the director concluded that the company had a reasonable prospect of avoiding insolvent liquidation and he took every reasonable step to minimise potential loss to the company's creditors (IA 1986, s.214(3)).

The test to be applied to the director's actions is an objective standard, but will also take into account the general knowledge, skill and experience that the director has (IA 1986, s.214(4)(a)). It is therefore both an objective and a subjective test (see *Re Produce Marketing Consortium Ltd (No.2)* [1989] BCLC 520; *Re DKG Contractors Ltd* [1990] BCC 903 for examples of the court looking to what the director knew and ought to have known/done as a result; and *Singla* v. *Hedman (No.2)* [2010] BCC 684 emphasising the objective analysis the court conducts).

The continuation of trading, and even obtaining additional credit past the point of inevitable insolvent liquidation, will not necessarily lead to liability (*Re Hawkes Hill Publishing Co. Ltd* [2007] BCC 937; *Roberts* v. *Froclich* [2011] 2 BCLC 625). In contrast, it should also be noted that as 'trading' is not used in the text to the Act (but only the head note to the section) it does not necessarily mean that further trading/activity needs to take place with further debts being incurred; it could equally be the case that the directors allow the company's assets to be depleted (e.g. by continuing to pay directors' salary).

To establish a claim, the liquidator must evidence that past the point of inevitable insolvency liquidation, loss was caused to creditors/the net deficiency to creditors increased up to the date of liquidation (*Re Marini Ltd* [2004] BCC 172), although the liquidator still needs to establish causation, i.e. that loss was caused by the directors' actions (*Re Brian D Pierson (Contractors) Ltd* [1999] BCC 26).

Despite the possibility that directors may escape a finding of wrongful trading, the directors should, however, be very cautious of any trading activity which, while not causing loss to the creditors as a whole, may be to the detriment of a creditor or class of creditor, as this may be deemed to be a breach of fiduciary duty. Furthermore, the directors may also face civil and criminal liability if they obtain credit knowing that it will not be paid.

The directors' obligation to take every step to minimise the potential loss to creditors places a great onus on the directors to justify their actions. They will need to show that they took reasonable steps, such as obtaining advice and keeping proper accounts, and that they were making a reasonable and well-informed decision when they decided to continue to trade (*Re Purpoint Ltd* [1991] BCC 121). Steps could also include meeting with and informing creditors of the situation, taking business restructuring measures, cost-cutting generally and considering the appointment of an insolvency practitioner to advise on whether to commence an insolvency process (see checklist in **11.3.1**). As mentioned above, the directors are judged not only according to their own knowledge, skill and experience, but also by an objective test, namely what would be expected from a reasonable person carrying on the same functions as that director? The onus of proof is on the liquidator on the balance of probabilities, i.e. more likely than not, rather than beyond all reasonable doubt.

Poor information before the directors is no excuse, because of the objective test which is applied. Directors should obtain the necessary degree of financial information and introduce reasonable financial controls in the circumstances (see *Re Kudos Business Solutions Ltd* [2011] EWHC 1436 (Ch) for an example of poor accounting records). Directors are not entitled to rely upon their own lack of skill and experience (see *DKG Contractors Ltd* [1990] BCC 903).

On obtaining further financial information, it may or may not be advisable to obtain further credit, or it may be the case that an informed view cannot be taken until professional advice has been obtained.

Often, one director may be alone in spotting the financial weakness of the company. It is his responsibility to ensure that the board is fully informed of the situation and to give his best efforts to persuade the board to introduce financial controls, change direction, obtain proper advice and/or cease trading. If his views are rejected, the director may consider it appropriate to resign. In doing so, his attempts to persuade the board to take a different view and the reasons for his resignation should be properly recorded. A director who has simply walked away from the difficulties faced by a company still bears a responsibility. A director who has done all he can to alter the situation may be absolved from responsibility (see, however, *Lexi Holdings plc* v. *Luqman* [2008] 2 BCLC 725 in which non-executive directors had not acted to prevent a fraud by the managing director of the company but were not held liable for causing the loss to the company).

One of the most difficult issues in a wrongful trading case is the identification by the liquidator as to when there was no reasonable prospect of the company avoiding insolvent liquidation.

Checklist

Warning signs that directors may be wrongfully trading

1. Dishonoured cheques.
2. Company providing post-dated cheques to meet current liabilities.
3. Trading in breach of bank facility/overdraft.
4. Request to divert credit payments to different bank accounts.
5. Unusual change in banks.
6. Unmet letters of demand.
7. Claims being issued and judgments in default.
8. Winding-up petitions, even where withdrawn.
9. Executions levied – walking possession agreements.
10. Distraint by landlords.
11. Enforcement action by creditors.
12. Unusual entries/restrictions at HM Land Registry.
13. Assets transferred to connected companies.
14. Unusual switching of suppliers.
15. Poor credit rating.
16. Directors seeking instalments options or time to pay debts.
17. Time to pay arrangements entered into with HMRC.
18. Qualified accounts and accountants' warnings.
19. Unusual reduction of guaranteed debts.
20. Failing to meet budget forecasts/promises of payment.

While alternative dates as to when the company had no reasonable prospect of avoiding insolvent liquidation may be pleaded (*Rubin* v. *Gunner* [2004] 2 BCLC 110), multiple alternative dates may be viewed as oppressive, and on the failure to make a case on the date pleaded the liquidator would not be allowed to substitute a new date (*Re Sherborne Associates Ltd* [1995] BCC 40 and *Singer* v. *Beckett* [2001] BPIR 733).

The amount that a director may be ordered to pay by way of the contribution on a finding of wrongful trading is left entirely to the court's discretion. As a starting point, one may look at the amount of funds which have been depleted since the date that the company directors should have foreseen that the company was insolvent and had no reasonable prospect of paying its debts (see *Re Produce Marketing Consortium Ltd* (1989) 5 BCC 569). The directors' liability to pay is not punitive but compensatory (*Morphitis* v. *Bernasconi* [2003] 2 WLR 1521) and several not joint (*Re Continental Assurance Co. of London plc* [2001] BPIR 733).

Any payment received by the liquidator pursuant to an application under IA 1986, s.214 will not be caught by a floating charge; instead, it will be available to the unsecured creditors. The reason for this is that the cause of action is not 'company property' (*Re Oasis Merchandising Services Ltd* [1997] 2 WLR 764) and therefore not caught within the charge. A further effect of this is that the cause of action is personal to the liquidator and cannot be assigned (sold).

The consent of the creditors, or the court, is required before the liquidator can commence such proceedings (IA 1986, Sched.4, Part I, para.3A). This overcomes the problems caused by the Court of Appeal's decision in *Re Floor Fourteen Ltd; Lewis* v. *Commissioner of Inland Revenue* [2001] 3 All ER 499, which held that the costs incurred in pursuing an action for wrongful trading were not incurred in preserving, realising or getting in any assets of the company and hence were not recoverable expenses. If consent is obtained, the costs of pursuing such proceedings are treated as expenses of the liquidation.

11.3.3 Fraudulent trading

If, in the course of the winding up of the company, it appears that any of the business of the company has been carried on with an intent to defraud creditors or for any other fraudulent purpose, the court may on application by the liquidator declare that any persons who have knowingly been a party to this shall make such contribution to the company's assets as the court thinks proper (IA 1986, s.213).

Fraudulent trading has a longer history than wrongful trading, and bears both criminal liability (Fraud Act 2006) and civil liability (CA 2006, s.993). Criminal charges can be brought against a director whether or not the company has been, or is in the course of being, wound up, and upon conviction imprisonment of up to 10 years and a fine may be imposed.

Fraudulent trading is significantly more difficult to prove than wrongful trading, as there needs to be proof of actual intent to defraud, actual dishonesty involving real moral blame, wilful blindness or reckless indifference (see *Re Patrick and Lyon Ltd* [1933] Ch 786; *Bernasconi* v. *Nicholas Bennett & Co.* [2000] BCC 921; and *Atkinson* v. *Corcoran* [2011] EWHC 3484 (Ch) which confirmed that the onus to prove dishonesty is on the liquidator). As a result, proceedings are much less common than wrongful trading proceedings.

Fraudulent trading is also different from wrongful trading in that proceedings may be commenced against any person, not just a director or shadow director. Fraudulent trading actions have been brought against a creditor of an insolvent company and against the controlling directors of the creditor company (see *Re Gerald Cooper Chemicals Ltd* [1978] 2 All ER 49); *Bank of India* v. *Morris* [2005] BCC 739).

Proceedings may only be commenced by a liquidator and may be taken even if only one creditor has been defrauded (see *Morphitis* v. *Bernasconi* [2003] BCC 540 which outlined the possibility of such a claim but pointed to the creditor's own remedy, *Contex Drouzhba* v. *Wiseman* [2008] BCC 301 and contrast with *Re L Todd (Swanscombe) Ltd* [1990] BCC 125, regarding evasion of VAT), and may be in respect of fraud on potential creditors (*R.* v. *Kemp* [1988] QB 645).

The Limitation Act period runs from the date of the winding up (i.e. when the cause of action accrues) not from an earlier date, such as when the action complained of occurred (see *Re Overnight Ltd* [2010] BCC 787). Any fraudulent trading action commenced by the liquidator is for the benefit of all creditors, not just those defrauded.

11.3.4 Misfeasance

During the course of the winding up of the company, if it appears that a director of the company or a person who has taken part in the promotion, formation or management of the company, has:

(a)   misapplied, retained or become accountable for monies or property of the company; or

(b)   been guilty of any misfeasance or breach of fiduciary or other duty in relation to the company,

the court may, on application by the Official Receiver, liquidator, creditor or contributory (with permission of the court) (see *Irwin* v. *Lynch and another* [2011] 1 WLR 1364, where it was held that the administrator does not have standing but may bring the action in the name of the company), order that person to repay, restore or account for money or property or any part of it with interest as the court thinks fit, or contribute to the company's assets by way of compensation with respect to the misfeasance or breach of fiduciary or other duty (IA 1986, s.212).

This summary remedy may be sought against a director, a former director, or a *de facto* director (see *Holland* v. *HMRC, Re Paycheck Services 3 Ltd* [2011] 1 BCLC 141, which also casts considerable doubt on whether the section applies to shadow directors) where the officer of the company has been in breach of common law, fiduciary duties or other duties to the company (see *Re D'Jan of London Ltd* [1993] BCC 646; *Re Continental Assurance Co. of London plc* [2001] BPIR 733; *Kinlan* v. *Crimmin* [2007] BCC 106). As a result, it is effectively the company's claim against the individual director for loss and damage caused as a result of a breach of duty.

This statutory remedy is not a bar to common law remedies in contract (e.g. breach of contract) or tort (e.g. breach of fiduciary duty, negligence); indeed, it does not create any new separate cause of action (see *A & J Fabrications (Batley) Ltd* v. *Grant Thornton* [1999] BCC 807). It is, however, a speedy and convenient way to proceed where otherwise the issue of a claim form in ordinary proceedings would be necessary.

However, the remedy has its limitations. It is not available to enforce a contractual debt (*Re Etic Ltd* [1928] Ch 861), nor can it be used to overcome difficulties that would be encountered in pursuing an alternative form of claim (see *Re Continental Assurance Co. of London plc* [2001] BPIR 733 regarding the improper use of the remedy to get around the difficulties in establishing a preference claim). It is open for directors being pursued under this section to join into the proceedings third parties who may have contributed/caused the loss such as professional advisers on whose advice the directors relied (*Re International Championship Management Ltd* [2007] BCC 95). Most significantly, a director can avail himself of the defence that, despite the breach of duty/action complained of causing loss and damage to the company, liability should not fall personally on the individual as he had acted honestly and reasonably (see CA 2006, s.1157; *Re Continental Assurance Co. of London plc (No.4)* [2007] 2 BCLC 287; *Re Ortega Associates Ltd* [2008] BCC 256).

An award of compensation is within the discretion of the court (*Gil* v. *Baygreen Properties Ltd* [2005] BPIR 95), although the court may be guided by the loss that has been caused to the company (*Re Derek Randall Enterprises Ltd* [1990] BCC 749). The finding of any liability requires an assessment of all the surrounding circumstances, taking into account whether the actions were honest and reasonable, applying both an objective and a subjective test (as in IA 1986, s.214; see **11.3.2**).

The claim and any realisations from a successful claim are treated as company property and are therefore subject to any secured creditor's rights over the company's cause of action (*Re Anglo-Austrian Printing and Publishing Union (No.3)* [1895] 2 Ch 891) and where not caught by such security, can be sold and assigned (*Re Oasis Merchandising Services Ltd* [1997] 2 WLR 764). Following an order and award made against the director, the director cannot set off liability so arising against sums purportedly due from the company to the director (*Manson* v. *Smith (liquidator of Thomas Christy Ltd)* [1997] 2 BCLC 161).

11.3.5   Misuse of company name

Where a company has gone into insolvent liquidation and a person was a director or shadow director of that company at any time within the 12 months prior to that date, that person cannot, except with leave of the court, be a director of any other company that is known by a prohibited name, for a period of five years. Furthermore, that person cannot be involved directly or indirectly in the promotion or formation of a company with a prohibited name or be concerned in the carrying out of business of that company (IA 1986, s.216).

A prohibited name is one by which the liquidated company was known at any time within the previous 12 months, or is similar enough to suggest an association with that company. The test to be applied as to whether the name is similar is an objective one (see *Archer Structures Ltd* v. *Griffiths* [2004] BCC 156), and applies to trade names as well as business names (see *Inland Revenue Commissioners* v. *Nash* [2003] BPIR 1138) and to acronyms that had been used to identify the company (*ESS Productions Ltd* v. *Sully* [2005] BCC 435).

Any contravention of this section may make the director liable to imprisonment or a fine. The offence is one of strict liability (see *R.* v. *Doring* [2002] BCC 838; *Ricketts* v. *Ad Valorem Factors Ltd* [2004] BCC 164) and the director may be responsible for the relevant debts of the new company (IA 1986, s.217(2)).

'Relevant debts' are those liabilities of the new company incurred where that person was involved in management of the new company and such debts and liabilities were incurred at the time when the new company was acting or was willing to act on his instructions (*Thorne* v. *Silverleaf* [1994] 1 BCLC 637). This provision pierces the corporate veil and makes liable any director or any 'front man' who is acting on the instruction of that person. Liability is a primary liability (jointly and severally with the company), and the individual has no right of indemnity from other persons liable for the debt under IA 1986, s.217 (*HMRC* v. *Yousef* [2008] BCC 805).

The purpose of IA 1986, s.216 is to avoid abuse of the insolvency process by setting up 'phoenix companies', where the same business and trade are effectively carried on by the former directors of an insolvent company but free of the debts of the first. The section also catches the potential misuse by the director of the first company of a nominee, involved in management (of the second company) and who acts or is willing to act on instructions given (without leave of the court) by that first director (IA 1986, s.217(1)(b)). Where the nominee is aware that the individual for whom he is acting is in contravention of s.216, both can find they are liable.

It is common, however, for an insolvent company to be sold with any remaining elements of goodwill, which may well include the name of the company. This section does not bar the reuse of the company name, only the use of that name by the former directors of the insolvent company (without permission of the court).

Reuse of the company name by a director is likely to be permitted where the failure of the initial company was through no fault of the directors (see *Re Bonus Breaks Ltd* [1991] BCC 546). In considering whether to grant leave, the court will also consider the risks to creditors of the old company, e.g. whether the use of the company name will lead to expropriation out of the assets of the old company of goodwill or trade connections which could otherwise have been realised for the benefit of its creditors, or whether the creditors of the new company will be put at risk beyond that which is permitted under law (see *Penrose and another* v. *Secretary of State for Trade and Industry* [1996] 1 WLR 482). The court may also, when considering an application for leave under s.216, call on the liquidator or former liquidator of the liquidating company for a report of the circumstances in which that company became insolvent, and the extent, if any, of the applicant's apparent responsibility for its doing so (IR 1986, rule 4.227A).

Under IR 1986, rule 4.228 (as amended by the Insolvency (Amendment) Rules 2007, SI 2007/1974 following *First Independent Factors Ltd* v. *Churchill* [2006] EWCA Civ 1623), there are three circumstances where the section will not apply:

(a)   Where the whole or substantially the whole of the business of the insolvent company is acquired by a successor company under arrangements made by the liquidator or made before the company entered into insolvent liquidation by an administrator, administrative receiver or supervisor of a CVA and relevant notice is given to the creditors (IR 1986, rule 4.228). The notice must be given to every known creditor and published in the *London Gazette* no later than 28 days after completion of the acquisition. The notice in Form 4.73 must specify the name and number of the insolvent company, the circumstances under which it is being acquired, the name of the successor company and any change of name. A notice must name the persons to whom s.216 may apply, having been a director or shadow director of the insolvent company, and give particulars as to the nature and duration of that directorship.

(b)   Where an application has been made to court within seven days of the liquidation and the court grants leave not later than six weeks from that date (IR 1986, rule 4.229 is the provision for an interim order allowing continuation of trading where the full application is awaiting hearing).

(c)   Where the new company has been known by that name for 12 months ending with the date on which the liquidated company went into liquidation and has not at any time in those 12 months been dormant (IR 1986, rule 4.230).

The prohibition on the reuse of a prohibited name identifies and meets two elements of mischief: first, the danger that the business of the insolvent company has been acquired at an undervalue, or is otherwise to be expropriated, to the detriment of its creditors; and, secondly, the danger that creditors of the old company may be misled into the belief that there has been no change in the corporate vehicle (i.e. phoenix trading).

11.3.6   Criminal investigation and prosecution of malpractice

If it appears to the court during the course of the winding up that any past or present officer or member of the company has been guilty of any offence in relation to the company for which he is criminally liable, the court may direct the liquidator to refer the matter to the Secretary of State (IA 1986, s.218(1)).

It is not the duty of the liquidator to investigate criminal conduct, but if during the course of his investigation any such conduct comes to his attention, in a compulsory winding up he should report to the Official Receiver, and in a voluntary winding up he should report the matter to the Secretary of State. When the Official Receiver receives such information, he is entitled to pass it on to the appropriate authorities (*R. v. Brady* [2005] BCC 357) and the same applies to the Secretary of State.

These provisions are important and designed to ensure investigations by appropriate authorities in cases of criminal conduct by the directors of the company. Where criminal proceedings are instituted by the Director of Public Prosecutions, it is the duty of any liquidator and every officer or agent of the company, past and present, to give the Director of Public Prosecutions all reasonable assistance. Assistance should be provided in the same way to any other prosecuting authority. For this purpose, 'agent' includes any banker or solicitor of the company and any person employed as an auditor (IA 1986, s.219(3)).

11.4   ADJUSTMENTS OF PRIOR TRANSACTIONS

In the last section, the civil and criminal liabilities which a director could face on the insolvency of the company were considered. During the course of the liquidator's investigations, it may be discovered that certain transactions were in breach of various provisions of the insolvency legislation. Proceedings to adjust and/or set aside the transactions could lead to the augmentation of the company's assets and therefore a greater return to creditors.

Legislation dealing with the company's transactions and directors' conduct prior to insolvency has been in place since the sixteenth century, when fraudulent conveyances designed to keep assets out of the reach of creditors could be overturned. IA 1986 drew together provisions in the Bankruptcy Act 1914 which related to individuals, and provisions in various Companies Acts which dealt with corporate transactions. The intention of the insolvency legislation is to treat creditors equitably and ensure that a party has not benefited unfairly to the detriment of other creditors. If assets have been put beyond the reach of creditors in the months leading to the insolvency of the company, the 'ill-gotten gains' of the recipient can be ordered to be repaid to the company. The company may also have sought to distribute assets to connected companies, perhaps setting up phoenix companies prior to insolvency. The following legislation is specifically intended to police and deal with such actions:

- Transactions at an undervalue (IA 1986, s.238).
- Preferences (IA 1986, s.239).
- Extortionate credit transactions (IA 1986, s.244).
- Avoidance of floating charges in certain circumstances (IA 1986, s.245).
- Unenforceability of liens, etc. (IA 1986, s.246).
- Transactions defrauding creditors (IA 1986, s.423).

11.4.1 Transactions at an undervalue

A transaction at an undervalue occurs where the company:

(a) makes a gift to a person or otherwise enters into a transaction with that person on terms that provide that the company is to receive no consideration; or

(b) enters into a transaction with that person for a consideration, the value of which, in money or in money's worth, is significantly less than the value, in money or in money's worth, of the consideration provided by the company (IA 1986, s.238(4)).

However, the transaction can only be set aside where the company is in administration or liquidation. Proceedings may only be commenced by the office holder, the liquidator first requiring sanction from the creditors to bring the claim (IA 1986, Sched.4, para.3A).

The right of action is one that vests in the office holder, who consequently cannot assign the claim as it is not company property (*Re Oasis Merchandising Services Ltd* [1997] 2 WLR 764). As it is a right of the office holder and not the company, the proceeds of any claim are not caught by a floating charge holder's security and thus will be a return to unsecured creditors. It is for this reason that, generally, an action will be taken once the company has passed from administration into liquidation.

The transaction must also have occurred during a period of two years, ending with the onset of insolvency (IA 1986, s.240(1)(a)).

The onset of insolvency is defined as:

(a)   the date the administrator was appointed by court order;

(b)   the date on which the copy of the notice of intention to appoint the administrator was filed at court by a floating charge holder, the company or its directors or, in any other case, the date upon which the administrator's appointment takes effect;

(c)   the date the company entered into administration (or, if relevant, the date on which the administration order was made or a copy of the notice of intention was filed), where the company has gone into liquidation pursuant to an application by a liquidator in main proceedings in another EU Member State to convert an administration in the UK to a winding-up proceeding under Art.37 of Council Regulation 1346/2000/EC on Insolvency Proceedings;

(d)   the date on which the company entered into administration (or, if relevant, the date on which the application for the administration order was made or a copy of the notice of intention was filed) or, in the case of the company going into liquidation, on the appointment of the administrator ceasing to have effect;

(e)   in the case of the company going into compulsory liquidation, other than by any of the above, the winding up is deemed to commence at the time of the presentation of the petition for winding up; or

(f)   in the case of voluntary liquidation, the winding up is deemed to commence at the time of passing of the resolution for the winding up of the company.

Importantly, however, the time will not be treated as 'relevant time' for the purposes of IA 1986, s.238, unless at the time of the transaction the company was unable to pay its debts, or became unable to pay its debts as a consequence of the transaction (within the meaning of IA 1986, s.123). This may be proved by evidence, e.g. that the company had failed to pay invoices as and when due (*Re DKG Contractors Ltd* [1990] BCC 903). The requirement to prove 'insolvency' does not apply in respect of a transaction entered into after the making of an administration application, or the filing of a notice of intention to appoint (IA 1986, s.240(1)(c), (d)), provided administration of the company then follows.

In the case of a transaction with a person connected to the company, the liquidator is assisted by a presumption that the company was insolvent. A person 'connected' to the company is widely defined and a person is deemed to be connected to the company if he is a director or shadow director of the company, or an associate of such director or shadow director, or is an associate of the company (IA 1986, s.249).

The company is an 'associate' of another company if the same person has control of both, or the person has control of one and persons who are his associates, or he and persons who are his associates, have control of the other; or if a group of two or more persons have control of each company, and the group either consists of the same persons or could be regarded as consisting of the same persons by treating (in one or more cases) a member of either group as replaced by a person of whom he is an associate (IA 1986, s.435(6)).

A person is deemed to have 'control of the company' if he is a director of the company, or a director of another company which has control of it; or where it is the custom and practice of the company to act in accordance with his directions or instructions; or he is entitled to exercise, or control the exercise of, one-third or more of the voting power at any general meeting of the company; or he has voting rights of one-third or more in another company which has control of the company (IA 1986, s.435).

In the case where the transaction was entered into with an unconnected party, the office holder needs to prove to the satisfaction of the court that the company was unable to pay its debts at the time, or became unable to pay its debts as a result of the transaction (IA 1986, s.240(2)).

The court will not set aside the transaction if it is satisfied that the company has entered into a transaction in good faith for the purpose of carrying on its business, and that at the time it did so there were reasonable grounds for believing the transaction would benefit the company (IA 1986, s.238(5)). The burden of proof is on the party seeking to uphold the transaction (see *Re Barton Manufacturing Co. Ltd* [1999] 1 BCLC 740) and the court will need to be satisfied on an objective test of what would benefit the company (see *Lord* v. *Sinai Securities Ltd* [2004] BCC 986).

Examples of transactions at undervalue could include:

- a gift of property (*Singla* v. *Hedman (No.2)* [2010] BCC 684);
- purchase of property which is worth significantly less than the price paid for it;
- sale of assets for a price which is significantly less than their true value (*Stanley* v. *TMK Finance Ltd* [2011] BPIR 876);
- payment for services provided which is significantly more than the value of the services rendered (*Clement* v. *Henry Hadaway Organisation Ltd* [2008] 1 BCLC 223);
- alleged loans made to directors (*Re Barton Manufacturing Co. Ltd* [1998] BCC 827);
- provision of services at a price significantly less than the value of the services rendered;
- allowing a party to retain an asset in settlement of a debt, the value of which is significantly in excess of the value of the debt;
- conversion of an interest free loan to an interest bearing loan (*Re Shapland Inc* [2000] BCC 106); and
- releasing a creditor from a debt on terms which are significantly less valuable than the value of the debt.

Where the court is satisfied that there has been a transaction at an undervalue, it may make such order as it thinks fit, having regard to the non-exhaustive list of possible orders that can be made as set out in IA 1986, s.241 (see **11.4.3**).

11.4.2 Preferential transactions

The company gives a preference to a person if:

(a) that person is one of the company's creditors or a surety or guarantor for any of the company's debts or other liabilities; and

(b) the company does anything or suffers anything to be done which (in either case) has the effect, in the event of the company going into insolvent liquidation, of putting that person in a better position than he would have been in if that thing had not been done (IA 1986, s.239).

An order on application by a liquidator will only be made where the company gave the preference and in doing so was influenced in deciding to give it by a desire to produce, in relation to that person, the effect outlined above (IA 1986, s.239(5)). A liquidator requires sanction in order to bring a claim under this section (IA 1986, Sched.4, para.3A).

The preference must be made at the time the company was unable to pay its debts, or cause the company to become unable to pay its debts, and the transaction must have occurred within six months (or two years in the case of a connected person) of the onset of insolvency. Time runs not from the time of completion of the transaction, but from when the decision to prefer was taken (*Re MC Bacon Ltd (No.1)* [1990] BCC 78). However, there may be circumstances where at the time the decision was taken there was no question of preference, but at the time of completion the situation differs; in such a case it might still be incumbent on the company to reconsider its decision (*Re Brian Pierson (Contractors) Ltd* [1999] BCC 26).

As under IA 1986, s.238, it needs to be established that at the time of the decision to give effect to a transaction which has the effect of preferring a creditor, the company was insolvent (IA 1986, s.240) and the same considerations arise (see above).

The need to evidence creditor 'betterment' (i.e. being placed in a better position in the event of the company's insolvency than otherwise) is allied to a requirement to show that the company must have been influenced by a desire to produce that effect (which is a mandatory requirement: see *Doyle* v. *Saville* [2002] BPIR 947). This introduces a requirement to evidence 'intention' in the mind of the debtor company. If the company is responding to normal commercial pressure to make a payment or perform any other act, then arguably this cannot constitute preferential payment as there is no desire to carry out that act. The leading case on this point is *Re MC Bacon Ltd (No.1)* [1990] BCC 78. In this case, the office holder sought to challenge security granted by a company to its bank. The court held that:

(a) desire cannot be inferred simply from the fact that the recipient's position is improved: there must be some subjective evidence that the debtor company is motivated to produce that effect; and

(b) desire to improve the position need not be the dominant factor, but must have been influential on the minds of those making the decision.

The requisite element of desire was not found in cases where the company was commercially motivated to make the payments to keep its business running (see *Re Lewis's of Leicester Ltd* [1995] BCC 514; *Re New Generation Engineers* [1993] BCLC 435). The company may also feel it is necessary to retain the services of its professional advisers, namely accountants and solicitors, and pay off arrears to these creditors over the demands of other creditors (see *Re Ledingham-Smith* [1993] BCLC 635). It may also be willing to grant a debenture in respect of pre-existing debts in order to obtain a new advance to keep the business going (see *Re Fairway Magazines* [1992] BCC 924). Such considerations are not relevant, however, if it could be shown that the preference was given to a recipient who was already willing to provide working capital (*Re Conegrade Ltd* [2003] BPIR 358).

The fact that something has been done pursuant to an order of the court will not, without more, prevent the doing or suffering of that thing from constituting the giving of a preference (IA 1986, s.239(7)).

The company is presumed to have acted with the necessary mental element (i.e. intention/desire to prefer) in the case of a transaction with a connected person (e.g. director) or an associate of such a person.

Where the court is satisfied that a preferential payment has been made, it will make such order as it thinks fit to restore the position to what it would have been, if the company had not given that preference (IA 1986, s.239(3)). The court may make such order as it thinks fit, including those set out in the non-exhaustive list provided by IA 1986, s.241 (see below on the consequences of an order under IA 1986, ss.238 or 239).

The court will not set aside the preference given if entered into in good faith and without notice of the surrounding circumstances. In the circumstances, it is difficult for directors, controlling shareholders and their relatives and other group companies to retain the benefit of preferential payments made to them by the insolvent company, as they will almost certainly have had notice of the relevant circumstances (see *Weisgard* v. *Pilkington* [1995] BCC 1108; *Katz* v. *McNally* [1999] BCC 291; and contrast with *Re Fairway Magazines Ltd* [1992] BCC 924).

The following principles have been established through case law:

- There must be dealings between the parties requiring a positive act by the company, although omission (such as failure to pursue a debtor) may amount to a preference (see *Re Taylor Sinclair (Capital) Ltd* [2001] 2 BCLC 176).
- There must be some depletion of the company's assets or diminution in the value of the assets of the company (see *Re Mistral Finance Ltd* [2001] BCC 27, in which the granting of security for a previously unsecured advance was held not to be a transaction at undervalue, but rather capable of attack as a preference; see also *Re MC Bacon Ltd (No.1)* [1990] BCC 78 and *Re Lewis's of Leicester Ltd* [1995] BCC 514, where the sole creditor of a bank account created a trust in favour of various company creditors which was held not to constitute a transaction at an undervalue; these decisions must, however, be reviewed in light of *Re Nurkowski; Hill* v. *Spread Trustee Company Ltd* [2006]

BPIR 789 (CA), where Arden LJ was prepared to hold that the granting of security could constitute consideration and thus be capable of being set aside as a transaction at an undervalue).

- Valid consideration may be provided by a third party (*Phillips* v. *Brewin Dolphin Bell Lawrie Ltd* [2001] 1 WLR 143 (HL)).
- The insolvent company must be responsible for the transaction (*Re Parkside International Ltd* [2010] BCC 309, the assignment of a debt due from the insolvent company was not a transaction over which the insolvent company had control).
- In assessing the value of the consideration, the court can take into account an event which occurred after the transaction, in order to substitute the real value of the transaction as opposed to a speculative value at the time of the transaction (see *Re Thoars (Deceased)* [2003] 1 BCLC 499).
- The value given must be 'significantly' less than the value of the consideration provided by the company and this depends on the facts of each case (*Re London Local Residential Ltd (No.2)* [2005] BPIR 163, where a 7 per cent difference between sale value and expert value was held not to be significant; see also *Ramlort Ltd* v. *Reid* [2004] BPIR 985 and *Re Marini Ltd* [2004] BCC 172).

Examples of preferences include:

- granting security to secure an existing debt (see *Re Mistral Finance Ltd* [2001] BCC 27);
- repayment of a loan made by the directors to the company when the terms of the loan do not require immediate repayment;
- return of goods to a supplier where title has already passed;
- payment of a debt which is guaranteed by the directors;
- failing to take reasonable steps to protect the company's interest (possibly allowing a creditor to obtain a judgment and enforce by way of charging order); and
- payment to a creditor of the company who is an associate of the debtor company.

11.4.3 Consequences of an order under IA 1986, ss.238 or 239

Where all the conditions of the legislation are fulfilled, the court may make an order:

(a) requiring any property transferred as part of the transaction to be vested back in the company;

(b) where property has vested in a third party, as to the application of either the proceeds of sale of the property so transferred or of money so transferred;

(c) releasing or discharging (in whole or in part) any security given by the company;

(d) requiring any person to pay such sums to the office holder, in respect of benefits received by him from the company, as the court may direct;

(e)   providing for any surety or guarantor whose obligations to any person were released or discharged (in whole or in part) under the transaction, to be under such new or revived obligations to that person as the court thinks fit;

(f)   providing for security to be provided for the discharge of any obligation imposed by or arising under the order, for an obligation to be charged on any property, and for the security or the charge to have the same priority as the security or charge released or discharged (in whole or in part) under the transaction; or

(g)   providing for the extent to which the person whose property is re-vested by order in the company, or on whom obligations are imposed by the order, is to be able to prove in the winding up of the company for the debts or other liabilities which arose from, or were released or discharged, in whole or in part, under or by the transaction (IA 1986, s.241).

The court will endeavour to unravel the transaction such that the parties are put back in the position they were in before the transaction complained of and that the creditors as a whole are therefore not prejudiced. This is important as the aim prevents the unscrupulous from entering into a transaction with the thought that they can remedy the situation by simply paying damages, e.g. if a property was intentionally sold at an undervalue, if proceedings were commenced the transferee would pay the difference in value between that paid and market value.

However, the court's power to restore the company's position to the status quo, i.e. pre-transaction position, is subject to the safeguard that those persons who have acquired any interest in property of the company in good faith for value will obtain good title and will not be prejudiced by the making of an order. However, any actual party to the transaction at an undervalue or the party who has received the benefit of a preference is not so protected even if they act in good faith and for value (IA 1986, s.241(2)).

An order will only be made against a third party (i.e. not a party to the transaction) where it is necessary to restore the position to the pre-transaction position (*Re Oxford Pharmaceuticals Ltd* [2010] BCC 834).

A person is presumed to act in good faith unless he has notice of the relevant surrounding circumstances and of the relevant proceedings, or he is connected with or was an associate of either the company in question or the person with whom that company entered into the transaction, or to whom that company gave the preference (IA 1986, s.241(2A); see also *Re Sonatacus Ltd* [2007] BCC 186 confirming that the onus to prove good faith is on such persons).

It should be noted that in the case of a person who is not a 'connected person', the individual must have notice not only of the relevant surrounding circumstances (i.e. that the company entered into a transaction at an undervalue), but also notice of the relevant proceedings (i.e. administration order, notice of intention filed, winding-up petition being presented, the company having gone into liquidation). This revised section (post-Insolvency Act 1994, which came into force 26 July

1994) therefore provides greater protection to any party who has entered into the transaction in good faith.

11.4.4   Transactions to defraud creditors

Table 11.1   Advantages and disadvantages of Insolvency Act 1986, ss.238 and 423

Transactions at an undervalue: s.238	
Advantages	Disadvantages
• No need to show dishonesty on the part of the company or its directors	• Proceedings can only be taken on liquidation or administration of the company
• No need to show intention to procure the result of the transaction	• Two-year time limit
	• Application only by liquidator or administrator
Transactions to defraud creditors: s.423	
Advantages	Disadvantages
• No requirement that the company is/was insolvent	• Must show dishonesty, i.e. intention to put the assets out of reach of the creditors
• No time limit	
• Application can be made by the victim of the transaction	

IA 1986, s.423 has application to both individuals and companies (*Re Shilena Hosiery Co. Ltd* [1980] Ch 219), referring to 'persons' entering a transaction at an undervalue with the purpose:

(a)   of putting assets beyond the reach of a person making, or who may at some time make, a claim against him, or

(b)   of otherwise prejudicing the interests of such a person in relation to a claim which he is making or may make (IA 1986, s.423(3)).

Where so satisfied, the court may make such order as it thinks fit, restoring the position to that which it would have been if the transaction had not been entered into and protecting the interests of persons who are victims of the transaction (IA 1986, s.423(2)).

There is considerable overlap between IA 1986, s.238 and s.423. IA 1986, s.423, however, has considerably longer historical antecedents and is open to parties other than the liquidator, including a creditor of an insolvent company (*Re Ayala Holdings Ltd* [1993] BCLC 256; see also *Sands* v. *Clitheroe* [2006] BPIR 1000 on who might use the section). It should be noted that any application brought by a single creditor who has been prejudiced by the transaction is made on behalf of every victim of the transaction (IA 1986, s.424(2)), the meaning of the word 'victim' being wider than simply creditors (*Clydesdale* v. *Smailes* [2010] BPIR 77).

There is no requirement to prove insolvency at the time of the transaction and the company does not need to be in an insolvency process (*Trowbridge* v. *Trowbridge* [2003] BPIR 258).

However, it remains notoriously difficult to prove that the relevant transaction was entered into for the purposes of putting assets beyond the reach of a person who is making, or may at some time make, a claim or otherwise has prejudiced the position of trust of such a person (IA 1986, s.423(3)). The burden of proof lies with the applicant (*Habib Bank Ltd* v. *Ahmed* [2004] BPIR 35) and, unlike IA 1986, ss.238 and 239 proceedings, there are no statutory presumptions to assist the applicant. The test to be applied is whether an intention to put the assets beyond the reach of creditors was a substantial purpose of the transaction, not a mere result or by-product of the transaction (*Inland Revenue Commissioners* v. *Hashmi* [2002] BPIR 974, replacing the former 'dominant' purpose test in *Chohan* v. *Saggar* [1994] BCC 134).

A transaction to defraud creditors may be a gift, or entered into where the consideration is significantly less than the value, in money or money's worth, of the consideration provided by the company.

Despite the fact that there is no time limit in IA 1986, s.423 (i.e. the transaction may have arisen many years before), the courts have shown some reluctance to reopen transactions going back many years (see *Law Society* v. *Southall* [2002] BPIR 336). In *Re Nurkowski* [2006] BPIR 789, the court considered the application of the Limitation Act 1980 and held that it did apply to IA 1986, s.423, the period being six years if monetary relief is claimed but 12 years for any other form of relief (i.e. a specialty). The court also pointed out that a creditor would have six or 12 years from the date of the transaction to apply, whereas an office holder would have six or 12 years from the date of the commencement of the insolvency. The fact that differing Limitation Act periods arose was not considered objectionable.

On an application, the court will make an order on being satisfied that the company has entered into a transaction at an undervalue where the dominant/ substantial purpose was as set out in IA 1986, s.423(2), i.e. to defraud or prejudice creditors (*Chohan* v. *Saggar* [1994] BCC 134 which talks of a dominant purpose; and contrast with *4Eng Ltd* v. *Harper* [2010] BPIR 1 which, as per IA 1986, s.238, talks of a substantial purpose). See also *Papanicola* v. *Fagan* [2009] BPIR 320 where it was held that although the purpose of the transaction was to help save the debtor's marriage, the result of the transaction was to defeat the claims of creditors.

An order may lead to payment to the company or potentially to the specific creditor who has been defrauded, although the applicant cannot be put in a better position than he would have been in had the transaction not occurred (*Ram* v. *Ram (No.1)* [2005] BPIR 616).

An order for restoration will generally take into account the value of the interest the respondent had in the property prior to the transaction (*Chohan* v. *Saggar* [1994] BCC 134).

Where a person is a bona fide purchaser for value without notice of the relevant circumstances, his interests cannot be prejudiced (IA 1986, s.425(2)).

Examples of transactions to defraud creditors include:

- the creation of a sham family trust to protect the debtor's assets in the event of the business failure (see *Midland Bank* v. *Wyatt* [1996] BPIR 288);
- declaration of an agricultural tenancy in order to defeat a claim by a mortgagee (see *Agricultural Mortgage Corporation plc* v. *Woodward* [1994] BCC 688);
- the transfer of a property to defeat the possible obtaining by the creditor of a charge over the property (see *Beckenham MC Ltd* v. *Centralex Ltd* [2004] BPIR 1112); and
- the forging of a will with consequent payments (see *HM Treasury Solicitor* v. *Doveton* [2009] BPIR 352).

Even where legal advice has been obtained, it does not necessarily prevent a successful action by a creditor (see *Arbuthnot Leasing International Ltd* v. *Havelet Leasing Ltd (No.2)* [1990] BCC 636), and it is possible where issues of motive are in question for the court to order disclosure of professionally privileged material (*Barclays Bank* v. *Eustice* [1995] BCC 978).

Table 11.2   Summary antecedent transactions

Type of transaction	Period in which transaction took place	Insolvency of company at time of transaction	Presumption of insolvency	Intention of company directors	Presumption of intention
Transaction at an undervalue to a connected person	In last 2 years	✔	✔	✕	✕
Transaction at an undervalue to unconnected persons	In last 2 years	✔	✕	✕	✕
Transaction at an undervalue to put assets beyond reach of creditor(s)	At any time	✕	✕	✔	✕

Type of trans-action	Period in which transaction took place	Insol-vency of company at time of transac-tion	Presump-tion of insolvency	Intention of com-pany directors	Presumption of intention
Preference to connected person	In last 2 years	✔	×	✔	✔
Preference to uncon-nected per-son	In last 6 months	✔	×	✔	×

11.4.5 Extortionate credit transactions

A liquidator may apply to court for an order reopening any credit transaction that is extortionate, which was entered into in the period of three years ending on the date on which the company entered into administration or went into liquidation (IA 1986, s.244(2)). There is no requirement that the company was or became insolvent as a result of the transaction.

A credit transaction is deemed extortionate, having regard to the risk accepted by the person providing the credit, where the terms of it are, or were, such as to require grossly exorbitant payments to be made, whether unconditionally or on certain contingencies arising, and otherwise grossly contravene ordinary principles of fair dealing. The burden of proof to show that a rate is not extortionate is thus on those claiming interest.

Case law in this area suggests, however, that a very high rate of interest will be necessary before it is considered extortionate (see *Ketley Ltd* v. *Scott* [1981] ICR 241 where a rate of 48 per cent per annum was found not to be extortionate). Where the parties are of equal bargaining power and the borrower has made a free and informed decision as to credit, with the interest rate being set out clearly, the court will remain reluctant to intervene; the test as to whether the rate is extortionate being described as a 'stringent' (see *Paragon Finance plc (formerly National Home Loans Corp)* v. *Nash* [2002] 1 WLR 685 and *White* v. *Davenham Trust Ltd* [2011] BCC 77).

The court, if satisfied that the transaction was extortionate, may make such order as it thinks fit, including:

(a) setting aside the whole or part of the obligations created by the transaction;

(b) varying the terms of the transaction or varying the terms on which any security for the purpose of the transaction is held;

(c) requiring any person who is or was a party to the transaction to pay the office holder any sum paid to that person by virtue of the transaction by the company;

(d)   requiring any person to surrender to the office holder any property held by him as security for the purpose of the transaction; or

(e)   directing that an account be taken of the dealings between the parties to the transaction.

In every case, the onus to prove that the transaction was not extortionate is upon the company or person providing credit.

11.4.6 Avoidance of certain floating charges

A floating charge is one 'which, as created, was a floating charge' (IA 1986, s.251). This means that one looks at the effect of the charge as at the date of creation (i.e. prior to crystallisation) (*Re Beam Tube Products Ltd* [2006] BCC 615); it does not matter that due to events provided for in the charge it has later become fixed. However, a floating charge is not otherwise defined and has been the subject of much judicial debate (leading up to *Re Spectrum Plus Ltd* [2005] BCC 694). The essential character of a floating charge is the company's freedom to deal with the assets (which can be future assets) that are subject to the charge.

If a floating charge was created by the company within 12 months prior to the commencement of insolvency proceedings (or where the charge was created in favour of a person connected with the company, within two years), it is invalid if the company goes into liquidation or administration, unless the floating charge was created in consideration of new value, supplied at the same time as or after the creation of the charge.

In the case of a floating charge being granted to an unconnected party, the charge will not be set aside unless the company was insolvent at the time the charge was created, 'insolvent' meaning that the company was unable to pay its debts, or becomes unable to pay its debts as a consequence of the transaction (IA 1986, s.245(4)). The wording of the section does not make clear if it is for the charge holder or office holder to prove solvency/insolvency.

In the case of a floating charge created in favour of a company connected to the company, there is no such requirement to prove insolvency.

If the charge was created for pre-security debts and also provided for new value, the security is subject to pro rata valuation, i.e. it is valid only in respect of the new money. Whether the advance is made at the same time as the creation of the charge or thereafter is a matter of fact determined by the court (see *Re Shoe Lace Ltd* [1993] BCC 609). Contemporaneous creation and advance is satisfied if a binding agreement creates an immediate equitable charge made at or before the making of the advance, irrespective of whether formal execution of the debenture takes place at a later date. However, if there is no agreement, and if the advance precedes execution, unless the interval is *de minimis*, it will not be regarded as contemporaneous.

Where an equitable charge has been created (i.e. a promise to execute a debenture) and monies have been advanced in reliance on the agreement, any delay between the advance and the execution of a formal charge is immaterial (see

Rehman v. *Chamberlain* [2011] EWHC 2318 (Ch) for an unsuccessful attempt to argue that an equitable charge had been created). It should, however, be remembered that as at the date the equitable charge arises, it should have been registered and the lender could lose its rights should it have failed to register the charge within the statutory required period (i.e. 21 days) (CA 2006, ss.860(1), 861(5), 870(1), 874(1)).

IA 1986, s.245 (and the provisions relating to registration, see **11.4.8**) has no application for a charge created or arising under a financial collateral arrangement (Financial Collateral Arrangements (No.2) Regulations 2003, SI 2003/3226; see *Gray* v. *G-T-P Group* [2011] BCC 869 and *In the Matter of Lehman Brothers International (Europe) Ltd (in administration)* [2012] EWHC 2997 (Ch)).

11.4.7 Unenforceability of liens on books, etc.

Where the company enters into administration, liquidation or a provisional liquidator is appointed, any lien or other right to retain books, papers or records of the company is unenforceable, to the extent that the enforcement would deny possession of any books, papers or records to the office holder (IA 1986, s.246).

Liens are often claimed over files and deeds by professional advisers, such as solicitors or accountants who are claiming outstanding fees. IA 1986, s.246 does not apply to goods (where a repairer has retained goods pending payment for services) or to documents which give title to property and are held as such (IA 1986, s.246(3)). This entitles the retention of property title deeds, which often is extremely valuable to solicitors claiming unpaid legal costs (*Re Carter Commercial Developments Ltd* [2002] BCC 803).

11.4.8 Registerable but unregistered charges

CA 2006, s.860 provides that where a charge (meaning any form of security interest (fixed or floating) over property, other than an interest arising by operation of law) is created by a company registered in England and Wales, which requires registration, and is not registered within 21 days of creation, it is void against the liquidator or the administrator or a creditor of the company. This section applies to any charge created after 1 October 2009; for any charge created prior to that date the previous provisions contained in CA 1985, ss.395–409 apply.

This provision remains an important part of corporate governance regulation in the UK and is part of the filing obligations on the company to ensure that particulars regarding the affairs of the corporate body are available to potential trading partners on the records at Companies House. An important aspect of this is the registration of secured interests so that when trading with a limited company, creditors may make their own judgments on the credit risk involved.

Should the charge fail to be registered in time, the court may on application by the company or the charge holder make an order extending the time for registration (CA 2006, s.873(2)). The court may make such order as it thinks just and expedient. The court will need to be satisfied that there was a reasonable excuse for failing to register on time and the company was not insolvent at the time the charge was created or as at the date of the order, and/or that the late registration will not otherwise prejudice the position of the company's creditors and shareholders. Any attempt to get round the provisions by taking a new charge instead of applying for an extension in the time to register an existing charge is liable to be struck down (see *Re Telomatic Ltd* [1993] BCC 404).

The non-registration of any charge does not affect the position of the charge holders to enforce their rights against the company prior to its winding up or administration. Consequently, charge holders who have realised their security or obtained payment pursuant to that security prior to the company's insolvency or administration are unaffected and the payment cannot be set aside.

CA 2006, s.860 has no application for a charge created or arising under a financial collateral arrangement (Financial Collateral Arrangements (No.2) Regulations 2003, SI 2003/3226), although it is common practice still to register security that may be governed by these provisions.

11.5 COMPANY DIRECTORS DISQUALIFICATION ACT (CDDA) 1986 PROCEEDINGS

11.5.1 History and purpose of the Act

Since the Companies Act 1947, the courts have had the power to disqualify an individual from holding the post of a director of a company. CDDA 1986 brought together different legislation that had evolved dealing with directors, conduct and disqualification and introduced a new provision whereby a director could be disqualified where his conduct has been such as to render him unfit to be a director.

The legislation, by preventing directors from holding office in any other company without leave of the court, fulfils a number of differing functions. It is a punishment (*R. v. Young* [1990] BCC 549), a deterrent to potentially dishonest directors (*Re Blackspur Group plc* [1998] BCC 11) and is intended to have the effect of raising commercial probity generally (*Secretary of State for Trade and Industry v. McTighe* [1997] BCC 224). It also provides a degree of protection for the public at large. Limited liability is a unique privilege, and in cases where a director has been guilty of gross negligence, dishonesty or total incompetence, the courts are bound to disqualify that director, so protecting the public at large from further potential losses (*Re Lo-Line Electric Motors Ltd* [1988] Ch 47; *R. v. Secretary of State for Trade and Industry Ex p. Lonrho plc* [1992] BCC 325).

Prior to the reform of CDDA 1986 introduced in IA 2000, in theory, every disqualification proceeding required assessment of the evidence by a court. This resulted in undue delay and expense which militated against wider use of the procedures. There was, however, some judicial innovation which resulted in a summary procedure to deal with uncontested cases (see *Re Carecraft Construction Co. Ltd* [1994] 1 WLR 172).

IA 2000 amended CDDA 1986 and enabled the Secretary of State to accept undertakings from directors. The disqualification undertakings have the same effect as court orders, but are consensual agreements reached between the director and the Secretary of State (via the Disqualification Unit of DBIS). Following this amendment, most disqualification proceedings result in an undertaking being given rather than an order being made.

However, it should be borne in mind when advising a director that the chances of successfully defeating any potential CDDA 1986 proceedings are usually relatively slim and the procedures for contesting a hearing are long, drawn-out and costly. In the circumstances of financial failure, the director may well have little or no resources available to fund a legal defence. Public funding from the Legal Services Commission is unavailable for defending such proceedings. It is perhaps unsurprising that the majority of proceedings remain uncontested and the 'conviction rate' is very high.

Proceedings can only be commenced by the Secretary of State. From 1986, the DTI (now DBIS) set up a special Directors Disqualification Unit, which considers reports made by liquidators, administrative receivers and administrators on the conduct of directors in every case of corporate insolvency. While a director can be disqualified in respect of a solvent company, the majority of disqualifications are made after a failure of the company and by reason of the directors' conduct being such as to render them unfit.

11.5.2 Application and effect of the Act

Appointed directors, shadow directors, *de facto* directors, partners of insolvent partnerships, members of an insolvent limited liability partnership and a company or corporate body may be subject to CDDA 1986 proceedings.

Anybody who is the subject of a disqualification order, or the subject of an undertaking, must not be a director of a company, act as receiver of a company's property or in any way, whether directly or indirectly, be concerned or take part in the promotion, formation or management of a company unless (in each case) he has leave of the court (CDDA 1986, s.1(1)(a)).

It is not open to the court to make an order which only prohibits certain of the listed activities (*Re Cannonquest Ltd* [1997] BCC 644), although such considerations come into play where an application is made by the director for leave (despite the order) to be concerned with another company, nor is the court able to make the prohibition in respect only of certain companies (see *R. v. Ward* [2002] BCC 953 on an unsuccessful attempt to limit the prohibition only to public companies).

The period of disqualification will commence 21 days from the date of the order. This 21-day period allows the director a short period of time in which to put the affairs of the company in order, i.e. appoint alternative directors in his place.

The legislation is worded widely to prohibit not only an appointment (as registered at Companies House), but also indirect control over the management of a company, either internally or externally (*R. v. Austen* (1985) 1 BCC 99). This has been held to include acting as an adviser/management consultant to the board (*Re Campbell* [1984] BCLC 83). However, each case will depend on its own circumstances and it might be that the individual could act as an adviser if he was not actually involved in the decision making of the company (*CCA v. Brecht* [1989] 7 ACLC 40, an Australian authority) or vote as a majority shareholder on matters concerning the management of the company (*Re Magna Alloys and Research Pty Ltd* (1975) CLC 40-227, another Australian authority). Whether a person thus has management control is a question of fact not title (see *Re Clasper Group Services Ltd* (1988) 4 BCC 673; *Drew v. Lord Advocate* (1996) SLT 1062; and *Re Market Wizard Systems (UK) Ltd* [1998] 2 BCLC 282).

If an individual is disqualified, there is nothing to stop that individual acting as an employee of a company at the direction of the board of directors. What is not permissible is for the individual to continue to hold himself out as a director to the outside world, or (a more common instance in small companies) to appoint a relative and exercise indirect control over the company.

An individual who has been disqualified from acting, but contravenes the order, commits a criminal offence (CDDA 1986, s.13); the penalty, on indictment, is a maximum of two years' imprisonment and unlimited fine, and on summary conviction, six months' imprisonment and a fine subject to the statutory maximum (currently £5,000). Furthermore, the former director may be held personally liable for the debts of the company in whose management he has become concerned. This liability is joint and several with the new company (CDDA 1986, s.15).

A register of disqualified directors or those granted leave to act is kept by the DBIS (CDDA 1986, s.18) and the register is open to inspection at **www.companieshouse.gov.uk**. Where an appeal is pending against a disqualification order, it is possible for the court to order the Registrar of Companies not to make an entry while that appeal is heard (*Cathie v. Secretary of State for Business, Innovation and Skills* [2011] EWHC 2234 (Ch)). Since January 1988, the DBIS has maintained a Directors Disqualification Act hotline (tel.: 0845 601 3546) to invite members of the public to report those directors who have previously been disqualified and are acting in contravention of CDDA 1986.

11.5.3 Permission of the court to act as a director despite disqualification

Under CDDA 1986, s.17, any person who is disqualified may apply for leave from the court to act as a director in respect of a company (or companies). It is preferable for such an application to be brought at the same time as the CDDA 1986 proceedings.

In the application for leave, the court will weigh the interests of the company of which the individual wishes to be a director against the interests of the public at large and, in particular, whether adequate protection from abuse is available (see *Re*

Verby Print for Advertising Ltd [1998] BCC 652). The court's wish to protect 'the public' runs through much of the case law in this area, and such protection is given a wide meaning, to include protection of shareholders, employees, lenders, customers and creditors (*Re Tech Textiles Ltd* [1998] 1 BCLC 259).

The court will look at all the circumstances of the case, balancing the issue of public protection against the consideration of whether it is in the interest of the company that the applicant is concerned in its management and control (e.g. is it essential for the business? Would employees lose their jobs or livelihoods?). However, in the case of dishonesty or illegal conduct, protection of the public will outweigh these other considerations (see *Re Amaron Ltd* [1998] BCC 264; *Re Westminster Property Management Ltd (No.2)* [2001] BCC 305); similarly, where the company is wholly or substantially owned by the applicant (*Re Britannia Homes Centres Ltd* [2001] 2 BCLC 63) the needs of 'the company' are less likely to be given much weight.

The court retains an absolute discretion as to whether or not to grant leave (*Shuttleworth* v. *Secretary of State for Trade and Industry* [2000] BCC 204), but some guidelines have been laid down which give an indication as to the kinds of considerations taken into account (*Re Tech Textiles Ltd* [1998] 1 BCLC 259):

(a)   Relevance of the ground of unfitness, particularly if the case involved dishonesty.
(b)   The character, honesty and reliability of the individual.
(c)   Previous history and character of the individual.
(d)   Whether the individual has been subject to any previous disqualification.
(e)   The size of the company, nature of the role and risk of further abuse.
(f)   Likelihood of re-offence.

In contrast an individual's honesty and evidence of good character is not admissible when the Court considers whether or not to make a disqualification order (*Re Verby Print for Advertising* [1998] BCC 652); similarly the fact the applicants management of other companies may have been blameless is not taken into account (*Re Servaccomm Redhall Ltd* [2006] 1 BCLC 1), as has the fact that the applicant's management of other companies may have been blameless (*Re Servaccomm Redhall Ltd* [2006] 1 BCLC 1). Both, however, may well be relevant on the application under CDDA 1986, s.17.

The court has been willing to grant permission for an individual to continue as a director of another company despite the disqualification order, attaching conditions such as:

(a)   providing for the appointment of another director with voting control over the company (see *Re Lo-Line Electric Motors Ltd* [1988] Ch 477);
(b)   limitation as to the role and duties in the new company (*Re TLL Realisations Ltd* [2000] BCC 988);
(c)   providing for the appointment of a financial director to take financial control

of the new company and ensure that accounts and annual returns are kept up to date (see *Re Majestic Recording Studios Ltd* (1998) 4 BCC 519);

(d)   removing an individual from financial control over the company or requiring an individual to agree not to undertake executive duties (see *Re Barings plc (No.5)* [1999] BCC 960);

(e)   the holding of monthly board meetings attended by the auditor's representatives (see *Re Chartmore Ltd* [1990] BCLC 673);

(f)   providing safeguards such as the requirement for cheque counter-signature, that the applicants not be allowed to seek repayment of directors' loan accounts or seek security for the same (see *Re Gibson Davies Chemists Ltd* [1995] BCC 11); or

(g)   no loans to be made to associated companies (*Secretary of State for Trade and Industry* v. *Arif* [1996] BCC 960).

Where an order is made or an undertaking given, the court has no power to order, and the DBIS has no power to grant, permission to an individual to continue acting as a director, generally or in respect of a specific company (*R.* v. *Goodman* [1992] BCC 625), or that the individual be subject to only part of the restrictions imposed under CDDA 1986, s.1(1)(a). Application to the court under CDDA 1986, s.17 is always required should the individual wish to be involved in the control, management or promotion of another company.

11.5.4   Grounds for disqualification

Conviction of an indictable offence (CDDA 1986, s.2)

An individual may be disqualified if convicted of an indictable offence, whether on indictment or summarily, in connection with the promotion, formation, management, liquidation or striking off a company. The maximum period of disqualification on summary conviction is five years, in other cases, 15 years.

Examples of the application of this section, while primarily relating to the actions of an individual director against his own company, have included convictions of defrauding other companies and insider trading (see *R.* v. *Corbin* (1984) 6 Cr App R (S) 17; *R.* v. *Goodman* [1992] BCC 625). See also *R.* v. *Georgiou* (1988) 4 BCC 322 where disqualification followed the respondent's conviction for carrying on an unauthorised insurance business, although there was no actual finding of misconduct in relation to the company's affairs.

The order may be made by the court in which the individual is convicted of the offence or on an application to another court. The fact that the court which has imposed the criminal conviction does not proceed to disqualify the director is no fetter on proceedings later being conducted by the Secretary of State (*Re Denis Hilton Ltd* [2002] 1 BCLC 302).

Persistent breach of company legislation (CDDA 1986, s.3)

A person may be disqualified if he has been persistently in default of company legislation requiring any return, account or other documents to be filed or delivered on notice of any matter to be given to the Registrar of Companies. 'Persistently' has been held to mean some degree of continuance or repetition (*Re Arctic Engineering Ltd* [1986] 1 WLR 686).

The maximum period of disqualification under this section is five years. Proceedings may also lead to a civil fine.

Fraudulent trading (CDDA 1986, s.4)

The court may make a disqualification order in the course of the winding up of a company, if it appears that an individual has been guilty of the offence of fraudulent trading under CA 2006, s.993(1)–(3) or has been guilty of fraud in relation to the company or any breach of duty. The reference to a breach of duty does not cover breaches which are trivial or a result of a mistake (*Re Adbury Estates Ltd* [2003] BCC 696).

In the matter of *Asegaai Consultants Ltd & 43 others (in liquidation)*, sub nom. *Wood and Earp* v. *Mistry* [2012] EWHC 1899 (Ch) it was held that a liquidator could be disqualified under this provision for grossly improper conduct in relation to his conduct of a liquidation. Interestingly, the replacement liquidators sought the order and it was held that despite their lack of financial interest in the disqualification, they had sufficient interest to bring the proceedings.

The maximum period of disqualification is 15 years and, unlike other grounds of disqualification, the winding up of a company is necessary to commence such proceedings.

Disqualification on summary conviction (CDDA 1986, s.5)

An individual may be disqualified if, during the five years ending on the date of the conviction, he has been convicted of a total of no fewer than three default orders relating to the provision of company returns, accounts and documents, etc. which are required to be filed with the Registrar of Companies.

The maximum period of disqualification is five years and can arise in circumstances of persistent default, irrespective of whether the company is being wound up or not.

Finding by the court of director's unfitness (CDDA 1986, s.6)

A court shall make a disqualification order if satisfied that the individual has been a director (or shadow director) of the company which has become insolvent (whether he was a director at that time or otherwise) and his conduct as a director of the company (either taken alone or together with conduct of any other company in which he was involved) makes him unfit to be concerned in the management of a company (CDDA 1986, s.6(1)).

A company becomes insolvent when it enters into insolvent liquidation or administration, or when an administrative receiver is appointed (it is therefore not a question of financial viability such as that found in IA 1986, s.214 on wrongful trading), and conduct as a director means conduct in respect of the company or connected with the company that has entered into insolvency (CDDA 1986, s.6(2)).

The court having competent jurisdiction is the court where the company was wound up, or which has jurisdiction to wind up (if in voluntary liquidation, administration or administrative receivership) (CDDA 1986, s.6(3); see also CDDA 1986, s.6(3A), (3B), introduced to overcome procedural difficulties regarding jurisdiction where the company may have been dissolved, or changed registered office; even if proceedings are initiated in the wrong court it should not invalidate the proceedings (*Secretary of State for Trade and Industry* v. *Arnold* [2008] BCC 119)).

A period of disqualification under this section can only be sought by the Secretary of State, and the period of disqualification will range between two and 15 years (CDDA 1986, s.6(4)).

The director's conduct in relation to the insolvent company must in itself constitute unfitness. If there is no finding of unfitness in respect of the lead company, the court cannot then consider the director's conduct in respect of companies where there has not been any insolvency (see *Secretary of State for Trade and Industry* v. *Tillman* [1999] BCC 703 and *Re Diamond Computers Systems Ltd* [1997] 1 BCLC 174 where leave to amend was refused where the focus of the misconduct was to shift from one company to another). However, the court will consider the cumulative effect of the conduct of a director in both the insolvent company and previous companies to assess the reasonable period of disqualification.

This ground for disqualification is by far the most commonly used and may result in an order or an undertaking, with undertakings now being far more common than court orders.

Each case will depend upon its own facts, although some guidance was delivered by the Court of Appeal in *Re Sevenoaks Stationers (Retail) Ltd* [1991] 3 All ER 578, which put forward a three-tier approach:

- 10 to 15 years for 'particularly serious cases', which include where a director has previously been disqualified.
- Six to 10 years for serious cases which do not merit the most severe penalty.
- Two to five years where the case is not considered very serious, although disqualification is a mandatory requirement where evidence of unfitness has been found by the court.

Unless the court otherwise gives leave, the application must be brought within two years of the date of insolvency (CDDA 1986, s.7(2) and *Secretary of State for Trade and Industry* v. *Vohora* [2009] BCC 369 confirming that an application is made when it is lodged at court). In considering whether to allow an application to be brought out of time, the court will consider the length of delay, the reasons for delay, the strength of the case, the prejudicial effect on the directors caused by the delay, the seriousness of the allegations and the directors' responsibility for the delay (*Secretary of State for Trade and Industry* v. *Desai* [1992] BCC 110; *Secretary of State for Trade and Industry* v. *Ellis (No.2)* [1993] BCC 890; *Re Manlon Trading Ltd* [1995] BCC 579; *Secretary of State for Trade and Industry* v. *Davies* [1996] 4 All ER 289; *Secretary of State for Trade and Industry* v. *McTighe* [1997] BCC 224; and *Instant Access Properties Ltd* [2011] EWHC 3022 (Ch)).

If liquidation follows on from an administrative receivership, the date of insolvency runs from the first event (see *Re Tasbian Ltd (No.1)* [1990] BCC 318).

Once the proceedings are commenced, the Secretary of State must guard against delay which could lead to dismissal of the claim (*Secretary of State for Trade and Industry* v. *Tjolle* [1998] BCC 282 and *EDC* v. *UK (Application No.24433/94)* [1998] BCC 370, the latter case concerning a successful human rights challenge that a seven-year stay of proceedings pending determination of a criminal trial was excessive; to be contrasted with *Re Blackspur Group plc (No.3) Secretary of State for Trade and Industry* v. *Eastaway* [2003] BCC 520) or striking out for want of prosecution (*Official Receiver* v. *B Ltd* [1994] 2 BCLC 1).

It remains a duty of every liquidator, administrative receiver or administrator to report on the conduct of the director to the DBIS; thereafter the Secretary of State may require the insolvency practitioner to provide such information and assistance as deemed necessary (CDDA 1986, s.7(3)). The report made by the insolvency practitioner is not privileged and is open to disclosure if proceedings are commenced (see *Secretary of State for Trade and Industry* v. *Baker (No.2)* [1998] Ch 356) and *Re Astra Holdings plc* [1999] BCC 121 regarding the disclosure of internal notes and memorandum (held not discloseable) in contrast to a letter between the Secretary of State and the inspectors (held discloseable)).

In determining whether an individual's conduct in relation to a particular company or companies makes him unfit to be concerned in the management of the company, the court has regard to matters determining unfitness as laid down in the Act (CDDA 1986, s.9(1) and Sched.1) and considers evidence before it on the balance of probabilities (*Re Living Images Ltd* [1996] BCC 112).

Matters applicable in all cases

The following will be considered in all cases:

(a) Any misfeasance or breach of any fiduciary or other duty by the director in relation to the company.

(b) Any misapplication or retention by the director of, or any conduct by the director giving rise to an obligation to account for, any money or other property of the company.

(c) The extent of the director's responsibility for the company entering into any transaction liable to be set aside under IA 1986, Part XVI (provisions against tax avoidance, IA 1986, s.423).

(d)   The extent of the director's responsibility for any failure by the company to comply with various provisions of the Companies Acts (e.g. the company's obligation to keep proper accounting records; maintain registers of directors, members and charges; file annual accounts and returns, etc.).

Matters applicable where the company has been insolvent

The court will consider the extent of the director's responsibility for the causes of the company becoming insolvent, including factors such as:

(a)   any failure by the company to supply any goods or services which have been paid for (in whole or in part);

(b)   the company having entered into any transaction or the giving of any preference which is liable to be set aside (IA 1986, ss.127, 238 and 240);

(c)   any failure by the directors of the company to comply with IA 1986, s.98 (i.e. duty to hold a creditors' meeting in creditors' voluntary winding-up proceedings);

(d)   any failure by the director to comply with various obligations imposed under IA 1986 (IA 1986, ss.22, 47, 66, 99, 131, 234, 235 and 253, including provision regarding the statement of affairs, duty to deliver up company property and to co-operate with the liquidator, etc.); and

(e)   any other matters that are deemed appropriate by the court (*Re Amaron Ltd* [1998] BCC 264).

If a finding of unfitness is made, it is irrelevant that this was a one-off case and that past conduct shows that in all other cases the director has been exemplary, or that he has now mended his ways (see *Re Grayan Building Services* [1995] BCC 554). Character evidence is not admissible (*Re Verby Print for Advertising Ltd* [1998] BCC 652).

It should be noted that a finding of fact made in early civil legal proceedings, such as wrongful trading, is not admissible in the disqualification proceedings (*Secretary of State for Trade and Industry* v. *Bairstow* [2003] BCC 682), although this should be contrasted with *Official Receiver* v. *Stojevic* [2007] EWHC 1186 (Ch) where it was held that a judgment in which the director was found guilty of fraud could be adduced as evidence in disqualification proceedings.

As each case will differ and depend on its own facts, with the burden of proof resting on the applicant, it is difficult to draw any hard and fast conclusions as to when the courts are likely to consider disqualification appropriate. Case law provides some guidance, as do the provisions contained within CDDA 1986 outlined above.

The following factors have been considered relevant:

- The need to punish the individual and provide protection to the public at large (*Re Sevenoaks Stationers (Retail) Ltd* [1991] Ch 164; although the disqualification does not need to be in the public interest: *Re Grayan Building Services Ltd* [1995] Ch 241).
- Commercial misjudgment by a director is not generally enough on its own (*Re McNulty's Intercharge Ltd* [1989] BCLC 709); usually, the court will need to be satisfied of gross negligence or total incompetence (see *Re Lo-Line Electric Motors Ltd* [1988] Ch 477) and evidence of 'serious' misconduct (*Re Polly Peck International plc, Secretary of State for Trade and Industry* v. *Ellis (No.2)* [1993] BCC 890).
- Whether the company has suffered from unforeseeable misfortune outside the directors' control (e.g. *Re Bath Glass Ltd* (1988) 4 BCC 130, an unexpected loss of a key member of staff; *Re Cladrose Ltd* [1990] BCLC 204, the sudden loss of a profitable contract).
- The director's honesty, probity and competence (see *Re Landhurst Leasing plc* [1999] 1 BCLC 286).
- Whether the directors have discriminated between creditors, perhaps failing to pay so-called 'involuntary creditors', such as HMRC, preferring to pay themselves or associates (see *Secretary of State Trade and Industry* v. *McTighe (No.2)* [1996] 2 BCLC 477 regarding directors' loans, and contrast with *Re Keypak (Homecare) Ltd (No.2)* [1990] BCLC 440 on the question of directors' due remuneration and *Official Receiver* v. *Dhaliwall* [2006] 1 BCLC 285).
- Whether there has been negotiation with creditors and/or full disclosure of information leading up to the insolvency (*Re Funtime Ltd* [2000] 1 BCLC 247; *Cathie* v. *Secretary of State for Business, Innovation and Skills* [2011] EWHC 3026 (Ch)).
- The position that the director has held and role taken on the board (*Re Austinsuite Furniture Ltd* [1992] BCLC 1047).
- What would reasonably be expected of a director of that age, experience and position within the company (*Re Chartmore Ltd* [1990] BCLC 673).
- Failing to take steps to prevent misconduct (of others) or making oneself absent will not provide a defence (see *Re Peppermint Park Ltd* [1998] BCC 23). If an individual director considers that the board is taking an incorrect view, perhaps in respect of wrongful trading, it is that director's responsibility to ensure that these views are noted and he should endeavour to dissuade the directors from taking that course of action. If ultimately he is unsuccessful in persuading the directors to take a particular course, he should consider resignation, although failure to resign is not necessarily fatal to his position.
- Whether the director has properly and reasonably delegated (*Re Burnham Marketing Services; Secretary of State for Trade and Industry* v. *Harper* [1993] BCC 518).
- Whether the individual has taken proper advice, and obtained regular budgets and forecasts of the company's position (see *Re Bath Glass Ltd* (1988) 4 BCC 130; *Re UNO plc and World of Leather plc* [2004] EWHC 933 (Ch)).

- If the directors have made a heavy financial commitment or suffered heavy financial loss as a result of commercial misfortune and have admitted responsibility, any finding of unfitness may lead to a shorter period of disqualification (see *Re Aldermanbury Trust plc* [1993] BCC 598 and *Re Cargo Agency Ltd* [1992] BCC 388, in which it was stressed that this is not a defence but can be a mitigating factor).
- If the director has received assurances from a third party, such as a parent company, that funding will be made available, or a director is reasonably entitled to hold the view that if the company went into liquidation its assets would be sufficient to cover its liabilities, a disqualification order will not be made (see *Re CU Fittings Ltd* (1989) 5 BCC 210; *Re Imperial Board Products Ltd* [2004] EWHC 2096 (Ch)).
- Previous conduct and involvement in prior insolvent companies (*Re Migration Services International* [2000] BCC 1095).
- Misrepresentation to customers and suppliers (*Secretary of State for Business Innovation and Skills* v. *Sullman* [2010] BCC 500) and/or creating false accounts, invoices and financial information (*Kappler* v. *Secretary of State for Trade and Industry* [2006] BCC 845).
- Misappropriation of company property (*Secretary of State for Trade and Industry* v. *Blunt* [2006] BCC 112; *Secretary of State for Business Innovation and Skills* v. *Doffman* [2010] EWHC 3175 (Ch)) or entering into a transaction at an undervalue (*Secretary of State for Business, Enterprise and Regulatory Reform* v. *Poulter* [2009] BCC 608).

It is not relevant that the director may have honestly believed that he was acting properly; conduct is assessed objectively (*Goldberg* v. *Secretary of State for Trade and Industry* [2004] 1 BCLC 597), although the court may have regard to the director's personal commitment to the company and the degree to which he has suffered personal financial loss (*Re Douglas Construction Services Ltd* (1988) 4 BCC 553; *Re Swift 736 Ltd* [1993] BCC 312).

On consideration of the facts of the case, as reported to it by the liquidator, the Directors Disqualification Unit of DBIS will consider if it is in the public interest for a disqualification order to be made on grounds of unfitness. If it is considered an order should be made, an application will be made in the name of the Secretary of State, or the Official Receiver at the direction of the Secretary of State (CDDA 1986, s.7(1)).

If the individual served with the proceedings is willing to provide a disqualification undertaking, the Secretary of State may in his discretion accept the undertaking if it appears expedient in the public interest to do so (CDDA 1986, s.7(2A)). This makes it clear that it is a matter for the Secretary of State to determine whether an undertaking should be given and acceptance is not mandatory. Indeed, it may be considered right and proper for the matter to be tried at a court hearing, particularly if there is public interest in the resulting publicity, or there is a matter of public interest which requires court determination. The undertaking is subject to the same period of disqualification as a court order, namely two to 15 years, and the same penalties arise if there is a breach.

A disqualification order usually carries with it an order to pay the costs and expenses of the Secretary of State or the Official Receiver, or both. Costs will be significantly reduced should an undertaking be offered and accepted. However, an agreed statement of conduct will still need to be settled.

If it appears to the Secretary of State that the conditions relating to unfitness set out in CDDA 1986, s.6(1) are made out in respect of any person who is willing to offer a disqualification undertaking, this may be accepted if it is expedient in the public interest to avoid applying for and proceeding with an application for an order (CDDA 1986, s.7(2A)).

Where an undertaking is offered before proceedings, costs will not usually be sought, which is a strong incentive to any individual to provide the undertaking.

However, it is not mandatory for the Secretary of State to accept an undertaking (*Re Blackspur Group plc (No.3)* [2002] 2 BCLC 263), as he may wish proceedings to be commenced if it is in the public interest for the issues to be aired in court and/or where the individual has refused to accept a statement of agreed facts.

Guide to procedure: director's disqualification proceedings

1. The Secretary of State will issue a claim form with evidence in support. (Although it is not strictly required, the insolvency practitioner is likely to provide an affidavit in support of the Secretary of State's application.) The statement settled by the Secretary of State in support is drawn up with the co-operation of the insolvency practitioner, who is likely to be the key witness in most cases.
2. The individual is served with the claim form and has 14 days in which to acknowledge service.
3. Twenty-eight days after service the individual should file evidence in opposition, if possible before the hearing.
4. All claims are allocated to the multi-track.
5. The registrar will hear the first hearing and may be able to deal with the application summarily, imposing a period of disqualification of up to five years.
6. If thought appropriate, the registrar may adjourn the hearing to a judge or to himself on making further directions (such as may relate to disclosure and expert evidence).
7. Further evidence may be filed by affidavit, including expert evidence. (However, both parties should avoid including excessive detail in their evidence. See *Re Pamstock Ltd* [1994] BCC 264.)
8. The final hearing takes place, at which evidence is put before the court by the applicant and respondent and any matter considered relevant. If necessary, witnesses are called and cross-examined and the court makes a determination.
9. The costs of the proceedings are generally awarded to the successful party.
10. If a disqualification order is made, it shall be registered by the Secretary of State.

Disqualification after investigation of the company (CDDA 1986, s.8)

Various investigations of the Secretary of State for Business, Innovation and Skills outside any insolvency procedure may lead to investigations being made of the company (CDDA 1986, s.8; CA 1985, s.437; Financial Services and Markets Act 2000, ss.167–168, 169, 284) and could result in an application to wind up the affairs of the company on a public interest petition.

If, during the course of these inspections, information or documentation is obtained which satisfies the Secretary of State that there is conduct in relation to the company making the directors unfit to be concerned with the management of the company, an application may be made to court.

Examples of the use of this section include attempted manipulation of the share register (*Re Looe Fish Ltd* [1993] BCC 348), breaches of company law, the City Code on Takeovers and Mergers and fiduciary duties (*Re Aldermanbury Trust plc* [1993] BCC 598).

The maximum period of disqualification for any offence discovered is 15 years.

Disqualification in respect of a breach of competition law (CDDA 1986, s.9A)

If a director or shadow director has been in breach of both domestic and EU competition law (see Competition Act 1998) and the court considers his conduct as a director makes him unfit to be concerned in the management of a company, he may be disqualified for up to 15 years, although no minimum period is prescribed.

Application for an order under this provision is made by the Office of Fair Trading, which is also empowered to accept undertakings (CDDA 1986 s.9B).

Disqualification in respect of fraudulent or wrongful trading (CDDA 1986, s.10)

If an application alleging fraudulent or wrongful trading is made, an individual is liable to make a contribution to the company's assets. If the court thinks fit, it may also make a disqualification order against that individual for a period of up to 15 years (IA 1986, ss.213, 214) (see *Re Brian D Pierson (Contractors) Ltd* [1999] BCC 26 where an order was made and contrast with *Re Idessa (UK) Ltd* [2011] EWHC 804 (Ch) where the court referred the matter to the Secretary of State).

11.6 DIRECTOR'S DUTIES AND OFFENCES DURING THE INSOLVENCY PROCESS

As we have seen above, if a former director of the company fails to comply with any obligation imposed by IA 1986, this can lead to disqualification. A director found guilty of an offence contained within the Act may also be liable for imprisonment and/or a fine.

11.6.1 Duty to provide statement of affairs

Central to any insolvency process is the investigation of the company's affairs and disclosure of this information to its creditors. The directors, a single director or former director(s) may be obliged to provide the office holder with a statement of affairs pursuant to the following provisions:

1. IA 1986, s.47 – to the administrative receiver.
2. IA 1986, s.99 – to the meeting of creditors in a voluntary liquidation.
3. IA 1986, s.131 – to the Official Receiver on compulsory winding up.
4. IA 1986, Sched.B1, para.48(1) – to the administrator.

An administrative receiver or an administrator may serve notice on any person who is or was a director of the company to provide a statement of affairs of the company. The statement of affairs should set out the company's debts and liabilities, its creditors, securities held by the creditors and dates when security was given. A person served with notice must comply within 21 days in the case of receivership and 11 days in the case of administration. The time for compliance with this provision may be extended by agreement with the office holder or on application to the court.

In the case of voluntary winding up, it is a director's duty to attend and lay a statement of affairs before creditors at the duly convened meeting (IA 1986, s.98). A director who without reasonable excuse fails to provide a statement of affairs and/or attend the creditors' meeting is guilty of an offence.

Similar provisions apply where a court has made a winding-up order or appointed a provisional liquidator. The Official Receiver may request that any director or former director provides a statement of affairs and that person has 21 days from the date of notice to comply, unless released by the Official Receiver or given an extension of time from the Official Receiver or by court order (see *Re Wallace Smith Trust Co. Ltd* [1992] BCC 707 where the Official Receiver in the absence of a response obtained *ex parte* an order for the public examination of the director. The court held that although such an action was not an abuse of process, it was more appropriate to proceed by way of specific order for delivery up of a statement under IR 1986, rule 7.20).

A person who without reasonable excuse fails to comply with the requirements of any of the office holders to provide a statement of affairs commits an offence (IA 1986, Sched.10: punishable on indictment with an unlimited fine; on summary conviction, a maximum £5,000 fine and default rate of £500 per day).

11.6.2 Duty to co-operate with office holder

Getting in company property

Where the company is in administration, an administrative receiver is appointed, or the company is in liquidation or a provisional liquidator is appointed, a person (including an office holder) who has in his possession or control any property, books, papers or records to which the company appears to be entitled, may be ordered by the court forthwith to pay, deliver, convey or surrender books, property or records to the office holder (IA 1986, s.234).

The office holder makes the application in his own name, but if suing a party for unlawfully retaining possession of company property (the tort of conversion) the claim would be in the name of the company (*Smith* v. *Bridgend County Borough Council* [2002] 1 AC 336). It should be noted that the office holder can take proceedings in respect of property to which the company 'appears to be entitled'; the office holder does not need first to 'prove' ownership (*Euro Commercial Leasing Ltd* v. *Cartwright & Lewis* [1995] BCC 830). Save in exceptional circumstances, proceedings should be made on notice (*Re First Express Ltd* [1991] BCC 782).

The office holder is entitled to seek delivery up only where it is in exercise of his statutory functions (see *Sutton* v. *GE Capital Finance Ltd* [2004] 2 BCLC 662 where it was held that the administrative receiver's request for delivery up of documents held by a solicitors' firm was to assist a secured creditor in its action against a third party).

If the office holder seizes or disposes of property which is not in fact property of the company, provided the office holder has reasonable grounds for his belief in his entitlement, he will not be liable for loss or damage, provided that loss or damage was not caused by the office holder's own negligence (IA 1986, s.234(4)). However, this protection does not extend to choses in action (*Welsh Development Agency Ltd* v. *Export Finance Co.* [1992] BCC 270).

A common issue that arises in corporate insolvencies is where a retention of title claim is asserted by a supplier; if the office holder has notice of the claim (or should have notice), he may well be held negligent for disposal of those goods. As a result the office holder is better advised to seek agreement with those claiming retention of title (perhaps agreeing to hold the proceeds of sale in a separate escrow account pending determination of the claim) or to seek directions of the court in cases of dispute.

Duty to provide information and attend before office holder

An officer, director, employee or former director of the company is under a specific duty to give to the office holder such information concerning the company and its promotion, formation or business dealings, affairs or property as the office holder may at any time require (IA 1986, s.235(2)(a)).

The individual is also under a duty to attend the office holder at such time as may be reasonably required (IA 1986, s.235(2)(b)). This is often an informal meeting, but the director should be aware that the meeting may be recorded or a note made. Statements made in such meetings may be used in director disqualification proceedings (*Re Polly Peck International plc* [1994] BCC 15) or disclosed to relevant authorities (*R.* v. *Brady* [2004] BPIR 962).

A person who without reasonable excuse fails to comply with any request or obligation under this section will be liable to a fine (IA 1986, Sched.10: on indictment, an unlimited fine; on summary conviction, a maximum £5,000 fine and a default rate of £500 per day).

Private examination procedure

A more formal means of obtaining the co-operation of a director or former director of the company to assist in the office holder's investigations and enquiries is the use of the private examination procedure outlined in IA 1986, s.236.

This section provides that the court may, on application of the office holder (or Official Receiver where the company is being wound up), summon before it any officer of the company, or any person known or suspected to have in his possession any property of the company, who is or is supposed to be indebted to the company; or any person whom the court thinks capable of giving information concerning the promotion, formation or business dealings and affairs and property of the company. The scope of this provision was shown in *Re Delberry Ltd* [2008] BCC 653 where an order on the application of a liquidator was made against the former administrative receiver of the company to deliver up documents regarding the receiver's conduct of a sale of the company's business and assets.

An application under this section is sought where the informal approaches under IA 1986, s.235 have been unsuccessful in obtaining co-operation, perhaps because the individual has failed to attend the office holder and/or where the office holder determines that a more formal method of compulsion is necessary.

A person so ordered may be required to submit an affidavit to account for his dealings with the company and/or produce any books or records in his custody or control relating to the company (IA 1986, s.236(3)).

If a person without reasonable excuse fails to appear before the court, or there are reasonable grounds for believing he has absconded, the court has a power of arrest, which includes seizure of any books, papers, records, money or goods in that person's possession (IA 1986, s.236(5)).

In weighing up whether to exercise its discretion, the court will not act in a way which is oppressive or unfair to the respondent, although this does not mean that the office holder is first obliged to provide the respondent with a list of questions or topics that will be dealt with (see *Re Embassy Art Products Ltd* (1987) 3 BCC 292).

The office holder cannot use this procedure simply to obtain evidence which might be useful during the course of litigation (see *Re Sasea Finance Ltd* [1999] BCC 103), or to determine a proof of debt (*Bellmex International Ltd* v. *Green* [2001] BCC 253), but the court may order an examination even if the purpose is only to support the issue of disqualification proceedings (*Re Pantmaenog Timber Co. Ltd* [2004] 1 AC 158) and may do so even if legal proceedings alleging fraud have already been commenced (*Shierson* v. *Rastogi* [2003] BPIR 148).

The court will not make an order where the request is opportunistic, i.e. such as where the office holder is fishing for evidence or where the office holder has already settled on a course of action (see *Re RBG Resources plc* [2002] BCC 1005). The court will also refuse to make an order if it considers the examination unnecessary or unreasonable or otherwise oppressive (*Long* v. *Farrer & Co.* [2004] BPIR 1218). While the making of an order may in itself be inconvenient to the respondent, the difficulties and cost which would be incurred by the respondent in dealing with the request are, however, not regarded as unreasonable (see *British and Commonwealth Holdings plc [Joint Administrators]* v. *Spicer Oppenheim (No.2)* [1992] BCC 977).

The fact that the examination may reveal self-incriminating information does not prevent an order being made against a director or former officer of the company (*Re Bishopsgate Investment Management Ltd* v. *Maxwell* [1992] 1 BCC 222).

In view of these factors, it is very often advisable for the office holder first to set out the information that he would wish to obtain on examination, seeking co-operation under IA 1986, s.235 (*Re Barlow Clowes Gilt Managers Ltd* [1992] Ch 208). On refusal and/or failure to reply, an application to court then should be considered.

In making the application, the grounds relied on should be set out in writing (IR 1986, rule 9.2(1)) and may be made without notice, although good reason for such an approach must be shown (*Re PFTZM Ltd* [1995] BCC 280). Save where it would be unfair and would not enable the application to be disposed of properly, the document setting out the grounds on which the order is being sought is confidential and should not be disclosed to any person save with leave of the court, including the person against whom the order is sought. The reasoning for this is that the document will deal with matters regarding the office holder's investigations, why he considers an examination is necessary to enable him to fulfil his functions and thus disclosure may be prejudicial (*Re Gold Co.* (1879) 12 Ch D 77 and *Re British and Commonwealth Holdings plc (No.1)* [1992] BCC 165).

A person who without reasonable excuse fails to comply with the obligations under IA 1986, s.236 is liable to a fine (IA 1986, Sched.10: on indictment, an unlimited fine; on summary conviction, a £5,000 fine).

If, during the course of the private examination, it appears to the court that any person has in his possession any company property, on application by the office holder the court can order that person to deliver up such property on such terms as it sees fit (IA 1986, s.237(1)).

If, during the course of the private examination, it appears to the court that any person is indebted to the company, on application by the office holder the court may order that person to make payment to the office holder on such terms as it thinks fit (IA 1986, s.237(2)).

These two provisions are a useful means of summary determination of issues that would otherwise require separate proceedings.

11.6.3 Insolvency Act offences

Fraud in anticipation of winding up (IA 1986, s.206)

When a company is ordered to be wound up by the court or passes a resolution for voluntary winding up, any past or present officer of the company is deemed to have committed a (criminal) offence if within the 12 months prior to the commencement of the winding up he has:

(a) concealed any part of the company's property in excess of £500 or more;

(b) concealed any debt due to or from the company;

(c) fraudulently removed any part of the company's property to the value of £500 or more (this includes diversion of funds to the account of a third party: see *R. v. Robinson* [1990] BCC 656);

(d) concealed, destroyed, mutilated or falsified any book or paper affecting or relating to the company's property or affairs (including computer records: see *R. v. Taylor* [2011] 1 WLR 1809);

(e) made any false entry in any book or paper affecting or relating to the company's property or affairs ('officer' has been held to include an auditor: see *Re Thomas Gerrard & Sons Ltd* [1968] Ch 455);

(f) fraudulently parted with, altered or made any omission in any document affecting or relating to the company's property or affairs; or

(g) pawned, pledged or disposed of any property of the company which has been obtained on credit and which has not been paid for unless the pawning, pledging or disposal was in the ordinary course of the company's business.

As any of these is a criminal offence, civil proceedings for recovery may be stayed pending determination of the prosecution (*Re DPR Futures Ltd* [1989] 1 WLR 778).

A defence is open to the director or shadow director if he is able to prove he had no intent to defraud creditors or had no intention of concealing the state of affairs of the company or of impeding the legal process. However, in accordance with the European Convention on Human Rights, Art.6(2), it is enough for the defendant to raise the issue that he had no intent to defraud and it is then for the prosecution to prove beyond all reasonable doubt that an offence was committed (*R. v. Carass* [2002] 1 WLR 1714).

A person guilty of an offence under this section is liable to imprisonment or a fine or both (IA 1986, Sched.10: on indictment, a maximum term of imprisonment of seven years and/or an unlimited fine; on summary conviction, six months' imprisonment and/or a £5,000 fine).

Transactions in fraud of creditors (IA 1986, s.207)

If a company is wound up by court order or passes a resolution for winding up, a person is deemed to have committed a (criminal) offence if he, being at the time an officer of the company:

(a) made or caused to be made any gift or transfer of, or charge on, or caused or connived at the levying of any execution against, the company's property; or

(b) has concealed or removed any part of the company's property since, or within two months before, the date of any unsatisfied judgment or order for the payment of money obtained against the company.

A person is not guilty of such an offence if the action which would otherwise have been an offence occurred more than five years prior to the commencement of the winding up or, at the time of the conduct, the individual had no intent to defraud the company's creditors. See evidential burden of proof above.

A person guilty of an offence under this section is liable to imprisonment or a fine or both (IA 1986, Sched.10: on indictment, a maximum term of imprisonment of two years and/or an unlimited fine; on summary conviction, six months' imprisonment and a £5,000 fine).

Misconduct in the course of winding up (IA 1986, s.208)

Under IA 1986, s.208, where a company is being wound up by a court order or voluntarily, any person being a past or present officer of the company commits a (criminal) offence if he:

(a) does not to the best of his knowledge and belief fully divulge to the liquidator all the company's property and how and to whom and for what consideration and when the company disposed of any part of that property, except where the property was disposed of in the ordinary course of business;

(b) does not deliver to the liquidator as directed, all or such part of the company's property as is in his custody, or under his control, which he is required by law to deliver up;

(c) does not deliver up to the liquidator (or as the liquidator directs), books and papers in his custody, or under his control, belonging to the company and which he is required by law to deliver up;

(d) knowing or believing that a false debt has been proved by any person in the winding up, fails to inform the liquidator as soon as practicable; or

(e) after commencement of the winding up, prevents the production of any books or papers affecting or relating to the company's property or affairs.

A director is under a positive and ongoing obligation to disclose the existence of company property, it is not enough simply to react to enquiries (*R. v. McCredie* [2000] 2 BCLC 438).

A person has a defence to this provision if he can prove that he had no intention to defraud the creditors and/or had no intention of concealing the company's state of affairs or of defeating the process of law (see evidential burden of proof above and *R. (Griffin)* v. *Richmond Magistrates' Court* [2008] 1 BCLC 681).

A person guilty of an offence under this section is liable to imprisonment or a fine or both (IA 1986, Sched.10: on indictment, a maximum imprisonment term of seven years and/or an unlimited fine; on summary conviction, a maximum term of six months' imprisonment and/or a £5,000 fine).

Falsification of company books (IA 1986, s.209)

Under IA 1986, s.209, where a company is being wound up a person (being an officer of the company or contributory) commits a (criminal) offence if he destroys, mutilates, alters or falsifies any books, papers or securities, or makes or is privy to the making of any false or fraudulent entry in any register, book, account or document belonging to the company with intent to defraud or deceive any person.

A person guilty of an offence under this section is liable to imprisonment and/or a fine (IA 1986, Sched.10: on indictment, a maximum imprisonment term of seven years and/or an unlimited fine; on summary conviction, six months' imprisonment and/or a £5,000 fine).

Material omission from statement relating to company's affairs (IA 1986, s.210)

Under IA 1986, s.210, when a company is being wound up, whether by the court or voluntarily, any person being a past or present officer of the company commits a (criminal) offence if he makes any material omission in any statement relating to the company's affairs. This includes information contained in the statement of affairs, but is not limited to it (see *R. v. Taylor* [2011] 1 WLR 1809 where a director was found guilty of dishonest concealment).

A person has a defence to this provision if it is proved that he had no intention to defraud creditors. A person guilty of an offence under this section is liable to imprisonment and/or a fine (IA 1986, Sched.10: on indictment, a maximum imprisonment term of seven years and/or an unlimited fine; on summary conviction, six months' imprisonment and/or a £5,000 fine).

False representation to creditors (IA 1986, s.211)

Under IA 1986, s.211, when a company is being wound up any person being a past or present officer of the company (including a shadow director) commits a (criminal) offence if he makes any false representation or commits any fraud for the purpose of obtaining the consent of the company's creditors, or any of them, to an agreement with reference to the company's affairs or to the winding up. This section applies to misrepresentations, whereas IA 1986, s.210 deals with omissions.

A person guilty of an offence under this section is liable to imprisonment and/or a fine (IA 1986, Sched.10: on indictment, seven years' imprisonment and/or an unlimited fine; on summary conviction, six months' imprisonment and/or a £5,000 fine).

CHAPTER 12

The creditor's position during the personal insolvency process

12.1 DISTRIBUTION TO CREDITORS

12.1.1 Proof of debt

The insolvency regime in the UK is designed to provide a balance between the interests of the debtor and the interests of the creditors, and also to ensure equity and fairness as between respective creditors. This does not mean that all creditors are treated the same. The rights of creditors are determined according to the unique status that they hold as against the debtor: rights acquired by contract, statute or in equity.

As we have seen, the effect of the bankruptcy order being made is to provide a stay of action in respect of any debt which is provable in the bankruptcy. On the discharge from bankruptcy, the bankrupt is released from all debts provable in the bankruptcy, irrespective of whether the creditor claimed in the bankruptcy or not.

It is therefore important to ascertain what debts may be claimed in the bankruptcy (i.e. proved), the process and procedures for doing so and how this will lead to a potential distribution, after the costs and expenses of the bankruptcy are deducted and net realisations are available.

The proof of debt process is effectively to establish 'but for' the bankruptcy what would have been owed by the bankrupt to the creditor as of the date of bankruptcy, and, secondly, how the estate would be distributed among creditors, of the same class, in proportion to their respective claims. Equal treatment on a rateable basis, the *pari passu* principle, is the foundation stone on which much of insolvency law is based.

All claims by creditors are provable as debts as against the bankrupt, whether they are present or future, certain or contingent, ascertained or sounding only in damages (IR 1986, rule 12.3(1)).

This wide definition of what is a provable debt means that for certain creditors, i.e. those whose claims arise in the future or are contingent, additional statutory guidance is required to quantify those claims (see **12.1.2**) so as to not postpone indefinitely the realisation and prospective distribution of the bankruptcy estate.

Certain claims are not provable:

- Any fine (see Magistrates' Court Act 1980).
- An obligation pursuant to family proceedings (see Matrimonial and Family Proceedings Act 1984).
- An obligation arising under a confiscation order (see Drug Trafficking Offences Act 1986, Criminal Justice Act 1988 and Proceeds of Crime Act 2002).

This list (see IR 1986, rule 12.3(2)), drawn up in the light of public policy considerations, sets out those debts from which the legislature considers it would be unacceptable for the debtor to be released by reason of bankruptcy. It is also necessary to consider IA 1986, s.382(1) and the definition of a 'bankruptcy debt', which includes:

(a)   any debt or liability to which the bankrupt is subject at the commencement of the bankruptcy;

(b)   any debt or liability to which the bankrupt may become subject any time after the commencement of the bankruptcy, provided that the obligation was incurred before the commencement of the bankruptcy.

However, a tortious liability may still constitute a bankruptcy debt provided that the obligation (i.e. the cause of action) accrued before the commencement of the bankruptcy (IA 1986, s.382(2)).

This definition means that a party with a future tortious claim may be at a singular disadvantage on the bankruptcy of a potential tortfeasor. In the case of *Re T & N Ltd* [2006] BPIR 532 it was held that a future tort claimant was not a creditor with a provable debt under IA 1986, s.382, while in *Re Wisepark Ltd* [1994] BCC 221 (confirmed by the Court of Appeal in *Glenister* v. *Rowe* [2000] Ch 76) it was held that a claim for costs was a contingent claim which did not exist until the costs order was made. In either case, the claimant will have the right to proceed against the bankrupt to establish a claim, although in practice the value of a judgment/order leading to a second bankruptcy may be questioned. As an aside, the fact that such future potential creditors are excluded may make an IVA unworkable.

Case law has also developed to distinguish what may be regarded as a contingent claim from one which is merely a possibility (see *R. (on the application of Steele)* v. *Birmingham City Council and Secretary of State for Work and Pensions* [2006] BPIR 856; *Casson and Wales* v. *Law Society* [2009] EWHC 1943 (Admin)). However, this distinction is sometimes a difficult one to make and appears to be case specific and reliant on an 'accident of timing' (contrast the above cases with *Secretary of State for Work and Pensions* v. *Balding* [2007] BPIR 1669).

A 'liability' means 'a liability to pay money or money's worth, including any liability under an enactment, any liability for breach of trust, any liability in contract, tort or bailment and any liability arising out of an obligation to make restitution' (IA 1986, s.382(4)).

Unless otherwise ordered by the court, a person claiming to be a creditor of the bankrupt who wishes to recover his debt in whole or in part must submit a proof of debt to the Official Receiver or trustee in bankruptcy in Form 6.37 (IR 1986, rule 6.96).

The trustee should investigate each claim and does so by requiring each creditor to prove for his debt. The trustee may admit a proof for dividend purposes in whole or in part. If he rejects the proof, he is required to prepare a statement setting out his reasons for doing so (IR 1986, rule 6.104(2)).

In order to investigate each proof, the trustee may have regard to the bankrupt's statement of affairs; however, the trustee is entitled to reject a claim even where the bankrupt has admitted to the claim in a sworn statement (*Re Browne, ex. p Official Receiver* v. *Thompson* [1960] 2 All ER 625).

The trustee is also entitled to go behind a judgment debt (*Re Menastar Finance Ltd* [2003] 1 BCLC 338). He may also reopen a settlement if it was not reached in good faith (*Re a Debtor (No.12 of 1958)* [1968] 2 All ER 425). This issue is looked at in the context of matrimonial disputes and settlement below. The trustee is not, however, entitled to go behind an assessment reached by HMRC; the assessment of HMRC stands unless appealed successfully to the Commissioners of Revenue (*Re Moschi B, ex p. Moschi* v. *IRC* (1953) 35 TC 92).

The determination of claims by the trustee can lead the trustee into difficult and complex areas of law and fact. It is, however, to be noted that the trustee can ultimately apply to the court in such circumstances and seek appropriate direction as to how he should treat the claim (IA 1986, s.363).

Depending on whether the trustee considers that a distribution is possible, the proof of debt form may be sent by the trustee to every creditor of the bankrupt known to the trustee, or identified in the bankrupt's statement of affairs, and will accompany:

(a) the notice of the Official Receiver's decision not to call a meeting of creditors under IA 1986, s.293(2);
(b) the notice of the first meeting; or
(c) where a trustee has been appointed by the court, the notice of the trustee's appointment.

A form of proof will be sent to any creditor who so requires it (IR 1986, rule 6.91).
    A creditor's proof of debt must contain:

(a) the creditor's name and address;
(b) the total of the claim, including VAT, as at the date of the bankruptcy order;
(c) whether or not the amount includes any outstanding and capitalised interest;
(d) particulars of how and when the debt was incurred by the debtor;
(e) particulars of any security held and the date given and value;
(f) details of any reservation of title in respect of goods to which the debt refers; and

(g)   the name and address and authority of the person authenticating the proof, if other than the creditor.

Where a debt is due to the Crown, the proof of debt need not be in prescribed form (i.e. Form 6.37).

There is no time limit within which a creditor must submit a proof. However, in order to improve the general administration of the estate, the trustee may from time to time seek to impose a cut-off date by which creditors must submit a proof. The trustee may therefore provide that creditors must prove by a specified date in order to receive a potential distribution. The failure by a creditor to prove by a specified date does not prevent the creditor putting in a claim while the debtor's liability continues, although it may have lost the right to receive a dividend declared prior to its proving for the debt (*Re Smith, ex p. Bress* (1833) 3 Deac & Ch 283).

In such circumstances, the creditor has no right to disturb any dividend paid or to be paid (*Re Fenton, ex p. Day* (1831) Mont 212). If it proves after an interim dividend has been paid, it is entitled to receive a dividend attributable to the rateable value of its claim in any subsequent dividend. It is even possible to prove after the administration of the estate has been completed and a final dividend declared (*Re Westby, ex p. Lancaster Banking Corp.* (1879) 10 Ch D 776).

In exercise of his duty in admitting and rejecting a proof of debt, the trustee may be liable for misfeasance if he fails to investigate the creditor's claim reasonably and/or makes a distribution without proper regard to the creditor's claims (*Re Home and Colonial Insurance Co.* [1930] 1 Ch 102).

The creditor should submit documents sufficient to prove his debt, and the trustee may call for such documents to substantiate the whole or part of the claim (IR 1986, rule 6.98(3)). While the cost of proving the debt is borne by the creditor, the trustee's costs in admitting/rejecting claims are to be treated as an expense of the bankruptcy (IR 1986, rule 6.100(1), (2)).

If the claim is rejected by the trustee in whole or in part, the trustee should send a written statement of his reason for doing so to the creditor (IR 1986, rule 6.104(2)). On receipt of this notice, the creditor has 21 days in which to object and apply to the court for the decision to be reversed or varied (IR 1986, rule 6.105(1)). The court has power to extend the time limit for contesting the decision (IA 1986, s.376).

It is also open to the bankrupt or any other creditor dissatisfied with the trustee's decision to apply to the court to vary the trustee's decision, within 21 days from when they became aware of the trustee's decision.

The court will fix a venue for the hearing, and notice should be sent to the trustee, creditor and if applicable, other applicant(s). The trustee then files at court the proof and the written statement rejecting the proof. The court on hearing the application is not restricted to the evidence available to the trustee (*Re Trepca Mines Ltd* [1960] 1 WLR 1273) and may reverse, or vary, the trustee's decision in any way it sees fit (*Cadwell* v. *Jackson* [2001] BPIR 966), or uphold the trustee's decision on different grounds from those set out in the written statement (*Re Thomas Christy Ltd* [1994] 2

BCLC 527). The court can order disclosure of documentation and cross-examination of witnesses (*Re Bank of Credit and Commerce SA (No.7)* [1994] 1 BCLC 455).

The creditor's proof may be withdrawn or varied by agreement between the creditor and trustee (IR 1986, rule 6.106). In most cases, the value of the creditor's claim is agreed after investigation and then negotiation.

On application by the trustee or a creditor, the court may expunge a proof or reduce the amount by which the creditor has been admitted, if the proof has been improperly admitted or where it ought to be reduced (IR 1986, rule 6.107). If the proof is expunged or reduced, a creditor may, however, still retain any dividend previously received (*Re Browne (a Bankrupt)* [1960] 1 WLR 692).

12.1.2 Quantification of claims

Contingent claims

Where a debt is subject to any contingency, or contingencies, or for any other reason it lacks a certain value, the trustee must estimate its value as at the commencement of the bankruptcy (IA 1986, s.322(3)). However, the trustee is to have regard to events which occur after the date of bankruptcy (*MS Fashions Ltd* v. *BCCI* [1993] Ch 425). The 'hindsight principle' thus means that the trustee can take into account subsequent events which have made the contingency more or less likely, and so enable him to quantify the claim.

Debt owed on a negotiable instrument

Unless the trustee otherwise allows, a proof in respect of monies owed on a bill of exchange, promissory note, cheque or other negotiable instrument or security cannot be admitted unless the document or a certified copy of it is produced (IR 1986, rule 6.108).

Debt due to a secured creditor

If a secured creditor realises his security, he may prove for the unpaid balance (IR 1986, rule 6.109(1)).

Interest arising on a secured debt after the date of the bankruptcy order cannot be claimed by a secured creditor that has realised its security and in respect of such element the secured creditor may submit a proof (*Re London, Windsor and Greenwich Hotels Co.* [1892] 1 Ch 639). Interest is only recoverable after the payment of all preferential and unsecured creditors (IA 1986, s.328(4)).

In any other case, in order to claim a dividend the secured creditor is required either voluntarily to surrender its security and to prove for the whole debt as if unsecured, or to value the security and prove for the unsecured element of the claim alone (IR 1986, rule 6.109(2)). The secured creditor must therefore think very carefully about submitting a proof and can be seen to have voluntarily surrendered the security by doing so and failing to mention the existence of the security. The secured creditor can seek relief from the effects of this provision only if the omission was inadvertent (*Re Small; Westminster Bank* v. *Trustee* [1934] Ch 541), 'inadvertent' being accidental or the result of an honest mistake (IR 1986, rule 6.116(1)).

It is also open to the trustee to redeem the security at the value put on it by the secured creditor after first serving a 28-day notice (IR 1986, rule 6.117). Within 21 days of the service of the notice the secured creditor may revalue its security with leave of the court where IR 1986, rule 6.115(2) applies. Alternatively, it is open to the secured creditor to serve notice on the trustee, giving the trustee three months within which to determine whether to redeem the security at the value placed on the security by the creditor (IR 1986, rule 6.117(4)).

Where there has been no revaluation of the security approved by the court, the trustee, if dissatisfied with the value put on the security, may require the property charged with the security to be put up for sale, and the trustee on behalf of the estate (or creditor on his behalf) may bid for the property at auction. Once the property has been sold, the actual amount realised replaces the valuation previously put on it (IR 1986, rules 6.118, 6.119).

For further consideration of the secured creditor's position in bankruptcy see **12.4.1**.

Debts subject to discounts

Trade discounts which would otherwise be applicable, but for the bankruptcy, will be taken into account by the trustee, save where that discount was attributable to immediate, early or cash settlement (IR 1986, rule 6.110).

Debts in a foreign currency

Debts incurred in a foreign currency will be converted to sterling at the official exchange rate as at the date of the bankruptcy order (IR 1986, rule 6.111(1)).

Debts subject to rights of set-off

One of the important considerations for a trustee in evaluating a creditor's position (and for that matter a debtor of the bankrupt) is rights of set-off (IA 1986, s.323), whereby account is taken of what is due from each party to the other as at the date of bankruptcy.

IA 1986, s.323 provides that where, before the commencement of the bankruptcy, there have been mutual credits, debts or other dealings between the bankrupt and any creditor proving in the bankruptcy, an account will be taken and sums due from one party to the other will be set off against sums due from the other.

In *Stein* v. *Blake* [1996] AC 243 it was held that the operation of set-off is mandatory. It cannot be contracted out of and applies irrespective of whether the creditor submits a proof. The effect of this on the creditor is examined more closely at **12.4.5**.

Debts due periodically

In the case of rent or other payments of a periodic nature, the creditor may prove only for amounts that are due and unpaid as at the date of bankruptcy, not future or prospective liabilities (IR 1986, rule 6.112). If the landlord is willing to treat the lease as at an end, a claim for loss and damage may be appropriate (*Re Panther Lead Co.* [1896] 1 Ch 978; see also *Re Park Air Services plc* [2000] 2 AC 172 for quantification of a landlord's claim post disclaimer (IA 1986, s.378)).

Interest

A creditor's claim may in certain circumstances include interest on the debt up to the date of bankruptcy (IR 1986, rule 6.113), namely if the debt is due by virtue of a written instrument and interest is payable at a certain time, it may be claimed, or where a formal demand setting out the interest claimed has been sent to the debtor at a rate not exceeding that specified in the Judgments Act 1838, s.17 (currently 8 per cent per annum).

Debts payable in the future

If the debt has not fallen due as at the date of bankruptcy, this must be made clear by the creditor, and although that creditor will be entitled to a dividend, for the purpose of calculating the eventual dividend payment (and for no other purpose), the amount of a creditor's admitted proof will be reduced by a percentage calculated (as set out in IR 1986, rule 11.13, as amended by the Insolvency (Amendment) Rules 2005, SI 2005/527, with effect from 1 April 2005) as follows:

$$X \div 1.05n$$

Where:

$X =$ the value of the admitted proof.
$n =$ the period beginning with the relevant date (the date of the bankruptcy order) and ending with the date on which the payment of the creditor's debt would otherwise be due expressed in years and months in a decimalised form.

Prior to 1 April 2005, the discount for accelerated receipt was set at a rate of 5 per cent per annum on the full amount. This meant that a debt due in 20 years or more was valued at nil for dividend purposes. This rule was criticised in *Re Park Air Services Ltd* [2000] 2 AC 172, a case concerning a liability under a long leasehold, as being 'seriously defective'. The amended rule means that the future debt will always have a value (i.e. a debt due in 20 years is discounted by 62.3 per cent rather than 100 per cent).

12.2 DIVIDEND AND DISTRIBUTION TO CREDITORS

12.2.1 Dividend payments

Where the trustee has sufficient funds to cover all costs and expenses of the bankruptcy, any remaining sum will be subject to a declaration and distribution of dividends among the creditors in respect of bankruptcy debts which they have proved (IA 1986, s.324(1)). As we have seen (at **12.1**), a creditor who has failed to prove or has a non-provable debt will not receive a dividend and the trustee does not owe it any duties (*Levy* v. *Legal Services Commission* [2000] BPIR 1065).

In some rare cases the trustee may, with the permission of the creditors' committee, make a distribution of property *in specie* (IA 1986, s.326). This may relate to unusual property which may not be readily or advantageously sold.

Notice of dividend payment

Before a dividend is declared by the trustee, notice of intention to distribute will be given by the trustee to all creditors whose addresses are known to him and who have not yet proved their debt (IR 1986, rule 11.2). Unless it has been previously advertised, the trustee must advertise the bankruptcy and invite proofs of debt, giving notice of intended distribution by public advertisement, i.e. by advertising in the *London Gazette* and in such other manner as the trustee thinks fit (IR 1986, rule 11.2(1A)).

The trustee must give creditors at least 21 days' notice of intended distribution and in his notice state that it is his intention to declare a dividend within two months from the last date of proving (IR 1986, rule 11.2(3)).

The trustee will, within five business days of the last date of proving, deal with all creditors' proofs unless he has already done so, accepting or rejecting the same.

The trustee has discretion to deal with proofs of debt that are lodged late (*Painter* v. *Hutchison* [2008] BPIR 170). If during the two-month period a creditor seeks to vary or reverse the decision of the trustee by court application, the trustee may postpone or cancel the dividend payment (IR 1986, rule 11.4). If the trustee considers it appropriate, pending the determination, he may make an interim distribution with leave of the court (see *Lomax Leisure Ltd* v. *Miller* [2008] BCC 686).

Payment of dividend

If at the end of two months the trustee has no reason to postpone or cancel the dividend payment, the dividend payment will be made, with a notice given to all creditors who have proved their debt, a statement of amounts realised, expenses related to the administration of the insolvent estate, provisions for unsettled claims or retention of any sums and the total amount to be payable by dividend (IR 1986, rule 11.6). It is possible for the trustee to make a number of distributions.

Where no distribution is intended, nor any further dividend is to be paid, notice to that effect must be sent to the creditors (IR 1986, rule 11.7). If after the payment of the dividend the creditor's proof increases, the creditor is not entitled to disturb the distribution of the dividend; creditors are, however, entitled to payment from any further dividend and can then receive any dividends they previously failed to receive (IR 1986, rule 11.8).

No action lies against the trustee for payment of a dividend; however, if the trustee has unreasonably refused to deal with a creditor's claim and has failed to pay a dividend that was otherwise due, he may on application of the creditor be ordered to pay the claim, interest and costs personally (IA 1986, s.325(2)).

Final dividend and final meeting

Where the trustee has realised as much of the bankrupt's estate as he thinks possible without needlessly protracting the trusteeship, he must give notice of his intention to declare a final dividend, or, if appropriate, give notice that no dividend or further dividend will be declared (IA 1986, s.330). Provided no creditor has applied to postpone the final date (IA 1986, s.330(3)), after the final date the trustee will proceed to:

(a) defray any outstanding expense of the bankruptcy out of the estate;
(b) declare and distribute the final dividend without regard to those who have failed to prove; and
(c) pay any surplus after payment of all claims, interest and costs to the bankrupt.

Where the trustee is not the Official Receiver, he is required to summon a final meeting of creditors to receive his report on the administration of the estate and determine whether he should have his release (IA 1986, s.331) (see **6.7** for further details).

12.2.2 Priority of payments

In making a distribution of the bankrupt's estate, the trustee is to have regard to IA 1986, s.328 (priority of preferential debts) and IR 1986, rule 6.224 (priority of expenses).

Checklist

Priority of distribution in bankruptcy (IA 1986, s.328)

- Costs and expenses of preserving and realising secured assets.
- Secured creditors as against secured property.
- Expenses of bankruptcy including remuneration of trustee (see IR 1986, rule 6.224 for the rule as to priority of expenses).
- Preferential creditors.
- Unsecured creditors.
- Post-insolvency interest on debts.
- Deferred/postponed debts (e.g. debts owed to spouses; see IA 1986, s.329).

The expenses of the bankruptcy will be treated as a first charge against any realised funds. IR 1986, rule 6.224(1) sets out an order of priority for the payment of bankruptcy expenses, including, near the rear of the list, the remuneration of the trustee. As was pointed out in **Chapter 4**, a creditor who has initiated the bankruptcy process by petitioning is in no better position than any other creditor; however, the petition costs are payable as expenses of the bankruptcy.

There are some unusual, largely historic, provisions that ensure that a small number of unique classes of creditors have priority over the generally recognised class of preferential creditors:

- By virtue of IA 1986, s.348, apprentices or articled clerks of the bankrupt who have paid a premium for apprenticeship will have repaid to them such sum as the trustee thinks reasonable; the trustee may, however, transfer the apprenticeship to some other person.
- Where the bankrupt has in his possession money or property of a friendly society, the trustees of the friendly society have a first right of recovery in respect of the money (Friendly Societies Act 1974, s.59; see *Re Miller* [1893] 1 QB 327).
- Where the bankrupt has died, the reasonable funeral, testamentary and administration expenses are treated as pre-preferential debts (Administration of Insolvent Estates of Deceased Persons Order 1986, SI 1986/1999).

Preferential debts are those set out in IA 1986, Sched.6, which has been substantially amended following the Enterprise Act 2002 reforms (which came into force on 15 September 2003), the major change being the removal of Crown debt priority, which has had significant impact on bankruptcies commenced after 15 September 2003. There are now three remaining categories of preferential debt:

- Contributions to occupational pension schemes (Pension Schemes Act 1993, Sched.4).
- Remuneration of employees (subject to various limits).
- Levies on coal and steel production (ECSC Treaty, Arts.40(3), 49, 50).

The preferential debt must have been due at the date of the bankruptcy order or, in the more unusual circumstances where an interim receiver was in office, when he was first appointed (IA 1986, s.387(6)(b)).

The payment to unsecured creditors is to those who have proved for their debt in the bankruptcy, and they will receive distribution on a *pari passu* basis. Interest is payable on all preferential and unsecured debts at a prescribed rate (currently 8 per cent) or the rate applicable to the debt apart from bankruptcy, whichever is the higher (IA 1986, s.328(5)).

Postponed debts include the following:

- Debts between spouses: where a loan was provided by a person who was the spouse of the bankrupt (or civil partner, see Civil Partnership Act 2004, s.263(10)(b) from 5 December 2005) at the commencement of the bankruptcy, the debt is only payable after all other creditors' claims have been dealt with. This provision operates irrespective of whether the loan was given for personal or business reasons (IA 1986, s.329).
- Loans falling with the Partnership Act 1890: where a loan is made and repayable according to the profits of the business, or a share of the profits is paid as interest, or a share of the profits is to be paid in consideration of a sale of the goodwill of the business, the lender's debt is postponed. (See *Re Meade* [1951] Ch 774, where it was expressly held that the lender need not be a partner of the business nor share directly in profits provided there is some element of 'investment' on the part of the lender.)
- The claims of any beneficiaries under a settlement made by the bankrupt that has subsequently been avoided under IA 1986, s.339.

After all of the above claims have been satisfied in full, any surplus is available to the bankrupt. This is unlikely, although it is possible where realisations of assets have been greater than was anticipated. In such cases, the individual could seek annulment of the bankruptcy (see **10.10**). In practice, if realisations were likely to exceed liabilities, the bankrupt would have been better advised to seek the approval of creditors to an IVA proposal during the course of the bankruptcy.

12.3 CLAIMS ON PROPERTY IN THE POSSESSION OF BANKRUPT

An unsecured creditor is likely to receive only a limited return as a result of the bankruptcy process. Most bankrupts will be non-traders, so-called consumer debtors (85 per cent in 2010), a significant proportion will be unemployed (36 per cent in 2005) and only a small percentage will have an interest in a property (9 per cent in 2005) (source: DTI, *Tackling Over Indebtedness* (Annual Report, 2006)). This is also putting to one side the rise and now predominance of debtors who are subject to a DRO as opposed to bankruptcy. The rise of 'NINJA debtors' (no income, no job, no assets) has had significant impact on the way that bankruptcy is viewed and the use of it by creditors as an effective means of repayment of debt.

Generally, the best that may be anticipated by an unsecured creditor is a small dividend, i.e. a proportion of their debt payable on a rateable value among all unsecured creditors. Exceptions to this general rule might occur where on investigation the debtor is in fact solvent, as on a balance sheet basis his assets exceed his liabilities, or where the trustee has taken proceedings against the bankrupt and/or third parties for recovery of property and/or for damages.

Due to the potential poor return during the insolvency process, a creditor should endeavour to exhaust all possible routes of enforcement against the debtor. Where the creditor has obtained payment from the debtor prior to commencement of the insolvency process, it is entitled to retain this sum. There are, however, specific rules regarding executions that remain uncompleted as at the date of bankruptcy.

An alternative for the creditor is to claim some proprietorial right of ownership over property or assets of the bankrupt. Such claims may act as an alternative remedy for unsecured creditors, who may stand to receive little in the way of dividend payments. Those who have such claims will need to think very carefully as to whether they are to prove in the bankruptcy as they may be forgoing rights to receive a dividend.

Checklist

A creditor may be able to improve his position by:

- obtaining a judgment debt;
- completing execution prior to commencement of bankruptcy;
- claiming security for the debt;
- claiming that goods in debtor's possession are held on trust for the benefit of the creditor;
- claiming a retention of title;
- claiming additional rights exercisable irrespective of bankruptcy, e.g. landlord.

12.3.1   Execution attachments

Where a creditor has issued a warrant of execution against goods or land of an individual or attached a debt due to that person from another person and the individual is subsequently adjudged bankrupt, the creditor is not entitled to retain any benefit of the execution or attachment as against the Official Receiver or trustee unless the execution or attachment has been completed before commencement of the bankruptcy (IA 1986, s.346).

In applying this rule, a number of factors must be borne in mind:

1. The bankruptcy of an individual commences on the date the order is made by the court, not the date the petition was presented. It should be remembered, however, that when proceedings on a bankruptcy petition are pending, the court may stay any action, execution or other legal process against the property or person of the debtor (IA 1986, s.285(1)).

2. Where, before completion of the execution, notice is given to a High Court enforcement officer, or other officer charged with execution, that the individual debtor has been adjudged bankrupt, the High Court enforcement officer will on request deliver to the Official Receiver, or trustee in bankruptcy, the goods and any money seized, although the costs of execution are a first charge on those goods or monies delivered (IA 1986, s.346(2)).

3. Where any execution is for a judgment debt in excess of £1,000 and the goods of the individual are sold or monies paid by the debtor in order to avoid sale, the High Court enforcement officer will deduct the cost of execution from the proceeds of sale and retain the balance for 14 days (Insolvency Proceedings (Monetary Limits) (Amendment) Order 2004, SI 2004/547). If, within that time, notice is served that a bankruptcy petition has been presented and thereafter a bankruptcy order is made on that petition, the balance of the proceeds of sale or monies paid will pass to the Official Receiver or trustee in bankruptcy (IA 1986, s.346(4)).

4. An execution against goods is completed by seizure and sale or by the making of a charging order (Charging Orders Act 1979, s.1). Execution against land is completed by seizure, or by appointment of a receiver, or by the making of a charging order. A charging order must be a final order and not merely the interim order (see *Roberts Petroleum Ltd* v. *Bernard Kenny Ltd* [1983] 2 AC 192; *Nationwide Building Society* v. *Wright* [2009] BPIR 1047) (IA 1986, s.346(5)(a), (b)).

5. An attachment of debt is completed by receipt of that debt. The right of the Official Receiver or trustee in bankruptcy to set aside the creditors' rights attained upon execution may be set aside by court order (IA 1986, s.346(5)(c)).

6. In exceptional circumstances, the court may allow a creditor to retain the benefit of an incomplete execution or attachment (IA 1986, s.346(6); see *Re Buckingham International plc* [1998] BCC 943).

7. Bona fide purchasers for value who have obtained goods in good faith from the High Court enforcement officer under a sale agreement will be entitled to retain the same (IA 1986, s.346(7)).

8. In respect of any after-acquired property, execution against this property will be effected by claims from the Official Receiver or trustee under IA 1986, s.307. A copy of the notice given under that section must be served upon the High Court enforcement officer or other officer charged with execution (IA 1986, s.346(8)).

12.3.2 Trust claims

Assets held by the bankrupt (or by an insolvent company) but which belong to a third party are not available to the trustee to realise for the benefit of the creditors of the debtor. Conversely, if it can be established that the debtor has no beneficial interest in the property, then the creditor may be able to claim that property/money, rather than prove for a debt in the bankruptcy or liquidation.

IA 1986, s.283(3)(a) specifically provides that property held on trust by the bankrupt for another person does not pass into the bankrupt's estate. This applies to assets that have never belonged to the debtor and assets held on trust for the benefit of a third party, as well as to assets where the debtor's interest has expired, e.g. expiry of a rental period or lease.

Property has been held to be excluded from the insolvent estate by virtue of express, implied, constructive or '*Quistclose*' resulting trusts in favour of a third party.

Express/implied trust

To establish a trust relationship there need to be three certainties (*Re Kayford* [1975] 1 WLR 279):

1. Certainty of words, i.e. there must be demonstrated a sufficient intention to create a trust; express use of the word 'trust' is not essential and save where the property subject to the trust is land, the trust does not need to be in writing.
2. Certainty of subject matter, i.e. the property within the trust must be sufficiently ascertainable and identifiable.
3. Certainty of object, i.e. the beneficiary of the trust must be clear and ascertained.

Constructive trust

A constructive trust arises where a party receives money in circumstances where it is unconscionable for that party to retain the money, such as where there is a payment made by mistake and the receiving party knows that the money is due/belongs to another. (See *Chase Manhattan Bank NA* v. *Israel-British Bank (London) Ltd* [1979] 3 All ER 1025, where a bank mistakenly paid another bank twice on behalf of a customer. When the recipient bank went into liquidation it was held that the mistaken payment was held on a constructive trust in favour of the customer.)

Quistclose trust

This form of resulting trust derives from the case of *Barclays Bank* v. *Quistclose Investments Ltd* [1970] AC 567, in which it was held that where payments were made by a party for a specific purpose and where that purpose subsequently could not be fulfilled, the money paid over for that specific purpose was held on resulting trust for the paying party. In that case, a loan had been made by a bank to a company for the purposes of paying a dividend to shareholders; it was held by the company solely for that purpose and was thus deemed to be held on a resulting trust in favour of the bank.

12.3.3   Retention of title

A creditor of the debtor may be able to claim that until payment of its debt it retains title to goods supplied to and in the possession of the bankrupt. This has less application in the case of a bankruptcy than in corporate insolvency, but may be of relevance if the bankrupt was in trade and received goods/stock on credit (i.e. not cash on delivery).

Title to goods will generally pass on the handing over of possession, in consideration of which the buyer is likely to owe a debt to the seller. However, it is possible for a contractual term between the buyer and seller to depart from this normal course of events and for the seller to retain an equitable (beneficial) interest in identifiable assets in the hands of the buyer, unless or until the goods are paid for or until some other conditions are met (see Sale of Goods Act 1979, ss.17(1), 19(1) and leading case *Aluminium Industrie Vaassen BV* v. *Romalpa Aluminium Ltd* [1976] 2 All ER 552).

A retention of title agreement depends not only on the contractual language and the form of the contractual term, but also on the substance of the transaction. Although the intention of the parties is not determinative (*Welsh Development Agency* v. *Export Finance Co.* [1992] BCC 270), as a general rule, the more simple the clause the more likely it is to succeed.

The seller must establish that the retention of title was incorporated into the contract of supply, that the goods supplied can be identified and distinguished from other such assets in the hands of buyer, and that they have a right to take back possession of the goods supplied.

A fuller analysis of retention of title is contained in **Chapter 13**.

12.4   CREDITORS POSSESSING A UNIQUE POSITION

In addition to creditors who can bring claims over specific assets held in the hands of the bankrupt, there are certain creditors who, as a result of their unique status and position, enjoy additional rights over ordinary unsecured creditors. In certain instances, these rights can be exercised during the insolvency process. The following section focuses on the position of secured creditors, the bankrupt's landlord and employees of the bankrupt.

12.4.1   Secured creditors

A secured creditor cannot petition for the bankruptcy of an individual debtor. A debt is secured where a person holds any security for the debt, whether a mortgage, charge, lien or other security over any property of the person by whom the debt is owed (IA 1986, s.383(2)). As we have seen at **12.1.2**, a secured creditor may, however, petition for the bankruptcy of an individual should it relinquish its security, or estimate the value of its security, showing an unsecured shortfall in respect of which it is entitled to petition (IA 1986, s.269(1)(a), (b)). A secured creditor is under no obligation to participate in the bankruptcy process and may rely solely on its security. However, as we shall see, a creditor who has or is likely to suffer a shortfall on realisation of its security may find it appropriate to submit a proof of debt. It should be remembered that on submitting a proof of debt, every creditor is obliged to state whether it holds any security in respect of the debt (IR 1986, rule 6.98(1)(g)). The security must be identified and the trustee in bankruptcy may require the creditor to produce the instrument of the security (IR 1986, rule 6.108). If the creditor fails to disclose the security, the trustee in bankruptcy or Official Receiver may treat the property as unencumbered and may deal with it accordingly, unless the secured creditor applies for relief on the grounds that omitting to disclose the security was the result of an honest mistake (IR 1986, rule 6.116(2)).

A secured creditor thus has a number of choices:

- Realise its security and prove for the balance.
- Surrender its security and prove for the full amount.
- Value its security and prove for the unsecured element.
- Rely solely on its security and take no part in the bankruptcy.

After valuing the security, the creditor may, with the agreement of the trustee or with leave of the court, revise the valuation of the security (IR 1986, rules 6.115 and 6.117(2)). However, where the secured creditor has valued the security for the purposes of petitioning for an unsecured debt, or where the secured creditor has voted in respect of the unsecured balance, any revision of its valuation can only be made with the permission of the court.

If the trustee is dissatisfied with the valuation put forward by the secured creditor in respect of the security, whether in his proof or by revaluation, he may, on election, require the property comprised in the security to be offered for sale (IR 1986, rule 6.118(1)).

The terms of sale are such as to be agreed between the creditor and the trustee, or as the court may direct. If the sale is by auction, the trustee on behalf of the estate, and the creditor on its own behalf, may appear and bid.

At any stage, the trustee may give notice to the creditor requiring redemption of the security. The security will be redeemed at the valuation given by the creditor at the expiration of 28 days (IR 1986, rule 6.117). The creditor has 21 days, or such longer time as the trustee may allow, to exercise the right of revaluation. A secured creditor may at any time with prior notice call upon the trustee to elect whether or not he will exercise the power to redeem at the value placed upon it. The trustee then has three months in which to exercise its power of redemption or determine not to exercise it (IR 1986, rule 6.117(4)).

If a creditor has valued its security, but subsequently realises it, the net amount realised will be substituted for the value previously estimated by the creditor (IR 1986, rule 6.119). On realisation of the security, the secured creditor may apply the proceeds to other debts owed to it by the debtor, but not otherwise secured (see *Re William Hall (Contractors) Ltd* [1967] 2 All ER 1150). This will not disturb dividends already paid or votes taken.

It should be noted that during the course of the bankruptcy, the secured creditor is entitled to realise its security at any time. The trustee in bankruptcy has no interest in the secured property as it falls outside the bankrupt's estate. However, should the trustee consider there is available equity and wish to deal with the secured assets, he can use the provisions regarding notice and redemption as outlined above. The most common situation where this occurs is where there is a matrimonial home that is subject to security, but the equity of redemption vests in the trustee in bankruptcy. Where by court order, or by agreement, the property is sold, the trustee in bankruptcy will receive only that proportion of the bankrupt's interest in the proceeds as remains unsecured. The trustee would thus need to account to the secured creditor for the value of the secured creditor's debt. As a consequence, close co-operation between the trustee and the secured creditor needs to take place when secured assets are sold.

12.4.2 Landlords

We have looked previously at how a creditor seeking payment of rent or other periodic payments may prove for the debt in the bankruptcy. However, landlords, or other lessors of property, whose property is in possession of the bankrupt have certain additional rights that may be exercised despite insolvency. Indeed, it is very common for a lease to contain provisions for forfeiture on the event of the insolvency of the tenant. These terms are generally widely drawn and 'insolvency' can mean third party claims which cannot be met by the insolvent tenant.

The rights for the landlord to commence proceedings, distrain upon goods of the tenant, to effect forfeiture by peaceable re-entry or take legal proceedings in respect of the arrears of rent are not removed as a result of the bankruptcy of the tenant. However, the rights are subject to application to the court for leave to continue with such proceedings.

After the making of a bankruptcy order, it is a general rule that no creditor of the bankrupt may, before discharge of the bankrupt, commence any action or legal proceedings against the bankrupt except with leave of the court and it then does so on such terms as the court may impose (IA 1986, s.285(3)(b)).

A landlord's right to distrain over the bankrupt's goods and property is limited by the provisions of IA 1986, s.347. This confirms the right of a landlord to distrain upon goods and property of the undischarged bankrupt for rent due only in respect of six months' rent accrued due before the commencement of the bankruptcy. Any sum recovered in excess of six months' rent arrears will be part of the bankrupt's estate. One caveat to this is that where distress has been completed within three months of the date of the bankruptcy, so much of the goods and effects, or proceeds of sale, not otherwise held in the bankrupt's estate, must be charged for the benefit of the bankrupt's estate with the preferential debts of the bankrupt to the extent that the bankrupt's estate is insufficient for meeting those debts (IA 1986, s.347(3)). Prior to 15 September 2003 and the abolition of Crown preference, this section had some considerable scope and effect. With the abolition of Crown preference, the effect of preferential creditors' claims on personal bankruptcies will be limited.

A landlord is not permitted to distrain for rent after the bankrupt's discharge for any arrears of rent which were owed as at the date of bankruptcy. This does not prevent the landlord from exercising rights in respect of rent arrears accruing after the date of bankruptcy, although the landlord should take note that the bankrupt may have few if any available assets, as property owned as at the date of bankruptcy will have vested in the trustee (IA 1986, s.306). The bankrupt's property and assets may therefore be limited to such after-acquired property as has not been claimed by the trustee (IA 1986, s.307). As the majority of bankrupts will be discharged from bankruptcy within one year, in many cases within a matter of weeks, the landlord's right to distrain has to be very carefully thought out and may be more readily used.

The right to distrain against property can be exercised notwithstanding that the property is vested in the trustee, and notwithstanding that the landlord has a right to prove in the bankruptcy in respect of the arrears of rent (IA 1986, s.347(9)), but once the landlord has received a dividend he is considered to have elected not to distrain (*Holmes* v. *Watt* [1935] 2 KB 300), and once the bankrupt has been discharged from bankruptcy the landlord can no longer distrain (IA 1986, s.347(5)).

In respect of taking legal proceedings for arrears of rent, once a bankruptcy order has been made as stated above, the landlord is prevented from commencing any legal proceedings without leave of the court. In the normal course of events, the trustee in bankruptcy will discuss the payment of the arrears with the landlord. This might be required if the lease has value, or the business carried out by the individual bankrupt is in leased premises. In such circumstances, the trustee may agree to pay the arrears of rent as an expense of the estate, to prevent the landlord from exercising rights of distraint or forfeiture. Where the rent cannot be paid, and/or there is no value in the lease for the estate, the trustee is likely to give consent to forfeiture, or may agree formal/informal surrender.

Table 12.1 The landlord's position in personal insolvency

	Bankruptcy without leave	Bankruptcy with leave
Distraint	✔*	
Forfeiture	✔	
Sue for arrears		✔
Disclaimer available to insolvency practitioner	✔	

* See IA 1986, s.347(1).

12.4.3 Employees

If an individual is employed by a person who subsequently becomes bankrupt, e.g. where the bankrupt operates a business as a sole trader or in partnership, the employee's contract of employment does not automatically terminate. However, it is highly unlikely that a bankrupt will be able to trade his business in such circumstances, as all property and assets of the bankrupt will have vested in the trustee in bankruptcy (IA 1986, s.306). Furthermore, any income received by the bankrupt could be subject to an IPO. The bankrupt cannot obtain credit, either solely or jointly, in excess of £500 without first disclosing his bankruptcy (Insolvency Proceedings (Monetary Limits) (Amendment) Order 2004, SI 2004/547; IA 1986, s.360). For these practical reasons, it is most likely that the insolvent employer will be unable to pay the employee further. There is also a possibility that payments made could constitute preferential payments and could be set aside.

In the situation that the employee's wages remain unpaid, or the employee is dismissed or made redundant, the employee's claims will generally be unsecured claims in the bankruptcy, save for specified amounts which are regarded as preferential debts (IA 1986, Sched.6, Category 5). These amounts are limited to so much of any amount that is owed by the debtor to the present or former employee by way of remuneration throughout the whole or part of the period of four months prior to the commencement of bankruptcy. This sum is, however, subject to a prescribed maximum level set by the Secretary of State (currently £800: Insolvency Proceedings (Monetary Limits) Order 1986, SI 1986/1996). This amount has remained unchanged for almost 30 years. Preferential status is also accorded to any sums accrued by way of holiday pay for any period and these are not subject to a monetary limit. Since 15 September 2003, employee claims remain the most significant preferential debt in any insolvency. However, as can be seen, the monetary value of the claims is limited.

12.4.4 Bankrupt's spouse

From 5 December 2005, reference in the insolvency legislation to the bankrupt's spouse includes a civil partner (Civil Partnership Act 2004, s.263(10)(b)) and all references to spouse or former spouse in this section have equal application to a civil partner.

We have looked at the position of a spouse as a co-owner of the family home (in **Chapter 10**) and of course it follows that a spouse's own financial affairs and assets are unaffected by the other spouse's bankruptcy. It is not uncommon to find that a bankrupt's spouse may well be in the position of a creditor of the bankrupt. However, any debt owed to a spouse is treated as a deferred debt (IA 1986, s.329), meaning it ranks lowest in the order of priorities.

However, it is often found that the stress and strain of financial difficulty and bankruptcy will be accompanied by marriage breakdown. The inherent conflict between matrimonial and bankruptcy jurisdiction presents a significant challenge, with the family court balancing the interests of the spouses and giving primacy to the interests of the children in a marriage (and therefore often the non-bankrupt spouse), whereas the bankruptcy court seeks to give primacy to the interests of creditors (as seen at **10.9**).

Quite obviously, each situation is unique, but for the purposes of this section we will assume that the husband is the debtor and there has been a transfer of his equity in the matrimonial home to his wife (ex-wife) and/or maintenance paid.

Prior to his bankruptcy, the husband may have transferred property or made maintenance payments, either pursuant to an order of the court made in matrimonial proceedings or in contemplation of marriage breakdown. The creditors may feel that they have been prejudiced by this transfer; there may even be suspicion that the marriage breakdown has been used as an excuse to move assets out of the husband's name. In some circumstances, the wife may feel that the husband is using bankruptcy to avoid the consequences of matrimonial proceedings and may well need to proceed to annul the bankruptcy in order to obtain effective relief.

Transfer/payments made pre-bankruptcy without court order

If a lump sum payment, a transfer of property or a payment of maintenance was made outside the terms of family proceedings, then at common law, this is said to suspend the wife's common law and statutory rights to claim maintenance. On the husband's bankruptcy, the agreement comes to an end and any unpaid arrears can be claimed in the bankruptcy (they are a 'provable' debt) (IR 1986, rule 12.3). The bankruptcy determines the agreement and reinstates the wife's right to claim maintenance under statute (under the Matrimonial and Family Proceedings Act 1984). However, this right is unlikely to be of much value to the wife if the husband is then made bankrupt (see *Dewe* v. *Dewe* [1928] P 113).

If the husband has, within five years of the date of bankruptcy, made a transfer to his wife in consideration of the marriage, or where the value of the consideration in money or money's worth is significantly less than the value of the transfer, then if at the date of the transfer the husband was insolvent, or if he made himself insolvent as a result of the transfer, the transfer may be set aside as a transaction at an undervalue (IA 1986, s.339). A presumption of insolvency is deemed in the case of a 'transfer to an associate' (i.e. the wife), but this remains a rebuttable presumption (IA 1986, s.435(2)).

Furthermore, if the bankrupt has, within two years of the date of bankruptcy, carried out a transaction resulting in his wife being in a better position in the event of bankruptcy than she would have been in had the event not taken place, and did so being influenced by a desire to produce that result, then the transaction can be set aside as a preference (IA 1986, s.340).

A transfer of property or action which prefers a spouse pre-bankruptcy outside matrimonial proceedings can thus be challenged by the trustee.

Transfers/payments made pre-bankruptcy with court order

Maintenance paid pursuant to an order made in family proceedings is treated very differently from payments made pursuant to an agreement reached between husband and wife without a court order. Payments due under 'family proceedings' (as defined in IA 1986, s.281(8)) cannot be claimed in a bankruptcy as they are 'non-provable' debts (IR 1986, rule 12.3(2)(a)). These include awards of costs which may have been made during the proceedings (see *Levy* v. *Legal Services Commission* [2000] BPIR 1065).

As a result, despite bankruptcy, debts arising pursuant to family proceedings continue to be due and payable. The wife can therefore bring enforcement proceedings, even though the husband is bankrupt. This could, in certain circumstances, lead to committal proceedings and/or an application for an attachment of earnings order (Debtors Act 1869, s.5; Magistrates' Courts Act 1980, s.76). It should, however, be remembered that the husband would most likely seek relief in the family proceedings (based on his bankruptcy) and the court will have regard to the creditors' interests in assessing the case.

Despite any debt being owed pursuant to an order in family proceedings potentially being one which is not provable in bankruptcy, the wife can in fact petition for the husband's bankruptcy, as she is a creditor. A bankruptcy order is, however, likely to be made only in unusual circumstances, where, e.g. the husband is using bankruptcy proceedings as a shield against the wife's claim in family proceedings and/or where investigations by the Official Receiver's office are deemed appropriate (*Russell* v. *Russell* [1998] 1 FLR 936).

As a result of the debt being non-provable, however, the wife will not be entitled to any dividend in the bankruptcy as a result of any unpaid sums due under family proceedings.

The fact that the payment is made pursuant to an order of the court (within or outside matrimonial proceedings) causes some different considerations to arise.

In *Hill and Bangham* v. *Haines* [2007] EWHC 1012 (Ch), a property adjustment order made after a fully contested hearing was overturned at first instance as being a transaction at an undervalue. Following the reasoning in *Xydhias* v. *Xydhias* [1999] 2 All ER 386, *G* v. *G (financial provisions: equal division)* [2002] 2 FLR 1143 and *McMinn* v. *McMinn* [2003] 2 FLR 823, the court held that 'the position is the same whether the Matrimonial Court makes an order following a contested hearing or following a compromise agreement – in neither case does the receiving party give, nor the paying party receive, consideration' (per Pelling J, at [23]).

On appeal ([2007] BPIR 1280), the Court of Appeal took an entirely different view, holding that valuable consideration was provided for the transfer by the wife giving up her claim for ancillary relief, although the court did not go on to quantify the value of the consideration. This has led some commentators to take the view that a distinction could be made between cases where a property transfer followed a consent order, and possible collusion and/or a sham divorce between the bankrupt and his former wife. While such an argument was rejected in *Re Jones* [2008] BPIR

1051, it remains possible that in certain circumstances the trustee (and the court) will look closely at consent orders made in matrimonial proceedings.

In the same vein, a trustee may also wish to consider whether maintenance payments could be viewed as preferential payments (IA 1986, s.340). The key question to determine is whether in making such a payment the husband sought to put his wife/ex-wife in a better position than other creditors. In the case of an order by consent, the requisite element of desire may be easier to make out than if the order was made to compel payments following a contested hearing.

12.4.5 Creditor with right of set-off

Where before the commencement of the bankruptcy there have been mutual credits, mutual debts or other mutual dealings between the bankrupt and any creditor of the bankrupt claiming to prove for a bankruptcy debt, an account should be taken of what is due from each party to the other, and the sums due from one party will be set off against the sums due from the other (IA 1986, s.323).

The ability to set off, instead of having to prove and recover a dividend, allows the creditor to recover 'pound for pound'. The statutory right of set-off derives from common law (see e.g. *Foster* v. *Wilson* (1843) 2 M & W 191). It is a right triggered by bankruptcy and is not dependent on the creditor having a contractual right of set-off.

Where the set-off operates such that the bankrupt's claim exceeds that of the creditor, the trustee may take proceedings for recovery of the balance.

Where the set-off operates such that the creditor's claim exceeds that of the bankrupt, the creditor is entitled to prove for the balance of the debt (IA 1986, s.323(4)).

The statutory right of set-off:

- cannot be contracted out of, or waived (*British Eagle International Airlines Ltd* v. *Compagnie Nationale Air France* [1975] 2 All ER 390 and *Re Cushla Ltd* [1979] 3 All ER 415);
- arises even when the money is owed by the creditor, or is stated to be held on trust (*Re ILG Travel Ltd* [1996] BCC 21);
- cannot be disapplied by the court (*Re Bank of Credit and Commerce International SA (No.8)* [1998] 1 BCLC 68);
- is applied as at the date of the commencement of bankruptcy (*Stein* v. *Blake* [1995] 2 All ER 961) and is not available in respect of debts arising after the date of commencement, nor in consequence of any obligation in being at the date of commencement (*Bradley-Hole* v. *Cuzen* [1953] 1 QB 300); and
- cannot be extended to third parties, even by consent (*Re Bank of Credit Commerce and International SA (No.8)* [1998] 1 BCLC 68).

Mutuality

The debts must be due from the creditor to the debtor, and the debtor to the creditor, in respect of the same rights and capacity, i.e. if a creditor is holding monies on trust for the bankrupt, the creditor cannot set off claims that it may personally have against the bankrupt against the sum held on trust (*Elgood* v. *Harris* [1896] 2 QB 491).

Mutuality is judged objectively as at the commencement of the bankruptcy in light of all the circumstances (*Re ILG Travel Ltd* [1996] BCC 21).

The debt need not, however, be liquidated before the commencement of the bankruptcy, so the right of set-off may be applied to sums payable in the future, whether the obligation is certain or contingent, whether the sum is fixed or liquidated (see *Secretary of State for Trade and Industry* v. *Frid* [2004] 2 All ER 1042).

As a result, provided that the debt is provable, the debt is capable of being set off where there have been mutual dealings between the creditor and the bankrupt (*Re Charge Card Services Ltd* [1986] 3 All ER 289).

'Mutual dealings' covers transactions giving rise to rights and liabilities between the bankrupt and the creditor, resulting in pecuniary liabilities in respect of which an account may be taken (*Rose* v. *Hart* (1818) 8 Taunt 499).

Where there is a set-off between a present liability and a future/contingent debt as at the commencement of the bankruptcy, the trustee is entitled to apply the 'hindsight principle', i.e. to assess the value as at the date of the account had the contingency arisen. If, however, it is impractical to wait for the contingency to arise or the future date to occur, the trustee may estimate the value of the bankruptcy debt (IA 1986, s.322(3)).

However, the reverse does not apply, namely the trustee may not estimate sums due to the bankruptcy estate, i.e. accelerate the creditor's liability (*Stein* v. *Blake* [1996] AC 243).

CHAPTER 13

The creditor's position during the corporate insolvency process

13.1 INTRODUCTION

Underpinning all collective insolvency processes is the principle of *pari passu* distribution, namely that creditors of the same type or class are dealt with equally and any distributions made are at a rateable value. In corporate insolvency, however, the role of the secured creditors has much greater importance, with secured lending to companies being commonplace and security taken over the company being both fixed and floating. The position of preferential creditors (while less central to the process since the abolition of Crown preference from 15 September 2003) is also important. In this chapter we look at the treatment of creditors during the corporate insolvency process.

In doing so, it should be remembered that while it is possible for an administrator to make distributions during the course of the administration (IA 1986, Sched.B1, para.65(1); and see *Re GHE Realisations Ltd* [2006] BCC 139 and *Re HPJ UK Ltd* [2007] BCC 284 respectively for guidance and an example where permission of the court for an administrator to make a distribution was granted), primarily distributions made to unsecured creditors remain through a liquidation process.

A receiver appointed to enforce a floating charge has an obligation to meet preferential claims (IA 1986, s.40), a responsibility that continues irrespective of whether the secured creditor has been repaid (*Re Pearl Maintenance Services Ltd* [1995] BCC 657). Save for this obligation, it is not the role of a receiver to distribute to any creditors, other than to those who possess security, although it should be noted that both administrators and receivers are subject to the provisions of IA 1986, s.176A, a measure introduced to seek to ensure that some return is made to unsecured creditors where there is floating charge security.

At the commencement of the winding up, there is a theoretical determination of claims and thereafter realisation and distribution of company assets to satisfy those claims (*Wight* v. *Eckhardt Marine GmbH* [2004] 1 AC 147).

13.2   CREDITORS' CLAIMS DURING THE CORPORATE INSOLVENCY PROCESS

13.2.1   Proof of debt

Compulsory liquidation

A creditor that wishes to recover its debt in whole or in part must (except where the court otherwise orders) submit a claim in writing to the liquidator (IR 1986, rule 4.73(1)). The submission of a written claim must be in prescribed Form 4.25 (a proof of debt).

Since 1 April 2004, there has been no requirement on the Official Receiver or liquidator in the instance of compulsory liquidation to send to every creditor a proof of debt form, only an obligation to send the form to creditors that request one (Insolvency (Amendment) Rules 2004, SI 2004/584).

While the liquidator has discretion as to whether to send out a proof of debt form, guidance has been issued to Official Receivers to send a proof of debt form where:

- there is to be a creditors' meeting;
- a dividend is to be paid; or
- it would aid investigation.

A liquidator in private practice is likely to follow the same guidance. It should be noted that unless permitted by the liquidator within his discretion, a creditor cannot vote at any creditors' meeting unless he has submitted a proof (IR 1986, rule 4.67(1)).

No time is fixed for when the proving of debts should be commenced or completed, this being a power of the court delegated to the liquidator (IA 1986, s.160(1)(e)). However, the court may fix a time or times within which creditors are to prove their debts or claims or be excluded from the benefit of any distributions made before those debts are proved (IA 1986, s.153). It is general practice, however, for the liquidator to allow late proving of a debt, but in doing so not allow any prior distribution to creditors to be disturbed (see *Harrison* v. *Kirk* [1904] AC 1). In any subsequent distribution, the non-payment of the earlier dividend will be taken into account.

Voluntary liquidation

The liquidator may require a creditor wishing to recover its debt in whole or in part to submit a claim in writing (IR 1986, rule 4.73(2)). The creditor's claim must be in writing but the proof may be in any form (IR 1986, rule 4.73(6)). The liquidator may, if necessary, request the creditor to provide such details as deemed necessary to substantiate the claim (IR 1986, rule 4.76).

Where winding up is preceded by administration, any creditor who has submitted a claim in the administration is deemed to have proved in the winding up (IR 1986, rule 4.73(a)). A proof is necessary for the liquidator to establish the creditor's claim.

Administration

As we have seen in **Chapter 7**, it is possible for the administrator to make a distribution to a creditor of the company (IA 1986, Sched.B1, para.65(1)). However, it should be noted that permission of the court will be required for any distributions to be made to unsecured creditors (IA 1986, Sched.B1, para.65(3)). In granting permission, the court will need to be satisfied that the distribution is in the best interests of the creditors as a whole, and will consider, *inter alia*, whether the distribution is conducive to the objectives set out in the administrator's proposals, whether the creditors have approved the proposed distribution, whether proper provision has been made for the secured and preferential creditors, and the impact that any distribution may have on the exit from administration (*Re GHE Realisations Ltd* [2006] BCC 139 and *Re MG Rover Belux SA/NV* [2007] BCC 446).

An administrator is also able to make a payment to a creditor, other than through the process outlined above, if the payment is likely to assist the administrator in achieving the purpose of the administration (IA 1986, Sched.B1, para.66). The administrator in the exercise of his discretion may make a payment, e.g. to a key 'ransom' supplier that may be refusing to supply essential goods and materials without payment of any debt owed by the company pre-administration. This provision has been utilised in cross-border insolvencies to make payments to employees in another Member State, where the payments would not need to be made in the UK, so avoiding the need for secondary proceedings in the second Member State (*Re MG Rover Espana SA* [2006] BCC 599; *Re MG Rover Belux SA/NV* [2007] BCC 446).

As a result of the ability given to administrators to make distributions to creditors, there are a raft of rules governing the exercise of that power (IR 1986, rules 2.68–2.105), which in the main mirror the rules relating to proving debts and the quantification of claims in liquidation. However, the administration process will be used as a means of facilitating distributions to unsecured creditors only in exceptional circumstances; this was certainly indicated in the parliamentary debates on the Enterprise Act 2002. As a result, in this section of the book the separate rules that govern the proving and quantification of debts in administration will not be expressly referred to, as liquidation is likely to be the process which results in distribution most commonly encountered by unsecured creditors and the procedures under administration are very similar.

Admission, rejection of proof and appeal

A proof may be admitted for dividend purposes for the whole amount or in part (IR 1986, rule 4.82(1)). The cost of proving a debt is borne by the creditor (IR 1986, rule 4.78(1)). The liquidator's costs in admitting/rejecting claims are to be treated as a liquidation expense (IR 1986, rule 4.78(2)). After obtaining the proofs of debt from the creditors, the liquidator should allow inspection of proofs lodged with him to any creditor or contributory (IR 1986, rule 4.79).

On receipt of the proof, the liquidator may:

- accept the proof in total;
- accept only part of the proof; or
- reject the proof in total.

The liquidator should examine every proof and must consider the validity of the claim being made by the creditor (*Re Home and Colonial Insurance Co.* [1930] 1 Ch 102) and its true value (*Re Exchange Securities and Commodities Ltd* [1988] Ch 46). This exercise must still be carried out irrespective of whether the claim is based on a judgment or account stated (*Re Van Laun* [1907] 2 KB 23; *Re Menastar Finance Ltd* [2003] BCC 404; *Re Shruth Ltd* [2007] BCC 960).

If the liquidator rejects the proof in whole or in part, he is required to send a written statement outlining his reasons for doing so, as soon as reasonably practicable, to the creditor (IR 1986, rule 4.82(2)).

If the creditor who submitted the proof, a contributory or any other creditor is dissatisfied with the decision in respect of the proof, it may apply to court for the decision to be reviewed and must do so within 21 days of receiving the statement or on becoming aware of the liquidator's decision. However, the court will reject any application made by a contributory unless it can show that there is likely to be a surplus available after payment to creditors (i.e. it has an economic interest in the determination) (IR 1986, rule 4.83 (4A)).

This application to court is not, however, an appeal, and the court is free to consider evidence which was not before the liquidator and similarly may accept reasons that were not put into the written statement (*Re Kentwood Construction Ltd* [1960] 2 All ER 655). It should be remembered that the liquidator is fulfilling an administrative function and not a quasi-judicial one; the liquidator is not a lawyer (although he may obtain a legal opinion on the quantification of claims). Furthermore, the court may order the applicant to provide security for the liquidator's costs (*Re Pretoria Pietersburg Rly Co.* [1904] 2 Ch 359).

On an application being made, the court will fix a venue and notice will be sent to the liquidator and creditor. On receipt of the notice of application the liquidator will file at court the relevant proof, together with, if appropriate, a copy of the statement of rejection (IR 1986, rule 4.83(3), (4)).

A creditor's proof may at any time be withdrawn or varied by agreement between the creditor and the liquidator (IR 1986, rule 4.84). In practice, after assessment of the proof, the liquidator is likely to seek to agree/negotiate with the creditor the value of the claim.

The liquidator shall on receipt of notice of application, file at court the proof and the relevant statement (IR 1986, rule 4.83(4)). After the hearing, unless the proof is wholly disallowed it shall be returned by the court to the liquidator (IR 1986, rule 4.83(5)).

On the hearing of the application, the court may also expunge the proof, or reduce the amount by which the creditor has been admitted, if it considers the proof has been improperly admitted, or that it ought to be reduced (IR 1986, rule 4.85). The court will consider this on the balance of probabilities (the civil test) (*Re Global Legal Services Ltd* [2002] BCC 858). Where the proof is expunged or reduced, any dividend already obtained may be retained (*Re Browne* [1960] 1 WLR 692), and although there is no time limit on when a challenge can be made, delay on the part of the applicant means that the liquidator's decision is less likely to be overturned (*Re Allard Holdings Ltd* [2001] BCLC 404).

The Official Receiver is not personally liable for the costs incurred by the applicant in reviewing the decision and a liquidator (if not the Official Receiver) will not be liable unless the court specifically provides. If the liquidator has acted reasonably (albeit the court disagreed with the determination), it is highly unlikely that costs would be awarded against him (IR 1986, rule 4.83(6)). The liquidator's role in assessing a proof of debt is not that of a court of law; as office holder he must act fairly and not in a partisan manner unduly relying on the rule of law (the 'rule in *Ex parte James*'); but he must make a reasonable assessment on the information before him, expending a proportionate use of time and resource in reaching a determination.

Checklist

Completing a proof of debt

1. Is the debt legally due as at the date of liquidation?
2. If the debt is expressed in a foreign currency, convert the debt into sterling at the exchange rate prevailing at the date of liquidation, contract or statute.
3. Consider whether interest is payable – pursuant to what, and at what rate? If interest is payable, it can be claimed on the debt up to the date of liquidation.
4. Does the debt include VAT? If so, it may be possible to claim VAT bad debt relief.
5. Is the debt or part of the debt preferential?
6. Is the debt or part of the debt secured? Is the security to be relinquished? Valued?
7. Is there any reservation of title claimed over goods in the possession of the company in liquidation?
8. Is there any available evidence to substantiate the debt, e.g. contract, invoice, etc.?

13.2.2   Quantification of claim

Procedure

We have looked at when a creditor may claim that a debt is payable in circumstances which will entitle the creditor to commence an insolvency procedure (be it winding up, administration or bankruptcy); the rules applied in this assessment are very similar to when a creditor is able to prove for a debt. The debt must be *prima facie* provable in insolvency, whether present or future, certain or contingent, ascertained or sounding only in damages (IR 1986, rule 12.3(1)). Furthermore, the debt:

- must not be statute-barred (see *Re Joshua Shaw and Sons Ltd* (1989) 5 BCC 188; *Re General Rolling Stock Co, Joint Stock Discount Company's claim* [1872] 7 Ch App 646);
- may not be proved if in respect of any obligation arising under a confiscation order (Drug Trafficking Offences Act 1986, s.1; Criminal Justice Act 1988, s.71; Proceeds of Crime Act 2002, Parts 2, 3 or 4);
- cannot be claimed in respect of certain claims by virtue of the Financial Services Act 1986, s.61(3)(c) or the Banking Act 1987, s.49; and
- must be unsecured (see IR 1986, rules 4.88, 4.95 and the ability of a secured creditor to realise or surrender his security allowing the creditor to prove; see *Re PAL SC Realisations 2007 Ltd* [2011] BCC 93).

A liquidator may be called on to value a debt where, by reason of it being subject to any contingency, or where it is an unliquidated amount, it does not bear a certain value. The liquidator has an ability to place an estimate on the value of the debt and may revise any estimate previously made if he thinks fit, by reference to any change of circumstances, or where additional information been provided. He must then inform the creditor of his estimate and the revision (IR 1986, rule 4.86(1)).

In cases where there is a difficult assessment in respect of a contingent or unliquidated debt, the liquidator may seek the court's direction (IA 1986, s.168(3)). It should be remembered that while the liability must exist as at the date of commencement of the winding up, it does not need to be shown that the debt is payable at that date. In such circumstances the liquidator is called on to value the debt, and valuations are reckoned as at the date of liquidation (*Re Global Trader Europe Ltd* [2010] BCC 729).

In assessing the claim, unless the liquidator otherwise allows, any debts owed on bills of exchange, promissory notes, cheques or other negotiable securities cannot be admitted, unless the instrument of security itself, or a certified copy, is produced to the liquidator (IR 1986, rule 4.87).

Trade discounts which would otherwise be applicable (but for the liquidation) are also taken into account by the liquidator in assessing the claim, except where the discount is due in respect of an immediate or early cash settlement (IR 1986, rule 4.89).

One of the most important assessments to be made on the valuation of a claim by the liquidator is the value of any set-off which a creditor may possess. Where, before the company goes into liquidation, there have been mutual credits, debts or other dealings between the company and any other creditor of the company seeking to prove in the liquidation, account is taken of mutual dealings and set-off (IR 1986, rule 4.90). The relevant date for the assessment of the set-off is when the company goes into liquidation, i.e. when the resolution has been passed by the members to enter into voluntary liquidation or when an order for compulsory winding up has been made by the court (IA 1986, s.247(2)).

Mutual debts and creditors do not include those debts acquired by assignment after the date the creditor has notice of a meeting of creditors under s.98 or a petition to wind up. If, however, the debts are acquired after such dates but in accordance with an agreement entered into at an earlier date, they are considered to be mutual dealings capable of set-off (IR 1986, rule 4.90(2)).

13.2.3 Quantification of specific types of debt

Debts due to more than one creditor

The rule against double proof prevents more than one proof being admitted in respect of the same debt, e.g. if a debt is owed to a principal creditor and to a party with the benefit of a guarantee (see *Re Kaupthing Singer & Friedlander Ltd, Mills* v. *HSBC Trustee (CI) Ltd* [2012] BCC 1). However, it is not an abuse of process to submit a proof of debt if the debt has already been claimed in foreign proceedings (see *Rawlinson & Hunter Trustees SA* v. *Kaupthing Bank HF* [2011] 2 BCLC 682).

Debts due under a negotiable instrument

Unless permitted by the liquidator, a proof in respect of money owed on a bill of exchange, promissory note, cheque or other negotiable instrument or security will not be admitted unless the instrument or security or a certified copy is produced with it (IR 1986, rule 4.87).

Debts due to a secured creditor

If a secured creditor realises its security, it may prove for the unpaid balance (IR 1986, rule 4.88(1)) and may do so without bringing into account rules of equitable accounting (i.e. hotch-pot) (see *Cleaver* v. *Delta American Reinsurance Co.* [2001] 1 BCLC 482).

Interest arising on a secured debt after the date of the commencement of the winding up cannot be claimed by a secured creditor that realises its security post commencement, although in respect of such an element the secured creditor may submit a proof (*Re William Hall (Contractors) Ltd* [1967] 1 WLR 948). Profits that are obtained from unrealised security may, however, be set off against interest that arises post liquidation (*Re Savin* (1872) 7 Ch App 760).

In any other case, in order to claim a dividend the secured creditor is required either voluntarily to surrender its security to prove for the whole debt, as if unsecured, or to value the security and prove for the unsecured element of the claim alone (IR 1986, rule 4.88(2)). A creditor who has surrendered its security may share in the prescribed part available to unsecured creditors under IA 1986, s.176A (*Re PAL SC Realisations 2007 Ltd* [2011] BCC 93).

A secured creditor must therefore think very carefully about submitting a proof, and can be seen to have voluntarily surrendered the security by doing so and failing to mention the existence of the security (IR 1986, rule 4.96) (see *LCP Retail Ltd* v. *Richard Andrew Segal* [2007] BCC 584 for an example – a landlord who had levied distress and obtained a walking possession agreement was treated as having abandoned security for submitting a proof of debt without identifying this element of security). The secured creditor can seek relief from the effects of this provision only if the omission was inadvertent or an honest mistake

A secured creditor that has valued its security may at any time revalue the security with the agreement of the liquidator or leave of the court. However, if the creditor is the petitioning creditor and has valued its security for the purposes of the petition or has voted in respect of the unsecured balance, the security can only be revalued with leave of the court (IR 1986, rule 4.95).

It is open to the liquidator to redeem the security at the value put on it by the secured creditor after first serving 28 days' notice (IR 1986, rule 4.97). Within 21 days of the service of the notice, the secured creditor may revalue its security with leave of the court if IR 1986, rule 4.95(2) applies. Alternatively, it is open to the secured creditor to serve notice on the liquidator, giving the liquidator six months within which to determine whether to redeem the security at the value placed on the security by the creditor (IR 1986, rule 4.97(4)).

Where there has been no revaluation of the security approved by the court, the liquidator, if dissatisfied with the value put on the security, may require the property charged with the security to be put up for sale, and the liquidator may bid for the property at auction on behalf of the estate (or the creditor may bid on its behalf). Once the property has been sold, the amount realised replaces the valuation previously put on it (IR 1986, rules 4.98 and 4.99).

Debts subject to discount

Any trade or other discount which was available to the company must also be deducted by the liquidator in qualifying the claim, except discounts for immediate, early or cash settlement (IR 1986, rule 4.89).

Debts subject to a right of set-off

The purpose of the set-off provisions is to do justice between the parties. It would be wrong for a liquidator to be able to claim from a party the whole of the debt due to the insolvent company if that party were also a creditor of the company in liquidation and could at best only expect to receive a dividend. Instead, there is a mutual set-off where the parties are in the same position as against one another, i.e. creditor and creditor (see *Re ILG Travel Ltd* [1996] BCC 21; *Re Griffins Trading Co.* [1999] BPIR 256).

As a result, an account is taken of what is due from each party and to the other in respect of mutual dealings, and the sums due from one party are set off against sums due from the other (IR 1986, rule 4.90(3)). The dealings do not have to arise out of or be referable to the same transaction (*Secretary of State for Trade and Industry* v. *Frid* [2004] 2 AC 506); the obligations merely have to be incurred by the same parties in the same right of capacity (see *BCCI* v. *Al-Saud* [1997] BCC 63).

The process of set-off is mandatory and cannot be excluded by contract. It is applied more widely than other contractual or statutory rights of set-off (see *National Westminster Bank* v. *Halesowen Presswork and Assemblies Ltd* [1972] AC 785 and *Re Kaupthing Singer & Friedlander Ltd, Mills* v. *HSBC Trustee (CI) Ltd* [2012] BCC 1 which confirmed that the equitable accounting principle – known as the rule in *Cherry* v. *Boultbee* (1839) 4 My & C 442, that a person who has an entitlement with others to a share in a fund cannot receive payment until he has paid into the fund that which he owes – is disapplied). Conversely, the parties cannot confer a right of set-off in the event of insolvency where it would not otherwise have arisen (see *British Eagle International Airlines Ltd* v. *Compagnie Nationale Air France* [1975] 2 All ER 390; *Re BCCI* [1998] AC 214).

A sum cannot be set off if at the time the debt was incurred:

- the creditor had notice of the s.98 meeting (i.e. voluntary liquidation) or petition for the winding up (i.e. compulsory liquidation) (IR 1986, rule 4.90(2)(a));
- if liquidation was immediately preceded by administration and the creditor had notice of the application or notice of intention to appoint (IR 1986, rule 4.90(2)(b));
- during a period of administration which preceded the liquidation (IR 1986, rule 4.90(2)(c)); or
- if the debt was acquired by assignment or agreement and that assignment or agreement was entered into with notice of the liquidation/administration as set out above (IR 1986, rule 4.90(2)(d); see *Re Parkside International Ltd* [2009] BPIR 549).

A sum is regarded as being 'due' to the company if:

- it is payable at present or in the future;
- the obligation by virtue of which it is payable is certain or contingent; or
- its amount is fixed or liquidated, or is capable of being ascertained by fixed rules or as a matter of opinion (see IR 1986, rule 4.90(4)).

Sums that may therefore be owed to, or from, the company and may either arise on a contingent basis or be payable in the future are brought into account. As a consequence, where a balance is due to a creditor with a future or contingent claim, the creditor will be able to participate in the dividend ahead of the due date/liability arising, the rules operating to accelerate payment. In respect of liabilities arising which are contingent or arising in the future, the liquidator must estimate their value (IR 1986, rule 4.90(5) for contingent liabilities, and see below for future liabilities).

However, after set-off, if a balance is due from the debtor to the insolvent company the sum is only payable after the contractual date for payment or on the contingency arising (IR 1986, rule 4.90(8); see *Revenue and Customs Commissioners* v. *Millichap* [2011] BPIR 145).

However, the area of set-off in respect of future and contingent debt is still fraught with uncertainty and is an area of interplay between a simple administrative act required to give effect to the ease of realisation and distribution of assets and a legal and/or actuarial assessment requiring expert advice. In practice, the office holder may seek to reach a compromise with the creditor and seek approval of a creditors' committee to any proposed action, but until more cases reach court we are still left with questions such as: What happens if the contingency never arises? What happens if the estimate put on the debt by the liquidator differs on the contingency arising? Even if it can be corrected by a revised subsequent dividend or final dividend, it is clear that the creditor may have been disadvantaged by the artificial acceleration of the debt.

Debts in a foreign currency

If the debt has been incurred in a foreign currency, the creditor should convert the debt into sterling at the official exchange rate on the date the company went into liquidation (IR 1986, rule 4.91(1)). The official exchange rate is the middle exchange rate on the London Foreign Exchange Market on close of business as published on the date in question (IR 1986, rule 4.91(2)).

Debts due periodically

In the case of rent or other payments of a periodical nature, a creditor may prove for any amount due and unpaid up to the date the company entered into liquidation (IR 1986, rule 4.92(1)).

Debts bearing interest

Where a debt proved in the liquidation bears interest, the interest is provable as part of the debt up to the date that the company went into liquidation (IR 1986, rule 4.93).

A debt bears interest if a written instrument so provides or if a demand had been made and the notice provided that interest would be payable from the date of demand to payment. The rate of interest is that payable under the Judgments Act 1832, currently 8 per cent (Judgment Debts (Rate of Interest) Order, SI 1993/564). If the debt carries a higher rate of interest by reason of contractual agreement, that higher rate is payable.

Interest cannot be claimed if it only becomes due after the date of the winding up (*Re Amalgamated Investment and Property Co. Ltd* [1985] Ch 349), but it should be remembered that if there are sufficient monies available to discharge all creditor claims, statutory interest due to creditors on their debt post liquidation will be payable.

Debts payable in the future

A creditor may also claim in respect of future payments which are not due as at the date of liquidation, subject to adjustment of the dividend payment (IR 1986, rule 4.94).

If the debt has not fallen due as at the date of liquidation, the creditor will still be entitled to a dividend and, for the purpose of calculating the eventual dividend payment (and for no other purpose), the amount of a creditor's admitted proof will be reduced by a percentage calculated (as set out in IR 1986, rule 11.13, amended by the Insolvency (Amendment) Rules 2005 with effect from 1 April 2005) as follows:

$$X/1.05n$$

where:

$X =$ the value of the admitted proof
$n =$ the period beginning with the relevant date (see IR 1986 11.13(3)) and ending with the date on which the payment of the creditor's debt would otherwise be due expressed in years and months in a decimalised form.

Prior to 1 April 2005, the discount for accelerated receipt was at a rate of 5 per cent per annum on the full amount, which meant that a debt due in 20 years or more was valued at nil for dividend purposes. This rule was criticised in *Re Park Air Services Ltd* [2000] 2 AC 172, a case concerning a liability under a long leasehold, as being 'seriously defective'. The amended rule means that the future debt will always have a value (e.g. a debt due in 20 years will be discounted by 62.3 per cent rather than 100 per cent).

Debts subject to a contingency

As set out above, the liquidator will assess the value of the claim and in doing so will take into account the likelihood of the contingency arising, etc. (IR 1986, rule 4.86).

Where after operation of set-off an amount is found to be due to the company arising from a contingent debt, the amount will become payable by the debtor to the company in liquidation if the debt becomes due and payable, i.e. the contingent event arises (IR 1986, rule 4.90(8)).

13.2.4 Distribution of assets

In the words of Templeman LJ: 'Unsecured creditors rank after preferential creditors, mortgagees and the holders of floating charges and they receive a raw deal' (*Borden (UK) Ltd* v. *Scottish Timber Products Ltd* [1981] Ch 25 at 42F).

After realising available assets and before making a distribution, the insolvency office holder must consider the effect of any security held over the company, any creditors holding a special position and, importantly, the costs and expenses of the insolvency process.

This process often involves a degree of negotiation and co-operation between the secured creditors and a subsequently appointed liquidator, with the secured creditors allowing the liquidator to conduct the sale of the assets subject to the security. By dealing with all the assets of the company, the liquidator may be able to realise more and/or the costs of sale are subject to enhanced economies of scale. Clearly, however, the secured creditor's consent to the release of its security will remain dependent on the liquidator obtaining a satisfactory offer. In such circumstances, the liquidator is able to recover costs and expenses incurred in preserving and realising the secured assets in priority to any floating charge holder's claim.

However, the liquidator is not entitled to recover general liquidation costs and expenses from the funds obtained in realising the asset subject to the fixed charge. On a practical note, this may mean that liquidators will need to agree their fees and the course of conduct with the charge holder prior to appointment. Very careful regard may need to be had pre-realisation as to what assets are held, which fall into the fixed charge and which into the floating charge. The strategy adopted will then depend on the likely realisations, and is it probable that the secured creditor will be paid in full.

In regard to the costs and expense of liquidation, IA 1986, s.176ZA provides that these costs will be drawn from the monies otherwise distributable to the unsecured creditors. Where, however, there are insufficient realisations available to meet the costs of the liquidation, the costs may be drawn from floating charge realisations. Where costs are to be drawn from floating charge realisations (not including assets set aside for the prescribed part: IA 1986, s.176A), regard must be had to the rules which restrict the liquidator's ability to recover costs from such funds (IR 1986, rules 4.218A–4.218E, see below).

Checklist

Priority of distribution in liquidation – before introduction of IA 1986, s.176ZA reform (6 April 2008)

1. Assets subject to a floating charge:

    - The costs of preserving and realising the assets.
    - The receiver's remuneration and proper costs and expenses of the receivership;
    - Preferential debts.
    - If security created after 15 September 2003 – prescribed part, IA 1986, s.176A.
    - Principal and interest secured by the floating charge.
    - The company (i.e. return to the liquidator in an insolvent liquidator).

2. The company's free assets:

- The costs of preserving and realising the assets.
- The liquidator's remuneration and proper costs and expenses of winding up (see IR 1986, rule 5.218 for the order of priority of expenses).
- Preferential debts.
- The charge holder to the extent that preferential debts have been paid out of the assets subject to the floating charge.
- Unsecured creditors.
- Post-insolvency interest on debts.
- Deferred debts.
- The balance, if any, to the contributors.

Priority of distribution in liquidation – after IA 1986, s.176ZA reform

- The costs of preserving and realising fixed charged assets.
- The principal and interest secured by the fixed charge.
- The liquidator's remuneration and proper costs and expenses of winding up preferential debts.
- If security created after 15 September 2003 – prescribed part, IA 1986, s.176A.
- Principal and interest secured by the floating charge.
- The floating charge holder to the extent that preferential debts have been paid out of the assets subject to the floating charge.
- Unsecured creditors.
- Post-insolvency interest on debts.
- Deferred debts.
- The balance, if any, to the contributors.

Liquidation costs and expenses

As we have seen, in general a liquidator cannot overreach the interests of a secured creditor holding fixed charge security. The liquidator deals only with unencumbered assets unless duly authorised. In this regard, the House of Lords determination in the case of *Re Leyland Daf Ltd, Buchler* v. *Talbot* [2004] BCC 214 caused great difficulty for liquidators and overturned over 20 years of accepted practice. In this case it was held the company's assets from which liquidation costs and expenses could be deducted did not included assets subject to a floating charge; liquidation costs and expenses thus ranked behind the claims of the floating charge holder. As modern corporate finance documentation ensures that there are few, if any, unencumbered assets and/or higher gearing, the secured debt was close to the value of the company's assets, and following the judgment the onus was placed on the liquidator to agree fees with the secured creditor where there was an anticipated shortfall. The other effect of the judgment was that the possibility of pursuing office holder-type litigation (e.g. wrongful trading actions) for the benefit of the creditors as a whole was much reduced.

As a result of the effect of *Leyland Daf*, legislative reform introduced a new provision (IA 1986, s.176ZA), which applies to any liquidation commenced after 6 April 2008. The reform swung the balance of the conflict towards the liquidator (acting in the interests of the creditors as a whole) and away from creditors, with a specific interest in the floating charge assets, as (subject to IR 1986, rules 4.218A–4.218E) the liquidator was able to take not only the cost of realising a particular secured asset, but also general costs and expenses associated with the liquidation for the realisation of secured assets.

However, this ability is tempered by the fact that where it is proposed that a company goes into voluntary liquidation, notice must first be served on a qualifying floating charge holder (IA 1986, s.84(2A)). The charge holder is then given at least five business days to decide if it wishes to realise its security by appointing an administrator. In practice, the costs effect will be much the same, with the administrator's costs drawn from the floating charge realisations; however, the charge holder may feel more in control of the process by 'appointing their own man'.

Rules 4.218A–4.218E

In addition, specific rules restricting the liquidator's ability to recover costs from floating charge realisations came into effect at the same time as the new provision. In particular, the rules deal with expenses incurred by the liquidator in pursuing certain categories of legal proceeding by litigation, arbitration or other form of alternative dispute resolution which may not be recovered from the floating charge realisations without approval of the parties having a claim over such funds (i.e. floating charge holders, preferential creditors) or, failing such approval, sanction of the court.

The legal proceedings to which these rules apply are those which can be brought by the office holder, but only if the proceeds are incapable of being caught by a floating charge (*Re Oasis Merchandising Ltd* [1997] BCC 282), namely IA 1986, ss.212, 213, 214, 238, 239, 244 and 423.

Approval or authorisation is required if the claim of the preferential or floating charge creditor will not be met in full. Requests for approval from such creditors may be made in Form 4.74 or otherwise and must include a statement outlining the nature of the legal proceedings; where the power to bring proceedings is subject to sanction, a statement that the sanction has been obtained or undertaking that sanction will be sought; the amount of litigation expense sought; and notice that a reply must be made within 28 days (IR 1986, rule 4.218C(1)). The liquidator may have regard to issues of confidentiality and seek to bind the creditors in respect of the same.

If the actual or anticipated litigation expenses exceed £5,000, authorisation is required (IR 1986, rule 4.218A(1)(d)(ii)). Failure to obtain authorisation will result in a loss of the priority afforded by IA 1986, s.176 ZA.

In the absence of approval, in urgent cases or where the specified creditor may be a defendant to legal proceedings (e.g. a secured creditor where the liquidator believes that the granting of security was a preferential transaction), the liquidator may seek the court's approval (IR 1986, rule 4.218E).

Distribution to unsecured creditors

On the assumption that the liquidator has sufficient available funds to make a distribution to unsecured creditors, he must, subject to the retention of necessary expenses of the winding up, declare and distribute dividends to creditors that have proved for their debts (IR 1986, rule 4.180(1)).

The liquidator must give notice of the intended distribution to all creditors, stating how the dividend is proposed to be distributed and giving sufficient particulars of the company, its assets and its affairs to enable the creditors to understand the calculation of the dividend (IR 1986, rule 4.180(3)).

Unless the liquidator has already invited the creditors to prove their debts by public advertisement, before declaring a dividend the liquidator must publicly advertise (by notice in the *Gazette* and in such other manner as he thinks fit: IR 1986, rule 11.2 (1A)) his intention to pay a dividend, giving potential creditors a date which allows not less than 21 days in which to lodge a proof. The dividend should then be paid within two months of that date, which should also be stated in the advertisement (IR 1986, rule 11.2).

Unsecured debts rank equally among themselves and abate in equal proportions between themselves (IA 1986, s.107 (voluntary liquidations), IR 1986, rule 4.181(1) (compulsory liquidations): the *pari passu* principle). It is not possible for parties to contract out of this effect in the event of insolvency (*British Eagle International Airlines* v. *Compagnie Nationale Air France* [1975] 1 WLR 758; see, however, the effect of certain pre-insolvency agreements in *Mistral Finance Ltd* [2001] BCC 27); this does not affect debt subordination agreements (*Re Maxwell Communications Corporation Ltd* [1993] 1 WLR 1402).

The liquidator should also take account of potential claims not yet brought or determined and claims that remain disputed, if it appears by reason of distance that the creditor has now had insufficient time to establish its proof (IR 1986, rule 4.182(1)(a)) and make necessary provision.

A creditor (that has failed to prove prior to the distribution) cannot disturb the distribution once it is made, but is entitled to payment from any further distribution (IR 1986, rule 4.182(2)). However, this does not prevent a creditor seeking direction of the court if the liquidator has failed to discharge his duties, perhaps negligently failing to notify creditors (IR 1986, rule 4.182(3)). In such cases, the liquidator could be made personally liable to pay the dividend (*James Smith & Sons (Norwood) Ltd* v. *Goodman* [1936] Ch 216). The extent of the liquidator's duties and obligations as regards the payment of a dividend are, however, limited, as seen in the case of *Lomax Leisure Ltd* [2008] BCC 686. In this case, a creditor successfully appealed against the rejection of his claim, although the notice of the application was received after the liquidator had declared a final dividend and sent out cheques to the other creditors. Recognising the effect of the now substantiated claim, the liquidator stopped the cheques. It was held that the creditors who had received the cheques had no right to enforce payment as no consideration was given from the creditor to the liquidator and, secondly, a creditor's ability to recover a dividend was governed by the ability to seek an order under IR 1986, rule 4.182(3), which, despite the fact it can lead to a payment out of the liquidator's own money, still means it is not possible to sue a liquidator for payment of a dividend.

Any property of a peculiar nature which cannot be readily or advantageously sold may be distributed to the creditors (IR 1986, rule 4.183) with permission of the liquidation committee.

When the liquidator has reasonably concluded that he has realised all of the assets of the company or obtained the most value he is reasonably likely to achieve for them within a reasonable time, he should give notice of a final dividend, or notice that no dividend or further dividend will be declared (IR 1986, rule 4.186).

The liquidator will, within five business days from the last date for proving, deal with the proofs in so far as they have not yet been dealt with, admitting or rejecting in whole or part. The liquidator is not obliged to deal with proofs submitted late, but may do so if he thinks fit (IR 1986, rule 11.3; see *Painter* v. *Hutchinson* [2008] BPIR 170).

The notice of final dividend should contain details of the company's assets and affairs and specify a final date for any claims to be submitted (IR 1986, rule 4.186(2)). If there is a possibility of future claimants arising (perhaps contingent creditors that have not proved in the liquidation), the liquidator can apply to the court for directions regarding the setting up of a contingency fund to avoid keeping the liquidation open, perhaps indefinitely (*Tombs* v. *Moulinex* [2004] 2 BCLC 397).

The court may, on the application of any person, postpone the date specified in the notice (IR 1986, rule 4.186(4)).

13.2.5 'Prescribed part': IA 1986, s.176A

During the consultation period leading to the Enterprise Act 2002 reforms, one of the major criticisms of the insolvency regime was that the poor returns often provided to unsecured creditors resulted in a lack of creditor interest and involvement in the insolvency process. The government's response was to introduce the ring-fenced sum provision.

The provision is itself a *quid pro quo* for the abolition of Crown preference (and the floating charge holders' subsequent gain), and leads to the ring-fencing from floating charge realisations of a 'prescribed part' for the benefit of a company's unsecured creditors if the company has gone into liquidation, administration, provisional liquidation or receivership.

The legislation provides that the liquidator, administrator or receiver must make a prescribed part of the company's net property available for the satisfaction of unsecured debts and not distribute that part to the proprietor of the floating charge except in so far as it exceeds the amount required in satisfaction of unsecured debts (IA 1986, s.176A(2)).

The 'prescribed part' is a percentage of the company's net property, set on a sliding scale of 50 per cent of the first £10,000 and 20 per cent thereafter up to a maximum prescribed part of £600,000 (Insolvency Act 1986 (Prescribed Part) Order 2003, SI 2003/2097).

Where the company's net property does not exceed £10,000 and the liquidator, administrator or receiver thinks that the cost of making the distribution would be disproportionate to the benefits, the office holder can elect not to make a prescribed part available to the unsecured creditors. As can be seen in many of the Enterprise Act 2002 reforms, the obligation is on the office holder to determine whether it is appropriate to take this course of action. The word 'thinks' produces a subjective element which is unlikely to be challenged by the court unless the office holder has taken a course which no reasonable office holder would have taken.

Where the net property exceeds £10,000 but the liquidator, administrator or receiver considers that the cost of making a distribution would be disproportionate, e.g. if there are many hundreds of creditors, a court order can be sought to disapply this provision (see *Re Hydroserve Ltd* [2008] BCC 175, *Re Courts plc* [2008] BCC 917 and *Re International Sections Ltd* [2009] BCC 574 for examples of applications for such leave). Generally, the courts have been reluctant to disallow the provision, even if the cost of effecting the distribution to some smaller creditors exceeds the value of the dividend or the dividend itself is minimal. The provision will be disapplied as an exception, not as a rule.

'Net property' is defined as the amount of property available after discharge of:

- sums secured pursuant to a fixed charge;
- cost of realising the company's assets; and
- preferential claims (IA 1986, s.176A(6)).

Importantly, this provision only applies to floating charges created after 15 September 2003 (IA 1986, s.176A(10)).

It is also settled law that a secured creditor is not entitled to participate in the distribution available to the unsecured creditors by way of the prescribed part in respect of any unsecured surplus (*Re Permacell Finesse Ltd* [2008] BCC 208 and *Airbase Services (UK) Ltd* [2008] BCC 213). As we have seen, however, it is open to a secured creditor to abandon its security so to be treated as an unsecured creditor and participate in the prescribed part distribution (*Re PAL SC Realisations 2007 Ltd* [2011] BCC 93).

In practice, the introduction of the ring-fenced sum provision has not as yet encouraged unsecured creditors to become more involved in the insolvency process. Secured creditors seek very wide fixed charges over the company's assets, meaning that often very little falls into the definition of floating charge. However, one area of significant judicial development in recent years has been the loss of the fixed charge over book debts in standard corporate banking arrangements (*Re Spectrum Plus Ltd* [2005] UKHL 41). This should have meant that more funds fall under the floating charge, meaning a wider application of the prescribed part provisions.

13.3 CLAIMS ON PROPERTY IN POSSESSION OF THE CORPORATE DEBTOR

Checklist

Can the creditor improve his position by:

- completing execution of a judgment debt prior to the commencement of the liquidation?
- claiming security for the debt?
- claiming that goods/assets in the debtor's possession are held on trust for the benefit of the creditors?
- claiming retention of title?
- claiming additional rights exercisable irrespective of liquidation, etc., e.g. landlords, employees, etc.?

13.3.1 Execution attachments

Special rules apply where creditors have commenced, but failed to complete, enforcement proceedings prior to the commencement of the insolvency procedure. As a general rule, if a creditor has completed an enforcement process prior to the commencement of the insolvency proceedings, it is entitled to retain the proceeds. As previously discussed, it is therefore advisable for creditors to explore the possibilities of enforcing their claims by other means, before the commencement of any insolvency procedure.

Where a creditor has issued a warrant of execution against the company's goods or land or has attached any debt due to it and the company is subsequently wound up, the creditor is not entitled to any benefit of the execution or attachment against the liquidator unless the execution or attachment had been completed before commencement of the winding up (IA 1986, s.183(1)).

The winding up is deemed to commence in the case of a voluntary winding up when the creditor has notice of the meeting at which the resolution to wind up is to be proposed (IA 1986, s.183(2)(a)), meaning, however, the date of notice rather than the date of actual receipt of notice (*Trow* v. *Ind Coope (West Midlands) Ltd* [1967] 2 QB 899).

Any attachment, sequestration, distress or execution put in force against the estate or the effects of the company after the commencement of the winding up is void (IA 1986, s.128). In the case of compulsory liquidation, the commencement date is the date of the presentation of the petition (IA 1986, s.129(2)).

In applying this rule, however, a number of factors must be borne in mind:

(a) if the creditor has notice of a meeting at which the resolution for winding up has been called, it is not entitled to retain the benefit of any execution or attachment uncompleted from the date on which it received notice (IA 1986, s.183(2)(a));

(b)   a person who purchases in good faith under a sale by a High Court enforcement officer any goods of the company on which execution has been levied in all cases acquires good title to it against the liquidator (IA 1986, s.183(2)(b));

(c)   an execution against goods is completed by seizure and sale (seizure alone is insufficient: *Re Standard Manufacturing Co.* [1891] 1 Ch 627), or by the making of a charging order absolute under the Charging Orders Act 1979, s.1 (*Roberts Petroleum Ltd* v. *Bernard Kenny Ltd* [1983] 2 AC 192);

(d)   an attachment of debt is completed by the receipt of the debt and execution against land is completed by the seizure, by appointment of the receiver, or by the making of a charging order; money received prior to commencement is unaffected (*Re Caribbean Products (Yam Importers) Ltd* [1966] Ch 331);

(e)   this rule has no application in respect of distress levied against goods by a landlord or by HMRC (see *Re Bellaglade* [1977] 1 All ER 319 and *Re Modern Jet Support Centre Ltd* [2005] 1 WLR 3880) (see **13.4.2** for further details on landlords' rights of action);

(f)   the right of the liquidator to claim any sum obtained by the creditor's rights on execution may nevertheless be set aside by the court in the exercise of its discretion. However, exceptional circumstances must be shown by the creditor for a court otherwise to interfere with the general principle of *pari passu* (see *Re Caribbean Products (Yam Importers) Ltd* [1966] Ch 331);

(g)   where goods are taken in execution and before their sale or completion of the execution (by receipt or recovery of the full amount of the levy), notice is served on the High Court enforcement officer (formerly known as sheriff) that a resolution for winding up has been passed, or an order for compulsory winding up made. The High Court enforcement officer must deliver up the goods or money seized. However, the costs of execution are a first charge on the goods or money and the liquidator must sell the goods sufficiently to discharge such charge (IA 1986, s.184(2)); and

(h)   on any execution in respect of a judgment debt in excess of £500 and where goods of the company are sold or monies paid by the debtor in order to avoid a sale, the High Court enforcement officer will deduct the cost of the execution from the proceeds of sale and retain the balance for 14 days. If within that time notice is served and a winding-up petition is presented, or a meeting is called for a voluntary winding up and an order is thereafter made, or resolution passed, the High Court enforcement officer must pay the balance to the liquidator. If no notice is served within the 14-day period, the creditor is entitled to the balance.

13.3.2 Trust claims

Claims that can be brought by third parties over assets in the possession of the bankrupt, such as trust claims, were considered in **Chapter 12**. Trust claims have similar application in cases of corporate insolvency, and property may be excluded from the company's assets by virtue of an express, implied, constructive or resulting trust in favour of a third party (see **12.3.2** for further details).

The party seeking to establish the existence of a trust relationship must establish that there was an intention to create a trust, certainty of trust property and certainty as to the beneficiary of the trust (*Re Kayford Ltd* [1975] 1 All ER 604 setting out the 'three certainties' and *Multi Guarantee Co. Ltd* [1987] BCLC 257). The fact that monies may have been held by a company in a separate account and used only for a particular purpose may be evidence of the existence of a trust, but it is not conclusive and each case will rest on its own facts (*Carreras Rothmans Ltd* v. *Freeman Matthews Trease Ltd* [1985] Ch 207).

Where an insolvency practitioner is dealing with property and a third party is claiming an equitable interest (i.e. the company was holding the asset on trust for the party's benefit), the court may allow costs incurred in connection with the administration of that property to be recovered by the office holder (see *Re Berkeley Applegate (Investments Consultants) Ltd* [1989] 1 Ch 32). Such jurisdiction will be sparingly exercised (*Green* v. *Bramston* [2010] EWHC 3106 (Ch)).

13.3.3 Retention of title

A retention or reservation of title claim, sometimes referred to as a *Romalpa* clause (a name derived from the leading case of *Aluminium Industrie Vaassen BV* v. *Romalpa Aluminium Ltd* [1976] 2 All ER 552), is commonly used by suppliers to protect themselves in the event of a customer's non-payment. Title to goods will generally pass on the handing over of possession, in consideration of which the buyer is likely to owe a debt to the seller. A retention of title claim derives from contractual agreement between seller and buyer which departs from this normal course of events, and where the seller retains equitable (beneficial) title to identifiable assets in the possession of the buyer (such contractual provision being permitted by virtue of the Sale of Goods Act 1979, ss.17(1), 19(1)). The effect of the clause is that the buyer cannot deal with or dispose of the goods supplied (save as permitted by the supplier) until they are paid for, or until other conditions are first met. This has important consequences if and when the buyer goes into an insolvency process.

The tension that arises in an insolvency from the use of such clauses is that such contrary equitable ownership to the goods is not easily identifiable (nor does it require registration), so that other creditors dealing with the company are likely to extend credit to the company in ignorance of other creditors' (in this case suppliers) prior claims. In addition, in liquidation the realisation of available assets and in administration the continued ability to trade the business, is made significantly more difficult if stock held by the insolvent business is subject to claims from 'ransom' creditors (i.e. they will not allow it to be disposed of unless their debt is paid in full).

It should be noted that where an administrator is faced with a retention of title agreement, he has the ability to apply to court to dispose of the goods as if the rights of ownership were vested in the company (IA 1986, Sched.B1, para.72 regarding goods subject to a hire purchase agreement and IA 1986, Sched.B1, para.111(1) if the definition of hire purchase agreement is said to include a retention of title agreement). The use of such provision is limited to cases where the court is persuaded that the purpose of the administration will be furthered by the disposal and where the administrator accounts to the supplier for the net proceeds and any additional money so to produce a return for the supplier in line with market value. In practice, rather than rely on this statutory provision an administrator is more likely to sell the company's stock (which may or may not be subject to a retention of title) without title, warranty or representation and in the sale and purchase agreement provide that the buyer of the stock deals with retention of title claimants/hands back the goods/indemnifies the administrator against claims. In instances where the administrator is made aware of the supplier's claim prior to disposal, he may be more cautious and seek to reach an amicable solution with the supplier, i.e. account to the supplier for an agreed sum from the total sales proceeds. In this way the supplier avoids the need to take back the goods where the value may be much diminished by being 'second hand' and potentially obtains a better return,

In cases where such agreement cannot be reached, a significant body of case law has grown up in which the courts have sought to balance the competing interests of the supplier against the interests of creditors as a whole.

Types of retention of title clauses

Retention of title clauses are either:

(a) *simple*: claiming title only over the goods supplied, unpaid for and still in the possession of the buyer; or
(b) *extended*: including claims that cover all monies, proceeds of sale or tracing into finished products.

The retention of title depends not only on the language and form of the contractual term, but also on the substance of the transaction. Each case depends on its own facts. The intention of the parties is a guide, although the real question in each case is the true nature of the substantive rights of the parties. If the rights exercised over the assets by the buyer are inconsistent with retention by the seller, there will be no retention of title (see *Welsh Development Agency* v. *Export Finance Co.* [1992] BCC 270).

As a general rule, the simpler the clause, the more likely it is to succeed. The classic example of a successful retention of title is a milk bottle marked with the words 'This bottle remains the property of the dairy'. Clauses which reserve title of goods until payment of all liabilities, so-called 'all monies' or 'rolling account clauses', have been approved (see *Specialist Plant Services Ltd* v. *Braithwaite Ltd* (1987) 3 BCC 119), but clauses which attempt to catch proceeds of sale will generally fail, in that they will amount to a registerable charge and are likely to be void for want of registration (CA 2006, ss.860(1), 861(5), 870(1) and 874(1)).

A retention of title clause remains valid despite any implied or express right of the buyer to sell to third parties, or an ability of the seller to repossess the assets only in specific circumstances.

Identification of goods supplied

The problem for a supplier relying on a 'simple' retention of title claim is that it is not always easy to identify whether the particular goods held by the buyer have been paid for or not. While the buyer may still owe money to the seller, it may not be clearly identifiable whether the goods which remain in his possession are those which remain unpaid for, or whether the seller has disposed of unpaid goods but retained those he has paid for (see e.g. *Re London Wine Company (Shippers)* [1986] PCC 121 and *Re Goldcorp Exchange Ltd* [1994] 2 All ER 806, where identity could not be established; and contrast these cases with, e.g. *Re Stapylton Fletcher Ltd; Re Ellis, Sun & Vidler Ltd* [1995] 1 All ER 192 and *Re Kayford Ltd* [1975] 1 WLR 279, where separate storage and identification could be evidenced).

The problem of identification may be overcome if the parties operated a running account; otherwise, evidence will need to be adduced to discover in what order the goods received by the buyer were used and disposed of (see the rule in *Clayton's Case; Devaynes* v. *Noble* (1816) 1 Mer 572, a banking authority concerning the payment of monies into a current account which established the principle of 'first in, first out').

To overcome the simple retention of title problem of storage and identity, it is possible to create an all monies floating retention (see *Armour* v. *Thyssen Edelstahl-werke AG* [1990] 3 All ER 481, an authority for establishing the validity of an all monies clause).

Repossession of the goods supplied

A party claiming retention of title will, on notice of the liquidation, assert the claim and demand delivery up or seek consent to enter the company property to take back the goods subject to the retention. An insolvency office holder who has notice of such claim but deals with the assets in contravention of the supplier's rights of ownership will potentially be personally liable for damages arising from the tort of conversion.

A liquidator may have practical difficulty in refusing or barring access to premises where goods are stored (even where the supplier has not reserved an express right of re-entry in its agreement with the insolvent buyer). Furthermore, personal liability may be incurred in the case of unreasonable refusal (see *6 Arlington Street Investments* v. *NJ Benson* (unreported, 1979)).

Loss of identity: segregation

A retention of title claim will be defeated if the buyer has been given power to deal with or change the identity of the goods (see *Re Peachdart* [1984] Ch 131, where leather was made into leather products, and *Chaigley Farms Ltd* v. *Crawford Kaye & Grayshire Ltd* [1996] BCC 957, where livestock was slaughtered; in both cases the goods had changed identity).

The buyer must therefore be under a duty to segregate and keep the products distinct, which creates some form of fiduciary relationship, one which is more than merely that of buyer and seller. In *Re Andrabell Ltd* [1984] 3 All ER 407, the court held that as there was no obligation on the buyer to store the goods supplied (in this case travel bags) separately from other stock and no obligation to keep the proceeds of sale separate from general company funds, there was no such fiduciary relationship.

Loss of identity: incorporation

The seller of goods may lose retention of title where the goods have been incorporated into other goods or have been made into a new object altogether (see *Borden (UK)* v. *Scottish Timber Products Ltd* [1981] Ch 25, where title to resin became meaningless once it had become amalgamated into chipboard, i.e. its identity could not be traced into the new product; *Chaigley Farms Ltd* v. *Crawford Kaye & Grayshire Ltd* [1996] BCC 957, where title to animals was lost upon slaughter, because the meat became a new object; *Re Peachdart* [1984] Ch 131, leather losing identity on manufacture into leather goods).

Where a product has been wrongly mixed with goods belonging to another and the goods are of substantially the same nature and quality (e.g. oil) and they cannot be separated for practical purposes, the mixture is held in common for both parties and the innocent party is entitled to receive from the mixture a quantity equal to the value of its goods (see *Indian Oil Corp. Ltd* v. *Greenstone Shipping* [1998] QB 345; Sale of Goods (Amendment) Act 1995). If, however, separation of the mixed goods involves damage, the seller's ownership may be lost (see *Appleby* v. *Myers* (1866–67) LR 2 CP 651); in contrast, where skill and labour have been expended on materials and become a major component of their value, the courts tend to find that title vests in the maker (see *Re Peachdart* [1984] Ch 131). In general, where materials have become incorporated into real property so as to become part of that real property, title will pass by operation of law. However, much will rest on the nature of the incorporation and how easy it is to reverse the process of incorporation (see *Hendy Lennox (Industrial Engines) Ltd* v. *Grahame Puttick Ltd* [1984] 1 WLR 485).

Loss of title on sale to a third party

The Sale of Goods Act 1979, s.25, provides that a purchaser in good faith without notice of lien or other rights of the original seller in respect of the goods obtains good title. A seller may, however, be entitled to claim retention of title if the sale and subsale are both subject to a retention of title (see *W Hanson* v. *Rapid Civil Engineering* (1987) 38 BLR 106; *Re Highway Foods International Ltd* [1995] 1 BCLC 209; and *ICI New Zealand* v. *Agnew* [1998] 2 NZLR 129).

The seller may also be able to claim retention of title if it can be proved that the sub-buyer was aware of the retention of title. The sub-buyer cannot establish ownership since it has not received the goods in good faith and without notice of the original seller's ownership (see *Re Interview Ltd* [1975] IR 382 (Irish case) and *Feuer Leather Corporation* v. *Johnstone & Sons* [1981] Com. LR 251). The equitable doctrine of constructive notice cannot be imported into a commercial transaction; the court is concerned with actual and not constructive notice. The burden of proving good faith and the absence of notice rests on the person receiving the goods. There is no general duty on the buyer of goods in ordinary commercial transactions to make enquiries as to the right of the seller to dispose of the goods. However, the test to be applied is an objective one, that is to say what, in the circumstances, the buyer, as a reasonable man, should have known (*Heap* v. *Motorists' Advisory Agency Ltd* [1923] 1 KB 577; *Forsythe International (UK) Ltd* v. *Silver Shipping Co. Ltd* [1994] 1 All ER 851).

The ability of the buyer to resell goods subject to a retention was also seen as fatal to the validity of a retention clause in *Re Mark One (in Administration)* [2010] EWHC B17 1936 (Mercantile). In this case, the supplier had stayed silent, allowing the company in administration to sell the goods and not seeking return of the goods, instead seeking to rely on a claim for the sales proceeds of the goods sold by the administrator. The failure of the supplier in this case is a reminder that where a right exists it must be exercised and the administrator put on notice of the consequences of dealing in a manner averse to ownership.

Clauses that extend to proceeds of sale

To overcome the problem that arises where the buyer has dealt, or perhaps needs to deal, with the goods supplied in the ordinary course of business, in some agreements the buyer is permitted to resell the goods if it accounts to the seller for the proceeds. In *E Pfeiffer* v. *Arbuthnot Factors Ltd* (1987) 3 BCC 608, it was held that while the seller had effectively retained title to wine supplied to the buyer, where it had been sold on to a sub-buyer, the supplier's claim over the proceeds of sale was defeated on the basis that the provisions in the retention of title clause were inconsistent with a fiduciary duty and the true relationship was debtor/creditor, with an interest by way of security in respect of the debts created by subsale. It was therefore a registerable charge void for want of registration.

Indeed, despite *Aluminium Industrie Vaassen BV* v. *Romalpa Aluminium Ltd* [1976] 2 All ER 552 opening up the possibility for a retention of title clause to extend to cover proceeds of sale, it now appears that the courts have been able to distinguish *Romalpa* virtually out of existence.

Invariably, claims over proceeds will be struck out as a charge on book debts void for want of registration, with the court taking a purposive view as to what is intended by the clause (see *Re Bond Worth Ltd* [1980] Ch 228, in which it was held that as the purpose of the clause was to provide the seller with security for payment of funds, it must be a charge).

An effective claim over proceeds is still theoretically possible if the original buyer is not only accountable for sale proceeds, but the agreement also provides that the original buyer acts as trustee/bailee for the seller and is under a duty to keep a separate account of the proceeds of the subsale identifiable and held on trust for the benefit of the seller. This must arise in substance as well as by the form of the agreement. It should also be noted that not all bailees or agents have fiduciary duties, so it would be desirable explicitly to state this and have an express provision denying the buyer the free use of the proceeds of sale. The clause should also specify that the buyer will hold the proceeds as trustee or fiduciary (see *Re Andrabell Ltd* [1984] 3 All ER 407; *Re Shulman Enterprises*, 744 F.2d 397 (1983); *E Pfeiffer* v. *Arbuthnot Factors Ltd* (1987) 3 BCC 608; *Compaq Computer Ltd* v. *Abercorn Group Ltd* [1991] BCC 484).

Where the legal property in goods remains in or is passed back to the seller, a charge will be a legal charge. However, if the legal property is passed to the company and remains with it, the charge will be an equitable charge (see *Re Charge Card Services Ltd (No.2)* [1987] Ch 150). Where the seller takes a charge from a company over goods sold to it or over the proceeds of resale of such goods, the charge will usually fail as one requiring registration.

Claims that extend to ownership of finished goods

Clauses claiming title to finished products are open to significant doubt.

A relationship of bailee and bailor must be established, and also an obligation for the goods to be stored separately. Case law shows that in the majority of cases this will create a charge which, if unregistered, will be void for want of registration (see *Re Peachdart* [1984] 1 Ch 131; *Clough Mill* v. *Martin* [1985] 1 WLR 111).

In *Associated Alloys Pty Ltd* v. *CAN* (2000) 171 ALR 568 (an Australian authority), it was held that steel manufactured into various steel products could be subject to retention of title, as the relationship between buyer and seller was fiduciary agent and bailee (although the claim was defeated on the facts). The court distinguished existing authorities on the basis that the parties were subject to a trust relationship. However, this must be open to some doubt in light of other authorities, for the trust seems to have created a security which would be void for want of registration.

Checklist

Considerations on evaluating a retention of title claim

1. Is the clause incorporated into the contract?
2. Does the clause extend to both legal and beneficial ownership?
3. Is the clause simple or extended?
4. If the clause is simple, are the goods identifiable, namely:

    - stored separately from other goods?
    - easily identifiable?
    - easily separated and not mixed with other goods?

5. If the clause is extended:

    - does this create a registerable equitable charge?
    - is the claim over the proceeds of sale?

6. Have the goods been sold on to a third party?
7. Does the buyer possess a right of repossession?

13.4 CREDITORS POSSESSING A UNIQUE POSITION

In addition to creditors that can bring a claim over specific assets held in the hands of the insolvent company, there are certain creditors that as a result of their unique status and position enjoy additional rights over ordinary unsecured creditors. In certain instances, these rights can be exercised during the insolvency process. The following section focuses on the position of secured creditors, landlords of lease-hold property in the possession of the insolvent company and employees of the insolvent company.

13.4.1 Secured creditors

While in general any property secured by mortgage or charge cannot be dealt with in a way which prejudices the secured creditor, in certain corporate insolvencies it is important that the office holder has an ability to deal with the secured assets. This may be necessary to effect a sale of the business and its assets. For instance, the company may operate from premises which are subject to security. If the business is to be sold as a going concern, not only do the goodwill, tools and machinery, etc. need to be transferred, but also the trading premises may need to be retained (and sold) if the business is to have any effective value.

The administrator of the company may therefore dispose of or take action relating to property which is subject to a floating charge as if it were not subject to charge. In doing so, the floating charge holder does not lose priority over the proceeds or other property acquired by the administrator (IA 1986, Sched.B1,

Figure 13.1   Establishing a retention of title (ROT) claim

para.70). In respect of assets subject to fixed charge security, the administrator can only deal with the assets subject to order of the court (IA 1986, Sched.B1, para.71). In practice, the administrator will proceed with the consent of the charge holder (e.g. seek its agreement to sale) rather than apply to court. For further details of the administrator's ability to deal with charged property, see **7.3.3**.

A liquidator may similarly by agreement deal with secured property, if the secured creditor has not appointed an administrative receiver (pre-15 September 2003 security) or an administrator (post-15 September 2003 security) or appointed an LPA receiver over specific property secured under a mortgage or charge. The liquidator is likely to do so only if there is potential equity in the property under charge or a sale of the charged property is required as part of the sale of the whole business and assets of the company. In dealing with the charged property in this manner, the liquidator will also need to seek approval of his fees for so dealing (see *Buchler* v. *Talbot*; *Re Leyland DAF* [2004] UKHL 9 and the consequent reform of IA 1986, s.176ZA).

As well as provisions which allow the insolvency practitioner to deal with secured assets, there are provisions to prevent secured creditors from taking actions which would otherwise prejudice the interests of the creditors as a whole, primarily evident through the administration process.

The initiation of the administration procedure provides the company with a moratorium against secured creditors' enforcement rights. A secured creditor may still enforce its security, but will first require leave of the court or the administrator. While the administration process is taking place, the office holder can investigate and ascertain whether the business can be rescued.

Once the company is in administration, the secured creditor may not appoint an administrative receiver. It is for this reason that the holder of a qualifying floating charge must be provided with notice of intention to appoint an administrator. If the creditor possesses security created before 15 September 2003, it has the right to appoint an administrative receiver, or an administrator. In respect of security created after 15 September 2003, it will generally only be able to appoint its own choice of administrator.

In the case of liquidation, a secured creditor with security created before September 2003 retains a right to appoint an administrative receiver. Although, as we have seen, administrative receivership is not a collective insolvency process, it is very often the beginning of the process of the winding up of the company. After a receiver has completed his duties, it is likely that the company will enter into liquidation.

If the security is created after September 2003, there is no ability to appoint an administrator by an out-of-court route when the company is in liquidation. As a consequence, notice of intended voluntary winding up must be provided to secured creditors, which may exercise their right to appoint an administrator (IA 1986, s.84(2A)). Should they fail to appoint an administrator within five business days of the notice and the company passes into liquidation, the secured creditors may only place the company into administration by application to the court.

13.4.2 Lessors of leasehold property

Where a tenant falls into arrears of rent a landlord, in accordance with the terms of the lease, is likely to have the right to forfeit, a common law right to distrain over the tenant's chattels or an ability to sue for the arrears. A landlord's important ability to issue a rent diversion notice to a sub-tenant is not, however, affected by the tenant entering into an insolvency process. If the landlord had such a right before the tenant's insolvency event, it will continue to have such a right after the tenant's insolvency event. It should be noted, however, that the landlord's right to take proceedings against the tenant and/or seek to deal with the head lease are affected, and are dependant upon the nature of the insolvency process that the tenant enters into.

The landlord's position vis-à-vis a receiver

As LPA receivership, fixed charge receivership and administrative receivership are remedies exercised by a secured creditor to recover monies advanced, they are not strictly insolvency processes. However, in practice receivership is often a prelude to the company's demise.

One important consequence of the nature of receivership is that the receiver has no statutory power to resist claims made by the landlord against the tenant company. The landlord is therefore entitled to take such proceedings as deemed necessary in order to seek payment for arrears of rent (be that to sue for arrears, distrain over company assets, forfeit the lease by peaceable re-entry and/or serve a rent diversion notice on an under-tenant).

The receiver therefore needs to come to an arrangement with the landlord as a matter of urgency. The landlord may well be willing to accept payment of rent during the course of the receivership if there is a possibility that the receiver may find a new tenant for the property or the company will be returned to profitability. While the receiver may find a prospective new tenant, it is entirely at the discretion of the landlord as to whether to accept the new tenant, consenting to an assignment of the lease or, alternatively, by entering into entirely new lease terms with the new tenant.

Due to the strong position held by the landlord during the course of receivership, there is a disadvantage to using the procedure as a form of corporate rescue where there is a need to trade the business from its existing leasehold premises. As a result, administration holds many advantages over receivership where a landlord is owed substantial arrears of rent.

The landlord's position vis-à-vis a liquidator of a company in voluntary liquidation

The landlord's rights to commence proceedings are unaffected by voluntary liquidation. However, the liquidator may apply to restrain any proceedings being commenced against a company in liquidation. The court will need to weigh up the interests of the landlord against the interests of the creditors as a whole. However, if the tenant company is in liquidation there is unlikely to be any necessity for the company to retain its leasehold premises. The company would generally have ceased trading and its assets will be realised. In practical terms, there might be an agreement between the liquidator and the landlord to hand over to the liquidator goods belonging to the company which are held at the premises and/or arrange for the orderly clearance of the premises. The head lease may thus be dealt with by forfeiture or surrender.

In regard to any sub-tenant, following forfeiture/surrender of the head lease it is entirely a matter for the landlord as to whether it wishes to reach agreement with the sub-tenant regarding continuing occupation.

If, however, the landlord does not exercise rights of forfeiture in liquidation, it is open to the liquidator to disclaim the tenant company's interest in the lease (IA 1986, s.178). This right can be exercised notwithstanding that the liquidator has taken possession of the property, endeavoured to sell it or otherwise exercised rights of ownership in relation to it. However, a liquidator does not acquire personal liability if he does not disclaim the lease (*Stead, Hazel & Co.* v. *Cooper* [1933] 1 KB 840).

Until 6 April 2010, the liquidator's right to forfeit was one available only with leave of the court. However, the process became essentially an administrative one, with a requirement to file and have stamped copies for service on interested parties. It is now open to a liquidator to disclaim without leave of the court, and the court will only become involved if a party affected by the disclaimer makes application to court. A notice of disclaimer must be in prescribed form (IR 1986, rule 4.187, Form 4.53) and must be authenticated (signed) and dated by the liquidator. As soon as reasonably practicable, the notice must be sent to the Registrar of Companies and, where in respect of registered land, the Chief Land Registrar (IR 1986, rule 4.187(3A)).

The disclaimer operates so as to determine, as at the date of the disclaimer, the rights, interest and liability of the company in respect of the property disclaimed, but does not release the company from any liability or affect the rights and liabilities of any other person, such as a guarantor or surety of future liabilities under the lease (*Hindcastle Ltd* v. *Barbara Attenborough Associates Ltd* [1997] AC 70; and see also *Shaw* v. *Doleman* [2009] EWCA Civ 279) or effect a third party charge (*Hughes* v. *Groveholt Ltd* [2005] BPIR 1345).

The disclaimer of a lease has the effect of destroying any underlease (see *Re ITM Corp Ltd (in liquidation)* [1997] BCC 554 and below). As a result, a disclaimer does not take effect in respect of the leasehold property, unless a copy of the disclaimer has been served (so far as the liquidator is aware) on the addresses of any person claiming under the company as underlessee or mortgagee and no vesting order has been sought by any person within 14 days of being given notice of the same (IA 1986, s.179). The disclaimer is presumed valid and effective unless proved otherwise, and the liquidator's decision cannot be interfered with unless it is deemed to be perverse or taken in bad faith (*Re Hans Place Ltd (in liquidation)* [1993] BCLC 768).

Where there has been a disclaimer, the landlord is entitled to claim in the liquidation as an unsecured creditor for the loss and damage resulting from the earlier termination of the tenant's liability (see *Re Park Air Services plc* [2000] AC 172 regarding the issue of calculating compensation and taking into account accelerated receipt). However, the landlord is under a duty to mitigate loss and may need to take into account the rent received or capable of being received from the sub-tenant.

The court may not make a vesting order, except on the terms that the sub-tenant (underlessee) takes on the same liabilities and obligations as the insolvent company under the lease or, if the court thinks fit, subject to the same liabilities and obligations as that person would be subject to if the lease had been assigned prior to commencement of winding up (IA 1986, s.182) (see *Re A E Realisations* [1987] 3 All ER 83 and *Re ITM Corp Ltd (in liquidation)* [1997] BCC 554 which concerned an application by a landlord to seek a vesting order with the benefit of the existing sub-leases entered into by the insolvent tenant, i.e. stepping into the shoes of the insolvent tenant. In this latter case, the court held that a vesting order could not be made until all those with an interest and ability to seek a vesting order had been cleared away and in any event a vesting order in favour of a landlord could only be made where freed of the sub-lessees' interests).

As a result, on disclaimer of the head lease, it is for the underlessee to decide if it wishes to apply for a vesting order. If it does not, it will have no right to occupy and it is open for the landlord to take such action as deemed fit.

The landlord's position vis-à-vis a liquidator of a company in compulsory liquidation

The same rights are available to the landlord as are available in voluntary liquidation. However, in the case of compulsory liquidation, it should be noted that the landlord must have leave of the court to take any action or proceedings (IA 1986, s.130(2)).

The court, in being asked to grant leave, will weigh up the interests of the creditors as a whole against the interests of the specific creditor seeking leave. The courts are more prepared to allow a creditor a right to continue with the process of execution or attachment where there has been some act of deception or evasion by the debtor company (see *Re Grosvenor Metal Co. Ltd* [1950] Ch 63). However, in general, the court needs to be persuaded that there is significant reason to depart from the general principle of *pari passu*.

In this context, distress has been subject to different judicial interpretation. However, it now appears settled that distress will be subject to IA 1986, s.130(2), and it cannot be proceeded with and must have been completed by the sale of the distressed goods before the winding-up order has been made (see *Re Memco Engineering Ltd* [1986] Ch 86).

However, it has been held that peaceable re-entry of the premises by the landlord is not an action or legal proceeding within the purposes of s.130(2) (see *Ezekiel* v. *Orakpo* [1977] QB 260). In practice, where the tenant company is in compulsory liquidation, this is the most likely course to be taken.

As a result, leave to seek possession is likely to be granted should the liquidator proceed in a way which otherwise prejudices the landlord's claims, e.g. the liquidator will not be allowed to retain possession of the leasehold premises if he has no intention of paying the rent. As a consequence, general agreement between the landlord and the liquidator regarding the payment of the rent, or at least a part payment, or licence to occupy is often reached where the liquidator needs to occupy the premises for a short period (the Lundy Granite 'salvage' principles as regards costs and expenses applying: see *Re Lundy Granite Co., ex p. Heavan* (1871) 6 Ch

App 462, where the liability for rent will be treated as a cost and expense of the liquidation if the premises are being used to further the purposes of the liquidation).

Where the landlord does not take the property, the liquidator has a power to disclaim the tenant's interest in the property as outlined above.

The landlord's position vis-à-vis an administration

Administration has one considerable advantage over receivership in that it prevents the landlord, which may be owed arrears of rent, from exercising rights of action without leave of the court or the administrator.

Administration (since the reforms of IA 2000) offers a full moratorium against the actions that could be taken by a landlord, namely suing for arrears, distraint or forfeiture. The court will consider whether to grant leave on the same principles as when there is a compulsory liquidator in office. The court will balance the interests of the landlord against the interests of the creditors as a whole, taking into account all circumstances of the case (see *Re Atlantic Computers Systems plc (No.1)* [1992] 2 WLR 367).

In practice, if rent cannot be paid during the administration period it may be preferable for the potential administrator to seek an agreement with the landlord prior to entering into administration regarding an affordable level of rent during the course of the administration, if the landlord is to be prevented from exercising its right to forfeit with leave of the court. However, this can be a dangerous course of action as the landlord may exercise available rights on hearing of the potential insolvency of the tenant. In practice, therefore, such discussion often needs to ensue after the filing of a notice of intention (when the interim moratorium takes effect) but before the commencement of the administration proper.

A problem arises where the administrator cannot reach reasonable terms with the landlord. In contrast to a liquidator, an administrator does not have a power to disclaim the lease.

Where the administrator (as agent for the company) is in occupation of premises, he is liable to the landlord for payment of the rent, as a cost and expense of the administration (see *Re Trident Fashions plc* [2007] EWHC 400 (Ch)). Where the administrator has quit the premises (and in particular where the landlord has not agreed to forfeit or accept a surrender of the lease), the position is less certain.

Administrators initially drew comfort from the decision of *Innovate Logistics Ltd (in administration)* v. *Sunberry Properties Ltd* [2008] EWCA Civ 1321, a case which concerned a landlord's unsuccessful application to terminate a licensee's right of occupation granted by the administrator without consent of the landlord. In that case, it was stated *obiter* that a landlord had no automatic right to the rent as an administration expense, and as regards rent falling due after the date of administration, the landlord would be treated as an unsecured creditor of the tenant company. If the rent was unpaid, then that was a major factor to be considered by the court in deciding whether to grant the landlord permission to forfeit the lease.

However, this case was followed by *Goldacre (Offices) Ltd* v. *Nortel Networks UK Ltd (in administration)* [2009] EWHC 3389 (Ch). In this case, Judge Purle QC identified that the *Innovate* case and the comments made on rent, etc., were provided on the basis of a concession granted by counsel for both parties and that therefore he was not strictly bound to follow this Court of Appeal ruling.

Instead, he determined that the court should adapt the long-established *Lundy Granite* 'salvage principle'. This is the established proposition that in liquidation one should assess whether a liability is an expense of the liquidation, by virtue of whether the asset/contract under which the liability arises is adopted for the beneficial conduct of the liquidation. In short, if one is using the premises for the beneficial conduct of the liquidation, i.e. continuing to trade from the premises, then a liquidator should bear the rent and other liabilities as a cost and expense of the liquidation.

Judge Purle QC said (at [20]):

> ... a liquidator electing to hold leasehold premises can do so only on the terms and conditions contained in the lease, and ... *any liability* incurred while the lease is being enjoyed or retained for the benefit of the liquidation is payable in full as a liquidation expense. The same principle in my judgment applies in an administration. As Lord Hoffmann recognised in *Toshoku* at para.28, the liability to pay rent is not treated as an expense having priority until (and lasts only so long as) the office holder makes use of or decides to retain the property. Subject to that, any such liability accruing during that period is in my judgment to be treated as an expense having the requisite priority.

Judge Purle QC went on to determine if that the rent was payable quarterly in advance, it continued to be payable so long as the administrators retained or used part of the premises demised; it could not be apportioned. He went on to say (at [29]):

> If of course they vacate the property demised under one of the leases entirely, the rental liability under that lease, but not under the other, will cease to be payable as an administration expense. If they vacate the other demised property as well, the rental liabilities under both leases will cease to be payable as administration expenses.

As a corollary to that, it follows that rent can no longer be regarded as a cost and expense of the administration once the administrator has determined to vacate and informed the landlord by offering the surrender of the lease, etc. It should be remembered that the administrators have no course other than to offer a surrender of the lease, hand back the keys, etc., and cannot force the landlord to forfeit. Indeed, it could well be the case that the landlord refuses to take back possession (business rate liability for empty premises being a consideration). If this occurs, the administrator is best advised to seek to regularise the relationship and/or provide notice that the tenant has vacated and has no use for the premises.

Goldacre has been further clarified in the case of *Leisure (Norwich) II Ltd* v. *Luminar Lava Ignite Ltd (in administration)* [2012] EWHC 951 (Ch) in March 2012. In this case, Judge Pelling QC held that where rent was payable in advance and fell due prior to the commencement of the administration (or liquidation), it was not payable as a cost and expense of the administration (or liquidation). While the rent remained due, it was solely a debt which could be proved in the administration (or liquidation).

However, this decision was not all good news for insolvency practitioners, as Judge Pelling QC went on to hold that where the administrator retained the property for the purposes of the administration and rent became due during that period, the entire rental payment for the forthcoming period became due and payable as a cost and expense of the administration, irrespective of whether the administrator intended to or did vacate the property before the expiry of the period for which the advance payment was due.

This has led to the situation that administration can be timed to commence after the quarter date and the administrator can occupy, effectively rent free, until the eve of the next due quarter. The more equitable solution that administrators reached with landlords to 'pay as you go', possibly even on a daily rate basis, has been replaced by a hard but certain rule. It is, however, questionable whether the timing of an insolvency process should be so dependent on the interests/prejudice that can be caused to the landlord. We wait to see if legislative amendment or further judicial clarification will bring reform in this area.

The landlord's position vis-à-vis a company voluntary arrangement (CVA)

As we have seen, a CVA is a form of statutory binding on the company's unsecured creditors, binding all unsecured creditors to a compromise or scheme of arrangement where 75 per cent in value of creditors voting have approved the terms of the proposal. There is therefore a possibility that a CVA can be used to try to bind a landlord's rights of action as against an insolvent tenant.

Although, as we have seen, the CVA process remains comparatively little used, it has in recent years been used in a number of high-profile cases concerning 'insolvent' tenants with multiple premises as part of an exercise in corporate reconstruction.

Careful negotiation should then ensue between the tenant company, the nominee and the landlord, as it is clear that the terms of the CVA may affect the landlord's position in regard to arrears of rent, future rent and general rights of action arising from the tenant company's default (see *Re Lomax Leisure* [2000] BCC 352 – a landlord's right to forfeit is not a secured right and hence a landlord can be bound to the terms of a CVA in respect of arrears and future rent).

The use of a CVA as part of a reconstruction strategy (see contrasting CVA proposals for *Stylo plc (Barratt Shoes)*, *JJB Sports* and, more recently, *Miss Sixty* below) is an alternative to administration and pre-pack administration sales, and with careful negotiation and drafting can be seen to be a fairer and more effective means of dealing with the landlords of unwanted sites.

Whether the landlord has a right to challenge the approved CVA on the ground that it unfairly prejudices the interests of a creditor (i.e. itself as landlord) (see IA

1986, s.6(1) and Sched.A1, para.38(1)) is, however, a matter to be determined on a case-by-case basis. Certain recent case law has offered some guidance.

In the case of *Thomas* v. *Ken Thomas Ltd* [2006] EWCA Civ 1504, the relationship between a CVA and the landlord's right to forfeit for non-payment of rent was examined by the Court of Appeal. The court considered two first instance positions, that of *Re Naeem (a Bankrupt) (No.18 of 1988)* [1990] 1 WLR 48 and *March Estates plc* v. *Gunmark Ltd* [1996] 2 BCLC 1. In both instances, the court had determined that a voluntary arrangement did not affect a landlord's proprietary right to forfeit.

However, the Court of Appeal held the following:

1. A CVA is concerned with obligations not remedies. If the rent obligation is consumed within the CVA, all remedies must be modified.
2. To allow the landlord the right to commence proceedings for forfeiture in respect of sums payable within the terms of a CVA was inconsistent with a rescue culture.
3. The effect of the CVA meant that the rent was no longer owing from the tenant to the landlord and there was therefore no right to forfeit.
4. The landlord's right to forfeit is not a secured right and therefore as an unsecured creditor the landlord was bound within the terms of the CVA.

As a result, the tenant's obligations are as per the CVA. However, it should be noted that this case concerned accrued rent and not future rent and was for a relatively small amount of arrears.

Prudential Assurance Co. Ltd v. *PRG Powerhouse Ltd* [2007] EWHC 1002 (Ch) concerned a restructuring plan for an insolvent electrical retailer which proposed to save 53 stores using a CVA, the terms of which were that employees, local authorities and other creditors (including landlords) of the closed stores would share a pot of money provided by the parent company of £1.5 million. The remaining creditors would be paid out of the trading receipts of the reconstructed business.

The reasoning behind this proposal was that the business was hopelessly insolvent and the landlords would receive nothing from liquidation due to the huge deficiency owed to the secured parent company. The £1.5 million payment therefore allowed the landlords time to re-let and saved the core of the company's business. Importantly for some of the landlords, the CVA proposals also sought to release the parent company from liability in respect of a guarantee given on granting of the lease to its subsidiary. It was argued that if the guarantees were called upon the parent might be unable to support the newly reconstructed business.

The CVA was approved at the creditors' meeting, but the landlords of the closed stores immediately challenged it.

The court was asked to determine two preliminary issues:

1. Were the guarantees given by the parent released by reason of the CVA?
2. If so, was this unfairly prejudicial?

It was common ground that IA 1986 does not deal expressly with the position of guarantors and co-debtors. However, the position is reasonably clear under common law. Once a debt is released, a guarantor will no longer be liable to discharge it (*Commercial Bank of Tasmania* v. *Jones* [1893] AC 313). However, if the guarantee contains an express provision that the guarantee would be unaffected by indulgence/release of the principal debtor, there is no automatic release.

The treatment of guarantors under the terms of a voluntary arrangement was considered in *Johnson* v. *Davies* [1999] Ch 117. This case established the principle that a voluntary arrangement does not have the effect of automatically releasing a co-debtor, but that the terms of a voluntary arrangement could be such as to effect the release of a guarantee without the creditor's consent. The practice since then has therefore been to look closely at the terms of the CVA to see how guarantors are treated.

It was held that each creditor was a party to the CVA as a creditor of the company and that a CVA is a special form of contract between the debtor and the creditors. It is not a contract between one creditor and another, or between a creditor and a third party. As a result, the terms of the CVA cannot affect the rights and obligations between a creditor and a third party; the terms of the CVA did not therefore give rise to an automatic release of the guarantees.

The court held that it is entirely possible for a CVA to provide that a creditor cannot take steps to claim from a third party where that third party may have a right of recourse against the debtor, i.e. the fact that the guarantor could then claim repayment from the debtor may defeat the purpose of the CVA. While such a clause has no direct effect as between the creditor and the third party, it could in theory be enforced by the debtor to block claims against the guarantor.

After determining that the Powerhouse CVA did indeed release the parent company from its guarantees, the court went on to question whether this was unfairly prejudicial, affording the landlords a right of challenge capable of overturning the CVA. The court held that there was no single test for unfairness and instead it needed to look at all circumstances of the case in the exercise of its discretion. Etherton J carried out both a vertical comparison, i.e. what is the effect of the CVA as opposed to other insolvency procedures, and a horizontal comparison, i.e. what is the treatment of other creditors under the CVA?

Generally, the debtor needs to establish that the CVA offers the best available alternative and that creditors are being treated fairly. The fact that one creditor is being treated differently is not in itself enough for the CVA to be deemed unfair; instead, the court should move on to balance the interests of that creditor against the interests of the creditors as a whole.

In the *Powerhouse* case, it was held that the landlords of the closed stores were left in a worse position: in the case of liquidation they had lost a potential valuable guarantee against a solvent third party (namely the parent company guarantor); under a s.425 Companies Act scheme of arrangement they would have been treated as a separate class of creditor. They were also being treated unfairly when compared with other creditors in that their dividend was calculated without reference to the value of the guarantees. The effect of the CVA was therefore unfairly prejudicial.

The case of *Mourant & Co. Trustees Ltd* v. *Sixty UK Ltd (in administration)* [2010] EWHC 1890 (Ch) concerned Miss Sixty, a women's fashion retail chain, where a CVA used as an exit route from administration was challenged on the grounds of unfair prejudice and material irregularity by the landlords of two retail units.

The CVA sought to distinguish open store landlords, which would effectively have been unaffected by the proposal, from closed store landlords, which would receive a sum in the CVA that should have been a genuine estimate of the surrender value of the leases.

As in the *Powerhouse* case, the parent company, which had provided guarantees to the landlords, was willing to fund the CVA provided it was released from the guarantees for a one-off compensatory payment of £300,000 (it said this represented the company's liability on surrender).

At the hearing, Henderson J applied the vertical and horizontal analysis provided in *Powerhouse*, finding the following:

1. In the event of liquidation, the landlords of the closed stores would have had a continuing ability to call on the parent company guarantee and hence the CVA was unfairly prejudicial to their position (vertical analysis).
2. In contrast with other creditors (the parent and connected companies were not bound by the terms of the CVA), the landlords of the closed stores were treated unfairly (horizontal analysis).

The *Miss Sixty* case followed the *Powerhouse* approach and is a salutary reminder to insolvency practitioners that despite the proposal being one put forward by the debtor, the nominee needs to remain objective and to consider the interests of all the creditors in putting forward a CVA proposal for consideration, and should not simply be led by the commercial imperative of the debtor and its potential funding party.

Table 13.1 Landlord's right of action

	Administrative receivership		Voluntary liqui- dation		Compulsory liquidation		Administration	
	Without leave	With leave	Without leave	With leave	Without leave	With leave	Without leave	With leave
Distraint	Yes	N/A	Yes*	N/A	No	Yes	No	Yes
Forfeiture	Yes	N/A	Yes*	N/A	Yes**	Yes	No	Yes
Sue for arrears	Yes	N/A	Yes*?	N/A	No	Yes?	No	Yes

Table 13.2   Insolvency practitioner's right of action

	Administrative receivership	Voluntary liqui- dation	Compulsory liquidation	Administration
Disclaimer available to insolvency practitioner	No	Yes	Yes	No

* Insolvency practitioner may apply for a stay of proceedings.

** Where forfeit by peaceable re-entry.

? Remedy available but almost certainly better advised proving for debt.

13.4.3   Employee's position during the insolvency process

The position of an employee during the insolvency process depends on whether the business is likely to continue to trade. If there is some element of corporate rescue, possibly with transfer of the business, it could well be that the employee's position is unaffected, the employment rights and liabilities being transferred as a matter of law to a new employer under the Transfer of Undertakings (Protection of Employment) Regulations 2006, SI 2006/246 (TUPE), which replaced the 1981 Regulations from 6 April 2007.

Employee's rights on TUPE transfer

Of companies entering into an insolvency process, the preservation rate of the businesses carried on by those companies (and therefore employee jobs) is estimated to be some 30 per cent (source: DTI, *Final Regulatory Impact Assessment – Employment Rights Directorate* (January 2006)). In the majority of those cases, the business will be transferred and carried on by a new company.

TUPE is designed to safeguard employees' rights when the business in which they work changes hands between employers. Potentially, the purchaser of the insolvent business steps into the shoes of the old employer, inheriting the acquired rights and liabilities connected with the employees' contracts of employment (TUPE, reg.4). The employer's liabilities for arrears of wages, redundancy pay, etc. will pass to the new owner, and except in special circumstances, the dismissal of any employee for reasons connected with the transfer will be deemed automatically unfair.

However, TUPE has been accused of hampering the rescue of insolvent businesses in that it prevents a company restructuring its workforce in a way to make it more attractive to buyers. It should also be remembered that the insolvency practitioner will not be prepared to provide any indemnities or warranties to a proposed purchaser, which therefore takes on the potential risk of a disgruntled ex-employee claiming that there has been a TUPE transfer. Significant regulation exists to ensure that employee liability information is given to the new transferee employer. Buyers may therefore face a potentially complex and uncertain situation in that issues relating to employee rights are very often determined in employment tribunals, and inconsistencies of approach are not uncommon. As a result, the price that the purchaser is prepared to pay for the business (and as a consequence the return to creditors) is reduced as it will want the TUPE liabilities taken into account. TUPE thus has the effect of reducing the return to unsecured creditors while ensuring that employees (part of whose claims are likely to be unsecured) are preferred.

TUPE applies to the sale or transfer of an undertaking, which is defined as any trade or business situated before transfer in the UK. The dismissal of an employee with more than one year's continuous employment is automatically unfair where the sole or principal reason for the dismissal is 'the relevant transfer' or the reason connected with the relevant transfer is not an economic, technical or organisational (ETO) reason entailing changes in the workforce (TUPE, reg.7(1)).

Where a dismissal occurs before the transfer of the business, it is deemed automatically unfair and the liability for the transfer passes to the transferee, as the employee is treated as being employed 'immediately before the transfer' or would have been so employed but for the unfair dismissal (see *Lister* v. *Forth Dry Dock* [1996] 1 AC 546; now codified in TUPE, reg.4(3)). As a result of TUPE, a proposed purchaser of a business cannot ask an insolvency practitioner to dismiss staff as a condition of purchasing the business.

For some years following the introduction of the previous employment protection regulations in 1981, the situation was less clear where an insolvency practitioner dismisses the staff for an ETO reason, such as an inability to fund the wages during the insolvency process, but did so also with a view to the ultimate sale of the business, i.e. making it more attractive to buyers. Case law established that the employment tribunal will look at each case on its own facts to see whether there was a legitimate ETO reason (*Ward* v. *Beresford and Hicks Furniture Ltd* (1996) EAT 860/95, 16 December) or whether the dismissal was at the request of the purchaser for a reason connected with the transfer (*IBEX Trading Co. Ltd* v. *Walton* [1994] IRLR 564, to be contrasted with *Logden and Paisley* v. *Ferrari Ltd* [1994] IRLR 157). If the insolvency practitioner considered the sale of the business was unlikely and dismissed the staff, it seems unlikely that this would be treated as a dismissal connected with the transfer (*Secretary of State for Employment* v. *Spence* [1987] QB 179).

In *Spaceright Europe Ltd* v. *Baillavoine* [2011] EWCA Civ 1565, however, the Court of Appeal was asked to consider the situation where an employee was dismissed on the day that administration commenced (a not uncommon scenario), but where the business was sold and thereby transferred after marketing, etc. over a month later. Clearly, a sale to that particular buyer had not been contemplated at the time of the dismissal and it was argued that the dismissal was therefore for an ETO reason. The Court of Appeal held in favour of the employee: where any sale is anticipated and the dismissal of an employee is to make the purchase more attractive, it will be automatically unfair. A logical extension to the judgment was that to make the dismissal unfair a transfer of the business did eventually need to take place; the employee was therefore left to wait and see whether a transfer took place. Generally, an employee will have three months in which to bring a claim, and as a result where the administration continues past that point it could be deemed to make a potentially unfair dismissal 'fair'. However, it is possible for an employee to bring a claim after three months where it was not reasonably practicable to bring a claim within the first three months (see *Machine Tool Industry Research Association* v. *Simpson* [1988] IRLR 212). It therefore seems possible that an employee could claim unfair dismissal in any case where eventually the business is sold by an administrator.

Timing therefore still appears important in considering whether the dismissal was for a reason connected with the transfer or for an ETO reason. Although the insolvency practitioner may be limiting the costs and expenses of the insolvency process, he may also be doing so with a view to slimming down the workforce to make the business more attractive to any potential purchaser. The sooner that the insolvency practitioner does this and the further away it is from any proposed transfer, the less likely it is that any potential purchaser will incur TUPE liability. This, of course, has the practical effect of reducing employee job security, while job security is ultimately the purpose behind TUPE.

The reform of TUPE in 2006 and more recent Court of Appeal decisions such as that in *Spaceright* seem have to have tipped the balance in favour of the employees. One of the key aims of the TUPE 2006 reforms was said to be a promotion of rescue culture, to save businesses and jobs that would otherwise be lost. The following provisions were therefore introduced:

- When insolvency proceedings are commenced with a view to liquidation of the assets of the company, the transfer and dismissal provisions contained within TUPE, regs.4 and 7 do not apply.
- The obligation to pay some pre-existing debts due to the employees will remain with the transferor company or the DBIS through the National Insurance Fund. A transferee employer will only be liable for debts which are due over and above payments made by the insolvent employer/DBIS.
- New terms and conditions of employment in respect of a transferred employee can be imposed by the new employer, provided that:
    - it is a permitted variation agreed with an employee representative;
    - where the employee representative is not a union, the agreement to vary must be in writing and signed by the representative, and before signature the employee(s) must have a copy of the agreement with appropriate guidance provided;
    - the variation must not be in breach of any other statute (e.g. minimum wage); and
    - the variation must be made with the intention of safeguarding employment

> opportunities by ensuring the survival of the undertaking or business or part of the undertaking or business.

Under TUPE, reg.8(7), the transfer and dismissal provisions contained in TUPE, regs.4 and 7 do not apply to any relevant transfer where:

(a)   the transferor is the subject of bankruptcy proceedings or any analogous insolvency proceedings which had been instituted with a view to the liquidation of the assets of the transferor; and

(b)   the proceedings are 'under the supervision of an insolvency practitioner'.

This wording was taken directly from the European Acquired Rights Directive 2001, which importantly does not list which insolvency processes it applies to. Instead, the DTI issued guidance in June 2006 (*Redundancy and Insolvency Payments*, URN 06/1368), stating what it considered would be the application of TUPE in various specific insolvency proceedings, and case law in this area has also subsequently clarified the application of TUPE.

COMPULSORY LIQUIDATION

If a company is wound up by an order of a court on the grounds that it is unable to pay its debts, TUPE, regs.4 and 7 do not apply.

The reasoning behind this is that the company's business is highly unlikely to be sold as a going concern, and compulsory winding up is a process analogous to bankruptcy proceedings.

As a result, the employees would be entitled to claim certain payments from the National Insurance Fund in accordance with the provisions of the Employment Rights Act 1996 (see below regarding employee rights).

CREDITORS' VOLUNTARY LIQUIDATION

A transfer of the business by a company that is in creditors' voluntary liquidation will not be a TUPE transfer (to which regs.4 and 7 apply) unless prior to the transfer there was an agreement between the liquidator, purchaser and employees that the purchaser would be substituted as the employer.

In the absence of such an agreement, the employees are deemed to be dismissed and they will be entitled to claim certain payments from the National Insurance Fund.

MEMBERS' VOLUNTARY LIQUIDATION

As a members' voluntary liquidation is the winding up of a solvent company, it is not an insolvency proceeding and consequently TUPE will apply.

ADMINISTRATION

Where there is a relevant transfer, it will be regarded as a TUPE transfer (regs.4 and 7 applying).

The DTI June 2006 guidance stated that the main purpose of administration is not one analogous to bankruptcy proceedings, i.e. it is not commenced with a view to realisation of assets and distribution of proceeds to creditors, and it is necessary to look to the purpose of the procedure at its commencement, not its outcome. Despite this guidance, certain Employment Appeals Tribunal authorities seem to indicate that an analysis of the intention behind the appointment of the administrator (was it to save the business/was a sale anticipated?) was necessary (see *Oakwood* v. *Wellswood (Yorkshire) Ltd* [2009] IRLR 250, although not followed in *OTG Ltd* v. *Burke* [2011] IRLR 272). However, such intent was not always clear and there was uncertainty as to whether a transfer by an administrator could in certain circumstances ever be a transfer to which TUPE did not apply.

In *Key2Law (Surrey) LLP* v. *Gaynor De'Antiquis* [2011] EWCA Civ 1567 the Court of Appeal made clear that administration will always be a relevant insolvency proceeding, meaning that on any sale of the business by an administrator TUPE will apply. This avoids the necessity of looking at the intention of the administrator, the appointor's motive or the outcome, as administration is to be regarded always as a rescue procedure since the primary objective is to rescue the company as a going concern.

Where there is a TUPE transfer, the new employer/transferee will not, however, be liable for certain transferring employee liabilities (those under the Employment Rights Act 1996, Part XII).

ADMINISTRATIVE RECEIVERSHIP

Where there is a relevant transfer, it will be regarded as a TUPE transfer (regs.4 and 7 will apply). The reasoning is that such proceedings are neither collective proceedings nor analogous to bankruptcy proceedings.

Where there is a relevant transfer, the Employment Rights Act 1996, Part XII liabilities will be paid by the National Insurance Fund.

LPA RECEIVERSHIP

Where there is a relevant transfer, it will be regarded as a TUPE transfer (the reasoning as above).

Any liabilities for arrears of wages, etc. will be the responsibility of the purchasing transferee.

EMPLOYEE ENTITLEMENTS

Employees may claim the following from the National Insurance Fund:

- Statutory redundancy pay.
- Arrears of pay (up to eight weeks), subject to a current statutory maximum (of £45 per week from 1 February 2013).
- An amount due for failure to give the statutory period of notice.
- Any holiday pay entitlement (up to six weeks) which accrued during the 12 months prior to the appropriate date.
- Any basic award of compensation for unfair dismissal (not the compensatory award).
- Any reasonable sum by way of reimbursement for any fee or premium paid by any apprentice or articled clerk.

The employee's ability to claim from the Fund will depend upon the circumstance of the case; the Insolvency Service issued a statement of intended practice to insolvency practitioners on 3 April 2006. This provided the following guidance.

WHERE THE EMPLOYEES TRANSFER TO A NEW EMPLOYER

The National Insurance Fund will pay unpaid wages and holiday pay up to the statutory limits. No redundancy pay, accrued holiday entitlement or notice pay will be paid as there has been no dismissal.

WHERE THE EMPLOYEES ARE UNFAIRLY DISMISSED BY REASON OF THE TRANSFER

The National Insurance Fund will pay unpaid wages and holiday pay up to statutory limits.

No redundancy pay or notice pay will be paid as the employees will not be treated as dismissed by reasons of redundancy. This situation is most likely to occur in an administration rather than a liquidation of the insolvent employer company (see above). In such circumstances, the employee may seek to claim for unfair dismissal and breach of contract against the insolvent business or, more likely, the new transferee business.

WHERE THE EMPLOYEE IS DISMISSED FOR AN ETO REASON

The Redundancy Payment Office will pay redundancy pay, arrears of wages and holiday pay (if it is in respect of accrued entitlement). This situation is most likely to occur where the employee has been dismissed on the liquidation of the company or where an administrator has dismissed the staff for an ETO reason rather than for reasons connected with the transfer.

The National Insurance Fund will pay unpaid wages and holiday pay up to the statutory maximum. Redundancy pay and notice pay will not be paid as the employee is not treated as redundant and instead is treated as having left employment of his own accord.

While it is clear that some burden has been lifted from potential new employers on taking on transferring employee liabilities, substantial liabilities such as obligations for non-statutory redundancy pay will continue to pass to the new employer. This will be particularly relevant in the case of senior management staff, who very often are the type of employee whom the new employer does not want to take on in the new business.

While changes to terms and conditions on transfer are in theory made easier, in practice the conditions imposed may make the concessions introduced by the 2006 TUPE reforms unworkable. There is often very little time available during the company's insolvency to find employee representatives, conduct negotiations and give relevant notice to each employee. It is difficult to see how an insolvency practitioner would be able to conduct negotiations between employee representatives and competing bidders for a business, where the bids may be dependent on differing terms and conditions being attached to the transferred workforce.

While the 2006 TUPE reforms were intended to encourage business rescue, reluctantly one is forced to conclude that the reforms will be of only marginal assistance in facilitating business rescue and that the current level of uncertainty regarding the application of the new regulations makes corporate reconstruction planning particularly difficult.

Employer insolvency with no TUPE transfer

Where corporate rescue is unavailable, the employee is likely to have a claim against the company for unfair dismissal and/or for arrears of wages. An employee's claim and treatment as either a preferential or an unsecured creditor depends upon a number of factors and, clearly and most importantly, the type of insolvency procedure.

EMPLOYEE'S POSITION ON LIQUIDATION OF EMPLOYER

On voluntary liquidation, there is no automatic termination of any contract of employment (see *Fowler* v. *Commercial Timber Co. Ltd* [1930] 2 KB 1). However, the company is highly likely to cease to carry on its business, except so far as is beneficial for its winding up (IA 1986, s.87(1)). As a result, the liquidator in exercise of the powers of the company is likely to dismiss the employees, save in exceptional circumstances. The employees will therefore become creditors of the company and they can claim preferential status in respect of part of their debt, if applicable (IA 1986, ss.387, 396 and Sched.6, Chapter 5; e.g. an amount payable in respect of remuneration payable within four months of the relevant date not exceeding £800 plus holiday and sickness pay, etc.).

In the case of compulsory liquidation, the contracts of employment with employees or agents are automatically terminated (see *Gosling* v. *Gaskell* [1897] AC 575). As a consequence, in compulsory liquidation, the employee is likely to claim as an unsecured creditor for damages (i.e. failure to pay during the notice period) and for any arrears in pay, subject to any part of that debt which may be preferential.

EMPLOYEE'S POSITION ON EMPLOYER ENTERING INTO ADMINISTRATIVE RECEIVERSHIP

The appointment of an administrative receiver does not terminate any of the employee's contracts of employment. The administrative receiver acts as an agent of the company and may carry on its business. Indeed, this is often the reason why an administrative receiver has been appointed. In the few instances where an administrative receiver is appointed pursuant to a debenture which does not provide for the administrative receiver acting as agent of the company, the administrative receiver will not be carrying on business of the company and dismissal will result.

There are certain employees whose continued employment may be inconsistent with the appointment of a receiver to control and manage the business, which might include members of senior board management, such as a managing director. However, it is quite possible for the administrative receiver to require the managing director and other senior staff to remain in office, although their role and responsibilities may be limited. They may, however, be able to claim unfair dismissal in such circumstances (see *Griffiths* v. *Secretary of State for Social Services* [1973] 3 All ER 1184).

A receiver (other than an administrative receiver) is personally liable for any contracts of employment adopted by him in performance of his functions, although he is entitled to an indemnity out of the assets in respect of such liability (IA 1986, s.37(1)). A receiver is not, however, taken to have adopted a contract of employment by reason of anything done or omitted to be done within 14 days of his appointment. The receiver therefore has 14 days to decide whether or not to adopt a contract. Should he do so, liability will be imposed on him.

In the 1980s, it was a common practice for receivers to send out a standard letter to employees stating that they did not adopt any contract of employment. They would thereafter seek the employees' agreement to continue working. This practice was thrown into disarray by a decision in *Powdrill* v. *Watson, Re Paramount Airways Ltd (No.3)* [1995] 2 All ER 65 (HL).

However, there is some relief for administrative receivers as opposed to receivers. This is derived from the emergency legislation introduced in IA 1994, which followed the *Re Paramount Airways* decision. Like a receiver, an administrative receiver is personally liable on any contracts of employment adopted by him; the administrative receiver is taken not to have adopted a contract of employment by reason of anything done or omitted to be done within 14 days of appointment (IA 1986, s.44). However, the administrative receiver's liability is limited to qualifying liabilities, namely:

(a) liability to pay by way of wages or salary or contribution to an occupational pension scheme, incurred while the administrative receiver is in office; and

(b) liabilities in respect of services rendered wholly or partly after the adoption of the contract.

Following IA 1994, this provision applies to all contracts of employment adopted on or after 15 March 1994.

EMPLOYEE'S POSITION ON EMPLOYER ENTERING INTO ADMINISTRATION

Like an administrative receiver, an administrator cannot be personally liable for any liability arising out of a contract of employment, provided an administrator has not taken a step to adopt the contract of employment. Where an administrator has adopted the contract of employment, no liability arises in respect of anything before the adoption of the contract and, similarly, an administrator is taken not to have adopted a contract of employment by reason of anything done or omitted to be done within 14 days of appointment. No account will be taken of any liability to make payment other than for the wages or salary (IA 1986, Sched.B1, para.99(5)).

Importantly, the administrator's liability to employees under this section is treated as an expense of the administration, which has priority over all other expenses of the administration, including the administrator's remuneration.

The administrator should therefore think very carefully before agreeing to continue the employees' employment. It is a careful balancing act in each case to determine whether the employees are needed for the purpose of selling the business as a going concern, or whether costs can be saved by reducing the workforce. It is often the case that retaining employees is a problem for the insolvency practitioner. The employees are unsettled by the employer's insolvency and may seek alternative employment as a matter of urgency. In such circumstances, the administrator may offer a bonus or incentives to the employees to stay on, pending negotiations for a sale of the business. 'Golden handcuff' agreements are therefore not uncommon for those employees who are essential to the business.

CHAPTER 14

The future of insolvency law and practice

14.1 STRIKING THE RIGHT BALANCE

When the Chinese statesman Zhou Enlai was asked to comment on the significance of the French Revolution, he is reputed to have replied: 'It's too early to tell.'

The Enterprise Act 2002 reforms to corporate insolvency law and practice came into force on 15 September 2003 and the personal insolvency reforms on 1 April 2004. As a result this third edition of the Handbook is published as we approach a decade since these fundamental reforms. It would be good to report that the reformed insolvency regime has now bedded down, that the law is clear and free of ambiguity and provides a perfect balance between creditor and debtor, that the rescue of businesses with sustainable enterprise value is commonplace and that there is fair and equitable treatment of all stakeholders where there is an orderly wind down of those businesses that have no future. If only it were thus!

The balance of interests between creditor and debtor explored at the beginning of this book is never constant, with the influence of socio-economic conditions being as important to trends in insolvency law and practice as legislative reform. Problems have emerged through the use (and possible abuse) of the reformed system; we have seen in operation the law of unintended consequences and the unexpected rise in certain insolvency processes. It is, however, proffered that these changes are perhaps more a reflection of the economic imperatives arising during the last decade rather than legislative change.

A successful free market economy will ensure that individuals and businesses are appropriately rewarded for enterprise and entrepreneurial activity, allowing the most efficient and competitive businesses to succeed and flourish. An inevitable consequence of this economic 'survival of the fittest' is the failure of certain enterprises. It is often the case that those enterprises most at peril are smaller and/or start-up type businesses, which may be more susceptible to market downturns, even if such downturns are temporary and not a result of long-term structural changes. A fear of failure and the consequent insolvency process that may result must not, however, be allowed to inhibit economic activity, and a balance must be struck between reward and sanction. Responsible entrepreneurial risk-taking is essential to a growing and dynamic economy.

A free marketer may argue that it is the responsibility of the creditor to undertake his own checks and balances, and to seek appropriate reward for the risk in providing credit; it is not for the law to intervene and regulate, control, and potentially stifle economic activity. In the UK, however, the market is regulated to ensure a further balance is struck between creditors receiving fair and reasonable treatment and being allowed freely and openly to negotiate the terms and rewards for providing credit, on the one hand, against the imposition of harsh, oppressive or unfair terms of credit which may discourage entrepreneurial activity because of fear of sanction, personal liability and ultimately bankruptcy, on the other.

This balance is provided by a vast array of regulatory and legislative provisions, a major component of which are those arising on insolvency. Insolvency laws thus intervene in economic activity to regulate the affairs between insolvent debtors and their creditors and as between the creditors themselves; to provide fair and equitable treatment; balancing the rights and interests of the debtor to obtain financial rehabilitation against the rights of creditors to receive a return against their debt. Insolvency law and practice are thus primarily intended to deal with economic interests – only on the margins do they deal with punishment (e.g. director disqualification, bankruptcy restrictions), and even then such punishment is generally imposed to safeguard the public (the free market). The balance between debtor and creditor and as between creditors that is sought to be struck is a fine one, dictated by legislation and judicial interpretation, both of which in turn are influenced by the current socio-economic climate. Undoubtedly, over the last 30 years attitudes towards debt, risk and reward have shifted significantly, and this has shifted the balance.

Behind the Enterprise Act 2002 reforms were the stated aims of removing the stigma of bankruptcy and allowing businesses and individuals a second chance; part of the government's intention was specifically to encourage an entrepreneurial culture. The reforms were also set against a background of changing public attitude towards debt, and up until the credit crunch of 2007/08, credit provision and increasing debt burdens were accompanied by an expanding and prosperous economy and an 'end to boom and bust'. This rise in available and cheap credit, with lending opportunities (in a variety of new guises) being made ever more readily available both to the corporate and to the individual, was, however, a 'liquidity bubble' which burst.

In the more straitened times post credit crunch, attitudes towards debt have been redefined and continue to receive critical analysis. One must always take into account that insolvency arises on the failure to satisfy debt; the loss is not of the debtor's own money but that of others' money. Insolvency is thus set apart from poverty in that the debtor has in some way spent or utilised the money of a third party rather than simply spent his own. Enterprise failure may thus result in hardship for the individual, but it is the creditors who have suffered the loss. This is undoubtedly so in the case of limited liability companies and is perhaps the principal reason why the balance between creditor and debtor is being recalibrated, with ever greater personal demands being made on debtors if they are to take on credit in regard to an enterprise which enjoys limited liability.

It should also be noted that there are more companies in the UK economy than at any time in its history; indeed, in the UK half a million new companies have been created in the last decade. As a result, a highly unusual feature of the post-credit crunch double-dip recession is the fact that this economic decline has not been accompanied by an equally proportionate rise in unemployment levels. Anecdotally, it appears that individuals are starting up their own businesses, often multiple businesses, often low tech with low capital requirement. There are now a record 4.13 million people who are termed self-employed, with a move towards part-time working, individuals having multiple employers and a huge growth in owner-managed small enterprise start-ups. The emergence of this increasingly entrepreneurial culture appears thus to have resulted from changing economic conditions. The emergence of powerful IT/communication platforms available at low cost to individuals has created a more level playing field for new entrants into most market sectors, meaning that less initial capital investment (such as premises, machinery and equipment) is required to start up an enterprise. Media promotion and acceptance of those such as Richard Branson engaged in successful entrepreneurial activity, and a raft of programmes such as *Dragons' Den* and *The Apprentice*, have all gone some way to change the public perception of entrepreneurial activity. Legislative reform in the area of insolvency is thus seen less as a catalyst for change and more as a reflection of changing attitudes towards debt, risk and reward.

Another factor that cannot be underplayed is the fact those undertaking a new enterprise do so for the opportunity for reward. Indeed, studies into the so-called Laffer curve concept (the point at which increasing tax revenue is reduced by an increase in tax rates) show that the rate at which an effective tax rate becomes a disincentive to further work is a rate of around 70 per cent, but this can be considerably higher in countries with differing socio-economic conditions. Human nature means that people will work and seek to obtain reward even if the return is small. Does the contrary apply: are individuals disincentivised by fear of failure and the personal risks that will befall them on enterprise failure? Again, human nature is such that it is the optimistic individuals who are likely to undertake new enterprise activity and are less inclined to consider the consequences of failure. Insolvency law is there to regulate and moderate inappropriate risk taking; it should ensure that precautionary measures are taken. However, despite the best efforts of the insolvency profession, it seems to play little part in business planning and the undertaking of new enterprises.

Other stakeholders providing credit must also balance their own business requirements against concerns over the financial stability of the borrower. A supplier wishing to expand its customer base and a landlord that would rather a property was tenanted, must take into account the possibility of enterprise failure and that the customer or tenant will leave debt. In the circumstances, landlords with long-term lets are likely to insist on personal guarantees or rent deposits, while suppliers may impose onerous conditions to supply, particularly making use of reservation of title clauses and the use or otherwise of the goods being supplied pending payment.

HMRC is of course classed as an involuntary creditor, as the accumulation of tax liability (be it PAYE, VAT or income or corporation tax) is incurred prior to HMRC's ability to collect. HMRC faces a central challenge to maximise tax revenues while seeking to enforce payment of tax fairly and proportionately, so as not to depress the economy still further. While time to pay arrangements provided assistance to some businesses post credit crunch, this was only ever a short-term fix, as it simply deferred the problem of indebtedness. As the general economy shows at the time of writing little sign of significant growth, time to pay arrangements are being phased out and a more aggressive collection policy, such as the more ready use of distraint, seems to be being reinstated. At the same time, there have been some high-profile attacks on overly aggressive tax planning schemes and a move to stamp out not just tax evasion but also tax avoidance. However, a tax regime which is unduly punitive will potentially discourage entrepreneurial activity and may cause high net worth individuals and foreign investors to settle and invest else-where. The balance between encouraging entrepreneurial activity and collecting sufficient tax revenue is, as ever, a difficult one.

Post credit crunch, we have seen a return to more prudent lending practices, with lenders, particularly in the small and medium-sized enterprise (SME) market, seeking to impose personal guarantees and/or seek security over personal assets. With tightening credit criteria, increasing transactional costs and fees for obtaining debt funding, it is often portrayed that the current funding crisis and the inability of the banks to meet lending targets (and SMEs' willingness to seek debt funding) is the fault of the banks in imposing draconian lending terms, which in turn is prohibiting entrepreneurial activity and, ultimately, overall economic growth.

This is a rather simplistic view and one that does not take into account the changing socio-economic conditions in the UK. Prior to the 1980s, the UK economy was dominated by a smaller number of employers employing the majority of the UK's workforce. These big industrial/manufacturing employers were accom-panied by a large number of sole traders and partnerships that had, by reason of their business, unlimited personal liability. Today, the economy is very different, with a huge growth in limited liability companies and limited liability partnerships remov-ing the risk for those setting up a business enterprise in the event of failure.

While often the use of such corporate structures has been tax driven, the increasing use of corporate structures to conduct business enterprise has meant a change in social attitude, with limited liability being regarded as less of a privilege and more a right. Limited liability is, however, a right that can be abused and lead to imprudent decision making; the thought of losing someone else's money is perhaps not quite as bad as the risk of losing one's own. While insolvency law is intended to police director conduct and inhibit the reckless treatment of creditors, these laws deal with problems post failure; they do not directly regulate the affairs of the business prior to the insolvency, which remain a matter for the creditors alone. As a result, post credit crunch, it is unsurprising that creditors, be they lenders, landlords or suppliers, wish to see a debtor share not only the reward of their enterprise but also the risk of its failure.

It should of course also be remembered that the credit crunch was a consequence of a banking crisis of unprecedented proportions. Bank balance sheets have required significant restructuring and as never before lenders are acutely conscious that they need to return profit on their investments (lending). If, as a result of the current economic climate, they cannot back SMEs, other sources of funding need to be found.

Undoubtedly, despite best intentions, for an individual setting up a business the number of current schemes and initiatives must be bewildering. However, the current difficulties for businesses arise not necessarily because of the lack of available funding (be that through traditional bank lending, venture capital trusts/enterprise investment schemes, asset-based lending or government or private sector initiatives) or as a result of the potential spectre of personal liability; rather, it is a result of the economic climate. The fear of enterprise failure and associated personal risk is thus a symptom not a cause of the UK's current economic difficulties. To change economic course, one will need to see both borrower and lender confidence return to the mid-market. Confidence, however, has an ephemeral elusive quality: hard won, it is easily lost, and post credit crunch it has proved frustratingly slow to return.

14.2 PERSONAL INSOLVENCY: LOOKING INTO THE CRYSTAL BALL

14.2.1 Socio-economic change

Traditional explanations as to the causes of bankruptcy focus on the debtor and the occurrence of an unforeseen event that has an impact on the individual's financial position that cannot be corrected. Such factors include unemployment, health issues and matrimonial breakdown. However, bankruptcy can equally be caused by general poor economic conditions, which may affect interest rates, asset values and credit availability. These external factors interlink with the first, and influence whether the downturn in the current financial situation and prospects of the individual can be corrected, e.g. by borrowing, selling available assets or expectation of future income. External factors such as the economic condition of the country also play a major part in confidence and whether it is reasonable to believe that short-term difficulty can be overcome. As a result, when a country is in recession one should see a rise in personal insolvency levels and when the country is prospering, personal insolvency levels should fall. What we have seen in the last 20 years runs contrary to this simple hypothesis. Personal insolvency rates have escalated dramatically (during a period of sustained economic growth) but have been falling in recent times (during the period of recession/economic stagnation).

It appears therefore that the rise in personal insolvency levels may be accounted for by a third element, namely a cost/benefit analysis undertaken by the debtor in deciding whether it is appropriate to become bankrupt (or attempt to overcome the difficulty). Into this analysis will come considerations as to what happens to the debtor's assets (family home, pensions), how much control will be imposed and what will be the day-to-day effect (duration and disabilities) and a more ephemeral view of the stigma that may be associated with the use of the process. It has been suggested, therefore, that the liberalisation of the bankruptcy regime from 2004 and, more recently, the introduction of the DRO process have caused a rise in personal insolvency levels.

Again, these factors may play a part but this explanation ignores the more fundamental social and demographic changes that society has undergone and which explain why a rise in personal insolvency levels has not been particularly affected by the period post credit crunch. Changing social attitudes towards debt and financial failure have been significant; we are no longer a nation of prudent shopkeepers and instead have become a nation of consumers and borrowers. Obtaining credit has become easy, with the range of lenders ever increasing; in particular, the sub-prime lending market rapidly expanded, and debt became an accepted part of everyday life. As bankruptcy becomes ever more common, individuals continue to have more personal experience of the procedure, perhaps knowing of a friend or relative who has undergone the process. Bankruptcy has to some extent lost, and will increasingly lose, its stigma and become an 'accepted' risk of personal economic activity.

Not only have attitudes towards debt and bankruptcy changed, but the profile of those entering into a process has changed. In the last few years acres of newsprint have been taken up reporting on the rise in personal debt levels. On a macro-economic level, this situation was perhaps less of a concern to the growth of the economy (which was in reality sustained on a decade-long consumer spending spree) more a social one, leading to unsustainable debt levels among demographic groups who previously may not even have had access to credit. These groups (e.g. the young, the asset poor) will have less ability to overcome an unexpected financial event and, arguably, with less fear of stigma/less to lose (i.e. no house), it is perhaps unsurprising to find the use of the personal insolvency processes has become prevalent.

This trend is borne out by the fact that, where once bankruptcy was seen as a creditor's remedy and used predominately to recover business debts from sole traders, it is now predominately commenced by the debtor, with fewer assets being available to creditors resulting in a poorer return to creditors. It should also be factored in that the huge rise in the use of the IVA accounts for those debtors who may have assets.

Personal insolvency trends 2004–2012 may be summarised as follows:

- Continuing predominance of consumer debtors.
- Increasing bankruptcy numbers until 2009 and then relative fall.

- The emergence of debt relief order, exceeding bankruptcy numbers by mid-2012.
- A rise of the IVA process.
- Bankrupts having fewer available assets, lower returns for creditors.
- Increasing personal insolvency viewed as a debtor-led administrative rather than a creditor-led court process.

14.2.2 Bankruptcy tourism

The stated aim of the Enterprise Act 2002 as expressed in the Government White Paper of July 2001 by the then Secretary of State for Trade and Industry, Patricia Hewitt, was as follows: 'We want an enterprising economy to make the UK the best place in the world to do business.'

Important in achieving this aim was to allow the non-culpable debtor a second chance, to try again without the fear and stigma of failure. As we have seen, a key reform targeted to achieve this aim was the reduction in the duration of bankruptcies for the majority to less than one year. This period is considerably shorter than periods of bankruptcy in many other countries.

With membership of the EU allowing free movement of workers across Member States, an unintended consequence has been the migration of insolvent individuals to the UK. This movement has been particularly marked in recent years from Germany and Ireland, both countries having a personal insolvency regime regarded as more penal and certainly of longer duration.

For an individual to establish a right to petition for his own bankruptcy in the UK, he will need to establish that his COMI for the purposes of the EC Regulation 1346/2000/EC on Insolvency Proceedings is in the UK. As we have seen, COMI is not defined; in the preamble to the Regulation it is stated that it 'should correspond to the place where the debtor conducts the administration of his interests on a regular basis and is therefore ascertainable by third parties'. As can be seen, therefore, the choice of jurisdiction rests with the location of the debtor, not with his creditors.

The case of *Sparkasse Hilden Ratingen Velbert* v. *Benk and Another* [2012] EWHC 2432 (Ch) was similar on its facts to many others. Here, a German national who had been suspended from his notarial position in Germany and whose properties in Germany had been repossessed, moved to England, rented a flat, opened a bank account, bought a car and claimed that he was working as a sports photographer. While he was initially successful in his petition for bankruptcy, this was overturned. On the facts, it was found that the debtor had previously made himself bankrupt in the UK but that this bankruptcy had been annulled on the petition of a creditor (IA 1986, s.282(1)(a)), the case turning on the fact that the debtor did not own a camera despite claiming to have found a new vocation. In his judgment, Purle J provided guidance on the considerations that the court must have where a debtor has purported to change COMI in the face of foreign creditor claims. In each case, the court should consider the activities and actions of the debtor other than at the date of presentation of the petition. This requires careful case-by-case analysis of the facts pertaining to the individual. Considerations may include whether the economic activities carried on in the UK are genuine, whether the debtor returns to his family in the foreign jurisdiction, who he is supported by and where his creditors consider his place of residence to be.

While this judgment provides welcome clarification, it does mean that litigating such matters is fact-heavy, therefore complex and likely to be uncertain and costly. In the majority of cases, the foreign creditors are unlikely to want to go to the cost and expense of seeking an annulment where it is already likely that the debtor has no ability to meet the creditor claims in full.

The judgment is also addressed at those cases where the debtor is seeking to mislead the UK court, where the move of COMI is a sham. It is not intended to stop those who have genuinely moved COMI to use the UK regime. Is this wrong?

This is clearly a policy issue rather than a legal one; is it right that individuals in the EU should avail themselves of a regime that is perceived to be more liberal despite the fact that the creditors may object? It is of course often forgotten in this debate that despite the duration of the bankruptcy being shorter, all property of the bankrupt will vest in the trustee (IA 1986, s.306). The trustee is then free to realise that property, wherever situated, and, save for the bankrupt's principal residence (IA 1986, s.283A and the three-year re-vesting), there is no restriction on the time in which he can realise that property. As an aside, the fact that the bankrupt may have moved to rented accommodation in the UK may mean that the former residence situated abroad is not one falling under s.283A. As a result, it may be the case that rather than focusing on the fact that the discharge from bankruptcy arises earlier in the UK, creditors in whatever country are persuaded that the rigorous and effective actions of the UK insolvency practitioner acting as trustee will see a better return for the creditors as a whole. It would be good to see a balance returned and rather than bankruptcy tourism being seen as a debtor-friendly measure and an unwelcome, unintended consequence of the interaction between the Enterprise Act reforms and the EC Regulation, we ensure that the UK regime provides a better return to creditors than any other jurisdiction.

As will be explored further when considering COMI in the context of multi-jurisdictional restructuring, while there is different application of insolvency laws in each Member State, the free movement of companies and individuals across Member States to avail themselves of perceived more favourable regimes will continue. Perhaps this is proof that the UK has made itself 'the best place in the world to do business'.

14.2.3   Tackling indebtedness – the rise of debt relief orders (DROs)

Cheap credit, a change in attitude towards debt and a 'spend now' consumer culture fuelled by cheap exports from the emerging economies caused historic levels of personal indebtedness in the UK. In the DTI's annual report of 2006 (*Tackling Over Indebtedness*), a strategic priority of the government was said to be to reduce debt cases brought before the court and for debtors and creditors to seek an early resolution of debt problems. The rise in debt and bankruptcy numbers was seen to be socially unacceptable.

More effective than any government-introduced measure in controlling consumer spending has, however, been the economic conditions since 2007/08. The initial stages of the credit crunch saw a huge rise in the cost of inter-bank borrowing, and such stresses on the financial system itself that government intervention across the world was required to shore up funding gaps. The cost to governments is still being felt, and the need for austerity measures has led to the slashing of public spending. Consumer confidence has undoubtedly been shaken while these seismic events occur in the worldwide economy. Coupled with credit restrictions and a return to prudent lending practice based on ability to pay, consumers have been seen to be paying down debt with unsecured debt reducing from £165 billion to £156 billion between 2010 and 2011 (source: **www.creditaction.org.uk**). However, in August 2012, total household indebtedness still stood at £1.412 trillion, a figure close to the entire economic output of the UK in 2011. It is clear that despite changes in attitude to debt, personal debt levels in the UK still remain unsustainable.

It is perhaps surprising therefore that, at the time of writing, personal insolvency levels have not continued to rise and, indeed, at the time of writing, the numbers are just down on those seen in the wake of the credit crunch. The reasons for this are manifold, but include continuing low interest rates, the ability to service interest (if not the principal debt), lender reluctance to take (and be seen to take) enforcement action and the fact that corporate insolvency levels and unemployment rates, despite the double-dip recession, have remained surprisingly low.

Against the background of changing economic conditions, on 6 April 2009 a new form of personal insolvency process was introduced. The debt relief order (DRO) provisions were contained in the Tribunals, Courts and Enforcement Act 2007 and have had a significant impact on the treatment of individuals facing insolvency. The DRO has removed those who are on low income (less than £50 a month surplus income) and have a low asset value (less than £300) who owe less than £15,000 to their debtors from the bankruptcy regime. At the time of writing, the number of individuals entering into a DRO exceeds those entering bankruptcy.

The DRO is administered by the Insolvency Service through the Official Receiver's office, and the effect of an order is, like bankruptcy, to provide a moratorium from enforcement of debts during the duration of the order and to discharge the individual from all qualifying debts after 12 months (non-qualifying debts include secured debts, court fines, student loans and family maintenance payments).

The call for a DRO arises from concern that bankruptcy is unavailable to those on a very low income given the high petitioning costs (the Official Receiver's deposit). While the DRO is still subject to a non-refundable fee (£90 as at time of writing) to cover the costs of the initiation of the procedure, this is significantly lower than the court fee and Official Receiver's fee payable on a debtor petitioning for his own bankruptcy.

The process is also administrative as opposed to court-led, and sees the debtor submitting an application for a DRO to the Official Receiver's office via an approved intermediary authorised by a competent authority (IA 1986, ss.251B, 251U). The intermediary's role is to assess the liabilities, assets and income of the debtor and therefore his eligibility for the scheme. The application must contain certain specified information (complying with IR 1986, rule 5A.3) and then is submitted electronically to the Official Receiver, who considers the application to ensure that the requirements of IA 1986, s.251B, Sched.4ZA are met, that any queries are answered and that the debtor has not made false representations (IR 1986, rule 5A.4).

A register of DROs is maintained and the ease, low cost and efficiency of the process are proving attractive to those individuals who have poor prospects of clearing their debts. It is also to be noted that the age profile of those seeking a DRO is understandably younger when compared with bankruptcy (one in four individuals are aged between 25 and 34), with women also taking up a proportionately larger share.

The Tribunals, Courts and Enforcement Act 2007 also contained a series of proposals regarding the approval of one or more non-court based debt management schemes. Approved debt management schemes will be open to non-business debtors whose debts and assets are under a prescribed maximum. The debtor will be able to make a request of an authorised scheme operator for a debt repayment plan to be arranged for him. If approved by the court on application, the debtor would be discharged from the debt specified in the plan when all required payments have been made.

The reason for proposed reform in this area was the proliferation of companies seeking to provide debt management services. Often, such companies were associated with premium lending providers, which may offer to consolidate the individual's debt or, at the 'bottom end of the market', seek to charge administration fees on payments being offered to debtors which were disproportionate and/or greatly extended the term of eventual payments.

While reform and greater regulation of both the sub-prime lending market (including pay day loans and other high interest unsecured loan alternatives) and the debt management sector are overdue, the proposals outlined in the Act appear to have been mothballed. The emergence of the DRO has provided an attractive alternative to those on low income with few assets and it is perhaps felt that at this current time over-regulation of this sector (and removing such sources of funding for those with a low income) would cause an unwelcome strain on social services.

As a coda, the increasingly held view of personal insolvency as an administrative, debtor-led process, as opposed to a court-driven one commenced by creditors, led to government proposals in October 2012 to make bankruptcy on the petition of the debtor akin to debt relief. This will see the removal of the need to petition in respect of an individual and the necessity of judicial scrutiny and court order. Like the DROs the process will be dealt with by the Insolvency Service. Opponents point to the abuse that could arise from such 'easy' entry into bankruptcy and that the lack of resources at the Official Receiver's office will mean a lack of proper scrutiny. See DBIS: *Consultation on Reform of the Process to Apply for Bankruptcy and Compulsory Winding Up: Government response statement* (9 October 2012) and the Enterprise and Regulatory Reform Bill 2012.

14.2.4 The rise and rise of IVAs

Perhaps the most unexpected trend in insolvency since 2004 has been the rise in the level of IVAs. On the liberalisation of the bankruptcy regime, there were some commentators (this one included) who felt that the successful introduction in IA 1986 of the IVA procedure as an alternative to bankruptcy was imperilled. Why enter into an IVA when one could be released from bankruptcy debts within a maximum of a year?

While in 2003 there were 8,307 IVAs, accounting for 23 per cent of all individual insolvencies, by 2006 there were 44,332, accounting for 41 per cent of all individual insolvencies. Since the introduction of the DRO and consequent fall in use of bankruptcy, the IVA is now the single most used process in instances of personal insolvency. In 2011 there were 49,056 IVAs, accounting for 41 per cent of all processes, as compared with 41,886 bankruptcies (35 per cent) and 29,019 DROs (24 per cent).

It should also be noted that the rise in the use of IVAs was at a time when relatively benign economic conditions prevailed. It therefore seems somewhat counterintuitive that when there is a more 'attractive' debtor-friendly bankruptcy regime, at a time of economic growth, there was such a rise in IVA numbers.

The IVA process was introduced in 1986 to provide a rescue mechanism for indebted businessmen and entrepreneurs. It should be remembered that, historically, the majority of personal insolvencies were those of people in trade, and when the IVA process is examined it can be seen that it was designed for such trade debtors. For instance, the IVA is proposed by the debtor after formulating his own proposal and is simply sponsored by a nominee, who will become supervisor of the arrangement if he considers it appropriate. The content of the IVA is left open, reflecting the bespoke nature of the arrangement, and envisages close co-operation between the debtor and his creditors in formulating that proposal. Since 1986, however, the ready availability of consumer credit led to rising levels of unsecured personal debt. Indeed, the credit boom (and growth in consumer spending) was the stimulus for much economic growth throughout the late 1990s onwards. As a result of the problem of consumer over-indebtedness, some 90 per cent of those now entering IVAs are doing so for non-business-related debts, although it is noted that a more recent trend in 2011/12 has been a move by consumers to use the DRO process if the consumer/credit card debt is below £15,000.

The change in spending patterns has provided an opportunity for a new breed of firm which specialises in debt management services and provision of IVAs. The firms have been able to invest heavily in IT systems and are now able effectively and cheaply to run large volumes of IVAs. They also had the opportunity of being able aggressively to advertise their services on television and, increasingly, on the internet. Once 'advised', individuals may find themselves directed towards a plan supervised by an insolvency practitioner who specialises in nothing but IVAs. During this process, the individual is highly unlikely to meet the insolvency practitioner who may be the supervisor on this arrangement, and the insolvency practitioner may in turn be supervising 1,500–2,000 similar types of arrangement. Each will be remarkably similar, run on a system requiring minimal input.

The rise in the use of this form of IVA caused some concern to creditor groups on account of the costs of the process and returns to creditors being offered. Increasingly, banks and some credit card companies sought to vary the proposals, seeking higher levels of return and/or insisting on smaller fees for nominees and supervisors as a condition of approval. These steps imperilled the commercial model of the IVA for the providers. On the other side was the concern of regulators that consumer debtors may not have been provided with the best advice. These tensions led to extensive negotiations from representative bodies acting for debtors, lenders, insolvency practitioners and regulators and the eventual emergence in 2008 of an IVA protocol.

The IVA protocol is a voluntary framework for dealing with straightforward, consumer-based IVAs, and is aimed at increasing trust and confidence between the participants in an IVA and also improving the efficiency of the IVA process. The ongoing effectiveness of the protocol will be overseen by a standing committee, resulting in new versions of the protocol being released each year. The protocol deals with standard fees and provision for return and central to this was the British Banking Association's confirmation that its members will be expected to support protocol-compliant IVAs.

The emergence of the IVA protocol led to the abandonment of plans by the government via the Insolvency Service to introduce a new form of 'simple IVA' (see September 2004 Insolvency Service paper, *Improving Individual Voluntary Arrangements*), which was intended to deal with the growing demand for consumer IVAs.

14.2.5 The culpable bankrupt

The government's White Paper which preceded the Enterprise Act 2002 was revealingly entitled *Insolvency: Second Chance*. In the White Paper, the government's commitment to reforming insolvency law and procedure was identified as an important part of economic policy, and the stated aim of the reforms was to give both businesses and individuals a second chance after business failure. In turn, this would encourage a dynamic entrepreneurial risk-taking culture with consequent economic benefits for the economy as a whole.

When the Enterprise Act reforms were eventually revealed, it could be seen that a fundamental aspect of the reforms of personal insolvency law was an intention that the stigma of bankruptcy should be lessened. The White Paper had shown that the government viewed bankruptcy in the majority of cases as a consequence of individual financial misfortune arising through no fault of the individual, rather than as a consequence of recklessness or imprudence. As a result, the majority of bankrupts should not be fettered in their ability to have a fresh second chance after a newly shortened period of bankruptcy.

To counter the procedural liberalisation of the bankruptcy regime, the government introduced a two-tier system, distinguishing for the first time between the treatment of culpable and non-culpable bankrupts. The introduction of the bankruptcy restrictions order (BRO) regime was seen as central to the policing of debtor behaviour and the means of stopping the irresponsible and reckless. However, since 2004 the BRO regime has arguably been underused and is not seen as an effective punishment or necessary deterrent. In 2005, 387 restrictions (through orders and undertakings) were imposed, representing only 0.8 per cent of all persons entering bankruptcy. This did rise in 2006 to some 2.9 per cent, but since the high water mark of 2006/07, numbers have been falling. In 2010/11, 1,796 restrictions were imposed and in 2011/12, 873 (source: Insolvency Service, *Annual Report 2011–12*). While this decrease was attributable to a fall in bankruptcy numbers and a loss of senior investigation staff in the Insolvency Service, this number represents only a small fraction of the approximately 70,000 individuals per year entering into bankruptcy (or a DRO). It also falls woefully short of the estimated 7–10 per cent of potentially culpable bankrupts identified in the White Paper.

Fostering responsible risk-taking and encouraging a dynamic entrepreneurial culture can be seen to have a cost. It should always be remembered that a bankrupt has lost not only his own money but that of other people, i.e. his creditors. In doing so he has taken a risk with other people's money and failed. While risk-taking is an essential part of the dynamic entrepreneurial culture, is it really relevant to the majority of consumer bankrupts? Furthermore, a responsible risk-taker balances the risk of loss against the chances of reward, perhaps building in contingencies, insurances and reserves before taking any risks. As a consequence, while the reasons for an individual's bankruptcy may be many and varied and the bankruptcy often caused by circumstances initially outside the control of the individual, this does not necessarily lead to the inevitable conclusion that the individual is not responsible for his own financial failure. The individual has failed to take account of the degree of risk associated with his own economic activity and has not provided for contingencies or reserves to cover the risk of failure. Is such an individual blameless for losing other people's money?

As the BRO regime has applied only to a small majority of bankrupts and in the most part only to those who have been willing to give a BRU (about 80 per cent of restrictions come through undertakings), there must be some doubt as to whether the restrictions and disabilities imposed during the duration of a BRO or BRU are of any deterrent to individuals not engaged in business. Whether a result or an effect of the liberalisation of bankruptcy laws or not, there has undoubtedly been a huge rise in bankruptcy numbers and a change in culture whereby bankruptcy is seen as a socially acceptable option, with little personal consequence for the individual debtor. The social and economic cost of increasing bankruptcy numbers may,

THE FUTURE OF INSOLVENCY LAW AND PRACTICE

however, for a period have been outweighed by the economic advantages of a sustained consumer boom and greater entrepreneurial flare shown by a minority of individuals. In more straightened times, the need to live within one's means and a changing attitude toward debt may mean that this view needs to be reappraised.

14.2.6 Diminishing creditor returns?

Unfortunately, the returns made to creditors following the debtor's bankruptcy are often poor. This is perhaps unsurprising in view of the fact that only a small percentage of those entering into insolvency (about 8 per cent) have a beneficial interest in their own home and in recent time much equity value has been destroyed. In addition, in the majority of cases an individual's pension is now unavailable to the trustee in bankruptcy and very often the bankrupt is unemployed.

One improvement for creditors since 2004 has, however, been the increasing use of income payment orders (IPOs). Up until 2002, the level of IPOs was running at 1,500–2,000 per annum, and the introduction of the income payment agreement (IPA) procedure has seen a massive escalation in use. In 2011 there were 10,643 IPO/IPAs, and while this is a fall from the 2009 high point of 15,401, this reflects the increased determination by the Insolvency Service to ensure that debtors make some return to creditors during their bankruptcy and the ease of the post-2004 undertaking procedure as opposed to the former IPO regime.

Much of the success of the current insolvency legislation is, however, dependent upon the continued scrutiny and interest of creditors in the insolvency process. Unfortunately, with the poor levels of return that can be expected, creditors' interest in the process often very quickly dissipates. One significant trend, however, in recent years has been an increased level of trading in so-called 'distressed debt'. While this move was initially confined to the corporate debt market, increasingly there have been moves into the personal debt market, with firms/funds being set up to purchase the debt owed to institutions from large numbers of debtors/bankrupts. Using economies of scale and exercising specialist knowledge of debt recovery, these funds are increasingly becoming more vocal in negotiations with insolvency practitioners, particularly regarding proposed IVAs. One trend that we may also see is these funds becoming more interested in trustees commencing proceedings against the bankrupt and/or associates as a means of obtaining a greater return.

A significant move in recent years for many firms of insolvency practitioners has been to set up specialist asset recovery departments. This is because initial instructions to seek recoveries are increasingly being led by creditors such as HMRC and other institutions. In the past, trustees were often appointed by the Official Receiver by 'rota'; the trustee would investigate and report to creditors on possible recovery proceedings. The delays that occurred would often mean that creditors showed little interest and/or there was insufficient funding in the estate to justify further steps being taken. Increasingly, however, it is the case that trustee appointments will be taken on a conditional fee agreement basis with a view/mandate to seek recoveries (hence the need for departments which specialise and utilise economies of scale).

The trustee is also increasingly able to obtain insurance to cover adverse costs and disbursements and will seek to engage solicitors and counsel on similar no-win, no-fee conditional fee arrangements. At the time of writing, there continues to be debate as to whether reforms as to the recovery of conditional fees (see the Jackson Report on Civil Justice (2010)) will apply to insolvency cases. There is fear that if there is no exclusion, recoveries from the unsuccessful party of the conditional fee element (and payment from the awards) will reduce returns to creditors such that the legal proceedings become disproportionate and uneconomic and this pro-creditor development will be imperilled.

14.3 CORPORATE INSOLVENCY: LOOKING INTO THE CRYSTAL BALL

14.3.1 Economic climate

As has been explored when considering the effect of economic conditions on personal insolvency (**14.2.1**), an unusual feature of the post-credit crunch business landscape has been the failure to see at a time of economic stagnation and recession a significant rise in the use of corporate insolvency processes. Economic growth has stalled for the best part of four years, during which time we have experienced a double-dip recession and yet have not seen corporate insolvencies at anything like the levels experienced in the early 1980s and the 1990s.

Policymakers may credit a basket of measures, a reigning in of public expenditure, a base rate of 0.5 per cent since April 2009, quantitative easing and other fiscal stimulus measures with causing an economic soft landing and an ability to 'kick the can down the road', thereby avoiding an economic depression which was seen as a clear and present danger in the wake of the Lehman's collapse and the consequent instability of the global financial system. Also important in considering the economic consequences of what was a worldwide crisis is the cause of that crisis.

As has been explored, for the best part of 20 years debt levels soared as credit was made ever more readily available. This huge expansion in available credit was in part a result of 1980s de-regulation and then a systemic effect arising from the prevalence in capital markets of financial product innovations introduced from the late 1990s, such as collateralised debt obligations (CDOs) and mortgage backed securities (MBS) (which are bundles of debt derived from funds made available to mortgage providers and other financial institutions) with accompanying forms of credit insurance, such as credit default swaps. Such financial product innovation played a central role in the creation in the USA of a housing bubble and in turn the availability of funds back into the banking system. In effect, the trading of such instruments created a shadow banking system driven by large investment banks obtaining funds from the sale of CDOs and MBS, which in turn required debt to feed new CDOs and MBS, which in turn caused the release of funding back into the banking system. As the debt derived from standard mortgages was extinguished, the increasingly strong demand for CDOs drove down the quality of the debt to sub-prime levels. This drive down in quality was not acknowledged by investors, regulators or rating agencies as the investment risk was seen to derive from the relative positioning as amongst investors (holding bonds) when a return was made/a default occurred. The spread of risk and uncertainty as to the value of the underlying assets was to cause market paralysis following the US housing market bubble burst of 2006.

Together with uncertainty as to losses arising from investment in CDOs and MBS was the need for certain financial institutions to repay obligations, resulting in asset disposal and an acceleration of the solvency crisis. This in turn stopped the flow of funds to initially those financial institutions involved in construction and mortgage lending and concern as to those financial institutions who were over-geared and/or dependent on the short-term capital markets for funding. The collapse of such lenders led to the collapse of large financial institutions and the need for national banks to bail out their banking sectors. At the time of writing, the cost of this bailout, and the failure of the world economy to rebound from the events of 2008, have caused a sovereign debt crisis, the effects of which are unparalleled and unpredictable.

In the UK and Ireland, due to the bailouts of 2008, a number of banks came under effective state ownership. This and the continuing pressure/uncertainty on the banking system, and the need for banks to re-balance their own finances, has caused an imbalance in the relationship of creditor and debtor.

The old saying, 'owe the bank £100 it is your problem, owe the bank £1 million it is the bank's problem' is writ large across the current banking system. It is the financial institutions that are holding huge debts, but unlike the position in other recessions, this time there is great difficultly in crystallising that debt. First, there is the size of the debt burden; if collateral was released to repay that debt the glut of assets on to the market would depress the realisable price. The fear of oversupply arises because of reminders of the early 1990s property crash and the recessionary spiral caused by banks releasing more property on to the market. Secondly, there is the political imperative at play; governments have bailed out the banking sector and do not want to see banks putting fragile enterprises to the wall. Time is needed for businesses to restructure in light of the economic downturn. Thirdly, there is the need for banks to sort out their own balance sheets; the size of the problem means that, for some, bundling up their debt into assignable packages to third parties is preferable to seeking to manage the whole debt book. Fourthly is the historically low interest base rate, meaning that the ability to service debt (if not repay it) is a factor for many heavily indebted enterprises. Lastly is the lack of available debt funding in the market and/or where an offer of funding is made it is deemed unattractive to investors. This last factor is coupled with a lack of investor confidence; why invest/borrow in circumstances where enterprise value may be wiped out by global economic events? This means that there are few willing (and funded) purchasers in the market, which discourages those with distressed assets from releasing them into the market.

The result of this is that secured creditors frequently do not wish to act when a debtor cannot pay the principal debt, often preferring to amend the existing facility to allow more time. The cynical have dubbed such agreement 'amend and pretend', hoping that by extending terms it will allow the business time to restructure and acquire an ability to repay the debt. The effect of this is, however, that, increasingly, struggling businesses are seen to go through numerous rounds of restructuring, sometimes using an insolvency process to 'wash out some debt' or restructure a property portfolio. At each round, enterprise value is diminished until eventually the company, suffering 'death by a thousand cuts', succumbs and falls into a process with few if any valuable assets other than those available to secured creditors (which have been monitoring the process).

Whether this is preferable is a moot point. Many venture capitalists would argue that the exposure of the business to the market at an early stage would lead to more fundamental changes: a change of management, new capital and a greater opportunity for turnaround. Allowing weak and effectively doomed companies to fail is important in ensuring that the market functions efficiently. Against this is the contrary argument that management of debt allows the principal creditors time to obtain a better return (remembering that the banks can ill afford to bear losses). The transfer of value away from creditors by means of an insolvency process has been stultified; is this a consequences of the Enterprise Act reforms?

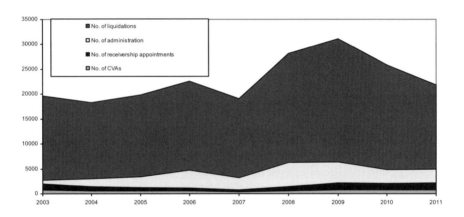

Figure 14.1   Corporate insolvency numbers 2003–2011

Corporate insolvency trends 2003–2012 may be summarised as follows:

* The expected decrease in administrative receivership but the return of receivership.
* The rise and the fall in administrations.
* A fall in the use of creditors' voluntary liquidations.

- Continuing use of the CVA procedure, but emergence of its use for retailers with large property portfolios.

14.3.2   Restructuring not insolvency?

Irrespective of whatever economic conditions are prevalent, there will always be corporate failures. It is in the nature of any competitive market that certain businesses will become uncompetitive as competing businesses profit at their expense. It is also the case that the majority of corporate insolvencies are caused by bad management: human failings, boardroom disputes and poor decision making all contribute towards a failing business.

One cultural change, however, has been an increasing drift away from formal insolvency procedures to turnaround and restructuring work. This is partly driven for the reasons outlined above by the banks and other secured lenders, the wish not to crystallise loss or expose the distressed assets to the market. Irrespective of this reason, the use of restructuring gives all stakeholders a chance to turn around the decline in the company's position.

Pre-credit crunch, a solution to distress was often seen to be an increase in capital (debt), with the lender offering new money but demanding that professionals be parachuted into the management of the company. This demand was fed by a developing turnaround industry, marketing its services to all stakeholders in a distressed business, not just the secured creditors. Within the industry a wide variety of different services are being offered, ranging from those of a company doctor/ management consultant to the offering/brokering of corporate finance for distressed businesses. Some professionals will also take executive appointments on the board of the distressed company, perhaps as a chief restructuring officer. This sector has taken its lead from the US experience, and the growth of a dedicated turnaround profession consisting of a wide range of professionals (not just insolvency practitioners) can be seen in the membership of both the Turnaround Management Association and the Society of Turnaround Professionals.

The growth of this sector (particularly in the mid-market) has, however, been halted post credit crunch. One of the key reasons is the fact that the introduction of business consultants to a distressed business comes at a cost and additional lending (refinancing) is often seen as throwing good money after bad. This is to be regretted as the use of dedicated turnaround professionals can be of assistance in rectifying the shortcomings of management and can lead to more fundamental long-term restructuring. It is, however, clear that as there is less demand for insolvency practitioners to provide an insolvency process, much of the profession is engaged in providing advisory services. This has seen many insolvency practitioners take on turnaround professionals into their practice and/or specialise in providing advice pre-appointment. The move of the insolvency profession away from 'insolvency' is likely to continue for the foreseeable future.

14.3.3 The role of the secured creditor

After the Enterprise Act 2002, unsurprisingly, there was a fall in the use of receiverships and a consequent rise in the use of administration. In recent years this trend has been reversed. Why?

With assets proving difficult to dispose of, it is often the case that a lender will look to hold on to the asset in the hope that prices will improve in the future. This strategy is particularly appropriate in regard to the treatment of property, where sites can be 'mothballed'. In such circumstances the appointment of a receiver is seen as considerably cheaper and less burdensome to the lender, remembering that the lender would not wish directly to take on the costs and expenses arising from the site (where the lender becomes mortgagee in possession).

Increasingly common in fixed charge security provisions are specific powers to enable receivers to carry on the business carried out by the company on the secured property. This has particular application for businesses such as hotels, restaurants and pubs, where property agents, who, when previously appointed as LPA receivers, would simply have marketed the property, are now often carrying out the kinds of trading activities once associated only with insolvency practitioners. Alternatively, banks and other secured creditors are increasingly appointing insolvency practitioners to be LPA receivers. The dividing line is becoming ever smaller.

In contrast (and as we shall explore in **14.3.4**), there are difficulties with the use of the administration process which militate against its use and in recent times account for its relative unpopularity.

One feature of the use of the administration process is that it is most commonly commenced by the company/its directors. It would seem therefore at first glance that the role of the secured creditor post the Enterprise Act 2002 has diminished. A very interesting analysis undertaken by Alan Katz and Michael Mumford on behalf of the R3 General Technical Committee (Study of Administration Cases for the Year 2004, *Insolvency Law and Practice*, vol.23, no.2 (2007)) has revealed that while a floating charge security existed in 67 per cent of all cases of administration, only 14 per cent of appointments were made by a floating charge holder.

However, the commencement of the process by the directors often masks the reality. Banks may be reluctant to make appointments and encounter the consequent bad publicity attached from 'pulling the rug' on their customer and will instead 'encourage' their customers to make an appointment of an administrator. The choice of the administrator is still often dictated by the bank, which not only will have notice of the intention of the appointment, but also, importantly, can prevent the administrator dealing with secured property and/or can control cash flow into the insolvent company. Unless it is clear that the secured debt will be cleared, the economic interests of the secured creditor will predominate.

The banks learned much from the experiences of the last major recession in the early 1990s and set up special units to deal with the unique problems arising from businesses facing insolvency. Generally, these units work quickly to ensure that the situation is not worsened by providing specialist advice and assistance to customers, offering restructuring advice and/or refinancing if appropriate. This may also lead to the appointment of insolvency practitioners to report on the viability of the business to service its secured debts (a so-called security review). Where insolvency is unavoidable, the secured creditor in such cases will have had more prior notice, may have been able to manage down liabilities and will have the power and influence to dictate to the company the choice and timing of the initiation of the insolvency process.

The reluctance to appoint is also a partial response to political pressure. During the debate leading up to the Enterprise Act 2002, various proposals would have significantly reduced the powers of secured lenders. To forestall draconian measures being taken which would have limited their powers, secured creditors have made a number of non-binding commitments (practice statements) as to the approach they will adopt in regard to businesses in distress; at the same time, there has been a marked decrease in the use of insolvency procedures by secured creditors.

Despite the above, and while the Enterprise Act 2002 was heralded as a major step towards reducing the powers of the secured creditors in the UK, it must still be noted that the insolvency regime in the UK remains one of the most secured-creditor-friendly regimes in the major industrialised world (the continued existence of the floating charge as a means of corporate security is unique to the UK and other Commonwealth countries). In particular, secured creditors retain influence over the choice of insolvency procedure (they can effectively veto any choice by the directors of an administrator or appoint an administrator where a creditors' voluntary liquidation is being proposed) and, more importantly, they still hold a key role in the remuneration and control of expenses in any given insolvency procedure. Behind the scenes of most corporate insolvencies, the secured creditor remains the key stakeholder.

14.3.4   Administration – pre-pack

The stated principal aim of the Enterprise Act 2002 insolvency reforms was to give businesses a 'second chance' by introducing a series of measures that would facilitate the increasing use of corporate rescue procedures, leading to more companies being saved. The reform of the administration procedure was a key component of these measures, with the intention of making a cheaper and more efficient administration procedure designed to be attractive to all companies, large or small.

Following the reforms, the use of the administration process quickly escalated and it was certainly seen that administration was, as intended, being used by small companies utilising the out-of-court appointment procedures to effect a quick and easy commencement of an insolvency process. This use of administration has not, however, resulted in an increase in the number of rescued companies. Instead, in the majority of cases, the administrator will sell such of the company's assets as he is able to, if at all possible selling the company's business as a going concern. At best this may lead to the rescue of the business, but almost invariably it will result in the demise of the company.

Case law has also made it quite clear that a sale by the administrator prior to a meeting of creditors is permissible (see *Re T & D Industries plc* [2000] 1 All ER 333, a case determined pre-Enterprise Act 2002, although it acts as a reminder that the court would not seek to intervene in what it viewed as a commercial decision of the administrator, who in turn could not use the court as 'bomb shelter' from subsequent creditor criticism; *Re Transbus International Ltd* [2004] EWHC 932 (Ch) and *Re DKLL Solicitors* v. *HMRC* [2007] EWHC 2067 (Ch), cases determined post Enterprise Act 2002, in which it was held even where there might be (majority) creditor objection, the court would not intervene where a pre-pack administration sale was an appropriate approach to procure business rescue). The ability to sell the business prior to the creditors' meeting is a power that must be exercised in genuine furtherance of the purpose of the administration (*Innovate Logistics* v. *Sunberry Properties Ltd* [2008] EWCA Civ 1321).

One consequence of the ease of use of the administration process was the fall in the use of voluntary liquidation (and a sale of the assets of the business on a break-up basis). A payment for the business (i.e. the goodwill) is the critical factor for an office holder that justifies the use of administration as opposed to liquidation. Some go further and argue that as the use of the administration process in this manner was not an intended consequence of the Enterprise Act reforms, it is therefore an abuse of a court process. Those more critical commentators also point to the fact that the use of administration is a means to avoid a creditors' meeting and possible replacement of the proposed office holder prior to the sale and effectively ensures control of the insolvency process by the existing management.

The creditors' role in any corporate insolvency in policing the conduct of the insolvent company, its directors and the insolvency process itself remains vital if standards of business efficacy are to be maintained. However, the use of the pre-pack administration can mean that creditors have little to no involvement in the process (meetings can also be dispensed with and can be conducted by correspondence) or that their involvement is limited to a time when the key steps (i.e. sale of the business) have already been taken. It is also the case that creditors generally lose interest in an insolvency procedure after a very short period. If they learn that the assets and value of the business have already been dissipated by the time they have received notification of the company's insolvency, they will have even less inclination to become involved in the insolvency process.

The pre-pack administration sale has thus been viewed by some commentators as, at best, an unintended consequence of the legislative changes, at worst an abuse of process. The debate around this topic was fierce, with calls to legislate and prevent the sale of the business pre-creditors' meeting at least to connected parties without creditor scrutiny. One proposal put forward was a three-day notice period to creditors of such a sale, giving them the right to challenge through court application the proposed sale. These proposals were dropped after consultation, for fear that a delay in completing the sale of the business could result in uncertainty and damage and/or result in ransom creditors demanding payment/preferential treatment in order to 'approve' the transaction.

The introduction of the Statement of Insolvency Practice No.16 (SIP 16), which came into effect on 1 January 2009, was, however, the industry response to the criticism levelled at the pre-pack. A failure to comply with the requirements of SIP 16 is a regulatory and disciplinary issue, with immediate obligations being imposed on the administrator to report to the creditors and to the Insolvency Service on the entering into of a pre-pack sale. There are 17 heads of information that must, save in exceptional circumstances, be disclosed. These include the source of the administrator's initial introduction, the extent of the administrator's involvement prior to appointment, the marketing activities carried out, the valuations obtained, the alternatives considered and differing financial outcomes, the consultation conducted with stakeholders, and details of the sale, including price, timing and purchaser. SIP 16 is intended to provide transparency to the deal and ultimately put the administrator to proof that the pre-pack was justifiable and in the best interests of the creditors as a whole.

An abuse of the process can arise if insufficient steps are taken by the insolvency practitioner prior to appointment to ensure that the sale which will take place on appointment is one which is to the best advantage of the creditors as a whole. Full public marketing of the business is unlikely; if the insolvency practitioner or the company indicates that the company's business is for sale (possibly at a discounted rate due to its distressed state) this may well defeat the very purpose of the pre-pack administration sale (i.e. retaining the goodwill). Alternatively, if potential purchasers of the business are approached on a discreet private basis, it may well be the case that they are unwilling to express any interest owing to any number of structural issues which may make a purchase unattractive (it is of course a business which is failing). However, if that same purchaser was approached and told that it could buy the business from an administrator perhaps cherry-picking certain assets and parts of the business it might be willing to offer a better price.

There is a risk that the business will not be properly marketed pre-administration since the insolvency practitioner may have needed to work hard to obtain the confidence and co-operation of the existing management, who may have initiated his appointment. Very often, the existing management is interested in forming a new vehicle to buy the business of the company; if the insolvency practitioner is seeking to sell the business to new owners/managers this may lead to conflict. In such instances, the management is unlikely to provide a great deal of assistance to potential rival bidders for the business. As a result, the insolvency practitioner may become unduly influenced and overly supportive of the management's proposals to rescue the business. Alternatively, the management may well persuade a more naive insolvency practitioner that they are in fact the only potential purchaser of the business, whereas in reality the market is much wider.

While the difficulties caused by these factors are not necessarily alleviated by a practitioner following SIP 16, it does, however, mean that criticism of any deal is likely to come much earlier in the process. Further, the process is more open to scrutiny (IA 1986, Sched.B1, para.74 (unfair harm), para.75 (misfeasance)), with the practitioner having regard to the need for transparency of the process. Ultimately, the fact that an administrator may comply with SIP 16 does not mean that he is free from scrutiny or challenge if the administration process has been abused.

Arguably, however, the additional regulatory requirements around the pre-pack have come at a cost. By its very nature it will be more time-consuming and thereby costly, and this may mean that it is uneconomic for smaller businesses. As a result, such businesses may fail to use the pre-pack route and instead indulge in what may be regarded as quasi-phoenix trading, namely that, pre-liquidation, a company will cease trading and its business (i.e. contact base, existing contracts) may be effectively 'picked up' by the owner/management through a new trading vehicle. When the old company goes into liquidation, while there is a risk the liquidator may question whether the business has been acquired for nothing and seek recovery, the new company will argue that the business was valueless and/or there was no alternative. At worst, the new company may find it needs to settle on the liquidator some compensatory payment. Certainly, since 2009 we have seen a return to liquidation from the use (overuse?) of administration.

14.3.5 Administration – trading

The most significant reason for the predominant use of the pre-pack is, however, the fact that trading administrations (i.e. where the administrator takes control of the company and carries on its business pending sale) have become increasingly difficult to fund. Instead, the administrator is likely either to close down the business, dismiss the staff and seek to sell the business on a break-up basis, or, as outlined above, find a potential purchaser of the business prior to appointment, and on becoming the administrator sell the business as a going concern to that party.

During the consultation process leading to the Enterprise Act 2002, many of the proposals would have led to a more radically reformed administration process, perhaps more akin to US Chapter 11 proceedings. Instead, the reforms resulted in a process which continues to have problems which, in part, can explain why pre-pack administration sales have proved popular.

The first difficulty is the overriding role of the administrator in the UK procedure. It is often difficult for the managers of the company to relinquish control of the situation, sometimes to face up to the realities of 'their' company's insolvency. The initiation of the insolvency procedure in the UK, even if it is one which effects corporate rescue, is often misinterpreted as an end, not a chance for a new beginning. While there has been a shift in culture over the last decade with some positive press reporting and director awareness of administration as a means of corporate rescue, there is still a marked reluctance for directors to give up control and management of the company to an administrator. This partially explains why a pre-pack administration sale to a management buy-out team is understandably attractive to them.

In the USA, the Chapter 11 procedure ensures that the control and management of the company remain with the existing management (so-called 'debtor in possession'). Chapter 11 is therefore seen as a valuable tool by the management of the company to obtain a moratorium from creditor action and an ability to 'cram down' debt, although critics say the procedure is resorted to far too easily. The central role of the directors of the company in the Chapter 11 procedure does, however, encourage its use.

In contrast, in the UK, the control and management of the company are almost entirely handed over to the administrator, who will only delegate certain powers to the existing management if it is to further the purpose of the administration. This passing of control and management of the company can be a very expensive process and it is not unusual for a large team of accountants to take over the day-to-day running of each part of the business while an administrator formulates proposals to creditors. In the UK, directors and senior management are often excluded from the process and are therefore disinclined to commence administration at an early stage, when company rescue is still possible.

The second problem for administrators is the funding of the process. If the company enters into administration, there may be significant cash flow difficulties, with suppliers demanding cash on delivery or imposing stringent credit terms. Allied to this is an obligation on the administrator to ensure during the administration process that the ongoing expenses of the company are paid and, at very least, that the position of creditors is made no worse by the process of administration. It may be the case that trading profits of the company will cover the overheads of the business and the administration expenses, but this is not always the case. Indeed, it is a brave/foolhardy administrator who commences an administration, trading the business, retaining the workforce and maintaining its business activities where the administrator is not clear how expenses will be paid and/or relying on poor forecasts from the failed management team. Very often the administrator will only take the appointment if he receives some form of funding or indemnity from a third party.

In the USA, the Chapter 11 procedure provides for 'debtor in possession financing'. This gives, subject to the court approval, certain 'super-priorities' to those willing to fund companies in distress. While such provisions were considered in the UK, it was determined that the banking industry was best able to judge whether administration would be of benefit and effect greater realisation. In the UK, it is therefore for banks to judge whether to finance a company during administration and no priority is obtained.

This conclusion, however, misses a significant point in that secured creditors are often neutral as to whether to company goes into administration, particularly if they have sufficient assets to cover their security on a break-up basis. They are therefore unlikely to provide funding unless they see an advantage to themselves. It is often for the benefit of unsecured creditors alone that the business needs to trade as a going concern, although unsecured creditors are likely to be reluctant to provide funding or additional credit when they are lowest on the list of priorities and the last to benefit from any potential gain.

The courts, however, have indicated that in appropriate cases they will treat funding made available to the administrator as an expense of the administration, thereby giving the funder some priority. This has gone some way to address the lack of 'debtor in possession financing' that is afforded in the USA.

The third difficulty is the ongoing problems related to what is and what is not an administration expense. This issue was ignited by the *Trident Fashions* case ([2007] EWCH 400 (Ch)) (concerning the liability to pay taxes and local authority rates) and the determination by the court that IR 1986, rule 2.67(4) has imparted the inflexible liquidation doctrine of expenses and that administrators and courts are not allowed to exercise their discretion to achieve a balance allowed for by the decision in *Re Atlantic Computers Systems* [1992] Ch 505. The case has been followed by those relating to rent (*Goldacre (Offices) Ltd* v. *Nortel Networks UK Ltd (in administration)* [2009] EWHC 3389 (Ch); *Leisure Norwich (II) Ltd* v. *Luminar Lava Ignite Ltd* [2012] EWHC 951 (Ch)), the latter case confirming that if an insolvent company retains or uses a third party's asset for the benefit of the company's creditors, the company in administration should pay for that use as a cost and expense of the administration (the so-called '*Lundy Granite* principle'): see *Re Lundy Granite Co., ex p. Heavan* (1871) 6 Ch App 462. See also *Lomas* v. *RAB Market Cycles (Master) Fund Ltd* [2009] EWHC 2545 (Ch) and the *Nortel case of Bloom* v. *The Pensions Regulator* [2011] EWCA Civ 1124 regarding pension liabilities imposed by a financial support direction being regarded as an administration expense.

While confirmation that the *Lundy Granite* principle has application in cases of administration offers some comfort, significant problems still arise. What constitutes 'use' for the benefit of the company's creditors? Furthermore, it should be remembered that the administrator has no choice over the contracts and obligations incurred by the company, as the administrator has no power of disclaimer. It also erodes the principle outlined in IA 1986, Sched.B1, para.99 that it is only those liabilities incurred by the administrator and not those incurred by the company for which the administrator will be responsible.

The problem that is posed by administration expenses is fundamental and has resulted in the position that insolvency practitioners are less willing to commence trading administrations. While at the same time there is scrutiny, criticism and a restriction on pre-pack administration sales, successful corporate rescues of businesses are increasingly difficult for mid-market and small companies – the very companies the Enterprise Act reforms sought to assist by the reform of the administration procedure.

14.3.6 Company voluntary arrangement – use in retail restructuring

Since 2008, with crushing regularity, the passing of each rent quarter day brings further news of crisis on the UK high streets. It has been evident for some time that many businesses with large long-term leasehold property portfolios, often negotiated in a more benign economic climate, are encountering difficulty. For retailers, changes in consumer spending patterns, weaker demand and a move to online purchasing mean that less floor space is required and a fundamental structural change to the retail sector is in operation. Pitching into this volatile changing landscape is the restructuring profession.

The timing of any attempted restructuring process will, by reason of the *Goldacre* and *Luminar Leisure* cases (see *Goldacre (Offices) Ltd* v. *Nortel Networks UK Ltd (in administration)* [2009] EWHC 3389 (Ch); *Leisure Norwich (II) Ltd* v. *Luminar Lava Ignite Ltd* [2012] EWHC 951 (Ch)), often be driven by when rent falls due, a situation that can create unfairness for landlords and may even be of hindrance to those seeking to restructure the business. The timing of what is a collective process, for the benefit of the creditors as a whole, should not be so influenced by the rights of one stakeholder. Unfortunately, we must wait for judicial or, more likely, legislative intervention to remedy this inequality.

The reconstruction industry rightly prides itself on innovation and an ability to provide solutions for key stakeholders, be they the existing owner/management and/or principal funders. As an alternative to administration we have in recent years seen a number of attempts to restructure property portfolios by use of a CVA process; these have included JJB Sports, Blacks Leisure, Focus DIY, Speciality Retail and more recently La Tasca restaurants and Travelodge.

A landlord is a creditor in a unique position; even if not owed rent at the time of the tenant restructuring, it will in any event be a future/contingent creditor. It will also have unique rights pursuant to the lease to forfeit on an event of default, invariably for non-payment of rent, generally on the insolvency of a tenant. For some years landlords largely remained unaffected by a CVA, with two first instance decisions, that of *Re Naeem (a Bankrupt) (No.18 of 1988)* [1990] 1 WLR 48 and *March Estates plc* v. *Gunmark Ltd* [1996] 2 BCLC 1. holding that a voluntary arrangement did not affect a landlord's proprietary right to forfeit.

In *Thomas* v. *Ken Thomas Ltd* [2006] EWCA Civ 504, the Court of Appeal, however, held that a CVA is concerned with obligations not remedies. If the rent obligation is consumed within the CVA, then all remedies must be modified. To allow the landlord the right to commence proceedings for forfeiture in respect of sums payable within the terms of a CVA was inconsistent with a rescue culture. The effect of the CVA meant that the rent was no longer owed from the tenant to the landlord; consequently there was therefore no right to forfeit. As the landlord's right to forfeit is not a secured right, the landlord is therefore an unsecured creditor and bound within the terms of the CVA. (See also *Re Lomax Leisure* [2000] BCC 352.)

As a result, the use of a CVA was opened up as an alternative to administration (which of course stays the landlord's rights of action). The use of the CVA as a means of restructuring an overburdened leasehold property portfolio has developed apace, although with some notable failures along the way.

In *Prudential Assurance Co. Ltd* v. *PRG Powerhouse Ltd* [2007] EWHC 1002 (Ch) the terms of the proposed CVA provided that employees, local authorities and other creditors (including landlords) of closed stores would share a pot of £1.5

million provided by the parent company. The remaining creditors would be unaffected and paid out of the trading receipts of the reconstructed business, a typical form of CVA proposal in this area.

Although the CVA was approved, the 'minority', landlords immediately challenged the CVA. After determining as a matter of construction that the Powerhouse CVA released the parent company from its guarantees to the landlords, the court went on to question whether this was unfairly prejudicial. Mr Justice Etherton held that there was no single test for unfairness; instead in exercise of the court's discretion all circumstances of the case must be examined and a vertical comparison (i.e. What is the effect of the CVA as opposed to other insolvency procedures?) and a horizontal comparison (i.e. What is the treatment of other creditors under the CVA?) must be carried out.

Generally, the debtor will need to establish that the CVA offers the best available alternative and that creditors are being treated fairly. The fact that one creditor is being treated differently does not in itself constitute unfair treatment; instead the court should move on to balance the interests of that creditor against the interests of the creditors as a whole.

In the *Powerhouse* case it was held that the landlords of the closed stores were left in a worse position; in contrast to what would have been the position in a liquidation, they had lost a potentially valuable right of guarantee against a solvent third party (namely the parent company guarantor). Furthermore, if a Companies Act scheme of arrangement had been proposed, they would have been treated as a separate class of creditor. They were also being treated unfairly when compared with other creditors in that their dividend was calculated without reference to the value of the guarantees. The effect of the CVA was therefore held unfairly prejudicial.

In the case of the Miss Sixty (*Mourant & Co. Trustees Ltd* v. *Sixty UK Ltd (in administration)* [2010] EWHC 1890 (Ch)), a women's fashion retail chain sought to use a CVA as an exit route from administration, but was challenged on the grounds of unfair prejudice and material irregularity by the landlords of two retail units.

The CVA sought to distinguish open store landlords, which would effectively have been unaffected by the proposal, from closed store landlords, which would receive a sum in the CVA equivalent to the estimated surrender value of the leases. As in the *Powerhouse* case, the parent company, which had provided guarantees to the landlords, was willing to fund the CVA provided it was released from the guarantees in return for a one-off 'compensatory' payment of £300,000 (it said this represented the company's liability on surrender).

At the hearing Henderson J applied the vertical and horizontal analysis provided in *Powerhouse*, finding that:

1.   In the event of liquidation, the landlords of the closed stores would have had a continuing ability to call on the parent company guarantee and hence the CVA was unfairly prejudicial to their position (vertical analysis).

2.   In contrast with other creditors (the parent and connected companies were not

bound by the terms of the CVA), the landlords of the closed stores were treated unfairly (horizontal analysis).

Lessons were clearly learnt from these legal challenges and earlier skirmishes with landlords (e.g. the failure of the Stylo plc and Oddbins CVAs). Clearly, a better dialogue with key landlords and a more realistic expectation from them led to a number of successful restructuring of property portfolios via a CVA process. However, the collapse of JJB Sports after two previous CVAs is attracting controversy. This, accompanied by the subsequent failures also experienced in Blacks Leisure, Focus DIY and Speciality Retail, has led to an accusation that the use of the CVA is a sticking plaster when radical surgery is required.

Criticism is also mounting from landlords who note that they are being treated differently, not only from other creditors, but also from other landlords, with some CVAs providing for a range of different outcomes for various classes of landlord. Whether this differing treatment is unfairly prejudicial on a horizontal analysis is a moot point, although in practice it is clear that these landlords have the weakest economic interest and will feel that going through an expensive and uncertain challenge process is unlikely to yield a willing solvent tenant. This is particularly evident where the funders to the business, be they banks or private equity funds, will expect the landlords, or at least certain classes of landlord, to bear an element of pain; often it is made clear that the company will not be refinanced and will pass into administration (with the closure of many stores) unless the CVA proposal is accepted.

Is the use of the rescue procedure in these circumstances causing secured creditors to 'kick the can along the road' and thereby allowing uncompetitive businesses to remain in operation? Such rescue processes may have the effect of avoiding an unwelcome jolt to the economy, but is it potentially delaying necessary corrective structural change? One also needs to face the criticism that such rescue procedures may deprive those with greater efficiencies and more coherent long-term strategies of the opportunity to invest in or buy up such failing businesses.

It is perhaps inevitable that key stakeholders, be they secured creditors, employees or suppliers to the business, will much prefer to see the rescue of the business. If nothing else, a softer landing is provided if the business is allowed to gently decline. It is also correct to say that, at least in the short term, the CVA will almost certainly offer a better return to creditors as a whole. Indeed, if the majority of creditors accept what is of course the company's/directors' proposal, what place has an insolvency practitioner to say that the business is one that is doomed to eventual fail? Few of us are blessed with such foresight. In addition, it could well be said that the failure of those businesses that have undergone a property portfolio restructuring is due to unprecedented economic conditions.

A balance, however, needs to be struck. The reputation of our profession rests upon its credibility. If rescue procedures are ultimately seen not to work, where the existing management and key stakeholders remain unaffected and the business dies by a thousand cuts, is it not inevitable that criticism will result and potentially lead to erosion in confidence in rescue techniques? We must always ask what has changed in the business that will mean it should succeed in the future. If the business remains over-geared and/or requires fundamental remodelling, should it not be put out of its misery?

14.3.7 Increasing numbers of stakeholders

One trend that has arisen over the last few years is the increasing number of stakeholders in any distressed business scenario.

There has been a significant increase in the number of institutions/funds willing to trade in distressed debt. In some instances these parties are willing to buy bank debt and while this was originally associated with activities within the higher-end financial markets, there has been a move in recent years into the mid-market corporate level. In some instances, those seeking to buy distressed debt may be looking to inject turnaround techniques into the business, restructure it, repackage it and sell it on at a profit. Some, however, may be looking to strip assets away from the distressed company, particularly if it has an undervalued property portfolio, while others have simply bought debt to exercise leverage in a corporate reconstruction. This latter kind of activity has been particularly prevalent in the USA, where bond holders have often taken a particularly aggressive stance in any proposed corporate reconstruction, in effect acting as ransom creditors willing to prevent the restructuring of the company unless their position is improved.

A trend commented on previously has been the reluctance of secured creditors to crystallise debt and instead offer to extend facilities. Ultimately, successive refinancing and high leverage reduces the available assets for unsecured creditors, particularly when the company has at each stage taken advantage of an ability to securitise available assets. This is particularly true of asset-based lenders, which are likely to take a very different approach to the restructuring of a company from that of a 'traditional' secured bank creditor.

14.3.8 International reconstruction

Given ever rising levels of global economic activity, there are increasing numbers of international cross-border insolvencies. One of the more encouraging trends in recent times has been the noticeable development in co-operation between different jurisdictions to effect global reconstruction.

The EC Regulation on Insolvency Proceedings (Council Regulation 1346/2000/EC of 29 May 2000) has been adopted in the EU outside Denmark and became operative in the UK on 31 May 2002.

The Cross-Border Insolvency Regulations 2006, SI 2006/1030 came into force on 4 April 2006. These brought into effect in the UK the United Nations Commission on International Trade Law (UNCITRAL) model law, which has primary application in countries outside the EU (of particular note is the fact that the USA is a co-signatory: see US Bankruptcy Code, Chapter 15).

Neither set of regulations seeks to impose the application of a single insolvency regime across signatory states. Instead, their aims are threefold:

1. Co-operation: and in particular the recognition of foreign representatives who conduct insolvency procedures. On obtaining recognition from the court of the foreign insolvency proceeding, the foreign representative (office holder) will have at his disposal the array of court-sanctioned powers that are available to a local office holder.
2. Communication: and the ability for courts to request information from foreign courts or foreign representatives.
3. Coordination: being the agreement that main insolvency proceedings will be conducted in the jurisdiction where the individual or corporate has its COMI.

As a result of these regulations, we are seeing a great deal of co-operation between insolvency professionals across different jurisdictions to effect the best means of restructuring any given business. This has in turn has led to so-called forum shopping with, if necessary, the company moving its COMI to a jurisdiction that best suits the reconstruction of that business asset (COMI migration).

In the UK, the courts have confirmed that an administrator in dealing with a multi-jurisdictional group company can treat creditors in other jurisdictions according to the local laws applicable regarding creditor priority and treatment (*Re Collins & Aikman Europe SA* [2006] EWHC 1343 (Ch)). This practical interpretation of administration powers is an example of the courts' willingness in the UK to assist measures which will effect international corporate reconstruction. As a result, the UK is increasingly seen as being a desirable jurisdiction to effect corporate reconstruction and there have certainly been moves for companies in Germany to move COMI to the UK to allow for restructuring, a move which could be replicated in the USA.

Chapter 11 procedures have in the past proved a model for the UK administration process, but in more recent times Chapter 11 has increasingly been criticised as being a cumbersome process which takes too long; as a court-driven process it is also proving incredibly costly and therefore only available to large corporations. Chapter 11 is also criticised in that it does not deal with the underlying causes of the business failure and seldom leads to the business being restructured (and a change of management/ownership); instead the procedure simply allows for a moratorium, an ability to lose unprofitable contracts and cram down debts, which may well give the company an uncompetitive advantage. As a result of these criticisms, it could be that the UK will continue to attract businesses seeking to restructure.

With growing inter-jurisdictional co-operation and determination of COMI as a means of identifying where main proceedings may be commenced, one consequence is that one country will be identified as being, if not the best place, at least the most appropriate place to restructure a business. As a result, one trend that has arisen from COMI identification is a move to so-called 'universalism'. This is the concept that one set of insolvency proceedings in relation to a company should apply worldwide, so that all creditors (wherever situated) can prove for their debt in that insolvency. This avoids the necessity of secondary proceedings being commenced in a variety of other jurisdictions, which in turn makes restructuring more difficult.

On 24 October 2012, arguably this trend was slowed when the Supreme Court handed down its judgment in the cases of *Rubin* v. *Eurofinance SA* and *New Cap Reinsurance Corporation (in liquidation)* v. *Grant* [2012] UKSC 46. At its heart, the *Rubin* case concerned an attempt by a receiver appointed in the USA to enforce a judgment obtained in the USA against individuals situated in the UK, where those individuals had not submitted to the jurisdiction of the US court and the judgments were obtained in their absence and without defence.

The Supreme Court took note of the fact that not only was there a pressing need for international co-operation in cross-border insolvencies, but that it was in the interests of all creditors to tackle the transfer of assets cross-border to evade and defraud creditors. However, when considering the significance of universalism, it was felt that this was a trend arising from non-contentious applications by foreign courts for the assistance of the English court. In seeking to effect the international cross-border restructuring of a business, this clearly had merit, but the Supreme Court felt the judgment in the *Rubin* case at Court of Appeal level was not an incremental development of existing principles, but instead a radical departure from substantially settled law.

In overturning the Court of Appeal decision, the Supreme Court by majority held that the UNCITRAL model law does not relate, either expressly or by implication, to the recognition or enforcement of foreign judgments against third parties. Accordingly, the Cross-Border Insolvency Regulations 2006, which implement the model law in the UK, cannot be used to enforce a foreign judgment against an individual. The rules that govern the courts' powers (at common law and by statute) to enforce foreign judgments are intentionally limited in scope. To expand the rules such that a foreign judgment obtained in insolvency proceedings could be automatically enforced in the UK was a matter for Parliament, not the courts. As a matter of policy, the court further held that there was no reason why the rules for the enforcement of foreign judgments in insolvency proceedings should differ from judgments made outside insolvency proceedings.

Some commentators have seen the *Rubin* case as a major reverse for the concept of universalism. However, it is submitted that while the Court of Appeal decision in *Rubin* may come to be seen as the high water mark of the trend, the EC Regulation and UNCITRAL model law were not attempts to override the rules and procedures applicable in any state not having conduct of the main proceedings. Neither is there any attempt to have a single law applicable to insolvent companies irrespective of where they are located, and to do so would override an individual country's cultural, historical and economic treatment of debt and credit. Although globalisation of international business is continuing apace and the European currency crisis is drawing some countries towards a more centralised economic control, to see a move towards a single unified insolvency law or the principle that COMI determination leads to that Member State's law having predominance, was not intended. The general principle of EU law, as reiterated in both the Treaty of Maastricht and the

Treaty of Lisbon, is that of subsidiarity, i.e. the EU will only make laws where the proposed action cannot be made by laws of a Member State at central, regional or local levels.

While one can see the attraction of having one set of insolvency laws and certainty in an international structuring as to how to treat creditors and debtors, this is unrealistic and instead one needs to continue to rely on recognition and co-operation between courts in differing jurisdictions. It is hoped that, as such, co-operation becomes commonplace and greater certainty is introduced into any cross-border restructuring process.

14.3.9 Where next?

In the second edition of this Handbook, the following conclusion was reached:

> While administration may be recognised as an effective tool for large-scale corporate reconstructions, particularly any with a cross-border element, we may find however that the 'one size fits all' process is inappropriate if it once again becomes increasingly unavailable to small and medium-size enterprises.

This has certainly come to pass in regard to the use of administration for its intended purpose, namely to allow a company breathing space to put forward a plan of reconstruction and implement an agreed proposal to save the company. Trading administrations have become rare and are simply too risky to be contemplated as a rescue technique for most SME businesses. Instead, we have administration used as a means to sell the business quickly before enterprise value is dissipated by means of the pre-pack.

Without reform of the cost and expense rule and/or an ability to disclaim onerous contracts, this use of administration will continue to be hamstrung. Reconsideration as to the effect and intent of the post-reform administration procedure is necessary, and is overdue. With appropriate judicial clarification together with statutory reform, a robust, cost-effective administration procedure could become both a primary international reconstruction tool and, domestically, the predominant corporate insolvency procedure.

On consideration of what lay in store for insolvency law and practice in 2004, the first edition of this book concluded with the now legendary words of wisdom from the then US Secretary of Defence, Donald Rumsfeld; they remain as true now as they were then.

> We know there are known knowns; these are the things we know. We also know there are known unknowns; that is to say we know there are some things we do not know. But there are also unknown unknowns; the ones we don't know we don't know.

Index